HEALTH AND THE HUMAN CONDITION

HEALTH AND THE HUMAN CONDITION

Perspectives
on Medical
Anthropology

Michael H. Logan

University of Tennessee

Edward E. Hunt, Jr.

Pennsylvania State University

DUXBURY PRESS   *North Scituate, Massachusetts*

Library of Congress Cataloging in Publication Data

Main entry under title:

Health and the human condition.

    Bibliography: p.
    1. Medical anthropology—Addresses, essays, lectures.
2. Folk medicine—Addresses, essays, lectures.
3. Medicine, Primitive—Addresses, essays, lectures.
I. Logan, Michael H. II. Hunt, Edward E.
[DNLM: 1. Adaptation, Biological. 2. Anthropology,
Cultural. 3. Ecology. 4. Cross-Cultural comparison.
QH541 L831h]
GN296.H42   362.1   77-22936
ISBN 0-87872-140-1

Duxbury Press
A Division of Wadsworth Publishing Company, Inc.

©1978 by Wadsworth Publishing Company, Inc., Belmont, California 94002. All
rights reserved. No part of this book may be reproduced, stored in a retrieval system,
or transcribed, in any form or by any means, electronic, mechanical, photocopying,
recording, or otherwise, without the prior written permission of the publisher,
Duxbury Press, a division of Wadsworth Publishing Company, Inc., Belmont,
California.

Health and the Human Condition: Perspectives on Medical Anthropology was edited
and prepared for composition by Eleanor Gilbert. Interior design was provided by
Jane Lovinger and the cover was designed by Patricia Sustendal.

L.C. Cat. Card No.: 77-22936
ISBN 0-87872-140-1
Printed in the United States of America
1 2 3 4 5 6 7 8 9 - 81 80 79 78 77

Contents

SECTION IV
Culture and Mental Health
247

Preface

There is little question that medical anthropology is the fastest growing area of specialization within anthropology. As recently as ten years ago there was not a single graduate program in medical anthropology in the United States. There are now at least ten American universities offering advanced degree programs in medical anthropology, and no doubt this number will continue to increase. In the past ten years there has been a similar, though more pronounced, jump in the number of anthropologists who teach undergraduate courses in medical anthropology or who serve outside academia as intermediaries between anthropology and the health sciences. However, to date there is no comprehensive textbook in this field. We offer the present volume as an interim solution to the problem of introducing anthropological aspects of medicine to an increasing readership.

We anticipate that the readership will be broad. Medical anthropology may well appeal to students and professionals in psychology, history, sociology, and geography as well as to those in other branches of anthropology. Its relevance to demography, medical ecology, and epidemiology is virtually self-evident, since medical anthropology shares with these disciplines a view of population and disease from wide geographical and historical perspectives. Since health care is a primary facet of social services, medical anthropology may well reach students and practitioners in a variety of service professions. Indeed, health care personnel, whether in clinical, educational, or community settings, may find this reader useful, particularly toward understanding the significant role that culture plays in the etiology of disease, patient behavior, therapy, nutrition, family planning, drug and alcohol abuse, nursing, and other related subject fields.

Certain problems are inherent, however, in a book of this nature. We have made no attempt, nor do we imply, that the selections cover all facets of medical anthropology. Rather we try to introduce the reader to materials that in our opinion selectively represent some of the major perspectives within the discipline. Thus primary attention is given to three areas of research: the evolution and ecology of disease, medical beliefs and practices in non-Western cultures, and the complexities of health care delivery in pluralistic societies. At the end of this book are suggested reference and audiovisual resources. For reasons of space we have moved most of the references that appeared at the ends of the articles into one alphabetical list at the end of the book, and we have followed the *American Anthropologist* style for the references in the text and in the reference list. There are a few articles that retain the references as endnotes because they use number notes.

The articles chosen for this book vary considerably with respect to subject, scope, geographical location, and degree of technical specialization. In the general introduction and in each section introduction, we provide a synthesis of these articles in an attempt to show that there is a highly relevant theme pervading all the materials in the present collection. This theme is unquestionably anthropological: health, disease, and medicine are integral parts of culture.

It has become increasingly clear to us from teaching medical anthropology that students frequently find some required readings to be, in their words, dry, too difficult, and not interesting. Moreover, we have found that many physicians, nurses, and other modern health specialists have only a vague understanding of what medical anthropology is, and how it can contribute to improving the attainment of their professional goals. Hopefully this book will actively stimulate student and professional alike to a further interest in medical anthropology—an interest centered on understanding the complexities of culture's influence on health and health care.

We heartily thank all the contributors to this volume. Any weakness, however, in the book's format, style, interpretation, or representation of medical anthropology is our responsibility alone. We also wish to acknowledge the cooperation of the many organizations that granted permission to republish copyrighted holdings and allowed us to move the citations in the individual articles and compile a general reference list at the end of the book. Our last word of thanks goes to Duxbury Press and its anthropology editor, Jeremiah Lyons, who was instrumental in the conception and completion of this book, and to Katharine Gregg, a tireless and skillful editor.

The editors' royalties from the sale of this book will be donated to the Carroll Behrhorst Clinic and Hospital, Chimaltenango, Guatemala.

M.H.L.
E.E.H.

Introduction

Disease and health care are common to all societies. But the types of disease that afflict a given people, and in turn how they perceive and treat their afflictions, are indeed variable. Many Americans die from cardiovascular failure. Yet for Mayan Indians this pathology is far overshadowed by tuberculosis and dysentery, conditions of only minor occurrence in our society. And just as they treat illnesses by taking herbal concoctions, we consume vast quantities of barbituates, steroids and antibiotics. Although disease and health care are universal, they are always marked by variability. The reason is that culture largely determines why people suffer from what they do, and why treatment follows a particular course and not another.

The growing awareness of culture's role in health has been responsible for the development of medical anthropology, which can be defined as the comparative and holistic study of culture and its influence on disease and health care. Several words in our definition need clarification. A comparative approach considers two or more units of analysis in terms of their contrasts or similarities. These units, for example, may be entire societies, health programs, death rates, medical systems, gene frequencies, or theories of disease causation and therapy. A holistic approach emphasizes the study of a multiplicity of interacting factors that affect what is under investigation. The medical anthropologist looks at the evolution and geographic distribution of disease, the means by which societies have learned to cope with illness, and ways to improve the delivery of modern medicine in traditional settings.

The importance of comparative and holistic research in medical anthropology is well illustrated by studies of the relationship between malaria and the sickle-cell trait (Allison 1954; Livingstone 1958, 1969). Falciparium malaria has disabled or killed millions of people. Although this disease is particularly severe in parts of black Africa, some inhabitants are largely immune to malaria because they possess a genetic condition responsible for the production of abnormally shaped or "sickled" red blood cells. These cells, unlike ordinary red blood cells, are not adversely affected by the malarial parasite. Even though the sickle-cell trait has evolutionary advantages against malaria, it does not occur uniformly among indigenous African populations. This uneven distribution was revealed through comparative research and can be explained by a holistic examination of history, environment, and culture in the African tropics.

Until 5,000 years ago, this region was inhabited by people who lived by hunting, fishing, and gathering of plant foods. One of the greatest revolutions in the history of Africa was the adoption of slash-and-burn agriculture. The environment was transformed by cutting and clearing trees and bushes to create garden plots. The pools of stagnant water that formed in cleared fields after rain provided ideal breeding places for mosquitoes that transmit the malarial parasite. In regions of low rainfall or localities where pools of water seldom persist, human populations show little malaria and few carriers of the sickle-cell trait. Elsewhere, the local frequency for the sickle-cell gene can generally be explained historically. Where an African group in a malarial region has only recently adopted agriculture, the gene is usually rare. After centuries of exposure to the disease, however, a considerable proportion of the population exhibits the gene, even outside of Africa. From this example we see that comparative research was used to record differences in the occurrence of the sickle-cell trait, while a holistic approach served effectively to explain why such differences have developed.

Equally important to medical anthropology is the concept of culture. Many definitions of culture have been advanced (Kroeber and Kluckhohn 1952), although they differ little from an early and famous definition proposed by Sir Edward Burnett Tylor (1871:1), who wrote that culture is "that complex whole which includes knowledge, belief, art, morals, law, custom, and any other capabilities and habits acquired by man as a member of society." Culture includes virtually all of the observed behavior of human beings, including our language, symbolism, and technological accomplishments. To Robert Carneiro (1968:551), culture is "something which man interposes between himself and his environment in order to insure his security and survival."

The primary objective of this book, and the principal concern of medical anthropology, is to reveal the importance of culture in health and health care. Materials in this volume illustrate that culture governs to a considerable extent (1) the type and frequency of disease in a population; (2) the way people explain and treat disease; and (3) the manner in which persons respond to the delivery of modern medicine.

Concerning the first point it should be stressed that culture isolates and exposes humans to disease. In rapidly growing populations, for example, the capacity to increase food supply will have a significant impact on the nutritional status of those involved. If food needs are met, the general health of a people will obviously be better than during times of shortage. In this respect, culture isolates people from disease associated with malnutrition. Moreover, when food intake is adequate, the body is not as susceptible to bacterial and viral infections as when it is malnourished. But if people fertilize crops with human wastes to increase food supply, as has often been the case, intestinal parasites and fecal-related diseases become an increasing threat. Culture is now exposing humans to disease. Therefore, it plays a dual role in our health, isolating us from some diseases and exposing us to others.

The way people define and respond to illness is learned and varies from society to society. In our culture we recognize that the body exhibits certain symptoms when malnourished. We have learned this, as well as diets appropriate to restore health. In other cultures, however, the same symptoms might be attributed to a large number of causes, none of which is related to food. Ghosts, evil winds, fright, sin, or breach of taboo might be identified as the source of misfortune. In American culture the physician is the primary health specialist, one who prescribes a therapeutic diet. Elsewhere the specialist may be a shaman who applies a butchered toad to the heels of a patient to draw out and absorb a malevolent force. Because of culture people learn to view and treat their illnesses in different ways.

Another important aspect of culture is its effect on health-care delivery. Frequently medical aid programs fail because differences in the culture of those receiving and giving assistance create barriers to effective communication, education, and treatment (Foster 1962; Paul 1955). The health of persons in traditional societies cannot be improved simply by exporting medical knowledge and then assuming that those in the recipient group will change their ways to adopt advocated procedure. An understanding of the cultural context of delivery is absolutely necessary. And if such an understanding is absent, the goals of a medical program are likely to be jeopardized. The field of nutrition again provides a useful example.

Americans enjoy drinking cow's milk. In our culture it is considered essential for sound nutrition and good health, particularly for those in their earlier years. To improve dietary standards of people elsewhere in the world we think we need only to give them shipments of nature's more perfect food, milk. In fact, this has been done repeatedly but with highly negative results. Milk in many cultures is viewed with disgust and is often given a status comparable to blood or urine. Moreover, some people cannot metabolize milk because they lack an enzyme (lactase) needed to break down milk sugar (lactose). Africans, Asians, Greeks, and American Indians frequently develop diarrhea and stomach cramps after drinking milk. Even though there are barriers to using milk as a nutrition supplement, this food is still delivered to millions of people in foreign countries. Chile, for example, recently received 107 million pounds of powdered milk to use in a nutrition program for rural peasants. Such aid must be seriously questioned when it is considered that Guatemalan and Columbian villagers involved in a similar program refused to drink milk and instead used it to whitewash their huts (McCracken 1971). The nutrition of a population can only be improved when the imported food is acceptable to those in the recipient group. Milk is fine for Americans and Europeans, but not for a large proportion of the world's people.

The articles in this book expand on the purpose, history, methods, findings, and applications of medical anthropology. Although each article is concerned with a specialized topic, the collection of papers provides the range of factual information needed to gain not only an understanding of medical anthropology as a discipline, but an appreciation of the ways in which culture influences health in diverse settings.

The purpose of the first section is to establish a foundation that the reader can use to interpret more meaningfully the materials in the rest of the book. In this section medical anthropology is related to anthropology in general, emphasizing their similar use of methods and theories. Medical anthropology is defined and its objectives are clarified by comparing it to a closely related field, medical sociology. Much of the current research being done in medical anthropology is an outgrowth of developmental trends in the larger discipline of ethnology. An understanding of this should aid the reader in recognizing why certain topics and societies are studied in a particular manner.

The second section of the book emphasizes human biological adaptability, cultural evolution, and disease stress. The reader can begin to appreciate the difficulty of researching health in terms of the interrelationships uniting biology, the environment, and culture change over time. The incomplete but valuable record of paleopathology tells us a great deal about the longevity and injuries of early people and about the diseases that have left diagnosable marks on human bones, teeth, or mummified remains. Until about 10,000 years ago, all societies lived by hunting, gathering, and fishing. A few small communities still live by these means today and afford a tantalizing glimpse of what the health conditions of our early ancestors may have been like. Since then, however, gradual but profound changes in demography, subsistence, and technology have greatly altered the diseases affecting human beings. Although new developments in scientific medicine and public health have increased survivorship and longevity, the health problems of modern society are drastically different from those that affected early human beings. For the remainder of the book our focus shifts to an examination of the cultural aspects of health-care practices in traditional and modernizing societies.

In the third section we present ethnomedicine and the healer in cross-cultural perspective. An important universal among the world's people is their attempt to understand and cure sickness. Ethnomedicine is the study of non-Western medical beliefs and practices. The articles in this section cover a variety of subjects ranging from primitive surgery and *materia medica* to theories of disease and types of curers.

All societies have members that specialize to one degree or another in the diagnosis and treatment of illness. An essential part of the human struggle against disease is found in the healer's use of suggestion, medicinal agents, and—to a limited extent—surgery. As the reader will learn, healers fill a spiritual or religious need as well as a physical one. Many of their efforts are medically sound. The spiritual aspect of healing is also important because it often improves mental health and morale. The health beliefs and practices of traditional peoples can be important factors not only in terms of biological adaptations but in the control of individual behavior as well.

The fourth section deals more specifically with mental illness and psychotherapy. Because members of society share ideas and beliefs about health and disease, the classification of mental illness and the means by which it is recognized, treated, or alleviated are affected significantly by the collective sentiments of the group. Although the occurrence and patterning of mental illness vary considerably from culture to culture, certain psychobehavioral pathologies seem to be universal in human beings.

One's perception of illness has profound effects not only on health care but on one's reaction to modern medicine and public health practices. The fifth and final section of this book addresses this theme in a wide variety of settings. At present, the world is modernizing so rapidly that all but a few societies are at least minimally in contact with modern drugs and health services. The degree to which modern health resources are utilized depends on many things. Often cost dictates choice, particularly when pharmacies, clinics, or hospitals are more expensive than the traditional ways of healing and when potential patients are poor. The clinic may be far away and the traditional healer nearby. Transportation may be a consideration. Poorer patients may have to wait for hours in a modern clinic, while the traditional curer offers immediate and personal solicitude. Accordingly, the healer may be viewed as a friendly or familiar figure but the clinic as a house full of discourteous strangers or enemy aliens. Perhaps the most important factor, however, is the cultural base from which patients draw their understanding of what causes disease and what constitutes appropriate therapy. The competition between traditional or folk medicine and modern medicine is virtually worldwide and is so important in medical anthropology that it is repeatedly discussed in this book.

Because anthropologists typically do field work among people whose culture is quite different from Western societies, they can often function as "culture brokers" or intermediaries between modern clinicians and patients of foreign cultural heritage. The more different the backgrounds of the health professionals and the sick, the more useful is the anthropological role of the culture broker. Since effective communication between healers and patients is essential for effective treatment and health education, the final section illustrates the importance of medical anthropology as an applied science.

HEALTH AND THE
HUMAN CONDITION

Perspectives and Approaches in Medical Anthropology

The aim of this section is to illustrate and define the position of medical anthropology in relation to the behavioral, social, biological, and medical sciences.

The papers by George Foster and Virginia Olesen are relevant for their comparisons of medical anthropology and medical sociology. Each discipline, while ultimately concerned with studying health and human behavior, employs different research populations, methodologies, assumptions, and theories. The principal difference separating the two is that the anthropologist typically sees problems and data in terms of a cultural context, while the sociologist sees them in a social context.

Hasan's article was written as a comment on the Foster and Olesen papers. It provides a needed perspective on medical anthropology as a biomedical field. He shows how medical anthropology has grown from the research and contributions of anatomists, dentists, historians of medicine, specialists in forensic medicine and pediatrics, and workers in community medicine, public health, nutrition, population studies, psychology, and psychiatry. From the three articles one gains a useful understanding of the salient points which unite and separate medical anthropology from other sciences. Although medical anthropology is highly eclectic, it finds unification in the concept of culture.

This concept has been dealt with in different ways during the short history of anthropology. The paper by Edward Wellin explores some of the historical developments in anthropological theory and relates them to particular approaches in medical anthropology. His article is useful for it provides a framework for understanding why ethnographic, environmental, and biological data in disease and health-ways have been examined differently in the field of medical anthropology. This is seen not only in the papers by Foster, Olesen, and Hasan, but is equally clear in the rest of the articles contained in this book.

George M. Foster

Medical anthropology: some contrasts with medical sociology

Introduction

During the past three decades anthropology and sociology have witnessed a parallel development of interest in health and disease as major categories in culture and society, as well as a concern for the ways in which the special knowledge of these disciplines can contribute to the solution of health problems. Both fields now formally recognize subcategories—medical anthropology and medical sociology—as legitimate units denoting areas of research and teaching, and increasing numbers of behavioral scientists describe themselves as "medical anthropologists" or "medical sociologist." Medical anthropologists and medical sociologists find employment in schools of medicine, nursing, and public health; in hospitals and health departments; and in traditional university departments as well. They do research on such topics as definitions of health and disease, social and cultural factors in the cause and incidence of disease, epidemiology, the training of medical personnel, medical bureaucracies, hospitals, communication problems between doctors and patients, innovation and change in medical beliefs and practices, mental health, and drug addiction. In their professional formation, anthropologists and sociologists (including those whose chief interests lie in the health field) have been exposed to essentially the same formal and informal training and socialization processes, they share common bodies of theory and conceptualization, and they know and often use each others research methodologies.

At first glance the similarities between medical anthropology and medical sociology seem so patently obvious that one wonders whether, in fact, the division represents more than historical accident, the simultaneous spawning of new subdivisions by related but formally distinct disciplines. Murray Wax, who among sociologists is especially close to anthropology and anthropologists, appears to believe that the distinction is more apparent than real. Writing in *Anthropology and the Behavioral and Health Sciences*, he says,

> *In terms of a logical and systematic division of social-scientific labor, much of sociology and anthropology should be grouped together. For example, social psychology, ethnopsychology, and psychological sociology are actually one field, and the attempts to justify their disparateness are almost comical [Wax 1970:41].*

Reproduced by permission of the Society for Medical Anthropology from *Medical Anthropology Newsletter*, 6 (1), 1974.

Undeniably the similarities between medical anthropology and medical sociology are pronounced, and it is quite possible that the two fields will continue to be viewed as more similar than different. At the same time, there *are* significant differences between the two, in origin, in identification with the actors in health dramas, in research methodologies, in research topics, and in basic conceptual approaches to problems. It is to these differences, rather than the similarities, that I address myself.

Origins

The roots of contemporary medical anthropology can be traced to three rather different sources: (1) the traditional ethnographic interest in primitive medicine, including witchcraft and magic; (2) the culture and personality movement of the late 1930's and 1940's, with collaboration between psychiatrists and anthropologists; and (3) the international public health movement after World War II.

The subdivision of medical anthropology today called "ethnomedicine" is the lineal descendant of the early interest of anthropologists in the medical institutions of non-Western peoples. Since the beginnings of our discipline we have viewed medical beliefs and practices as a part of the total cultural repertoire of the peoples we study, and we have routinely gathered data on them in the same way, and for the same reason, that we have gathered data on all other aspects of culture: to have as complete an ethnographic record as possible. The diligence of early anthropologists in this endeavor is illustrated by Clements (1932) who, in the first comparative worldwide survey of beliefs about disease causation, cites 229 sources, a high proportion of them ethnographic. Needless to say, in those days few if any anthropologists routinely collecting data on medical institutions were greatly concerned with the bearing of their findings on health problems of the people being studied; they would have been astonished had they been told that they were engaged in medical anthropological research.

I see relatively little direct influence from early studies of non-Western medical beliefs and practices on the first stages of development of contemporary medical anthropology. Rather, it is the other way around. Anthropologists who today work in the health fields have "recaptured" and given a formal name to ethnomedicine, and made it a part of their specialty. As medical anthropology has developed, especially in the broad areas of international public health and transcultural psychiatry, the practical as well as theoretical importance to these topics of knowledge about non-Western medical systems has become apparent. This recognition has sparked renewed interest in ethnomedical research, elevating it to major importance in medical anthropology.

Except for these early studies of non-Western medicine, done largely as a part of tribal studies, and except for the historical-comparative articles about primitive medicine by the physician-ethnologist Ackerknecht, most health related publications by anthropologists prior to 1950 deal with psychological and psychiatric phenomena (e.g., Bunzel 1940; Demerath 1942; Devereaux 1940; Gillin 1948;

Hallowell 1934; Henry 1949; A. H. and D. C. Leighton 1941; Mead 1947; Opler 1936). Rare indeed are the items that deal with the social and cultural context of health behavior per se, or of the cultural chasm separating practitioners of Western medicine and their non-Western patients (e.g., Devereaux 1944; Joseph 1942; A. H. and D. C. Leighton 1944; and Schneider 1947). Even much of this work is cast in a psychiatric or mental health context. It is interesting to speculate about what medical anthropology would be today if this early interest in psychoanalytic theory in cross cultural settings had remained the principal impetus in the field. Fortunately, a third vigorous impetus was to be given to medical anthropology.

Although the Rockefeller Foundation had been engaged in international public health work since the early years of this century (e.g., Philips 1955, on the 1916-1922 hookworm campaign in Ceylon), it was only in 1942 that the United States government initiated cooperative health programs with the governments of a number of Latin American countries as a part of a broader technical assistance program. With the end of the war, with the establishment of the Point IV program, and with the founding of the World Health Organization, major bilateral and multilateral public health programs in developing nations became a part of the world picture. Health workers in cross-cultural settings came to see far sooner than those working within their own cultures, and particularly those involved in clinical medicine, that health and disease are as much social and cultural phenomena as they are biological. They quickly realized that the health needs of developing countries could not be met simply by transplanting the health services of industrialized countries.

The corpus of data on primitive and peasant medical beliefs and practices which had been gathered by cultural anthropologists in earlier years, their information on cultural values and social forms, and their knowledge about the dynamics of social stability and change, provided the key that was needed to many of the problems encountered in these early public health programs. Anthropologists were in a position to explain to health personnel how traditional beliefs and practices conflicted with Western medical assumptions, how social factors influenced health care decisions, and how health and disease are simply aspects of total culture patterns, which change only in the company of broader and more comprehensive socio-cultural changes.

Beginning in the early 1950's, anthropologists were able to demonstrate the practical utility of their knowledge (and of their research methods as well) to international public health personnel, many of whom welcomed anthropologists with open arms. Anthropology provided insight into why many programs were less successful than had been hoped, and in some instances anthropologists were able to suggest ways to improve programs. The anthropological approach was acceptable to public health personnel, too, because it did not threaten them as professionals. They saw it as a *safe* approach, in that it defined the problems of resistance to change as lying largely with the recipient peoples.

During most of the 1950's both anthropologists and health personnel were content to believe that with adequate socio-cultural information on target groups, health programs could be designed and carried out in ways that would lead people to accept modern medicine. It was only later that we began to realize that we need equal information about the premises, values, and practices of members of the health professions themselves, and that we began to question seriously whether all of these premises and values are, in fact, valid. In any event, whatever shortcomings we now perceive in this early definition of the problem, international public health was a hospitable field for anthropologists, and the working relationships between early medical anthropologists and health personnel were perhaps the best in the history of applied anthropology.

It is important to stress that throughout the 1950's most anthropologists working in health and medical fields assumed they were engaged in applied work, an area of interest described by Caudill as "Applied Anthropology in Medicine" (Caudill 1953). The term "medical anthropology" did not come into common use until the early 1960's (cf. Scotch 1963a). One of the advantages of the new label is that it permits us to see that there are both theoretical and applied sides to the field, which conform to Straus' distinction between "sociology *of* medicine" (the theoretical, the study of medical behavior) and "sociology *in* medicine" (the applied, the use of sociology in ameliorating health problems) (Straus 1957).

Although the roots of medical anthropology are quite distinct, all three are cross cultural and comparative. Most of the proto-psychiatric medical anthropology articles and books deal, not with American society, but with such groups as the Navaho, the Apache, the Salteaux, the Pilaga, and the Indians of Guatemala. Today's expression, "transcultural psychiatry," has a legitimate ancestry. To this day concern with cross cultural phenomena remains a major feature distinguishing medical anthropology from medical sociology. Not all medical anthropology, of course, is cross cultural, nor does medical sociology ignore intercultural situations. Nevertheless, the major interests of the two groups can be divided on this point.

In the pages that follow some of the other differences between medical anthropology and medical sociology, as I interpret the evidence, will be explored.

The Identification of the Researcher

Anthropologists traditionally have identified with, and felt sympathy for, the peoples they study. Most of these peoples have been underdogs, the powerless: North American Indians, Mexican peasants, African tribesmen in colonial settings. Not surprisingly, this identification is reflected in medical anthropology, where research problems, however they may have been determined, tend to be viewed from the side of the patient, and perhaps of low status medical personnel, rather than from that of the physician and the other high status personnel. Today anthropologists increasingly are inclined to see the barriers to improving health care as rooted in medical personnel and bureaucratic systems rather than in the patient and his beliefs. When we observe a Mexican-American mother with little control of English in the office of an Anglo physician, we empathize with her, and we wonder why the physician often has so little understanding of the linguistic and cultural barriers that separate him from his patient. Anthropologists are, it may be said, "consumer advocates."

Medical sociologists, in contrast, tend to identify with, and view problems from, the point of view of the medical establishment. Rodney Coe puts it this way:

> *Since medical sociology is an applied field, it is incumbent upon sociologists to demonstrate their value by solving problems which result in a product with a clear practical utility for their "client"—in this case, the medical profession (Coe 1970:23).*

And from Eliot Freidson we learn

> *By and large . . . medical sociology has focused on the areas that the medical practitioner himself has considered problematic, adopting the conception of what is problematic from the profession itself without raising questions about the perspective from which the problem is defined . . . . In addition . . . even when sociological studies have turned their attention to the health worker himself, they have adopted the perspective of the worker in that they have emphasized the health worker's own conception of what is problematic about his own occupations with which he has worked (Freidson 1970a:48).*

Freidson sees this tendency as in part "produced by relying on the survey question-nair as the prime method of collecting data—an occupational disease of the sociologist that is present in all fields" (1970:48).

The sociologist Julius Roth has labeled this identification "management bias," and in a study of a TB hospital, he shows how the sociologist unconsciously defines problems from the point of view of medical personnel. A common question asked by staff of social scientists is, "Why do patients leave the hospital against medical advice?" The fact that the question is asked in this form, rather than "Why do patients stay in the hospital?" represents a bias in favor of the staff rather than the patient. Yet, says Roth,

> *It is unfortunate . . . that social scientists have accepted the viewpoint of medical authority as norm and have used it as a reference point for their studies and action programs in TB hospitals" (1962:47).*

The social scientist studying tenant farming, education, and family relations would not think of letting the landlord, the school administrator, or the parents set his research problems, says Roth. In like fashion,

> *he should not accept the values, the questions, the problems of physicians and hospital and public health officials as the proper reference points when making a study of medical treatment. (Yet this is what sociologists tend to do.) (1962:48-49).*

The contrast between what I believe is a marked *tendency* (but by no means an absolute) for the sociologist to identify with "management", (i.e., medical personnel), and for the anthropologist to identify with the patient, is nicely illustrated by Glaser, who writes,

> *Occasionally social scientists have observed the relationships between doctor and patient . . . the class differences between doctor and patient have been found to affect the success of their clinical relationship: since the less edu-cated patient is less able to communicate with the doctor* in the latter's own vocabulary, *he is asked to give fewer reports, and he receives fewer explana-tions and fewer instructions for home care than do patients of higher social classes (Glaser 1968:95-96; emphasis added).*

I interpret this passage as placing the responsibility for a poor therapeutic interview on the patient who fails to communicate with the physician on the latter's terms. In contrast, and to illustrate, in Margaret Clark's account of medical problems of Mexican Americans in a California city, we are led to see how the patient's cultural background makes it difficult for him fully to benefit from contemporary Ameri-can medical care (Clark 1959:215). The reader's attention is focused on the patient, and not on the physician.

Methodology

The bulk of medical anthropology research has been based on a systems approach, a holistic view of health and disease in the context of cultural systems. As in other anthropological community research, participant observation emphasizing qualita-tive data has been the most productive research method. In contrast, a majority of medical sociologists utilize survey research as their main method, augmented by statistical and other quantitative information. Yet interestingly, when studying whole systems—especially hospitals—medical sociologists often more nearly approximate anthropologists in their research methods than they do other soci-ologists. For example, in *Boys in White*, Becker and his associates describe research that is purely ethnographical:

> *We had no well-worked-out set of hypotheses to be tested, no data-gathering instruments purposely designed to secure information relevant to these hypotheses, no set of analytic procedures specified in advance (Becker et al. 1961:17).*

Further,

> *We concentrated on* what *students learned as well as on* how *they learned it. Both of these assumptions committed us to working with an open theoretical scheme in which variables were to be discovered rather than with a scheme in which variables decided on in advance would be located and their consequences isolated and measured (1961:18).*

Participant observation was the principal research method, and the emphasis was on "student culture."

Olesen and Whittaker, in their analysis of a school of nursing, frankly recognize their anthropological approach: "Some readers may assert that in the best anthropological tradition we 'went native,' at least in a psychological sense" (Olesen and Whittaker 1968:xi). But, they say, "Our rationale was that the best way to understand a process was to become part of it" (1968:19). And Merton, in *The Student-Physician*, notes the anthropological approach used in that study:

> *Particularly in the early part of the present investigation, and to some extent throughout its course, field observers have been conducting what is tantamount to a social anthropological study of the medical school and of associated sectors of the teaching hospital. The field workers have observed the behavior of students, faculty, patients, and associated staff in the natural, that is to say, the social setting. They have made observations in lecture halls and laboratories; have, upon invitation, accompanied physicians and students on rounds to note the social interaction there; have spent time observing the kinds of relationships which develop between student and patient, and between student and teacher. These many hours of observation have been recorded in several thousand pages of field notes, making up a detailed account of recurrent patterns of students' experience" (Merton et al. 1957:43).*

Bloom, describing his research for *Power and Dissent in the Medical School*, writes, "The most salient question, it was decided, concerned the collective character of the institution, and not its separate, more readily measurable assets" (Bloom 1973:11). "To answer such questions," he continues,

> *the first step logically appeared to be in the tradition of ethnography–to observe, interview and participate–to become immersed in the environment and follow the flow of its currents of opinion and behavior (1973:12).*

The evidence suggests that the problem—rather more than narrow professional training—dictates the research methodology to be used. Just as anthropologists who work in urban areas make greater use of survey and statistical methods than do those who work in small communities, so do medical sociologists concerned with major social systems rely heavily on participant observation and related qualitative measures.

Although, as pointed out in the first paragraph of this paper, medical anthropologists and medical sociologists are concerned with many of the same research topics, there are other areas that are totally or largely the domain of one or the other of the two disciplines. In medical anthropology, nonwestern medical systems, and biocultural phenomena such as evolutionary adaptation and nutrition, are among the specialties one notes.

Nonwestern Medical Systems

Most medical sociologists are concerned only with American and European medical systems. Coe, who devotes an entire chapter in *Sociology of Medicine* to "Systems of medical beliefs and practices" is the rare exception (Coe 1970:119-161). Freidson more nearly represents the sociological point of view. He acknowledges that a great deal of information on "popular" knowledge about and attitudes toward health has been gathered by anthropologists and sociologists, but believes that

> *The greatest proportion of that literature is grossly descriptive [and that] by and large both anthropological studies using the idea of culture and sociological surveys of "popular knowledge" in industrial societies have been singularly vague (Freidson 1970:10).*

Most such studies, he continues, focus on particular illnesses, and are essentially catalogues "often without a classified index" (1970:10).

In contrast, medical anthropologists are vitally concerned with nonwestern medical systems, with what has come to be called "ethnomedicine." They would take issue with Freidson, arguing that traditional Chinese medicine, Indian Ayurvedic medicine, and Greek humoral pathology and its contemporary forms in Latin America are indeed true systems, whether they come with a classified index or not. Medical anthropologists believe *all* medical systems are worth studying, for their intrinsic interest, for their contributions to the improvement of health levels, and because of what they tell us about the wider views of the people concerned. We agree with Pellegrino who believes that

> *Medicine is an exquisitely sensitive indicator of the dominant cultural characteristics of any era, for man's behavior before the threats and realities of illness is necessarily rooted in the conception he has constructed of himself and his universe (Pellegrino 1963:10).*

Like Pellegrino, we believe that

> *Every culture has developed a system of medicine which bears an indissoluble and reciprocal relationship to the prevailing world view. The medical behavior of individuals and groups is incomprehensible apart from general cultural history (1963:10).*

And, we would add, cultural patterns.

Biocultural Phenomena

Since anthropology is a biological as well as a social science, it is not surprising that medical anthropology has embraced biological phenomena. Particularly important

in this context are such things as the problem of adaptation in cultural and biological evolution (e.g., Alland 1966, 1970; Baker and Weiner 1966), the origin
and spread of the sickle-cell trait as influenced by cultural practices (e.g., Livingstone 1958: Wiesenfeld 1967), and the meaning of lactase deficiency in dietary
evolution (e.g., McCracken 1971).

Nutrition

The interest of many medical anthropologists in the cultural and social aspects of
nutrition and diet stand in striking contrast to the absence of interest in this topic
among medical sociologists. Anthropologists, not surprisingly, look upon food and
eating as one of the most important of all cultural categories, with biological,
health, social and psychological implications. They are interested in relating beliefs
and practices concerning food to the other major social and cultural institutions,
and they know that medical systems and health levels—including those in our own
society—cannot fully be understood with reference to food. The symbolic significance of food, of food exchanges, of the offering of food as an expression of
perceived social relationships—these, and many other matters dealing with nutrition and diet have interested, and will continue to interest, medical anthropologists.

Summary

In summarizing the differences between medical anthropology and medical sociology, the basic concepts of the sister disciplines—culture and society—hold the key.
The anthropologist, consciously and subconsciously, sees problems and data in a
cultural context, while the sociologist sees them in a social context. A systems
approach, a holistic view, the question, "How do these data fit into the whole
picture?" underlies most medical anthropological research. The anthropologist
begins his research by asking about the ethnic and cultural affiliation of the people
concerned, about their beliefs and practices, their values and premises. The sociologist thinks first of social and class differences, of economic levels and standards
of living, of role and status, of professions and professionalization, of dependent and
independent variables. Although they research many of the same topics, the basic
professional orientations of medical anthropologists and medical sociologists will
be reflected in their approach to the problem, the data they gather, and the conclusions they reach. In the doctor-patient relationship, for example, the sociologist
is concerned with status differences, the sick role, and perhaps illness as a form of
deviancy. The anthropologist, in contrast, sees cultural rather more than social
differences as separating doctor and patient, and he emphasizes communication and
perception problems, and the differing role expectations that stem from different
cultural backgrounds.

Both approaches are valid; both are important. From the two together, we
learn more than from either one singly. And this, it seems to me, is the rationale for
separate but allied medical behavioral science specializations. Precisely because we

ask different questions, seek out different data, and come to conclusions that reflect our professional biases, our total understanding of medical and health phenomena is richer and more varied than if the task were left to a single discipline. We are in complementary, and not competitive, lines of work. We learn from each other, and we teach each other. Our society needs both of us.

Virginia L. Olesen

Convergences and divergences: anthropology and sociology in health care

To compare medical anthropology and medical sociology is not unlike a kinship exercise wherein the analyst scrutinizes two look-alike relatives from different branches of the same family. Under the family resemblances lie many critical differences generated from family history and social change. Those differences and their implications are the topics of this necessarily brief essay which the author hopes will include all appropriate materials, but will not misread "family" history.

Before examining those differences, it may be noted that both these disciplines profit and suffer from the term "medical." This label inhibits conceptualization of problems and brackets issues which concern both disciplines, though scholars in each have transcended some barriers imposed by the adjective. Sociolgists have studied other parts of the health care system, while anthropologists have exploited their traditional interests in non-medical healing systems. Nevertheless, such terms as the anthropology or sociology of health and illness, of health care or of healing systems appear preferable as ways to convey the work of these disciplines, while avoiding the constrictions of the term "medical." Such a change, however, may be more easily desired than accomplished, for periodic attempts in the Medical Sociology Section of the American Sociological Association to change the name have thus far come to naught. This essay will utilize the various terms suggested above, as well as those of medical sociology and medical anthropology.

The medical label does highlight certain shared problems deriving from the applied orientation in these fields and the pressures which beset institutions of health care. Members of both disciplines, for instance, receive some of the opprobrium accorded applied sociology and anthropology by colleagues whose aims

Reproduced by permission of the Society for Medical Anthropology from *Medical Anthropology Newsletter,* 6 (1), 1974.

are more scholarly or academic. From the health care side of the picture they encounter demands that they explain, if not answer, urgent questions. They may also meet uneasiness or hostility from health professionals who are unacquainted with, or unwilling to understand, the social science orientation or who are threatened by that perspective (Pattishall 1972).

Origins

Some early sociological classics, for example Henry Mayhew's *London Labour and the London Poor* (1861) with chapters on vermin catchers, hospitals for fallen women, etc., or Faris and Dunham's *Mental Disorders in Urban Areas* (1939), would now be regarded as work in medical sociology, though they were clearly not done under this rubric nor are they now a part of a body of work labelled as medical social science. What appears to be the case historically is that a number of disparate intellectual activities, the interest in sociology of medicine stimulated in the 1930's by L. J. Henderson at Harvard, the writings of scholars in the 1920's and 1930's in social medicine, and the influential interest of Harry Stack Sullivan in the social sciences constituted developments which were to forecast the emergence of medical sociology in the 1940's and 1950's (Badgley and Bloom 1972:191-192). It was that period when the field, labelled as such, witnessed substantial numbers of studies in the social epidemiology of disease, patient-practitioner relations, health care occupations, the structure of medical practice (Badgley and Bloom 1972; Caudill 1953; Freeman, Levine, and Reeder 1972; Clausen 1959; Reader and Goss 1959; Freidson 1961-62; Graham 1964; Hyman 1967; Mechanic 1967). That period also saw the employment of the first full-time sociologist by a college of medicine when Odin W. Aderson in 1949 was appointed to the Department of Psychiatry and Preventive Medicine at the University of Western Ontario (Badgley 1963).

It is thus apparent that the growth of a distinct sub-specialty within sociology is a most complex and intriguing issue in the sociology of social science knowledge that merits more intense scrutiny on another occasion. What may be done briefly here is to indicate broadly a number of social influences, in addition to the intellectual factors above, which suggest that complex history.

In the 1940's and 1950's sociology's long-standing concerns with social amelioration of human problems had not died out, in spite of earlier efforts to disassociate the discipline from the applied problems of social work and to become "more scientific." Sociologists had had long-standing relationships with policy makers in Washington dating to the Depression and World War II. These older lines of communication provided new channels to policies and funds in government agencies such as various branches of HEW when attention turned to such problems as mental health in the 1950's. The early collaboration between sociologists and psychiatrists on problems of mental health (Stanton and Schwartz 1954; Hollingshead and Redlich 1958) suggests not only the influence of funding policies surrounding the mental health movement on the development of medical sociology, but also points to a critical locus of many medical sociologists, namely departments of psychiatry. A 1970 survey of sociologists with appointments in medical schools showed that most were affiliated with departments of public health or psychiatry (*Medical Sociology Newsletter*, Vol. VI, No. 4, Winter, 1970).

The nursing profession, which had enjoyed professional and intellectual expansion during and after World War II with extensive training and research programs, was also highly receptive to anthropology and sociology in the 1950's, a departure from the earlier and narrower influences of educational psychology. Two front rank sociologists, Everett Hughes of the University of Chicago and Robert K. Merton, both served as influential consultants to major nursing organizations in this period. (Currently there is an active committee on Anthropology and Nursing in the American Anthropological Association, but no parallel committee exists within the American Sociological Association or the Medical Sociology Section.)

Also influential were the interests of such foundations as the Russell Sage Foundation, the Milbank Memorial Fund and the Commonwealth Fund which have supported scholars, training programs, demonstration public health programs and research into medical education. In particular, the Russell Sage Foundation's Department of Studies in the Professions, influenced since the beginning in 1944 by the anthropologist Esther Lucille Brown, herself highly influential for nursing education and practice, promoted the contributions of sociologists to medicine (Badgley and Bloom 1972:194).

Each of these sound developments served to create fresh interest in sociological concerns about health care and to provide specific social roles (for example, the Russell Sage Fellows in medical sociology), or opportunities to lay down the parameters of a field which would by 1959 be formally recognized as "medical sociology." That year that the American Sociological Association formally acknowledged a section by that name, this section having grown from an informal Committee on Medical Sociology organized in 1955 by August Hollingshead and his colleagues at Yale. The growth and wide acceptance of the new sub-specialty was indicated in the establishment in 1965 of the *Journal of Health and Human Behavior*, later the *Journal of Health and Social Behavior*, an official ASA journal.

Subsequently, a medical sociology section within the International Sociological Association was set up, providing the opportunity for interested scholars to communicate across political boundaries which would have otherwise separated them. In particular, Polish and East German medical sociologists have been active therein, as well as in the bi-annual International Social Science and Medicine Conferences held in the British Isles, Scandinavia and in the future, The Netherlands under the sponsorship of Peter McEwan, a British physician and sociologist, and his group. (Medical sociology in Britain has substantial following. Medical sociologists hold their own meetings in addition to the annual British Sociological Association conclaves. A parallel growth of interest in medical anthropology among British anthropologists has apparently not occurred.)

Aside from these social influences, certain factors within the history of American sociology contributed to the growth of medical sociology and endowed it with particular concepts which differentiate it from medical anthropology. Not surprisingly, the four major sociology departments in the country in the 1940's and 1950's were among the first to train medical sociologists: Yale University, where the social class theorist August B. Hollingshead took an early interest, already noted here; Harvard University, where the structural functionalist interests of Talcott Parsons were applied to analyses of medicine in society (Parsons 1951, 1958); Columbia University, where the survey research techniques perfected at the Bureau for Applied Social Research (Coleman, Katz, and Menzel 1966) and the functionalist influence of Robert K. Merton were influential (Merton, Reader, and Kendall 1957); and the University of Chicago, where the long tradition of urban sociology which relies on theories of symbolic interaction and the related method of participant observation were applied to urban studies of health occupations, professional practice and patients' perspectives and concerns (Becker, Geer, Hughes, and Strauss 1961; Goffman 1961; Freidson 1961a, 1963; Davis 1963; Roth 1963).

These major institutional and departmental influences have understandably shaped and guided the concepts, theories and methods which medical sociologists have applied to their work, though there continues to be substantial borrowing across these traditions. "Stress," "socialization," "the professions," "complex social organization," "dominance," "the sick role," "illness behavior," "negotiation," "student culture," "patterned variables," "social system," and in particular in recent days, "deviance" have been widely used. Such theoretical work as has been advanced has occurred within traditional sociological or social psychological concerns, such as social organization, the professions, stress and illness behavior; and most of this within "middle range theory." The development of "grounded theory," as yet in its infancy, has clearly been rooted in medical sociological analysis of the social situations of dying patients (Glaser and Strauss 1967). In general, however, much remains to be done regarding theoretical advancement in medical sociology (Johnson 1974). The influence of major departments does not seem so apparent in medical anthropology at this writing.

These major departments have not only contributed to major methodological, conceptual and theoretical elements within medical sociology, but have also trained the bulk of medical sociologists. In particular, Chicago and Columbia have been dominant in this regard, for of all sociologists holding appointments in medical schools in 1970, most were from these schools. Yale and North Carolina followed closely (*Medical Sociology Newsletter*, Vol. VI, No. 4, Winter, 1970). The origins of the 957 members of the Medical Sociology Section would probably be similarly distributed, but would also reflect the emergence and influence of other universities, both public and private, which now educate well-trained medical sociologists. In these respects, namely, discernible intellectual traditions within the field which have generated distinct differences among scholars, medical sociology appears to be a discipline which has perhaps aged a bit more than medical anthropology. Whether aging can be equated with maturity is a question which lies outside this brief review.

The range of medical sociology, then, is very wide indeed: from studies utilizing participant observation with families of dying patients (Glaser and Strauss

1968) through those relying on survey methods of mental illness in urban settings (Srole et al. 1962); from phenomenological analyses of the meaning of timing in illness (Fox 1959) to epidemiological scrutiny of the distribution of cancer (Graham 1960); from poverty and health (Kosa, Antonovsky, Aaron, and Zola 1969) to the analysis of dominance within and by medicine (Freidson 1970a); from review of socio-cultural variables at play in individual experiences such as bereavement (Vokart 1957) through evaluation of the complex interplay of politics, medicine and social science (Mechanic 1974); through research on hospital wards (Coser 1962) to the context of nursing practice (Mauksch 1969).

Similarities and Differences

While the foregoing paragraphs are necessarily crude in their overview of medical sociology's origins and current status, they do establish a critical point in the comparison with medical anthropology: there are sectors of medical sociology that have much more in common with medical anthropology than with other parts of medical sociology, yet within the similarities with medical anthropology certain subtle differences still hold. For instance, two fieldworkers from these subdisciplines, both analyzing the labor and delivery room with data gathered via participant observation would ground their analysis in the views of their respondents or informants rather than testing derived hypothesis from theory. Both, if they were well-trained fieldworkers, would carefully attend to their own participation in the setting and the meaning of that participation to the data gathering processes. However, the concepts of the parent discipline might well separate their eventual reports to their colleagues, to health care professions, or to patient groups: the sociological fieldworker might well develop emergent concepts which were influenced by such sociological work-horses as "role"; Goffman's dramaturgical concepts of "front and back stage," "presentation of self," "stress," "hierarchy"; while the anthropologist observer might want to entertain concepts of "kinship," "ritual," "purity and danger," "contagions," "mythic properties of birth."

Differences between other sectors of medical sociology—those which rely on survey techniques or cohort analysis through time, or which borrow from demography and epidemiology—and medical anthropology are quite clear, even though the same topic (e.g., population) might well be selected by persons working in both fields. As anthropologists turn to these alternative methods, as indeed some already have, these differences, too, will diminish.

What then are some of the substantive differences between those who identify themselves in these subdisciplines? This comparison is perhaps enhanced by noting areas where the disciplines could profitably work together.

Sociologists have done considerable work on the area of *socialization* into health care professions, mostly nursing and medicine (Olesen and Whittaker 1968; Munford 1970), an area neglected by anthropologists who might well focus on socialization into these and other health occupations, e.g., orderlies, LVN's, pediatric nurse practitioners, etc.

For their part sociologists have failed to consider as either *alternatives* or *adjuncts to medical care systems* persons such as healers, practitioners in faiths such as Christian Science, whom the holistic perspective in anthropology would not exclude from the analysis of healing or socialization into healing roles. A few sociologists are starting to look at systems of health care delivery, focusing on modes in which patients take their care into their own hands either through attempts to "beat the system," through self-help movements such as women's clinics, through consumer's responses to health care (Nelson and Olesen 1974).

Curiously, *the study of diffusion of innovations or artifacts*, an area of great interest in anthropology has not had attention from medical anthropologists, though sociologists of health care have analyzed the diffusion patterns of new drugs and their adopters (Coleman et al. 1966).

Sociologists have done research on *drug taking* from various perspectives ranging from ingestion of everyday drugs, such as aspirin or digestive aids on through prescription drugs and hallucinogenic or narcotic substances (Lennard 1971), the latter being the only area where anthropologists thus far have examined this intriguing subject, and that largely in the context of rituals within cultures other than those in the U.S.

Issues in *rehabilitation* of the mentally ill, the crippled, have been dealt with in medical sociology (Sussman 1965), but not in general in medical anthropology.

A few medical sociologists (Zola 1974), have begun to examine the place of *medical systems in the systems of social control*, a topic to which anthropologists could bring insights following the leads in early ethnographies on roles of healers in smaller social systems.

Sociologists, but few anthropologists, have become concerned about *social policies planning* in the area of health care and the future of health care here and abroad (Mechanic 1974). At this writing a few scholars in medical anthropology or medical sociology have undertaken the analysis of how individuals, whatever their class or culture, *learn what it is to be well or sick* in the particular circumstances in which they grow to adulthood, in particular within ethnic groups or social classes in the U.S., how illnesses are managed through learning family, class or cultural patterns (Zborowski 1969).

Curiously, with scattered exceptions largely in the dramaturgical analyses of mental illness, neither field has examined the *moral implications of health care systems*, the impact and influences on definitions of self, the whole person, the human being, though they would appear ideally suited to do so, particularly in those sectors, noted above, where interests converge. Nor have these two disciplines examined from any perspective known to this author the *implications of genetic advances* which will place in man's hands the capacity to control not merely reproduction but the characteristics and nature of human life. Neither discipline has yet concerned itself with the *meaning and impact of the "ecology crisis"* on the health of individuals, its meaning to them and its implications for quality of life as imbedded in cultural and social arrangements.

Conclusion

Both medical anthropology and medical sociology have much to contribute and both could, quite successfully, yield new knowledge without reference to the efforts of the other discipline. However, if either or both disciplines are to make genuine contributions to the understanding of health and the contexts of health, cross-disciplinary communications and cooperation are highly desirable. In particular, sociologists concerned with health and health care can profit from closer exposure to the anthropological perspectives that render problematic much that is taken for granted in the American health care system. The work of anthropologists, it appears, would be enriched by further acquaintance with bodies of knowledge in medical sociology. Each discipline needs the other to help strengthen that self-esteem necessary for the demanding work in health care studies (Pflanz 1974) if that work is to enrich understandings of this aspect of the human lot.

Khwaja A. Hasan

What is medical anthropology?

The papers by George M. Foster and Virginia L. Olesen (M.A.N. 6(1), 1974) on the relationships between sociological and anthropological approaches to the study of health and medicine were essentially exercises in answering the age old question: What are the differences and similarities between *social anthropology* and sociology? Although the similarities and differences between medical anthropology and medical sociology described by Foster and Olesen are very valuable indeed in a narrow sense, the points of major difference between the two sub-categories within the framework of each discipline have been missed. The major focus of study in anthropology is *man* and the major focus of study in medicine and health is *also* man and anthropology shares this basic focus with medicine and health in a wider sense than does sociology. Sociologists do not usually receive the biological, archeological, and linguistic training that is so important to anthropologists. Medical anthropology, in fact, is a lot more than what Foster describes it to be. Furthermore, the roots of contemporary medical anthropology are much older than Foster has indicated in his paper.

History of Medical Anthropology

The roots of contemporary medical anthropology, in fact, are traceable to the

Reproduced by permission of the Society for Medical Anthropology from *Medical Anthropology Newsletter*, 6 (3), 1975.

development of anthropology itself. Furthermore, many medical men have contributed a great deal in expanding the horizons of the science of man. Physical anthropology as a scientific field of study was emerging in the 19th century. Many early physical anthropologists were medical men who were attempting to study the stages whereby primates emerged from lower mammalian forms, how they diversified and how they became slaves or masters of their environments. Early physical anthropologists showed keen interest in the study of paleoanatomy and paleopathology. The findings of a skull cap and some long bones in 1856 belonging to Neanderthal Man, and of *Pithecanthropus erectus* in 1891 by a Dutch physician, Eugene Dubois, attracted the interests of many medical men and anatomists of that time. The most remarkable aspects of these findings were the diagnosis of a healed fracture in the former and an exostosis of undoubtedly pathologic nature in the latter (Castiglioni 1947).

Early biologists were interested in the classification of man into races. For a long time serious disagreements among physical anthropologists prevailed as to how many races there were. A number of morphological criteria were devised by physical anthropologists by which they tried to classify *Homo sapiens* into so-called racial types. It is in the study of these criteria that some of the branches of physical anthropology such as anthropometry and anthroposcopy developed. Since human classification based on morphological characteristics alone encountered many difficulties, attempts were made to emphasize on traits that are known to be inherited. Thus, physical anthropologists paid increasing attention to serology and human genetics and talked more about human variations in terms of gene frequencies, and less about racial types based on overlapping morphological characteristics (Hasan 1964c).

The natural outcome of the interest in the study of human evolution, comparative anatomy, paleontology, serology, and human genetics was to devise methods by which (a) human body remains could be identified as distinct from those of other higher primates; (b) different physically identifiable ethnic groups could be established on the basis of distinguishing characteristics of bones (osteology, osteometry, and craniometry) hair, blood groups and so forth; (c) sex differences could be identified from bone and other material; and (d) age of the living human individual could be ascertained, and age at death could be estimated from the body remains. Forensic medicine, the science dealing with medico-legal problems, makes use of these techniques in human identification (Hasan 1964c).

Medical Anthropologists and Medical Specialties

Although medical anthropology today is regarded as a subcategory within anthropology, it is important to recognize the fact that there are many kinds of medical anthropologists as there are many specialties in medicine and health. Each branch of medicine, public health, dentistry, and nursing may find it useful to use the services of a special kind of anthropologist who is especially trained to meet its needs. Thus, we find that departments of anatomy in medical schools employ the services of those physical anthropologists who are interested in comparative anatomy, osteology, osteometry, and anthroposcopy. The schools of dentistry employ the services of those physical anthropologists who are interested in the study of teeth, facial anatomy and so forth. The departments of community dentistry employ the services of cultural-social anthropologists in the study of community dental health problems and the role of behavioral factors in dental health programs. The point that I am trying to stress here is that as a total study of man, anthropology has contributed valuable information and techniques to several branches of medicine and health, especially to nursing, dentistry, public health, anatomy, history of medicine, forensic medicine, social and preventive medicine, psychiatry, pediatrics, nutritional science, geriatrics, epidemiology, and many aspects of health related behavior (Hasan and Prasad 1959, 1960, 1961, 1962; Hasan, Prasad, and Chandra 1961; Hasan 1963, 1964a, 1964b, 1964c, 1965, 1966a, 1966b, 1967, 1968, 1971, 1973). What makes anthropology especially valuable to medical sciences and allied health professions is that anthropology combines in one discipline the approaches of the biological sciences, the social sciences, and the humanities.

Medical Anthropology as a Profession

Professional medical anthropologists today are found working in hospitals, clinics, research organizations, and government agencies. These applications of medical anthropology and the associated job opportunities are the result of research and teaching programs that have been developed in two academic settings. The first is the academic department of anthropology in a university or college where one or more courses in medical anthropology are taught. Medical anthropologists in this setting represent their field as a specialty as many of their colleagues represent other specialties such as economic anthropology, political anthropology, and so forth. The second setting is the school of medicine, dentistry, nursing, or public health. Anthropologists in this setting are engaged in teaching and research in specific departments of their respective schools or serve the needs of overlapping interests of two or more departments. The following brief account deals with some of the contributions that anthropology makes in teaching and research needs of the following departments or divisions in medicine, dentistry, nursing, and public health; and the list is by no means an exhaustive one:

Anatomy. Departments of anatomy in medical schools and facial and cranial anatomy in dental schools often employ those physical anthropologists who are interested in comparative anatomy, osteology, somatometry, and osteometry, for they provide valuable expertise for students of anatomy and serve the research needs of their specialties. Dental anthropologists are specialized in such areas as the evolution of face, jaw, dental arch, and the role of food habits in the wear and tear of teeth.

History of medicine.   Many schools of medicine have departments of history of medicine. One common subspecialty of both history of medicine and physical anthropology is paleopathology. This term was first defined by Ruffer (Quoted by Goldstein 1963) in 1921 as "the science of diseases which can be demonstrated in human and animal remains of ancient times." This subspecialty calls for close cooperation of physical anthropologists, archeologists, pathologists, anatomists, and medical historians (Hasan 1968). Virchow, a noted pathologist and physical anthropologist of the nineteenth century paid considerable attention to the pathology of fossil bones. In 1923, the noted anatomist and anthropologist, Roy L. Moodie, published the first comprehensive book on the subject, *Palaeopathology: An Introduction to the Ancient Evidence of Disease.* The same year Moodie published a short but more popular book, *The Antiquity of Disease.*

An important contribution of prehistoric archeology in the study of history of medicine is the study of early works of art of prehistoric man. Archeologists have been able to show that the earliest origins of medical thought and its developmental trends go back to prehistoric periods. We find figures suggestive of morbid conditions. We also find evidence of the first instruments used in surgery. Numerous arrowheads have been found embedded in vertebrae and extremities of Neolithic period and pre-Columbian America.

Anthropologists have also studied mummies for diagnosing pathological processes during ancient times (Hasan 1968). Polgar (1964) has shown that the disease picture at different stages of cultural and biological evolution of man differed considerably. Hudson (1965) has attempted tracing the history of trepanematosis, an infectious disease of man caused by a microscopic parasite.

Forensic medicine.   The refinement and differentiation of anthropometric procedures has proved to be of great value in legal medicine. These applications of physical anthropology lie in the areas of identification of sex, determination of age at death, and identification of ethnicity from skeletal remains (Hasan 1964c). Other aspects of physical anthropology applicable in legal medicine include practical applications of human genetics and serology in solving medico-legal problems such as the use of blood groups in cases of disputed paternity, and in the study of blood stains to trace criminals. Dermatoglyphics, the study of finger, palm, and sole print patterns, is also used for these purposes.

Pediatrics.   Pediatrics is the medical specialty of child care. It emphasizes preventive medicine requiring frequent checks of the growing child to keep him well and help him develop as a healthy adult both physically and emotionally. Anthropology has been closely related to pediatrics. Both physical anthropology and cultural-social anthropology make important contributions in the study of growth and development of infants and children.

Physical anthropologists use anthropometry and anthroposcopy in the study of growth and development of infants and children and in the nutritional assessment of infants and children in schools or other institutions. Social-cultural anthropologists, on the other hand, study the particular forms of social inter-action between persons and the derivatives of those interactions in particular cultures. The latter have, therefore, also influenced the field of pediatrics (Hasan, Prasad, and Chandra 1961). The pioneering studies of Margaret Mead (1928, 1930) on the role of carrying, feeding, cradling, etc., in moulding and developing the personality have shown the interaction of emotional and cultural forces in the growth and development of children.

Community medicine, social and preventive medicine and public health. The concept of multiple causes of disease is widely accepted today. This means that disease is not only a biological phenomenon but it is also a social and cultural phenomenon. In the medical profession there has been considerable confusion be-tween the terms "preventive medicine," "community medicine," "social medicine," and "public health." The reasons are historical as well as regional. Public health arose out of the urgency to control epidemic and communicable diseases and, in the early stages of its development, was mainly concerned with the sanitation of the environment (Leavell and Clark 1965:7-13). Social medicine developed in Western Europe where the role of environment—physical, biological, and socio-cultural—in health and disease was recognized. With the advancements in medicine and health, it is widely recognized today that the lines of demarcation between curative medi-cine and community measures to combat diseases has to be less sharp. Therefore, many schools of medicine in Europe and elsewhere have established departments of social and preventive medicine. In the United States and many other countries, similar departments are known as departments of community medicine. These departments emphasize the concepts of prevention, treatment, and rehabilitation in their teaching curricula and research programs.

Public health today is recognized to be a profession requiring teamwork. The public health team includes medical officers, sanitary scientists, epidemiolo-gists, statisticians, public health nurses, administrators, health educators, and social scientists. Since it is a widely accepted fact today that prevention of disease can not be achieved merely by the laboratory findings of the bio-chemical causes of disease but also on our ability to change culturally regulated behavior, the social-cultural anthropologist is often asked by the departments of social and preventive medicine (or community medicine, or schools of public health) and nursing to help in their teaching as well as research programs.

It is not my intention to leave the impression that other social scientists are not utilized in these situations. Indeed they are. Sociology, psychology, and social-cultural anthropology differ in their approaches to the study of health and other problems. Social psychologists provide us with experimental data related to group dynamics; sociologists lean heavily on the use of questionnaires and interviews, mostly single interviews of many people, while social-cultural anthropologists depend upon unstructured situations in the community based on personal observa-tion and, as a rule, on repeated and extensive interviews (Paul 1956).

Social-cultural anthropologists also often emphasize the microcosmic approach for it is of great value for accuracy of first hand observation. Anthropologists also emphasize comparison. Thus social-cultural anthropologists not only try to get a general pattern but also the degree of variation from it, and the reasons for such variation. They use the microcosm to illuminate the macrocosm—the particular to illustrate the general. Furthermore, anthropological enquiries also emphasize *holistic* approach. Social-cultural anthropologists may study a particular problem, but they try to see it in the total milieu, and the life of the human group concerned (Firth 1951).

Psychiatry and psychological medicine.   Social-cultural anthropologists are commonly utilized in teaching as well as research programs of departments of psychiatry or psychological medicine. Private organizations and governmental agencies connected with mental health also utilize the services of social-cultural anthropologists. The relationships of psychiatry, psychological medicine, and social-cultural anthropology have been very close. Numerous anthropological studies of nonliterate cultures have shown the importance of cultural factors in the psychosomatic diseases as well as the personality development of the individual (Montagu 1957). Ackerknecht (1944) has demonstrated the role of culture in his study of psychological and physical peculiarities of white children abducted and reared by North American Indians, and shown that such children in the process of growing up became Indians mentally and to a certain extent even physically.

Anthropological studies of acculturation have shown that acculturation, when rapid and extensive, has a damaging effect on mental health of the people (Leighton 1959). The rapid urbanization due either to industrialization or to other processes in many developing countries and areas provides situations whereby social-cultural anthropologists and psychiatrists could collaborate in the area of mental health. Today, departments of psychiatry in medical schools do employ the services of social-cultural anthropologists in their teaching and research programs and seek collaboration from them in such areas as studies of alcoholism, drug addiction, psychosomatic disorders and numerous other aspects of mental health where social and cultural stresses and strains are considered to be important.

Summary and Conclusion

Medical Anthropology is different from medical sociology in many ways. The basic focus of attention of the two disciplines—*man* (in anthropology) and *society* (in sociology)—holds the key to such differences. Anthropology shares the basic focus of its study, *man*, with medicine and health in a wider sense than does sociology, for physical anthropology and archeology provide valuable research problem areas, techniques, and data usually not covered by sociologists. Examples would be comparative anatomy and osteology, history of medicine, forensic medicine, pediatrics, and human genetics.

Anthropology combines in one discipline the approaches of the biological sciences, the social sciences, and the humanities. Thus, the biological and ecological approaches are common to anthropology, medicine, and health and provide valuable grounds for collaboration between medical scientists, health professionals, and anthropologists. As early as 1959, in collaboration with a public health specialist in India, Professor B. G. Prasad, I attempted to give a definition of the term "medical anthropology" as follows: "Medical anthropology may be defined as that branch of the 'science of man' which studies biological and cultural (including historical) aspects of man from the point of view of understanding the medical, medico-historical, medico-legal, medico-social and public health problems of human beings" (Hasan and Prasad 1959).

Edward Wellin

Theoretical orientations in medical anthropology: change and continuity over the past half-century

Although the term *medical anthropology* was not in general use before Scotch (1963a), work in many of the areas associated with the term has a considerably longer history. This paper examines the succession of theoretical orientations in medical anthropology over the past five or six decades, focusing on what each approach has tried to explain and on the shifts and continuities in theoretical emphasis. The aim is not to review the substance of developments in medical anthropology—this has been amply done in a series of summaries and syntheses by Caudill (1953), Polgar (1962, 1963), Scotch (1963a), Hughes (1968), Fábrega (1972), Lieban (1973), Colson and Selby (1974), and Foster (1974)—but to identify and compare the major conceptual models that underlie and frame substantive work in the field.

First, the continuities. To be sure, medical anthropology's historic roots are diverse (Foster 1974), and its current orientations and interests are varied (Lieban 1973). Nonetheless, one can identify a limited number of commonalities around which the discipline has developed. These commonalities consist of three empirical generalizations; that is, certain repeatedly observed regularities in nature that have been reference points for medical-anthropological study over the years. The three empirical generalizations, formulated in various ways by writers like Ackerknecht (1945a), Caudill (1953), Scotch (1963a), Polgar (1963), and Hughes (1968), might be stated as follows:

1. Disease is a universal fact of human life; it occurs in all known times, places, and societies.

2. All known human groups develop methods and allocate roles, congruent with their resources and structures, for coping with or responding to disease.

3. All known human groups develop some set of beliefs, cognitions, and perceptions consistent with their cultural matrices, for defining disease.

These basic generalizations constitute both the strength and weakness of medical anthropology. Their strength is that they summarize and order a large number of specific observations concerning and time, place, and people. Thus, they provide a rich empirical base and many points of departure for medical-anthropological research. Their weakness is that they can describe observed regularities in nature but cannot explain them.

This distinction between theories and theoretical orientations is deliberate. Merton (1967) observes that theory involves formulations that specify determinate relationships between particular variables. According to him, a theory is a set of logically interconnected propositions from which specific hypotheses are derived, which are prescribed by the theory and whose empirical testing must lead to confirming, modifying, or rejecting the theory. Put differently, a theory must attempt to explain something, and a well-formulated theory tries to explain that thing in terms of a causal sequence of interrelated variables capable of generating hypotheses that can put the theory to an empirical test. In this sense, we do not yet have much theory in anthropology generally or in medical anthropology specifically.

What we do have, as Kaplan and Manners note (1972), are theoretical orientations—broad postulates that involve characteristic ways of selecting, conceptualizing, and ordering data in response to certain sorts of questions. For example, functional orientation examines the interrelations among parts of a society, its culture, and perhaps even its ecosystem. A cognitive orientation deals with the modes of categorizing and structuring experiences that occur among different cultures and speech communities. Each orientation provides a general context for inquiry, identifies certain types of relevant variables, and serves to inspire hypotheses congruent with it. But while either approach can generate theories, neither is a theory. Rather, each is a broad theoretical orientation. In the same sense, the various approaches discussed in this paper are best viewed as theoretical orientations, not as theories.

As we examine theoretical approaches in medical anthropology, our core question is what has each of them tried to explain? More specifically, on what sorts of dependent variables have the different theoretical orientations attempted to shed light? Further, what explicit or implicit models have served as the framework of inquiry?

We proceed chronologically, starting with the work of W. H. R. Rivers and then analyzing the orientations and models in the contributions of Forrest Clements, Erwin Ackerknecht, Benjamin Paul, and a number of recent ecological scholars. Although all the foregoing workers have influenced the thinking and research of other anthropologists, their selection here does not mean to imply that they have been the only or most outstanding figures in medical anthropology over the past sixty years. They have been selected because each typifies a distinct and important theoretical orientation, representing a significant modification over the orientation of the preceding worker.

Rivers: Native Medicine as Part of Culture

William Hallam Rivers Rivers (1864-1922) is perhaps better known for his contributions to ethnography and social organization (1900, 1906, 1914a, 1914b) than for his work in medical anthropology. He was originally trained as a physician and practiced medicine at various stages of his career. His primary legacy to medical anthropology consists of *Medicine, Magic and Religion* (1924) and portions of *Psychology and Ethnology* (1926), both published posthumously.

Although Rivers was by no means the first anthropologist to report on the medical beliefs and practices of nonliterate peoples, he pioneered in developing a formal theoretical orientation for his work in medical anthropology and in attempting systematically to relate native medicine to other aspects of culture and social organization. His formal framework was based on two propositions. The first was that primitive medical practices follow logically from underlying medical beliefs, that is, that native medical practices "are not a medley of disconnected and meaningless customs . . . [but rather] . . . are inspired by definite ideas concerning the causation of disease" (1924:51). His second proposition was that native medical practices and beliefs, taken together, were parts of culture and constituted a "social institution . . . [to be studied in terms of the same] . . . principles or methods found to be of value in the study of social institutions in general" (1926:61).

On the basis of his propositions, Rivers formulates a set of general statements concerning the nature of primitive medicine. In line with a preoccupation of early twentieth-century anthropology, these statements revolve around efforts to classify manifestations of primitive medicine as either magical or religious.

Rivers's basic conceptual model consists of three sets of variables. His dependent variable is observed or reported behavior of native peoples in coping with disease. He recognizes only one independent or causal variable—the group's "attitude toward the world" or what modern workers might term world view. A subclass of the attitudinal variable is a derivative variable, that is, a society's beliefs and concepts regarding the nature and causes of disease. Rivers further categorizes world view into three classes—magical, religious, and naturalistic—each with an associated set of beliefs and mode of behavior. Figure 1 shows a diagram of his scheme as a whole.

Rivers confines himself largely to the first two world views, magical and religious, defining them essentially in Frazer's terms (1890). The magical outlook involves belief in man's ability to manipulate forces in the universe, and the religious world view concerns belief in the control of events by the will of some super-

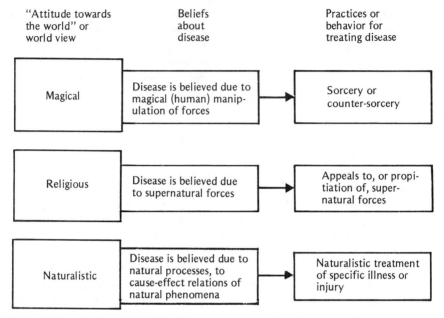

Figure 1. Rivers's Conceptual Model

natural power. Rivers deals only lightly with the third world view, the naturalistic. Defining it as the outlook that views phenomena as "subject to natural laws," he sees it as characteristic of the West and of modern medicine, not of primitive peoples. Although he acknowledges the occurrence among native groups of empirical and ostensibly naturalistic curing practices, he decides not to regard the latter as naturalistic within his terms of reference on the grounds that they are embedded in magical or religious matrices of belief.

Rivers also attempts to correlate the type of disease-related belief and behavior to an associated curer role. Thus, he sees the sorcerer as playing the key role where magic and sorcery predominate; the priest, where religious and supernatural explanations rule; and the leech (a generic term proposed by Rivers for traditional empirical curers), where the emphasis is on empirical techniques. However, this aspect of Rivers's scheme is wholly circular: he defines the type of medical belief and practice on the basis of role and the role on the basis of the prevailing set of disease-related beliefs and practices.

Although Rivers's model is essentially static, he does allow for change by placing the primary elements of his model on a change gradient, with the world views of native societies relatively fixed and unchanging, beliefs about the nature and causes of disease somewhat less impervious to modification, and medical practices most susceptible to change. He sees alterations in practices as occurring primarily through two processes: diffusion (cultural increments brought about through contact) and degeneration (cultural loss produced largely through cultural isolation).

Within Rivers's outlook, primitive and modern medicine constitute wholly separate universes of discourse. By focusing on world view and its linkages with belief and behavior, Rivers can find no way to accommodate magico-religious and naturalistic-scientific world views within the same domain of inquiry. As a result, Rivers's model precludes consideration of Western medicine and is limited to medicine among primitive groups.

Rivers deals with culture as though it were a closed system in which cultural facts can be explained only by recourse to other cultural facts with ultimate explanations to be sought in psychology. Despite his training as a physician, Rivers is indifferent to biological factors and allows no place in his model for them. Nor is he interested in adaptations to environment. Behavior is treated not as adaptive but as the product of beliefs that are in turn derived from a world-view.

Despite Rivers's constant and futile preoccupation with classifying manifestations of primitive medicine as either magical or religious, he provides an insight of fundamental and enduring significance: The elements of primitive medicine are not shreds and patches of inexplicable behavior but constitute a social institution, one as worthy of study as any of a people's institutions. In short, Rivers's contribution sets the stage for medical anthropology by pointing to the interrelationships between native medical practice and belief and by viewing both as integral parts of culture.

Clements: Primitive Medicine as Atomized Traits

Forrest Clements's monograph, *Primitive Concepts of Disease* (1932), involves an atomistic or "culture-trait" approach within a framework of historical particularism. Despite the work's conceptual and methodological muddiness, it is often cited as one of the classical studies in medical anthropology.

On an a priori basis, but without acknowledging that substantially the same classification had already been offered by Rivers (1924), Clements classifies disease-causation concepts among primitive peoples into five categories: sorcery, breach of taboo, intrusion by a disease object, intrusion by a spirit, and soul loss. He then proceeds to carry out two aims: charting the worldwide distributions of the separate traits as reported in the literature and, on the basis of charted distributions, inferring relative time sequences and routes by which each of the several traits spread.

Although references to Clements's scheme continue to turn up in the literature without critical comment, it should be noted that his classification of disease causes is a conceptual morass. To be sure, it includes two traits that can be categorized as causes: sorcery and breach of taboo. However, the remaining three—disease-object intrusion, spirit intrusion, and soul loss—are not causes but mechanisms. Each is a result of effect attributed to human, supernatural, or other causative action.

The heart of Clements's study consists of a lengthy tabulation of each of the five etiologic concepts according to the region, tribe, or local group for which one or more of the concepts have been reported. In all, about three hundred groups are listed. Clements then presents a series of world maps summarizing the distributions of the separate traits. The oldest trait is sorcery. He interprets the spatial distributions to indicate that some manifestations of sorcery go very far back in time, while others are relatively recent. The next oldest trait is object intrusion, followed by soul loss, spirit intrusion, and the most recent is breach of taboo.

However, one must be cautious in accepting the details of either Clements's trait-distributional data or his interpretations of time relationships and routes of spread. Years before Clements's work, Sapir had posed the same general question that Clements attempted to address: "How [are we to] inject a chronology into this confusing mass of purely descriptive fact?" (Sapir 1916, *in* Mandelbaum 1949:392). Sapir warned that there were conceptual hazards and methodological traps in charting the spatial distributions of traits and in making temporal inferences from them. Clements apparently ignored Sapir's admonitions.

Let us turn to Clements's model. Three assumptions that inform and underlie his entire study are implicit; they are not explicated. The first and most fundamental assumption is that were it not for the operation of diffusion brought about through geographic-historic factors (spatial propinquity, migration, and other modes of contact or spread), the distribution of traits would be essentially random. The second is that there are no functional relationships among any of the five traits and that the reported presence of two or more traits in the same society is a chance event. The third is that there are no necessary functional relationships between any of the traits and the economic, religious, sociopolitical, ecological, or other features of the societies in which they occur.

On the basis of these implicit assumptions, Clements constructs his conceptual model, diagrammed in figure 2. It holds that, other things being equal,

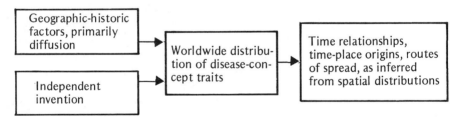

Figure 2. Clements's Trait-Distribution Model

diffusion and/or other historic-geographic events produce given profiles of distribution for each disease concept, and that relative time sequences and routes of spread—his dependent variables—can be inferred from the patterns of distribution. When the spatial occurrence of a trait makes diffusion an implausible explanation, that is, when other things seem not to be equal, Clements invokes the possibility of independent invention to account for the trait's presence. That is, a trait is developed separately in two different areas. In essence, the universe generated by Clements's conceptual model is one in which isolated cultural traits enjoy time-place itineraries governed by little more than cultural contact or propinquity and are largely unaffected by the cultural milieux or adaptive needs of their host peoples.

Despite Clements's unfruitful conceptual model, he does make a positive contribution to the anthropology of medicine through his efforts to document the worldwide distribution of disease concepts. He attempts to buttress the third of the previously discussed empirical generalizations—that societies everywhere develop some set of cognitions for defining disease.

Ackerknecht: Primitive Medicine as Culturally Patterned and Functionally Interrelated Elements within a Configuration

The essential shaping of medical anthropology as a modern subfield of anthropology is the result of the work of Erwin H. Ackerknecht. His considerable contributions to medical anthropology are embodied in publications extending over three decades, beginning in 1942 (1942a, 1942b, 1943a, 1943b, 1945a, 1945b, 1945c, 1946, 1947, 1948, 1949, 1958, 1965, 1971). During the same period he has also written extensively on a variety of topics in the history of medicine. Like Rivers, Ackerknecht was first a physician and later an anthropologist. Unlike Rivers, he has done little or no first-hand field research among non-Western peoples. His research has been primarily in libraries and with museum collections.

Ackerknecht (1942b, 1971) publicly acknowledges intellectual debts to the British functionalists, to several American workers representing various facets of the Boasian tradition, and, in particular, to "the theoretical and personal influence of Ruth Benedict" (1971:9). In a series of papers written during the 1940s (1942a, 1942b, 1945a, 1946), Ackerknecht presents his theoretical orientation, expressing it in the form of five generalizations. His five generalizations and some of the views with which they take issue are:

1. The significant unit of study in medical anthropology is not the single trait but the total cultural configuration of a society and the place that the "medical pattern" occupies within that totality. This generalization is a rejection of trait-list and noncontextual approaches, as typified by Clements.

2. There is not one primitive medicine, but many primitive medicines, perhaps as many as there are primitive cultures. This generalization extends Benedict's cultural relativism and her insistence of the uniqueness of each culture into the study of native medical patterns. It also counters the view of Garrison (1914, 1933)—one of the most influential medical historians during the first third of the twentieth century—that all forms of primitive medicine are identical.

3. The parts of the medical pattern, like those of the entire culture, are functionally interrelated, although the degree of functional integration of elements at both levels varies from one society to another. Ackerknecht's

latter qualification is a mild and implicit corrective for what he construes as Benedict's extreme position regarding the internal integration and consistency of a culture's parts.

4. Primitive medicine is best understood largely in terms of cultural belief and definition, that is, without consideration of biologic, epidemiologic, environmental, or material-culture factors. Ackerknecht questions the determinants or causes of native medical patterns only to explicitly reject what he calls the "great temptation to explain the causal necessity of things in terms of psycho-biology, environment or material culture ... " (1942b:574). Ackerknecht's view—that what non-Western peoples do and think about disease is relatively unaffected by the nature and distribution of disease or by considerations of adaptations to habitat, but that what they do and think is governed only or primarily by degree of fit with prevailing custom and belief—strongly shaped medical-anthropological inquiry during the 1940s and 1950s.

5. Finally, paralleling Rivers's and Clements's contentions, Ackerknecht insists that the varied manifestations of primitive medicine—however they differ and regardless of the acknowledged empirical efficacy of many primitive drugs and curing techniques—all constitute magic medicine. He denies the possibility of considering the medical patterns of primitive and of modern Western societies within a single universe of discourse on the grounds that "primitive medicine is primarily magico-religious, utilizing a few rational elements, while our [modern Western] medicine is predominantly rational and scientific employing a few magic elements" (1946:467).

Ackerknecht's conceptual model for dealing with primitive medicine, diagrammed in figure 3, is a sharply restricted one. He limits himself to two variables.

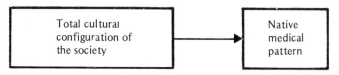

| Total cultural configuration of the society | → | Native medical pattern |

Figure 3.   Ackerknecht's Medical-Anthropological Model for Primitive Societies

His dependent variable is the complex of medical belief and behavior, that is, the prevailing medical pattern. He attempts to explain or account for it in terms of a single, global independent variable—the society's overall cultural configuration. His model also includes the postulate that the parts of the medical pattern stand in some degree of functional relationship to each other and to the total culture.

Essentially, Ackerknecht's orientation represents an explicit effort to integrate the two primary theoretical currents in the social-cultural anthropology of the time: American historicalism and cultural relativism, especially Benedict's configurational approach, and British functionalism.

Acknerknecht's model has undoubtedly been fruitful. By focusing on the importance of the totality of cultural behavior in shaping the society's medical elements, directing attention to the patterning of medical belief and practice, and emphasizing the functional interrelationships among the parts of the medical pattern and between the latter and the total culture, his orientation stimulated the development of medical-anthropological inquiry within the mainstream of social-cultural anthropology of the 1940s and early 1950s. At the same time, despite his recognition that the phenomena of health and disease were both cultural and biological (1945a), his approach helped to confine medical-anthropological study to a virtually exclusive focus on cultural parameters until the late 1950s.

Paul: System and System Change

The formulations of Rivers, Clements, and Ackerknecht address essentially basic rather than applied issues. In contrast, *Health, Culture and Community* (1955), edited by Benjamin D. Paul, is designed primarily as a contribution to applied anthropology and public health. The volume is both a reflection of and stimulus for the international public health movement of the late 1940s and 1950s. Paul's central concern is not to advance basic research or theory but to examine "the immediate situation where medicine and community meet" (1955:4). To do so, Paul utilizes a model that differs from those of his predecessors, one oriented around the concept of system.

The term *system* receives no special emphasis in Paul's volume, and the concept is not among those elucidated in a summary review of key concepts. Nonetheless, system constitutes Paul's strategic and integrating conceptual model. His system is manifest if, following Riley (1963:10-11), we adopt a minimal definition of system as (1) an entity that is (2) made up of identifiable parts, which are (3) mutually interdependent, so that each part tends to influence and be influenced by other parts, and (4) together the several parts and their interrelationships form the system as a whole. Two of Paul's integrative and interpretive statements illustrate the focus on system and system change.

> *The habits and beliefs of people in a given community are not separate items in a series but elements of a cultural system. The elements are not all equally integrated, however; some are central to the system, others peripheral. Hence, some cultural elements can be altered or replaced with little effort, others only by applying great force (1955:15).*
> *One way to learn what a particular organ contributes to the functioning of the whole organic system is to see what happens when that organ is altered or removed. The same method applies in the study of social systems (1955:325).*

Paul departs from Ackerknecht not in rejecting the latter's ideas but in taking them a step further. He does so by posing a set of questions that Ackerknecht had never addressed. If we view culture as a system and the medical pattern as one of its subsystems, what happens to the system and subsystem when they are disturbed, that is when new health-related elements are introduced? Further, what happens to newly introduced elements in the context of a given sociocultural system?

Two propostions are fundamental to Paul's approach:

1. The responses of a given sociocultural (and medical) system to the introduction of new elements are to be explained not solely by the nature of the system nor by the nature and mode of introduction of new elements, but by the complex interaction of both.

2. Reciprocal or feedback processes occur. The introduction of new health-related elements can be expected to affect the host sociocultural (and medical) system. In turn, the latter will also affect (shape or reinterpret) the new elements.

Figure 4 below embodies Paul's primary variables and basic propositions.

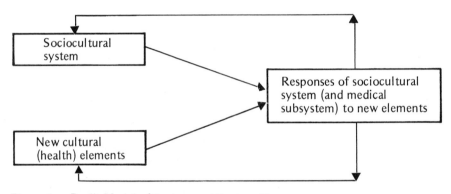

Figure 4.   Paul's Model of System and System Change

In at least two respects, Paul's model represents an important departure from the outlooks of Rivers, Clements, and Ackerknecht. For one, conceptual limitations in the models of his predecessors restrict medical-anthropological inquiry to traditional or relatively simple societies. In contrast, Paul's system model removes this constraint and permits the medical systems of modern or complex communities to be as appropriate for study as those of traditional groups. For another, despite differences in theoretical orientation, his three predecessors are similar in that they employ essentially static models—they dissect native medical systems at rest. Paul's orientation, on the other hand, requires a dynamic model, one that can deal with the nature and consequences of change.

In one respect, however, Paul's system model retains a significant feature of the orientations of Rivers, Clements, and Ackerknecht. Paul treats culture as though it were essentially a closed system and excludes from his model factors of biology and environmental pressure. While Paul acknowledges the fact and importance of broader ecological considerations, they are dealt with largely as background, and their interrelationships with social and cultural variables are only lightly explored.

We now turn to the final and most recent theoretical orientation, one that not only incorporates Paul's system approach but comprehends factors of biology and environmental exigency as well.

Ecological Approach with Cultural and Biological Parameters

Until about the 1960s, theoretical orientations in medical anthropology revolved exclusively around the ideas of scholars closely identified with a single sector of anthropological interest—the social-cultural. However, the expositors of an orientation that developed rapidly during the 1960s are more closely associated with biological rather than with social-cultural anthropology. The approach cannot readily be delineated by reference to a single author. An explicit and vigorous theoretical statement has been offered by Alland (1966, 1970), and notable contributions have been made by Livingstone (1958), Wiesenfeld (1967), Dunn (1968), McCracken (1971), Damon (1975), and others.

The orientation—for convenience let us call it "ecological"—is broadly concerned with dimensions of disease. Disease is often treated as a dependent variable, that is, how do factors of biology, culture, and/or environmental pressure influence the process and distribution of disease? Sometimes, however, disease is treated as an independent variable—what are the sociocultural, including the cognitive, consequences and concomitants of given diseases in particular groups? Anthropologists have given the approach various labels—dynamics of health status, ecology, medical ecology, epidemiology, social epidemiology (see Polgar 1962; Scotch 1963a; Fábrega 1972; Lieban 1973; Colson and Selby 1974). Alland refers to the orientation as "ecological with the focus on cultural and biological parameters" (1966). Its relative newness may be gauged by Scotch's observation, as recently as the early 1960s, that with some exceptions the area of sociocultural aspects of disease has been largely neglected in anthropological research and theory (1963).

The root of the ecological orientation is essentially a "scientific revolution" (see Kuhn 1962) in evolutionary biology that erupted along a broad front of biological disciplines during the 1940s and that laid the necessary theoretical foundations for dealing with human evolution and adaption as the complex interaction of cultural and biological factors under given environmental conditions. That biological more than social-cultural anthropologists have been centrally associated with the ecological approach in medical anthropology is by no means fortuitous. Because of the nature of the scientific revolution and its understandable consequence, the impact on anthropology was most immediate in the discipline's biological sector.

Until about the 1940s, as Dobzhansky (1951) observes, each biological science tended to produce ideas and conclusions about evolution that were distinct from and often inconsistent with those of other biological fields. Although workers from genetics, systematics, embryology, comparative anatomy, ecology, paleontology, zoology, botany, and other disciplines were interested in evolutionary problems, they had neither a common language nor many shared planes of discourse. Work in evolutionary biology tended to follow three primary lines, each involving a different and seemingly imcompatible theoretical orientation: natural selection, Mendelian genetics, and mutation.

By the early 1940s, it became evident to a growing number and variety of biological scholars that the three orientations and a host of separate developments among many biological fields were not only compatible but could shed more light on evolutionary processes in combination than was possible for any one approach or field alone. With relative suddenness during the decade, the scientific revolution occurred, that is, the three orientations were synthesized into a theory of evolution.

The theory proceeds on the proposition that populations—not genes, individual organisms, or species—are the basic units of evolutionary change, and it relies on the statistics of population dynamics as a primary tool for the study of evolutionary processes. The theory might be briefly stated as follows. Any population has a pool of hereditary characteristics and exists in an environment. Hereditary variation in the population is produced by two means. One is genetic combination and recombination essentially according to Mendelian laws of inheritance. The other is mutation, especially of the small and virtually imperceptible variety. The keystone evolutionary process is Darwinian natural selection, in which environmental exigencies result in differential selection of a population's hereditary characteristics, promoting or conferring advantage on some at the expense of others. No one of the processes singly is the cause of evolution; rather, evolution proceeds by the intricate interaction and complementarity of all three.

Within the broad framework of this theory humans are seen as evolutionarily unique, utilizing and transmitting culture as a prime and highly efficient instrument for adapting to and controlling their environments. Fundamentally, however, human adaptation, always with reference to given environmental parameters, is a mutually interactive cultural and biological process. Man changes his environment through culture. This changed environment then acts as a selective agent on man's physical structure as well as on his behavior (Alland 1970). Alland presents a general statement of the interrelatedness of culture, biology, environment, and disease in the adaptive process:

> In general, the incidence of disease is related to genetic and nongenetic factors. Any change in a behavioral system is likely to have medical consequences, some of which will produce changes in the genetic system. On the other hand, disease-induced changes in the genetic structure can affect the behavioral system. Such effects may be the result of population restructuring or the emergence of new immunological patterns which alter the possibilities for niche exploitation. In addition, induced or natural alterations in the environmental field provide new selective pressures relating to health and disease which must be met through a combination of somatic and nonsomatic adaptations (1970:49-50).

The ecological orientation conceptualizes health and disease, more or less in Lieban's terms, as "measures of the effectiveness with which human groups, combining biological and cultural resources, adapt to their environments" (1973:1031). The model also views health and disease as they affect culture and biology and as they respond to the environment.

Figure 5 is a highly generalized depiction of the ecological model. It does not describe any one piece of research with any specifity but attempts to set forth the broad and generic framework underlying much recent medical-anthropological research within the ecological approach.

The position of the box marked "medical system" in figure 5 varies with cultural evolution. In primitive and technologically simple societies past and present, medical theories and specific therapeutic procedures had and have less direct impact on the control of disease than those customs and behaviors outside the medical system, which serve to prevent or minimize disease through positive feedback from the environment (*see* Alland, 1970). However, among populations that possess advanced technology, full-time health practitioners, and a more or less systematic body of codified medical knowledge, the medical system comes to play an increasingly independent and significant therapeutic and preventive role in the total adaptive picture.

As noted, in medical anthropology empirical research utilizing the ecological approach was first contributed by workers with primary interests in biological problems and human evolution. Thus, Livingstone's classic study (1958) relates the distribution of the sickle-cell trait in West Africa to factors of cultural and biological evolution and their interplay under given environmental conditions. He attempts to account for the trait's different frequencies by recourse to the operation of multiple and interrelated variables: diffusion of new technology and crops, modification of tropical forest habitats, population increase, spread of malarial mosquitoes, and effects of malaria on populations and of the sickle-cell gene on malaria.

Subsequently, Wiesenfeld (1967) refines Livingstone's findings. Analyzing data from sixty societies in both East and West Africa, Wiesenfeld finds that the particular type of agricultural system significantly affects rates of the sickle-cell trait and of malaria. Specifically, he reports that reliance on the root and tree crops that go with the "Malaysian agricultural complex" (Murdock, 1959) creates a more malarious environment, leading to selective advantage for individuals with the sickle-cell trait and to changes in the population's gene pool over time. Wiesenfeld presents a hypothesis of biology and culture interacting together in a stepwise fashion. That is, given the intensely malarious environment and the given agricultural innovation, biological change in the gene pool helps maintain the cultural change that had previously led to the new cellular environmental change. The biological change allows further development of the cultural adaptation, and the latter in turn increases the selective pressure to maintain the biological change.

Dunn (1968) combines limited data with reasoned speculation about morbidity and mortality in relation to the ecology of hunter-gatherer life and raises significant issues regarding diseases as agents of natural selection and as dependent

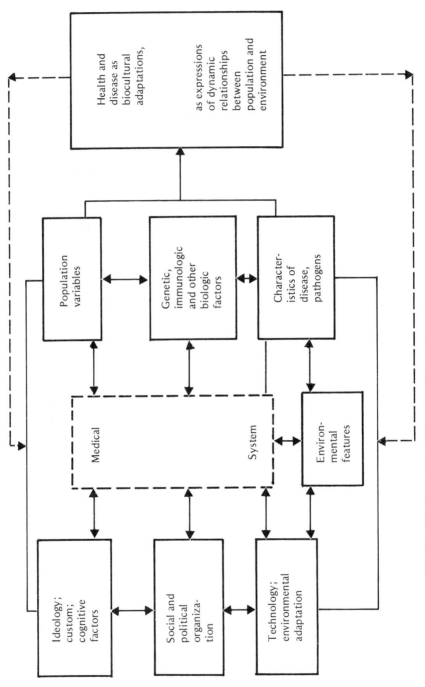

Figure 5.   Ecological Model with Cultural and Biological Parameters

and independent variables affecting population size and stability.

McCracken (1971) recasts in broad ecological terms a problem that anthropologists had formerly defined solely as one of cultural conditioning: the fact that some peoples have an aversion to milk. Testing the hypothesis that disliking milk is not simply a cultural but a biocultural trait, McCracken attempts to explain differentials in the worldwide distribution of lactase deficiency (or lactose intolerance). He postulates that lactase deficiency was the normal and universal adult condition prior to animal domestication and dairying and that the introduction of lactose into adult diets in certain cultures generated selective pressures among the populations concerned, favoring the genotype for adult lactose tolerance. To be sure, McCracken's evidence supports the notion that the long-term experience of populations with the production and consumption of milk is closely related to lactase deficiency rates. However, confirmation of McCracken's genetic hypothesis is still an open question. In any event, McCracken's effort to relate cultural evolution and cultural practices to the distribution of a biological trait is a provocative example of ecologically framed research on the interrelationships between cultural and biological variables.

In addition to medical-anthropological research related to evolutionary or diachronic issues, increasing attention is also being given to synchronic, cross-sectional, and contemporary problems within broad biocultural frameworks. Fabrega (1972) and Colson and Selby (1974) review some of the latter work, and Montgomery (1973) provides a succinct summary of recent research on ecological aspects of health and disease in local populations. Indeed, Montgomery's review indicates that the two things Bates (1953) called for more than twenty years ago—greater emphasis on the study of disease as an environmental factor influencing human development and the combining of medical and anthropological interests in single investigators or working teams—are now occurring. Other recent examples of this combining of interests are the studies of Boyden (1970) and Bahnson et al. (1974), in which medical workers and anthropologists (and other social scientists) deal with the interplay between disease and culture within broadly similar ecological frameworks.

Significantly, the broad ecological approach brings the single trait back into medical anthropology for the first time since Clements's work in the 1930s. Ackerknecht had argued forcefully in the 1940s that single traits have no meaning outside the context of their organization and patterning into larger wholes. Within the terms of his cultural-pattern-and-configuration model, Ackerknecht was right. However, modern workers—for example, Livingstone, Wiesenfeld, McCracken, Gadjusek (1963), and others—have been finding it conceptually and methodologically advantageous to focus on the frequencies and distributions of specific biological traits, relating them to more or less specific cultural practices and usages, always within the framework of broad ecological models.

It will be of great interest to observe how the combining of cultural and biological variables develops in medical anthropology in the years to come. Several workers view the prospects as highly promising. Alland contends that, given the broad ecological approach, medical anthropology is a major link between physical and cultural anthropology. Katz and Wallace predict that "biological and cultural anthropologists will soon deal with problems of behavior and disease in the same ecological framework . . . [involving the] . . . interactions of biology, the socio-cultural system, the environment [living and nonliving] , and population size and structure as continuously interacting and essential variables with various degrees of independence and dependence" (1974).

Discussion

There have been both continuities and shifts in theoretical orientations in medical anthropology over the past half-century. As noted, the common point of departure for the field over the years has consisted of three empirical generalizations: (1) the universality of disease as part of the human condition, (2) the fact that all human groups develop methods and roles for coping with disease, and (3) the fact that all human groups develop beliefs and perceptions for cognizing disease. All three have been recognized for a long time, but until relatively recently only the second and third generalizations—those dealing with sociocultural dimensions—have provided the subject matter for research. The first—involving biological parameters—has been held constant and thereby excluded from the purview of medical-anthropological study.

Thus, Rivers, before 1920, employed cultural practices or methods as his dependent variable and sought to explain the latter as a function of either magical or religious belief. Clements, in the early 1930s, focused on certain cultural beliefs—primitive concepts of disease causation—and, treating them as isolated culture traits, endeavored to chart their spatial distributions and relative time sequences. Ackerknecht, largely in the 1940s, built on Rivers's work by conceiving both belief and practice as components of a people's medical pattern and attempted to account for the latter in terms of its functional and historical linkages with the larger culture.

Although Ackerknecht's theoretical contribution dwarfed those of his prede-cessors, the orientations of Rivers, Clements, and Ackerknecht shared certain im-portant similarities. Each of the three viewed primitive and modern medicine in dichotomous terms, conceived the former as essentially magical or religious, focused on it to the virtual exclusion of modern or "rational" medicine, and dealt with it in conceptually static terms.

Paul's model, in the 1950s, ignored the work of Clements but represented both continuity with and departure from the approaches of Rivers and Acker-knecht. Paul proceeded cumulatively from Rivers's contribution by viewing health-related belief and practice as part of culture, and he also utilized Ackerknecht's postulates regarding the cultural patterning of medical elements and their func-tional interrelationships with other parts of the cultural totality. However, he diverged from his predecessors in accommodating their approaches to a system model and was thereby able to eliminate the conceptual gulf between primitive and modern medicine and to deal with problems of change. At the same time, Paul followed earlier workers in holding factors of biology and environmental exigency relatively constant and in limiting his parameters to cultural variables.

The final orientation reviewed here, an ecological approach involving cultural and biological parameters, differs from previous orientations in several respects. Whereas earlier approaches were derived from concepts in social-cultural anthropology and the social sciences, the ecological model by contrast owes its basic lineaments to revolutionary theoretical syntheses in the biological sciences, specifically in evolutionary biology. Moreover, the most important initial contributions based on this orientation have been made not by social-cultural anthropologists but by workers interested in biological and human evolutionary problems.

The orientation departs strikingly from previous models in that it comprehends biological variables, viewing health and disease (whether as dependent or independent variables) as expressions of dynamic relationships between populations, their cultures, and their environments. Thus, the scope of the ecological model includes societies and populations, the behavior of human groups and of microbiota, perceptions of the environment and primary environmental features, definitions of disease and disease itself, ethnomedicine (and traditional medical systems) and modern medicine.

At the same time, the ecological orientation enjoys definite continuity with and builds on preceding approaches. It accommodates Rivers's fundamental insight that medical beliefs and practices are part of culture. It even resurrects Clements's use of the single trait as a unit of study and comparison, but on a more viable conceptual and methodological basis. It incorporates Ackerknecht's emphasis on the cultural patterning of medical belief and behavior and the functional interdependence of medicine with other parts of the total culture. It embodies Paul's system approach and interest in change. However, previous insights are accommodated within a new framework. To be sure, cultural variables are seen to count, and to count heavily, but in terms of their interplay with biologic factors in multivariate ecological systems.

Human Adaptability, Culture, and Disease Stress

The articles in this section, while covering a wide range of subjects, collectively illustrate the importance of ecology in medical anthropology. Each paper discusses health and disease in terms of a complex system of interactions occurring between human groups and their physical, biological and cultural environments. Because these interactions vary, humans in different regions and societies are faced with different disease pressures and adaptive challenges. Several factors affect these ecological interactions. For example, climate, altitude, vegetation, animal life, the size and density of human populations, dietary habits, technological innovations, social stratification, and beliefs or values are but a few of the variables which influence patterns of health. What is important about the articles in this section is that they examine adaptation and disease in an ecological perspective, one which views the systematic interrelationships between man and his surroundings.

The opening paper, by Ellis Kerley and William Bass, explores paleopathology, the study of morbidity and mortality in prehistoric populations. This field provides the historical perspective needed to understand disease as a changing phenomenon. The article by Edward Hunt also adds a time dimension. By comparing longevity in contemporary chimpanzee and human populations we can reconstruct demographic principles of health and adaptation in the earliest human communities.

People everywhere must adapt to their environments. Our primary avenue of adaptation is culture, although there are many other ways by which humans survive. Gabriel Lasker's paper is important because it defines and illustrates genetic, physiological, and acclimatizational aspects of adaptation.

The diseases that affect human groups are products of ecological conditions, as illustrated in the paper by George Armelagos, Alan Goodman, and Kenneth Jacobs. These authors set forth a truly commendable model on the ecology of disease. This model is highly relevant to all articles in this section, particularly those appearing after their paper. The reader is encouraged to give considerable study to

41

this model, for it will improve one's understanding of subsequent materials on the effects of cultural variables on the epidemeology of disease.

George Armelagos and John Dewey provide data in the fifth article that strongly support and exemplify the model mentioned above. In this paper the authors examine cultural evolution as a process affecting both the type and frequency of infectious disease in human populations. Later papers complement and give more detailed examples of the main point in the Armelagos-Dewey article: as the complexity of a society changes so too will the diseases confronting that society.

Ecology emphasizes the analysis of interconnecting parts within a system. The utility of such analysis is seen in Edward Hunt's discussion of specific health problems in traditional non-Western societies. To understand any disease one must examine a multiplicity of interconnected factors, as shown with respect to sickle-cell, kuru, and other conditions.

The next five papers cover a central theme, one which is defined and amply illustrated in the previous articles. Culture is an integral component in the etiology of disease. These papers look at health problems in societies that differ markedly in terms of size, settlement pattern, subsistence, and internal social complexity. Because of these differences people in hunting-and-gathering societies, as shown in the article by Frederick Dunn, experience diseases uncommon in larger, agrarian-based communities. As people turned from hunting and gathering to agriculture their diseases also changed, a subject discussed by Gina Kolata. The Dunn and Kolata articles and the one by Francis Black, which concerns tribal societies in the Amazon Basin, provide interesting cases of why disease stress changes as characteristics of culture change. Their results are made particularly meaningful when compared to the research of Don Brothwell, who examines pollution and disease, and Denis Burkitt, who describes health problems common in modern civilizations.

An ecological approach enables the medical anthropologist to learn a great deal about disease in prehistoric populations, the effects of adaptations on the human body, and why cultural evolution and changing societal characteristics have played such key roles in the history and patterning of disease in diverse human communities.

Ellis R. Kerley
William M. Bass

Paleopathology:
meeting ground for many disciplines

Paleopathology is the study of prehistoric disease and, as such, deals predominantly with skeletal remains and prehistoric populations. In its broadest sense, paleopathology deals with diseases in animal as well as human tissues, and consequently it is a field of interest to many scientific disciplines. When infection, malfunction, or trauma affect bones and teeth, the lesions or other abnormalities can be observed and studied, and in many cases the cause can be determined.

Evidence of disease in prehistoric populations is obtained from (i) human and animal remains and (ii) prehistoric art. In the literature there are various reports of abnormalities in the bones of prehistoric animals, but the first serious controversy involving possible abnormality in a prehistoric human specimen occurred in 1896 when the eminent German pathologist Rudolf Virchow questioned the authenticity of the Neander Valley specimen, and of Neanderthal man as a human fossil population, and suggested that the Neanderthal specimens were the remains of abnormal modern men (1). From that time on, attempts to detect and interpret abnormalities in prehistoric specimens have increased, and in recent years the methods of investigating prehistoric disease have become more complex as new techniques have been developed. The publication in 1923 of Moodie's monumental treatise on the subject (2) was a milestone in paleopathology. An equally important contribution was Ruffer's study of disease among the ancient Egyptians (3), wherein he introduced the microscopic study of lesions in mummified tissue. Other authors have dealt with specific populations or diseases; Hooton (4), for example, dealt with the Pecos Pueblo, and Herbert Williams (5), with syphilis in the New World. Virchow himself was interested in the possibility of detecting prehistoric disease, despite his declarations against the authenticity of Neanderthal man. In the United States one of the most eminent champions of paleopathology was Aleš Hrdlička.

Since knowledge of the diseases, abnormalities, and epidemiology of prehistoric populations can shed light on hereditary relationships, on the adaptations of populations to disease environments, and on the times and routes of migration of peoples during prehistoric times, it is small wonder that anthropologists have long been interested in this field. Since not only skeletal material but disease itself is the subject matter of paleopathology, many disciplines find a meeting ground in these studies.

From *Science*, Vol. 157, pp. 638-644, 11 August 1967. Copyright 1967 by the American Association for the Advancement of Science.

Information That Can Be Derived from Paleopathology

Examination of individual skeletons can yield an indication of abnormalities, tumors, malformations, fractures (in particular, healing or healed fractures), and other skeletal pathology. One can document the number of skeletal abnormalities in any given population, keeping in mind the fact that not all disease is skeletal and that not all members of a population are found in any archeological site. Sometimes it is not possible to identify the disease even when the skeleton shows obvious abnormality. One cannot distinguish between severe infectious processes of relatively short duration, but it is usually possible to distinguish between infection, disturbances of growth, and simple reparative processes. It is almost always possible to distinguish between major categories of lesions, such as uncomplicated injury and infection. It is possible to distinguish between infections, malformations, tumors, metabolic disturbances, and the like. Though there are exceptions, usually a specimen can be assigned to a major disease category. Not infrequently the causative factor of a particular type of lesion can be determined. Certain types of inflammation are so distinctive that we can infer the causative factor to have been a lack of a specific vitamin. In the case of fractures. the time that has elapsed since injury occurred can be determined by the amount of healing that has taken place. Cut wounds of bone have a fairly distinctive appearance, and the direction of slice can be determined even after extensive healing has occurred. Projectile points penetrating bone leave matching wounds.

The disease pattern of a prehistoric population can be described statistically. In this procedure the number of individuals with a given lesion and the number of different types of abnormality found in the archeological population are recorded. The numbers of individuals having lesions of specific types should be recorded for each level of an archeological site. If many individuals at a given level were affected, one could infer probable famine, epidemic, or war, or, possibly, migration and first contact between populations. One might find, following migration and contact, new infectious diseases, or new hereditary diseases resulting from the introduction of new genes. Such introduced diseases would be found after the date of contact but not before. Diseases found evenly distributed throughout all archeological levels would probably be endemic, hereditary, or the result of traditional cultural practices.

Some environmental factors causing disease and death are seasonal. Famine occurs primarily in late winter and early spring, before new crops have been harvested and before edible animals become plentiful. Floods generally occur in the spring as the snow melts. Pneumonia tends to occur when the season is changing—in early winter and early spring. So it is of some importance to determine during what season the individual was buried. The presence of insect remains often provides the key; the presence of insect exuviae and of numerous maggot remains suggests summer burial (6), while their absence suggests that burial occurred in the winter.

Examination of a Skeleton

In paleopathologic studies the entire skeleton must be examined, not just the areas of obvious abnormality, and any skeletons found nearby in an archeological site should also be examined for possible bearing on the abnormality. For one thing, any abnormalities that affect the skeleton generally—such as osteoporosis, osteomalacia, or some of the anemias—can be misinterpreted if only one bone is examined. Some injuries and certain other disease conditions—such as Paget's disease, syphilis, and even leprosy—affect more than one bone. Sometimes the distribution of the lesions throughout the skeleton is important in diagnosis. This is particularly true in the case of syphilis, malnutrition, and certain types of atrophy. Gross examination is still the best general method for determining prehistoric disease.

Radiologic examination is essential for assessing abnormality in archeological material. It is possible to investigate the internal structure of bones and the nature of the disease process by means of radiographs. X-ray diffraction or microradiography may give some indication of the length of time a skeleton has been buried by giving information on the mineral content of the bone.

Microscopic examination of skeletal lesions is important, too, in interpreting structural changes in bones. At certain stages in fracture repair there is a considerable amount of resorption of the cortex adjacent to the fracture. At other stages there is a buildup of callus. In some diseases, also, there are resorptive and reparative phases, evidence of which can best be identified through microscopic inspection of ground sections of the affected bone. Also, alterations in the normal structural and growth patterns of bone can be determined microscopically, and the skeletal age of an individual can be determined through microscopic examination of cross-sections of the bones of the leg. In addition, hair is examined for the purpose of determining an individual's race or of detecting the presence of arsenic or other heavy metals, and skin from mummies is examined microscopically, particularly if there is any evidence of lesions, scars, tattoos, or the like. Fingernails, when present, are examined microscopically for evidences of injury or of fluctuations in the growth patterns of the nails.

It is possible in many cases to determine an individual's blood type from his skeleton by pulverizing the cancellous ends of the long bones or vertebrae and soaking the powder in saline solution before subjecting it to serologic techniques (8). In the future it may be possible to correlate certain anemias with certain serologic reactions in the skeleton, but at present only the ABO blood types can be determined in purely skeletal material. There are some indications that, under certain postmortem conditions, the antibody reactions to even these blood types can be misleading (9).

Microradiography in combination with light microscopy can show minute variations in calcification, in areas adjacent to skeletal abnormality, which result from arrested growth during periods of physiologic crisis. Radiographs may show these arrested growth lines near the ends of the long bones (10), and the time from severe illness to death (or to adulthood) can be calculated from the distance from the line of arrested growth to the epiphysial line (11). The electron microscope has not as yet been brought to bear on much archeologic material, partly because much of the organic structure has often been lost and partly because it is difficult to prepare purely skeletal material for electron-microscopic processing. It is probable, however, that this instrument will prove useful in assessing archeologic skeletal abnormality in the future, perhaps in the identification of specific viruses or bacteria.

Other Sources of Information

Information concerning the disease pattern in prehistoric populations is derived from paintings, figurines, and pottery, as well as from skeletons. Artifacts depicting certain types of disease have been found in Egypt, in parts of the Near East, and in Central and South America (12).

Therapeutic devices are often found near archeological skeletons; these include splints, braces, surgical instruments, and sometimes bone or stone figures. Of course, kidney stones and gallstones are occasionally found with skeletons (2).

Analysis of the climate and ecology that existed at the time an archeological population inhabited a particular area can be enlightening in terms of the disease pattern. Some parasites live only under certain climatic conditions or only in certain areas. One would not expect to find hookworm among the Eskimo. On the other hand, some diseases are endemic to certain regions, and probably also were in the past. Provided there has been no severe alteration of climate or environmental conditions, it is unlikely that a particular disease would have been endemic, in prehistoric times, in areas now very different from those where it is endemic today.

One major controversy in paleopathology has been the possibility that syphilis originated in the New World; among the skeletal specimens available there are some that support the view that it did (5). The problem of the origin of syphilis is an interesting example of the types of data that can be brought together to provide information concerning prehistoric disease patterns. Pre-Columbian skeletons from various parts of the New World exhibit lesions that resemble those of syphilis in modern populations. These range from lesions that might possibly have been luetic to others that are exact duplications of modern syphilitic bone lesions. For years many reputable scientists have interpreted these as evidence that syphilis was present in the New World before the time of Columbus and probably originated here. Other equally reputable scholars have maintained that one cannot be sure what these lesions represent, since the treponema spirochetes that are known to cause syphilis are no longer present in skeletons. They argue, further, that syphilis and yaws produce similar lesions, that both are spirochetal in origin, and that therefore one cannot be distinguished from the other. This view tends to confuse the disease syphilis, which had been known and recognized for centuries before the spirochete was discovered, with the diagnostic tests for syphilis devised by Wassermann and Kahn.

Syphilis, which was named for Fracastoro's tragic hero, was enjoyed by the populace of Europe without benefit of any knowledge concerning the causative microbe. History records the first occurrence of this disease in Barcelona in 1493, when de Isla treated Vincente Pinzón, captain of the *Pinta*, for the disease which later came to be known as the great pox that spread across Europe (13) with the advancing and retreating armies of France, Spain and Italy. The skeletal lesions of this disease were well known, and it is interesting to note that most of the early physicians who had wide experience in dealing with syphilis recognized the skeletal lesions in cases of known syphilis and in several of the pre-Columbian specimens (5). With the increased dependence on serologic tests as diagnostic tools and the advent of antibiotics came a decrease in the frequency of tertiary syphilis. Specimens of skeletal lues are seldom seen today except in older museum collections such as the extensive collections of the Armed Forces Institute of Pathology Medical Museum in Washington, D.C.

Some of the pre-Columbian New World skeletons have lesions which are typical of those caused by known and documented syphilis in some of the older pathologic collections. It may be said with certainty that syphilis *can* cause such lesions and that they usually have a particular distribution throughout the body, the frontal bone and the tibiae, fibulae, and distal humeri being the areas most commonly affected.

On the other hand, very few diseases other than syphilis are known to raise such lesions in bones. In some skeletons from the southeastern United States the lesions are found in the skeletal areas affected by syphilis, where destructive foci are surrounded by sclerotic bone. Other disease processes that might produce skeletal lesions similar to those found in these specimens would include the following:

1. Osteomyelitis, which is a rather active destruction of cortical and cancellous bone, accompanied by the formation of a sleeve of reactive involucrum. Only in cases of very low-grade infection does one find destruction and repair of bone so closely adjacent as in luetic skeletal specimens.

2. Tuberculosis. This is a low-grade inflammation, but it affects the spine with greatest frequency (which syphilis does not) and the epiphyseal regions of long bones.

3. Paget's disease. This affects the skull and tibiae as lues does, but Paget's disease expands the medullary cavity, whereas syphilis contracts it (14). In the skull, Paget's disease usually affects the parietals first, whereas syphilis most commonly strikes the frontal bone first and usually produces discrete foci of inflammation surrounded by sclerotic reparative bone.

4. Yaws (frambesia). This may produce bone lesions resembling those of syphilis, and it is caused by a spirochete closely related to the *Treponema pallidum* of syphilis. Some skeletal lesions could be the result of either yaws or lues, but certain lesions are distinctively syphilitic in appearance and distribution. These include the small, focal lesions of bone in areas of sclerotic reactive bone, the stellate scars of the frontal bone, and lesions having a

typical distribution in frontal bone, tibiae, distal humeri, and hands (15).

The epidemiologist contributes the additional information that, whereas syphilis is not limited by climate, since it is venereally contracted, yaws is a disease of the tropics and has never been endemic to the United States.

Quite often it is not possible to say with certainty that any given lesion represents a specific disease. However, if a lesion on a prehistoric bone is precisely similar to lesions known to be caused by a given disease in living individuals and if no other disease is known to cause similar lesions, it is reasonable to infer that the lesion on the prehistoric bone was caused by the same factor that causes such lesions in modern populations.

Interested Disciplines

Because of its varied aspects, paleopathology is of interest to workers in many disciplines.

Physicians in general are interested in the origins of diseases and in fluctuations in the prevalence and virulence of certain diseases in historic and prehistoric times. Having some knowledge of past history, one is better able to predict the course of future events.

Orthopedists in particular are interested in paleopathology, since it deals primarily with skeletal disease and skeletal evidence of disease. Such studies enable them to see the consequences of untreated fractures, injuries, growth abnormalities, and other diseases of the skeletal system and of untreated bone tumors and arthritis. Among the artifacts of certain prehistoric populations, such as the early Egyptians and some of the American Indian groups, are early forms of splints, braces, and other orthopedic devices, and orthopedists can compare the effectiveness of these early forms of treatment with that of modern methods.

The radiologist also finds much of interest in paleopathology. In dealing with prehistoric, as with modern, skeletal abnormalities, x-rays of affected areas are essential to an adequate diagnosis and understanding of the disease process involved. The radiologist is able to interpret bone diseases, as revealed by x-ray, whether they are prehistoric or recent. However, lesions in ancient bones often look quite different from similar lesions in living persons (or in fresh cadavers), and many orthopedists and radiologists welcome the opportunity to examine dry, macerated specimens of known pathology.

Epidemiologists study the temporal and geographic distribution of diseases and are interested in tracing evidence of disease in populations back into prehistoric times, particularly evidence of epidemic diseases such as leprosy, syphilis, malaria, and tuberculosis.

Many obstetricians are interested in the treatment of pregnancy and the methods of obstetric delivery in both prehistoric and modern primitive societies, and in abnormalities of fetal development. Abner Weisman, a New York obstetrician, has collected numerous prehistoric clay figurines from Mexico that depict possible abnormalities and treatment. Surgeons study the numerous specimens showing evidence of surgery which are to be found in archeological collections. Many of the pre-Inca and Inca skulls show evidence of trephining (16). The instruments used in such operations have been preserved, and the operations have been depicted in the art of the Incas and the Egyptians.

Prehistoric remains are usually skeletal, but mummified remains which show evidence of soft-tissue lesions are occasionally recovered. The skeleton itself can provide evidence of prolonged cardiac or pulmonary insufficiency, of tuberculosis, and of the anemias—all matters of interest to the internist as well as to the anthropologist.

Dentists (17) and orthodontists study the teeth of prehistoric peoples, particularly in populations that had a gritty diet. They are interested in the growth of untreated abnormal teeth, in the effects of diet upon teeth and tooth wear, in the alignment of teeth, and in the relation of dental caries to diet and drinking water. Orthodontists are particularly interested in the effects of tooth wear on the spacing of teeth and on the angulation of the rami of the mandibles in prehistoric populations where the wear was excessive.

Manifestations of the diseases of old age and of senility in primitive and prehistoric populations provide the gerontologist with information that has bearing on modern problems of biologic aging. A psychiatrist finds much of interest in the mutilations, scarifications and decorations of prehistoric peoples, and in burial customs and other cultural practices that have left their marks upon the skeleton or are depicted in stone or paint.

Among specialists in fields other than medicine, the physical anthropologist has an important role in these investigations. It is his task to describe the physical characteristics of archeological populations in terms of the approximate age at death of individuals, the sex ratio, the ages of survival for male and female, the general stature and physical appearance of the population, and the diseases manifested in the skeletons. He is particularly interested in the physical effects of cultural practices (effects such as cranial deformation or alterations of bone structure from squatting), in growth, and in the response of the skeleton to disease. Genetic skeletal characteristics and hereditary diseases that have affected the skeleton indicate hereditary differences or similarities between populations. So do growth patterns and differences in stature. Evidence of trauma is found in some of the earliest human remains where bone has formed in an injured muscle (myositis ossificans). The left femur of *Pithecanthropus erectus* shows an exostosis which probably originated in this way. Occasionally misinterpretation of a skeletal abnormality has led to an erroneous conclusion. One example is the reconstruction of Neanderthal posture from one skeleton which Straus and Cave show (18) to have been severely afflicted by osteoarthritis.

In the field of the history of medicine, the physical anthropologist has furnished much information on early amputations. Stewart (19) has found evidence of the removal of an arm in the Neanderthal skeleton from Shanidar, Iraq, dated about 40,000 B.C. Brothwell and Møller-Christensen (20) report a possible case of amputation in Egypt, in a skeleton dated about 2000 B.C. (19th Dynasty). Various explanations of amputation of parts of hands or limbs have been proposed: it may have been an expression of mourning, a result of battle injuries, surgical amputation required by infections, or a form of punishment, especially of thieves or prisoners. Brothwell and Møller-Christensen make a strong case for their conclusion, from study of the Egyptian skeleton of 2000 B.C., that amputation of the right hand was a means of recording the number of prisoners after a conflict; a scene painted on the walls of the temple of Rameses III shows this recording procedure.

The cultural anthropologist (a category which includes the archeologist) looks for the relationship of skeletal injuries and physical characteristics of skeletons at the archeological site to pictorial depiction of cultural practices, migrations, contacts with other archeologic populations, and warfare. The ethnologist is interested in prehistoric medical practices as well.

Geneticists are interested in the evolution and distribution of hereditary diseases in prehistoric populations, and in the possibility of evaluating the influences of heredity versus those of environment in producing certain effects upon the skeleton.

Human paleontologists and evolutionists study the selective force that certain injuries and diseases may exert on evolving populations (21). The relationship between malaria and sickle-cell anemia is of interest, since populations with high frequencies of sickle-cell genes may have a greater immunity to malaria than those lacking such genes. Sickle-cell anemia often prevents the effective breeding of homozygous individuals and may strongly affect the nature and course of evolution in a population.

Zoologists and vertebrate paleontologists investigate prehistoric distributions of skeletal lesions in extinct species, and life forms in the entire zoologic realm.

Historians are interested in the events leading up to the beginning of recorded history—for example, in the prehistoric occurrence of diseases, such as syphilis and leprosy, which became important during historical times.

Present and Future of Paleopathology

Thus, paleopathology is at present a field of interest to many disciplines rather than a science in itself. As such, it can call upon methods and techniques derived from many fields. Information is obtained from the orthopedic pathologist, the orthopedist, and the radiologist, each of whom examines prehistoric diseased material from his own specialized point of view. It is also obtained from the physical anthropologist, the archeologist, the ethnologist, the paleontologist, the geologist, and occasionally, the historian, for certain eras.

Each interested discipline contributes information to the general field and derives information from the general store of knowledge. In the future more techniques will be developed for examining diseased prehistoric material, but it is unlikely that there will ever be an adequate substitute for the comparison of lesions in prehistoric bones with gross radiographic and microscopic patterns associated with known diseases. If paleopathology is to provide useful information concerning the people in whose skeletons evidence of ancient diseases has been found, the disease process must be understood, not merely identified. Only in this way can such studies add to our knowledge of the daily lives, hereditary relationships, cultural practices, diets, and contacts of prehistoric peoples.

References and Notes

1. R. Virchow, "Beitrag zur Geschichte der Lues," Dermatol. Z. Berlin *6* (1896).

2. R. L. Moodie, *Paleopathology* (Univ. of Illinois Press, Urbana, 1923).

3. M. Ruffer, *Studies in the Paleopathology of Egypt* (Univ. of Chicago Press, Chicago, 1921).

4. E. A. Hooton, *The Indians of Pecos Pueblo* (Harvard Univ. Press, Cambridge, Mass., 1930).

5. H. U. Williams, *Arch. Pathol. 13,* 779 (1932); *ibid.,* p. 931.

6. B. M. Gilbert, *Plains Anthropologist 10,* 32 (1966); *ibid.* p. 172.

7. E. R. Kerley, *Amer. J. Phys. Anthropol. 23,* 149 (1965).

8. W. Boyd, *ibid. 25,* 421 (1939); P. B. Candela, *ibid.,* p. 187.

9. F. Thieme and C. Otten, *ibid. 15,* 387 (1957).

10. C. Wells, in *Science in Archaeology,* D. R. Brothwell and E. Higgs, eds. (Basic Books, New York, 1963), p. 406.

11. J. Blumberg and E. Kerley, in *Human Paleopathology,* S. Jarcho, ed. (Yale University Press, New Haven, 1966), p. 150.

12. A. Weisman, exhibit on pre-Columbian Medicine, at the 64th annual meeting of the American Anthropological Association, Denver, Colorado, 1965.

13. W. Pusey, *The History and Epidemiology of Syphilis* (Thomas, Springfield, Ill., 1933).

14. R. Knaggs, *The Inflammatory and Toxic Diseases of Bones* (Wright, Bristol, England, 1926).

15. C. J. Hackett, *Old Lesions of Yaws in Uganda* (Blackwell, Oxford, 1951).

16. R. Fletcher, "Contributions to North American Ethnology," No. 5, *U. S. Dept. Interior Pub.* (1882).

17. C. Moorrees, *The Aleut Dentition* (Harvard Univ. Press, Cambridge, Mass., 1957); A. Dahlberg, in *The Physical Anthropology of the American Indian,* W. L. Laughlin and S. L. Washburn, eds. (Viking Fund, New York, 1951).

18. W. Straus and A. Cave, *Quart. Rev. Biol. 32,* 348 (1957).

19. T. D. Stewart, *Yearbook Amer. Phil. Soc. 1959,* 274 (1959).

20. D. R. Brothwell and V. Møller-Christensen, *Man, 244,* 192 (1963).

21. F. Livingstone, in *Culture and the Evolution of Man,* M. F. Ashley Montagu, ed. (Oxford Univ. Press, New York, 1962).

Edward E. Hunt, Jr.

Evolutionary comparisons of the demography, life cycles, and health care of chimpanzee and human populations

As shown in the previous paper, paleopathology is a mine of information on the diseases and longevity of early human communities. Although fertility cannot be directly measured from ancient bones, it is clear that since the first appearance of human culture, our species has gradually overrun the earth. This numerical increase could only occur because human births have outnumbered deaths. By contrast our nearest animal relative, the chimpanzee, has experienced no such population explosion. This scarcity of the chimpanzee seems to have persisted partly because it is a poorer breeder than most women in the absence of cultural contraceptive practices, and partly because the health care of human children has improved considerably with the evolution of culture.

The data which document this position come from more extended papers (Teleki, Hunt, and Pfifferling 1976; Hunt 1977), which compare the physical and behavioral development, demography, and aging among these apes and human beings. Most of the data on the life cycles of chimpanzees come from research done at the Yerkes Laboratories of Primate Biology, such as the monograph on postural development in chimpanzee and human infants by Riesen and Kinder (1952). Most of the comparative evidence on human beings comes from white children in the United States (Sontag and Reynolds 1945). The data on wild chimpanzees come from a decade of observations at the Gombe National Park, Tanzania, initiated by Jane van Lawick-Goodall (1975) and her colleagues.

Human beings take longer to mature and grow old than do apes. Measured from conception, this prolongation, or retardation, of the human life cycle is greater in some organ systems than in others. If an event in human beings occurs 1.2 to 1.3 times later than in the chimpanzee, we speak of *minimal* human retardation. This pattern is seen in the length of our gestation period, the attainment of upright sitting and bipedal standing, and the age of menopause in the human female. Where an event occurs 1.4 to 1.7 times later, with a median of 1.6, we speak of *moderate* human retardation. This pattern is seen in most of the organs of the human body. It occurs in the attainment of one-quarter to three-fourths of adult brain size (Schultz 1940), quadrupedalism in the infant (Riesen and Kinder 1952), adolescence (Gavan 1953), and general senility (Riopelle 1963). *Major* human retardation (1.9 to 2.1 times the time of an event in a chimpanzee) is seen in the emergence of the deciduous and permanent molar teeth. *Maximal* retardation, where the human delay is 2.5 times the corresponding age in the chimpanzee, occurs when the brain reaches its adult size. Chimpanzees have a full-sized brain at about six years of age, soon after the young ape is weaned. Full brain size in human beings is reached late in adolescence (Coppoletta and Wolbach 1933).

Two other notable contrasts in retardation should be mentioned. Chimpanzees retain their milk teeth longer than children do, and the permanent incisors emerge in late childhood (Nissen and Riesen 1945, 1964). These anterior teeth emerge in captive animals from 5.6 to 6.7 years of age, just after the stage when wild chimpanzees are weaned. The second contrast is in menstruation. A few captive female apes have been kept alive well into senility, and when they are equivalent to a woman in her seventies, irregular menstruations and estrus (heat) may persist. One female that lived past 45 years of age ceased to menstruate, and her ovaries at autopsy were similar to those of women past menopause (Flint 1976).

Although some of the preceding evidence is based on captive chimpanzees, it sheds much light on the life cycles of wild apes at Gombe. The fertile ages of breeding females at Gombe are estimated to extend from 10 to 35 years. From midadolescence to definite senescence, the annual probability of a live birth per female remains constant at 0.188, based on 29 infants born from 1963 to 1973. Virtually no wild apes live much beyond 35 years of age, so that the final exhaustion of reproduction in the female, as suggested from the evidence on captives, is probably rare in their ancestral habitat.

The length of the menstrual cycle in Yerkes captive chimpanzees averages 37.3 days, and captives reach their first menstruation at a mean of 8.8 years (Gavan 1953). First menstruation at Gombe may be as late as 11 to 12 years, and the cycle may be longer than in captivity (about 42 days), according to Goodall (1975). Assuming that ovulations extend from 8.8 to about 45 years of age in a captive female, in the absence of pregnancy she could probably produce no more than about 350 ova. A woman, cycling every 29 days, could ovulate singly no more than about 460 times, assuming that both species have a total timespan of ovulation of about 36 years. As a result, the shorter menstrual cycle length in an average nonpregnant woman provides her with about 30 to 40 percent more ovulations in her lifespan than would be likely in the reproductive years of a chimpanzee. This shorter human cycle length, then, provides a woman with a genuine reproductive advantage.

Another important disadvantage of the female chimpanzee is a long interval between births. If a mother ape at Gombe had a spontaneous abortion, stillbirth, or an infant who died before the next was born, in 10 cases the minimal interval from that death to the next birth was 1 year, and the mean 1.6 years. However, in seven cases where the first infant was alive when the next was born, the minimal interval was three years. The mean age of weaning the first infant was 5.2 years, and the mean birth interval 5.6 years. Lactation is a very effective reproductive spacing device in the chimpanzee. In this ape, copulation rarely takes place unless the female is in estrus or heat, and the average nursing mother does not resume estrus and coitus for about four years after her infant is born if the youngster is still alive. Women, on the other hand, do not show estrus, and coitus may be resumed soon after the birth of a child. Even though lactation with minimal supplemental feeding of an infant will space human births, the mechanism seems to be less reliable than in the chimpanzee. Indeed, it is interesting to translate the mean interval between surviving, live births in the ape (5.6 years) into human terms, using the multiplier of moderate human retardation (1.6) as a yardstick. By this procedure, we get an interval between living human births of 9 years!

This long interval in the chimpanzee may be related to the size and lateness of emergence of the permanent incisor teeth. In general, the larger a tooth and the greater its height from its functional surface to the apex of the root or roots, the longer it takes to mineralize and the later its emergence will be (Gleiser and Hunt 1955). The permanent incisors in chimpanzees are much larger than those in human beings, and it is notable that these teeth in the ape emerge just after weaning. By then the young ape must find its entire supply of vegetable foods by its own efforts. In the common ancestors of human beings and chimpanzees, these teeth were probably smaller. In fact, the enlargement of the incisors and canines in the ancestral chimpanzees may have helped them to consume tough foods such as fibrous fruits, bark, and meat. As adults, males in particular use their canines and incisors, together with their bare hands, to butcher and gnaw on the small mammals that they sometimes prey upon. Small amounts of this meat in some cases are shared with other chimpanzees, both young and old (Teleki 1973).

Dental adaptation to a broader range of foods at maturity is apparently achieved at a reproductive cost to the chimpanzee. It results in late weaning and prolonged child spacing. Furthermore, these apes are weaned when their brains are near their adult size (Schultz 1940), which is true of most mammals, but not of human beings.

The chimpanzee may compensate for its low reproductive performance in young adulthood by prolonging fertility well into old age. This prolongation may be sustained in part because the breeding female is not monogamous. Estrous females at all ages may copulate with both young and old adult males, and even with adolescents. Even elderly females may be impregnated by males in their reproductive prime. Furthermore, males have unusually large testes for their body size, which in itself may provide enough sperms to improve the probability of conception at coitus.

The life cycle and reproduction of human beings differ in many respects from those of chimpanzees, notably in such features as brain development, bipedalism, tooth emergence, child care and demography. All of these features have facilitated the evolution of health care and the numerical increase of our species. The continuing growth of the human brain into adolescence reflects a dramatic prolongation of neurological differentiation that has much to do with our intelligence, some of which is applied to improving our health. Once upright posture and bipedalism became habitual in human evolution, the muzzle became more vertical and the head better balanced on the neck. The human face is vertical because its posterior growth centers are far less active than those in animals with muzzles. The human deciduous and permanent molar teeth all lie successively next to these centers during the development of the face, and their major retardation is most logically explained as a by-product of the loss of the human snout.

Bipedalism and upright sitting are so essential to human existence that our gestation has been curtailed to allow passage of the fetus through the confined human birth canal, which itself is a feature of the bipedal human pelvis. Correspondingly, the human infant is born with a much reduced percentage of adult brain size compared to the chimpanzee. Human children learn to sit and stand upright at a similarly reduced percentage of adult brain development, presumably because of stringent pressures of natural selection for their early acquisition. This minimal retardation of the brain in relation to birth and bipedalism is not true for human quadrupedalism, which is achieved at the same percentage of adult brain size in man as in the chimpanzee. Progression on all fours is not so important for human survival and culture as bipedalism is. Birth, sitting, and bipedalism in human infants occur at a retardation from conception, relative to the chimpanzee, on the average of about 1.26.

In human evolution, all of the anterior teeth probably became reduced, perhaps as an adaptation to a diet of seeds and other small food items in a grassland habitat. The fat human buttocks, too, may have reflected such a way of life. The only nonhuman primate with fat buttocks is the gelada baboon, which sits in the grass eating seeds and often hunches along on its rear end from one feeding place to the next (Jolly 1970).

As soon as human beings learned to make cutting tools and weapons, they were no longer obliged to kill prey and butcher meat with their bare hands and teeth. Indeed, the human anterior dentition may always have been too small for much skill in these tasks. Small incisors tend to emerge earlier in infancy and childhood in children than in young chimpanzees, since human incisors take less time to form. Biparental care and feeding of children, in particular, could have led to a far younger age of weaning and closer spacing of births in early human communities, especially if infants were given supplemental foods along with their mother's milk. On the other hand, the pair bonding between men and women that these practices imply might lead to a more rapid impairment of fertility with age in women, as they more often mated with older, less fecund men. The onset of menopause in middle age as opposed to old age in women may be explained by the absence of severe pressure of natural selection toward high reproduction in middle-aged human couples.

Because chimpanzees have no familial health care, the late weaning and emotional dependency of juveniles are real reproductive disadvantages. If a mother dies before her young reach adolescence, the orphan usually dies unless it is "adopted" by an older sibling. In human beings biparental child care probably evolved along with an elaboration of kinship recognition and mutual aid so that more members of a human group became available to adopt orphans. If successful adoption of all orphans occurred among the Gombe chimpanzees, such that their chances of survival were the same as for the children of living mothers, the number of young adolescents in this group of apes could be increased as much as 20 percent. Hence, adoption among human beings may be regarded as a major achievement in the early evolution of the health care of children.

A delay of 1.6 from conception to various ages in the lifespan (moderate human retardation) can be used to construct the expectations of life in early human populations from the life table of Gombe chimpanzees. Table 1, compiled by Weiss (1973) and by Acsádi and Nemeskéri (1970), presents evidence from paleopathology and from some living traditional human communities. In these comparisons, the expectation of life at nine years of age in the chimpanzee is taken as equivalent to that at fifteen years of age in the human species.

Table 1. Life expectancies of Gombe chimpanzees and comparative data from several human groups

Group	Number of Populations Studied	Mean Life Expectancies at Specific Ages			Range in Life Expectancy at 15 Years
		Birth	9 Years	15 Years	
Chimpanzees					
□ Gombe chimpanzees	1	11.9	15.5		—
□ Gombe x 1.6 (moderate human retardation)	1	19.0		24.8	—
Evidence from Paleopathological Study of Human Beings*					
□ Paleolithic	4	19.9		20.6	15.0 - 26.9
□ Mesolithic	4	31.4		26.9	15.0 - 34.8
□ Copper Age	5	28.4		22.2	15.2 - 28.4
□ Bronze Age	6	32.1		23.7	20.4 - 27.0
□ Iron Age	3	27.3		23.4	18.0 - 32.4
□ Classical period	19	27.2		24.7	15.0 - 34.5
□ Medieval Europe	23	28.1		25.3	18.0 - 34.0
Evidence from Living Traditional Human Communities**					
□ Australopithecines	1	—		12.7	—
□ Neanderthals	1	—		17.5	—
□ Hunter-gatherer averages	4	—		16.5	15.0 - 19.1
□ Proto-agricultural averages	22	—		19.8	15.0 - 28.7
□ Urban agricultural averages	8	—		25.3	16.9 - 34.6
□ Living primitive averages	14	—		26.3	19.2 - 34.0

*Acsadi, Gy., and J. Nemeskeri 1970 History of Human Life Span and Mortality. Budapest: Akademiai Kiado; **Weiss, K. M. 1973 Demographic Models for Anthropology. Memoirs of the Society for American Archaeology 27: 1-186.

Note: To compare with the human populations, the life expectancies at birth and 9 years have been multiplied by 1.6 (moderate human retardation).

If we consider the four Paleolithic populations from Acsádi and Nemeskéri (1970), as shown in table 1, the expectations of life at birth and at fifteen years are not unlike those from the transformed or "humanized" expectations from Gombe. In other words, before about fifteen thousand years ago, the cultural evolution of prehistoric human communities had not significantly improved the health care of children. Progress in this respect is evident from the data on all later populations.

At the onset of reproduction at fifteen years of age, life was more dangerous for the African man-apes (australopithecines) and for Neanderthal man, and even for some modern hunter-gatherers, than for chimpanzees, relative to their lifespans. In other words, human beings survived the first millions of years of their existence on earth because of superior fertility. Even in the simplest of human communities, however, this impressive fertility of women is balanced by a variety of cultural restraints on procreation, often rationalized by the people themselves as conducive to maternal and child health. The age of marriage may be later than the earliest possible time of impregnation during female adolescence. Sexual abstinence may be enjoined on couples for many religious and hygienic reasons. Some communities practice simple or even sophisticated contraceptive acts to avoid pregnancy, such as coitus interruptus, or sponges in the vaginal tract (Newman 1972). Infanticide sometimes takes place, especially of female infants, and discrimination against female children may diminish their probability of survival from birth to the age of reproduction (Cowgill and Hutchinson 1963).

As shown in table 1, the evidence from paleopathology indicates a quantum jump in the expectation of human life at birth in the Mesolithic stage of cultural evolution (about ten thousand years ago), followed by a plateau that lasted until medieval times. This increase during the Mesolithic may have resulted from better health care of children in relatively sedentary communities. After early adolescence, however, human survivorship continued to resemble the "humanized" chimpanzee pattern (Gombe survivorship in years multiplied by 1.6).

The human species has experienced an impressive numerical increase both because of the preservation of children and because women have been much better breeders than female chimpanzees, especially women in sedentary villages and towns. The foregoing evidence on the evolution of human health care helps to explain why chimpanzees are becoming an endangered species, and why human beings have a persistent problem of explosive fertility.

Gabriel W. Lasker

Human biological adaptability:
the ecological approach in physical anthropology

The theme of the U.S. effort in the International Biological Program is listed as "Man's survival in a changing world," and the whole of the International Biological Program has been described as focusing on ecology, especially human ecology.

The Human Adaptability Project is one of the principal aspects of the International Biological Program. Internationally about 50 nations are participating in the Human Adaptability Project studies of adaptation of many different peoples to a wide variety of environments. Of the integrated research programs constituting the U.S. contribution to the International Biological Program, five studies form the Human Adaptability group while eight constitute the environmental management group (1). The former consist of (i) the "International Study of Circumpolar Peoples Including Eskimos" involving adaptations to cold; (ii) the "Population Genetics of the American Indian" emphasizing adaptations to life under primitive conditions on the tributaries of the Amazon and Orinoco rivers; (iii) the "Biology of Human Populations at High Altitudes" in the Andes of Peru and in the Rockies but coordinated with studies in the Ethiopian highlands, and in the Himalayan and Tien Shan mountains; (iv) "Nutritional Adaptation to the Environment"; and (v) the "Ecology of Migrant Peoples." A sixth program in chronobiology is being prepared.

Because adaptation has a variety of connotations that are different in different disciplines, this surge of activity and the participation of so many physical anthropologists in it warrant an attempt to explain a physical anthropologist's view of human adaptation. I shall not attempt to review here man's adaptation to infectious diseases, man's cultural adaptations, the story of the evolution of man, or the abundant physiological literature on various homeostatic adaptations.

Adaptation is the change by which organisms surmount the challenges to life. In the broadest sense biological adaptation encompasses every necessary biological process: biochemical, physiological, and genetic. Adaptation can therefore be involved in (i) major evolutionary events, (ii) growth of the individual, and (iii) behavioral and physiological changes lasting only hours or minutes. Human adaptation covers both functional processes and the structures on which they depend. It differs from human biology as a whole chiefly by its limitation to the concern with how the organism relates to the circumstances it must meet to live.

From *Science*, Vol. 166, pp. 1480-1486, 19 December 1969. Copyright 1969 by the American Association for the Advancement of Science.

Adaptation implies its antithesis: if one way of functioning is adaptive, another is less adaptive or disadaptive under comparable circumstances. From this springs the idea of adaptive selection, the central theme of the Darwinian theory of evolution—the natural selection of better adapted organisms and the extinction of the less well adapted through reduced fertility or earlier death. In this sense adaptation is a modification in structure or function that enables an organism to survive and reproduce. The term can apply to a particular organ or the whole individual and to entire populations or whole species. The more different the individuals or species are, the more able we are to identify the relation of the anatomical differences to different behavior and different adaptation to the environment. Conversely, the peoples of the world today are so similar that it is often difficult to relate specific structural differences to the specific environmental differences man encounters throughout the world. Adaptation occurs at three levels: (i) selection of genotype, (ii) ontogenetic modification, and (iii) physiological and behavioral response. As one goes from interspecific differences to individual differences within the human species, the chief emphasis shifts from the first level to the second and third. This can be exemplified by anthropological studies of human adaptation to altitude, cold, heat, migration, and other circumstances.

Altitude Adaptation

Adaptation of man to high altitudes involves numerically a relatively small problem. Only about 25 million people (that is, less than 1 in 100) of the world's people live in high mountains. But high altitudes, with their low atmospheric oxygen tension, present an environmental problem that could not be modified by human inventions until the present century when bottled oxygen and other such therapies were available for treating mountain sickness. Men living in the mountains use drugs such as alcohol and coca (the plant that yields the narcotic cocaine) to lessen their psychological burden, and this may alter the nature of their response and hence the impact of the conditions. However, the extent to which these drugs ameliorate the physiological burden of the altitude seems to be slight although consumption of alcohol can raise the foot temperature of the highland Indian and increase his comfort during the cold of night (2).

When individuals climb from sea level to an elevation of 4000 meters or more, there are large differences in the extent of the response and some individuals may even die of pulmonary edema. However, a usual response is an increased rate of breathing and an increased pulse rate under comparable work loads. After a few days at that altitude there is some short-run "adaptation," including increase in hemoglobin concentrations, but there still are difficulties in working. Families who continue to live there incur increased risks of miscarriages, birth defects, and infant deaths. Individuals reared at these elevations achieve more adequate adaptation and the risks are lower. Those born into populations genetically adapted to the altitude apparently do better still. Newman and Collazos and, more recently, Baker (3) report that in the Peruvian Andes growth and skeletal maturation is retarded; the consequent relative stunting is possibly an advantage. Chest measurements do not follow this trend toward small dimensions, however; Indian boys in the high mountains of Peru, while developing more slowly than coastal dwellers in other respects, develop a larger thorax and greater lung capacity (4).

Mountain dwellers thus show the three chief modalities of adaptation: (i) short-run physiological changes; (ii) modifications during growth and development; and (iii) modification of the gene pool of the population. It is probable that the well-adapted mountain dweller suffers some relative shortcomings when at sea level, but since the Indians who migrate from the Andes to the cities on the coast suffer some of the same kinds of social disabilities as Appalachian Mountain folk do in the core cities of the United States, analysis of purely biological status is complicated by the concomitants of social status, and the results of studies of such people are difficult to interpret. One example of the fact that good genetic adaptation at one elevation may be bad at another is the case of sickle-cell and thalassemia traits. Heterozygosis confers a degree of immunity to endemic malaria in low-lying areas; but at very high elevations even the heterozygotes may have hemolytic crises.

Cold Adaptation

Man in the arctic provides another example of adaptations. In the arctic, however, people build houses, wear clothes, and light fires. These cultural traits constitute the predominant adaptations, and they are available for anyone to borrow. Thus the Eskimos have designed fine arctic clothing, and European and American explorers have copied their parkas and mukluks. Furthermore, Eskimos have developed behavioral patterns to meet crises. William Laughlin, F. A. Milan, and others are contributing much to our knowledge of Eskimo adaptations. If one Eskimo falls into the water, a companion will immediately share half his dry clothing—enough to get both men home, cold but alive.

Despite cultural adaptations there are times when biological differences count. Baker (5) gives an example of the Yahgan at the cold, southern tip of South America: we should not envision one native dying of exposure in a snowstorm while a better adapted companion survives: instead, cultural modes ordinarily modify the biological conditions: the family of the ill-adapted individual dies of starvation huddled at their campfire while the well-adapted counterparts comfortably collect shellfish in the frigid water. To study cold-adaptation in man one must take account of indoor as well as outdoor temperatures, and also of activities, clothing, and shelter.

For life, man must maintain a core temperature close to 37°C. In the cold he does this by reducing circulation to the extremities (which therefore drop to lower temperatures than the trunk). But the vessels of the extremities periodically dilate; this cold-induced "cycling" is a widespread phenomenon among mammals and must be adaptive in some way (perhaps through decreased chance of frostbite) although it costs loss of stored heat. Body heat is generated by metabolizing food, burning it up as fuel. Shivering is an involuntary activity that increases the production of heat. All peoples of all places respond to cold in much the same ways. However, some people from cold climates (notably the Central Australian aborigines) have been reported to meet cold sleeping conditions by having the extremities cool off more relative to the trunk, and also by lowering core temperatures; but the subjects of these studies chewed tobacco and the leaves of *Duboisia* which contains an alkaloid poison. This cultural practice rather than genetic constitution may account for the difference in response (6). The short-run adaptations differ somewhat in those inured to the cold and in those new to it, but it is not definitely known how much genetic capacity for acclimatization, if any, differs among peoples.

In other species of animals, arctic forms tend to differ in predictable ways from those found in more southerly areas. One of the differences, fur, has no counterpart in man. The Eskimos, for instance, are relatively devoid of body hair. Arctic forms have small body-surface area relative to body mass. Some heat is lost in breathing, but most heat loss is through the skin; therefore the surface area of the skin (and hence the size of the individual, which largely determines surface area) relates to dissipation of heat. Body mass consists of metabolizing tissues (which produce heat) and fat (much of it just beneath the skin where it may help to insulate); hence increases in weight cause increased heat production and retention. Newman applies to man the two rules (or laws) which express these relations between body size and form with temperature (7). Bergmann's rule (7) states that, in bodies of the same shape, the larger one has relatively smaller surface area; cold-adapted animals therefore tend to be large. Allen's rule (7) states that short extremities further increase the ratio of mass to surface area and that cold-adapted forms have relatively short limbs. In man, general body size as measured by weight or stature is, on the average, positively correlated with climate—especially the temperature in the coldest month. In continuous populations of large land areas of the Northern Hemisphere, including China, Europe, and the contiguous states of the United States, there is a gradient from larger average size in the north to smaller in the south (8). Nevertheless these dimensions vary considerably in any one place, and there are numerous exceptions to Bergmann's rule. For instance, Eskimos are small but squat and have relatively short limbs. Some people of East Africa provide an instructive example; they are very tall, but slim, and their limbs are exceptionally long (9). In any case, Roberts showed that the relation of weight to climate applies on a world scale, Schreider extended this to the ratio of surface area to weight, and Newman concluded that temperature accounts for almost 80 percent of the variance in average body mass of different populations throughout the world, when an appropriate allowance for stature is included (10). In mankind in general, tall stature is achieved primarily by growth of the limbs (trunk length being much less variable). The real test of the applicability of the rules of Bergmann and Allen to man should, therefore, come in genetically determined tendencies to depart from this nutritionally determined pattern, and to find large size with short limbs in the arctic and short stature with long limbs in the tropics.

Other details of morphology may also relate to heat balance. Nose form seems to be adapted to the degree of need to moisten the air one inhales. Noses are narrower in colder zones. Although correlations of nasal dimensions with degree of prognathism and shape of the dental arch complicate interpretation, the average ratio of the width to the length of the nose (nasal index) of populations throughout the world is highly correlated with climate—especially with vapor pressure, the amount of moisture in a given amount of air (11). Of the various Mongoloid peoples, Eskimos have the narrowest noses. But it is unwise to assume that every morphological feature found in Eskimos is directly a protection against cold. For instance, the large, broad Mongoloid face of the Eskimo is more exposed to cold than the smaller face of the European, but frostbite of the face is rarely serious in either people (12).

High altitudes are also cold, and altitude studies must deal with the influence of both altitude and temperature. Some individuals adapted to altitude and cold maintain warmer hands and feet than nonadapted controls. This may serve to maintain more oxygen in these tissues as well as meet the challenge of low temperature (13).

Heat Adaptation

The regulation of human responses to excessive heat involves at least two distinct types of environment—dry heat and humid heat. In a hot place when a person works hard, the temperature is extreme, the humidity is high, or the sunlight is excessive, it puts a strain on the temperature-regulation system of the body. After about a week of acclimatization to repeated heat stress a subject will improve his tolerance for these conditions through increased sweating and decreased cardiovascular strain (14).

Most species of primates live in tropical forest environments. In the view of many, man's ancestors at one stage also lived in a hot, humid zone with little movement of air and with little direct sunlight. Under those circumstances the heat is well tolerated during rest but hard work produces heat stress.

In drier and more open country at low latitudes, where it is possible that, at a later stage, man's progenitors evolved their upright posture and a hunting-gathering economy, sweat evaporates more readily but sunlight on man and on the objects about him add a severe radiant heat load to the problems of heat adaptation. Sweating remains important. The upright posture reduces the surface area exposed to direct sunlight compared to that of a quadruped. Whether hair, at least long, straight hair could be an added protection against heat is problematical. In any case nakedness, far from being an advantage, as some anthropologists have mistakenly claimed, would have prevented man from adapting to life under desert-like conditions until he achieved ready access to water through use of vessels or learned to wear loose clothing of some sort (15). Man cannot drink very much water at one time but can sweat more per hour than any other mammal so far tested. Before man learned how to carry water with him, human occupation of open plains and savanna therefore required behavior that would make it easy to reach drinking water frequently.

Although man is unique in his heat-adaptive mechanisms, there is little innate difference between human groups in their ability to respond to heat stress. Short-term acclimatization aside, there is little evidence of population differences. Since heat absorption and dissipation are surface phenomena, the search for possible population differences is logically concentrated on the area of the skin and the nature of its structures: pigment granules, hair, and sweat glands. Groups inhabiting the tropics are, as already noted, generally composed of small individuals. This increases the surface area relative to mass so that heat produced by activity can be more readily dissipated. Although even moderate activity in a hot environment normally results in some heat storage, excess heat must be dissipated sooner or later and this is more significant than the somewhat greater capacity for heat storage of larger individuals. In hot deserts the people are generally lean, another way of increasing the relative surface area and facilitating heat dissipation.

Pigment is not a simple question. Inhabitants of equatorial zones are dark. This is true of Melanesia, Australia, South India, and Africa, although in other respects the peoples of these areas are very different. Common adaptive modification rather than close common origins therefore accounts for the similarity in skin color. Numerous theories have been advanced to explain why dark skin color is adaptive in hot climates, and there is still no general agreement. Although light skin reflects more radiant heat, dark skin must protect the body better. Among other things dark skin inhibits sunburn, and sunburn interferes with the sweating response. Dark skin is also less susceptible to skin cancer, and it prevents the synthesis of too much vitamin D. In zones with much sun in summer, and little in the winter, the ability to tan in summer would therefore be an advantage. Marjorie Lee and I (16) subjected individuals of various groups to measured amounts of ultraviolet light and we measured changes in the amount of light of different wavelengths reflected from the skin. We found that the capacity to tan varies considerably between individuals—even those with similar initial pigmentation.

The chief pigment of skin is melanin, and control of its production is evidently polygenic but based on few alleles at few loci. Livingstone (17) shows by computer simulation that on these assumptions one can easily account for the sort of skin color distributions one encounters in going from north to south in Europe, the Near East, and Africa, if there is a small differential advantage of presence of dark color in tropical Africa and vice versa in Europe. His calculations include a variety of assumptions, including migrations between populations. They do not explain its basis, but they do show that adaptative natural selection for skin color reasonably accounts for the known skin color distribution. Low rates of selection and recent migration are consistent with the facts that after some hundreds of years Europeans in the tropics are still light and Negroes in the United States are still dark. After several thousand years, however, American Indians in the tropics are slightly darker than those of North America to about the extent Livingstone's calculations would predict. Furthermore, the selective advantages postulated in the model are of a relatively low order so it is hardly surprising that we still lack direct evidence of the nature and amount of selection that takes place.

The role of human differences in hair with respect to heat tolerance is hard to calculate. Sheep with thick wool can thereby stand very heavy exposure to direct sunlight. Perhaps the retention of head hair in human beings is related to the crown of the head being the most exposed part in the noonday sun, but the influence of hair of different color and form remains to be established experimentally. Essentially nothing is known concerning when man's progenitors began to have such bald bodies or whether this antedated the invention of cloaks and hats.

It was once believed that Negroes had more or more efficient sweat glands than whites. Careful counts of areas of skin show no such thing. The only known difference is that obese individuals have fewer sweat glands per given area of skin than thinner individuals. Persons of different body build seem to have approximately the same total number of sweat glands, however (18). After all, ability to maintain body temperature at a constant level is as important to an Eskimo trotting beside his sled dogs as to a caravaneer astride his camel.

Nutritional Adaptation

Nutritional adaptation not only depends on the resources available but also on the mode and degree of utilization. The utilization of food resources is a culturally determined matter. Hunters, fishermen, and food collectors select only certain of the available foodstuffs. Agriculture and animal husbandry in any one place is limited to a very small number of edible species by the knowledge and culturally determined technology of the group. We still know relatively little about differences in nutritional requirements between populations. There do seem to be some inherent differences of this kind. Size itself is the most significant variable. Furthermore basal metabolic rate seems to be inherently high in populations which have always had a diet of good quality and low in some poorly nourished populations. Thus in one region in South China where a meager diet, 90 percent of which was from grain (mostly polished rice), has been reported, basal metabolic rates are also low. Neither the immediate diet nor that usual in the population explain all the variability in metabolic rates, however (19). Newman, in considering human bodily adjustments to nutrition, reports several instances where ingestion of necessary nutrients is a very small fraction of the supposed minimum requirements (7). He concludes that tolerances must vary over the world and that some human populations have adapted to levels of intake that would be fatal in others. On the other hand, ability to get by on less food may be more general. Throughout history most populations of the world have been subjected to repeated famines, and mankind must therefore share adaptive mechanisms to meet food shortages.

In addition, time apparently has been adequate for some special adaptations in subpopulations. For instance, difficulty in digesting milk sugar (lactose) has been reported as occurring more frequently in some populations than in others, and the Chinese, whose cultural practices do not include use of milk from domestic animals, have a high rate of lactose intolerance; symptoms from ingesting monosodium glutamate, on the other hand, were reported not in those who have used this cooking powder for many generations but in Americans who call it "the Chinese restaurant syndrome" (20). One takes it for granted, on theoretical grounds at least, that where specific nutrients are scarce, populations with lower natural requirements for them would thrive, but this must be a minor advantage compared with the possession of adaptive cultural practices for acquiring such nutrients.

Lack of much food (hypocaloric diet) often occurs in the very environments, the tropics, where soils are leached of minerals and foods of animal origin are scarce. Furthermore, the food ingested must often feed parasites as well as the person. Thus the increase in body weight, from tropics to frigid zones, noted earlier under consideration of Bergmann's rule, may be a response to nutritional stress as well as to cold and heat stresses.

Plasticity

The adaptations discussed so far are mostly of two kinds; those genetically entrenched in the population by repeated natural selection and those dependent on a capacity to acclimatize in the short run (whether the capacity is equally shared by all subpopulations of the species or not). There is also a third intermediate type of alteration, modification of an individual during his growth and development. It may be thought of as a special case of acclimatization, but, since the process is essentially irreversible after adulthood, it deserves separate consideration and it may be separately designated as plasticity.

Early in the present century some anthropologists first asked whether the traits that were being used to characterize races could be influenced directly by environmental factors. They did not mean Lamarck's theory of inheritance of acquired characteristics, which had already been discredited; nor did they mean Darwin's description of the selectivity of the natural environment. The question was: Would people grow up to be physically different if they lived differently? In 1905, Walcher, a German obstetrician, showed that, when babies are regularly placed on the backs of their heads, they become broaderheaded than do babies who are customarily placed on their sides (21). In the same year, Fishberg compared measurements of the cephalic index and stature of Jews in various parts of Europe and in the United States and found that the two groups differed in these respects from each other (22). If cephalic index and stature could change in immigrants of at least one European group, how could these measurements be used as major criteria of race?

At this time many Americans were concerned with the assimilation of immigrants. Franz Boas exploited this concern in getting support from the United States Immigration Commission for a survey of the physical measurements of immigrants (23). Whatever may have been the expectations of the commission, Boas characteristically set himself a concrete problem and defined it operationally. Are the American-born children of European immigrants significantly different from their parents in such characteristics as cephalic index and stature? If so, do they also differ in the same respects from their immigrant brothers and sisters? Of the various groups Boas studied, his largest samples were of Central European Jews and Italians from Sicily. In both groups the offspring born in America tended to be taller than their parents; but in the Jews the cephalic index decreased, and in the Sicilians it increased. The measurements of the immigrant brothers and sisters, correlation with the length of the time the parents had been in the United States, and smaller studies of other nationalities led to the conclusion that the changes were the result of some aspect of the American environment that tends to bring about an American type with tall stature and medium cephalic index.

Some anthropologists attempted to explain Boas' findings on the basis of some selection, perhaps a self-selection of immigrants. To examine the possibility of such selection of immigrants, as well as the possibility of changes in the off-spring of immigrants, Shapiro, in collaboration with Hulse and Lessa, undertook studies of two national groups in Hawaii, the Chinese and Japanese. Besides migrants and persons born in Hawaii, his study included nonmigrants in the Orient, for whom Shapiro coined the word "sedentes." Of the Chinese study only a brief preliminary report ever appeared; the Japanese study, however, has been fully presented (24). The Japanese born in Hawaii were taller and broader-headed, and they differed significantly from Japanese immigrants in this and numerous other respects. However the immigrants were also different from the sedentes in many dimensions—including many in which those born in Hawaii differed from the immigrants. Shapiro explained the difference between sedentes and migrants on the basis of selection, and that between migrants and Hawaiian-born persons on the basis of factors in the environment during the growth period. The general findings of Boas and Shapiro have been confirmed by a number of studies (25).

Nevertheless, a number of problems remained. In the various studies, the im-migrants measured were older than the subjects born in America, and to some extent this fact might explain the differences. There is a tendency for individuals to decrease somewhat in height after the age of 30 or so, and, in addition, people have been getting taller from generation to generation all over the world; both in Japan and the United States, for example, adult sons are taller than their fathers (and also taller than their fathers were at the same age). Such increases have been going on for 100 years and possibly for 200 or more years. Bowles has shown that Harvard sons of Harvard fathers were taller than their fathers were at the same age. The sons are larger in most other bodily measurements also, markedly so in the length of their thighs and forearms. Damon has followed some of these same families for four generations and finds no further increase in stature in the last generations, however, and he suggests that it is a straw in the wind that the secular increase in height has ended for economically favored American men (26).

To take account of secular trends as well as the effects of migration, Gold-stein undertook a study in Mexico of Mexican parents and their adult children and a parallel study of Mexican immigrants to the United States and their adult children born in America (27). He found that the immigrants were larger in the usual respects than the sedentes, that the younger adults in Mexico were larger than their like-sexed parents, and that those born in the United States were larger than their parents. The last difference was the most pronounced, however, and seemed to indicate a growth factor that is especially strong in the United States.

Subsequent studies of Mexicans have confirmed that Mexicans who grow up in the United States are taller and larger in other ways than those brought up in Mexico and that this is not the result of initial differences between those who migrate and those who do not (28).

On the other hand, studies of Italian Swiss in Italy and California demonstrate three factors leading to increased dimensions in the United States: (i) A selective migration of larger individuals; (ii) a tendency for those whose parents come from different communities to be larger than offspring of endogamous marriages, a finding confirmed in some but not in all other studies of the question; and (iii) plasticity in response to environmental conditions that are different in the two locations (29).

What is there in the environment of the United States that accounts for the greater growth here? The pattern of plastic changes is constant in all the studies of migrants, but such studies do not isolate specific causes (30). Nevertheless there is little evidence of significant influences of variation in temperature, altitude, or hygiene. The biggest single factor is diet, and the most significant aspect of diet is not the quality nor the vitamin content but simply the quantity of food. In the United States hypercaloric diets (too much food) are apparently more of a problem for health than any shortage or dietary deficiency. Coronary heart disease and other circulatory disorders are one of the chief causes of death, and the life insurance companies have found that, on the average, persons of normal weight for height live longer than the overweight and that underweight individuals live still longer.

Large body size would seem to be an advantage in the face of hypercaloric diets; the extra size achieved during growth would provide a larger frame and more metabolizing tissue to consume high caloric diets in adulthood without creating an excess that can only turn to fat. This may be as important as a small size achieved through the growth period is to an adult who must survive on a diet of very few calories per day. But there are other factors in the equation. Individuals adjust their food intake, and even in times of scarcity individuals of different size may have different abilities to acquire food. Cultural factors are important, too, through the enforcement of various modes of food distribution and norms of rationing during shortages.

Growth

The adaptation of organisms is not only to adult form—important as viability of adults is to the survival of the population. Each developmental stage must also be viable, of course. In man growth itself requires considerable nutrients and is therefore part of the nutrient-energy economy. Tanner has surveyed the influence of environments on the growth process itself (31). During a period of starvation, a child slows down his growth, thereby conserving food energy. But he also tends to delay his maturation, thereby preserving the possibility of making up most of the loss if the period of deprivation is not too long and adequate food again becomes available. These temporary interruptions of growth in size with age may have little effect on body form. In virtually every country studied, growth of children was retarded as a result of the wartime food shortages of 1944-1945, but the characteristic population norms in proportion and eventual adult size were much less, if at all, affected.

Adverse conditions tend to retard growth, but not equally in all respects. Weight is, of course, immediately affected and height somewhat more slowly. As already noted, there is a general stunting and retardation of bony development in children in the Andes, but early and marked chest development occurs. Greulich found that in Japan children of all ages are, on the average, smaller than American white children in standing height, sitting height, and weight. The Japanese children are also slower in the ossification and maturation of specific bones. In these respects, however, North American-born children and also Brazilian-born Japanese children approach American standards (32).

Different criteria of maturation show different degrees of influence by nutrition and disease. Eruption of the teeth seems more resistant to modification than skeletal development (usually assessed on x-rays of the wrist). Sexual development, especially menarche (the age at which girls have their first menstruation) is retarded about 2 years in populations of lower social status or who for other reasons have poor nutrition; menarche occurs earlier as conditions ameliorate (33). There is always a positive correlation between different signs of growth and development, however. Growth is thus channelized by genetic factors—no doubt slightly different in different populations—and adaptation is achieved by retardation within the channel in the face of acute stresses on the growth process. When the stress is chronic there may also be some change in the channels.

Some individuals, viewing the way racial differences have been used in the past as an excuse to enslave or even to annihilate whole populations, try to deny the existence in man of any adaptive differences. But differences exist both between individuals within the population and, on the average, between populations. Adaptive variability is a great asset to the species, hence, at least potentially, to future generations of every population. Throughout evolutionary history, however, adaptive traits which were inherent in certain genotypes and differently distributed in various subpopulations have probably given way to species-wide plasticity—an adaptive capacity available to any member of the species if he is subjected to certain conditions during development. Plasticity in turn must tend to be supplanted by the capacity to ever more rapid adaptation and acclimatization. The ready reversibility of acclimatization in the individual and of plastic traits in the subpopulation permit adaptation of genetically similar individuals in diverse environments. This must have been a necessity for man as he became one of the most widely distributed species and as he frequently changed his environments with ever-increasing rapidity.

The three modes of adaptation (selection, plasticity, and acclimatization) overlap and intergrade in populations and in individuals. The increasing importance of ready response does not eliminate selective pressures. All three modes are still operating and, in this day of rapidly changing conditions, provide a safeguard for the species. At a time when human genetic engineering is discussed and may be implemented, it is well to understand the significance of human variability and human adaptability. Social and political policies that provide opportunities for all will best accommodate varying individuals according to their biological capacities and needs.

Summary

Adaptation is an aspect of virtually all questions of human biology. Besides their interest in evolution through adaptive selection of the primates, including man, physical anthropologists are concerned with biological adaptability as a human attribute. In this sense adaptation has been examined at three overlapping levels: (i) those represented by differences in the extent of inherent capacities in subpopulations long exposed to different conditions, such as differences in the inherited determinants of body form and skin pigment in peoples in different climatic zones; (ii) adaptations acquired during the growth period of the individual such as residual stunting and reduced caloric needs in individuals receiving low caloric diets throughout childhood; and (iii) reversible acclimatization to the immediate conditions such as the changes which make it easier to work at high altitudes after the first few days there. Greater resilience to change is achieved if adaptations are reversible in each generation or within a lifetime. This implies an evolutionary tendency to shift human adaptability from genetic selection to ontogenetic plasticity to reversible adaptability.

References and Notes

1. Research Studies Constituting the U. S. Contribution to the International Biological Program (National Academy of Sciences, Washington, D.C., 1968), part 2.
2. R. B. Mazess, E. Picon-Reategui. R. B. Thomas, M. A. Little., *Aerosp. Med* 39. 403 (1968); J. M. Hanna, "The effects of coca chewing on exercise in the Quechua of Peru," *Hum. Biol.*, in press; M. A. Little. "Effects of alcohol and coca on foot temperature responses of highland Peruvians during a localized cold exposure." *Amer. J. Phys. Anthropol.*, in press.
3. M. T. Newman and C. Collazos, *Amer. J. Phys. Anthropol.* 15. 421 (1957); P. Baker, *Science* 163. 1149 (1969).
4. A. R. Frisancho, "Human growth and pulmonary function of a high altitude Peruvian Quechua population." *Hum. Biol.*, in press.
5. P. T. Baker, *ibid.* 32. 3 (1960).
6. P. F. Scholander, H. T. Hammel, J. S. Hart, D. H. LeMessuria, J. Stem, *J. Appl. Physiol.* 13, 211 (1958); C. S. Hicks, *Perspect. Biol. Med.* 7, 39 (1963); R. W. Newman, personal communication: *J. Appl. Physiol.* 25, 277 (1968).
7. M. T. Newman, *Ann. N.Y. Acad. Sci.* 91, 617 (1961).
8. G. W. Lasker, *Anthropol. J. Inst. His. Plul.* (Chungking) 2, parts I and II, 58 (1941); C. S. Coon, *Races of Europe* (Macmillan, New York, 1939); R. W. Newman and Ella Munroe, *Amer. J. Phys. Anthropol.* 13. 1 (1955).
9. The great size of the Watusi is a notable exception to Bergmann's rule which Baker (5) thinks may be due to their having been a ruling caste—hence perhaps less subject to the stress of work in the heat. In any case, these and other data from Africans show the complexity of

the interaction between different ecological principles and quite unknown factors which must be integrated in the determination of physique, and which leads to many exceptions in the application of any one explanation. D. F. Roberts and D. R. Bainbridge, *Amer. J. Phys. Anthropol.* 21, 341 (1963); J. Hiernaux, *La Diversité Humaine en Afrique Subsaharienne* (Inst. Sociol. Univ. Libre. Bruxelles, 1968).

10. D. F. Roberts, *Amer. J. Phys. Anthropol.* 11, 533 (1953): E. Schreider, *Nature* 165, 286 (1950); E. Schreider, *ibid.* 167, 823 (1951): M. T. Newman, *Ann. N.Y. Acad. Sci.* 91. 617 (1961).

11. J. S. Weiner, *Amer. J. Phys. Anthropol.* 12. 615 (1954); M. H. Wolpoff, *ibid.* 29. 405 (1968); E. V. Glanville, *ibid.* 30. 29 (1969).

12. A. T. Steegmann, Jr., *Hum. Biol.* 39. 131 (1967); "Thermal responses to cold in Hawaii," *Amer. J. Phys. Anthropol.*, in press.

13. P. Baker, *Science* 163, 1149 (1969).

14. J. S. Weiner, *J. Roy. Anthropol. Inst. Gt. Brit. Ireland* 94, 230 (1964).

15. R. W. Newman, "Why man is such a sweaty and thirsty naked animal: A speculative review," *Hum. Biol.*, in press.

16. M. M. C. Lee and G. W. Lasker, *ibid.* 31, 252 (1959).

17. F. B. Livingstone, "Polygenic models for the evolution of human skin color differences," *ibid.*, in press.

18. A. S. Kip, "Measurement and regional distribution of functioning eccrine sweat glands in male and female Caucasians," *ibid.*, in press.

19. Reviews of the anthropological significance of basal metabolic rates by E. A. Wilson [*Amer. J. Phys. Anthropol. 3*, 1 (1945)]. N. A. Barnicot [*Sci. Progr. London* 153, 124 (1951)], and D. F. Roberts [*J. Roy. Anthropol. Inst. Gt. Brit. Ireland* 82, 169 (1962)] indicate that the world distribution of basal metabolic rates is inversely related to mean annual temperature even when due allowance is made for differences in stature and weight; there remains some doubt concerning what fraction of this adaptation is inherent, because rates change in migrants.

20. Among asymptomatic subjects, A. E. Davis and T. Bolin [*Nature* 216, 1244 (1967)] report that all 15 Chinese, 4 of 5 individuals from the Indian subcontinent, and 2 of 12 Caucasians had abdominal pain and diarrhea after ingesting 80 grams of lactose. The Chinese restaurant syndrome was described by H. H. Schaumburg, R. Byck, R. Gerstl, and J. H. Mashman [*Science* 163, 826 (1969)].

21. G. Walcher, *Zentraib Gynaekol.* 29, 193 (1905).

22. M. Fishberg, *Ann. N.Y. Acad. Sci.* 16, 155 (1905).

23. F. Boas, *Changes in Bodily Form of Descendants of Immigrants.* Senate document 208, 61st Congress, 2nd Session. Washington, D.C. (1910).

24. H. L. Shapiro, "The Chinese population in Hawaii." Preliminary paper prepared for the 4th general session of the Institute of Pacific Relations, New York (1931), pp. 3-29: *Migration and Environment* (Oxford Univ. Press, New York, 1939).

25. P. K. Ito, *Hum. Biol.* 14, 279 (1942): G. W. Lasker, *Amer. J. Phys. Anthropol.* 4, 273 (1946); F. P. Thieme, *Pap. Mich. Acad. Sci. Arts Lett.* 42, 249 (1957).

26. G. T. Bowles, *New Types of Old Americans at Harvard and at Eastern Women's Colleges* (Harvard Univ. Press, Cambridge, 1932); A. Damon, *Amer. J. Phys. Anthropol.* 29, 45 (1968).

27. M. S. Goldstein, *Demographic and Bodily Changes in Descendants of Mexican Immigrants* (Univ. of Texas, Inst. of Latin Amer. Studies, Austin, 1943).

28. G. W. Lasker, *Hum. Biol.* 24, 262 (1952); *ibid.* 26, 52 (1954); ――― and F. G. Evans, *Amer. J. Phys. Anthropol,* 19, 203 (1961).

29. F. S. Hulse, *Arch. Suisses Anthropol. Gen.* 22, 103 (1957).

30. B. A. Kaplan, *Amer. Anthropol.* 56, 780 (1954).

31. J. M. Tanner, in *The Biology of Human Adaptation*, P. T. Baker and J. S. Weiner, Eds. (Clarendon Press, Oxford, 1966), pp. 45-66.

32. W. W. Greulich, *Amer. J. Phys. Anthropol.* 15, 489 (1957); P. B. Eveleth and J. A. de Souza, *Hum. Biol.* 41, 176 (1969).

33. R. J. W. Burrell, M. J. R. Healy, J. M. Tanner, *Hum. Biol.* 33, 250 (1961); K. P. Sabharwal, S. Morales, J. Mendez, *ibid.* 38, 131 (1966); V. G. Vlastovsky, *ibid.* 38, 218 (1966); K. Bojlén and M. W. Bentzon, *ibid.* 40, 69 (1968); L. A. Malcolm, "The growth and development of the Bundi child of the New Guinea highlands," *ibid.*, in press.

George J. Armelagos
Alan Goodman
Kenneth H. Jacobs

The ecological perspective in disease

Introduction

The role of infectious disease in the evolution of human and non-human populations has long been of interest to historians, physicians, and anthropologists. While earlier scientists speculated on the significance of disease to the extinction of species (Young 1931:123) and races (Moodie 1917), Haldane (1949) developed the theoretical framework necessary to the study of the impact of culture on human epidemiology. Through an analysis of the effects of agriculture on human population, Haldane discussed the impact of disease on the biology of those groups. Research on this subject has intensified in recent years (Alland 1966, 1967, 1970; Armelagos 1967; Armelagos and Dewey 1970; Armelagos and McArdle 1975; May 1958, 1961; Montgomery 1973; Polgar 1964), but the basic perspective has not changed since Haldane. Models of the disease process continue to rely upon the traditional concept of a simple cause and effect relationship between pathogen (defined in the broad sense as any disease-causing agent) and host.

We will deal briefly with the historical roots of this concept and in more detail with its implications for the study of the evolution and ecology of disease. A model will be presented which attempts to relate in a systemic fashion the full spectrum of variables which influence the disease process. This model will enable researchers to focus on specific components of the disease-host complex in more detail, while retaining the ability to integrate such studies into a more comprehensive evolutionary and ecological framework than is now current.

The model will be discussed in two sections: the potential of various aspects of the inorganic, organic, and cultural environments to serve as insults to the organism and, thus to cause disease will be investigated; the impact of disease on the cultural system of the host population and the nature of the response to these insults will be discussed.

Steps toward an Ecology of Disease

If there is a common thread which runs through models of disease used by Western scientists, it is that which Dubos (1959) has identified as "the doctrine of specific etiology." Its basic tenet is that for every symptomatically identifiable disease

A revised and expanded version of "Disease and the Ecological Perspective," *The Ecologist*, 6 (2), 1976. Reprinted by permission.

there is a single factor which, acting upon the individual, destroys the equilibrium of health and creates a "dis-ease" state (Cohn 1960). This causal chain has remained sacrosanct whether implied within the context of theories of demoniac possession (Osterreich 1930) or of the germ theory of disease. In this view, a demon, upon entering the individual's body precipitated a clearly pathological condition; amelioration of this condition necessitated exorcism of the demon.

Replacing demons with microbes, the scientific expansion of the 17th and 18th centuries spawned an increasingly sophisticated classification of disease "entities" (DeKruif 1926). Stimulated by the apparent classificatory successes of the Linnaean taxonomy, and operating within a social context which placed a high value on description, definition and classification (Eiseley 1958), this view was influential in shaping the theories of subsequent workers. The tremendous importance of acute microbial diseases in the 19th century provided a context within which Pasteur, Koch and others would continue in this tradition and further developed the doctrine of "specific etiology" (Dubos 1959, 1965).

The basic assumptions of this "one germ-one disease" theory are optimized by Koch's famous postulates, each of which must be satisfied before any disease can be considered "classified." One must be able to isolate a pathogen from a diseased animal; this pathogen must then be grown on a culture medium; a sample from this new growth must cause the disease when injected into a laboratory animal; one must then be able to reisolate the pathogen from this second animal. For the vast majority of then-prevalent diseases, classification by these criteria was indeed possible. Furthermore, the identification of pathogenic agents which were associated with some of the major scourges of the period greatly aided in attempts to medically treat or prevent these disorders.

The germ theory continues to be of undisputed utility in the clinical area. With minor modifications to accommodate the *rickettsiae* and viruses, it is the foundation of much modern medical and public health practices. Medical intervention, in the form of antiobiotic therapy or vaccination, and public health measures, such as the draining of swamps in malaria control efforts, have done much to decrease the infectious disease load on modern populations. Yet the evolutionary study of disease requires a consideration of a wider array of variables than is usually possible within the theoretical confines of the germ theory. By definition, the germ theory accepts as the dominant, and in most cases the only relevant, variable the presence or absence of a pathogen. Emphasis upon this single variable is not satisfactory for many purposes.

Even the ancient Hippocratic doctrines, which had originally stressed the interrelationship of myriad environmental and internal factors (the four humours), were recast in a unicausal form. Despite the superficial similarity to Hippocrates' "Air, Water, and Places," the etiology of rampant swamp fever, for example, was confidently traced to the malefic influence of a single factor, the foul swamp air (Italian: *mal aria*).

The pace of success achieved by the earlier followers of the germ theory of disease has not been maintained. The germ theory is unable to help solve many health problems in modern groups. Burkitt has compiled a short list of ailments that "can be considered diseases of the modern economic development (1973: 141)"; the list is composed of the following ailments: coronary heart disease, cancer of the large intestine, appendicitis, diverticular disease of the large bowel, gallstones, varicose veins, obesity and dental cavities. From the attempts to cure these modern ailments it has become increasingly clear that not only are the important "pathogens" of this era of a different nature, but that the causality between pathogen and disease state is not as simplistic as once perceived. The efforts to isolate the cause of cancer as a singular entity should serve as an example (see section on applications).

That the doctrine of specific etiology should prove so tenacious should not be surprising. As noted by Monod (1971), an almost religious adherence to unicausal thinking is a necessary consequence of the belief in a teleological universe inherent to Western thought. Furthermore, in a practical sense, the germ theory of disease has been a useful paradigm in efforts to treat, cure, and eradicate numerous diseases. The drastic reduction in the major epidemics which were the proving ground for the early germ theorists continues to persuade many of the possibility of eliminating all disease (Dubos 1959; Cockburn 1971; Imperato 1975).

Yet the very simplicity which contributes to this model's practical utility makes it less than useful. Recognition of the wide variety of nutritional (Scrimshaw et al. 1968) and psychosocial (Moss 1973) factors which affect disease severity and identification of an increasingly large class of disorders which are not traceable to a single "cause" have convinced many of the necessity of a multifactorial approach. May (1960), expanding upon Sigerist's (1933) notion of an historic and geographic atlas of diseases, sought to formalize the role of the environment in the disease process. May suggested that the host, pathogen, and environment were equally important in the epidemiology of any population. His inclusion of culture under the category environment made his model of special significance to researchers interested in the evolution of human diseases (Polgar 1964; Armelagos and Dewey 1970; Armelagos and McArdle 1975).

Audy (1971) has attempted to transcend May's focus on disease involving organic pathogens by incorporating the notion of "insult" into his model. Insults are physical, chemical, infectious, psychological, or social stimuli which adversely affect the individual's or population's adjustment to the environment. In a later work, Audy and Dunn (1974:329) state that this effect may arise from either an excess or a dearth of a given stimulus (for example, excess social interaction versus social deprivation). These insults may be of external or internal origin. Often the insult of an inappropriate or excessive internal response will be added to that of the original external insult. In this context, disease is defined as a phase in the response to an insult in which the ability to cope (as with an additional insult) is lowered. Health, on the other hand, represents the continuing ability of the individual to rally from insults. Health and disease must therefore be considered on a continuum and not as an either/or situation.

There is much promise in such an approach; it recognizes the disease-causing potential of a wider variety of stimuli than is possible under the germ theory. It suggests ways in which the "Host-Insult-Environment" complex may be subjected to far more rigorous analyses than has been possible previously. As presented, however, it raises several important questions: in what ways are the various insults similar?; what are the implications of these similarities for the ability of the individual to respond?; what are the implications, at both the individual and population levels, for adaptation and evolution? It is to these sorts of questions that the present paper now turns.

The Environment

We have attempted to construct our model (Figure 1) of the environment in a way that would be amenable to evolutionary and ecological analysis. In so doing, the division of the environment into its inorganic, organic and cultural components has been found to be useful. Such a distinction is found in both ecological (Stewart 1955) and evolutionary (Huxley 1958; Dobzhansky 1962) studies, and emphasizes features which are essential to a holistic understanding of health and disease phenomena (Boyden 1973; May 1960).

Temperature, humidity, oxygen pressure, trace elements in the soil and water, ultra-violet and cosmic radiation are some of the many inorganic components of the environment which affect our species. Disorders associated with a lack or an excess of such inputs are familiar and need only briefly be discussed. For example, excess ultra-violet radiation may, at the most, promote dermal carcinoma or, at least, precipitate the destruction of dermal tissue, which may lead to edema, erythema, and severe secondary infections. Insufficient ultra-violet radiation may, in cultures without sufficient dietary sources of vitamin D, lead to rickets in children or osteomalacia in adults (Blum 1961; Loomis 1967). A similar situation exists for all such inorganic inputs. The individual is adapted to function at peak efficiency when each stimulus is within an optimum range. Deviation outside that range, in either direction, will invariably be associated with a deterioration in the individual's condition.

A large proportion of the input we face emanates from the organic component of the environment. However, as a species, we use a considerable portion of the organic input as a source for nutrition. Human adaptation may be viewed in this light as the process by which we obtain optimal caloric input in the face of caloric expenditure. Yet we ourselves provide energy for a wide range of predator species; these predators are not the large canivores familiar to other consuming species, but are, rather, innumerable protozoan, metazoan, bacterial, Rickettsial and viral organisms. Epidemiologists have long recognized that such "predators" bear responsibility for a majority of human ailments. Malaria, schistosomiasis, tuberculosis, scrub typhus and influenza are well-known examples from each of these categories.

The cultural component is comprised of our species' technological, social and ideological systems; it functions within the total environmental framework in two

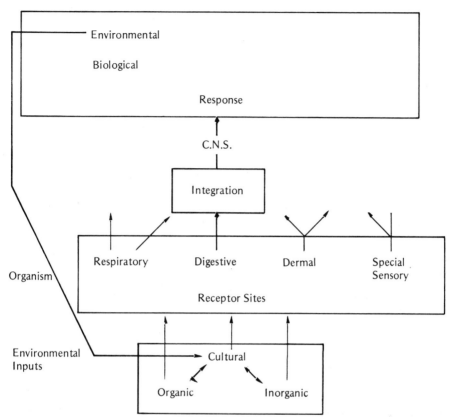

Figure 1. Ecological Model of Disease

ways. It may alter the frequency and intensity of exposure to inorganic and organic inputs. It may also create a set of informational inputs which are uniquely its own (Armelagos and McArdle 1975). The use of clothing, or the addition of vita- min D to dairy products, are both ways in which the social environment mediates a population's interaction with the (other parts of the) environment. The impact of ultra-violet radiation on the population will be altered. In a similar fashion, the clearing of tropical forest, and the subsequent use of slash-and-burn agricultural techniques, can be expected to alter a population's relationship with organic inputs. In this instance, an environment conducive to the development of endemic malaria will have been created (Livingstone 1958; Wisenfeld 1967).

In cases where there is already disease, social environment also functions, through medical practices, to influence the distribution and prevalence of the disease. It is most effective in cases where knowledge of the causative process of the disease has been achieved, i.e., in infectious diseases where a pathogen has been isolated. Even this is no guarantee of success, however, as other aspects of the social environment may be influencing the disease in the opposite direction. Such is the case with syphilis, for example. Knowledge of the pathogen, its life cycle, anti-biotic treatment, have as yet proved insufficient to the task of eradicating the disease, largely because social relations, and specifically sexual relations, are of a form which is highly favorable to the spread and persistence of the disease (Rose-bury 1971).

The perpetuation of culture depends upon the persistence of symbolic com-munication among members of the social unit. Even symbolic interaction is capable of producing stimuli in the form of information. Constantly changing relationships of the individual to the social and ideological systems, and thus constantly varying informational input, often create a situation in which the individual may undergo psychological or social stress (Moss 1973). An example of the consequences of such a situation may be schizophrenia; a socially precipitated "double bind" situation (the presentation of simultaneous contradictory messages, to which there is no correct response) may be crucial in the etiology of this disorder (Bateson et al. 1956; Singer and Wynne 1966).

In summary, in our model disease is seen as the result of an inappropriate constellation of inputs. Admittedly this constellation of inputs is complex. As will be seen, the organism instantly attempts to adjust to these inputs. Disease may arise in cases of under input, over input, improper input.

The Organism

Vital to a comprehension of the impact of the various inputs discussed above is an understanding of the ways in which these inputs are received by the organism. Previous ecological models have tended to de-emphasize this aspect of the Organ-ism-Environment complex. The environment is dealt with in all of its complexity, while the individual organism is treated very much like a "black box." It is assumed that, in the presence of inputs, the organism will react in an anticipated manner. Such a scheme neglects the intricacies of the reception and reaction processes. While we can never accommodate the total variety of such processes within our model, we hope they are divisible into meaningful categories. Thus, for reception, we have isolated four subsystems: respiratory, digestive, dermal and special sensory.

We interact with a wide variety of inorganic and organic inputs through our respiratory system. Most inorganic material is either integrated into the body tissue or expelled without noticeable trauma. One aspect of our cultural evolution, however, has been the development of new methods for the extraction of energy from the earth. A by-product of the use of these energy sources, for the most part fossil fuels, has been an increase in the amount and diversity of inorganic inputs to which we are exposed. This increased exposure to chemicals such as carbon monox-ide (Lave and Seskin 1970) and asbestos (Oliver 1974; Rohl et al. 1975) has conse-quences which are only beginning to become apparent. It seems increasingly likely that controlling inorganic inputs will be of far greater importance in maintaining our health status than has previously been the case. The respiratory system is also actively involved in our interaction with numerous organic inputs. Tuberculosis, bubonic plague, smallpox and influenza are only a few of the infectious diseases which are contracted through the respiratory system. Asthma, hay fever, and other allergic conditions also stem from respiratory contact with antigenic substances.

The normal input for the digestive system is quite obviously nutritive. The system is designed to extract useable energy from a variety of foods. Both organic and inorganic input is required, the former for the actual energy, which is released through digestive processes, and the latter are the essential mineral metabolites necessary for the organism's biochemical reactions. In either case, an excess or a lack of these stimuli leads to well-recognized problems. Zinc deficiencies (Weinberg 1972) and an excess of iron (Weinberg 1974) have been associated with an increase in the severity of infectious diseases. Vitamin deficiencies, such as pellagra or beri-beri, and more rarely, vitamin excesses, are associated with imbalances. Organic imbalance is reflected in obesity and its cardiovascular correlates in the case of overnutrition, and in syndromes such as marasmus and kwashiorkor, in instances of undernutrition. Disorders arising from sensitivity to a specific dietary stimulus are also common. They can be caused by a heritable lack of an essential digestive enzyme, as in lactase deficiency (McCracken 1971; Harrison 1975), or by an immunologically mediated allergy to a component of the diet, as in celeac disease. The digestive system may also be the focus of stimulation by many organic pathogens. Such pathogens may be of external origin, as with cholera or typhoid fever. In other cases, disruption of the intestinal environment may alter the pathogenicity of otherwise innocuous indigenous microbiota (Dubos 1965). Such a process seems to underlie disorders like Traveler's Diarrhea (Gorbach et al. 1975).

Our skin, or dermal system, is also in continuous contact with the environment. It harbors an intricate web of nervous tissue, whose function it is to monitor numerous inorganic inputs, such as temperature or solar radiation. It is a site where several essential physiological processes are carried out, for example the dissipation of excess body heat and the production of vitamin D, and also functions as a shield, preventing entry into the body of a wide variety of inputs. It is not, however, a perfect shield. Various organic inputs gain access to the body by penetrating the dermal system. Schistosomes are able to actively bore through dermal tissue; other diseases, such as malaria and yellow fever, also enter through the skin, albeit with the assistance of insect vectors.

The final method of reception combines our inputs from special sensory modalities: hearing, seeing, taste, smell, and touch are the most well known. Much of the information received through the special senses is channeled into the central nervous system. A great deal of nervous activity takes place in which the channels interact with each other and stored information. The strength of the inputs, their effect on the organism, may be varied by symbolic interpretation and perception. The often-noted psychological difficulties attending the development of institutionalized children are probably consequences of an under input of information (Gardner 1974). The possible association of the over input of complex and incongruous information with the etiology of schizophrenia has already been noted.

Integration and Response

As a dynamic homeostatic system, the organism constantly monitors its environment. As inputs interact with the receptor systems, the organism must seek to adjust itself in accordance with the nature of the various inputs. Inputs which fall within the environmental range for which the organism is adapted, and which thus cause little or no disturbance in the homeostatic state, demand a correspondingly minimal response, while inputs which produce considerable disruption of the organism's condition demand, and elicit, a considerably greater response (Selye 1956).

The organism, once subject to a disruptive input, may regain homeostable condition by either of two response mechanisms: 1) change biologically or 2)

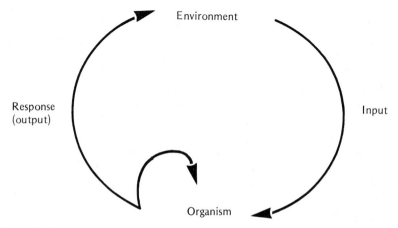

Figure 2. Simplified Environment-Organism Adjustment (Feedback) Loop

change the environment (see Figure 2). Biological changes or adjustments, changes that occur "below the skin" within the organism's body, will be discussed first. Eagan (1963) places delimitizations of the mechanisms of human adaptation into a temporal sequence of developmental acclimatization; long-term acclimatization, seasonal acclimatization, and short-term acclimatization. Stressing a slightly different response characteristic, Harrison delimits reversable versus inversable responses (1966). Both of these delimitations are methodologically useful and should be noted. These categorizations are functional in their relationship to duration of input to duration and energetic cost of response.

Natural selection, driving force of evolution, may be viewed as the genetic adjustment of organisms to the environment. Genetic adjustment takes place over generations of time and is a population's means of adjustment.

Whereas biological responses occur within the body of the individual organism, environmental responses are of an extra-somatic nature. They directly attack the root of disease by altering the environment, specifically the cultural component. Efforts to screen the appropriate inorganic or organic input may be intensified in response to a new disease state. Medical practices may be instituted which augment existing biological responses. There is however a growing concern for diseases (iatrogenic diseases) which are direct or indirect results of medical treatment (Burnet and White 1972). Thalidomide, chlortetracycline and oral contraceptives have resulted in unexpected effects for the users.

If the resources available to all of these potential responses are sufficient, the organism will persist. The disease state may be terminated, for example, if the pathogen is eliminated from the body or from the surrounding environment. In other cases, the relevant input may simply be incorporated into the system; if a balance is achieved, such a condition could only be termed disease in the strictest sense. If the resources are insufficient, the disruption will be fatal unless the proper stimuli are altered by factors external to the organism.

Application

The development of an ecological perspective is not new. There have been a number of excellent studies which have attempted to understand the importance of ecological factors in the disease process. In the present model we have considered the ecological perspective in more detail. There have been a number of studies which have demonstrated how insults cause disease, and how culture provides a buffer between these elements of the environment. There are however many instances in which culture increases the potential for disease. It was the understanding of the relationship of culture to disease which renewed interest in the ecology of disease.

Multifactorial Consideration of the Organism and the Insults

Although the analysis of the ecology of disease considered the relevant variables in the disease process, the previous models dealt with the organism as a black box. By treating the organism as a black box, the model fails to consider the organism as a variable in the disease process. In our model we viewed the relationship of the organism to disease in terms of the receptor sites and response. Furthermore the model attempts to expand the concept of disease to include a number of chemical, biological, social and psychological factors which can insult the organism, causing disease. Since the model isolates and integrates environmental factors, the disease receptor sites, and the response of the organism, the model is able to accommodate a vast array of disease associations. For a disease in which an insult has been isolated, it enables one to visualize the interrelationships of the various factors which influence the course of a disease. For disease of uncertain etiology, it suggests ways in which the etiology may best be viewed multifactorially. Atheriosclerosis, for example, can be analyzed from the perspective of the relevant input: organic imbalances of diet, internalized aggression, tension from symbolic input, and inorganic material such as trace element, and the genetic makeup of the individual may help to explain the inability to arrive at an adequate unifactorial explanation for atheriosclerosis.

Reconstruction of Prehistoric Population Epidemiology

This model is easily adaptable to the epidemiological reconstruction of prehistoric and historic populations. Evolving disease patterns through human history can be viewed in terms of the changing articulation of the components of the model. The relative importance of inorganic and organic inputs and the efficiency of the social environment as a screen can be analyzed. The effect of evolutionary changes on the exposure of the various receptor systems to new and varied inputs can be modeled. For example, dietary changes involved in the evolution of agricultural systems become important for their inevitable impact on the digestive system, and thus on the health status of the individual and the population. Increasing population size and density can be viewed in the light of their impact on the respiratory reception of pathogenic inputs. The use of various sorts of clothing would alter the exposure of the dermal system to the environment. Some inputs would be screened, as with ultra-violet radiation, while other factors might be increased, such as ecto-parasites. The influence of rapidly accelerating cultural complexity can be seen as having an impact on both the informational reception and the psychological and physiological responses of the organism. In short, then, it offers a means through which the disease status of various populations may be analyzed from an evolutionary perspective.

Impact of Disease on Cultural System

While the impact of culture on the disease process have been investigated extensively, there have been few studies which consider the influence of disease on the social system. It is true that disease has often been considered as a factor in the decline of great civilizations. Lead poisoning, for example, was suggested as a factor in the collapse of the Roman Empire (Boyden 1973; Gilfillan 1965). Although the evidence in this specific case is speculative, there is an abundance of well-documented literature on the controversy of the role which plague played on the economic, political, and social fabric of Europe. The epidemics of plague in the middle 1300's killed as many as one-third of the population. It has been argued that the peasant revolt and the reformation were caused by plague-induced population decline. Philip Ziegler (1969) has provided an excellent historical analysis of the importance of plague in Europe with respect to the peasant revolt and the reformation. While acknowledging the obvious disruption that was caused by the decimation of the population, the changes that led to the peasant revolt and reformation were occurring prior to the Black Death, and Ziegler suggests that the plague epidemics accelerated these changes.

Although historical studies of the great epidemics provide important information on the social and economic response to these catastrophic events, we need to know more about the impact of less catastrophic and more endemic diseases on population structure, technology, social organization and ideology of the group. The model which we have proposed will allow one to examine these changes.

Armelagos and McArdle (1975) have discussed in general terms the impact on small populations. Systematic studies of disease on social systems by Kunstadter (1972) and Neel et al. (1970) demonstrated that disease need not have a high mortality to disrupt the social system. Those individuals who become ill may not be able to fulfill their social obligations. Among the Yanomama, Neel and coworkers have demonstrated that measles, a disease which usually causes few deaths in technologically advanced groups, had a very high mortality rate. Death was not caused by a more virulent strain of the pathogen but by the social disruption caused by the measles among the Yanomama.

We are only beginning to investigate the effect of disease on the age structure of a population. Goodman, Jacobs and Armelagos (1975) have recently suggested that an epidemic effects all age segments in a virgin population, while an endemic or a recurring epidemic pathogen is more likely to involve younger and older segments of the population. Theoretically, the middle-age segment of the population has developed some resistance to the pathogen through previous contact, while the pathogen is novel to the younger age segment and the older age segment has lost its resistance with senility. In this sense, the segments of the population which are the primary producers are less affected and the society is more able to maintain itself. The survival of this age segment of the population also allows a rapid recovery since males and females in the reproductive age set are likely survivors and thus able to replenish the population.

It is a possibility that populations that are able to maintain pathogens endemically will not be as severely affected in their ability to increase as will populations of a lesser density; since small populations more frequently contact a pathogen novely, mortality is higher in the reproductive age segment of the group.

There are other methods which will allow one to test the impact of disease on a society. Haas and coworkers (1971) have measured energy to test impact of disease within a group. The formal application of energy flow (Thomas 1973, Rappaport 1971, Little and Moren 1976, Kemp 1971, Odum 1971) could provide one of the most useful tools in the study of disease. The cost of disease in energetic terms can be quantified and easily subjected to comparative analysis. Here the duration of responses both biological and environmental will gain increased importance.

Ecological Aspects of Ethnomedicine

The cultural response has traditionally focused on technological means for disease prevention, such as vaccines and social practice as quarantine to isolate disease. However, the ecological perspective must consider other aspects of the social and ideological response to disease. The ethnomedical approach which Fábrega defines is the way in which a culture defines disease, the way in which the group organizes themselves toward the treatment, and the social organization of the treatment. These ethnomedical factors should be considered in the ecology of disease. The ethnomedical approach has been an important area of study by medical anthropologists. It has, however, not been incorporated in most of the ecological studies of disease. In some sense, the ecological models have been used in the study of disease in technologically advanced societies. Disease is viewed in a biocultural perspective without attempting to analyze the ethnomedical response. The biocultural perspective examines the interaction of disease and cultural variables, but often fails to consider the impact that defining disease and the social organization of response and treatment has to the disease process. Our model attempts to resolve this shortcoming by focusing on the ethnomedical response as an aspect of disease ecology (1).

It would seem that if an ecological perspective is to be successful, it is necessary to incorporate the ethnomedical approach into the model. The incorporation of the ethnomedical approach will provide a link between the traditional studies of medical anthropology and medical ecology. In this way, ecological elements of disease as well as the ethnomedical response can be integrated, thus providing a more holistic approach.

The perception and definition of disease can have a significant impact on the ecological perspective. The perception of the disease is a reflection of social and historical factors, and the way in which a group defines disease can do much to shape the response which we make to disease. Zola (1972) and Fabrega (1975) note that a group defines a disease in order to combat it. The process of defining disease and the allocation of limited resources can be the means for exerting control which can affect the behavior of the group. Kunitz (1974) has shown that what is defined as a disease is not always the conditions which represent the greatest threat to the adaptation of the group, but often a reflection of social-political factors affecting the social unit.

There are various levels in which our model can be tested with a condition that has assumed relative importance in contemporary Western culture. Cancer is an excellent example of a disease in which the traditional models have not provided an adequate means for understanding and controlling this condition in the United States. Even a monumental governmental effort to "discover" the cause and develop a "cure" of cancer has not met with much success.

Strickland (1972) has presented an interesting analysis of the politics involved in the government's effort to control cancer. As early as 1928 there were outcries on the floor of the United States Senate to mount a national attack on cancer. There were attempts at developing a special governmental unit to wage a "war" on cancer and the Cancer Act of 1971 legislated the machinery for the organization to oversee the "fight" on cancer. Strickland (1972:260-290) describes the vast lobbying effort which even utilized Ann Landers to gain support for national legislation. Ultimately 1.59 billion dollars was authorized for a three-year period and developed a National Cancer board and a National Cancer Institute whose Director would be appointed by the President. Although the National Cancer Institute remained as a part of the National Institute of Health, its new status was elevated within the biomedical community.

The political and scientific attempts to develop a cancer cure have met with considerable criticism. The efforts to cure cancer have led to the fear that funds to control other diseases might decrease in order to support cancer research (Greenberg 1975). Even the scientific research has been criticized. Cairns (1975) points out that most of the basic cancer research involved attempts to discover a chemical which would control or inhibit the growth of cancer cells or an immunological procedure which would prevent its development rather than attempt to prevent it by changes in life style.

Cancer research has undoubtedly been influenced by a social setting with an advanced technology and a medical system whose professional status was in part based on its success in controlling infectious disease. It is noteworthy that the major research efforts have focused on a single cure for cancer with attempts to develop products of technology (chemotherapy and radiation) or vaccines. Since vaccines were so successful in early efforts for infectious disease (Cairns 1975), it was thought to be the most likely solution to cancer. While there has been some success in decreasing mortality from some forms of cancer (Frei 1975), over all mortality has increased from 1940-1973. We now realize that a "cure" for cancer is going to be difficult to obtain since there are over one hundred pathological conditions classified as cancer. The research efforts in cancer research are beginning to examine a myriad of environmental factors which are carcinogenic: diet, industrial pollutants such as heavy metals, organic compounds. A major factor in our difficulty in understanding which environmental factors produce cancer is the tremendous lapse in time of 10 to 20 years from exposure to the appearance of the cancer. An individual exposed to a carcinorganic agent for extended periods of time may not develop a lesion for many years.

Greenberg (1975:707-708) questions the accelerated support for cancer research based on developments in clinical as well as within basic science research. The fact that a cure of all cancers (including those effecting children) will increase life expectancy less than a year suggests that our research could be allocated differently. However, the fear of death from a malignancy which may linger for months or years seems to be a critical factor in the public support of cancer research.

The ecological perspective would suggest cancer might better be prevented than cured. The ability to change life style to minimize predisposing an individual to cancer or to prevent exposure to environmental carcinogens might be more successful than immunology, surgery or chemotherapy.

In summary, the traditional approaches to an understanding of the disease process in human population have been limited. Earlier approaches to the understanding of disease within contemporary and prehistoric human populations failed to consider ecological factors which played an important role in the disease profiles of these groups. The ecological perspective provides an integrative approach to understanding the interaction of the individual, the environment and the population in the disease process. It should be useful in the prediction of outcomes in specific clinical or epidemiological situations, and also in the reconstruction of homo sapiens' past disease experiences.

Note

1. The reason why the ecological perspective has failed to consider the ethnomedical factors is partially a result of historical factors. Since its inception, medical anthropology has traditionally viewed disease as a given and attempted to study the cultural response to disease in a closed system. For example. Ackerknecht's (1942b, 1945c) influential studies of the sociocultural response to disease argued that we need not consider the ecological factors such as biological adaptation of the host and pathogen. In his view, Ackerknecht seemed to make a distinction between primitive and Western views of disease. For example, in his analysis of disease in a Western group, Ackerknecht (1945b, 1946) incorporates the ecological and environmental factor as well as the biological response of the organism and pathogen into his model of disease. Yet in these studies, ethnomedical factors are not considered. In a similar manner, the ecological approach to disease reflected in the research of physicians and physical anthropologists (May 1960, Dubos 1965, Audy 1971) utilized a model which considered a "scientific" approach to disease in which the interaction of cultural and biological factors in the disease process were considered. While the investigation suggested how technological factors (Livingstone 1958), social organization (Hudson 1965), and ideological elements (Glasse 1970) may inhibit or enhance the disease ecology of a group, these studies seldom attempted to discuss the ethnomedical response to disease. Little effort is made to examine how our perception may influence the disease process.

Edward E. Hunt, Jr.

Ecological frameworks and hypothesis testing in medical anthropology

This paper is a historical review of ecological approaches in medical anthropology and related fields. Five examples of ecological research are given in some detail, together with a final section which discusses some newer theoretical positions and prospects for further activities in this area.

An important contrast is evident between field work by ethnologists and ecologists in medical anthropology. Ethnological research is typically undertaken by single investigators, who often use local assistants and amass a sizeable body of qualitative evidence from interviews and from close observations of the community under study. By contrast, ecologists in medical anthropology generally draw on more quantitative data, pay more attention to biological aspects of disease, and tend to be eclectic in their collection of evidence. Many ecological studies have resulted from the collaboration of teams of investigators from a variety of disciplines.

In contrast to the practice of many cultural anthropologists, especially in the past, ecologists in the health field tend to focus on explicit and testable hypotheses and to be attracted to newer scientific fashions, such as systems theory and computer simulation. Although these multivariate approaches do not invariably specify dependent variables, the ecologist may use them as devices to specify the likely direction of causation in an ecosystem. Indeed, many of the variables in the ecology of health and health care come from the triad of sciences of population: demography, evolutionary genetics, and epidemiology. The five studies to be reviewed in this paper all focus on populations, sometimes drawing on more than one of the population sciences in a single investigation.

Although interest in the ecology of health and disease is greater now than in the past, the idea that a people's health is related to its environment is thousands of years old. It can be argued, for example, that Moses used his ecological knowledge to the advantage of his Hebrew followers. He grew up in Egypt, a nation heavily burdened by environmental pollution (Dixon 1972). After an episode of unusually severe water pollution, which even the frogs could not tolerate, Moses predicted a series of further disasters to the health and well-being of the Egyptians and capitalized on ethnic differences in resistance to disease in liberating the Hebrews from bondage (Exodus 1-12). The ancient Greeks, too, applied ecological principles to public health. Ackerknecht (1965) states that the philosopher Empedocles seems to have had a system of drainage canals built in the Sicilian city of Selinus as a means of controlling malaria. In his treatise *About Airs, Waters and Places*, attributed to Hippocrates and his school (ca. 400 B.C.), evidence is presented on the effects of local climates on human health in different Greek city-states (Rosen 1958).

The intellectual climate of Greek, Roman, Arabic, and Western civilization ever since has repeatedly given rise to writings on the effects of environment on human health (Ackerknecht 1965). By the nineteenth century, medical ecologists considered geography and history as closely parallel disciplines (Sarton 1952). This unity is still evident in the work of some scholars. For example, Erwin Ackerknecht, who has contributed to the present volume, is a medical geographer, a historian of medicine, and a medical anthropologist.

Until late in the nineteenth century, the Mosaic or Hippocratic science of medical ecology was very much alive. One of its major advocates was the influential pathologist, anthropologist and statesman, Rudolf Virchow. He not only fostered general anthropology in Germany, but medical geography as well (Hirsch 1883-1886).

As medicine became more effective both in the laboratory and in the clinic in the late nineteenth century, medical geography and ecological public health declined except in two important areas. One was the sanitation and medical care of colonial peoples, or tropical public health, which clung to its geographic and ecological frameworks. The second area was environmental and occupational health, which for many decades has studied the diseases of men and women in the environment of the work place (V. R. Hunt 1975).

In the eighteenth and nineteenth centuries, although most biological anthropologists were physicians, their contributions to medical anthropology were often limited to the diagnosis of disease in skeletal remains, or paleopathology. Virchow (1872), for example, is remembered in this context as having erred in diagnosing a Neanderthal skull as pathological instead of being an ordinary member of an ancient human population. Indeed, when the theories of organic evolution of Darwin (1859, 1873) and his successors reached the physical anthropologists of the time, these workers failed to use them effectively for studies of disease. Instead, until about 1950, they continued to classify human races and to speculate unproductively on their history (Hunt 1958).

Although not a physician, Darwin (1873) made the prophetic observation that when an isolated human group experienced a severe epidemic, natural selection was likely to favor the survival and reproduction of individuals resistant to the disease. He also mentioned ethnic differences in susceptibility to yellow fever and sunburn. To Darwin, disease was important in the evolutionary process, both in human beings and in other organisms.

Like many other fruitful ideas of the early Darwinians, the concurrent evolution of human beings and their diseases could not be studied effectively until several related lines of theory and evidence had been articulated. By the 1950s, this level of sophistication had been reached (Hunt 1958). As Dobzhansky (1970) sums up this scientific revolution, as soon as the alphabet of DNA had been deciphered and a sufficient number of protein molecules had been mapped, natural selection could be reconstructed both at the molecular level and in terms of the evolving gene pools of living populations of organisms. At this point, the time was ripe to unravel the evolution of human beings' resistance to disease, and even the evolution of infectious microorganisms themselves, in molecular detail and in rich ecological context.

Other disciplines have added much to the ecological study of disease, such as medical climatology and physiology, nutrition, and global epidemiology. Genuine Hippocratics were Huntington (1939) and Mills (1938), who studied the effects of climate on civilization, physiological adaptations, and diseases. Indeed, the work of Mills (1935) on the climatic stresses and diseases of black southerners in northern cities in the United States has not yet been superseded. Price (1939) studied the ill effects of nutritional acculturation in twelve regions of the globe. He showed that when traditional communities, regardless of ancestry, abandon their customary diets in favor of the cheapest of foreign foodstuffs, many ill effects result, including decayed teeth, malformed faces, pelvic deformities, and increased obstetrical complications.

World War II stimulated an urgent need for information on diseases in the combat zones. Simmons and his colleagues (1944-1954) wrote *Global Epidemiology* in response to that need. May (1958) initiated a bookshelf of unsurpassed ecological surveys of both nutritional and infectious diseases. He and his colleagues have now completed volumes on most of the tropical nations of the world. These works are precisely the kind of background information that a medical anthropologist may need on the local communities where field work is to be carried out.

The first of the five papers to be considered here illustrates how natural selection operates in a population subject to falciparum malaria: the Black Caribs of Belize. In this case, the disease produces a genetic equilibrium between fertility and mortality. The second and third papers illustrate what I call the *cascade approach*, which analyzes health problems through the successive elimination of possible explanations. The fourth paper describes an ecological analysis of the Australia antigen, a molecule rarely found in the residents of affluent countries, but common in developing nations. The last paper is a study of adaptive and health consequences of energy flow among the people of the Peruvian Andes.

An Equilibrium Model in Genetical Ecology

I. L. Firschein studied the population dynamics of the sickle-cell trait in residents of the Caribbean coast of Belize, formerly British Honduras (1961). These people, known as the Black Caribs, are descended mainly from African slaves and have undergone centuries of continuous exposure to falciparum malaria.

In developing his model, Firschein reasonably assumed that some of the African ancestors of the Black Caribs carried the sickle-cell gene and therefore transmitted it to their descendants in the New World. By the late 1950s, when he examined blood samples of several hundred Black Caribs, most individuals had normal hemoglobin, but a minority had the sickle-cell trait. Trait carriers inherit one sickling gene from one parent, and the normal equivalent from the other. Firschein found no one with double sickling genes, which gives rise to the disabling disease called sickle-cell anemia. He assumed that these unfortunates probably died before reaching reproductive age in Belize. The data which Firschein used for examining the pressures of natural selection in the Black Caribs are shown in table 1.

Table 1. Differential fertility, sex ratios, and sickling frequencies in Black Caribs of Belize

Maternal Type	No. Mothers	Mean No. Children	No. Mothers	Percent Male Children	Sex	No.	Percent Observed	Sicklers Expected at Equilibrium
Sickler	89	6.17	68	51.92	Males	192	27.1	28.2
Normal	254	4.25	95	43.18	Females	513	21.8	24.7

Relative reproductive performance: 6.17/4.25 = 1.45	Chi square (3 degrees of freedom) = 2.46 (p = 0.48)

Source: I. L. Firschein 1961 Population Dynamics of the Sickle-Cell Trait in the Black Caribs of British Honduras, Central America. American Journal of Human Genetics 13:233-254.

By means of the data in table 1, Firschein wished to examine the hypothesis that the differences in mean numbers of children and the percentages of males born to normal and sickling mothers were enough to explain the observed percentages of male and female carriers of the sickle-cell trait in the Black Carib population. He tested this hypothesis by a computer simulation that is so easy that one can set it up on a miniature programmable calculator. He and I have done this, in fact, as a classroom demonstration on such a machine.

This simulation uses a random mating system, with ordinary Mendelian outcomes of the matings of normal times normal and normal times sickling persons. The system is constrained by three rules: (1) sickle-cell anemics fail to reproduce in the next generation; (2) for mothers with sickle-cell trait, reproductive performance is augmened by a factor of 1.45 because of their superior fertility; (3) normal mothers have a reproductive performance specified by the factor of 1.00. The expected percentages of male children from normal and sickling mothers are given in the table.

The computer is allowed to repeat or iterate this kind of mating system through as many simulated generations as the researcher wishes. One may start with any initial percentages of normal and sickling males and females, so long as both types are represented in the imaginary population. Eventually the system will equilibrate with no further changes in the percentages of male and female trait carriers. This steady state is shown in the right-hand column of table 1. To the left of this column are the actual percentages of male and female carriers that Firschein found in his survey of Black Carib blood samples. It agrees closely with the percentages expected at equilibrium, and this similarity is well within the limits of sampling as shown in the chi-square test referred to in table 1. Even if one begins a simulation with only 2 percent of carriers, which is well below the usual frequency in the West African relatives of the Black Caribs today, the computer will reach equilibrium in fewer generations than this ethnic group has lived in the New World.

Firschein's research shows how strong the selective pressures may be on the sickling gene in regions where falciparum malaria is severe. Elsewhere, these pressures may be very different in magnitude, even where malaria occurs. In general, the prevalence of this gene in a single population is the outcome of very complex processes of evolution, including interactions with several other genes beside the normal one considered here. In fact, the study of the evolution of human resistance to diseases has had a brilliant past, and promises to have a most productive future (Wiesenfeld 1967).

A Cascade Model: Depopulation in an Island Ecosystem

The causes of depopulation in traditional communities has proceeded from many historical processes, including epidemics, social disorganization, and disruptive contacts with foreigners. One of the most concerted efforts to explain such a depopulation came from field work on the Micronesian island of Yap in the western Pacific. I describe this research as a cascade model, where the likeliest explanation of the depopulation is arrived at by the exclusion of more improbable ones. The data for this brief sketch come from Fujii (1934), Hunt et al. (1949), Hunt, Kidder, and Schneider (1954), Schneider (1955), Underwood (1973), and Hagaman (1974).

In the eighteenth century the Yapese may have numbered as many as 51,000 individuals. By their first census in 1899 they numbered only 7,808. With virtually no immigration or emigration, their numbers continued to decline from 1899 to 1946 at a rate of about 2.3 percent a year until there were only 2,582 islanders. By 1966 they had increased again to a total population of more than 4,000.

The succession of hypotheses intended to explain the depopulation follows:

1. Male absenteeism.   Before 1946, most Yapese men spent long years away from their homes as laborers for foreign commercial enterprises in other parts of Micronesia. It was suspected that among men over thirty years of age in 1946, absences of longer than five years reduced their potential for fatherhood below that of men who had stayed in Yap or who had been away for less than five years. In fact, the longer absentees had 2.2 recognized offspring on the average, and the less migratory Yapese men 1.9. Hypothesis rejected.

2. Physical degeneration.   As mentioned previously, Price (1939) noted that when traditional communities abandon their ancestral diets in favor of cheap foreign foods, many health problems ensue: facial deformities in both sexes, dental decay, and pelvic malformations in women. Price believed that these deformities might threaten female fertility. In reality, the Yapese retained a traditional diet, their teeth were usually in good alignment, and their childbriths were generally easy. Even today they are among the least acculturated peoples in Micronesia. Hypothesis rejected.

3. Intestinal parasites.   These organisms, which most often are found in the human gut, have been implicated in some reproductive problems. Hookworm has been found in about half of the stools of the Yapese. In other populations it has apparently contributed occasionally to male impotence. The pinworm has been encountered in some three percent of stools in Yap. Elsewhere in the world pinworms have been known to enter the peritoneal cavity of women by way of the reproductive tract. The hypothesis that intestinal parasites have been an important cause of infertility in Yap seems unlikely, especially since pinworms have been rare. Furthermore, fertility in the population rose after 1946 without dramatic improvements in sanitation or in the control of intestinal parasites. Hypothesis rejected.

4. Reproductive behavior.   As recently as 1971 Wolff, DeSanna, and Chaine (quoted by Underwood 1973) found that the ideal family size preferred by 189 Yapese women, of whom only 41 percent answered this question, was 3.7 children. This figure was the lowest total found in any Micronesian population that the authors studied and was lower still in the youngest Yapese women. Table 2, using the model of Rivers (see Wellin, pp. 26), seeks to relate ideal family size among the Yapese to other reproductive beliefs and practices, especially abortion.

Table 2. Rivers's model applied to reproductive customs in Yap

Beliefs and Ideals of Sexual Behavior	Sexual Practices	Reproductive Outcome
	Women under 30	
From menarche on, sexual affairs, repeated marriages, and minimal household work and gardening. Male role in conception is denied by some Yapese.	Frequent love affairs; male rubs penis on clitoris or copulates with female.	Pregnancy treated often by induced abortion, using dried leaves to dilate cervix with genital moisture and cervical laceration with sharp instrument.
	Women over 30	
Arduous gardening, cooking	Pregnancy much desired; women feel lonely without children	Too many abortions have destroyed fertility; 31-34% of women claim never to have been pregnant. This is concealment of abortions when young and an indication of subsequent sterility.
	Men	
Under 30, no political responsibilities. Close obedience to marriage rules by social class. By 40 years of age, men assume political or religious offices.	Coitus probably more infrequent than at corresponding ages in the United States. Coitus considered debilitating; taboos during mourning, canoe building, fishing. Fear of menses keep many men from copulating with women secluded in menstrual hut. Older traditional religious leaders expected to be sexually inactive or celibate.	

Countering the abortion hypothesis outlined in table 2, Underwood (1973) found in her census of 1966 that among fertile women, even those born as early as 1892, their mean age of first live birth was twenty-three years or less. Thus, the fertile majority of Yapese women failed to achieve their ideal of long-delayed childbearing by means of abortion. Indeed, these young maternal ages for the first live birth in Yap cast doubt on the major impact of abortion on the depopulation. Hypothesis rejected.

5. Venereal disease and yaws.   Fujii (1934) undertook pelvic examinations of 1,192 Yapese women and genital inspections of 1,252 Yapese men. He thought that 24.9 percent of the males and 42.8 percent of the females had gonorrhea. The prevalence of gonorrhea among women at the time reminded him of the situation in Japanese prostitutes. In addition, almost all of the islanders had active or past signs of yaws, a disfiguring skin disease that is generally spread by personal contact or by insects that pass from an infected sore to the injured skin of a healthy person. Yaws is caused by a microbe which seems to be the tropical form of the treponema of syphilis.

In 1946 the new United States administration of Yap, which had taken over from the Japanese at the end of World War II, began to treat the islanders' diseases with antibiotics. In addition, arsenicals were given to hundreds of adults to treat their yaws, and many children received penicillin. When a U.S. hospital ship visited Yap in 1949, only the scars of past yaws were seen on the inhabitants, and gonorrhea was rare in men undergoing genital examinations (McNair et al. 1949).

Using the data from the 1966 census of Yap by Underwood, Hagaman (1974) found additional support for the hypothesis of Fujii (1934) that venereal disease among the Yapese was the principal cause of the depopulation, perhaps augmented by the chronic consequences of nonvenereal yaws. Among women born before 1926, the more husbands they had, the fewer their pregnancies. Hagaman concludes that when venereal disease was widespread, the likelihood of infection and sterility increased with the number of sexual partners. Among women born since 1927, however, the number of spouses was insignificantly, but positively, correlated with the number of their pregnancies. Although 25.9 percent of the older women had never been pregnant, which approaches the higher percentages found by earlier workers (31 to 34 percent), only 8 percent of the women born after 1927 and recorded in the census of 1966 had never experienced pregnancy.

As mentioned before, the depopulation of Yap occurred from 1899 to 1946 at a rate of about -2.3 percent a year. The birth and death rates almost exactly reversed in the years from 1946 to 1966, with the population increasing at +2.3 percent a year. In fact, the 1966 crude birth rate was 47.4 per thousand (Underwood 1973). By 1971 Wolff, DeSanna, and Chaine, in fact, studied ideal family size in Yap out of a concern for future birth control programs on the island (Underwood 1973).

From the preceding evidence, the cascade of hypotheses on the depopulation of Yap moves through a series of sociocultural and medical explanations, but the likeliest one seems to have been reproductive failure due to venereal disease and yaws.

A Second Cascade Model: Kuru in Eastern New Guinea

A notably successful cascade approach in medical anthropology has been the study of a fatal neurological disease called kuru. As in the preceding work on the depopulation of Yap, research on kuru was replete with false leads. Its cause is now agreed on, however, and it is gradually being eliminated in the communities where it once was a serious health problem.

The victim of kuru gradually deteriorates over a period of several months,

with increasing trembling and loss of control of body movements. He dies in a helpless state with considerable brain damage. The disease is sharply localized in the
eastern highlands of New Guinea among a tribe called the Fore, and only 20 percent of its victims belong to adjacent groups who intermarry with the Fore. Zigas
and Gajdusek (1957) first reported on kuru, and later literature on it is voluminous.

The Fore number about 15,000 people, and before 1960 about one percent
of them died of kuru annually. Zigas and Gajdusek noted that of 154 cases most
victims were females. Some died in childhood, but the majority were young and
middle-aged women. These deaths created an acute shortage of marriageable females in the population. Only in late adolescence were males as likely to die of kuru
as females. Explanations of the historic pattern of the spread of kuru must account
for the fact that it seemingly struck the Fore early in the twentieth century,
reached a peak around 1959, and has been gradually disappearing since, to the
point where it has virtually vanished among children and adolescents and has been
reduced more than 50 percent in adults (Gajdusek and Alpers 1972).

The successive hypotheses on the causation of kuru are as follows:

1. Death by sorcery.   This possible explanation, advanced by Berndt (1958),
is represented in table 3, recalling Rivers' model of culture and disease.

Table 3. Sorcery death as a possible explanation of kuru

Way of Life	Beliefs about Disease	Practices or Behavior for Treating Disease
Fore have many small feuding districts. Sorcery is used to kill inhabitants of enemy districts, including wife's kin. A familial type of trembling is common among the Fore, and many cult activities exploit trembling fits resembling kuru symptoms.	Fore have 45 widely known kinds of sorcery and believe that sorcery is a major cause of disease and death. Of 457 deaths diagnosed by the Fore, 44.6 percent were attributed to sorcery. Kuru accounted for 70.3 percent of these alleged sorcery deaths (Glasse and Lindenbaum 1969).	Fore can diagnose kuru symptoms earlier than European physicians can. Disease progresses to death in about one year. Futile supportive care is given by relatives.

Objections to this hypothesis of death by sorcery are that in the early stages
of kuru, patients show no loss of appetite as might be expected if they were in
terror of witchcraft (Fischer and Fischer 1961). Furthermore, if kuru sorcery were
a form of displaced aggression, one might expect it to be more prevalent among
the peaceable northern Fore than in the warlike southern Fore. The opposite is
true. Hypothesis rejected.

2. Malnutrition. This hypothesis also failed because the inexorable and fatal course of kuru cannot be reversed by nutritional supplementation through Western health care (Fischer and Fischer 1961).

3. Environmental toxicity. This hypothesis attempts to explain the peculiar distribution of kuru cases by age and sex. Men eat and sleep separately from women and spend most of their time in male company. Women are found mainly in their gardens, cooking areas, dormitories and menstrual huts. This hypothesis posits a toxic substance in the female environment where it could be ingested or inhaled by the women or by the children in their care. Hypothesis failed (Fischer and Fischer 1961).

4. Heredity. Formal genetic analyses of the pedigrees of kuru victims have been undertaken, because many deaths from this disease are aggregated in families (Bennett, Rhodes, and Robson 1958, 1959; Bennett 1962a, 1962b; Williams et al. 1964). Bennett postulated a gene for kuru that was dominant in females and recessive in males. This model presents great problems for the evolutionary geneticist. It fails to explain the abrupt spread of the disease from its original endemic focus and its clear geographic boundaries. It is also difficult to see how a gene with such lethal consequences would be advantageous in terms of natural selection. McArthur (1964) showed that the demographic consequences of such a hypothetical gene would be considerable. Using a stationary life table, she showed that in an imaginary cohort of newborn male children, 50 percent would be alive at the age of forty years. Survivorship for newborn females to this age, however, would be only 10 percent. Even so, the fertility of the Fore was high enough so that kuru did not threaten their extinction. At best, a genetic hypothesis today may explain the great individual variations during the incubation period of kuru. This aspect of host resistance, which may have some ill-defined genetic basis, is not well worked out even today.

5. A slow virus, transmitted wholly or mainly by cannibalism. This hypothesis, which has displaced the others, was already under consideration early in the kuru research. Historically, cannibalism is remembered by the Fore as a fairly recent practice, introduced from villages to their north. It has failed to spread to the south of the Fore. Other cannibals in New Guinea, however, are free from kuru, which poses difficult problems for the geneticist interested in gene flow and micro-evolution in this region (Mathews, Glasse, and Lindenbaum 1968).

Actually, the patterns of cannibalism among the Fore agree well with the distribution of kuru cases by age, sex, and geographic location. Until this dietary practice was largely suppressed by the Australian government in the 1950s, kindred expressed their respect for a newly dead member by eating the corpse. Women and children were the main consumers, and adult males rarely ate adult females. Because the Fore live at high altitudes where water boils at a low temperature, food is often eaten raw or only slightly cooked. The participants at a Fore funeral would particularly relish the raw or slightly toasted brain of the deceased. Some families were reluctant to eat kuru victims, but the women in the South Fore region were more likely to do so than women in North Fore communities, among whom kuru was rarer. Occasionally, the Fore also ate an enemy.

We can explain the spread of an epidemic of kuru in most villages after the consumption of the first victim of the disease. After an incubation period of four to ten years, kuru would reappear in three to six secondary cases. By then, it would spread through an increasing network of cannibals. Villages where kuru victims were not eaten, or where cannibalism was not practiced, also showed the spread of the disease, but geographic or linguistic barriers that inhibited intermarriage between villages retarded the spread of kuru. Since the drastic curtailment of cannibalistic funerals in the 1950s, kuru has gradually disappeared among the immature Fore who have never eaten human flesh.

The final confirmation of the spread of kuru by cannibalism has been achieved by the culture of brain cells taken from kuru victims after their deaths. Filtered, bacteria-free suspensions of these cells will transmit kuru to at least fifteen species of nonhuman primates, and an infected animal can be used as a source of the kuru agent to initiate the disease in another primate. Both the symptoms and the brain damage in these animals are similar to those in human kuru victims. Unfortunately for the endangered primates used in this research, kuru has not yet been initiated in one of the cheaper, more prolific, and more expendable laboratory animals (Gajdusek and Gibbs 1975).

This major triumph is the outcome of long and arduous field work in New Guinea and years of the most exacting work in major laboratories. The man most responsible for this victory is Dr. D. Carleton Gajdusek of the U.S. National Institutes of Health, an intrepid and brilliant virologist, pediatrician, and medical anthropologist. He and his colleagues were the first medical scientists to prove that a chronic degenerative disease (kuru) is caused by a virus. The kuru agent, which lodges in the brain of its victim, is now one of several "slow viruses" that may enter an individual, remain dormant for years or even decades, and finally lead to a serious or even fatal disease. Several enigmatic diseases of old age are now thought to arise from slow viruses. Dr. Gajdusek's work on these agents has been so impressive that in October, 1976, he was awarded the Nobel Prize in physiology and medicine.

The Hepatitis B Surface Antigen: Its Ecology and Significance

Dr. Gajdusek actually shared this Nobel Prize with another notable medical anthropologist, Dr. Baruch S. Blumberg, who is the Associate Director for Clinical Research, Fox Chase Cancer Center, Philadelphia, Pennsylvania. Blumberg became a Nobel laureate for his discovery of the Hepatitis B surface antigen (HBsAg), also called the Australia antigen. The latter name is based on the fact that it was first discovered in the blood of an Australian aborigine (Blumberg and Hesser 1975). This antigen is often found in the blood of people in tribal groups, but in civilized communities it has a spotty distribution which greatly depends on their cultural practices.

The core of research on HBsAg is the fact that every person's genes form a set of "blueprints" for a unique collection of molecules—especially proteins—that make up the body structure and biochemical distinctiveness. This collection can only be matched if the person has an identical twin.

The aggregate of genes in a human community are called its gene pool. Sexual reproduction distributes these genes into the blueprints of each new generation. The proportion of genes that each person inherits gives rise to a unique genetic and biochemical molecular endowment. We speak of this endowment as a biochemical individuality.

From an immediate environment, every individual is constantly being exposed to the molecular constituents or products of other organisms, including those of other human beings. These molecules may enter us through the air we breathe, the foods or other substances we swallow, or through the skin or other membranes by punctures, animal bites, or the entry of parasites. These substances are alien to the biochemical "self," and may include viruses, portions of pollen grains, dusts, constituents of heart or kidney transplants, blood from transfusions, and a variety of living or dead portions of bacteria, protozoa, and other parasites. In this context, an antigen is any molecule which in appropriate circumstances can be recognized by the immune system of an organism as "nonself." The body defends itself against most antigens by producing antibodies. An antibody coats the irregularities on the surface of an antigen. The coated antigen is then essentially deactivated, and can be destroyed by the body and broken into small, harmless parts than can be recycled or excreted.

Blumberg's work assumes that the intensity of the antigenic bombardment of a human being is environmental in origin. In general, people in clean surroundings in affluent communities have fewer antigenic challenges than do the members of many traditional communities, where a broad spectrum of microorganisms, plants, and animals are in intimate contact with the human population. Table 4 displays many of the circumstances that can intensify or inhibit the antigenic challenges that a person can experience.

As shown in table 4, in traditional societies an individual may be tattooed, circumcised, or scarified by a tribal surgeon with unwashed instruments. A woman may transmit antigens to others through her menstrual blood, but this antigenic circulation may be somewhat inhibited if she is secluded from others in a menstrual hut. Childbirth is often an occasion when antigens may circulate among the mother, the midwife, and the infant. As with kuru, described earlier, cannibalism may spread alien microbes or molecules from the corpse to the consumers. Many contaminated foods or drinks may transmit antigenically active materials or microorganisms into the body of the consumer.

In advanced societies these challenges are moderated by high standards of cleanliness in foods, bathing, clothing, housing, and waste disposal, so that for most individuals the degree of antigenic exposure is low. But even in these communities

Table 4. Antigenic Challenges to Human Beings in Different Ecological Settings

| Type of Exposure | Degree of Exposure | | |
| | Advanced Communities | | Traditional Communities |
	Low	High	High
Tattooing, scarification, circumcision, wounds	−	+	++
Feces, vomitus, menstrual blood from infected persons	−	++	++
Pets, laboratory animals, zoo animals, livestock, prey	+	+++	+++
Biting insects, insects on wounds	−	+	+++
Cannibalism	−	−	±
Childbirth	+	++	+++
Drug abuse, especially self-injection, as with heroin addicts	−	+++	±
Blood transfusion	−	+++	−
Kidney dialysis	−	+++	−
Practice of dentistry and other out-patient surgery	−	+	+
Microbes, intestinal and other parasites	+	+++	+++

the poor may live in squalor and be hardly better protected against infection than someone in a traditional society. A poorly fed person may consume cheap, incomplete proteins in limited amounts. This shortage in turn makes it impossible to synthesize adequate amounts of antibodies in response to an antigenic challenge. As a result, all over the world poorly fed people are notably vulnerable to infectious diseases (Scrimshaw 1966). Such individuals may threaten the health of others by making paid donations of their infected blood, which is highly antigenic to its recipients. Drug addicts often inject themselves repeatedly with poorly purified narcotics, using antigenically contaminated needles. Dentists, surgeons, and their patients may exchange infectious antigens—especially during operative procedures in the mouth. Finally, laboratory scientists, veterinarians, and technicians are at risk of acquiring infections from the animals on which they work. Monkeys and apes are especially dangerous in this respect.

The preceding considerations led to Blumberg's work on HBsAg. In 1963 he and his colleagues undertook studies of antibodies in a group of patients with hemophilia, a disease in which the blood fails to clot normally. Hemophilic patients are often given repeated transfusions of alien blood to supply a missing clotting factor and to save their lives after accidents. Each transfusion from a new donor presents a potential set of antigenic challenges to the hemophilic recipient. In the laboratory, Blumberg used hemophilic blood to examine the antigenicity of blood samples from communities all over the world—especially those where conditions of sanitation were poor. He found important similarities between blood samples from some primitive groups—especially in the tropics—and those from the poor and disadvantaged in modern societies. In a sizeable minority of cases these blood samples contained HBsAg.

In both primitive and affluent communities most carriers of HBsAg show no illness from it. However, transmission of the agent by infection from a carrier to someone else can often lead to acute viral hepatitis (hepatitis B) in the recipient. During the acute phase of the disease, the antigen occurs on the outermost layer of the virus particle. This fact is the reason for its name. If the patient recovers, the antigen generally disappears. Acute viral hepatitis is especially common among heroin addicts, the recipients of blood transfusions, patients and staff members in kidney dialysis units, personnel and inmates of institutions for the mentally retarded, and scientists and technicians working with laboratory primates.

This antigen is currently suspected of leading a double life. Not only can it be transmitted on an infectious virus, but in some traditional communities where a large minority harbor it, HBsAg aggregates in families as though it were part of the genetic endowment transmitted from parents to offspring. The discovery of a particle that may possibly be both infectious and hereditary is a major challenge to modern biology and is under intense investigation in many laboratories, including Blumberg's own group.

People who carry HBsAg are unusually likely to contract a number of diseases, possibly because of impairment of their immunological defenses. These diseases include chronic kidney disorders, tumors of the liver, and special types of leukemia and leprosy. The commonest of the human chromosomal disorders, which occurs in mentally deficient persons with Down's syndrome (mongolism), is strongly associated with the presence of HBsAg. Indeed, it has been suggested that the antigen may actually give rise to chromosomal diseases during the formation of eggs or sperms, or after conception.

Blumberg and his associates have developed practical tests for HBsAg in transfused blood. In hospitals where carrier blood is diagnosed and discarded, cases of hepatitis in the recipients of transfusions are dramatically reduced. As in the work on kuru, the rapidly expanding frontier of research on HBsAg has contributed notably to both the basic and applied sciences of medicine.

Energy Flow and Health

Human societies use energy in many complex ways, but the energy most closely related to human life and health comes from foods. The amount and quality of food energy influences the growth, health, body size, fertility, and mortality of human populations. The culture of a group, which modulates its work capacity, finally determines total calorie production, as shown in figure 1, developed by

Baker (1974). Thomas (1973, 1976) has used this approach to analyze the flow of energy in a high Andean ecosystem. His work helps to explain many parameters of health in the local Quechua Indian population.

The high Andes constitute a cold and bleak environment. Oxygen is scarce in the rarefied air, and heating fuel is scanty. Andeans must take up and use oxygen more efficiently than do people at low altitudes and must consume extra calories to keep warm. These physiological stresses are especially evident in children. As they have a higher ratio of surface area to body mass than adults, children experience a relatively great loss of rectal temperature during sleep in their unheated houses. Despite these stresses, children contribute greatly to the Andean economy. They consume fewer calories than adults, and, at moderate caloric cost, even a small child can herd up to 100 sheep, alpacas and llamas. Hence, the major source of high-quality protein in this human population is produced by child labor, closing the loop in figure 1 from "Adult and Child Morphology" to "Population Work Capacity" to "Human Foods." This achievement is costly, however, in that cold and altitude impose a metabolic load on the young and retard their physical growth and onset of fertility to a degree that would be considered abnormal in the United States. Nonetheless, slow physical development in Andean children is adaptive in prolonging the years that they can be put to herding. Normality of health, then, is somewhat specific to the ecosystem in which a community lives.

Discussion

The success of ecological research today is greatly influenced by the size and boundaries of the populations under study. A relatively self-sufficient village in the Andes or an island in the Pacific is more often practicable for ecological research than are more open ecosystems in larger societies, which are more dependent on outside sources of energy, including the supplies and facilities for health care (Baker 1974; Hunt 1951; Thomas 1973, 1956). As a result, the opportunities for ecological research on health are optimal in many of the very communities that are the special expertise of anthropologists.

The future of medical anthropology very much depends on a revival of the evolutionary approach in cultural anthropology and its articulation with events in human biological evolution. For example, the demography, rates of physical maturation and aging, and epidemiology of wild chimpanzees are a platform on which the anthropologist can reconstruct what an early human ancestor may have experienced before the evolution of health-care systems. This reconstruction is furthered by the observations of Dunn (chapter 11) on prehistoric and recent hunter-gatherers. He notes that malnutrition, starvation, and chronic disease today are rare in these communities, but accidental and traumatic deaths are common. Furthermore, thanks to a revival of paleopathology (see chapters 5 and 6), direct estimates of age-specific mortality and skeletal diseases in ancient human groups serve as cross-checks on the health and longevity of living apes and hunter-gatherers.

From an evolutionary perspective, some of the biological characteristics and

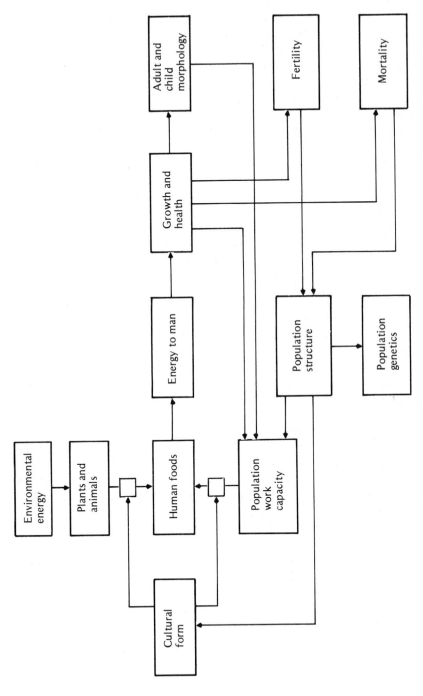

Figure 1. Energy Flow Determinants in Technologically Simple Societies

Source: P. T. Baker 1974 The Implications of Energy Flow Studies in Human Populations for Human Biology. *In* P. L. Jamison and S. M. Friedman, eds. Energy Flow in Human Communities. University Park, Pa., Human Adaptability Coordinating Office, U. S. International Biological Program and Committee on the Biological Bases of Social Behavior Social Science Research Council, p. 16.

susceptibilities to disease in people of northern European ancestry are anomalous compared to the rest of the human species. White skin, for example, is usually found in cold regions, perhaps in part because dark skin in susceptible to frostbite (Post, Daniels and Binford 1975). White skin is also advantageous for its enhanced ability to synthesize Vitamin D in cold, cloudy regions where not much of the body surface is exposed to the sun in winter (Loomis 1967). This argument on European peculiarities applies with special force to the ability to tolerate and digest fresh milk as an adult (McCracken 1971; Harrison 1975). Most depigmented Caucasians can synthesize an intestinal enzyme (lactase) in adult life, whereas most dark Caucasians and other human beings can produce it only in infancy and childhood. Lactase enables the individual to metabolize lactose, a useful carbohydrate in unfermented milk. The ability to digest fresh milk may have been valuable to early European farmers and herders when other nourishing foods were scarce, as in the winter and spring. Indeed, the critical nutrients in milk during these months may have been calcium and Vitamin D rather than calories from lactose per se.

Ecologists have brought the single trait method of study back into medical anthropology more often than at any time since the work of Clements (1932). He used trait distributions extensively in his work on traditional medical systems. Typically, the ecologist brings to bear evidence from both human communities and their environments to explain the prevalence of a single disease such as malaria, the frequency of a single gene such as the one for lactase production in adult life, or the duration and extent of childbearing in women at different ages (Livingstone 1958; Dunn 1965; Hudson 1965; Dumond 1975).

The missing ecological science that can confidently be expected to expand in the future of medical anthropology is environmental and occupational health. Aside from Thomas (1973, 1975), few workers have asked whether the division of labor in a given society is an efficient use of human resources. V. R. Hunt (1975) has pleaded for a greater concern for the costs of energy and healthfulness of traditional patterns of pregnancy, lactation, reproduction, and work. The comparative studies of birth spacing by Leridon (1973) and Dumond (1975) are cogent examples of what lies ahead in this area. Finally, Cowgill and Hutchinson (1963) have shown that in most traditional societies, females are more likely to die in childhood than are males. Explanations of this phenomenon in terms of nutrition, health care, and the psychological support of the two sexes are important tasks for future medical anthropologists. Several workers consider that the combining of cultural and biological variables in medical anthropology will be highly productive in the coming years. Alland contends that, given the broad ecological approach, "medical anthropology may serve as a major link between physical and cultural anthropology, particularly in the areas of biological and cultural evolution" (1966, p. 40). The major thrust of this section of the book has been to document this position.

George J. Armelagos
John R. Dewey

Evolutionary response to human infectious diseases

The study of the evolution of man seldom takes into consideration the role of disease in this development. This is understandable since the evidence available is essentially inferential and consequently open to interpretation. These inferences are based on the actual paleontological record with additional information provided by the historical accounts of disease. We are also able to speculate on the occurrence of disease in prehistoric populations from the disease patterns in contemporary *Homo sapiens* and nonhominid populations. This study is an attempt to discuss infectious diseases in human evolution.

There are three variables which we must consider in the study of infectious diseases—the host, the pathogen, and the environment (Cockburn, 1963). The study of diseases in man, then, would involve the interrelationship of these variables. Although there have been changes in the host (in this case, man) and the pathogen, some of the most significant changes are those in the environment (Armelagos, 1967). It is important to note that the environment of man includes not only biotic, climatic, geologic, and geographic elements, but also all aspects of his culture (Bates, 1953). This presents somewhat of a dilemma, since man has used culture as his major mode of adaptation in an attempt to control the other aspects of his environment. The study of man's culture—his technology, social system, and even his idealogy—must be considered if we are to understand the disease patterns of man.

The role of culture is so significant in understanding the disease process that May (1960) has constructed a model in which culture is dealt with as a separate factor, as are the environment (which includes the pathogen) and the host. May illustrates the role of culture with particular disease patterns in North Vietnam. North Vietnam has two relevant geomorphological features, fertile delta and the fertile hills. Although rice is grown in the hills, the major area of rice cultivation is in the delta. The rice growers in the delta build houses on the ground, with a stable on one side and a kitchen on the other. The hill people, on the other hand, build houses on stilts with living rooms about 8 to 10 ft. above the ground. The animals are kept underneath the houses, while the cooking is done in the living room.

The vector for malaria, *Anopheles minimus,* occurs in the hills, but the flight ceiling of this vector is about 8 or 9 ft. and, consequently, the *Anopheles* encounter

Reprinted, with permission, from the 1970 (157:638-644) *BioScience* published by the American Institute of Biological Sciences.

only the animals under the house. If the vector were to stray to the living room, fumes from the cooking would tend to drive it away. The malaria vector does not occur in the delta.

Some people have been forced to move to the hills under pressure of over-population in the delta. Typically, movement of the delta people to the hills has not resulted in the acceptance of the culture of the hill people. The delta tribes still build their houses on the ground, with the animals kept in the stables on the side. Food is cooked outside and brought into the house to be eaten in the smoke-free living room. This results in the *Anopheles minimus* feeding on the humans, whom they prefer to the nonhuman animals. This transfer results in the transmission of malaria to the new inhabitants. According to May, the people of the delta have been discouraged from relocating, feeling that the evil spirits in the hills do not like them. The intimate relationship between disease and culture noted by May is not unique; others (Hackett, 1937; Livingstone, 1958; Lambrecht, 1964; Alland, 1967; and Hudson, 1965) have presented similar interactions.

The changes in cultural adaptation, with the resulting increases in popula-tion size, population density, and changes in the ecological balance, altered the disease pattern of man. Polgar (1964) suggests five stages in the disease history of mankind: hunting and gathering, settled villages, preindustrial cities, industrial cities, and the present. Our discussion of infectious disease in human evolution will utilize Polgar's description of these stages.

The Hunting and Gathering Stage

For almost 2 million years man has subsisted on the animals he could hunt and on the edible plants he could gather. As one would expect, populations adapted to a hunting and gathering subsistence are small and are distributed over a wide area. In addition to their low density, these groups would have led a seminomadic existence. Small population size and low density would restrict the types of infectious disease which would have plagued them. Contagious diseases, for example, would not have had a large enough population base to have an impact on the evolution of these populations. Polgar suggests that the hunters and gatherers would have been afflict-ed with two types of disease—those which had adapted to the prehominids and per-sisted to infest them after speciation of the hominids, and those (zoonoses) which did not have human hosts but were accidentally transmitted to man. Such parasites as the head and body louse (*Pediculus humanus*), pinworms, yaws, and malaria would fall into the first category. Cockburn (1967b) would add that most of the internal protozoa found in modern man and bacteria such as *Salmonella typhi* and staphylococci would have been present. It is interesting to note that Livingstone (1958) would argue against malarial infections in early man. The small population size and bipedalism indicating a savannah adaptation would preclude the presence of malaria.

The second type of disease is that which has adapted to another host and is transmitted to man accidentally by insect bite, wounds, or from consuming meat of the infected animal. Sleeping sickness, scrub typhus, relapsing fever, tetanus, trichinosis, tularemia, leptospirosis, and schistosomiasis are examples of diseases which, Polgar speculates, may have been transmitted accidentally to man.

The range of the hunters and gatherers is a limiting factor for the kinds of parasites which would have been present. During the earlier period of the hunting and gathering stage, the hominids were restricted to the tropical zone. With an expansion of hominids into the temperature zone (by the time of *Homo erectus*), new and different parasites would have been present. It is important to note that by this time some food was being cooked, a process which would kill some of the parasites present.

Missing from the list of diseases which would have involved man prior to the Neolithic are contagious community diseases such as measles, influenza, smallpox, and mumps (Polgar, 1964). Burnet (1962) goes further and suggests that few viruses would have infected early man. Cockburn (1967a) disagrees strongly, since there are a number of viral infections found in monkeys. Although it is possible that monkeys studied may have contracted the viruses in captivity, the differences in the form of these viruses, according to Cockburn, are enough to argue against this.

The Settled Village Stage

The semi-sedentary encampments of the Mesolithic and sedentary villages of the Neolithic resulted in the concentration of populations in relatively small areas. As one could expect, this would create new and different problems. In hunting and gathering societies, the disposal of human excrement presents no great problem since nomadic travel would preclude the accumulation of human waste (Heinz, 1961). It should be pointed out that in some cases hunters and gatherers living in caves were forced to abandon them as the debris accumulated.

The sedentarism which is characteristic of the Mesolithic and Neolithic would provide new breeding places for many forms of life which harbor disease. In addition, domestication would have led to the herding of animals near the areas of habitation. Prior to this time, the dog was the only domesticated animal. *Salmonella* and *Ascaris* are carried by domesticated animals such as pigs, sheep, cattle, and fowl. C. A. Hoare (1957) has suggested that the trypanosomes were spread beyond the range of the normal host by domesticated animals. Polgar (1964) also suggests that the products of domesticated animals (milk, skin, hair) and the dust raised by the animals provide for the transmission of anthrax, Q Fever, brucellosis, and tuberculosis.

The expansion of agricultural societies into new environments created other problems. Audy (1961) has demonstrated that as new ground is broken for cultivation, scrub typhus increases. In this case, the agriculturalists exposed themselves to the bites of insects as they toiled in the fields. Livingstone (1958) has impressively illustrated the relationship between the spread of agriculture, malaria, and sickle-cell anemia. As the West African agriculturalists expanded into the forest and destroyed the trees in the preparation of ground for cultivation, they encroached on the environment of the pongids. The pongids, which were the primary host of the *Plasmodium falciparum* carried by *Anopheles gambiae,* were exterminated or forced further into the forest. The mosquitoes quickly transferred to the hominids for their meals. Livingstone points out that agricultural activity, which provides new breeding areas for mosquitoes and provides a large population for the mosquitoes to feed, led to malaria becoming an endemic disease. Populations in this area have developed a genetic polymorphism—sickle-cell trait—which gives those individual heterozygotes for the trait immunity to malaria. In other words, as the agriculturalists expanded, malaria would increase. In response to the increase in malaria, the frequency of the abnormal sickle-cell hemoglobin would increase.

Preindustrial Cities

The expansion of the population which began in the Neolithic continued with the development of large urban centers in the preindustrial cities. The problem which faced the settled communities of the Neolithic are present but are significantly more difficult to control. The concentration of a large population in a small area creates problems in supplying food and water and removing human waste. Since many cities dispose of waste via their water supply, serious health hazards developed. Cholera, for example, was transmitted by polluted water. Even with our advanced technology, pollution is still a serious concern.

The increased frequency of contact between members of the population resulted in the transmission of disease by contact. Typhus was transmitted by lice which moved from person to person. Plague bacillus which was originally spread by rodents could, with the high population density, be transmitted by inhalation. During the preindustrial stage, viral diseases such as measles, mumps, chickenpox, and smallpox were also transmitted by contact.

Social change resulting from urbanization was responsible for alteration in the expression of some of the diseases. Prior to urbanization, syphilis was a nonvenereal disease, but with the changes in family structure, crowding, and sexual promiscuity, syphilis became a venereal disease (Hudson, 1965).

It was during this period that exploration resulted in the introduction of disease into new areas.

Population during this period approached a size for the maintenance of diseases in an endemic form. Cockburn (1967b) has suggested that a population of about one million is necessary for measles to be maintained as an endemic disease.

Industrial Cities

Increase in population size and density was again a consequence of the cultural advances of the industrial revolution. The social and environmental changes were important. Industrial wastes increased pollution of water and air. Unsanitary conditions in the slums were ideal focal points for the spread of infectious diseases, and imperialistic expansion transported disease into new areas.

Epidemics also created havoc in the industrial populations. Typhus, typhoid, smallpox, diphtheria, measles, malaria, and yellow fever epidemics are well documented for the late 18th and early 19th centuries (Polgar, 1964). Tuberculosis and respiratory diseases such as pneumonia and bronchitis were enhanced by the crowding and harsh working conditions.

Perhaps the saddest consequence of the industrial period was the spread of epidemic diseases to populations which had not developed an immunity to them. Although contact had occurred earlier, in the preindustrial period, the impact was greater during the industrial period.

Present

The advances that have been made in recent times have been quite remarkable; our understanding of the relevant features of infectious diseases has allowed us to make significant strides in preventing and controlling some infectious diseases. Even with these advances, infectious diseases are still prevalent in many areas. Attempts to control disease are more difficult with rapid transportation. Infectious diseases may be transmitted in hours to populations which, 50 years ago, were 2 weeks distant.

The Evolutionary Response

The study of infectious diseases and their impact on human development is the host and the parasite (Motulsky, 1960). The duration of a human generation is much longer than that of the parasites which feed on man. This would favor evolutionary changes in the parasites leading to less severe manifestations of the disease. This is understandable since a parasite which causes the death of the host can then die from lack of a host.

The responses in the host were also significant. Haldane (1949) suggests that infectious diseases have been the most important selective factor in human evolution. Since the factors (i.e., large, dense population) which led to epidemic infectious diseases arose rapidly following the Neolithic revolution, the genetic factors would not have been present to provide immunity against these infectious diseases. In other words, the genotypes that were selected during the hunting and gathering stage would have provided little protection against the infectious diseases, but the genetic heterogeneity of the population would have been adequate to protect some individuals from the diseases. Lederberg (1963) disagrees, since many of the diseases which have animal reservoirs would be important in an epidemic sense. Instead of rapid selection acting on a large population, Lederberg suggests that the persistent application of small differentials over a long period of time, as characteristic of "reservoir disease," could have developed factors of genetic immunity.

Motulsky (1963) states that there are three areas of concern in disease susceptibility and resistance: (1) factors of immunity in the conventional antigen-antibody reaction; (2) generalized host factors; and (3) highly specific gene-determined factors which provide resistance.

Motulsky points out that there may be a genetic potential for antibody production, but it would be difficult to demonstrate in man. Lederberg (1959) has provided other data which would suggest a possible genetic variation in the response to antibody protection. Although not much is known about the inheritance of the nonspecific host factors in the response to infectious disease, they do appear to have a genetic basis. Efficiency of phagocytosis, levels of complements, antimicrobial factors in tissue, and serum inhibitors of microbial growth may have been important in providing immunity to diseases (Motulsky, 1963).

The highly specific genetic factors may have had a key role in the evolutionary response to infectious diseases. Although it would be impossible to demonstrate the genetic factors involved, populations appear to have developed a genetic immunity to disease. Motulsky (1960) states that when tuberculosis strikes a population which was not previously exposed to the disease, the mortality is high and the infection is acute. The individuals which are most susceptible to the disease would perish, while those with genetic characteristics which provide some resistance would survive. In subsequent episodes, the mortality is lower and infection is less severe. The differential susceptibility in different populations could result from a genetic difference. For example, American Indians and Eskimos developed a more acute tubercular infection. The evidence for genetic immunity is suggestive, however, since environmental differences in nutrition and sanitation may explain some of the population differences.

The evidence for highly specific genetic factors is more convincing in the metabolic polymorphisms which have evolved in response to disease (Motulsky, 1960). For example, the sickle-cell trait, which provides resistance to malaria, has been discussed. Other polymorphisms have evolved in areas where malaria is endemic. The hemoglobinopathy thalassemia and glucose-6-phosphate dehydrogenase dificiency also appear to provide protection against malaria (Motulsky, 1963).

The evolution of genetic protection against infectious disease would have been essential for the survival of population, since epidemic diseases could destroy large segments of the population. In some instances, infectious diseases may act as a factor inhibiting population growth. In those populations in which epidemic diseases are still an important factor, increases in population are evidence. Cultural practices tend to maintain population size. As cultural groups are better able to prevent and control infectious diseases, the population increases at an alarming rate. In order to combat this increase in population, Polgar (1964) suggests that public health programs which are designed to control and prevent infectious diseases in countries with high fertility rates should include programs to limit population increase.

In addition to the problem of the exploding population, the control of infectious diseases has helped to increase life expectancy. The increase in longevity would have created new problems for the older segments of the population; increase in degenerative disease would have been a consequence. In a population in which the oldest individuals live to 60 years of age, degenerative diseases are relatively unimportant. Neel (1958) states that in the state of Michigan, of the deaths in 1953 from arteriosclerotic, hypertensive, or degenerative heart disease (which constituted 33.1% of all deaths), 7.4% occurred prior to age 50. By the 60th year, approximately 25% have died of degenerative heart disease. The remaining 75% of deaths due to degenerative heart disease occur after 60 years of age.

Recently, we were able to demonstrate that osteoporosis (loss of bone mass with age) occurs earlier and is more severe in prehistoric Nubian populations when compared to bone loss in a modern population. In the prehistoric Nubian population, the frequency of fractures due to severe bone loss was not evident. An examination of the mortality pattern would indicate why this should be the case. Approximately 40% of the population die before their 40th year. Only 15% live past 40 years and all are dead before age 60. In the United States, 91% live past their 40th year, 75% past their 60th, 29% past their 80th, and 6% past their 90th year. Since many individuals live past age 60 and osteoporosis continues, the decrease in bone mass becomes great enough to predispose the neck of the femur to pathological fracture. It should be pointed out that since these degenerative conditions occur in that segment of the population which is past reproductive age, selective responses to degenerative conditions could not occur.

With the possibility that we may be able to control infectious diseases in some populations, concern with degenerative conditions (Spiegelman, 1956) and population control should be two areas of future research.

Acknowledgment

Partial support was received from a grant (H. D. AM02771–01) from the National Institute of Child Health and Human Development, United States Public Health Service.

Frederick L. Dunn

Epidemiological factors: health and disease in hunter-gatherers

Introduction

A series of generalizations concerning health, disease, and mortality in hunter-gatherers are reviewed and discussed in this paper. Some are long-established and widely accepted; others are proposed in the light of certain considerations of ecological diversity and complexity. I shall refer particularly to the published record for health and disease in the Bushman, the Australian aborigine, the Eskimo, the African Pygmy, and the Semang (Malayan Negrito). In the course of the discussion some epidemiological or "medical ecological" issues will be raised which pertain to the study of diseases: (1) as agents of natural selection, and (2) as dependent or independent variables influencing size and stability of human populations. I shall emphasize the role of disease in population regulation rather than in selection, but much that will be said relates to both areas of inquiry. Disease— particularly parasitic and infectious disease—has attracted considerable attention from human geneticists and anthropologists in recent years (Livingstone, 1960; Motulsky, 1960; Neel *et al.,* 1964; World Health Organization, 1968) but the role of disease in population regulation has been somewhat neglected.

Whether one's concern may be the destiny of the modern hunter-gatherer or the reconstruction of prehistoric hunting and gathering conditions, hunter-gatherer studies are really urgent today. This urgency is emphasized in a succinct World Health Organization report, "Research on human population genetics" (1968), which also outlines research needs, procedures, and the kinds of demographic, ethnographic, genetic, and biomedical data whose collection is so essential. These procedural matters need not be discussed here, but a brief review of the means available for gathering data and developing a picture of disease patterns in prehistoric hunter-gatherers may be useful. Only four approaches come to mind:

1. We may study health and disease in modern hunter-gatherers and project these findings into the past. This approach assumes that disease patterns in populations still removed from substantial contact with outsiders are to some extent similar to ancient disease patterns. The extensive pilot study of the Xavante Indians of the Brazilian Mato Grosso by Neel and his colleagues (1964) is a good example. Their report provides some tentative hypotheses of human genetic and evolutionary interest; many indications exist that additional studies along the same lines may also provide data of value in the interpretation of prehistoric populations and demographic conditions.

2. We may review first-contact records—historical and ethnographic within this century—for information about specific diseases and conditions of health. Much of our knowledge of aboriginal health conditions in the Americas has been built up in this way (Cook, 1955, for example).

3. We may make use of increasing refinement of archeological technique and extensive multidisciplinary collaboration in archeological investigations, which are beginning to provide extraordinary dividends in knowledge of the prehistoric environment. Paleoecological studies now make it possible to assess prehistoric environmental potentials for transmission of infectious and parasitic agents of disease. Paleopathological investigations are becoming increasingly sophisticated, and coprolite studies, which also provide valuable dietary and ecological information, have opened the way to epidemiological assessment of intestinal helminthiases in prehistoric populations (Callen and

Cameron, 1960; Samuels, 1965). Recently, in collaboration with Dr. Robert Heizer of the University of California I have had the opportunity to study a series of more than fifty coprolites from Lovelock Cave in Nevada. We found no eggs or larvae of parasitic helminths, but because of the extraordinary state of preservation of certain pseudoparasites—mites and nematodes—we were able to conclude, with a fair degree of certainty, that the ancient people represented by these specimens were in fact free of a whole series of intestinal helminths, including flukes, tapeworms, and important nematodes such as hookworm and *Ascaris*. This conclusion was not altogether surprising in the light of our knowledge of helminthiasis in modern Bushmen and other hunter-gatherers of arid regions.

   4. We may finally approach the study of prehistoric patterns of disease in man through the study of disease patterns in non-human primates today in a variety of ecological settings, some of which are shared with modern hunter-gatherers (Dunn, 1972). In this relatively unexplored field we can only expect to discern broad patterns of similarity for man and other primates. I shall return briefly to this approach when I discuss ecological complexity and diversity.

Disease in the Population Equation

To examine the role of disease in a human population, we may refer to the "equation of recruitment and loss" of Wynne-Edwards (1962), defining the variables contributing to the condition of population stability:

Recruit- ment Arising from Reproduction	+ Immi- gration	= Uncon- trollable Losses	+ Emi- gration	+ Social Mortality

   In this equation, "uncontrollable losses" are identified as the independent variable and include losses due to predation, parasitism (infectious and parasitic diseases), accidents, starvation and old age (chronic diseases, diseases associated with aging). Social mortality comprises that mortality arising from "social stress": strife, stress diseases, cannibalism, infanticide, war, homicide, suicide, etc. Wynne-Edwards, with an acknowledgement to Carr-Saunders (1922), discusses population stability in hunter-gatherer and subsistence agriculturalist societies in terms of this equation. Births and immigration are balanced by emigration and two kinds of mortality, the socially controllable (social mortality) and the socially uncontrollable (losses due to independent variables). Within the realm of controllable (sometimes even "acceptable") mortality is population regulation by abortion and infanticide, by reduction in numbers (sacrifice, cannibalism, head-hunting and other forms of warfare, geronticide, and even homicide and suicide), and by territoriality (rules regulating the utilization of space and resources, land tenure, marriage regulations, etc.). In a brief discussion of mortality due to predation and disease, Wynne-Edwards points out that neither of these variables can be considered wholly density-dependent or density-independent. Predation not only contributes to uncontrollable loss but is also density-dependent insofar as the prey may "cooperate" in making its surplus members available to predators. Similarly, infectious and parasitic diseases may be either uncontrollable or density-dependent, as socially stressed individuals are selected out by disease because of their "depressed" physiological state. Thus, as variables contributing to mortality, predation and disease due to parasitism are to some extent controllable and density-dependent, to some extent uncontrollable and independent. The disease variable is obviously important in the regulation of human population but its impact is constantly modified by sociocultural and ecological factors. Other variables in the demographic equation—notably accidents, predation, and certain forms of social mortality—may affect population size more profoundly than disease in certain settings.

Mortality and Disease in Hunter-Gatherers

Some of the characteristics of the hunting and gathering way of life (as seen today and in historic times) that may influence the prevalence and distribution of various diseases and other causes of mortality are these: the size of the social group is small, and contact between groups is limited, in part because of the relatively large area needed to support each small population unit; the group utilizes environmental resources intensively but with minimal permanent disturbance of the environment; the individuals are well adapted to the conditions of the ecosystem in which they belong; the individual lives in intimate contact with his fellows and the environment; the group is characteristically mobile, within certain territorial limits; dwellings are often rudimentary or temporary; the dietary range is relatively wide, at least potentially—less desirable foods are available as a reserve for times of hardship; in general the diet may be said to be well balanced in the sense that minimal nutritional requirements are apparently met; in the tropics and subtropics the vegetable component of the diet normally exceeds the animal component in quantity if not in quality; in the arctic and in certain maritime and riverine settings the animal component may bulk larger than the vegetable; occupational specialization except along lines of age and sex is relatively slight.

With these characteristics in mind we may consider some generalizations about health, disease, and mortality in hunting and gathering peoples (prehistoric, precontact, or isolated modern population).

   1. Patent (and perhaps even borderline) malnutrition is rare.   We should expect this in stable, well-adapted hunter-gatherer populations, modern or prehistoric. Dietary resources, even in arid environments, are diverse: typical sampling of these resources by modern hunter-gatherers in ecosystems relatively undisturbed by outsiders seems to provide at least the minimal protein, carbohydrate, fat, mineral, and vitamin requirements. Many workers have commented on the relatively good nutritional status of hunter-gatherers in comparison with neighboring agriculturalists or urban dwellers (for example: Ackerknecht, 1948; Maingard, 1937; Turnbull, 1965b; Woodburn, 1959). Neel (1962) postulated a dramatic gorging-and-fasting way of life for hunter-gatherers through "99 percent of hominid existence" in developing his hypotheses of the "thrifty" diabetic genotype. In the light of recent studies of the Bushman (Lee, 1965), this portrayal of major fluctuations in the quantity and quality of the hunter-gatherer diet is probably somewhat exaggerated.

2. Starvation occurs infrequently.   While hunter-gatherers are rarely exposed to *relative* dietary deficiencies leading to malnutrition, they may, exceptionally, be faced with *gross* deficits. In tropical and temperate regions of moderate to heavy rainfall, starvation has undoubtedly been the exception, occurring only in individuals incapacitated for other reasons (Turnbull, 1965b). In the arid tropics only an unusually prolonged drought may be expected to imperil the food supply, but failure of the water supply may select out the aged and sick before gross food shortages can have their effect. In the arctic and subarctic winter, on the other hand, starvation has probably always been a relatively important cause of death (Ackerknecht, 1948). In general it seems that agriculturalists, more or less dependent on one or several staple crops, are more liable to food supply failure and famine than are hunters and gatherers. Famine risk may even be increased as the effects of dry seasons are exaggerated through agricultural modification of the natural vegetational cover.

3. Chronic diseases, especially those associated with old age, are relatively infrequent.   Birth rates are high, but the population pyramid for hunter-gatherers is broad only at the base because life-expectancy at birth is low for males and even lower for females (Ackerknecht, 1948; Krogman, 1939; Krzwicki, 1934; Neel *et al.,* 1964; Polunin, 1953; Roney, 1959). Shorter female life expectancies presumably reflect maternal losses in childbirth, stresses associated with multiple pregnancies and deliveries, and in certain cultures male-female dietary disparities. Although life expectancies of hunter-gatherers are low by modern European or American standards, they compare favourably with expectancies for displaced hunter-gatherers, many subsistence agriculturalists, and impoverished urbanized people of the tropics today (Ackerknecht, 1948; Billington, 1960; Duguid, 1963; Dunn, 1972; Maingard, 1937; Polunin, 1953). Few hunter-gatherers survive long enough to develop clinical cardiovascular disease or cancer, major causes of mortality in America and Europe today. These diseases do occur infrequently, however, and preclinical manifestations of cardiovascular disorder may be detected in such populations (Mann *et al.,* 1962). Occasional writers have claimed that certain primitive populations are "cancer-free" or "heart disease-free," but sound evidence to support such contentions is lacking, and evidence to the contrary has been steadily accumulating. Chronic diseases of early onset, including genetic disorders, do of course occur regularly in all human populations; upon survey the more severe of

these appear less frequent in hunter-gatherers, probably because prolonged survival
of incapacitated individuals is less likely in mobile than in settled situations. Such
persons have sometimes been abandoned or killed, particularly in the Arctic
(Ackerknecht, 1948).

**4. Accidental and traumatic death rates vary greatly among hunter-gatherer
populations.** It is sometimes said that accidents constitute a major cause of death
in hunting and gathering societies. Although this is indeed the case for certain
peoples, it is not universally true for all hunter-gatherers, past and present. Deaths
due to drowning, burns, suffocation, exposure, and hunting accidents have probably always weighed heavily in the population equation for Eskimos and other
peoples of polar and subpolar regions (Ackerknecht, 1948; Hughes, 1965; World
Health Organization, 1963). The Australian aborigines and Bushmen, on the other
hand, cannot often drown or suffocate or fall from trees, and are physiologically
tolerant of an environment that is climatically "constant" compared to that of the
Eskimo. Turnbull (1965b) has recently commented on the low incidence of accidental injuries and deaths among the Mbuti Pygmies. He recorded falls from trees,
falls into campfires, attacks by animals, falling on a spear, bee stings, and snakebites
as Congo forest hazards. Similarly, Billington (1960) noted the infrequent occurrence of trauma among "settled" aborigines in Arnhem Land. Paleopathologists
have nevertheless demonstrated abundant traumatic pathology in skeletal series for
certain hunters and agriculturalists; most of these series have been recovered from
archeological sites outside the tropics.

**5. Predation, excluding snakebite, is a minor cause of death in modern hunt-
er-gatherers; predation may have been relatively more important in the past.** Haldane (1957) and Motulsky (1960) suggest that through much of hominid evolution
predation and other selective agencies were far more important than infectious and
parasitic diseases, which became major agents of natural selection only after the
introduction of agriculture with its concomitant increases in population density,
community size, and community contact. Livingstone (1958) has provided an interpretation of sickle cell gene distribution in West Africa that supports such an hypothesis, but little other evidence is available at this time to assist us in evaluating
Haldane's suggestion. We cannot rule out the possibility (a strong probability, in my
opinion) that some infectious and parasitic diseases were important selective agencies in prehistoric hunting and gathering populations, as they undoubtedly are and
have been in modern hunter-gatherer societies. Other parasites and microorganisms
have undoubtedly become important in selection only in recent millenia in response
to culturally induced environmental change. We do not know the relative importance of predators at various points in human evolution, although common sense
suggests that predators constituted a greater hazard for early man than for modern
hunter-gatherers. Accurate predation data for the great apes would be of interest in
this connection, but it would be rash to utilize these data in generalizing about
predation in early hominid life. In reviewing some of the literature on health in

hunter-gatherers, I have come upon occasional references to snakebite fatalities, which were apparently particularly frequent in Australia (Cleland, 1928), but references to animal attacks have been few, even for the Arctic (Ackerknecht, 1948; Turnbull, 1965b).

6. **Mental disorders of hunting and gathering peoples have been so little investigated that no generalizations about incidence can be justified.** Descriptions I have encountered of presumed mental disorder have been presented in terms of the psychological norms of the observer-recorder (for example, Cleland, 1928; Basedow, 1932). Ackerknecht (1948) and others have suggested that the rates for phobias and hysteria were higher for the precontact Eskimo than for other societies; discussions of mental disorder in other hunter-gatherers usually emphasize that mental health was good, at least in the aboriginal state. Facts to support such statements are essentially non-existent. Cawte and his colleagues in Australia are pioneering in their ethnopsychiatric investigations of acculturated and unacculturated aborigines. A few limited psychological investigations of Bushmen and Pygmies have been cited by Doob (1965).

7. **Ample evidence is available that "social mortality" has been and is significant in the population equation for any hunting and gathering society.** Cannibalism, infanticide, sacrifice, geronticide, head-hunting, and other forms of warfare have largely disappeared today, but the early contact records provide abundant evidence of the importance of these practices in many societies (for example, Ackerknecht, 1948; Krzwicki, 1934; Neel *et al.,* 1964; Radcliffe-Brown, 1933). Other forms of social mortality, such as homicide, suicide, and stress diseases, were apparently less frequent prior to contact; today they are replacing the old forms and increasing in frequency in displaced and acculturated hunter-gatherers as in so many other human societies (Doob, 1965; Duguid, 1963; Hughes, 1965; Polunin, 1953; World Health Organization, 1963).

8. **Parasitic and infectious disease rates of prevalence and incidence are related to ecosystem diversity and complexity. Although many of these diseases contribute substantially to mortality, no simple, single generalization is possible for all hunter-gatherers.**

A. **Introductory comments: Infection.** Infections by microorganisms and parasites (1) may be classified for epidemiological purposes in two primary subdivisions: *asexual infections* (organisms reproducing asexually) and *sexual infections* (organisms with some form of sexual reproduction; Macdonald, 1965). Each subdivision may be further divided into *direct* and *indirect* categories. An indirect infection requires some development outside the definitive host in normal transmission. This type of infection is therefore partially dependent upon conditions of environmental temperature and humidity; many but not all are specifically tropical.

Asexual infections may be introduced into a population by a single dose in a single individual. Multiplication in the community occurs most readily if the agent is *rare* in that community, and particularly if that agent has not circulated in the community previously. Malaria and yellow fever, whose agents are arthropod vector-transmitted, are good examples of indirect asexual infections. Direct asexual infections are numerous; they include many of the common viral and bacterial infections of mankind (measles, smallpox, diphtheria, etc.). Asexual infections often produce partial and sometimes complete acquired immunity to repeated infection.

Sexual infections cannot normally be introduced into new populations by single doses. The agents multiply and maintain themselves in the population more readily if they occur in large numbers in a high proportion of available hosts—that is, if the prevalence rate is high in the community and if the intensity of infection in the individual is great. Indirect sexual infections include many of the helminthiases: schistosomiasis, filariasis, hookworm infection, etc. Direct sexual infections are not numerous, but include such well-known parasitic helminths as the pinworm. Sexual infections stimulate poor to partial acquired immunity at best.

B. Introductory comments: Ecological diversity and complexity. The concepts of ecological diversity and complexity are well known to ecologists (Holdridge, 1965; Odum, 1959) but little attention has been paid to their epidemiological implications until recently. The starting point for discussion is the climax tropical rainforest, which is characterized by many species of plants and animals per unit area and by few individuals per species in the same unit area. A one-hectare plot in the Brazilian tropical rainforest, for example, contained 564 trees (greater than 10 cm. diameter at chest height) belonging to 60 species. Even the commonest species was represented by only 49 individuals, and 33 species were represented by single individuals (Dobzhansky, 1950). I need not stress the contrast with the tree species/individual relationships in boreal forest. As Dobzhansky (1950) has said, where diversity of inhabitants is great, the environment is rich in adaptive opportunities. This diversity in climax rain forest applies not only to trees, and to other plants, but of course also to birds, snakes, insects, mammals, and many other forms of life, not omitting potential or actual vectors, intermediate hosts, and alternative hosts for infective organisms. We are now beginning to see that this diversity also extends to parasites and microorganisms.

The ratio between the number of species and the number of individuals per species has been called the *diversity index* (Odum, 1959). In the tropical rain forest the diversity index is high; wherever man disturbs this forest the index is lower; wherever physical factors are severe and limiting, as in the Arctic, the desert, or at high altitude, the diversity index is very low—few species but large numbers of individuals per species. At an "edge," that is, the line of contact between a forest and a field, the diversity index may be somewhat higher than on either side of the line. Wherever man has substantially altered the environment, and the diversity is accordingly low, some of the species represented by large numbers of individuals are commonly called "weeds." Actually all plants and animals (including man) are weeds in such circumstances.

The *complexity index* recently developed by Holdridge (1965) provides a measure of vegetation complexity (and secondarily of other biological complexity), but should not be confused with the diversity index. The complexity index is based on height of forest stand, basal area of stand, number of trees, and number of tree species, but it does not take into account the number of trees per species. Holdridge has recently published a useful classification of world plant formations; it provides complexity indices for many of these formations (Holdridge 1965).

      C. Infection and ecological diversity and complexity: hypothetical conditions. We may now contrast two "ideal" and undisturbed ecosystems including human populations of similar group sizes, similarly dispersed (table I). One is complex—with high diversity and complexity indices; the other is simple—with low indices.

Table 1. Infection in Ecosystems of Contrasting Diversity and Complexity

Complex Ecosystem (example: tropical rain forest)	*Simple Ecosystem* (examples: subpolar tundra, desert bush, thorn woodland)
—*Many* species of plants and animals	—*Few* species of plants and animals
—*Few* individuals per species	—*Many* individuals per species
—*Many* species of parasitic and infectious organisms (in man and in other animals)	—*Few* species of parasitic and infectious organisms (in man and in other animals)
—*Many* species of potential vectors, intermediate hosts, and alternative hosts (to man) for parasitic and infectious organisms	—*Few* species of potential vectors, intermediate hosts, and alternative hosts (to man) for parasitic and infectious organisms
—*Low* potential transmission efficiency for indirect infections	—*High* potential transmission efficiency for those few indirect infections occurring in this ecosystem
—Sexual infections: *many* kinds due to many species of organisms	—Sexual infections: *few* kinds
—Sexual infections: *low* intensities of infection—*low* worm burdens—light infections	—Sexual infections: *greater* intensity of infection—*heavier* worm burdens
—Asexual infections: *many* kinds due to many species of organisms	—Asexual infections: *few* kinds
—Direct asexual infections producing good partial or permanent immunity: appearing in human population units at long intervals	—Direct asexual infections producing good partial or permanent immunity: appearing in human population units at long intervals
—Direct asexual infections producing little or no immunity: *low* prevalence	—Direct asexual infections producing little or no immunity: *high* prevalence
—Indirect asexual infections (except those producing substantial immunity): *low* prevalence	—Indirect asexual infections (except those producing substantial immunity): *high* prevalence
—(Also: many species but few individuals of venomous and noxious arthropods and reptiles = *low* incidence of bites)	—(Also: many individuals of a few species of venomous and noxious arthropods and reptiles = *high* incidence of bites)

D. Generalizations: infectious and parasitic disease in hunter-gatherers. The ideal conditions outlined in table I for a *complex* ecosystem are believed applicable in any consideration of infection in unacculturated, undisplaced Congo forest Pygmies or Malayan Negritos (Semang). The conditions for a *simple ecosystem* are presumably applicable to the Eskimo, the Bushman, or the Australian aborigine. These conditions should also be relevant in any epidemiological study of infection in non-human primates: in the more or less arboreal rain-forest species on the one hand, and in the more or less terrestrial open-country species on the other. I have recently reviewed records for parasitism in African primates, setting the findings against the conditions outlined above. The results are consistent with these conditions (Dunn, 1966). The epidemiological record for infection in hunter-gatherers is of course considerably "contaminated" by contact with outsiders, introductions of infections, environmental disturbances, and displacements. Careful study of historical and ethnographic records will probably provide additional data for examination against the hypothesized conditions. At the moment, however, I can offer only limited supporting data on helminthic and protozoan parasite species numbers in four hunting and gathering peoples (table II). Records for the Bushmen, Australians, and Pygmies have been extracted from the literature (primarily: Billington, 1960; Black, 1959; Bronte-Stewart *et al.,* 1960; Casley-Smith, 1959; Cleland, 1928;

Table 2. Parasitic Helminths and Protozoa in Four Hunting and Gathering Peoples
(summarizing all available records)

	Bushman Africa	Australian Aborigine — Entire Continent	Australian Aborigine — Central Australia	Semang Malaya	Pygmy Africa
PLANT FORMATION	Desert Desert Bush Thorn Woodland	Primarily: Desert Desert Bush Thorn Woodland	Desert Desert Bush	Tropical, Premontane & Lower Montane Rain-Forest	Tropical & Premontane Rain-Forest
Complexity Index (Holdridge)	5.6 or less	primarily less than 5.6	5.6 or less	270-405	270-405
No. Species Helminths	2	6	1	10	11
No. Species Intestinal Protozoa	–	1	–	9	6
No. Species Blood Protozoa	1	2	–	3	3
Total No. Species	3	9	1	22	20

Crotty and Webb, 1960; Heinz, 1961; Maingard, 1937; Mann *et al.,* 1962; Price *et al.,* 1963). Records for intestinal protozoa are probably incomplete; in other respects the records appear adequate. All available records for the Australian continent, representing a variety of habitats (mainly arid), are shown in one column; findings for one nomadic and isolated population in Central Australia are also shown separately. Semang data are based primarily upon my own surveys in 1962-64 (Dunn, 1972), and on the work of Wharton *et al.* (1963) and Polunin (1953). A few species of helminths and intestinal protozoa in modern acculturated, semi-urbanized Eskimos have been recorded, but I have not so far encountered any records of parasitological survey for truly isolated Eskimo populations.

E. Summary. The complexity and diversity of the ecosystem must influence—perhaps profoundly—the patterning of infection and disease in hunter-gatherer populations. Prevalence, incidence, intensity, distribution, transmission efficiency, vector abundance, intermediate or alternative host variety and abundance are all affected by these ecological factors. For some hunter-gatherers many kinds of parasitic and infectious diseases may be responsible for moderate rates of morbidity and mortality; for others only a few kinds of disease may be responsible for much morbidity, and even mortality; some diseases appear at long intervals, causing high mortality; others are ever present, causing more or less morbidity and mortality depending on a complex array of ecological and cultural factors. If diseases caused by parasites and microorganisms serve as agents of natural selection and population regulation, then any patterning of these diseases will mirror, or be mirrored by, similar patterning of disease-related selection pressures and population-regulating mechanisms.

Conclusion

The hunter-gatherer is an element in an ecosystem and cannot isolate himself from his environment. Little or no buffering stands between him and the other components of the system. His relationship to the land, to its flora and fauna, and to his fellow man is intimate. Although he is never perfectly adapted to the conditions in his environment, there is a degree of adaptive stability—of ecological conservatism—which does not exist in a modern urban setting. When forces of change appear, however, rapid and profound destabilization may follow. The medical sphere today provides many examples of this destabilization among the surviving hunting peoples as they encounter outsiders, lose their lands to agricultural and pastoral encroachment, and even suffer permanent displacement from these lands. "New" diseases and disorders appear, endemic diseases either disappear or become more prevalent and more damaging as social and ecological change enhances their transmissibility, and former causes of mortality are displaced by new causes.

Hunters today do not live in wholly aboriginal or "prehistoric" states of health, and historic or ethnographic records offer little data upon which to base speculations about prehistoric conditions of health. We can, however, take note of the *patterning* of present-day health problems among the surviving hunters. This patterning is inevitably affected by the ecological setting of the hunting group, for, as I have previously noted, the hunter lives in a truly intimate relationship with his surroundings. If we can determine and understand the factors that contribute to patterning of diseases and causes of death in modern peoples who live in an unbuffered relationship to their environment, we can apply this understanding to the interpretation of the prehistoric and evolutionary record, even in the absence of knowledge about which (specific) diseases may or may not have been present in an ancient population.

A discussion of epidemiological patterning for the infectious and parasitic diseases has been presented; this patterning is linked to ecological factors, including diversity and complexity. Elsewhere in this review I have mentioned striking differences in incidence for predation, accidents, and other causes of death for hunter-gatherers in various geographical settings. A few ecologically linked patterns of morbidity and mortality have emerged; others will no doubt be added as old information is screened and new data become available. The findings already emphasize the fallacy in generalizing about "hunter-gatherers" as though they were some kind of homogeneous cultural-genetic-ecological unity. They are *diverse*, their hunting territories are diverse, and so are their diseases and ways of death.

Note

1. Parasites, in the strict sense used here, comprise the protozoa, helminths, and ectoparasites of biomedical importance. Microorganisms (or infectious organisms) include the viruses, bacteria, rickettsia, and fungi.

Gina B. Kolata

!Kung hunter-gatherers: feminism, diet, and birth control

If results from recent studies of the !Kung* people apply to other societies, anthropologists may now have some new clues as to the social, dietary, and demographic changes that took place during the Neolithic Revolution when people forsook lives of hunting and gathering and began to farm and to keep herds of domestic animals. The !Kung have lived as hunters and gatherers in the Kalahari

*The exclamation point refers to an alveolarpalatal click. The tongue tip is pressed against the roof of the mouth and drawn sharply away, producing a hollow popping sound.

From *Science*, Vol. 185, pp. 932-934, 13 September 1974. Copyright 1974 by the American Association for the Advancement of Science.

Desert of South Africa for at least 11,000 years; but recently they have begun to live in agrarian villages near those of Bantus. Investigators who are documenting this change find that, among other things, the settled !Kung women are losing their egalitarian status, the children are no longer brought up to be nonaggressive, and the size of the !Kung population is rapidly increasing rather than remaining stable.

The !Kung's very existence is anomalous since they have lived by hunting and gathering since the Pleistocene. In his archeological studies, John Yellen of the Smithsonian Institution in Washington, D.C., finds artifacts from Late Stone Age hunter-gatherers, of about 11,000 years ago, at the same water holes where modern !Kung set up camp. According to Yellen, these prehistoric hunter-gatherers even hunted the same animals as the contemporary !Kung, including the nocturnal springhare which must be hunted by a special technique because it spends its days in a long deep burrow.

As recently as 10 years ago, many of the !Kung still lived by hunting and gathering. Now, however, less than 5 percent of the 30,000 !Kung live in this way; the remainder live in agricultural villages. This period of rapid social change coincided with extensive study of these people by numerous investigators throughout the world and from many disciplines.

It is difficult to distinguish between changes due to settling down and changes due to acculturation to Bantu society. Investigators have drawn on extensive long-term studies of the nomadic !Kung in their documentation of the effects of the !Kung's adoption of an agrarian life, but cannot conclusively state the causes of these effects.

One aspect of the settled !Kung society that has aroused considerable interest among social scientists is the role of women. Patricia Draper of the University of New Mexico reports that !Kung women who belong to the nomadic bands enjoy higher status, more autonomy, and greater ability to directly influence group decisions than do sedentary !Kung women. This loss of equality for the agrarian women, Draper believes, may be explained in terms of the social structure of nomadic, as compared to sedentary, groups.

Draper postulates that one reason for the higher status of !Kung hunter-gatherer women is that the women contribute, by gathering, at least 50 percent of the food consumed by a band. Since food gathered by women is so important to the group, the women, of necessity, are as mobile as the men (who hunt), and women and men leave the camp equally often to obtain food. Both the women and men who do not seek food on a given day remain in the camp and share in taking care of the children.

The women in sedentary !Kung societies have far less mobility than the men and contribute less to the food supply. The men leave the village to clear fields and raise crops and to care for the cattle of their Bantu neighbors. The women remain in the village where they prepare food and take care of the shelters. Since the men work for the Bantus, they learn the Bantu language. Thus when the Bantus deal with the !Kung, they deal exclusively with the men. This practice, together with the !Kung's emulation of the male dominated Bantu society, contributes to increasingly subservient roles for !Kung women.

Also contributing to a loss of female egalitarianism is the different way that agrarian, as compared to nomadic, !Kung bring up their children. Draper points out that the nomads live in bands consisting of very few people so that a child generally has no compainions of the same age. Thus play groups contain children of both sexes and a wide variety of ages. This discourages the development of distinct games and roles for boys and girls.

Unlike the nomadic children, the sedentary children play in groups consisting of children of the same sex and similar ages. The boys are expected to help herd cattle, so they leave the village where they are away from adults and on their own. The girls, according to Draper, have no comparable experience but remain in the village and help the adult women with chores.

In addition to promoting sexual egalitarianism by their child rearing practices, the nomadic !Kung also discourage aggression among their children. This is no longer the case when the !Kung become sedentary. The nomadic children observed by Draper do not play competitive games. She attributes this to the wide range of ages of children in a group which would make competitiveness difficult. Moreover, since these children are constantly watched by adults, the adults can and do quickly stop aggressive behavior among children. The children rarely observe aggressive behavior among adults because the nomadic !Kung have no way to deal with physical aggression and consciously avoid it. For example, according to Richard Lee of the University of Toronto, when conflict within a group of adults begins, families leave for other bands. Lee observed that the sendentary !Kung, who cannot easily pick up and leave, rely on their Bantu neighbors to mediate disputes.

In addition to studying social changes taking place when the !Kung settle down, investigators are studying dietary and demographic changes. The !Kung diet is of interest because the nomadic !Kung are exceedingly healthy and are free from many diseases thought to be associated with the diets of people in more complex societies. The sedentary !Kung have substantially altered their diets, thus providing investigators with a unique opportunity to document the effects of diet on the health of these people. The demographic changes taking place among the !Kung are of interest because the settled !Kung seem to have lost a natural check on their fertility rates.

The diet of the completely nomadic !Kung, which has been analyzed by geneticists, biochemists, and nutritionists, consists of nuts, vegetables, and meat and lacks milk and grains. All the investigators agree that the diet is nutritionally well balanced and provides an adequate number of calories. They found very few people with iron deficiency anemia, even when they included pregnant and lactating women in their sample. They also discovered that the nomadic !Kung have a very low incidence of deficiency of the vitamin folic acid and that the concentrations of vitamin B_{12} are higher in their serums as compared to concentrations considered normal for other populations. These findings led Henry Harpending of the University of New Mexico and his associates to suggest that Stone Age people probably had no deficiencies of these vitamins and that deficiencies first appeared when people settled down into agrarian societies.

In addition to being well nourished, the nomadic !Kung are free from many common diseases of old age. For example, Lee and others have found little degenerative disease among elderly !Kung, although it is commonplace for these people to live for at least 60 years and some live for as long as 80 years. A. Stewart Truswell of the University of London also finds that the nomadic !Kung are one of only about a dozen groups of people in the world whose blood pressure does not increase as they grow older.

The medical effects of the altered diet and way of life of the sedentary !Kung are not yet well established. In contrast to the hunter-gatherers, these people consume a great deal of cow's milk and grain. In his studies of a generation of !Kung brought up on such a diet, Lee finds that they are, on the average, taller, fatter, and heavier than the nomadic !Kung. Nancy Howell of the University of Toronto finds that the agrarian women have their first menstrual periods (menarches) earlier than the nomadic women.

The average age of menarche among nomadic !Kung is late—at least age 15.5 according to Howell. Although these women marry at puberty, they have their first children when they are, on the average, 19.5 years of age. This late start to reproductive life helps limit the growth of the population. However, a more significant curb on the size of nomadic populations is the low fertility of the women. Howell finds that the average length of time between giving birth for a nomadic !Kung woman is 4 years. These women have fewer children than any other women in societies that do not practice contraception or abortion. The low fertility of nomadic !Kung contradicts previously held theories that the sizes of hunter-gatherer populations were limited solely by high mortality rates. The !Kung population size remains stable because there are so few children born. Combining her studies of the fertility and mortality rates of !Kung hunter-gatherers, Howell concludes that the long-term growth rate for such a population is only 0.5 percent per year. This is in sharp contrast to the sedentary !Kung whose population is growing rapidly.

The population growth among the sedentary !Kung results from both a decrease in the age of menarche and a decrease in the average time between births. Lee has found that the birth intervals drop 30 percent when !Kung women become sedentary. The causes of these reproductive changes are unknown, but some investigators suspect that these decreased birth intervals may result from changes in nursing or dietary habits.

Nomadic !Kung women have no soft food to give their babies, and so they nurse them for 3 or 4 years, and during this time the women rarely conceive. Sedentary !Kung women, on the other hand, wean their babies much sooner by giving them grain meal and cow's milk. Irven DeVore of Harvard University believes that a contraceptive effect of the long lactation period is not unexpected, since investigators have observed the same phenomenon in many animals, including monkeys and the great apes. A woman who begins to supplement her infant's diet while the child is very young would not experience this effect because her child would require less and less milk.

Howell and Rose Frisch of the Harvard Center for Population Studies believe that an explanation of the decrease in the age of menarche and in the birth
intervals of sedentary !Kung women may involve the diet of the sedentary !Kung.
They base this idea on a study by Frisch and Janet McArthur of the Massachusetts
General Hospital in Boston. These investigators showed that the amount of body
fat must be above a certain minimum for the onset of menstruation and for its
maintenance after menarche. Howell points out that the !Kung hunter-gatherers
are thin, although well nourished. When women from these bands lactate, they need
about 1000 extra calories a day. Thus, during the 3 or 4 years that a woman nurses
a baby, she may have too little body fat for ovulation to take place. The shorter
birth intervals for sedentary !Kung women would follow from their shorter periods
of lactation and larger amounts of body fat. Howell notes that this explanation of
the low fertility of nomadic !Kung women cannot be verified until more extensive
medical studies are performed with these people.

Although no one claims that the changes taking place in the !Kung society
necessarily reflect those that took place when other hunter-gatherer societies became agrarian, studies of the !Kung are providing anthropologists with clues relative
to the origins of some features of modern societies. Many findings, such as the
social egalitarianism, lack of aggression, and low fertility of nomadic !Kung are
leading to new perspectives on the hunting and gathering way of life which was,
until 10,000 years ago, the way all humans lived.

Additional Reading

1. R. B. Lee and I. DeVore, Eds., *Kalahari Hunter-Gatherers* (Harvard Univ. Press, Cambridge,
   Mass., in press).

Francis L. Black

Infectious diseases in primitive societies

Infectious diseases have exerted some of the strongest of the pressures that
shaped the development of modern man (1, 2). Historic records give dramatic accounts of the role which disease played in the displacement of American Indian and
some Polynesian peoples from their lands (3), but more subtle effects of disease,
working over long periods, may have had greater evolutionary impact. The penetra-
tion of the gene for hemoglobin S into West Africa has been cited by Livingston (4)
as one instance in which disease has fostered the diffusion of a particular trait faster

From *Science*, Vol. 187, pp. 515-518, 14 February 1975. Copyright 1975 by the American
Association for the Advancement of Science.

than other characteristics of the people who introduced it.

There is reason to believe, however, that many of our modern diseases did not exist in primitive populations. Measles, for instance, requires a larger population for its maintenance than existed in any coherent group in Neolithic times (5). The spectrum of diseases that afflicted man through most of his development may have been much smaller than that to which we have been subject in historic times.

Fossil and Historic Records

Paleopathologists have attempted to identify diseases prevalent in early man through lesions in his bones. From this evidence, tuberculosis seems to have had a very long history (6), and lepromatous leprosy a relatively short one, with the earliest definite cases dating from about A.D. 500 (7). The antiquity of syphilis has been the subject of much controversy. Examination of human bones, however, sheds no light on the much more numerous diseases that affect only soft tissues. Ancient soft tissues are only available from a few desiccated or anaerobically preserved human remains from limited areas and from the mummies of the relatively advanced Egyptian civilization. These provide evidence of various metazoan and protozoan parasites (8), but the amount and quality of material available has been inadequate to provide convincing data on the incidence of other infectious diseases.

Hare (9) pointed out that the ability of an infectious agent to multiply in a nonhuman host or to persist in the infected person beyond the acute phase of disease would have determined its ability to persist in the small populations of antiquity. Hare analyzed historical accounts without finding convincing evidence of smallpox before the first century A.D., of measles before the sixth century, or of cholera before the sixteenth century. He does, however, accept Hippocrates' description of mumps and a first-century description of herpes zoster (shingles). Interpretation of historical accounts is fraught with problems in identifying disease names and limited by the ability of the writers of the time to distinguish between diseases.

Modern Primitive Societies

Polunin (10) has suggested that contemporary primitive societies perpetuate conditions which existed in ancient peoples. The populations he studied in Malaysia were not sufficiently isolated to be free of infectious agents conferred on them by more cosmopolitan peoples, but he found a relatively small number of diseases responsible for the bulk of their morbidity. Among infectious diseases, malaria, yaws, and the fungal infection *Tinea imricata* were most common. Polunin recognized that his methods measured prevalence rather than incidence, and that other infections might account for more acute disease.

The study of modern primitive cultures is complicated both by the introduction of foreign disease to readily accessible populations and by the difficulty of determining long-term incidence rates in isolated groups. Many infectious diseases, however, leave a lasting trace, sometimes, as with smallpox, in the form of permanent physical changes, but more often in the form of persisting specific antibody relatively settled villages of about 300 persons. Tribes of more than a few hundred are unstable and tend to split, often violently. The Kayapo tribes, which we have worked with, seem to have arisen by such a fissioning process (22). If the population of a tribe falls below 100 persons, other pressures come into play, particularly the problem of finding marital partners not forbidden by incest taboos. Two small tribes in northern Brazil have recently joined the Tiriyo for these reasons (23). The population of the Amazon periphery is very sparse, and 200 kilometers or more of forest may separate neighboring tribes. Even then, the only contact may be hostile.

Table 1. Immunological evidence of past infection with various disease agents in isolated Brazilian Indian tribes. Suia and others include data on the Suia and associated tribes of the southern Xingu Park from Baruzzi et al. (18). Data on the Xavante are from Neel et al. (17). The numbers in parentheses after the tribes' names are the total population and the specimens available.

Characteristic	Disease	Tiriyo (220, 200)	Ewar-hoyana (14, 9)	Kaxu-yana (40, 27)	Xikrin (123, 118)	Goro-tire (400, 219)	Kuben Kran Kegn (300, 57)	Mekra-noti (190, 175)	Suia and others (755, 258)	Xa-vante (1600, 412)	All (3€ 14
						Percentage of sample giving positive reaction					
Endemic—	Herpes	91	75		90			93			95
high inci-	Epstein-Barr virus	97	100		97			96			97
dence, low	Cytomegalovirus	43		95	72			96			54
morbidity	Hepatitis B	5			61			71			56
	Treponema*	0	0	0	19		85	62		0	32
Enzootic—	Yellow fever	14			37	4	0	5	5	3	8
low preva-	Mayaro	47			46	37	20	49	30	18	33
lence over	(arbovirus A)										
long time	Toxoplasmosis	43			46			52	52	100	57
Introduced—	Measles	4	11	89	3	98	33	0	78	86	45
explosive,	Mumps	29	11	73	23	73	33	22			33
transient	Rubella	95	11	74	0			1			32
	Influenza A	13	0	22	16			5	2	0	8
	Influenza B	0	0	0	0			0	42	13	13
	Parainfluenza 2	3	0	14	89						47
	Poliovirus 1				30		49	4		87	54
Introduced—	Tuberculosis				27			29	4	1	17
persistent	Malaria†				41			6	84	62	50

*Treponema is endemic only in the Kayapo tribes Xikrin, Kuben Kran Kegn, and Mekranoti, as tested by the FTA-ABS or the treponema palidum immobilization (TPI) test. †Positive tests are enlarged spleen in the Xikrin or fluorescent antibody in the Xavante.

Endemic Diseases

Serological test results and other evidence of past infection in South American Indian populations indicate that the prevalence of infectious disease may vary greatly titers. These traces can be determined with a single serum specimen or by a simple examination, and they can be used to estimate cumulated incidence rates for the total period covered by the life-span of the subjects. Where subjects of various ages are available for study, incidence rates for any period back to the birth of the oldest person can be estimated.

Paul *et al.* (11) used this approach to study poliomyelitis in a population of about 1000 north Alaskan Eskimos. By testing serums collected in 1949, they found a high incidence of type 2 poliovirus antibodies in persons born before 1930, but very few positive reactions in younger persons. Similarly, type 1 antibodies were confined to persons born after 1915, and type 3 to persons born after 1905. These results confirmed a history of a minor epidemic of paralysis in 1930 and a major one several years before 1921. Using this approach, they could not determine whether these viruses had been active in the community before the epidemic dates, but they could be confident that the viruses had not infected significant numbers of persons since the specified dates. It seems clear that, like measles in the Faroes (12) and the common cold in Spitzbergen (13), poliomyelitis spread in a small community with such efficiency that it soon killed or immunized so high a proportion of the population that the virus was unable to continue propagating. Since the virus is labile, when it could no longer replicate it died out from the community entirely.

The isolation of small oceanic island populations is often sufficient to give rise to long intervals between epidemics of individual diseases. It can be shown with many diseases that the intervals are due to the infectious agent dying out and that new epidemics start, not with activation of latent pathogen in an island population, but only when the agent is introduced from the outside. An exception to this pattern is varicella (chicken pox), epidemics of which were shown by Hope-Simpson (14) to have originated by activation of latent virus. Isolation by wide stretches of water has never been typical of the majority of mankind, and failure of certain diseases to persist in the islands had not been seen as relevant to the condition of the human race in general.

In fact, the isolation of primitive mainland groups from one another may be as profound as the isolation of island populations. The Eskimos studied by Paul *et al.* are a case in point. Also, Adels *et al.* (15) have shown that measles did not persist in certain isolated Australian and Papuan primitive communities, and Anderson and Mufson (16) found that reovirus type 3 failed to persist in an isolated African tribe. The largest area still inhabited by primitive cultures is on the periphery of the Amazon basin. Several workers, including the author, have looked at the epidemiology of infectious disease in the people of this area. Serological and clinical evidence of disease in the Xavante of Brazil was the subject of a major study by Neel *et al.* (17). Baruzzi and his colleagues (18, 19) have conducted various studies of the tribes of the Xingu Park, and Schaad (20) has studied two Surinam tribes. Black *et al.* (21) recently completed a study of seven Carib and Kayapo tribes in Brazil.

People of the Amazon, who retain their traditional social structures, are in Fenner's (2) second stage of human development, with incipient agriculture and with different diseases and in different tribes (table I). In one group of diseases, very high antibody prevalence rates were found in all but the very youngest age groups. We include in the category of endemic diseases those which showed a uniform proportion of positive test results in persons over 10 years of age, even if the proportion was considerably less than 100 percent, when it was known that the test being used was only sensitive enough to detect the higher titers. Herpes simplex, chicken pox, Epstein-Barr (infectious mononucleosis), hepatitis B, and cytomegalovirus diseases fall into this category. These are diseases that seemed to be very well adapted to persistence in primitive communities. Their prevalence in these communities was higher than commonly found in more advanced cultures, and no tribe was found free of them. They caused little apparent morbidity and did not threaten the continuance of their host population. The infectious agents of all these diseases are known to remain in infected persons for long periods of time and to be reactivable.

Evidence of treponemal infection was not found in the Surinam tribes, the Brazilian Tiriyo, or the Xavante, except in a few instances where contact with outsiders could be presumed. In the three Kayapo tribes tested, however, a very high prevalence of positive tests was found. Sixty percent of the adult members of these tribes were positive by both the standard flocculation (VDRL) test and the more specific fluorescent antibody (FTAABS) test, and another 19 percent were positive by one test or the other. No FTA positive reactions were found in children under 7 years of age, but there were several positive by both tests in the prepubertal age group. Clinical examination revealed no evidence of venereal or congenital syphilis, pinta, or yaws. The serological tests indicate that some treponema is very commonly encountered by these people. The absence of clinical signs suggests that it does minimal harm. Many authors have suggested that syphilis was indigenous to the Western Hemisphere, yet the pathological evidence in pre-Columbian bones is far from conclusive (24). If it were indigenous, it must certainly have been less virulent than the syphilis that appeared in Europe at the end of the 15th century. Either the agent active among the Kayapo is of low virulence or the people possess unusual resistance; for either reason, a stable relationship exists in this setting, which permits continuance of both parasite and host.

Another category of recurrent diseases are caused by agents whose chief host is some animal with a higher population density than man. The arboviruses of yellow fever and Mayaro are representative of this enzootic group. Toxoplasmosis and leishmaniasis are also in this category. The prevalence of antibody to these viruses varied from one tribe to another, presumably depending on the availability of some other host or vector in the immediate area. However, where antibody was found in the human population, the proportion positive increased gradually and steadily with increasing age. Apparently the risk of infection was proportional to duration of exposure, and the infections had not occurred in the form of major epidemics.

Introduced Diseases

When antibody to certain other disease agents was measured, a very high prevalence was found above a certain age in specific tribes; and there was practically no evidence of infection below that age. Where this was the case in one tribe, other tribes often exhibited no evidence of infection at all, except perhaps in a few of the most traveled individuals. This was true of measles, mumps, rubella, influenza, parainfluenza, and poliomyelitis. This group of diseases corresponds—with the exceptions that poliomyelitis is added and varicella-zoster is not included—to Hare's group (9) of "acute infections in which the organisms disappear when recovery or death occurs." If travelers are infected with one of these diseases while they are outside the tribal area, they are not likely to carry it home. If the diseases are brought in, they spread rapidly to essentially the whole population and then die out. Children born after the epidemic remain free of disease. This group includes many of the most prominent infectious diseases of cosmopolitan populations. However, because they do not persist in small populations, it is unlikely that, in their modern form, they were a problem to ancient man. Conversely, they are the diseases to which modern man may have had the least time to adapt.

Tuberculosis and malaria also seem to represent diseases that have been introduced to the Amazon tribes in recent time. As yet, none of the members of the Auca tribe of the Ecuadorian Amazon give positive tuberculin tests, but the incidence of positive tests is increasing in the Suia, Txukharamai (25), and Xikrin (21). There is no evidence in these tribes of hemoglobin S or the unusual glucose-6-phosphate dehydrogenase genes, which have been correlated with long-term selective pressures from malaria (26). Both these diseases entail long infectious periods and neither confers solid immunity after an acute attack. They, therefore, seem quite able to maintain themselves in these populations, and if they were not to be found in these groups prior to recent contact with outsiders, it may only reflect an accident of geography. However, both diseases cause high morbidity in the tribes, and there is serious concern that they may actually destroy the Indian populations. Thus, the persistence of these diseases may ultimately be no more certain than if the population became immune.

The geographical features that separated the South American Indians from important sources of evolving disease agents and the filtering effect of the Bering and Panamanian land bridges may have protected the people we studied from a number of diseases, including tuberculosis and malaria. However, another factor, their small population concentrations, would have protected them from many diseases even if the disease agents reached the area. The small population groupings that characterize the Amazon tribes are a very general phenomenon among primitive cultures, and similar groups have been studied with similar results in Australasia (15). It seems probable, moreover, that ancient man was also divided into small social groupings. Unless ancient conditions were fundamentally different from those of surviving primitive cultures, measles, influenza, smallpox, and poliomyelitis could not have been present during the period of human emergence nor through most of man's history. The time that we have had in which to adapt to these diseases is probably less than 200 generations.

Summary

Incidence of various infectious diseases in several Amazon Indian tribes has been determined serologically. Diseases that infect only man fall into two distinct categories. Those which can persist in an individual for a prolonged period are highly endemic, but those which are infectious only in the acute phase die out quickly after introduction. The suggestion is made that the latter diseases could not perpetuate themselves before the advent of advanced cultures and did not exert selective pressures on the human genetic constitution until relatively recently.

References and Notes

1. J. B. S. Haldane, *Acta Genet. Stat. Med.* 6, 321 (1957).
2. F. Fenner, in *The Impact of Civilization on the Biology of Man*, S. V. Boyden, Ed. (Univ. of Toronto Press, Toronto, 1970), pp. 48-68.
3. A. G. Motulsky, *Hum. Biol.* 32, 28 (1960).
4. F. B. Livingston, *Am. Anthropol.* 60, 533 (1958).
5. F. L. Black, *J. Theor. Biol.* 11, 207 (1966).
6. D. Morse, D. Brothwell, P. J. Ucko, *Am. Rev. Respir. Dis.* 90, 524 (1964); P. Bartels, *Arch. Anthropol.* 6, 243 (1907).
7. V. Möller-Christensen, in *Diseases in Antiquity*, D. Brothwell and A. T. Sandison, Eds. (Thomas, Springfield, Ill., 1967), pp. 295-306.
8. M. A. Ruffer, *Br. Med. J.* 16 (1910); T. Pizzi and H. Schenone, *Biol. Chil. Parasitol.* 9, 73 (1954); H. Helbaek, *Kuml* (1958), p. 83.
9. R. Hare, in *Diseases in Antiquity*, D. Brothwell and A. T. Sandison, Eds. (Thomas, Springfield, Ill., 1967), pp. 115-131.
10. I. V. Polunin, *Med. J. Malaya* 8, 55 (1953).
11. J. R. Paul, J. T. Riordan, J. L. Melnick, *Am. J. Hyg.* 54, 275 (1951).
12. P. L. Panum, *Observations Made during the Epidemic of Measles on the Faroe Islands in the Year 1846* (American Publishing Association, New York, 1940).
13. J. H. Paul and H. L. Freese, *Am. J. Hyg.* 17, 517 (1933).
14. R. E. Hope-Simpson, *Proc. R. Soc. Med.* 58, 9 (1965).
15. N. R. Adels, J. W. Francis, D. C. Gajdusek, *Am. J. Dis. Child.* 103, 255 (1962).
16. N. Anderson and M. A. Mufson, *Trop. Geogr. Med.* 24, 168 (1972).
17. J. V. Neel, F. M. Salzano, P. C. Junqueira, F. Keiter, D. Maybury-Lewis, *Hum. Genet.* 16, 52 (1964); J. V. Neel, A. H. P. Andrade, G. E. Brown, W. E. Eveland, E. D. Weinstein, A. H. Wheeler, *Am. J. Trop. Med.* 17, 486 (1968).
18. R. G. Baruzzi, M. D. Rodrigues, R. P. S. Carvalho, L. L. Souza Dias, *Rev. Inst. Med. Trop. São Paulo* 13, 356 (1971).
19. R. G. Baruzzi, *ibid.* 12, 93 (1970); H. G. Percira, R. G. Baruzzi, R. P. S. Carvalho, *ibid.*, p. 285.
20. J. D. G. Schaad, *Trop. Geogr. Med.* 12, 38 (1960).
21. F. L. Black, J. P. Woodall, A. S. Evans, H. Liebhaber, G. Henle, *Am. J. Epidemiol.* 91, 430 (1970); F. L. Black *et al.*, *ibid.* 100, 230 (1974).
22. F. M. Salzano, *Soc. Biol.* 18, 148 (1971).
23. P. Frikel, *Mus. Paraense Emilio Goeldi Publ. Avulsas* 14, 1 (1970).
24. C. J. Hackett, *Bull. W.H.O.* 29, 7 (1963).
25. N. Nutels, *Pan Am. Health Organ. Sci. Publ.* 165, 68 (1968).
26. F. M. Salzano, H. Gershowitz, P. C. Junqueira, J. P. Woodall, F. L. Black, W. J. Heirholzer, *Am. J. Phys. Anthropol.* 36, 417 (1972); F. M. Salzano, J. P. Woodall, F. L. Black, L. R. Weitkamp,

M. Helena, L. P. Franco, *Hum. Biol.* 46, 81 (1974).

27. Original data used in this article have mostly been published in the *American Journal of Epidemiology.* Tests were performed by F. P. Pinheiro, A. S. Evans, J. P. Woodall, W. J. Heirholzer, E. M. Opton, J. E. Emmons, B. S. West, and G. Wallace. Travel support was received from the Pan American Health Organization.

Don Brothwell

The question of pollution in earlier and less developed societies

In a study of the rehydrated feces of an early Amerindian community in Nevada, Heizer (1967) reflected, somewhat sadly, that his attempts to find corroborative information on the sanitary habits and attitudes of recent Amerindians had been mainly fruitless. Anthropologists have provided a great wealth of data on Amerindians, their politics, religion, economy—but clearly not all the day-to-day business of life has been recorded. In agreeing to prepare this contribution, I had innocently believed that a substantial supporting literature would be available for the task, but unknowingly, like Heizer, I had walked into barren lands. In fact all is not lost, for although there is little detailed information which can be given, it is certainly relevant to discuss in this volume the broader themes of pollution and less developed societies, with a view to demonstrating that pollution is not a new problem, and it is certainly not limited to advanced civilizations. The reason why the subject is now attracting international attention is because some detrimental aspects of pollution are cumulative, and we have reached a threshold which demands that long-term world action must now be taken. But the beginnings of the problem were established long ago.

A recent US government definition of pollution is

> *the unfavorable alteration of our surroundings, wholly or largely as a by-product of man's actions, through direct or indirect effects of changes in energy patterns, radiation levels, chemical and physical constitution and abundances of organisms. The changes may affect man directly, or through his supplies of water and of agricultural and other biological products, his physical objects or possessions, or his opportunities for recreation and appreciation of nature (Wolman, 1967).*

From P. R. Cox and J. Peel (eds.), *Population and Pollution* (London: Academic Press, 1972), pp. 15-27. Reprinted by permission of The Eugenics Society.

This environmental view of pollution perhaps needs some additional qualification. Although in the strict terms of health and biological stability, pollution may be referred to by means of standards, populations can in fact "rate" the various polluting factors differently. To Europeans, the long-term communal sounds in a Bornean long house, or the smells in a more squalid aboriginal settlement, or the local food delicacies of stinking durian fruit or rotten eggs, would offend one or other of the senses, but the indigenous communities may be well adapted to these things. In a similar way, visual pollution is rather relative to the attitudes of a community. War wrecks, such as those still in Scapa Flow, are a visual nuisance to some, but are considered excellent lobster breeding grounds to others. Hadrian's Wall, now a national monument, may nevertheless have been an eyesore to the post-Roman people of northern England! Perhaps I should say at the outset that I am well aware of the rather anthropocentric nature of this review, relative to the broader world environment issues of pollution. That pollution means far more than the detrimental effect of man upon his own cultural development and physical well being, is obvious. However, my task here is specifically to consider this question of to what extent man has polluted himself, prior to the emergence of advanced societies, and to what extent he may have been conscious of the problem and attempted to "adapt" to it.

Pollution is of course a man-made concept, but is behavior which tends to counteract it also purely distinctive of hominids? As yet, ethological studies have little to offer, but there is a certain amount of information to show that some in-built or learned animal behavior is geared towards basic sanitary and cleaning habits in various other animal groups. The badger, for instance, defecates in pits generally 20 yards or so from the set. Old bedding is periodically removed or the set may even be changed several times in a season. The female badger cleans her cubs and searches them for parasites. The result of such habits is that the wild badger is hardly ever infested with parasites but, significantly and in contrast to this, those kept in captivity for some time usually become verminous and unkempt (Neal, 1948).

Mutual grooming is of course a common phenomenon, including in the higher primates, and must assist the maintenance of good health. In some animal assemblages, a "cleaning symbiosis" is established; for example, the Pederson shrimp (*Periclimenes pedersoni*) cleans fish of various parasites and has been important in maintaining their health. Yet another mechanism of disease control is mutual wound licking, observed in mice. Healing occurred more rapidly in groups where licking could take place than in those prevented from doing so (Dubos, 1967). This sort of thing is a very long way from the pollution problem in man today, but nevertheless helps to emphasize that some of the basic habits concerned with cleanliness and the protection of health are of prehominid origin.

The history of our genus probably spans a million years, and, of this period, only one per cent of it is involved with the development of agriculture. During the Paleolithic phase of hunting and collecting, the world population may not have increased beyond ten million. As yet there is no evidence that the economy of the hunter could support concentrations of people. For most of human history, therefore, we are dealing with small bands who were unlikely to have hygiene problems beyond those for mammals in general. With the development of agriculture and urban communities, considerable changes took place, which affected the health and well-being of these populations.

Food

Foremost in the changes taking place during the so-called Neolithic phase, were those of food production and consumption. Plant and animal domestication, especially of cereals, cattle, caprovids and pigs, guaranteed sufficient food and probably also permitted considerable population increase. For the first time, human populations could concentrate, to form towns and then cities. But there were dangers in these early urban societies. Associated with the development of farming was probably a trend to reduce the range of wild foods eaten, and for the first time there may have been serious misuse of food, in the sense that too few foods were eaten. Some evidence of vitamin deficiencies are known from early records; night blindness possibly as early as 1600 B.C., and beriberi is perhaps indicated as early as 1000 B.C. Hippocrates and Pliny were acquainted with a condition which seems to be scurvy. Hippocrates also reports on lathyrism and says "At Ainos, all men and women who ate continuously peas became impotent in the legs and that state persisted." I appreciate that this type of evidence may seem to some to be outside the boundaries of the topic we are discussing. To me, however, it would seem reasonable to include as a form of pollution, modifications in the diet of a population which could seriously modify its health.

With the advent of the farming and urban revolution, and all this meant in terms of bulk supplies to the town communities, there were further dangers in food preparation, distribution and consumption. It probably also meant the wider distribution of any contaminants in the food. Plagues of ergotism would seem to have occurred in Europe during Medieval times, and there are possible references to ergot contamination in Babylonian and Assyrian texts many centuries earlier. Although this toxic plant could have been accidentally taken in with food even during Paleolithic times, it seems unlikely to have been a community threat until large-scale cereal cultivation was established.

Food storage must also have become an essential part of the agricultural economy, and may have produced contamination problems on a scale not previously known. Aflatoxin poisoning from the fungal attack of groundnuts is a problem which now concerns some African populations in particular, but what of its history in the groundnut-growing areas of the New World? It would certainly be an interesting exercise in scientific investigation to search for this fungus in early Amerindian food debris and coprolites. That evidence of this sort can be preserved is amply demonstrated by the occurrence of ergot sclerotica in the stomach contents of Grauballe Man, an Iron Age individual from a Danish peat bog.

The closer association of animal populations with earlier cultures also resulted in varying changes in the micro-environment surrounding human habitations. This association of domestic varieties with man permitted easy transfer of certain infections, such as brucellosis, bovine tuberculosis, anthrax and even dog hookworm. It also encouraged contact with insect vectors which may attack human hosts; ticks which carry spotted fever for example (Alland, 1970).

The agricultural revolution was thus a mixed blessing, guaranteeing not only greater availability of food all the year round and permitting increase in population size beyond previous levels, but at the same time perhaps heralding the beginnings of considerable food abuse and encouraging changes in disease patterns as a result of changes in the micro-environments directly surrounding man.

Town and House

Increase and concentration of population gave rise to new environments in the form of urban settlements, which imposed further adaptive problems and produced new stresses and health problems. During the evolution of these later prehistoric cultures, both in the Old World and the New, house and settlement design was clearly very variable. From the evidence of under-developed societies today, it is possible to see some of the pollution problems, albeit minor ones, which these earlier communities must have faced. These would be related to climate, economy, evolving traditions in terms of house and town planning, and general attitudes to cleanliness. At the village level, one might give two examples of the type of house micro-environment which must have been common.

In the Abor Hills of Assam, dwellings are of wood, and are raised on bamboo platforms at varying distances from the ground (depending upon local preferences). In the case of well-raised rooms, food debris and other waste is swept down through the wooden floor spaces, to be eaten by scavenging pigs and fowls underneath. However, where the flooring is low, waste materials tend to rot beneath it, and the smell can be offensive. No smoke outlet is built into the roof, so that wood smoke is a chronic nuisance and results in soot deposits on walls and "ceiling" (Gupta, 1953). Among the Shona of Southern Africa, the village huts have floors of dung, which may be periodically "re-surfaced". Again, smoke is a continuous problem and there is soot on walls and roof. Owing to the proximity of these huts to the cattle kraals, flies are prevalent, and in the older house pattern of having both humans and cattle "under one roof," this insect problem was probably far worse (Gelfand, 1964).

Increasing the density of this type of dwelling to some extent increases the problems of cleanliness and sanitation generally. Polunin (1953) has discussed the results of more densely settling the Malayan aborigines during the terrorist emergency. Serious water pollution occurred, and in combination with dietary insufficiency, liability to dysentery increased. In fact there was a general accentuation of the disease pattern, with an abnormal death ratio. In some early towns and cities, the concentration of housing and people was of course greater, and it is reasonable to question whether archaeological excavation has so far produced evidence to show that such populations were endeavoring to combat the micro-pollution problems and adapt to the more crowded environment of the larger settlement. For brevity, let us select one early Mexican site and another from the Indus Valley.

At the Central American site of Teotihuacàn, a wide range of structures are present, pyramids, palaces and "commoners" dwellings. Some indication of the way more ordinary people lived is given by a complex of ruins in the eastern part of the site, called Tlamimilolpa. Even from the partial excavation, the crowded cluster of rooms and alleys is obvious. These must in fact represent the multitude of traders, artisans and other non-food producers associated with an advanced society of this sort (Coe, 1962). The arrangement of these and other buildings at Teotihuacàn would suggest that planning and thought has gone into their lay-out and construction. In some there appear to be floor drains of varying sizes.

The early Indian city of Mohenjo-daro covered in the region of a square mile. Again, the lay-out is complex, with a network of roads and alleys. There had been much thought, presumably on the part of municipal authorities, for the sanitary needs and health of the population. An elaborate drainage system had been devised, with connections from the houses to the main street drains—which eventually linked with soak-pits. Rubbish chutes were also constructed, running out through house walls into brick-built bins outside (Piggott, 1950). In these two examples of early city development, placed in time between the third and first millennium B.C., we see evidence of population density linked with degrees of orderliness and organization which suggests that some aspects of pollution were fully appreciated and active steps to combat them—at least in a city environment—had been devised.

Air and Water

In view of the importance of air and water pollution as world problems today, perhaps separate mention can be made of them here.

When Juan Cabrillo visited California in 1542, and anchored in San Pedro Bay, he noted the mountain peaks but could not see their bases. This was the result of Amerindian fire smoke spreading as a sheet over the valley. The place was duly called the "Bay of Smokes" and in fact is not only a quaint example of early smoke pollution but also of the phenomenon known as thermal inversion (as unpleasantly exemplified now in Mexico City). I suppose, as Dubos (1967) says, atmospheric pollution began when man started to use fire. By the time chimneyless dwellings had evolved—of the kind already referred to—then smoke was a certain health hazard in the environment of the home. Anthracosis, resulting from pollution of this kind has been noted in Egyptian mummies, and there is a particularly good example of this disease in an ancient Guanche body (Brothwell *et al.,* 1969).

Evidence concerning the use of water in rural or urban areas may give three types of information which is relevant here. It can indicate something of the attitudes to general hygiene in a community. It may show the degree to which a population is concerned with the cleanliness of its drinking water; and finally, man-made changes in water-use might be relatable to changing patterns of disease.

Although information is as yet meager, there is I think enough to show that in at least some earlier urban cultures, there was an obvious need to avoid water pollution or ensure a clean supply for drinking. When I say "clean," of course, I simply mean water which does not smell, hasn't obvious impurities and tastes reasonable! In *Exodus* we have the comment that "All the waters that were in the river stank," which leaves no doubt as to its drinkability in this particular case. Obviously, surface water sources were used, but it is interesting that the development of wells, house water and water storage tanks have a long history in the Ancient East and Egypt. King Sennacherib was clearly far from satisfied with the water of the River Tigris and had fresh spring water brought to Nineveh from many miles away, by means of a wellconstructed canal (Vallentine, 1967). In the development of the Mexico City of the Aztecs, we have a further example of the concern of early communities for clean drinking water. King Ahuitzotl is known to have ordered the construction of a stone pipeline to bring spring water into the city (Duran, 1964). It is difficult to collect evidence of general washing habits, except where special bowls or baths are known. Even then, there are difficulties in interpretation. Bathing was established in early Greece and Rome, but in fact it was undertaken for its supposed healthiness and not to remove dirt (Wright, 1963). Baths had certainly evolved, presumably for a select few, by about 2000 B.C. in Syria and 1700 B.C. in Crete; however, by the second century B.C., there is some evidence from south-west Asia for their more common use. In the excavation of a small Phoenician town of Dar Essefi, whose inhabitants were clearly fishermen and murex purple dyers, evidence of baths with planned drainage was nevertheless found (Harden, 1962).

In contrast to what one might call these "anti-pollution" measures, the use of water in relation to early agriculture has probably been responsible for some detrimental changes in disease frequency. Early in the emergence of the farming economy, it was necessary in some areas to divert natural water courses and undertake controlled irrigation. By the third millennium B.C. irrigation practices were present in Mesopotamia and Egypt, and a little later had developed in the Indus Valley and possibly China. Schwabe (1964) comments on the interrelatedness of irrigation and increased schistosomiasis frequencies, a situation which could clearly have a long history. Increases of 15 per cent have been noted in Iraq, and of 70 per cent in Egypt, as a result of irrigation developments. It is therefore not so surprising to have possible references to this disease in ancient Mesopotamian and Chinese literature, or to have the eggs of this parasite in Egyptian mummies (Sandison, 1967).

Poisons: Home and Industry

To my knowledge, no one has yet considered in detail the plant use of primitive peoples from the point of view of the long-term damaging toxicity of any of the materials used. For instance, the use of peyotl cactus or varyingly-toxic fungi by some communities was by no means free of dangers. The taking of the yopo drug by Guaicas Indians, producing immediate severe nausea, followed by hallucinations (Botting, 1968), is another example of what has been tolerated in the plant lore of some communities. It is common knowledge that many plant poisons have also been utilized by primitive hunters, and this argues for considerable technological sophistication in such groups (Laughlin, 1968). However, one might well question whether, in the experimental stages of using these substances, recurrent poisonings occurred, either during extraction or from eating uncleaned meat from animals shot with a poisoned arrow. Even today, remedies may be kept for counteracting misfortunes of this kind. The use of poisons in fishing is widespread in the New World, and is known as early as Aztec times in Mexico (Vogel, 1970). There is considerable risk of decimating the fish in a locality by this means, and unless carefully operated, the entire fish population in an area might be lost. For this reason, a number of south American countries have forbidden the practice by law (Guppy, 1964), and perhaps now we shall never know the extent to which this poisoning of the environment has influenced long-term changes in the fish populations. Until recent years, most poisoning which has been associated with human activities, has been concerned with the mining or use of inorganic substances. In fact it must have been during the ancient mining and processing of metals and manufacture of certain pottery glazes, that the first cases of industrial poisoning occurred. Bentley (1971) suggests that expertise in handling poisonous mineral ores existed from early Chalcolithic times from the Near East to Central Europe. As she says,

> *Although both cinnabar and arsenic have a cumulative morbid effect on health this did not preclude their use by the ancient metallurgist in what appears to have been large quantities over a considerable period prior to and parallel with the first production of tin bronzes.*

In ancient Rome, there seems little doubt that lead was a long-standing pollutant. It was used for water pipes, in Roman pewter and as glazes on other vessels, and in the production of cosmetics. That old anti-pollutionist Pliny warned that fumes from heated lead were unhealthy. Vitruvius, another observer, remarks on the pallor of lead-worders (Balsdon, 1969). Without extending this argument further, it can be seen that the mishandling of poisonous substances has a long history. If some of the examples seem rather insignificant, this cannot be said of the chronic hazard of lead pollution in Roman society. Indeed, it is still a matter for debate as to whether population fertility might not have been significantly affected.

Health and Disease: Other Aspects

Mention has already been made of various diseases, and the way in which man's tampering with his environment has led to new health problems or the accentuation of old ones. I should like briefly to extend this question of population health, in order to emphasize more pointedly the variety of ways in which man, in changing his environment, has produced situations detrimental to himself.

First of all, the change to more advanced sedentary cultures during the last ten thousand years, has meant a lot more—in terms of community health changes— than simply diet abnormalities, water and drainage problems, and a more established disease corridor from domesticable animals to man. With the development of villages and towns, rodent infestation (especially of the rat) changed the "career prospects" of diseases such as plague. The invention of pottery, especially coarse unglazed ware, raised problems of cleaning which, if not met, would have encouraged enteric disorders. The use of artificial aids in infant feeding go back at least to 2000 B.C. (Lacaille, 1950), and pottery of this type may have been particularly dangerous if not cleaned well. In China, at least, "night soil" appears to have been used over a long period for cultivation purposes. The result has been the production, and the maintenance, of a high frequency of hookworm infection (Chang *et al.*, 1949). In some areas, forest clearance and shifting cultivation has changed the environment sufficiently to encourage the spread of malaria and mite-borne scrub typhus. As Garn (1963) has pointed out, population itself has favored disease by the very increase in numbers and by the increasing number of contacts with other populations.

Finally, the changes which have occurred in the social environment—with the profound changes in population size and settlement—have resulted in changes in the incidence of mental and behavioral disorders. Lambo (1967) sums up the position succinctly when he says:

> *The disturbances in which the influence of social development is most evident are the neuroses and the "socio-pathic" behavior disorders. In this connection it can be said that social development is, apparently, often a stress-producing factor and, as such, provokes anxiety and unhealthy psychological reactions.*

African studies comparing the differences in psychosomatic disorders (Leighton *et al.*, 1963) and blood pressures (Scotch, 1963b) between urban and rural communities, leave no doubt as to the ill-adapted nature of man in larger settlements.

Conclusions

Man has evolved from his position of an omnivorous mammal reasonably well fitted into the natural world, into a species tolerating the artificiality of overpopulated urban sprawls. What I have tried to do in this brief outline, is to show that pollution in its varied ramifications was present in, and to some extent evolved with, earlier human cultures, especially since the Neolithic cultural phase. Man has already had plenty of experience of living with the pollution problem.

Acknowledgments

I much appreciate information and helpful comments from Dr. G. Corbet, Dr. C. Gentry, Miss J. Ingles, Dr. R. J. Berry, Mr. H. Barker and Miss M. Bimson.

Denis P. Burkitt

Some diseases characteristic of modern Western civilization

A number of diseases of major importance are characteristic of modern Western civilization. These diseases are rare or unknown in communities who have deviated little from their traditional way of life, and a rise in their frequency follows adoption of Western customs. Available evidence suggests that all these diseases were rare or uncommon even in the Western world a century ago and that they are rare or unknown in undomesticated animals. Some appear or increase in frequency within a few years of exposure to a new environmental factor, others not until several decades later. The diseases to be considered in this connection are listed below, with indications of their prevalence and importance as causes of death and morbidity in Britain and the U.S.A., countries which represent the type of civilization with which these diseases are most closely associated.

Diseases in the Western World

Non-Infective Diseases of the Large Bowel

Appendicitis is one of the commonest abdominal emergencies. It has been estimated that over 300,000 appendixes are removed yearly in the United States. *Diverticular disease* is the commonest disorder of the large bowel and has been reported to be present in over a third of subjects over the age of 40 and in up to two-thirds of those over 80 years of age (1, 2). *Benign tumors* have been reported to be present in one-third of all necropsies on patients over the age of 20 (3). *Cancer of the large bowel* is, after bronchial carcinoma, the most common cause of death from cancer. It has been estimated that over 46,000 people would die from this form of cancer in the United States and that over 76,000 new cases would be recorded in 1972 (4). *Ulcerative colitis* has been reported to have a prevalence of about 80 per 100,000 population in Britain (5).

Common Venous Disorders

Varicose veins have been estimated to effect 10-17% of all adults (6-9). According to Alexander (10), over half of all urbanized Western people would develop varicose veins if they lived long enough. *Deep vein thrombosis* is believed to occur in 20-30% of all surgical patients and in over 40% of those undergoing major surgery (11, 12). *Pulmonary embolism* is responsible for over 2,500 deaths a year in Britain (13) and is believed to occur to some extent in half of all the patients who

Reprinted by permission of the authors and the Editor, *British Medical Journal*, Vol. 1 (February 1973), pp. 274-278.

develop ileofemoral thrombosis (14). *Hemorrhoids* are believed to be present to some degree in nearly half of all people over the age of 50.

Diseases Associated with Cholesterol Metabolism
These include *coronary heart disease,* which is the commonest cause of death, and *gall stones,* which are found at over 10% of all necropsies (15).

Obesity and Diabetes
Over 40% of the people in Britain are said to be overweight, and obesity has become so common in the United States that a variety of intestinal bypass operations are now being recommended for its relief.

It has been estimated that in affluent societies 3-10% of the population eventually develop known diabetes but that a much greater proportion have the disease undetected (16).

Hiatus Hernia
Zeppa and Polk (17) and Polk (18) found hiatus hernia in one of five in 35,000 patients undergoing radiological examination of the upper gastrointestinal tract.

Other Diseases
There are a number of other diseases, such as thyrotoxicosis, pernicious anemia, rheumatoid arthritis, multiple sclerosis, and celiac disease, which are common in the Western world but rare in developing countries, but they are not discussed here since no acceptable explanation has yet been suggested for their geographical distribution.

Racial Distribution
It is of particular significance that the prevalence of most of these diseases is now comparable in the white and colored communities in the United States. The incidence of fatal pulmonary embolism, which is very rare in Africa, is actually higher in American Negroes than in whites (19). In the few conditions where the prevalence is still lower in Negroes than in whites—for example, ulcerative colitis—it is much closer to that in white Americans than to that in Africans.

The Contrast in Developing Countries

All these diseases are rare or unknown in communities who still adhere to their traditional way of life. Many published reports have been confirmed by replies to questionnaires from, and by personal interviews with, doctors representing over 200 hospitals in developing countries in Africa and Asia. The rarity in these communities of diverticular disease (20-22); appendicitis (23, 24); bowel cancer (25); adenomatous polyps (21-26); ulcerative colitis (27-29); varicose veins, deep vein thrombosis, pulmonary embolism, and hemorrhoids (30); and hiatus hernia (31) has been documented. Cleave *et al.* (32) and Trowell (27), from an extensive survey of the literature and personal experience, drew attention to the rarity of these diseases in less economically developed communities.

Historical Emergence

Available evidence suggests that most of these diseases were rare even in the Western world before the present century and that the prevalence of each has greatly increased during the past 50 years. Obesity became prevalent at an earlier date, but evidence from art and literature indicates that it was rare in the common man in Europe before the late eighteenth century (33). The emergence of diabetes as a clinical problem is more difficult to assess but it was well recognized in the last century.

A rapid rise in frequency of pulmonary embolism seems to have occurred in the first quarter of this century (34), from which it may be inferred that deep vein thrombosis was uncommon half a century ago. Diverticular disease (20) and coronary heart disease (35) became prominent only after the first world war. The frequency of appendicitis was apparently rising steeply at the turn of the century (24).

It is highly significant that in the case of appendicitis (36, 37), diverticular disease (38), cancer (39, 40), polyps of the large bowel (41), and coronary heart disease (42) the prevalence in the Negro community some 30 years ago was much less than that among whites, whereas there is no appreciable difference in incidence in the two population groups today.

Rise in Incidence with Changing Environment

The prevalence of these diseases in populations of developing countries appears to relate to the extent of their departure from traditional patterns of life. In Africa and Asia most if not all these diseases first appear or become common in the upper socioeconomic groups and in urbanized communities. In Africa this has been evident in the case of appendicitis (23, 43), ischemic heart disease (44), diabetes (32, 45), obesity (32, 33), gall stones (46), varicose veins, venous thrombosis, and hemorrhoids (30, 43), all of which are more prevalent in the more Westernized communities.

Available information suggests a rapid rise in the incidence of these diseases in Japan since the 1939-45 war, particularly in urban communities. In the case of many of these diseases an increase in incidence has been observed among Japanese who have emigrated to Hawaii relative to that recorded in Japan. Stemmermann (47) estimated that adenomatous polyps of the large bowel are three times as common in the Hawaiian Japanese and that bowel cancer is at least seven times as common. Diverticular disease and ischemic heart disease are also much more prevalent in Hawaiian Japanese, but deep vein thrombosis and haitus hernia are still very rare in both countries.

Relation between Diseases

Many diseases characteristic of modern Western civilization are not only associated geographically but are also frequently found associated with one another in individual patients. Some have been recorded, but other associations which have not been specifically looked for may well exist. These diseases have also been related to one another in their time of emergence as important clinical entities, both historically in the Western world and, more recently, in developing countries. Moreover, the order in which the frequency of each rises in different communities following the adoption of a Western pattern of life appears to be relatively constant, and it is suggested that this reflects both the intensity of and the time of exposure to some new environmental factor which in time results in the appearance of clinical disease.

All the effects of a common cause tend to be associated with one another, each being most common where the causative factor is maximum and being rare or absent where the cause is minimal. All the effects of related causes will also tend to be associated. Conversely the recognition that certain diseases are more or less consistently related to one another suggests the possibility that they may be different results of common or related causes (26, 48).

A Possible Common Causative Factor

Epidemiological evidence indicates that environmental factors must be primarily responsible for the diseases being considered. It is therefore in the environment with which these diseases are related, both in their geographical distribution and chronological emergence, that clues to their causation must be sought. A carcass in the African bush is most easily discovered by locating the readily recognized and constantly associated telltale vultures. The same approach could be profitably followed in medical research, though it is often precluded by narrow specialization which does not encourage the following of guide lines provided by other fields of medical practice. Since a common cause can be suspected for diseases constantly associated with one another it seems wise, once such associations are recognized, to search first for the cause of the disease that can be more readily investigated, and I propose to start with the noninfective diseases of the large bowel.

The main environment of intestinal mucosa is the fecal content of the bowel, and in the colon and rectum this is largely determined by the undigested fiber in the diet. This is not digested by alimentary enzymes, so that it is scarcely altered during its passage through the small intestine. It is degraded partially by bacteria in the large bowel. Careful attention must therefore be paid to any changes in diet in the Western world towards the end of the last century which preceded the rise in incidence of non-infective diseases of the bowel and the changes now taking place in developing countries. Particular notice must be taken of alterations in fiber intake.

Dietary Changes 1860-1960

During the years 1860-1960 fat consumption increased by less than 50% and sugar consumption more than doubled (49). Though the greatest reduction in quantity of fiber consumed occurred during the eighteenth century, the proportionate fall between 1880 and 1960 was more than 90%. Robertson (50) estimated that the fiber content of white flour in 1860 was between 0.2 and 0.5% and that the amount of fiber supplied daily in bread was between 1.1 and 2.8 g. With bread consumption halved and the fiber content of white flour reduced to between 0.1% (50) and 0.01-0.04% (51) the daily fiber intake in bread is now reduced to about a tenth of the pre-1860 level. In addition porridge oats, which have a high fiber content, have been largely replaced by packaged cereals, some of which are poor in fiber.

Changes from Traditional Food

The first change in traditional food is usually the addition of sugar. This is followed by substituting white bread for part of the less processed cereals customarily eaten. Lubbe (52) showed that the greatest alterations in diet associated with a change from rural to urban life in South Africa are an increase in sugar and meat consumption and a fivefold reduction in consumption of fiber.

Effect of Fiber on Intestinal Behavior and Content

Since epidemiological evidence appears to point an incriminating finger at the lack of fiber in food it is essential to investigate the effect of this on intestinal content and behavior. It has been shown that intestinal transit times and stool weights and consistency are closely related to the content of fiber in food. Average transit times vary from some 35 hours in African villagers on a high-residue diet to over 70 hours in English volunteers on a low-residue diet. In the latter subjects transit times commonly exceed 100 hours. Stool weights and consistency are inversely related to transit times and often average 400-500 g of soft, unformed stool daily on high-residue diets and under 150 g of firm, formed stool on low residue diets. Communities on mixed diets, such as Indians, more Westernized Africans, and English vegetarians, have stool weights and intestinal transit times intermediate between the two extremes (25, 53-56).

It seems probable that the removal of the few grams of cereal fiber that remained in Western diets until about a century ago, part of which may be attributed to changes in milling techniques introduced between 1850 and 1890, could have been the last straw breaking the camel's back. This contention is supported by the evidence that in formerly constipated patients bowel habit can be restored and stools altered from hard to soft by restoring to the diet as little as 2 g of cereal fiber daily in the form of unprocessed bran (57). (A heaped dessertspoonful of bran contains rather more than a gram of fiber.)

Non-infective Diseases of the Large Bowel

Diverticular disease.   There is strong evidence that diverticular disease is the direct result of raised intraluminal pressures consequent on a low-residue diet (58-60). Not only is this disease virtually unknown in all communities examined on a high-residue diet and common in those who over a generation ago adopted a low-residue diet (20) but it can be produced experimentally in animals put on a fiber-free diet (61). It can in most cases be successfully treated in man by restoring as little as 2 g of cereal fiber to the diet (57).

Appendicitis.   This disease has likewise been attributed to raised intraluminal pressures beyond an abstruction due to fecalith or muscular contraction (23). Alterations in fecal bacteria resulting from changes in intestinal content or from fecal arrest may be a contributory factor (32).

Cancer.   The high incidence of cancer in Europe and North America has been attributed to carcinogens produced by the action on bile acids in the colon, of bacteria that are particularly prevalent in the feces of Western nations (62). Hill *et al.* (63) believe that increased fat in Western diets alters not only the bacterial composition but also the concentration of bile acids in the feces. Whether or not fat is the responsible dietary constituent the fecal arrest resultant on a low-residue diet will not only provide more time for bacterial proliferation and their degrading of bile acids but will result in carcinogens so formed being concentrated in a small fecal mass and retained for a prolonged time against the intestinal mucosa (25, 64, 65).

Polyps.   The close association between cancer and polyps, not only in geographical distribution (26) but also in anatomical and age distribution, and in their tendency to be associated in individuals (66), together with the fact that they can both be produced by the same experimental means (67, 68), suggests that they are merely differing manifestations of the same common cause (25, 69).

Ulcerative colitis.   The close association between this disease and bowel cancer both geographically and in individual patients suggests some common etiological factor. The commonly accepted explanation of a mere cause-and-effect relationship fails to account for the rarity of this condition in all known areas where the incidence of bowel cancer is low (25).

Venous Disorders Related to Fecal Arrest

Since a fiber-deficient diet has been shown to be closely related to the non-infective diseases of the large bowel the possibility first suggested by Cleave (70) that other associated diseases may also be causally related to fiber lack must be considered. Not only does fecal arrest result in raised intraluminal pressures, also in raised intra-abdominal pressures while straining to evacuate hard stools. These unnatural pressures could well be responsible for the following diseases, which are associated epidemiologically with low-residue diets.

Varicose veins.   It is well known that raised intra-abdominal pressures are readily transmitted down the superficial leg veins after the valves have become incompetent. An impulse detected on coughing is the classical clinical test for valve failure. Such pressures, which can exceed 200 mg Hg (71), must therefore be sustained by the valves when competent, and they may well be the cause of their failure and thus initiate the process which leads to varicosities (30).

Deep vein thrombosis.   It seems unlikely that venous changes resulting from valve incompetence would be confined to the visible superficial veins. Changes in the deep muscle plexuses with consequent venous stagnation that might predispose to thrombosis during enforced recumbency could account for the high incidence of deep vein thrombosis in the lower limb in communities with a corresponding high incidence of varicose veins. Though stool consistency is held to be of prime importance the squatting position adopted for defecation in all but Western countries is believed to be an additional factor protecting the veins in the leg against abdominal pressures. When the valves have become incompetent a cough impulse readily detected when standing is not transmitted in the squatting position.

Hemorrhoids.   It has been postulated that hemorrhoids are also the result of transmitted intra-abdominal pressures. The observation that the frequency of hemorrhoids in developing countries always appears to rise before that of varicose veins or deep vein thrombosis could be explained on the grounds that the hemorrhoidal veins lack the initial protection afforded to the leg veins both by their valves and by their occlusion when squatting (30).

Hiatus Hernia and Fecal Arrest

The close epidemiological relationship between hiatus hernia and a low-residue diet could well be accounted for by the raised intra-abdominal pressures consequent on such a diet. Constrictive clothing and adiposity have been considered to be causes of increased intra-abdominal pressures contributing to hiatus hernia, but these must cause insignificant pressure change compared with straining at stool.

Diseases Associated with Cholesterol Metabolism

Coronary Heart Disease

The geographical distribution of ischemic heart disease is very similar to that of diverticular disease. The former has been observed often without the latter, but not the reverse. Once again a common causative factor linking not only these diseases but also other diseases of economic development must be sought.

Trowell (72, 73), who drew attention to the close geographical relationship between intake of dietary fiber, serum cholesterol, and ischemic heart disease, reinterpreted certain dietary experiments planned for different purposes to show that serum cholesterol levels rose or fell while diminishing or increasing the amount of fiber consumed. Communities such as the Masai in East Africa, who adapted to a low fiber diet from time immemorial, are exceptions. These people metabolize their cholesterol differently (74). The mechanisms whereby dietary fiber influences serum cholesterol levels are open to question, but there is evidence that more bile acids are excreted in the large stools characteristic of an unrefined diet (75). Reabsorption of bile acids is thus reduced. Moreover, it seems likely that absorption of ingested cholesterol is reduced in the presence of a high fiber content in the feces (76).

It is, of course, admitted that many other factors almost certainly contribute to the development of ischemic heart disease. It is merely suggested that a fiber-depleted diet may be an important factor which has been overlooked.

Gall-Bladder Disease

Gall-bladder disease is not known to occur geographically in the absence of gall stones and the two are closely associated clinically. Cholesterol stones, the most frequent variety in the Western world, are in part dependent on the ratio of cholesterol to bile acids in the bile. It may well be that alterations in cholesterol metabolism associated with changes in dietary fiber are among the factors that influence gall-stone formation.

It has been suggested that both ischemic heart disease (32, 77) and gall-bladder disease (78) may be causally related to sugar intake. In this context Cleave's brilliant conception of an inverse relation between consumption of fiber on the one hand and of refined starch and sugar on the other is highly relevant (32).

Obesity and Diabetes

Cleave attributes the association between various diseases of modern civilization to different aspects of the two complementary results of refining carbohydrate foods—excess consumption of energy in the form of sugar and refined starch on the one hand and fiber depletion on the other (32, 70). He attributes obesity to overconsumption of refined carbohydrate foods, and diabetes to overconsumption as well as the increased rate of absorption of these foods which results when concentrated starch and sugar are consumed. In these circumstances, he argues, the pancreas is inevitably overloaded, with consequent pathological changes in some people. This could explain why the incidence of diabetes rises with the years during which the pancreas is subjected to this unnatural strain.

Obesity is primarily a disease of modern Western man and is rare, particularly in rural situations, in developing countries. It is the commonest form of malnutrition in the West and known to be associated with many of the diseases referred to here.

Conclusion

The close association geographically, chronologically, and in individual patients between many diseases characteristic of modern Western civilization could be explained on the basis of a deficiency of undigested fiber, in particular cereal fiber, in food. This supposition is a modification of the original hypothesis of Cleave, whose work was the main stimulus which initiated the studies and considerations outlined above. His emphasis is placed on the potential dangers of excess sugar consumption, whereas the complementary result of carbohydrate refining—fiber depletion—has been emphasized here. I endorse Sir Richard Doll's assessment of this work in his foreword to *Diabetes, Coronary Thrombosis and the Saccharine Disease* by Cleave *et al.* (32). Referring to the possibility that the predictions made may be proved correct, he affirmed that "If only a small part of them do, the authors will have made a bigger contribution to medicine than most university departments or medical research units make in the course of a generation."

It is, of course, not suggested that in any of the diseases discussed fiber deficiency is a sole causative factor, merely that it may be one important factor. The associations between these diseases may be more or less close according to the part played by lack of fiber in the etiology of each. Any hypothesis postulated to explain these diseases will be inadequate unless it accounts for (a) their geographical distribution, (b) their chronological emergence, and (c) their interrelationship.

If these observations can be further substantiated it may not be an exaggeration to predict that a return to a high-residue diet could have an effect on the health of Western nations as beneficial as would be the elimination of cigarette smoking.

Acknowledgment

I wish to express my gratitude to Miss Ella Wright for her help in preparing the text and to the many doctors in mission and other rural hospitals in Africa and elsewhere whose cooperation in epidemiological studies has been invaluable.

References and Notes

1. Parks, T. G., *Proceedings of the Royal Society of Medicine*, 1968, 61, 932.

2. Hughes, L. E., *Gut*, 1969, 10, 336.

3. Arminski, T. C., and McLean, D. W., *Diseases of the Colon and Rectum*, 1964, 7, 249.

4. Silverberg, E., and Holleb, A. I., *Ca-A Cancer Journal for Clinicians*, 1972, 22, 2.

5. De Dombal, F. T., *British Medical Journal*, 1971, 1, 649.

6. De Takatas, C., and Quint, M., *Surgery, Gynecology and Obstetrics*, 1930, 50, 545.

7. Dodd, H., and Cockett, F. B., *Pathology and Surgery of the Veins of the Lower Limb.* Edinburgh, Livingstone, 1956.

8. Martin, P., Lynn, P. B., Dible, J. H., and Aird, J., *Peripheral Vascular Disorders.* Edinburgh, Livingstone, 1956.

9. Davis, L., (editor), *Christopher's Textbook of Surgery*, 9th ed. Philadelphia, Saunders, 1968.

10. Alexander, C. J., *Medical Journal of Australia*, 1972, 1, 215.

11. Kakkar, V. V., Howe, C. T., Nicolaides, A. N., Renney, J. T. G., and Clarke, M. B., *American Journal of Surgery*, 1970, 120, 527.

12. Lambie, J. M., *et al.*, *British Medical Journal*, 1970, 2, 142.
13. General Register Office, *Statistical Review of England and Wales*, Part 1, Tables Medical. London, H.M.S.O., 1969.
14. Mavor, G. E., *British Medical Journal*, 1969, 4, 680.
15. Farooki, M. A., *Pakistan Medical Forum*, 1971, 6, 27.
16. West, K. M., in *Diabetes Mellitus*, ed. S. S. Fajans and K. E. Sussman. New York, American Diabetes Association, 1972.
17. Zeppa, R., and Polk, H. C., *Journal of the Florida Medical Association*, 1971, 58, 26.
18. Polk, H. C., personal communication, 1972.
19. Castranova, S., personal communication, 1972.
20. Painter, N. S., and Burkitt, D. P., *British Medical Journal*, 1971, 2, 450.
21. Bremner, C. G., and Ackerman, L. V., *Cancer*, 1970, 26, 991.
22. Kyle, J., Adesola, A. O., Tinckler, L. F., and de Beaux, J., *Scandinavian Journal of Gastroenterology*, 1967, 2, 77.
23. Burkitt, D. P., *British Journal of Surgery*, 1971, 58, 695.
24. Short, A. R., *British Journal of Surgery*, 1920, 8, 171.
25. Burkitt, D. P., *Cancer*, 1971, 28, 3.
26. Burkitt, D. P., *Lancet*, 1970, 2, 1237.
27. Trowell, H. C., *Non-infective Diseases in Africa*. London, Arnold, 1960.
28. Billinghurst, J. R., and Welchman, J. M., *British Medical Journal*, 1966, 1, 211.
29. Gelfand, M., *The Sick African*, 3rd ed., Johannesburg: Juta, 1967.
30. Burkitt, D. P., *British Medical Journal*, 1972, 2, 556.
31. Burkitt, D. P., *Medical Annual*, 1972. Bristol Wright.
32. Cleave, T. L., Campbell, G. D., and Painter, N. S., *Diabetes, Coronary Thrombosis and the Saccharine Disease*, 2nd ed. Bristol, Wright, 1969.
33. Trowell, H. C., personal communication, 1972.
34. Wilson, L. B., *Annals of Surgery*, 1912, 56, 809.
35. Sinclair, H., in *Just Consequences*, ed. R. Waller. Tonbridge, Knight, 1971.
36. Boland, F. K., *Annals of Surgery*, 1942, 115, 939.
37. Boyce, F. F., *Annals of Surgery*, 1951, 133, 631.
38. Kocour, E. J., *American Journal of Surgery*, 1937, 37, 430.
39. Steiner, P. E., *Cancer: Race and Geography*. Baltimore, Williams and Wilkins, 1954.
40. Quinland, W. S., and Cuff, J. R., *Archives of Pathology*, 1940, 30, 393.
41. Helwig, E. B., *Surgery, Gynecology and Obstetrics*, 1947, 84, 36.
42. Burch, C. E., personal communication, 1971.
43. Bremner, C. G., *South African Journal of Surgery*, 1971, 9, 127.
44. Seftel, H. C., Dew, M. C., and Bersohn, I., *South African Medical Journal*, 1970, 44, 8.
45. Goldberg, M. D., *et al.*, *South African Medical Journal*, 1969, 43, 733.
46. Bremner, C. G., personal communication, 1971.
47. Stemmermann, G. N., personal communication, 1971.
48. Burkitt, D. P., *Lancet*, 1969, 2, 1229.
49. Antar, M. A., Ohlson, M. A., and Hodges, R. E., *American Journal of Clinical Nutrition*, 1964, 14, 169.
50. Robertson, J., *Nature*, 1972, 238, 290.
51. Kent-Jones, D. W., and Amos, A. J., *Modern Cereal Chemistry*, 6th ed., p. 185. London, Food Trade Press, 1967.
52. Lubbe, A. M., *South African Medical Journal*, 1971, 45, 1289.
53. Walker, A. R. P., *South African Medical Journal*, 1947, 21, 590.
54. Walker, A. R. P., *South African Medical Journal*, 1971, 45, 377.
55. Cleave, T. L., and Campbell, G. D., *British Medical Journal*, 1968, 1, 579.
56. Burkitt, D. P., Walker, A. R. P., and Painter, N. S., *Lancet* 1972, 2, 1408.
57. Painter, N. S., Almeida, A. Z., and Colebourne, K. W., *British Medical Journal*, 1972, 2, 137.
58. Painter, N. S., *Annals of the Royal College of Surgeons of England*, 1964, 34, 98.
59. Painter, N. S., *American Journal of Digestive Diseases*, 1967, 12, 222.
60. Painter, N. S., *Proceedings of the Royal Society of Medicine*, 1970, 63, 144.

61. Hodgson, J., *British Journal of Surgery*, 1972, 59, 315.
62. Aries, V., Crowther, J., Drasar, B. S., Hill, M. J., and Williams, R. E. O., *Gut*, 1969, 10, 334.
63. Hill, M. J., *et al.*, *Lancet*, 1971, 1, 95.
64. Oettle, A. G., in *Tumours of the Alimentary Tracts in Africans*, Monograph 25, p. 97. Bethseda, National Cancer Institute, 1967.
65. Wynder, E. L., and Shigematsu, T., *Cancer*, 1967, 20, 1520.
66. Bockus, H. L., Tachdjian, V., Ferguson, L. K., Mouhran, Y., and Chamberlain, C., *Gastroenterology*, 1961, 41, 225.
67. Cleveland, J. C., Litvac, S. F., and Cole, J. W., *Cancer Research*, 1957, 27, 708.
68. Navarrete, A., and Spjut, H. J., *Cancer*, 1967, 20, 1466.
69. Morson, B. C., and Bussey, H. J. R., *Current Problems in Surgery*, Chicago, Year Book Publishers, 1970.
70. Cleave, T. L., *Journal of the Royal Navy Medical Service*, 1956, 42, 55.
71. Halpern, A., *et al.*, *Angiology*, 1960, 2, 426.
72. Trowell, H., *American Journal of Clinical Nutrition*, 1972, 25, 926.
73. Trowell, H., *European Journal of Clinical and Biological Research*, 1972, 17, 345.
74. Mann, G. V., Spoerry, A., Gray, M., and Jarashow, D., *American Journal of Epidemiology*, 1972, 95, 26.
75. Antonis, A., and Bersohn, I., *American Journal of Clinical Nutrition*, 1962, 11, 142.
76. Heaton, K. W., *Bile Acids in Health and Disease*. Edinburgh, Livingstone, 1972.
77. Yudkin, J., *British Journal of Hospital Medicine*, 1971, 5, 665.
78. Heaton, K. W., personal communication, 1972.

Folk Healers and Ethnomedicine

Humans have always been confronted with the threat of disease. But as shown in the previous section the types of diseases afflicting a population are largely determined by cultural factors. And just as disease varies because of culture, so, too, will the ways people define and treat their afflictions. A primary area of research in medical anthropology is ethnomedicine, a term referring to the health beliefs and practices of non-Western peoples. The articles in this section expose the reader to a sample of theories and treatments of disease found in traditional societies throughout the world. The opening paper by Charles Hughes establishes a base from which the reader can more meaningfully understand and interrelate the diverse factual information contained in the rest of the articles. His major point is that all societies possess a body of belief about the nature of disease, its causation and treatment, as well as health specialists or curers. Subsequent papers examine various aspects of ethnomedicine defined in the Hughes article, but in greater detail. The work by Pfifferling calls for the use of an epidemiological model in studying non-Western medical systems, an important methodological question not raised by Hughes. A case study employing such a method is found in the O'Nell and Selby article, which appears in section IV.

Therapy in ethnomedicine is based on both empirical and nonempirical or suggestive techniques. Erwin Ackerknecht, a physician and pioneer in the field of medical anthropology, surveys anatomical knowledge and surgical practices in a large number of traditional or preliterate societies. The next paper, by Michael Logan, deals with the use of plants as medicinal agents in a specific society, although cross-cultural generalizations are presented. The use of botanicals is not, however, a purely empirical matter, as shown in the study of Jivaro shamanism and drug use by Michael Harner. Plant stimulants often serve as a mechanism through which curers contact or achieve supernatural powers. In many cultures such powers are believed to be controllable by man, hence they can be employed to cause illness and death as well as to restore health.

The Harner study is complimented by Richard Lee's discussion of Bushmen ethnomedicine. In each article the supernatural basis of curing and disease causation is examined by reference to cultural aspects of the people in question. A true understanding of supernaturalism in health care can only be reached when the investigator views curing practices and theories of disease etiology in a cultural context. As Lee shows, supernaturalism is a reflection of daily social behavior, and as such it can serve effectively to transform the stresses and tensions of group life into a world of external sources of malevolence.

The papers by Carol McClain and David Landy expand on the function of the traditional curer, a subject given similar importance by the other authors contributing to this section. Injury, pain, and sickness are conditions which in all societies demand the attention of those with specialized or esoteric knowledge. The curer may be a surgeon, an herbalist, a bone setter, a shaman with supernatural powers or a midwife. The specialist of midwife is examined in detail by McClain, while Landy discusses the changing role of healers in societies undergoing modernization.

In the final paper of this section John McCullough reveals that certain ethnomedical beliefs and practices are biologically adaptive. His work, as well as that of the other authors, shows that health care in traditional societies is not by any means a curious collection of superstition or illogical behavior, but rather it represents a coherent, systematic, and effective means of responding to the universal threat of disease.

Charles C. Hughes

Medical care: ethnomedicine

Judging from paleopathological evidence, diseases of one kind or another have always afflicted man. Indeed, given the nature of life and the nature of disease, it could not be otherwise; for disease is but an expression of man's dynamic relationship with his environment. And even as there has always been sickness, accident, deformity, and anxiety to trouble man, so, too, has there been an organized, purposeful response by society to such threats. In all human groups, no matter how small or technologically primitive, there exists a body of belief about the nature of disease, its causation and cure, and its relations to other aspects of group life. There also exist therapeutic and preventive practices, many of which

"Medical Care: Ethnomedicine" by C. C. Hughes. Reprinted with permission of the publisher from the *International Encyclopedia of the Social Sciences*, David Sills, Editor. Volume 10, pages 87-92. Copyright © 1968 by Crowell Collier and Macmillan, Inc.

are empirically efficacious by standards of modern medicine, although often not for the reasons advanced by folk belief. The variability of societies and cultural systems impedes easy generalization about the nature of "primitive" or "folk" medicine (cf. Ackerknecht 1942b), but one common characteristic is its close integration with other institutions of the society. Religion, medicine, and morality are frequently found together in the behavioral act or event, and "folk medicine" becomes "social medicine" to an extent not found in industrialized societies.

The term "ethnomedicine" will be used to refer to those beliefs and practices relating to disease which are the products of indigenous cultural development and are not explicitly derived from the conceptual framework of modern medicine. In this light, most of the following discussion focuses on the non-Western, nonindustrialized societies of the world, although it is clear that in "modern" societies as well there exist beliefs and practices relating to disease and its treatment which are based on magical or religious conceptions rather than on those of scientific medicine.

Theory of Disease

Man, everywhere, devises or divines causes for the significant events in his life. The afflictions which beset body and mind are explained in both naturalistic and supernaturalistic terms. A cut finger, a broken limb, a snake bite, a fever, the halting speech and wandering mind of senility—all may be regarded as sometime hazards in life. To explain such events there is always some conceptual framework founded in common-sense empiricism. But often a wound does not heal, a sickness does not respond to treatment, and the normally expected and predictable does not happen. In such cases another order of explanation is employed, one which attempts to come to terms with the more basic meaning of the event in metaphysical perspective. For most non-Western societies this transcendent explanation for the occurrence of disease tends to figure more pervasively in the total body of medical lore and practice than does the empirical framework. One reason is the greater incapacitation and mortality from disease in the underdeveloped world than in highly industrialized societies. In addition, this reality is coupled with the comparative inadequacy of ethnomedical techniques and knowledge for dealing with these common threats to the existence of the group and the person.

Widespread throughout the world are five basic categories of events or situations which, in folk etiology, are believed responsible for illness: (1) sorcery; (2) breach of taboo; (3) intrusion of a disease object; (4) intrusion of a disease-causing spirit; and (5) loss of soul (Clements 1932). Not every society recognizes all five categories: indeed, many groups are selective in the emphasis placed upon one or a combination of causes. For example, the Eskimo most frequently trace the origin of diseases to soul loss and breach of taboo, while the malevolence of sorcerers or witches is especially emphasized in many African cultures. Usually, however, these categories are most useful in analytically characterizing the etiological beliefs of a particular group than in describing the content of an entire belief system. This would be the case where a disease is believed to be caused by the intrusion of an object which contains a spirit, and it is the latter to which primary causative influence is attributed (e.g., Hallowell 1935).

The Greeks were not alone in viewing disease as a manifestation of disharmony in man's overall relation to the universe. "Health" is rarely, if ever, a narrowly restricted conception having its locus only in the well-being of the individual body. In discussing conceptions of illness among a west African people, Price-Williams gives a modern illustration:

> *In common with a great many other people, Tiv do not regard "illness" or "disease" as a completely separate category distinct from misfortunes to compound and farm, from relationship between kin, and from more complicated matters relating to the control of land. But it would be completely erroneous to say that Tiv are not able, in a cognitive sense, to recognize disease. As Bohannan has said: "The concept of a disease is not foreign to the Tiv: mumps, smallpox, . . . yaws and gonorrhea are all common and each has a name." What is meant is that disease is seldom viewed in isolation. (1962, p. 125)*

Such a notion is widely found, as in certain American Indian groups, where bodily or mental affliction is often viewed as an indicator of moral transgression, in thought or in deed, against the norms of society. Indeed, man is frequently thought of as continuous with both the social and nonsocial aspects of his environment, and what happens in his surroundings affects his bodily well-being. Not only a person's own actions, therefore, but also those of kinsmen or neighbors can cause sickness. Such an etiological conception has obvious implications for treatment. For example, if the curative technique includes magically based dietary restrictions, they may apply to all members of the patient's family; a breach of the restriction by any of these people will undermine the patient's health. Similarly, as among the Thonga of South Africa, sexual relations between any of the inhabitants of the patient's village can aggravate his condition, and some Eskimo groups feel that the patient's family should do no work during the period of convalescence for fear of giving offense to the spirit causing the sickness.

The belief that by his own actions a man can influence the state of his fellow's health also has malevolent implications, as in the practice of witchcraft and sorcery. Frequently this may be an important factor deciding the success or failure of attempts at introducing new medical programs in underdeveloped societies. Cassel (1955) cites as an illustration the Zulu, who believe that only sorcerers and witches have the ability to transmit disease, particularly diseases which show themselves in symptoms normally associated with pulmonary tuberculosis. Progress in one community's acceptance of a Western-styled health program was brought to an abrupt halt when a physician tried to introduce the medical concept of contagion. He traced the course of tuberculosis through a family, showing how one person had been the original source of the disease in the group and had therefore been the agent responsible for sickness in all the others. The cautious cooperation of the family elder immediately turned into a hostile rejection, which was assuaged only after the doctor had retracted his apparent accusation that the daughter of the family was a witch.

A theory of disease implies a theory of normality. Yet the "normal" is in no way easy to define for all times and places. Aside from the questions of a "statistical" versus a "functional" basis for normality, there is the cultural definition. Afflictions common enough in a group to be endemic, though they be clinical deformities, may often be accepted simply as part of man's natural condition. Ackerknecht (1946), for example, has noted that the Thonga believe intestinal worms, with which they are pervasively affected, to be necessary for digestion; the Mano, also of Africa, feel that primary and secondary yaws are so common that they say, "That is no sickness; everybody has that." North Amazonian Indians, among whom dyschronic spirochetosis is prevalent, accept its endemicity to such an extent that its victims are thought to be normal, and individuals who have not had the disfiguring disease are said to be looked upon as pathological and consequently unable to contract marriage. It is culture, not nature, that defines disease, although it is usually culture and nature which foster disease.

Recent behavioral science research has attempted to go beyond a "phenomenological" orientation in investigation of cultural theories of disease and has sought analytic categories which would relate particular emphases in a theory of disease to other aspects of social and cultural life. A striking example of this type of investigation is the work of John Whiting and Irvin Child (1953). Using a wide sample from the ethnographic "laboratory," these investigators found high correlations between certain aspects of child-rearing practices and dominant themes in etiological beliefs related to disease, more particularly, between the hypothesized degree of anxiety generated during the socialization process—the degree of "negative fixation"—and a theory of disease which reflects these anxieties. Thus, harsh weaning is highly associated with oral explanations for onset of disease: these would include consumption of food, drink, or poison by the sick individual or oral activity on the part of others, such as incantations and spells. Societies in which independence training is characteristically fraught with emotional hazards tend also to have "dependence" explanations of illness. These include soul loss or spirit possession. "Aggression explanations" for disease are highly associated with societies in which training for handling aggressive impulses leaves a residue of unresolved anxiety, and they are expressed in theories which ascribe the cause of a disease to the patient's disobedience or aggression toward spirits, to aggressive wishes on the part of the patient or another person, to introjection of poison other than by mouth, or to harm by magical weapons or objects.

Theory and Practice of Treatment

Therapeutic practices in ethnomedicine address themselves to both supernatural and empirical theories of disease causation. Ackerknecht has said that primitive medicine is "magic medicine" (1942a); certainly much of it is, and, insofar as supernatural causes are involved, therapeutic regimes are based on countervailing supernatural powers or events. Thus, the powerful shaman or healer attempts to recover the soul lost or stolen by a human or supernatural agent. The intrusion of a disease object or disease-causing spirit is treated by extraction or exorcism, and diseases which come as punishment for breach of taboo are usually treated by divination or confession of the infraction. Forgiveness and re-establishment of harmony with the moral and supernatural order are thus important outcomes of the therapy.

In folk medicine, however, there is more to treatment than magical or religious ritualization, however effective this may be psychosocially in providing emotional catharsis and reassurance. All human groups have a pharmacopoeia and at least rudimentary medical techniques; some groups, indeed, are exceptional in their exploitation of the environment for medicinal purposes and in the degree of their diagnostic and surgical skills (Ackerknecht 1942a; Sigerist 1951; Laughlin 1963). The trephining done by the Inca, Masai surgery, the anatomical knowledge of the Aleut and the Eskimo, and the extensive drug repertory of west African tribes are familiar examples. In addition to trephining, numerous other types of surgery and bonesetting are found, as well as massages, blood-letting, dry cupping, bathing, inoculation, and cauterization. It has been estimated that from 25 to 50 percent of the non-Western pharmacopoeia is empirically effective. In fact, our knowledge of the therapeutic efficacy of a large number of modern drugs is derived from the experience of primitive peoples: opium, hashish, hemp, coca, cinchona, eucalyptus, sarsparilla, acacia, kousso, copaiba, guaiac, jalap, podophyllin, quassia, and many of the tranquilizers and psychotomimetics now used in psychiatric therapy and research.

A great part of the task of folk medicine, however, and especially of preventive medicine, is borne by cultural practices which, although oriented to different social purposes, have important functional implications for health. Thus, notable hygienic purposes are served by many religious and magical practices, such as avoidance of the house in which a death has occurred, theories of contagious "bad body humors" which necessitate daily bathing, distinctions of "hot" and "cold" food and water which require boiling or cooking, hiding of fecal and other bodily waste through fear of their use by sorcers or witches, and numerous others.

Other cultural practices inadvertently relevant to health have a more general ecological basis. These may include customs regarding cosmetics and clothing or house styles and settlement patterns. Regardless of their value to the archeologist, the middens of ancient sedentary communities have rather baleful implications for the public health of the times. Changing economic incentives and circumstances which disrupt the adaptation of a cultural activity to its environment frequently create health hazards. May (1960) provides a striking illustration of the intersection between cultural and ecological factors in North Vietnam. Dwellers on the plains lived in low, squat houses in which they sheltered their cattle on one side and did their cooking on the other. When these rice growers moved into the hills they constructed houses according to the same general plan. In the hills, however, the incidence of malaria among them became so high as to limit further such movement, despite governmental encouragement. The people themselves ascribed the calamity to the ill will of the hill dieties. In fact, however, the incidence of malaria was low among the indigenous hill people, who constructed their houses on stilts, sheltered their animals underneath, and did their cooking inside the house. Several factors were apparently instrumental in the latter case in keeping down the spread of malaria from the mosquito vector found in the hills; flight ceiling of Anopheles Minimus is restricted to about ten feet above the ground, and, despite its preference for human blood, the presence of animals underneath the house and of smoke inside the house (where the cooking was done) created an unrealized protection for human inhabitants.

The study of folk medicine has important theoretical implications for the persistent question of a "magical" versus a "scientific" orientation among non-Western peoples. Erasmus (1952), utilizing data from South American Indian populations, contends that the inductive epistemological framework of folk medicine is essentially similar in structure to that of modern scientific medicine, but that the latter differs chiefly in its amenity to generalization and degree of predictive success. In folk medicine the chances of "natural" recovery are in favor of predictive successes, but, more often than in modern medicine, the theoretical propositions lying behind such predictions are merely coincidentally rather than functionally related to the phenomenon in question. Thus, the recooking, before eating, of food that has been left standing overnight is done on the basis of the need to dispel the dangerous quality of "coldness" in the food, but in fact such recooking destroys enterotoxin-producing staphylococci.

The possible implications for a sociology of knowledge are apparent: so long as any activity or set of activities produces a sufficiently high proportion of predictive successes, there will be little elaboration or alteration of the conceptual framework orienting the activity. Cognitive frameworks relating to disease are instruments in the total process of adaptation; they change, evolve, and respond when their viability and acceptability are challenged. Only when folk etiology fails too often and in too many areas to give pragmatic and especially psychodynamic satisfaction does it yield to other frameworks, autochthonous or adopted from outside.

Disease, Medicine, and Culture

Some knowledge of diseases, their classification and etiology, is part of all cultural systems (e.g., Lieban 1962; Rubel 1960; Price-Williams 1962). Investigators have analyzed disease categories in an attempt to understand the structure of the conceptual world of different peoples. The use of componential analysis, the investigation of semantic interrelationships of terms, has been applied to words for sickness (cf. Frake 1961). Aside from illustrating the extent to which concern with disease is elaborated in a folk nosology, such work also emphasizes a more general point: an effective cultural response to disease requires patterned discrimination and categorization of disease symptoms, even if treatment is based largely on methods of trial and error. Diagnostic categories, however crude, serve the purpose of directing sustained attention and reflection to the appearance of disease syndromes, thus providing empirical data for inferences about the probable effectiveness of one type of treatment or another. Undoubtedly this constitutes a kind of inadvertent experimental approach (see, e.g., Laughlin 1963; Erasmus 1952).

Theories of disease generally have major relevance to the moral order, that is, to the control of man's behavior in society. Disease is frequently seen as a warning sign, a visitation from punishing agents for a broken taboo, a hostile impulse, or an aberrant urge to depart from the approved way. In a series of classical papers, Hallowell (e.g., 1963) has analyzed the function of anxieties over sickness among the Ojibwa Indians of North America, and other investigators have looked at the same problem in different cultural settings (e.g., Lieban 1962). Sickness is often interpreted as the supernaturals' way of indicating an act or intention of socially disruptive behavior. Especially in societies lacking strong centralized sociopolitical institutions, the occurrence and imminence of disease— with the belief that it represents punishment for aberrant, dissocial impulse or action—can be functionally important in maintaining group cohesion and restraining disruptive tendencies.

The therapeutic practices attendant upon occurrence of disease may also have socially cohesive results. Although such therapy may often be medically effective, it may serve ancillary functions in the total organization of the society. Typically, the curative session (and often the diagnostic occasion as well) involves not only the patient and the healer, but also the patient's family and neighbors. Often the therapy involves confession by the patient, and under such conditions the confession may well relieve him of diffuse as well as focused anxieties and guilt. When followed by concrete expiatory acts, it may also give him a chance to participate in his own treatment through action. (It is doubtful whether such curative rites do more than provide temporary symptom relief—but the same can be said of much modern psychotherapy.) At the same time group cohesion is often enhanced, for such confessions dramatize fundamental social values by illustrating the harm that can come from social deviance. They provide a setting in which all participants are enveloped in the aura of forgiveness and, through stress on the protection afforded by adherence to group values, assurance of good health. In short, the therapeutic context is usually explicitly a social context, and during the course of the theraphy the reciprocal psychosocial involvement of the patient with his fellows is ritually underscored. As noted above, if therapeutic directives for behavior are issued, they frequently apply to the group, or selected members of the group, as well as to the patient; and if successful recovery is as dependent upon good thoughts as upon effective techniques—as frequently happens—then the assembled company must be devoid of ill wishes and hostilities toward not only the patient but also each other. The curative rite thus may serve in multiple ways as an occasion for reintegration of the group around common social values.

The practice of folk medicine is variously institutionalized. In all societies some rudimentary medical knowledge is an aspect of enculturation, but beyond this general protection there is always a specialist. Sometimes the specialist's role is a full-time activity, but more frequently it is combined with other principal roles appropriate for the practitioner. In some societies there are more complex social arrangements than the simple dyadic relationship between healer and patient. Even as the kin and covillagers of the patient may be explicitly involved in the curative process, so too there may be a society of healers or several societies of healers devoted to diagnosis and cure of various diseases. In west Africa there are found, for example, specialized associations of healers of smallpox or snake bite; each association possesses its own rules of qualification, initiation, and procedure (Hardley 1941).

Folk Medicine in Change

Folk medicine does not easily change under the impact of sustained contact with the industrialized world, or even as a result of deliberate attempts to introduce new conceptions of disease and hygiene. Paul (1955), Foster (1962), and others have documented the variety of factors that may impede or altogether prevent the successful introduction of a modern health program, even of so simple an innovation as the boiling of drinking water. Such factors include ecological considerations, as well as functional efficiency in domestic tasks, the social structure, the status and prestige of the innovator, and the perception of threat or advantage to the recipient. The proper role of the healer may be differently defined; in India, for example, the medical practitioner must assure the patient of recovery, and any admission of uncertainty (even couched in the form of probability) is not allowed. Rudimentary physical testing may be impossible or difficult in a non-Western context. In societies where blood, for example, is thought of as a nonregenerative substance, to take samples for testing is tantamount to inflicting deliberate harm.

It has been found to be easier to introduce behavioral changes than changes in belief about the nature of illness, its cause, and prevention. Domestic hygiene and community health may be bettered by the public health worker who influences a change in habits while not disturbing the underlying belief system. One reason for this has been mentioned above: belief systems, particularly those centered on critical areas of social value, serve more than a single cognitive function. Because they interrelate with religious and magical systems, as well as with the moral order of the society, they impart a deeper sense of resignation and acceptance of events than does an alien concept treating of a germ theory of illness. The value system of a culture provides a more satisfying answer to the question, "Why did I and not my neighbor get sick?" than does an explanation phrased in terms of communicability of a disease, threshholds of resistance, host, agent, and environment.

Yet in many instances modern medicine does get accepted; and one of the reasons is its demonstrably greater effectiveness in the treatment and prevention of many diseases. But even such acceptance is often compromised by the existence of alternative diagnostic and therapeutic frameworks: One relating to those diseases for which it is felt modern medicine is more effective, and the second relating to diseases conceived to be unamenable to modern medical treatment. The first is often applied to sicknesses introduced by the Europeans (such as tuberculosis, measles, smallpox, and others of a communicable nature), while in the second group are traditionally endemic diseases and, especially, ailments having a large component of psychological or psychophysiological involvement.

But in the extremity of fear for a patient's life even such distinctions as these are often disregarded, and the ill person may be taken to a modern medical facility after indigenous healers have done their best—taken either to be cured or left to die. Every hospital, and not just those in non-Western, "underdeveloped" countries, will admit patients brought too late for the course of disease to be halted even by the most advanced techniques of scientific medicine. Disease being an unequivocal threat to life, adaptive responses are many and sometimes override ingrained belief, either of folk medicine on the one hand or modern medicine on the other. In this light, given the avowedly limited role of scientific medicine in society—together with the inevitability of disease—elements of folk medicine will no doubt everywhere persist, even as they do in Europe and the United States, so long as there is uncertainty of outcome or technical ineffectiveness in alleviating pain, prolonging life, and guaranteeing cure.

John-Henry Pfifferling

Some issues in the consideration of non-Western and Western folk practices as epidemiologic data

It is becoming increasingly obvious to physicians that the causal factor(s) in disease are to be found in physical *and* social domains. A reliance on the concept of the single etiologic agent as *the* causative pathogen is no longer tenable for the manifestations and the behavior of the diseased host. However, the behavior of the physician in treating disease is still primarily mechanistically oriented [1].

Anthropologists have discovered that the role of social factors in disease occurrence reinforces their belief that cultural factors are also integral in conceptualizing the reality of host-disease interaction.

Reprinted with permission from J.H. Pfifferling, "Some Issues in the Consideration of Non-Western and Western Folk Practices as Epidemiologic Data," *Social Science and Medicine* 9: 655-658, © 1975, Pergamon Press Ltd.

Clinical medicine by adopting the epidemiologic perspective has convergently discovered the ethnography of illness. Each independently realizing that the tools of epidemiology are cross-disciplinary. Anthropologists find it hard to believe that the central focus of epidemiology, "the relation of a disease process to a population living or working in a natural environment" [2] is a hallmark of another discipline.

The epidemiologist by attempting to describe geographic pathology: the determinants and distribution of disease entities, has discovered the major role of social factors in disease. Social, and now cultural, factors are no longer clues to disease but part of the cause of the morbid episode [3, 4].

Some of the elements that are essential in the process of causal decision-making, in the health sciences, have not yet been systematically utilized in ethno-medical research design. For example the Surgeon General's Report on Smoking (1964) has specified five variables that are crucial in assessing sound method. They are, (1) the temporal sequence of variables, (2) the consistency of association on replication, (3) the strength of associations, (4) the specificity of association and (5) the coherency of explanation [5].

The relationship of these five variables in the explanation of disease manifest-ation and the accurate plotting of incidence and prevalence frequency measures, are methodological tools that are inadequately employed in anthropological descriptions of illness. It is time that techniques from epidemiology are in-corporated in anthropological research.

Since a majority of the people in the world are exposed and relate to folk formulations of disease, such as the *Susto* complex in the Hispano-American world, it is important to produce a sound description of the folk diseases under scrutiny. Unfortunately it is infrequent that either physicians, trained in Western nosology, or epidemiologists participate in anthropological fieldwork.

The incorporation of epidemiologic methods in the non-Western, or folk society, can be beneficial at many levels. As many writers have shown the patient's perspective, if not utilized by the clinician, will usually produce non-compliance to a treatment regimen [6]. If incidence and prevalence rates for folk syndromes are produced by the anthropologist then useful baselines are available for comparison to Western nosologic rates. The rates produced from the folk perspective will help in the construction of a folk-perceived "morbidity" profile for the community [7]. Analysis of this profile, by demographic and other epidemiologic parameters, should produce evidence for the inclusion of particular behavioral actions (what we call psychosocial stressors) as clues in the etiology of illness.

By noting the way the folk classify and respond to locally acceptable treat-ment regimens and by determining their prevalence (both the entity and its cure) we should be able to pave the way for inclusion of some elements of the non-Western armamentarium into the Western delivery of health care services. Useful efforts in this direction have been made by Bergman among the Navaho [8, 9] and by Wintrobe among Puerto-Ricans in Hartford, Connecticut [10]. The epidemiology of folk disease will help to objectify, where possible, folk defined etiology. It will also help to clarify for the health professional the utility of blending folk and professional conceptual categories.

In the analysis of folk epidemiologic rates specific possible independent variables may consist of the following items: life cycle events, migration, fertility, infertility, climacteric, entrance into school, etc. These are all events that may co-occur with a folk defined illness. Some, or all of these may predispose, or be causally related to illness. The job of the ethnographer is to tease out the specific relationship. The astute ethnographer's advantage over visiting clinicians is that he has knowledge of the affect associated with these particular rites-of-passage or most importantly the folk perception of the emotional load associated with these situations. The distribution of illness among groups, the sexes, residential location, etc. has proved extremely useful in traditional epidemiological studies. Our plea is that the anthropologist and the clinician be aware of folk defined episodes of folk defined illnesses.

By borrowing the disease transmission model and applying it to the folk world we may identify one method for achieving folk epidemiology. In regard to each named illness, data indicating onset, duration, severity and termination should be collected. Where applicable, data should be collected on the putative agent (folk defined), the condition of the host, including peer/or relative evaluations.

For transmission to occur in the population, we postulate that a necessary but not sufficient condition is exposure to illness causing situations (i.e. stress *qua* "infectious material"). At any given time the specified population may be divided into at least four main classes in relation to the "infectious" risk. One, they may be *infectives.* Two, they may be *susceptibles,* those who can change from a susceptible state to an infective state, on exposure to a potentially pathogenic situation. A third class is that of *removals.* These may have been removed from the natural population because of death, immunity, hospitalization (cultural isolation), etc. A fourth class is the *protected* who never manifest the illness. (Consider in our culture, those who never have "headaches".)

This last category we may wish to call the psychosocially protected. Maybe these people have some sort of acquired protection. Within a particular pathogenic environment certain individuals do not succumb to the pathogen (e.g. non-smokers, non-drinkers, non-child abusers, etc.) Explanations based on previous exposure, immunity and family protection do not seem to explain why these individuals do not become infectives [11].

This postulated mechanism of protection, when clearly isolated, will surely be a mode of adaptation. Its opposite variable, stress, has been shown in both human and animal studies to cause reproductive casualities [12]. If we can find associations between demographic parameters and psychosocial stress than we may be able to "measure" social stress on reproduction. The interrelationships among stressors, health and illness, associated with the persistence of certain cultural practices, will contribute to the understanding of human adaptability [13].

The clusters of variables that probably comprise the psychosocial protective mechanisms are clearly found in Man's perception of his environment. Consider for example the cross-cultural relevance of Hinkle's observation, "there seems to be a very significant relation between a man's evaluation of his life situation, his reaction to it, and the number of illnesses that he experiences" [11]. Among many shaman their post-apprentice illness load is considerably less than prior to shaman-hood [14]. Anecdotally, among cancer patients, in our limited observations, there is a leveling off of perceived pain with the delivery of an understood terminal diagnosis.

The ramifications of this orientation, if it is valid, extend to many disciplines. Medical teaching could, perhaps should, search for the psychosocial protective devices. Health delivery could continue to attempt to correct overt pathology, but the emphasis would be on the reinforcement of those adaptive features that have been isolated. Medical education rather than being pervaded by pathological clinical material would extoll *Hygeia* [15]. "Healthful" cases could be presented at rounds to complement the diseased samples traditionally used at clinical conferences.

If we can identify stressors (both folk professionally and folk non-professionally defined) then we can attempt to ease undue stress which causes illness [16]. If we can accurately describe health and illness behavior from the patient's perspective, we can begin to formulate public health plans that will not conflict with local values [17, 18]. These intervention studies can be incorporated into generalizations about sickness and health [19, 20]. These studies would rely on neighborhood control populations rather than on subsets of "diseased" populations.

If our biases have been produced because of professional distance, culminating in medical nosology, then the incorporation of folk taxonomy and perception should more closely mirror the reality we wish so much to describe. Let us use folk taxonomy, but apply the methodological rigour of epidemiology to determine the distribution of those categories. The cross-checks of a formal methodology applied to a currently informal field should help us elucidate meaningful relationships.

Possible Paradoxes in the Preceding Discussion

Implicit in the categories of language that we use to describe illness is a notion of closure; that is the illnesses are invariably described retrospectively. So much data that are relevant to the understanding of the illness are lost by basing our search for causation on retrospective data collection. When one is culturally and/or linguistically different from the patient this distance is further increased. A method used to resolve this problem is advocated by Fabrega [21]. He recommends case-history collection using a culturally aware technique.

He does not clarify whether the putative etiologic agent, in producing a folk illness, should be based on a Western disease orientation or on a folk orientation. Several other questions arise in this context. From a native viewpoint, whether in Great Sankey, Lancashire or among the Sungei Kapit in Borneo, what degree of consensus, within the cultural group, should serve as a baseline for accepting native putative agents? In describing illness episodes, how do you decide what is part and what is not a part of the episode? What is *seen* depends upon who did the seeing, and a host of other factors. What is culturally seen is very different than what is professionally seen (unfortunately often to the disadvantage of the patient) [1].

In a similar domain, how do you decide on when an illness starts and ends? Among the Iban of Borneo, illness may end several times, depending on the status of the patient and the type of attempted divination (Pfifferling, unpublished field observation). Among other groups, like the Colla of the high altitude *Puna* in Argentina, most people are perpetually ill, except when they are undergoing a curing ceremony (Pfifferling, unpublished field observation, 1969); an almost identical example is given by Coles among the U.S. urban poor [22].

A commonly used phrase in Western medicine is outcome. Depending on the perspective of the observer, the status of the patient, the type of care facility the patient is in and a host of other considerations, outcome may be a measure or a state. Outcome may be process or discharge, short or long-term, final or not so final. The professional medical care evaluation literature, for the last decade, has wrestled unsuccessfully with the definition of an outcome measure.

The language of illness description is fraught with linguistic ambiguity. For example what is onset, resolution, or disease progression? These concepts appear clear to very few health professionals and less to consumers. They are used with a cavalier clarity but on closer inspection are enormously vague. How does one determine what the "natural course" of a disease is? In anthropological observations the natural course is locally defined and usually mirrors that culture's concept of time and item relationships. If life has a rhythm that is harmonious and blending then illnesses will run a course of disassociation and reassociation (the Navaho are a classic example of this concept.)

To the Western medical laity, notions such as discharge or medical outcome are reified far beyond what is generally understood by practitioners. Finality and concreteness are values that are borrowed from the ideals of medical practice to the vocabulary of the physician-patient interchange. There is currently no acceptable criterion for outcome in our medical culture so why should we expect this for other cultures or sub-cultures? If, after investigation, one discovers that community consensus does exist concerning illness resolution, what significance does this have for Medicine or Anthropology? Where there is a schism between the community's perception of illness and the clinician's perception one can expect a difficult re-incorporation for the patient. Stigmas associated with longterm hospitalization are common and illustrate the different language of "wellness".

Fabrega recommends that ethnomedical data should be analyzed in reference to external systems of meaning (Western Medicine) and that these systems bear directly on folk illness. We ask, do they *have* to be compared and is our Western classification system any less arbitrary or nomothetic than any local system. It is strange that there should be little investigation by anthropologists of the Western classificatory system. When one compares terminology used in different decades of the 20th century, a remarkable amount of faddism is noted. This is also associated with treatment. Our classification system variously uses, body parts, organ systems, modes of transmission, disease agent(s), psychological phases, and a host of other arbitrary labeling devices [22, 23].

If we seriously consider comparing "non-comparable" categories we raise some epistemological ghosts.

The Western physician, by adopting an epidemiologic perspective, including an awareness of cultural factors, may be able to approach patients with multiple problems in a less constrained way. And, as cultural blinders are lifted, social and psychiatric problems should no longer be considered as alien but as integral in handling total health care.

The combined perspectives of anthropology and epidemiology should lead us to a rethinking of classification, etiology and the role of social factors in illness. By perceiving all illness from a biosocial orientation, the multicausal framework is seen as a needed theoretical model. The role of social science in medicine is thus practical and theoretical [23, 24].

References

1. Duff R. S. and Hollingshead A.B. *Sickness and Society.* Harper & Row, New York, 1968.
2. Scrimshaw N. S., Taylor C. E. and Gordon J. E. *Interactions of Nutrition and Infection,* WHO, Geneva, 1968.
3. Scotch N. Medical Anthropology: A Review of the Literature from 1960—1962. *Biennial Review of Anthropology* (Edited by Siegal B.) 1963.
4. Kosa J. and Robertson L. The Social Aspects of Health and Illness. *Poverty and Health, A Sociological Analysis,* (Edited by Kosa J. et. al.)
5. Susser M. *Causal Thinking in the Health Sciences.* UP, London, 1973.
6. Becker M. H. The health belief model and personal health behavior, *Hlth Educ. Monogr.* 2, (4), 1974.
7. Recent research on the importance of the folk language associated with illness, and on the folk perception of illness, is now crystalizing into a field called "symptom classification". We have recently been invited to a spring 1976 meeting, hosted by the National Institutes of Health, on symptom classification schemes.
8. Leighton D. C. Cultural determinants of behavior: a neglected area. *Am. J. Psychiat.* 128, 1003, 1972.
9. Bergman R. *Personal communication,* 1973.
10. Wintrobe R. *Personal communication,* 1974.
11. Hinkle L. J. and Wolff G.: (a) The nature of man's adaptation to his total environment. *Arch. Int. Med.* 99, 442, 1957. (b) Ecologic investigations of the relationship between illness, life experience, and the social environment. *Ann. Int. Med.* 49, 1373, 1958. (c) Ecologic observations of the relation of physical illness, mental illness and the social environment. *Psychosom. Med.* 23, 288. 1961.
12. Stott D. H. Cultural and natural checks on population growth. In *Environment and Cultural Behavior* (Edited by Vayda A. P.) 1969.
13. Morris M. Book review of Adaptation in Cultural Evolution: An Approach to Medical Anthropology by Alland A. *Am. Anthropol.* 73, 1299, 1971.
14. Febrega H. Jr. Medical anthropology. *Biennial Review of Anthropology,* 1972.
15. Dubos R. *Man Adapting.* Yale University Press, New Haven, 1965.
16. Leininger M. *Nursing and Anthropology: Two Worlds to Blend.* Wiley, New York, 1970.
17. Paul B. J. Health. In *Culture and Community.* Russell Sage Foundation, 1955.
18. Simons O. G. Popular and modern medicine in Mestizo communities of coastal Peru and Chile. *J. Am. Folklore* 66, 57, 1953.

19. Kiev A. *Curanderismo, Mexican-American Folk Psychiatry.* Free Press, Glencoe, IL, 1968.
20. Mechanic D. Illness and cure. In *Poverty and Health: A sociological Analysis.* (Edited by Kosa J. et al,). 1967.
21. Febrega H. *Personal communication,* 1973.
22. Coles R. *The South Goes North.* Little, Brown, Atlantic, 1971.
23. MacMahon B. and Pugh T. *Epidemiology, Principles and Methods.* Little, Brown, Atlantic, 1970.
24. Cassell J. Social science theory as a source of hypothesis in epidemiological research. *Am. J. publ. Hlth* 54, 1482, 1964.

Erwin H. Ackerknecht

Primitive surgery *

Speaking of "primitive surgery" is one of those arbitrary procedures which are to a certain extent unavoidable if we try to analyze primitive phenomena for a better understanding of our own cultural processes, and which are justifiable as long as we remain aware of their arbitrary character. Not before the second half of the Middle Ages were surgery and its practitioners regarded as different from or inferior to other methods or practitioners of the healing art. Then for 700 years they remained separated from the body of medicine. In modern society "surgery" has again become part of medicine—but as one of its "specialties." This again is without precedent. Though we find "specialists" also in primitive and archaic medicine (Egyptian, Peruvian, etc.), specialization there has other reasons and proceeds along dividing lines different from those observed in modern scientific medicine (1). Surgery is, therefore, not a special field defined by the primitives themselves. We simply deal in the following with such procedures as would be mainly in the domain of the surgeon in our society. Practically, it means that we deal primarily with therapeutic measures which are of a definite technological interest.

Wound Treatment

There is no tribe on record which does not in some way or other treat wounds. It would lead us too far to go into details here of the hundreds of different treatments recorded, the principles of which are very similar. Herbs or roots, often with astringent or disinfectant qualities, are applied to the wound in form of powders,

*Parts of this article were given as a paper at a Viking Dinner Conference on March 22, 1946. I wrote this article while working in the Institute of Human Morphology (Department of Anthropology, American Museum of Natural History, New York), a project financed by a grant from the Viking Fund. I am glad to express on this occasion my appreciation to the Fund and to its Director of Research, Dr. Paul Fejos.

Reproduced by permission of the American Anthropological Association from the *American Anthropologist*, 49 (1), 1947.

infusions, or poultices. In rare cases animal substances, like powdered insects or cow dung, are used. Heat is rather widely employed to speed the healing process (2). Wound treatment by primitives is in general regarded as "good."

> *"In the treatment of wounds the Cherokee doctors exhibit a considerable degree of skill, but as far as any internal ailment is concerned the average farmer's wife is worth all the doctors in the whole tribe (3)."*

Similar appreciative judgments can be easily collected from Oceania (4), South America (5), or Africa (6). They are, of course, mainly based on the prompt healing of wounds, which can be explained equally well through the constitution of the patients or the absence of the highly "cultivated" germs of our cities and hospitals. To evaluate wound treatment in primitive society in such a general way is all the more difficult when we see in our own medicine rather different treatments applied with about similar results. Reports of deaths occurring during initiation rites in Melanesia and Africa (7) from infected scarification wounds should not be omitted from a general picture.

It is easier to appreciate certain isolated technical procedures in the course of wound treatment. For instance, the suturing of wounds [with sinews among North American Indians like the Carrier, Mescalero, Dakota, Winnebago (8); with thorns among the Masai and Akamba (9), and with the heads of termites among the Somali and Brazilian Indians (10)] is a very respectable accomplishment. Wound drainage too is reported from North American Indians (11).

The stopping of blood vessels is a difficult problem for primitives. That they do not know the ligature (12) is not surprising, as it appeared in our own culture only with Celsus (1st century A.D.) and was rediscovered by Ambroïse Paré (1510-90). Primitives do use, more or less successfully, such diverse materials as powdered gum, charcoal, ashes, eagles' down, and bandages of bark or coconut fibre. Tourniquets are known in Africa, North America, and Oceania (13). One of the best styptic methods is cauterization, practiced in Africa, America (14), and Oceania (15). The only tribe known to suture *vessels* (with tendons) is the Masai (16). We will encounter the Masai again and again as the primitive master surgeons. They are atypical, as their surgery is incomparably superior not only to that of all other primitive tribes reported, but also to the surgery of most civilized peoples up to the Renaissance. That even this highly developed surgery is not free from magic becomes obvious from such examples as the Masai, putting a dead fly into the wound, and binding one testicle around the left anterior leg of their cattle after castration so that the wound might close more quickly (16a).

Occasionally, deep-seated arrows seem to be extracted skillfully and successfully (17). In a limited area in East Africa, natives are *even able to sulture intestines* opened by arrows or spears (18). Intestinal wounds may heal sometimes (19), but treatment in general seems inept (20). Incarcerated hernias die. Umbilical hernias are, in many places, regarded as a sign of beauty. In North America hernias are occasionally bandaged (21). The Dene bring a prolapsed uterus back into its original position and bandage it (22).

The oldest document in the German language, the so-called "Merseburger Zaubersprüche," is wound incantations. Homer's "Odyssey" (XIX, 457) mentions an incantation against bleeding. It is, therefore, not surprising that in addition to dressing, wounds are treated with magic songs among, e.g., the Apache (23), Havasupai (24), or Creek (25). The Creek submit the wounded to the same kind of isolation as women after childbirth (26). The wounded among the Banyankole can be nursed only by women without sexual relations (27). The latex used in the treatment of wounds among the Mania plays a magic role (28). The Maori exorcised arrowheads which they could not touch (29). Heat used in the treatment of wounds, be it in the form of the "moxa" or not, has often a symbolical meaning and makes the disease spirit fly away (30).

Fractures and Dislocations

To base judgments concerning the quality of primitive surgery on mere excavation material has become impossible since Adolph Schultz has shown that well-healed fractures are numerous among wild gibbons and other primates which are not likely to enjoy treatment by professional bonesetters (31).

As in the case of wounds, numerous reports emphasize again the good treatment of fractures, e.g., among the Creek, Winnebago (32), the Barundi (33), Bavenda (34), Duke of York Islanders (35), and Maori (36). From these, and from the following tribes, the use of splints is reported: Chippewa (37), Nez-Percé (38), Hottentot (38a), Tahitians (39), Eskimo (40). Original casts, made from leather, chicle, or clay, are used by the Shoshone (41), the Lango (42), the Jívaro (43), and South Australian tribes (44). That splints do not prevent bad healing was already emphasized by Martius (45). Morice (46) sees the reason for such failures in the absence of proper setting of the fragments. As experience in Nias shows, even relocation does not always seem to prevent bad results (47). The Cherokee (48) and the Dakota (49) are credited with poor fracture treatment, without further comment. When on the other hand fracture treatment is associated with systematic traction [Liberian Manos (50)] or absolute immobilization, the limb being fixed to the floor with pegs [Akamba (51)], it is most likely to be successful. The absence of splints in fracture treatment is by no means rare. The Polynesian Tubnai (52) give only medicine and recommend immobility. The Murngin use only poultices and heat (53). The Tanala apply heavy bandages, but no splints (54). Dislocations are reduced, e.g., in North America (55), Oceania (56), and Africa (57). There is much less enthusiasm among observers about the treatment of dislocations than about fracture and wound treatment.

Fracture treatment of primitives seems to be more active than ours. Massaging seems to start relatively early (58). As the use of massage is by no means restricted to surgical cases among primitives and is not a surgical procedure, properly speaking, we prefer not to deal with this subject in detail in this connection. Massage as a therapeutic procedure seems to be almost universal (59). This is not surprising in view of the fact that it can be easily derived from the behavior of sick animals (scratching, rubbing) and presupposes no technological acomplishments whatsoever.

Fracture treatment like any other primitive treatment is, even if objectively effective, pervaded with magic elements. The plants used so frequently as internal medicaments or poultices have implications of magic power (60). Gio bonesetters use much mimic magic in setting bones (61). The success of an otherwise "rational" fracture treatment depends entirely on the fate of a chicken whose bones are broken and treated like those of the patient (62). A blacksmith tong is employed magically for reducing a dislocated mandible (63). The bonesetters among the Azande use splints, massage, and "mystic" ointments (64). Magic fracture treatment is reported from the Ubena (65) and the Tanala (66). At Nias, fractures and dislocations are preferably reduced by those born with their feet forward (67), among the Zuni by those struck by lightning (67a). The Tarahumare apply peyote and bind the heads of lizards around the fracture (68). The Havasupai use splints—and songs (69).

Blood-Letting

Though not used primarily in surgical diseases, bleeding is a surgical procedure itself. Bleeding again is an almost universal trait in primitive medicine. As we automatically identify bleeding with venesection, which is actually not too frequent among primitives, we tend to have a somewhat exalted idea of the technical excellence of primitive bleeding. The confusion between venesection (phlebotomy) and blood-letting makes a proper evaluation of source material difficult. If a source says that a tribe does not practice phlebotomy, does that mean that there is no bleeding at all? If a source speaks of "blood-letting" in general, we do not know which technique is really used.

Actually, there exist four bleeding techniques in primitive cultures: scarification, cupping, venesection, and leeching. Scarification is undoubtedly the technique most widely used. In some regions scarification is used so freely that everybody is covered with scars resulting from the treatment (70). A great variety of instruments is employed (70a). Scarification is reported particularly from Oceania (e.g., Samoa, d'Entrecasteaux Islands, Nias, Australia, New Guinea) and America [e.g., the Tlingit, Ten'a, Chippewa, Omaha, Cherokee; Central America and Brazil (70b)]. Cupping with a horn over incisions is so generally applied in Africa (71) that it has almost completely replaced scarification for bleeding, and sucking for the production of local hyperemia. Outside Africa cupping is found but rarely, e.g., in British Columbia and Nias (72). Venesection is not very frequent and is mostly found in America [Alaska, California, Honduras, Peru; the Déné, Chippewa, Carajá (73)]; though in some places the technique may be adopted from the whites—at least for Peru it is certain that the custom was pre-Columbian (74). Venesection is found occasionally in Africa (75) and Oceania (76). Leeching is extremely rare (77). A queer variation of bleeding techniques is the shooting of little arrows into the skin, reported from New Guinea (78) Africa (78a), Central and South America (79), and Greece (!) (79a); it is probably magical in origin (80). The magico-religious background of bleeding in primitive culture has so often been commented upon that it seems unnecessary to deal with this question here in detail (81).

Incision

Not so widespread as the above-mentioned practices, but still fairly frequent, are operations by incision. Technically akin to scarification and venesection, such operations are still conservative and not concerned with anatomical change, but they come much closer to "active" surgery. The most frequent one is, of course, the opening of boils and abscesses with a great variety of instruments. Boils are lanced, e.g., among the Eskimo (82), the Thompson Indians (83), and Zuni (84), among the Barundi, Akamba and Dama (85), in the Shan states (86), in New Guinea, Samoa, Tahiti, and Vaitupu (87). The Masai operate even on abscesses of the liver and spleen (88). In the same direction lies the lancing of a hydrocele in Vaitupu (89) or of an inflamed testis in Uvea. Fatal outcome of the incision of a hernia is reported by the same author (90). Rare operations along similar lines are the opening of an empyema (Great Lakes) (91); pneumothorax by cautery in pleurisy and pneumonia in Uganda (92); scarification of inflamed tonsils by the Masai (93); multiple piercing of goiters (94), and tenotomy (95).

Medical Amputation and Excision

With these operations we enter the field of the very rare. Observers of even the more surgery-minded tribes in America (96), as well as in Africa (97) and Oceania (98), emphasize the absence of amputation. Amputation seems most likely where nature, by freezing limbs, has already prepared the procedure. Thus we hear of the (very crude) amputation of frozen fingers among the Eskimo and Chippewa (99). The Dama represent an isolated case of amputating crippled fingers and toes (100). Whether the penis amputation photographed by Neuhauss (101) is of a medical nature is doubtful. The Masai enucleate eyes and, for instance, amputate limbs with hopelessly complicated fractures with great skill (102). They even have protheses (103). They are thus apparently the only primitives to equal in this field the accomplishments of the ancient Peruvians (104) who, according to Roy Moodie, were far better surgeons than "any other primitive or ancient race of people (105)." We are not dealing further with the surgery of the ancient Peruvians because neither can they be regarded as "primitives," nor is it clear whether the numerous mutilations of nose, lips, and extremities seen on Peruvian pottery are spontaneous (a consequence of lepra, syphilis, or, most likely, leishmaniasis), or, if artificial, whether they are of a medical, religious or juridical nature (106).

A remarkable local surgical accomplishment, reported by six different authors, is the excision of neck glands by native African doctors in the case of sleeping disease (trypanosomiasis) (107). Neck tumors are cauterized in Rhodesia (108). The Galla and the Akamba remove the uvula (109). The Tembu and Fingu operate vaginal polyps (110).

I have been able to find only one place outside of Africa where surgery equals similar levels, Vaitupu (Ellice Islands) in Polynesia. There subcutaneous lipomata, the elephantoid scrotum, tubercular glands in the neck, old leprotic or yaw ulcers are removed successfully (111). While the Africans at least have iron knives at their disposal, these Polynesians operate exclusively with shark teeth.

I would regard with the greatest distrust the marvelous stories of the abdominal surgery of the Araucanians, based on old sources (112). We know now that the shamanism of the Araucanians shows the closest resemblances to Siberian shamanism. The Araucanians practice the rare postmortem opening of the body, typical of Siberia (113), as well as the old shamanistic trick of opening the body and cleaning the intestines (114). It is most likely that early observers have mistaken both customs for operations.

Equally spurious are reports on primitive "cataract operations (115)." The only clear-cut case in the literature is no less clearly of Arabic provenience (116). If a case is described in sufficient detail, as by Morice (117), it becomes obvious that we are not dealing with the operation of a cataract but of a pterygium! Actually, I do not think that the one report on ovariotomy in Australia (117a) justifies counting this operation among the accomplishments of primitive surgery.

Caesarean Section

The Caesarean section is technically even more difficult than the operations mentioned above. It may be very old, but the earliest authentic reports of it stem from the 16th century, and only during the last sixty years has it become a routine procedure. One is thus inclined to dismiss reports of primitive Caesareans as mere fable or misunderstanding. Neither self-inflicted rippings of the belly by desperate mothers, as have occurred even in our time (118), nor the widely practiced cutting out of the fetus when the mother has died can qualify as "surgery." The latter measure was prescribed by law in Rome as early as 715 B.C., and seems to be rather common in parts of Africa (119) and Oceania (120). This performance, based mostly on magic representations, leads by no means automatically to the true Caesarean section. We might even disregard van der Burgt's repeated statements that the Kurundi do practice Caesarean section (121), and dismiss primitive Caesarean section with a shrug of our shoulders if there did not exist a well-dated, most detailed, and most positive description of a Caesarean section coming from an observer whose reliability has, to our knowledge, never been challenged. The skill with which the operator acted leaves no doubt that he did not improvise, but followed a well-established procedure.

The observer was Robert Felkin and he saw the operation performed upon a 20-year old woman in Kahura in Uganda in 1879 (122). Banana wine served as an anesthetic and disinfectant. Hemorrhage was checked with a red-hot iron. The incision was made in the midline, between symphysis and umbilicus, and closed with iron nails. Temperature never rose above 101°F in the postoperative stage, and the wound was closed on the eleventh day.

Unfortunately, I feel unable to explain why in 1879 there existed in Kahura in Uganda a black surgeon performing the Caesarean section safely and, in some respects, better than many of his contemporary white colleagues. It is suggested that, as we have already seen, East Africa shows generally a better surgery than any other region inhabited by primitives; that the widespread embryotomy (123) seems particularly frequent in East Africa (124); but all this, of course, does not constitute a real answer to our question.

Trepanation

The common surgical procedures described in the 1st to 4th sections, and even the rare ones noted in the 5th and 6th, create a picture of primitive surgery which would be fairly consistent if we did not encounter among primitives, and not rarely but fairly frequently, an operation which up to the second half of the 19th century was regarded by modern surgeons as extremely dangerous and difficult: trephining of the skull. It is, of course, neither possible to survey here the extensive literature on primitive and prehistoric trephining, nor is it necessary for our purpose. We need not deal with technical details, and we can almost entirely omit European prehistoric trephining as not belonging properly to our subject. (In another context this material is of the highest importance as it is the sole existing tangible evidence of prehistoric medicine.) Peruvian trephining I have included to a limited extent. I do not think that Inca medicine can be called "primitive (125)," but trephining in the Andean region preceded Inca civilization (126) and survived it into the 20th century (127).

The practice of trephining has been directly observed among the following tribes and nations: in the Balkans, in Daghestan (128), and among the Berber; in Abyssinia (129), Uganda (130), and Nigeria (131). It seems to be particularly frequent in Oceania (New Caledonia (132), New Zealand (133), New Guinea (134), Uvea and the Loyalty Islands (135), the Gazelle Peninsula and New Ireland (136), New Britain (137), the Solomons (138), and Tahiti (139). The center of trephining in the Americas was undoubtedly the Peruvian highlands. But isolated evidences of trephining have been found all over North, Central and South America, from British Columbia down to Chile (140). In the latter respect the situation is similar to the one encountered in European neolithic trephining: besides numerous finds in France, we encounter isolated ones from Russia to Spain, from Sweden to North Africa. Although success in this complicated operation is explainable where it is a routine procedure, genesis and success of such isolated operations are hard to understand.

Prehistoric trephining was interpreted by Broca and many subsequent authors as largely magical (to liberate the disease spirit). Wölfel, on the other hand, regards trephining as a purely surgical measure in the case of skull fracture, caused mainly by two weapons—the slingshot and the club. The little we know of actual motivations of primitive trephining, however, does not allow a clear-cut decision.

In New Britain the operation obviously is used in the case of combat fractures of the skull—and yet it is also a means to obtain longevity (141). In New Ireland, trepanation is applied in the case of skull fractures, as well as against "headaches" and "epilepsy" (both magically explained), and in children as a prophylactic against ill health in general (142). In the Gazelle Peninsula the indication is surgical, but success depends entirely on magic remedies (143). In Tahiti the indication seems purely surgical; in Uvea, purely magico-medical ("headache"). Almost all men are trephined there. The Uveans also trephine the tibia and ulna in cases of rheumatism (144). In most Peruvian trephinings, the slingshot, club, or accident seems to have been the causative agent. Yet the form of some trephinings suggests "medical" indication, a fact which is admitted even by Wölfel (145). Sometimes tumors or gummata seem to have been the reason for the operation (146). It is remarkable that even such an apparently rational procedure as the Peruvian one was so carefully hidden by the natives for almost four hundred years that no chronicler or traveler recorded it before Bandelier (1904).

It has been shown repeatedly that diverse pathological conditions may produce lesions very similar to trephining (147). That the bulk of our archaeological material consists nonetheless of true trephinings is suggested by the numerous unhealed trepanations which can be easily identified, and by the ethnographic record.

For Oceania, survival has been estimated by observers as high as 50 (148), or even 80 or 90 percent (149). For Peru, McGee concludes from his series of skulls a survival rate of 50 percent, which is equal to European results in the second half of the 19th century (150). The results of Tello and McCurdy are even more favorable (151).

Ritual and Judiciary Mutilations

With trephinings we have reached the limits of surgery proper in primitive societies, but by no means the limits of activities which, objectively, are on the same level with amputations and incisions. On the contrary, in numerous places we see the same primitives who only rarely use a knife in the case of disease or traumatism fall into a veritable frenzy of cutting and chopping off when ritual or judiciary motives are involved (152). Of this enormous field of ritual and judiciary mutilation I can here, of course, give only a very sketchy survey which, however, I hope will help us to a better understanding of primitive surgery.

I need scarcely mention such minor interventions as dental mutilations, ritual cicatrization, or head deformation. Amputation of the fingers for ritual reasons is well known to us from South and North American Indians (153). The custom seems even more widespread in Africa and Oceania. In an excellent survey, Lagercrantz mentions no less than fourteen tribes in black Africa practising ritual finger mutilation (154). Söderström gives almost the same number for Oceania (155). Next to the fingers, the genitalia seem to offer a convenient target for religious zeal. No less than fourteen methods of operating upon the male genitalia are known (156). There is no need to give details on circumcision and its variations (157).

Subincision, the opening of the male urethra, is, curiously enough, eminently unsuccessful when practiced for purely medical reasons (158). Its medical character in Fiji and Tonga is, to say the least, somewhat confused. Its magic character in Australia is clear. So far the most satisfactory explanation for its true nature has been brought forth by Dr. Ashley Montagu (159). A surgically most remarkable genital mutilation, monorchy, the removal of one testicle, has been reported from the Hottentot, the Dama, from Abyssinia, the Loyalty Islands, the Carolines, Tonga, etc. (160). The female genitalia are submitted to clitoridectomy, infibulation, etc. (161).

For punishment, the fingers again become convenient objects (162) if the whole hand is not sacrificed (163). The Seneca Indians performed a very neat amputation of half the foot upon their captives (164). Offenders may be deprived of their tongues (165), or of their genitalia in case of adultery (166). Compared to the rare incisions and even rarer amputations, ritual and judiciary mutilations are of an almost universal character in primitive societies.

The Surgical Personnel

Unfortunately most observers have failed to inform us about the not unimportant item of who actually performs the operations described.

Only among the Masai (167) do we hear of a definite class of surgeons (treating humans and animals alike). In West Africa surgery is not in the hands of the witch doctors, but of the herbalists (mostly female), who operate with the mysterious assistance of a white fowl (168). One of the religious societies of the Kiowa, the Buffalo Doctors, specialized in the treatment of wounds (169). The Omaha Buffalo Society concentrated upon the magic treatment of accidents (170).

It seems less surgery which is set apart as a specialty than bonesetting. We hear of Zuni bonesetters (mostly people struck by lightning (171); of a clan of bonesetters among the Azande, using splints, massage, and mystic ointments (172); of efficient, though much magic-using bonesetters among the Gio and Manos (173); of bonesetters in Melanesia (174), and at Ontong Java (175).

Most frequently surgery seems to be done by the otherwise supernaturalistic medicine-man. It is the "wizard" who trephines in New Britain (176), as well as in Bolivia (177). The famous abscess opening among the Zuni is done by the "theurgist (178)." One of the first things a Creek medicine-man learns is how to treat gun-shot wounds with "songs" and medicines (179). Paviotso shamans cure wounds and injuries as well as illness (180). Jíbaro medicine-men set bones (180a). In Kenya, surgery and bonesetting are in the hands of the medicine-man (181), and in Uganda the medicine-man first chops the limbs off as an executioner, to treat the wounds later as a surgeon (182).

It would lead too far to go here into the characteristics of medical specialization among primitives in general which differs considerably from medical specialization in our society. As far as the separation between medicine and surgery is concerned, it seems not to have advanced very far, if we are to judge from our scanty material. Our picture of the primitive surgeon as being probably more realistic and socially inferior is strongly influenced by the later medieval and early modern situation in our own society. Such an expectation does not seem to be confirmed by the data available (183).

Discussion and Conclusions

Primitive surgery has never reached the level of, for example, Alexandrian surgery as it is reflected in Celsus (1st century, A.D.). Celsus speaks of the excision of tumors, of operation for aneurism, hernia, and stone, of plastic surgery, of the amputation of the larger limbs and the resection of bones (the jaw included). The typical "surgery" of a Guarani tribe consists of cutting the umbilical cord, perforating the earlobe and the lower lip, and of opening abscesses (184). Tribes with a very developed medicine, like the Liberian Manos; "are extremely conservative when it comes to surgery (185)." Their surgery is limited to bonesetting, blood-letting by small shallow incisions, circumcision and scarification of tribal marks (186). There is no surgery in the Bhar-el-Ghazal (187); neither surgery nor autopsies in Madagascar (188). "Surgical cases are treated in the worst possible way, any intervention with a knife being looked on as absurd if not culpable. . . . Medical cases are generally treated more rationally than surgical cases (189)." There is no substantial difference between such isolated judgments of observers and the results of our foregoing survey. *Primitive surgery is indeed poor in scope and quality*. Only in the more southern parts of East Africa and in certain Polynesian localities do we encounter a relatively well-developed surgery. The East African focus of good surgery is not limited to the Masai. Among their neighbors we have found such outstanding accomplishments as Caesarean section, intestinal suture, trepanation, excision of glands, etc. It is to be hoped that regional specialists will be able to throw more light on the reasons why we find these two local centers of a more highly developed surgery.

Logically there exist four possibilities why primitive surgery has not advanced further: that there was no need of surgery; that primitives lack technical skill; that they lack certain elements of knowledge; that other elements of their socio-mental makeup have been unfavorable to the development of surgery among them. All these possibilities undoubtedly play a certain role, but their relative importance is by no means the same. It is a fact that one of the main objects of our surgical endeavors, cancer, is rare among primitives, whether for racial reasons, or simply because most of them never reach the cancer age. On the other hand, the ills to which the savages are not exempt are sufficiently numerous to have furnished enough incentive for a more developed surgery.

Surgery undoubtedly presupposes a considerable manual skill. But many primitives show such skill and yet, like the Eskimos, are very poor surgeons.

The great progress in modern surgery was made possible by an enormous increase in our knowledge concerning anatomy, anesthesia and asepsis. *The anatomical knowledge of most primitives is notoriously bad* (190). Yet explaining the lack of surgery by the lack of anatomy is only reformulating the problem in other terms. The lack of anatomy is undoubtedly due to certain objective limitations. Anatomical knowledge becomes valuable only when organized. The possibilities of organizing knowledge depend largely on the structure of society in general. Not accidentally have ideas concerning the social body so often colored anatomical ideas, and vice versa. And many primitive societies are rather amorphous. But this is only part of the truth. The knowledge of people is not only a question of what they are able to learn, but also one of what they want to learn—a question of interests and values. In this respect a comparison between the anatomical knowledge of primitives who make autopsies and those who do not has been very revealing to me. Surprisingly enough, both categories are equally ignorant of anatomy (191), because even the dissectors are so strongly under the influence of supernaturalistic ideas that they overlook the anatomically obvious (192). Anatomical ignorance of primitives seems mainly due to their supernaturalistic orientation. We must not forget that our own way of looking at the human body and bodily functions is rather unique compared to the attitude not only of primitives but also of most ancient civilizations.

The absence of anesthesia and asepsis in the modern sense is perhaps less important in the lag of primitive surgery than it appears at first sight. In spite of the lack of anesthesia and a very rudimentary asepsis, the Masai have developed a quite creditable surgery. Many primitives have a considerable number of general and local anesthetics at their disposal (193). All observers agree upon the relative ease with which primitives overcome wound infection (194). It is immaterial here whether this increased resistance is primarily constitutional or, as I am inclined to think, primarily due to the fact that no hospitals are at the disposal of primitives for the cultivation of particularly virulent strains of strepto- and staphylococci. The fact remains that primitives do, as far as wound infection is concerned, labor under less odds than did modern surgery in its beginning, and this might explain their comparatively excellent results in complicated operations like trephining whenever they did attempt them.

It seems, therefore, that the most satisfactory explanation for the particular character of primitive surgery lies in the direction of the limiting influence which supernaturalistic ideas among primitives exert upon the development of the operator's art. It seems the only way to explain the "mystery" of primitive surgery (195), that is, the occurrence of major operations such as trephining and of wholesale ritual and judicial mutilation among people who otherwise possess but the rudiments of surgery.

We have mentioned already the presence of magico-religious elements in surgical practice in their proper place. We hope that it has become obvious that primitive surgery is, as little as primitive midwifery, the purely empirical half of primitive medicine, and different in principle from a much more supernaturalistic internal medicine (as to a certain extent it is in Egyptian medicine). "Superstition affected more or less all surgical operations (196)." Yet this active role of the magico-religious in primitive surgery is only a part, and perhaps the smaller one, of the influence of magico-religious representations on primitive surgery in general.

The negative influence of supernaturalistic ideas on surgery is very clear in all those cases where bodily mutilation in general is dreaded because of its detrimental influence in the future life of the ghost. "A Central African will not consent to an operation (not even tooth extraction), as it conflicts with the anticipation of his dismembered spirit (197). For the same reason, the Tanala have no fear of death, but are very much afraid of mutilation (198). To the Arab and Shawia, death is preferable to the loss of a limb (199). It is obvious that amputation or other major surgery can hardly develop or be "diffused" under such circumstances. It is also clear that punishment by bodily mutilation in such tribes is damaging far beyond the physical disability it leaves. And it is understandable that in regions where mutilation is a customary form of punishment, people will dislike to undergo operations which externally would identify them with criminals (200). Such attitudes of fear are not restricted to primitive societies. The Chinese, for instance, dislike for magic reasons the spilling of blood to such an extent that they did not adopt blood-letting or a quite excellent surgery from the Hindus, though they did learn a great many other medical practices from them (201).

Yet, as we have seen, this fear of mutilation is not general. In numerous tribes ritual mutilation is widely practiced, and yet these tribes generally fail to develop medical amputation or other major surgery (202). The same holds good for most of those who practice trephining. It is most likely that ritual mutilation is so far removed in their thoughts from practical considerations, their general orientation and their thinking about the human body and the most appropriate ways of treatment so different from ours, that it just never occurs to them that this mutilating technique might be useful or even life-saving when applied to infected complicated fractures, focuses of septicemia, tumors, etc. (203). The medical use of trephining or Caesarean section seems to be arrived at not as a result of a general approach, but on magic or empiric grounds in such an isolated way that it cannot influence the general status of surgery. The fact that relatively high technical accomplishments remain isolated without influencing the general level or orientation is rather frequent in primitive societies and by no means restricted to surgery. It is mysterious only as long as we suppose such technical accomplishments to be the result of more or less scientific thought or research as they would be in our society. In the case of the non-operating, ritual mutilators or trephiners, we deal, as in the case of the dissectors who were unable to learn anatomy, with a particular brand of "ignorance," an ignorance not of technical means, but existing in spite of technical means through different orientation, interests, and values. We must realize that such behavior is primarily dictated by magico-religious ideas and is not merely "irrational." (In some respects, it is even very logical.) Irrational behavior is a general psychological mechanism in humans like, for example, suggestibility, and modern empiricist surgeons can be subject to it as well as primitive trephiners (204), while the supernaturalistic approach has been almost entirely eliminated from modern scientific surgery.

Notes

1. Rosen, 1944, p. 5ff.; Ackerknecht, 1945a, p. 37; Ackerknecht, 1946, 479ff.
2. Martius, 1844, p. 182; Harley, 1941, pp. 220, 222; Warner, p. 221.
3. Mooney, 1891, p. 323.
4. Landtman, 1927, p. 227.
5. Koch-Grunberg, 1923, III, p. 274.
6. Driberg, 1923, p. 55.
7. Linton, 1945, p. 301; Harley, 1941, p. 131.
8. Morice, 1900-01, p. 22; Stone, 1932, p. 76.
9. Lindblom, 1920, p. 312; Merker, 1910, p. 181.
10. Pardal, 1937, pp. 50, 161; Monfreid in Stephen-Chauvet, 1936, p. 76.
11. Stone, 1932, p. 76.
12. The ligature of an artery with copper wire among the Ba-Yaka mentioned by Tardy and Joyce, 1906, p. 50, and ligature of North Carolina Indians are likely to be borrowed from the whites.
13. Malcolm, 1934, p. 200.
14. Bartels, 1893, pp. 282, 287.
15. Hagen, 1899, p. 285.
16. Merker, 1919, p. 181.
16a. *Id.*, p. 159.
17. E.g., Chartier in Stephen-Chauvet, 1936, p. 76; Routledge in Harley, 1941, p. 221; Grinnell, II, p. 147.
18. Merker, 1910, p. 181; Monfreid and Maurice in Stephen-Chauvet, 1936, 76-80; Roscoe and Talbot in Harley, 1941, p. 222.
19. Bartels, 1893, p. 284.
20. Webb, 1933-34, p. 95; Catlin, 1876, I, p. 39.
21. Morice, 1900-01, p. 23; Opler, 1941, p. 217; Malcolm, 1934, p. 200.
22. Morice, 1900-01, p. 24.
23. Opler, 1941, p. 349.
24. Spier, 1928, p. 284.
25. Swanton, 1928, p. 617.
26. Swanton, 1928, p. 625.
27. Roscoe, 1923, p. 161.
28. Vergiat, 1937, p. 171.
29. Parham, 1943, VI.
30. Morice, 1900-01, p. 20; Sieroshewski, 1901, p. 105.
31. Schultz, 1939, p. 571ff.; *id.*, 1944, p. 115ff. Dr. Schultz' publications have very important implications on the problems of primitive pathology in general and natural selection, with which I have been unable to deal in this context. They should be perused by all interested in these problems.
32. Bartels, 1893, p. 290.
33. Meyer, 1916, p. 142.
34. Stayt, 1931, p. 273.
35. Brown, 1910, p. 185.
36. Parham, 1943, p. VI.
37. Densmore, 1928, p. 334.
38. Spinden, 1908, p. 257.
38a. Schapera, 1930, p. 408.
39. Ellis, 1853, III, p. 42.
40. Weyer, 1932, p. 329.
41. Stone, 1932, p. 82.
42. Driberg, 1923, p. 56.

43. Stirling, 1938, p. 120.
44. Bartels, 1893, p. 290.
45. Martius, 1844, p. 182.
46. Morice, 1900-01, p. 22.
47. Kleiweg, 1913, p. 133.
48. Olbrechts, 1932, p. 71.
49. Bartels, 1893, p. 290.
50. Harley, 1941, p. 95.
51. Lindblom, 1920, p. 311.
52. Aitken, 1930, p. 89.
53. Warner, 1937, p. 221.
54. Linton, 1933, p. 225.
55. Morice, 1900-01, p. 22.
56. Ellis, 1853, p. 42; Aitken, 1930, p. 89.
57. Schapera, 1930, p. 408.
58. E.g., Harley, 1941, p. 95.
59. See Sumner-Keller, 1927, II, p. 1401ff.; IV, p. 799ff.
60. Vergiat, 1937, p. 166.
61. Harley, 1941, p. 17.
62. *Id.*, p. 95.
63. *Id.*, p. 118.
64. Evans-Pritchard, 1937, p. 498.
65. Culwick, 1935, p. 397.
66. Linton, 1933, p. 225.
67. Kleiweg, 1913, pp. 132, 203.
67a. Spier, 1928, p. 285.
68. Hrdlicka, 1908, p. 250.
69. Spier, 1928, p. 284.
70. Ehrenreich, 1891, II, p. 33; Haddon, p. 113.
70a. Lillico, 1940, p. 135.
70b. Sumner-Keller, 1927, II, p. 1401; IV, p. 801ff.; Haddon, 1901, p. 113; Hagen, 1899,
    p. 257; Martius, 1844, p. 182; Fletcher-La Flesche, 1911, p. 582; Kleiweg, 1913, p. 133;
    Lillico, 1940, p. 135ff.
71. Harley, 1941, p. 217.
72. Sumner-Keller, 1927, IV, p. 799; Kleiweg, 1913, p. 133.
73. Bartels, 1893, p. 209; Morice, 1900-01, p. 18; Martius, 1844, p. 182.
74. Pardal, 1937, p. 49-50.
75. E.g., Smith and Dale, 1920, p. 231.
76. E.g., Ray, 1917, p. 273; Haddon, 1901, p. 223; Lillico, 1940, p. 137ff.
77. Lillico, 1940, p. 135.
78. Haddon, 190, p. 223.
78a. Merker, 1910, p. 182; Driberg, 1930.
79. Karsten, 1926, p. 159; Wafer (1699), 1934, p. 18.
79a. Heger, 1928, p. 275.
80. Karsten, 1926, p. 160.
81. *Id.*, p. 155ff.; Lillico, p. 133; Sumner-Keller, 1927, II, p. 1403.
82. Weyer, 1932, p. 328.
83. Teit, 1900, p. 370.
84. Freeman, 1924, p. 32; a masterly description of the opening of an abscess in Stevenson,
    1904, p. 386.
85. Meyer, 1932, p. 142; Lindblom, 1920, p. 314; Vedder, 1923, II, p. 90.
86. Milne, 1924, p. 251.
87. Whiting, 1941, p. 52; Turner, 1884, p. 141; Ellis, 1853, p. 44; Kennedy, 1931, p. 241.

88. Merker, 1910, p. 183.
89. Kennedy, 1931, p. 241.
90. Ella, 1874, p. 50.
91. Stone, 1932, p. 84.
92. Harley, 1941, p. 222.
93. Merker, 1910, p. 190.
94. Milne, 1924, p. 251.
95. Kaysser in Neuhauss, 1911, III, p. 77.
96. Morice, 1900-01, p. 22; Grinnell, 1923, II, p. 147; Swanton, 1928, p. 625.
97. Meyer, 1932, p. 142; Van der Burgt, 1903, p. 363.
98. Ella, 1874, p. 50.
99. Weyer, 1932, p. 328; Densmore, 1928, p. 333.
100. Vedder, 1923, II, p. 90.
101. Neuhauss, 1911, I, p. 436.
102. Johnston, 1902, II, p. 829; Merker, 1910, p. 193.
103. Merker, 1910, p. 196.
104. Pardal, 1937, p. 160.
105. Moodie, 1927, p. 278.
106. Pardal, 1937, Chapter VII, p. 217, 234.
107. Bartels, 1893, p. 300; Harley, 1941, pp. 45, 219.
108. Harley, 1941, p. 222.
109. Paulitschke, 1896, I, p. 184; Lindblom, 1920, p. 312.
110. Laubscher, 1937, p. 11.
111. Kennedy, 1931, p. 241ff.
112. E.g., Corlett, 1935, p. 242.
113. Ackerknecht, 1943a, p. 336.
114. Czaplicka, 1914, p. 233.
115. E.g., Teit, 1900, p. 370.
116: Harley, 1941, p. 38.
117. Morice, 1900-01, p. 27.
117a. Miklucho-Maclay, 1882, p. 26.
118. Young, 1944, p. 12ff.
119. Balima Unjoro (Emin Bey, 1879, p. 393); Barundi (Meyer, 1916, p. 442); Kisiba (Rehse, 1910, p. 117); Thonga (Junod, 1927, II, p. 332).
120. Mead, 1924, pp. 133, 156; Mackenzie, 1927, p. 333; Ploss-Bartels, 1899, II, p. 310.
121. Van der Burgt, 1903, p. 363.
122. Felkin, 1884, p. 928ff.
123. Ploss-Bartels, 1895, p. 306; Parham, 1943, p. VI.
124. Ploss-Bartels, 1895, p. 307; Roscoe, 1911, p. 54; *id.* 1924, p. 121.
125. See my article on the medical practices of the South American Indian in Vol. V of the forthcoming Handbook of the South American Indian, Smithsonian Institution.
126. Means, 1931, p. 446. My colleague, Junius Bird, was kind enough to inform me that the trephined skulls found at Paracas most likely come from the beginnings of the Christian era.
127. Bandelier, 1904, p. 442.
128. Guiard, 1930.
129. Wölfel, 1925, p. 1.
130. Roscoe, 1921, p. 147; *id.*, 1923, p. 161.
131. Driberg, 1929, p. 63.
132. Guiard, 1930.
133. Wolfel, 1925, p. 14.
134. Hagen, 1899, p. 257.
135. Ella, 1874, p. 51; Ray, 1917, p. 273.

136. Parkinson, 1907, p. 108; Crump, 1901, p. 167.
137. Crump, 1901, p. 167.
138. Wolfel, 1925, p. 10.
139. Ellis, 1853, p. 43.
140. Leechman, 1944; Shapiro, 1927; Wölfel, 1925, p. 19ff.
141. Crump, 1901, p. 168.
142. Parkinson, 1907, p. 113; Crump, 1901, p. 168.
143. Parkinson, 1907, p. 110.
144. Ella, 1874, p. 51.
145. Tello, 1913, p. 81; McCurdy, 1923, p. 251; Wölfel, 1925, p. 32.
146. Freeman, 1924, p. 24; Wölfel, 1925, p. 14; Tello, 1913, p. 79.
147. Alajouanine and Thure, 1945, p. 71ff.
148. Ella, 1874, p. 51.
149. Crump, 1901, p. 168.
150. Shapiro, 1927, p. 266.
151. Tello, 1913, p. 83; McCurdy, p. 259.
152. In this respect trephining fits much better into the ritual than into the medical field, and this is one of the reasons why I would feel hesitant to discard Broca's old hypothesis as eagerly as Wölfel did.
153. Dembo-Imbelloni, 1938, p. 203; Morice, 1900-01, p. 23; Grinnell, 1923, II, p. 196; Karsten, 1926, p. 186; Preuss, 1890.
154. Lagercrantz, 1935, p. 129ff.
155. Söderström, 1938, p. 24ff.
156. Malcolm, 1934, p. 200.
157. Hastings Encyclopedia of Religion and Ethics, III, p. 659ff.
158. Steinen, 1886, p. 129; Harley, 1941, p. 59.
159. Montagu, 1937, p. 193ff.
160. Lagercrantz, 1938, p. 199ff.
161. Hastings Encyclopedia of Religion and Ethics, III, p. 659ff.
162. Eleven African tribes mentioned by Lagercrantz, 1935, p. 129ff.; for Oceania see Söderström, 1938.
163. Uganda (Roscoe, 1921, p. 278); Bahr-el-Ghazal (Anderson, 1911).
164. Packard, 1901, p. 29.
165. Malcolm, 1934, p. 200.
166. Hrdlička, 1908, p. 251; Lagercrantz, 1935, p. 132.
167. Merker, 1910, p. 181.
168. Kingsley, 1899, p. 157.
169. Marriott, 1945, p. V.
170. Fletcher-La Flesche, 1911, p. 487ff.
171. Spier, 1928, p. 285.
172. Evans-Pritchard, 1937, p. 498.
173. Harley, 1941, pp. 17, 93.
174. Codrington, 1891, p. 199.
175. Hogbin, 1930-31, p. 165.
176. Crump, 1901, p. 167.
177. Bandelier, 1904, p. 442ff.
178. Stevenson, 1904, p. 386.
179. Swanton, 1928, p. 617ff.
180. Park, 1938, p. 59.
180a. Stirling, 1938, p. 120.
181. Barton, 1923, p. 74.
182. Roscoe, 1911, p. 278.
183. See Rosen, 1944, p. 5ff.; Ackerknecht, 1946, p. 479ff.

184. F. Muller, 1928, p. 502.
185. Harley, 1941, p. 74.
186. *Id.*, p. 40.
187. Anderson, 1911, p. 264.
188. Grandidier, 1908, IV, p. 428.
189. Junod, 1927, II, pp. 458-459.
190. E.g., Déné (Morice, 1900-01, p. 21); Omaha (Fletcher-La Flesche, 1911, p. 107); Chorti
     (Wisdom, 1940, p. 307); Brazilian Indians (Martius, 1844, p. 128); Pangwe (Tessmann,
     1913, II, p. 128); Thonga (Junod, 1927, II, p. 332); Ba-Ila (Smith and Dale, 1920, I, p.
     224); Kiwai Papuans (Laudtman, 1927, p. 281); Sinaugolo (Seligman, 1902, p. 301.)
191. Ackerknecht, 1943a, p. 338.
192. Mere dissection did not improve medieval anatomy either. More than 200 years of dissect-
     ing before Vesalius under scholastic auspices did not reveal the obvious errors of Galenic
     anatomy till the Renaissance shattered the authoritarian principle in science and replaced
     it by observation.
193. Ellis, 1945. See also, Stevenson, 1904, p. 386; Bandelier, 1909, p. 445; Freeman, 1924, p.
     32; Harley, 1941, p. 70; Felkin, 1884, p. 928; Angus, 1897-98, p. 324.
194. Malcolm, 1934, p. 201; Bartels, 1893, p. 307.
195. Bartels, 1893, p. 281.
196. Morice, 1900-01, p. 22.
197. Johnston, J., 1893, p. 335.
198. Linton, 1933, p. 314.
199. Hilton-Simpson, 1913, p. 717.
200. E.g., Abyssinia, Janus, 6:289, 1902.
201. Rivers, 1923, p. 95.
202. I am indebted to Dr. David Bidney who drew my attention to the fact that lack of surgery
     in those instances which cannot be accounted for by supernaturalistic fear of mutilation
     can be explained on the basis of my hypothesis of a general supernaturalistic orientation
     of primitives in medicine (see Ackerknecht, 1946).
203. One of the many ritual mutilators reluctant to adopt medical amputation are the Chey-
     enne (Grinnell, 1923, II, p. 147). I am obliged to Dr. E. A. Hoebel for drawing my atten-
     tion to the fact that, nevertheless, one case of medical amputation among the Cheyenne
     is on record (Llewellyn and Hoebel, 1941, pp. 122-123).
204. Leriche, 1944.

Michael H. Logan

Digestive disorders and plant medicinals in highland Guatemala

Introduction

Many of the plant medicinals comprising the pharmacopeia of rural highland
Guatemala are employed to treat ailments of the digestive system. Epidemiological
surveys (Shattuck 1938; Bruch 1963; Gordon 1964) have clearly shown that for

From *Anthropos*, 68, 1973, pp. 538-547. Reprinted by permission.

Guatemala, diseases of the digestive system are endemic and continue to be the leading cause of illness and mortality, especially in early childhood.

Continuation of traditional folk remedies has perpetuated an extensive knowledge of medicinal botany in Ladino and Maya communities throughout Guatemala (Blake 1922; Villacorta 1926; Roys 1931; Dieseldorff 1939; Standley 1946; Gillin 1951; Adams 1952, 1967; Woods 1968; Rodriguez 1969). The high percentage of digestive medicinals encountered in rural Guatemala is a manifestation of the peasant's attempt to counteract the illnesses which so greatly affect his health.

The Guatemalan peasant rarely makes use of the services of the modern medical doctor. Choice, financial and social barriers, as well as the prevailing scarcity of trained physicians in rural areas, have made treatment of illness in many cases a matter of traditional diagnosis calling for the appropriate cure, which habitually. involves a concoction of specific plant materials.

Much can be gained from studying the pharmacopeia and medicinal practices of non-industrialized or preliterate societies. Until well into the 1900's, 80% of all medicines in the Western world were obtained from roots, barks, and leaves. Of the 300 million prescriptions written during 1963 in the United States, 47% contained a drug of natural origin and the yearly world market for medicinal plants has been established at $300,000,000 (Krieg 1964: 7-8). The case examples involving the competitive efforts of individuals, pharmaceutical firms, and even nations to acquire monopolies on such useful native drug plants as *Cinchona, Digitalis, Dioscorea,* and *Strophantus* are well known and convincingly point out the possible usefulness of research on the remaining enclaves of preliterate medicinal knowledge.

Aside from the medical and economic motives for investigating folk-medicine, many previously unknown species have been identified as a result of ethnobotanical research (Schultes 1962). Medicinal botany is also of use in studying cognitive patterns and folk taxonomies (Conklin 1954; Berlin 1966, 1968), archaeology (Dimbleby 1967), ethnohistory (Emmart 1940), human migration (Barrau 1963), paleobotany (Just 1959), non-Western concepts of disease (Clements 1932; Erasmus 1952; Laughlin 1962; Rubel 1960; Fábrega 1971), divination (Castaneda 1967), medical anthropology (Alland 1966), psychological conditions of folk-therapy (Gillin 1951; Holland 1962, 1964; Kiev 1968), or as an index of acculturation.

Because all human beings are essentially the same anatomically and physiologically, and often succumb to similar diseases and disorders regardless of culture, the behavioral scientist may gain a useful comparative tool by examining differential social adaptations to one specified illness or set of symptoms. As recently noted by Hanson (1970: 1446) "Variations in theories of health, normal body functioning, disease, diagnosis, and treatment may be isolated and understood against a common anatomical, physiological, and pathological background . . . . Thus, folk medicine holds the potential for rigorous comparative study of human thought systems."

The purpose of this paper is to review briefly the significance of one pathological complex endemic in highland Guatemala and to present a correlated inventory of native plants employed by "Ladino" peasants in the treatment of digestive
disorders. Aside from consulting published material, the botanical specimens (1)
and ethnographic data underlying this report were collected over a four-month
period in 1970 (2) during which I resided in numerous Guatemalan communities
(3). Additional specimens were purchased from vendors in local markets and
the vendors, known as "hierbateros," consistently proved to be an invaluable source
for information concerning the socio-medicinal uses of plants.

Of the 122 medicinal species collected, 34% are used as specifics for digestive
ailments. The proportionately large representation of digestive medicinals in our
sample is compatible with, and offers additional support to an analysis (von Reis
1962) from which the percentage of digestive medicinals in preliterate pharmacopeias was established by sampling the materia medica housed in the collections
of the Harvard Herbarium. Sixty-one percent of the specimens in her sample were
obtained from Central and South America, Mexico, and the Philippines. By
examining the 3700 species within the sample, and the attached field notes of the
original collector, the calculation reached by von Reis is that 18% of the medicinals
comprising the pharmacopeias of preliterate and peasant societies in the above
countries are employed solely to treat complaints of the digestive tract. This study,
unfortunately, does not separate the pharmacopeias of local human groups to as-
certain the range of this digestive percentage in different parts of the former Spanish empire.

Digestive Disorders

Digestive malfunctions in Guatemala range from indigestion to acute diarrhea and
parasitic infestations. The etiologies of these disorders include enteric infections,
hyponutrition and malnutrition, host-reactions to parasites, alterations of dietary
patterns such as weaning, and in some cases, emotional disturbances. Clinical
diagnoses of the specific diseases involved and their associated etiologies are beyond
the scope of this report, but common symptoms include cramps, excessive acidity
and flatulence, nausea, blood in the stools, the passing of worms, and the dehydration and weakness resulting from dysentery and diarrhea.

For Guatemala, "diarrheal disorders are the first cause of death and the highest for any Latin American country" (Gordon 1964: 16). The death rate, per
10,000 population, attributed to diarrhea and intestinal parasites for all ages in
Guatemala between 1922-1927 was 76, as compared to 53 for Mexico and 8 for
Massachusetts (Hilferty 1938: 30). The death rate from diarrhea in early childhood,
0 to 5 years, during the same period was 394 per 10,000, but only 28 for Massachusetts *(ibid.:* 29). More extreme statistics from a recent study of three Guatemalan settlements (cumulative population 106,000) show that the percentage of
deaths from diarrhea per 1,000 population of one-year infants was 41%, two-year
olds 53%, three-year olds 43%, and at four years of age, 55% of all deaths were

caused by diarrhea (Gordon 1964: 16). The importance of these figures is perhaps better understood when compared with the frequencies prevailing in more in-dustrialized societies. For infants under one year, the death rate resulting from diarrhea in the Gordon study was 25 times that for infants in the United States. For preschool group it was 519 times greater; and for the general population, death from diarrhea was 115 times greater in Guatemala than in the United States (*ibid.:* 17). Clearly, diseases of the digestive tract are paramount in Guatemala.

Disease, Its Diagnosis and Treatment

Generally, peasants of Mesoamerica attribute illness and disease to four main sources: natural injury such as snake bite or burns; disruption of the internal harmony of the body; intrusion of foreign objects or organisms into the body; and malevolent activity of human or supernatural agencies underlying witchcraft, soul loss, evil eye and evil winds (Clements 1932; Redfield 1940; Foster 1953; Rubel 1960; Adams 1967).

Although western medical concepts are now becoming better understood in some rural areas, the peasant's knowledge of epidemiology remains limited (cf. Paul 1955). That is, his awareness of pathogens, contagion, nutrition, sanitation and hygiene "clinically" associated with particular disease patterns is extremely slight. For example, the importance of proper fecal disposal, nutrition, and general sanitation in controlling diarrhea is not well recognized by most Guatemalan villagers (Gordon 1964: 25-26, 33). It has been reported that in other Latin American populations, even human urine and excrement were used as medicinals by some peasant groups in Yucatan (Roys 1931: 23, Redfield 1940: 67, 71), Sinaloa (Werner 1970: 63), and Guatemala (Woods 1968: 126).

Folk-definition of illness and disease is largely a practice of symptom recognition, where the patient's complaints, recent behavior, foods eaten, and observable characteristics (fever, diarrhea, etc.) are joined with causation in the formulation of a diagnosis (cf. Adams 1967).

Fever, for instance, may be attributed to the disruption of the body's "internal harmony," this imbalance resulting from the patient's neglect of dietary regulations concerning the inherent humoral "temperature" quality of foods (Foster 1953: Currier 1966).

Throughout Latin America, peasants view particular foods as disease-causing agents. That is, over-consumption of foods "hot" in nature (4) (beans, beef, poultry, etc.) will upset the body's internal temperature balance, thus causing fever. Careless consumption of "cold" foods (corn, eggs, oranges, etc.) can produce chills and coughing. The remedy for treating hot-induced ailments is to increase the proportion of cold foods in the diet, and vice versa. The administration of herbal decoctions frequently accompanies the change in diet. Adherence to this binary system of humoral medicine may produce beneficial effects in controlling some nutritional diseases (Logan 1972).

Diarrhea "is not considered to be a disease but a symptom of disease"

(Gonzales 1963: 422). This condition may result from fright, overconsumption of "cold" foods; the drinking of "dirty" water, or from the intrusion of objects into the body, as with parasites. Treatment is directed equally at eliminating the causes and reducing the symptoms. In some cases, both attempts may prove harmful to the patient. For example, strong purgatives and vermifuges are at times administered to children in the mistaken belief that the ascarids so frequently expelled by children in early diarrhea are the "real" cause of the disorder (Gordon 1964: 40). In treating the symptoms of passing fluid feces, severe dietary restrictions on food and liquids are thought to "solidify" wastes, but this practice only promotes harmful dehydration. These practices, according to Gordon, "are the main reason for the high mortality from diarrheal disease in rural Guatemala" (1964: 40).

The following plants comprise the majority of digestive medicinals in the Guatemalan pharmacopeia.

Aguacate—*Persea americana,* Miller. Use: diarrhea. Part used: roasted seeds of fruit. Sold in markets.

Alata (Alcotan)—*Cissampelos pareira,* L. Use: cramps, diarrhea. Part used: roots.

Albahaca—*Ocimum micranthum,* Willd. Use: cramps and diarrhea. Part used: entire plant. Sold in markets.

Altamisa—*Ambrosia cumanensis,* H. B. K. Use: stomach cramps, diarrhea. Part used: leaves and stem. Sold in markets.

Anis—*Pimpinella anisum,* L. Use: stomach cramps. Part used: whole plant, except roots. Sold in markets.

Anona—*Annona reticulata,* L. Use: dysentery or diarrhea. Part used: dried, powdered fruit. Sold in markets.

Apasin—*Petiveria alliacea,* L. Use: stomach cramps, diarrhea. Part used: entire plant. Sold in markets.

Chinchin—*Crotolaria incana,* L. Use: diarrhea. Part used: leaves.

Contrahierba—*Dorstenia contrajerva,* L. Use: dysentery or diarrhea. Part used: leaves. Sold in markets.

Copalillo—*Bursera graveolens,* (H. B. K.) Triana. Use: stomach ache. Part used: leaves and stem.

Eneldo—*Foeniculum vulgare,* L. Use: diarrhea. Part used: leaves. Sold in markets.

Esencia del Monte—specimen not identifiable. (5) Use: intestinal parasites. Part used: leaves.

Granada—*Punica granatum,* L. Use: minor indigestion. Part used: fruit.

Guayaba—*Psidium guajava,* L. Use: cramps, diarrhea, indigestion. Part used: dried, powdered fruit. Sold in markets.

Guayacan—*Guaiacum guatemalense,* Planchon. Use: stomach inflammation. Part used: leaves.

Hierba Buena—*Lippia reptans,* H. B. K. Use: indigestion, diarrhea. Part used: leaves.

Hierba del Cancer—*Acalypha sp.* Use: stomach ache, to improve the blood. Part used: entire plant.

Hierba del Pollo—*Zebrina pendula,* Schnizl. Use: stomach inflammation, dysentery or diarrhea. Part used: leaves and stem.

Hierba del Toro—*Tridax procumbens,* L. Use: stomach pain, diarrhea. Part used: leaves. Sold in markets.

Higuerillo—*Ricinus communis,* L. Use: indigestion, cramps. Part used: leaves.

Hoja del Aire—*Bryophyllum pinnatum,* (L.) Kurz. Use: indigestion, diarrhea. Part used: leaves.

Huehuecho—*Aristolochia grandiflora,* Swartz. Use: stomach cramps. Part used: leaves.

Llanten—*Plantago major,* L. Use: stomach cramps, intestinal worms. Part used: leaves. Sold in markets.

Laurel—*Litsea glaucescens,* H. B. K. Use: inflammation, stomach cramps. Part used: leaves. Sold in markets.

Loroco—*Urechites karwinskii,* Mueller. Use: stomach cramps, inflammation. Part used: leaves.

Malba (Malva)—market specimen not identifiable. (5) Use: to induce vomiting, intestinal worms. Part used: leaves and stem. Sold in markets.

Malvavisca—*Malvaviscus abelomoschata.* Use: stomach ache, cramps. Part used: leaves.

Mansanilla—*Matricaria sp.* Use: stomach pains, diarrhea. Part used: leaves. Sold in markets.

Mejorana—*Ageratum conyzoides,* L. Use: intestinal worms. Part used: leaves.

Melon—*Cucumis melo,* L. Use: intestinal worms. Part used: crushed dried seeds. Sold in markets.

Misto—specimen not identifiable. Use: stomach cramps, gas, diarrhea. Part used: leaves and stem.

Palo Jiote—*Bursera simaruba,* L. Use: stomach cramps, diarrhea, inflammation. Part used: bark. Sold in markets.

Pericon—*Tagetes lucida,* Cav. Use: stomach ache, indigestion, gas, diarrhea. Part used: entire plant. Sold in markets.

Piñon—*Jatropha curcas,* L. Use: dysentery or diarrhea. Part used: leaves.

Raiz de Calaguala—*Polypodium sp.* Use: stomach cramps, gas. Part used: roots. Sold in markets.

Raiz de Valeriana—market specimen not identifiable. Use: intestinal worms. Part used: roots. Sold in markets.

Rosa Jamaica—*Hibiscus sp.* Use: stomach cramps. Part used: leaves. Sold in markets.

Salviasija—*Lippia sp.* Use: stomach pains, cramps. Part used: leaves.

Siguapate—*Pluchea odorata,* (L.) Cassini. Use: stomach cramps. Part used: leaves.

Suquinai—*Veronia patens,* H. B. K. Use: stomach inflammation, ulcers. Part used: leaves. Sold in markets.

Te Limon—*Cymbopogon citratus,* (DC.) Stapf. Use: stomach ache, gas, hangover, tonic. Part used: leaves. Sold in markets.

Zarza—*Smilax sp.* Use: stomach cramps. Part used: leaves.

Many of the foregoing plants are used frequently as medicinals elsewhere in tropical America (cf. Martinez 1936; Roig y Mesa 1945; Standley 1926, 1946), and some are of economic importance in the peasant market systems. At least half of the digestive medicinals mentioned above appear, along with dozens of other plants of medical significance, in the village and city market places throughout highland Guatemala.

After the desired plants are collected from the "monte" or bush, they are usually sun-dried and then lashed together with strands of a grass to form small bundles which are sold by the few who specialize in this trade. The "hierbateros" constitute a numerical minority in the market places because most peasants know which plants are useful for specific ailments and they simply collect their own when in need, or when the plant is in season. The market bundles are purchased for the standard price of five cents, as are the small sacks of "Romero" needles (*Rosmarinus officinalis*) used to treat body aches and the long pods of "Cana de Fistula" *(Cassia fistula)* employed as a specific against typhoid fever.

Of the medicinal plants of economic importance, "Pericon" *(Tagetes lucida)* deserves special mention. This plant, which is prescribed for cramps, indigestion, and diarrhea, is the most frequently seen medicinal in all Guatemalan markets and its sale accounts for more than half of the "hierbateros" income derived, in part, from the selling of plant remedials. "Pericon," furthermore, is the best known plant medicinal in both peasant and urban populations. In the latter, it is frequently the only native plant remedy known and used regularly.

Preparation of the various teas and tonics, analgesics, purgatives, and vermifuges used in treatment invariably are made by boiling the desired plant materials to produce a broth. This infusion is then taken internally. Frequently the entire plant is prepared, although particular sections of the plant may be used selectively depending upon the specific remedy. In addition to this method, dried plant materials may be added to soups or other condiments in the diet when treating minor ailments to improve one's stamina and resistance, or to "cleanse one's blood".

Conclusion

Guatemalan peasants, unlike their urban contemporaries, have developed and still retain an extensive botanical knowledge not only of medicinal plants, but of all usable wild flora and domestic crops. The accumulation and retention of this knowledge is a product of their life-way, where almost all subsist solely on the produce grown or collected locally. Construction material for houses, corrals, fences, most utensils, and fuel for cooking is taken from the "monte". The daily corn-based diet acquires diversity through the addition of wild greens, fruits, spices and flavorings. The prevalance of an endemic health problem, the general absence of modern medical services, and the social, political, and economic barriers to acculturation, have all contributed to the maintenance of the peasant's botanical knowledge, wherein some plant medicinals upon analyses may posses properties of significant medical value.

The proportionately large quantity of digestive medicinals in the Guatemalan pharmacopeia may be viewed as an index illustrating the severity and high frequency of an endemic pathological condition affecting peasant life. Diarrhea alone accounts for more deaths among the young in Guatemala than any other source of mortality. The "trinity" of dysentery, diarrhea, and intestinal parasites is reported as the major cause of death in the Guatemalan population at large. This health problem appears to be a primary catalyst of social adaptation via folk medicine.

By extension, in areas where verereal diseases are rampant, we would expect to find an extensive inventory of medicinals prescribed for treatment of these disorders. Furthermore, the inventory is likely to be larger than the average or mean number of venereal medicinals occurring in other preliterate societies exposed to differing disease stresses. Plant medicinals, therefore, may serve as possible indicators reflecting general health problems, whether they be associated with hepatitis, malaria, syphilis, or as in Guatemala, diarrhea and other digestive disorders.

Through recognizing the severity of digestive pathologies affecting the Guatemalan population and by providing their inventory of appropriate plant medicinals, we have seen one way in which the peasant has responded to his health needs. Although he is frequently unaware of the causes underlying most ailments of the digestive tract, he is, nonetheless, attempting to counteract the prominence of these health problems by resorting to traditional belief and the use of native plant medicinals, even though some practices are distinctly harmful. The psychological effects resulting from the peasant's trust in traditional folkways and the possible beneficial properties of some plant remedies have perpetuated knowledge of medicinal botany in Guatemala through experimentation, selection, and adaptation.

Notes

1. I am truly grateful to Dr. Anton J. Kovar, Departments of Botany and Anthropology, The Pennsylvania State University, for providing the taxonomic identification of specimens.
2. Field research was sponsored by the Kaminaljuyu Project, Department of Anthropology, The Pennsylvania State University. I am indebted to the directors of the project, Drs. William T. Sanders and Joseph W. Michels, for the opportunities made available to me while a member of the project. Acknowledgement is also due to Drs. Edward E. Hunt and Warren T. Morrill for their criticism of earlier drafts of this report.
3. Amatitlan, Barcenas, Boca del Monte, Chichicastenango, De los Reyes, Don Justo, El Pajon, El Tablon, Guatemala, Huehuetenango, Las Animas, Panajachel, Quetzaltenango, Ramirez, San Jose Pinula, San Miguel Petapa, Santa Catarina, Solola, and Villa Canales.
4. The terms "hot" and "cold" do not refer to actual qualities of temperature produced by cooking food or to pungent tastes as found in peppers.
5. A few market and field specimens lacked the diagnostic structures needed for complete and positive identification. These specimens were not identified, or only the generic name

was given, because it is an unsound practice to base the identification of any plant solely by resorting to homonymous usage of common names so frequently encountered in the botanical literature of tropical Amercia (cf. Mead 1970:180-190).

Michael J. Harner

The sound of rushing water

He had drunk, and now he softly sang. Gradually, faint lines and forms began to appear in the darkness, and the shrill music of the *tsentsak*, the spirit helpers, arose around him. The power of the drink fed them. He called, and they came. First, *pangi,* the anaconda, coiled about his head, transmuted into a crown of gold. Then *wampang,* the giant butterfly, hovered above his shoulder and sang to him with its wings. Snakes, spiders, birds, and bats danced in the air above him. On his arms appeared a thousand eyes as his demon helpers emerged to search the night for enemies.

The sound of rushing water filled his ears, and listening to its roar, he knew he possessed the power of *tsungi,* the first shaman. Now he could see. Now he could find the truth. He stared at the stomach of the sick man. Slowly, it became transparent like a shallow mountain stream, and he saw within it, coiling and uncoiling, *makanchi,* the poisonous serpent, who had been sent by the enemy shaman. The real cause of the illness had been found.

The Jívaro Indians of the Ecuadorian Amazon believe that witchcraft is the cause of the vast majority of illnesses and non-violent deaths. The normal waking life, for the Jívaro, is simply "a lie," or illusion, while the true forces that determine daily events are supernatural and can only be seen and manipulated with the aid of hallucinogenic drugs. A reality view of this kind creates a particularly strong demand for specialists who can cross over into the supernatural world at will to deal with the forces that influence and even determine the events of the waking life.

These specialists, called "shamans" by anthropologists, are recognized by the Jívaro as being of two types: bewitching shamans or curing shamans. Both kinds take a hallucinogenic drink, whose Jívaro name is *natema,* in order to enter the supernatural world. This brew, commonly called *yagé,* or *yajé,* in Colombia, *ayahuasca* (Inca "vine of the dead") in Ecuador and Peru, and *caapi* in Brazil, is prepared from segments of a species of the vine *Banisteriopsis,* a genus belonging to the Malpighiaceae. The Jívaro boil it with the leaves of a similar vine, which probably is also a species of *Banisteriopsis,* to produce a tea that contains the powerful hallucinogenic alkaloids harmaline, harmine, d-tetrahydroharmine, and quite possibly dimethyltryptamine (DMT). These compounds have chemical structures and effects similar, but not identical, to LSD, mescaline of the peyote cactus, and psilocybin of the psychotropic Mexican mushroom.

When I first undertook research among the Jívaro in 1956-57, I did not fully appreciate the psychological impact of the *Banisteriopsis* drink upon the native view of reality, but in 1961 I had occasion to drink the hallucinogen in the course of field work with another Upper Amazon Basin tribe. For several hours after drinking the brew, I found myself, although awake, in a world literally beyond my wildest dreams. I met bird-headed people, as well as dragon-like creatures who explained that they were the true gods of this world. I enlisted the services of other spirit helpers in attempting to fly through the far reaches of the Galaxy. Transported into a trance where the supernatural seemed natural, I realized that anthropologists, including myself, had profoundly underestimated the importance of the drug in affecting native ideology. Therefore, in 1964 I returned to the Jívaro to give particular attention to the drug's use by the Jívaro shaman.

The use of the hallucinogenic *natema* drink among the Jívaro makes it possible for almost anyone to achieve the trance state essential for the practice of shamanism. Given the presence of the drug and the felt need to contact the "real," or supernatural, world, it is not surprising that approximately one out of every four Jívaro men is a shaman. Any adult, male or female, who desires to become such a practitioner, simply presents a gift to an already practicing shaman, who administers the *Banisteriopsis* drink and gives some of his own supernatural power—in the form of spirit helpers, or *tsentsak*—to the apprentice. These spirit helpers, or "darts," are the main supernatural forces believed to cause illness and death in daily life. To the non-shaman they are normally invisible, and even shamans can perceive them only under the influence of *natema.*

Shamans send these spirit helpers into the victims' bodies to make them ill or to kill them. At other times, they may suck spirits sent by enemy shamans from the bodies of tribesmen suffering from witchcraft-induced illness. The spirit helpers also form shields that protect their shaman masters from attacks. The following account presents the ideology of Jívaro witchcraft from the point of view of the Indians themselves.

To give the novice some *tsentsak,* the practicing shaman regurgitates what appears to be—to those who have taken *natema*—a brilliant substance in which the spirit helpers are contained. He cuts part of it off with a machete and gives it to the novice to swallow. The recipient experiences pain upon taking it into his stomach and stays on his bed for ten days, repeatedly drinking *natema.* The Jívaro believe they can keep magical darts in their stomachs indefinitely and regurgitate them at will. The shaman donating the *tsentsak* periodically blows and rubs all over the body of the novice, apparently to increase the power of the transfer.

The novice must remain inactive and not engage in sexual intercourse for at least three months. If he fails in self-discipline, as some do, he will not become a successful shaman. At the end of the first month, a *tsentsak* emerges from his mouth. With this magical dart at his disposal, the new shaman experiences a tremendous desire to bewitch. If he casts his *tsentsak* to fulfill this desire, he will become a bewitching shaman. If, on the other hand, the novice can control his impulse and reswallow this first *tsentsak,* he will become a curing shaman.

If the shaman who gave the *tsentsak* to the new man was primarily a bewitcher, rather than a curer, the novice likewise will tend to become a bewitcher. This is because a bewitcher's magical darts have such a desire to kill that their new owner will be strongly inclined to adopt their attitude. One informant said that the urge to kill felt by bewitching shamans came to them with a strength and frequency similar to that of hunger.

Only if the novice shaman is able to abstain from sexual intercourse for five months, will he have the power to kill a man (if he is a bewitcher) or cure a victim (if he is a curer). A full year's abstinence is considered necessary to become a really effective bewitcher or curer.

During the period of sexual abstinence, the new shaman collects all kinds of insects, plants, and other objects, which he now has the power to convert into *tsentsak.* Almost any object, including living insects and worms, can become a *tsentsak* if it is small enough to be swallowed by a shaman. Different types of *tsentsak* are used to cause different kinds and degrees of illness. The greater the variety of these objects that a shaman has in his body, the greater is his ability.

According to Jívaro concepts, each *tsentsak* has a natural and supernatural aspect. The magical dart's natural aspect is that of an ordinary material object as seen without drinking the drug *natema.* But the supernatural and "true" aspect of the *tsentsak* is revealed to the shaman by taking *natema.* When he does this, the magical darts appear in new forms as demons and with new names. In their supernatural aspects, the *tsentsak* are not simply objects but spirit helpers in various forms, such as giant butterflies, jaguars, or monkeys, who actively assist the shaman in his tasks.

Bewitching is carried out against a specific, known individual and thus is almost always done to neighbors or, at the most, fellow tribesmen. Normally, as is the case with intratribal assassination, bewitching is done to avenge a particular offense committed against one's family or friends. Both bewitching and individual assassination contrast with the large-scale headhunting raids for which the Jívaro have become famous, and which were conducted against entire neighborhoods of enemy tribes.

To bewitch, the shaman takes *natema* and secretly approaches the house of his victim. Just out of sight in the forest, he drinks green tobacco juice, enabling him to regurgitate a *tsentsak,* which he throws at his victim as he comes out of his house. If the *tsentsak* is strong enough and is thrown with sufficient force, it will pass all the way through the victim's body causing death within a period of a few days to several weeks. More often, however, the magical dart simply lodges in the victim's body. If the shaman, in his hiding place, fails to see the intended victim, he may instead bewitch any member of the intended victim's family who appears, usually a wife or child. When the shaman's mission is accomplished, he returns secretly to his own home.

One of the distinguishing characteristics of the bewitching process among the Jívaro is that, as far as I could learn, the victim is given no specific indication that someone is bewitching him. The bewitcher does not want his victim to be aware that he is being supernaturally attacked, lest he take protective measures by immediately procuring the services of a curing shaman. Nonetheless, shamans and laymen alike with whom I talked noted that illness invariably follows the bewitchment, although the degree of the illness can vary considerably.

A special kind of spirit helper, called a *pasuk,* can aid the bewitching shaman by remaining near the victim in the guise of an insect or animal of the forest after the bewitcher has left. This spirit helper has his own objects to shoot into the victim should a curing shaman succeed in sucking out the *tsentsak* sent earlier by the bewitcher who is the owner of the *pasuk.*

In addition, the bewitcher can enlist the aid of a *wakani* ("soul," or "spirit") bird. Shamans have the power to call these birds and use them as spirit helpers in bewitching victims. The shaman blows on the *wakani* birds and then sends them to the house of the victim to fly around and around the man, frightening him. This is believed to cause fever and insanity, with death resulting shortly thereafter.

After he returns home from bewitching, the shaman may send a *wakani* bird to perch near the house of the victim. Then if a curing shaman sucks out the intruding object, the bewitching shaman sends the *wakani* bird more *tsentsak* to throw from its beak into the victim. By continually resupplying the *wakani* bird with new *tsentsak,* the sorcerer makes it impossible for the curer to rid his patient permanently of the magical darts.

While the *wakani* birds are supernatural servants available to anyone who wishes to use them, the *pasuk,* chief among the spirit helpers, serves only a single shaman. Likewise a shaman possesses only one *pasuk.* The *pasuk,* being specialized for the service of bewitching, has a protective shield to guard it from counterattack by the curing shaman. The curing shaman, under the influence of *natema,* sees the *pasuk* of the bewitcher in human form and size, but "covered with iron except for its eyes." The curing shaman can kill this *pasuk* only by shooting a *tsentsak* into its eyes, the sole vulnerable area in the *pasuk's* armor. To the person who has not taken the hallucinogenic drink, the *pasuk* usually appears to be simply a tarantula.

Shamans also may kill or injure a person by using magical darts, *anamuk,* to create supernatural animals that attack a victim. If a shaman has a small, pointed armadillo bone *tsentsak,* he can shoot this into a river while the victim is crossing it on a balsa raft or in a canoe. Under the water, this bone manifests itself in its supernatural aspect as an anaconda, which rises up and overturns the craft, causing the victim to drown. The shaman can similarly use a tooth from a killed snake as a *tsentsak,* creating a poisonous serpent to bite his victim. In more or less the same manner, shamans can create jaguars and pumas to kill their victims.

About five years after receiving his *tsentsak,* a bewitching shaman undergoes a test to see if he still retains enough *tsentsak* power to continue to kill successfully. This test involves bewitching a tree. The shaman, under the influence of *natema,* attempts to throw a *tsentsak* through the tree at the point where its two main branches join. If his strength and aim are adequate, the tree appears to split the moment the *tsentsak* is sent into it. The splitting, however, is invisible to an observer who is not under the influence of the hallucinogen. If the shaman fails, he knows that he is incapable of killing a human victim. This means that, as soon as possible, he must go to a strong shaman and purchase a new supply of *tsentsak.* Until he has the goods with which to pay for this new supply, he is in constant danger, in his proved weakened condition, of being seriously bewitched by other shamans. Therefore, each day, he drinks large quantities of *natema,* tobacco juice, and the extract of yet another drug, *piripiri.* He also rests on his bed at home to conserve his strength, but tries to conceal his weakened condition from his enemies. When he purchases a new supply of *tsentsak,* he can safely cut down on his consumption of these other substances.

The degree of illness produced in a witchcraft victim is a function of both the force with which the *tsentsak* is shot into the body, and also of the character of the magical dart itself. If a *tsentsak* is shot all the way through the body of a victim, then "there is nothing for a curing shaman to suck out," and the patient dies. If the magical dart lodges within the body, however, it is theoretically possible to cure the victim by sucking. But in actual practice, the sucking is not always considered successful.

The work of the curing shaman is complementary to that of a bewitcher. When a curing shaman is called in to treat a patient, his first task is to see if the illness is due to witchcraft. The usual diagnosis and treatment begin with the curing shaman drinking *natema,* tobacco juice, and *piripiri* in the late afternoon and early evening. These drugs permit him to see into the body of the patient as though it were glass. If the illness is due to sorcery, the curing shaman will see the intruding object within the patient's body clearly enough to determine whether or not he can cure the sickness.

A shaman sucks magical darts from a patient's body only at night, and in a dark area of the house, for it is only in the dark that he can perceive the drug-induced visions that are the supernatural reality. With the setting of the sun, he alerts his *tsentsak* by whistling the tune of the curing song; after about a quarter of an hour, he starts singing. When he is ready to suck, the shaman regurgitates two *tsentsak* into the sides of his throat and mouth. These must be identical to the one he has seen in the patient's body. He holds one of these in the front of the mouth and the other in the rear. They are expected to catch the supernatural aspect of the magical dart that the shaman sucks out of the patient's body. The *tsentsak* nearest the shaman's lips is supposed to incorporate the sucked-out *tsentsak* essence within itself. If, however, this supernatural essence should get past it, the second magical dart in the mouth blocks the throat so that the intruder cannot enter the interior of the shaman's body. If the curer's two *tsentsak* were to fail to catch the supernatural essence of the *tsentsak,* it would pass down into the shaman's stomach and kill him. Trapped thus within the mouth, this essence is shortly caught by, and incorporated into, the material substance of one of the curing shaman's *tsentsak*. He then "vomits" out this object and displays it to the patient and his family saying, "Now I have sucked it out. Here it is."

The non-shamans think that the material object itself is what has been sucked out, and the shaman does not disillusion them. At the same time, he is not lying, because he knows that the only important thing about a *tsentsak* is its supernatural aspect, or essence, which he sincerely believes he has removed from the patient's body. To explain to the layman that he already had these objects in his mouth would serve no fruitful purpose and would prevent him from displaying such an object as proof that he had effected the cure. Without incontrovertible evidence, he would not be able to convince the patient and his family that he had effected the cure and must be paid.

The ability of the shaman to suck depends largely upon the quantity and strength of his own *tsentsak,* of which he may have hundreds. His magical darts assume their supernatural aspect as spirit helpers when he is under the influence of *natema,* and he sees them as a variety of zoomorphic forms hovering over him, perching on his shoulders, and sticking out of his skin. He sees them helping to suck the patient's body. He must drink tobacco juice every few hours to "keep them fed" so that they will not leave him.

The curing shaman must also deal with any *pasuk* that may be in the patient's vicinity for the purpose of casting more darts. He drinks additional amounts of *natema* in order to see them and engages in *tsentsak* duels with them if they are present. While the *pasuk* is enclosed in iron armor, the shaman himself has his own armor composed of his many *tsentsak.* As long as he is under the influence of *natema,* these magical darts cover his body as a protective shield, and are on the lookout for any enemy *tsentsak* headed toward their master. When these *tsentsak* see such a missile coming, they immediately close up together at the point where the enemy dart is attempting to penetrate, and thereby repel it.

If the curer finds *tsentsak* entering the body of his patient after he has killed *pasuk,* he suspects the presence of a *wakani* bird. The shaman drinks *maikua (Datura* sp.), an hallucinogen even more powerful than *natema,* as well as tobacco juice, and silently sneaks into the forest to hunt and kill the bird with *tsentsak.* When he succeeds, the curer returns to the patient's home, blows all over the house to get rid of the "atmosphere" created by the numerous *tsentsak* sent by the bird, and completes his sucking of the patient. Even after all the *tsentsak* are extracted, the shaman may remain another night at the house to suck out any "dirtiness" *(pahuri)* still inside. In the cures which I have witnessed, this sucking is a most noisy process, accompanied by deep, but dry, vomiting.

After sucking out a *tsentsak,* the shaman puts it into a little container. He does not swallow it because it is not his own magical dart and would therefore kill him. Later, he throws the *tsentsak* into the air, and it flies back to the shaman who sent it originally into the patient. *Tsentsak* also fly back to a shaman at the death of a former apprentice who had originally received them from him. Besides receiving "old" magical darts unexpectedly in this manner, the shaman may have *tsentsak* thrown at him by a bewitcher. Accordingly, shamans constantly drink tobacco juice at all hours of the day and night. Although the tobacco juice is not truly hallucinogenic, it produces a narcotized state, which is believed necessary to keep one's *tsentsak* ready to repel any other magical darts. A shaman does not even dare go for a walk without taking along the green tobacco leaves with which he prepares the juice that keeps his spirit helpers alert. Less frequently, but regularly, he must drink *natema* for the same purpose and to keep in touch with the supernatural reality.

While curing under the influence of *natema,* the curing shaman "sees" the shaman who bewitched his patient. Generally, he can recognize the person, unless it is a shaman who lives far away or in another tribe. The patient's family knows this, and demands to be told the identity of the bewitcher, particularly if the sick person dies. At one curing session I attended, the shaman could not identify the person he had seen in his vision. The brother of the dead man then accused the shaman himself of being responsible. Under such pressure, there is a strong tendency for the curing shaman to attribute each case to a particular bewitcher.

Shamans gradually become weak and must purchase *tsentsak* again and again. Curers tend to become weak in power, especially after curing a patient bewitched by a shaman who has recently received a new supply of magical darts. Thus, the most powerful shamans are those who can repeatedly purchase new supplies of *tsentsak* from other shamans.

Shamans can take back *tsentsak* from others to whom they have previously given them. To accomplish this, the shaman drinks *natema,* and, using his *tsentsak,* creates a "bridge" in the form of a rainbow between himself and the other shaman. Then he shoots a *tsentsak* along this rainbow. This strikes the ground beside the other shaman with an explosion and flash likened to a lightning bolt. The purpose of this is to surprise the other shaman so that he temporarily forgets to maintain his guard over his magical darts, thus permitting the other shaman to suck them back along the rainbow. A shaman who has had his *tsentsak* taken away in this manner will discover that "nothing happens" when he drinks *natema.* The sudden loss of his *tsentsak* will tend to make him ill, but ordinarily the illness is not fatal unless a bewitcher shoots a magical dart into him while he is in this weakened condition. If he has not become disillusioned by his experience, he can again purchase *tsentsak* from some other shaman and resume his calling. Fortunately for anthropology some of these men have chosen to give up shamanism and therefore can be persuaded to reveal their knowledge, no longer having a vested interest in the profession. This divulgence, however, does not serve as a significant threat to practitioners, for words alone can never adequately convey the realities of shamanism. These can only be approached with the aid of *natema,* the chemical door to the invisible world of the Jívaro shaman.

Richard B. Lee

Trance cure of the !Kung Bushmen

"Bushman medicine is put into the body through the backbone. It boils in my belly and boils up to my head like beer. When the women start singing and I start dancing, at first I feel quite all right. Then in the middle, the medicine begins to rise from my stomach. After that I see all the people like very small birds, the whole place will be spinning around and that is why we run around. The trees will be circling also. You feel your blood become very hot just like blood boiling on a fire and then you start healing. When I am like this [telling the story] I am just a person. The thing comes up after a dance, then when I lay hands on a sick person, the medicine in me will go into him and cure him."

The speaker, whose words I have translated, is a Bushman. The !Kung Bushmen, a non-Bantu, click-speaking (the exclamation point stands for a click sound) people of the Kalahari Desert in Botswana, are one of the last peoples of the world to maintain a hunting and gathering way of life—until 10,000 years ago, the universal mode of human organization. According to the Bushman belief, each tribe and race in the world has a distinctive kind of medicine. The Bantu medicine consists of witchcraft and sorcery. The European medicine is contained in pills and in hypodermic syringes. The Bushman medicine, or *n/um,* is a physical substance that lies in the pit of the stomach of the *n/um kausi,* or "medicine owner." Medicine was given by God to Bushmen in the beginning, but men can transfer medicine from one body to another; this, in fact, is the main reason why Bushman trance dancers cure by laying on of hands on patients or subjects and by rubbing sweat. Normally medicine lies dormant. It is necessary to dance in order to heat it up. In their view, dancing makes the body hot. When the medicine reaches the boiling point, the vapors rise up through the spinal column, and when the vapors reach the brain, the dancer enters trance.

The dance ordinarily begins in the evening when a handful of women light a central fire and begin to sing. The dancing circle has a tight, symbolic organization. In the center is the fire, representing medicine, which must be kept burning throughout the all-night dances. Surrounding the fire and within the circumference of the circle, the women sit shoulder to shoulder facing inward. The women are primarily singers, dancing only occasionally. The men dance in an outer, circular rut, stamping around and around hour after hour, now clockwise, now counter-clockwise. Beyond these two tight circles of singers and dancers sit the spectators—the children and those dancers who have paused and are temporarily resting.

The songs are sung without words, in the form of yodeling accompanied by syncopated hand clapping. There is a generally known repertoire of about ten named songs, each commemorating game animals or natural phenomena, such as the giraffe, rain, God, and mongongo nuts. Each has a recognizable tune and associated dance steps. However they do not attempt in the dance to imitate the behavior or locomotion of animals.

Phase I—Working Up Chaxni Chi (*"dance and song"*)

Soon after the women begin singing, some of the men enter the circle to dance. They maintain a tightly hunched posture, arms close to the sides and semiflexed, there is a parsimony of movement, and the body is held stiff from the waist up. Short, heavy footfalls describe complex rhythmic figures built on quarter- and eighth-notes and formed into five- and seven-beat phrases. Artifacts of the dance include chains of rattles tied around the ankles, a walking stick to support the torso, and an indispensable fly whisk.

A dance lasts from five to ten minutes, with a short break followed by another dance of equal length. The women determine the beginning and end of each number and the choice of songs. For the first two hours of dancing the atmosphere is casual, even jovial.

Phase II—Entering a Trance n/um n/i n!uma (*"causing medicine to boil"*)

Several of the dancers appear to be concentrating intently; they look down at their feet or stare ahead without orienting to distractions around them. The body is tense and rigid. The footfalls are heavy and the shock waves can be seen rippling through the body. The chest is heaving, veins are standing out on the neck and forehead, and there is profuse sweating. This phase lasts for thirty to sixty minutes.

The actual entrance into trance can be gradual or it can come suddenly. In the first instance the trancer staggers and almost loses balance. Then other men, who are not in trances, come to his aid and lead him around in tandem until the trancer shouts and falls down in a comatose state—called "half-death" by the Bushmen. The sudden entrance is characterized by a violent leap or somersault and an instant collapse into the half-death.

Phase III—Half-Death Kwi ! ! (*"like dead"*)

Now the trancer is stretched out on the ground outside the dance circle. While the others continue dancing, some men work over the trancer. They rub his body with their hands and with their heads so that the body is kept warm and made to shine with sweat. The trance performer is rigid, arms stiff at the sides or extended. His body may tremble, and he moans and utters short shrieks.

Phase IV—Active Curing n/um (*"medicine"*)

The culmination of the trance episode occurs when the performer rises up to move among the participants and spectators to "cure." The technique used is laying on of hands. The performer's eyes are half-closed. He rubs the subject with trembling hands and utters moans of rising intensity, punctuated by abrupt, piercing shrieks. The trance performer goes from person to person repeating this action, ensuring that every person present is treated. He may break off curing to dance for a few minutes. This appears to reinforce the tranced state and to forestall a premature return to a normal state. If there is a sick person present at the dance each trance performer will make a special effort, often giving ten or fifteen minutes worth of treatment to this one individual.

Phase V—Return to a Normal State

The active curing phase lasts about an hour, after which the trance performer usually lies down and falls asleep. It is common for medicine men to have two trance episodes per night, one about midnight and the other just after dawn. The dance continues all night, reaching a peak intensity between midnight and 2:00 A.M. when the maximum number of medicine men are in trance. It slackens off in the predawn hours and then builds up to full strength again at sunrise with a renewed round of trances. The dance continues until midmorning and usually terminates by 10:00 or 11:00 A.M. Some memorable dances, however, continue throughout the day and into the following night, terminating thirty-six hours after they have started. What makes these marathon dances possible is the change-over of personnel. Although there are always ten to thirty people actively participating in the dance, individuals are constantly entering and leaving the circle in four- to six-hour shifts.

Apart from a male initiation ceremony, called *choma*, which takes place every four or five years during the winter, the Bushmen have no ceremony that is tied to the annual cycle, such as the first fruits rituals of the Australian aborigines. The Bushmen dance at all seasons of the year, winter and summer, with no discernible changes in frequency. There are, however, marked differences between separate Bushman camps in the frequency of occurrence of dances. Small camps of fewer than twenty people hold dances about once a month. Large camps with forty to sixty people dance about once a week. At one camp, which had a reputation for fine music, dances occurred as often as four nights a week. There is some indication that the Bushmen prefer to dance at the time of the full moon, but I could discover no reason for this preference beyond the simple fact that the light is better. A dance is a major all-night affair that involves the majority of the adult members of the camp. It is worth noting that the dance is a social and recreational event as well as an opportunity for trance performance. Many of the younger men dance for no more profound reason than to show off their fancy footwork. There is a juxtaposition of the sacred and the profane in the dance, with the intense involvement of the trance performers contrasting with a background of casual social chatter, laughter, and flirtation.

A dance will spring up spontaneously if the informal organizers can talk up enthusiasm for it. Three kinds of circumstances favor its initiation: the presence of meat in a camp, the arrival of visitors, and the presence of sickness in a camp.

The trance phenomenon of the Bushman is a culturally stereotyped set of behaviors that induces an altered state of consciousness by means of autosuggestion, rhythmic dancing, intense concentration, and hyperventilation. These exertions produce symptoms of dizziness, spatial disorientation, hallucinations, and muscular spasms. The Bushmen were never observed to use any drug or other external chemical means of inducing these states. The social functions of the trancers are to cure the sick, influence the supernatural, and provide mystical protection for all members of the group.

The key symbols and metaphors that are found in the Bushman trance complex are the concepts of boiling, fire, heat, and sweat.

Boiling (*n!um*—to boil) refers not only to the boiling of water on the fire but also to the ripening of plants. Water, like medicine, is dormant when cold, but powerful when hot. Similarly plant foods are dormant when young and unripe but become nutritionally potent when ripe. Thus there is a symbolic association of boiling water, cooked meat, ripened berries, and activated medicine. Sometimes this metaphor is extended, in a joking manner, to nubile maidens who have reached menarche. These young women are now considered "ripe" for intercourse and impregnation.

Fire *(da)* is the source of heat *(khwi)* for boiling water, cooking meat, and for activating medicine. The central fire symbolizes medicine, and rubbing of live coals on the body, which is often done, was interpreted by one informant as a means of rapidly incorporating the sources of medicine. Another informant interpreted fire rubbing as a means of heating up internal medicine. These two views are not necessarily contradictory. Trance performers use the same word *(da)* to describe both the central dance fire and the fire within their own bodies, which heats up the medicine.

Sweat *(cho)* is the most important of the trance symbols for it is the palpable and visible expression of medicine on the surface of the body. Sweat is symbolically equated with the steam rising from boiling water and with the vapors that rise from the medicine boiling in the pit of the stomach.

The production and transmission of sweat is the key element in the curing ritual. Illness is lodged at sites on the body of the sick person and can be driven out by the implanting of medicine.

There is an important contrast to be made between Bushman sweat symbolism and that of the sweat lodge and sweat house religions of North American Indians. In these rituals sweating is interpreted as a means of purification of the body. The perspiration, therefore, carries the negative or harmful substances out of the body. The Bushman belief specifies the opposite—the sweat is itself the positive and life-giving substance. In the sweat house it is necessary for the patient to perspire in order to be cured. In the Bushman case only the curer must sweat in order for the medicine to be effective.

The act of curing involves the laying on of hands, and the rubbing of medicinal sweat onto and into the body of the sick person. If the patient complains of chest trouble, the curer's attention will be focused there; similarly with other complaints located in specific organs, the curer will work on the afflicted part. In this ritual it is not necessary for the patient to enter trance in order for the cure to be effective. Often three or four curers will work simultaneously or in shifts on the body of a sick person. Thus there is no concept of individual responsibility if the cure is successful or unsuccessful. A demand of payment for the curer's service is not a common feature among the Bushmen, although some curers do receive payment when they are called in to give treatment to neighboring Bantu peoples.

In addition to healing, another class of powers attributed to the trance performer is the ability to see the ghosts of ancestors, to see at a distance, and X-ray vision.

Spirits of the dead may be responsible for causing sickness. The ritual curer in trance is able to see the shade hovering at the edge of the dance circle. These shades are invisible to all but the most experienced curers. Having diagnosed the source of the illness the curer then pleads with the ghost to make it go away. The following chant is used:

> *Why do you bother this one?*
> *Go away and don't trouble us;*
> *We love this man.*
> *What have we done to you?*

Some trance performers claim the ability to see distant scenes. On one occasion a performer stopped curing, walked to the edge of the circle of firelight and facing north described the scene at a Bantu village forty miles away. On another occasion a performer pointed to the horizon and announced that trouble was coming from the west. (As far as I know it never materialized.) This power was commonly attributed to trance performers, although I rarely observed it to be exercised.

X-ray vision takes the form of determining the sex of infants *in utero.* I lack a statistically significant sample of these predictions (only ten births occurred during the study period), so I cannot judge the effectiveness of this technique.

The Bushmen believe that, in the past, a few of the very powerful curers had the ability to transform themselves into lions and to stalk the desert in search of human prey. Lions ordinarily do not attack men, and hunters occasionally drive lions off fresh kills in order to scavenge the meat. On the several occasions when a lion has attacked a man, the Bushmen attributed the attack to a human curer-turned-lion. Since such incidents occur perhaps once or twice in a decade, there is little reinforcement for the belief in the malevolence of trance performers.

It is instructive that, apart from this belief, all of the !Kung folk beliefs about trance performers assign to them a benevolent, positive, and socially constructive role.

This positive evaluation of the trance performer's role is most clearly demonstrated in the offering of mystical protection. It is the performer's duty to lay hands on all who are present at a dance, including men, women, children, and young infants. Thus one sees the curers moving around the dance circle and through the spectators, treating each individual in turn, even though there is no sickness in the camp.

The !Kung Bushman trance complex resembles in some ways the classic shamanism of Siberia and native North America. Both the Bushman and the shaman complexes emphasize individual trance as a means of activating extraordinary healing powers. In addition the trance complex as a system of explanation of misfortune has some correspondence to the institution of witchcraft found in many non-European societies. However, the Bushman case differs from shamanism and witchcraft in critical areas.

The well-known distinction between the shaman, whose powers derive from direct contact with the supernatural, and the priest, who learns a codified body of ritual knowledge from older priests, is blurred in the Bushman context. Unlike the shaman who contracts directly with the spirit world, the Bushman trance performer derives his power from within the social body itself.

The Siberian shaman, to take one example, is a lone figure whose power comes from "spirit possession." This supernatural contract—he has entered into a pact with the supernatural—tends to alienate the shaman from his community, and it is significant that the shamanistic role serves as an outlet for emotionally unstable individuals. In American Indian societies, such as the Pawnee, the shamans as a group are set off from the community in a formal fraternity of medicine men. In a number of African societies the shaman may assume the role of an authoritarian prophet figure and may gather a considerable following around him. In all these cases the medicine men are collectively and individually regarded by the laity as awesome and potentially dangerous.

The Bushman trance performer, by contrast, maintains strong social ties with the community. Indeed, recruitment and training of performers forges bonds of affection between the novice and his mentors, and between the curers as a group and the rest of the community. The Bushman curers do not form an exclusive minority of unusually gifted men, nor are they organized into a secret society with special access to the mysteries. The ability to enter trance and cure is possessed by half of the adult men (and by a number of the women).

This close identification of the trance performer with the community at large becomes evident when we consider the logic underlying the Bushman conception of the sources of healing power and the sources of misfortune. The Bushmen regard the healing power as being derived from other living men. Illness and misfortune, however, are brought mainly by the spirits of the dead and other forces external to the living. In other words they seek within the social body for benevolent powers, but project the blame for malevolence to forces outside of the social body. Such a conception of health and disease serves to bind together the living in a common front against hostile external forces.

Societies in which sorcery, shamanism, and witchcraft are prevalent divide good and evil into a radically different projective system. In these societies, malevolence springs from within the social body as well as from without. Witches, sorcerers, and wizards are all conceived of as living humans who (willfully or not) cause harm. To combat this malevolence, the individual may resort to the services of another sorcerer sympathetic to his cause. It is true that in witch-oriented societies not all evil is defined as coming from the living. However, the logic of the system leads inevitably to such features as good and bad shamans, good and bad sorcerers, and a spiral of magical attack and counterattack.

When misfortune strikes a member of a witch-oriented culture, he is likely to seek its source among the living members of the community. In many cases the prime suspects are the individual's close relatives. The hostility that is an inevitable by-product of interpersonal relations is thus translated from the profane into the realm of the sacred. Nevertheless the hostility must be absorbed largely by the social body. The Bushmen, simply by attributing misfortune to an external source, have evolved a projective system that dissipates, rather than intensifies, interpersonal hostility.

It would be misleading to allow the reader to draw the conclusion that all the problems of social living are resolved by the Bushmen in the trance performance and its associated system of explanation. Although the role of "witch" is not an institution of Bushman society, there is a prevalent belief that a living man can (willfully or unknowingly) cause harm to others by neglecting to propitiate his ancestors.

I cite a case in which two old men, Kumsa and Neysi, had been feuding with each other over a period of years. Once, when Kumsa became ill, he complained that Neysi was indirectly the source of his difficulty. This accusation of witchcraft took the following form.

> *Neysi has spoken ill of me. His ancestors have overheard these words and now they have come to bother me. Why can't Neysi control his ancestors?*

In order to clear himself of the charge, Neysi was required to come to Kumsa's bedside and to plead publicly with his offending ancestors to leave Kumsa in peace. In this ritual of reconciliation Neysi used an incantation that is similar to that used by a trance performer when he sees a ghost hovering at a dance.

> *This territory here is ours to share. Now the ghosts should just go away and let this man live in peace. . . . Because of my words the ghosts are trying to kill Kumsa. Now I say—Kumsa is my child. Ghosts! Go away!*

However, this incident was an isolated occurrence; by far the more common attribution of malevolence was to a ghost who was acting entirely of its own volition—uninfluenced by human manipulation.

In conclusion, the attainment of a trance is a co-operative enterprise involving both women and men. The trance performance itself is characterized by a lack of secrecy and a high degree of mutual aid. The psychological rewards of the trance experience are available to a high percentage of the adult men of the community. All members including women and children enjoy the benefits offered by the mystical protection of the curer. The socially positive evaluation of the trance performer's role in society is congruent with the Bushman belief that misfortune springs largely from the dead, and not from the agency of living men. The !Kung Bushman trance performance can be regarded as a drama in which the stresses and tensions of social life are transformed into a common struggle against the external sources of malevolence.

Carol McClain

Ethno-obstetrics in Ajijic

Ajijic is a community of about 8000 people (1) in Jalisco, Mexico. It is situated on the north shore of Lake Chapala at a distance of about forty kilometers from Guadalajara, Mexico's second largest metropolis. Originally a village of Nahuatl speaking Indians, Ajijic became mestizoized, probably before the beginning of the nineteenth century, and completely lost its Indian identity. Within the past two decades, it has played host to an increasing number of both middle and upper class Guadalajarans and North Americans. Presently, the *pueblo* is literally surrounded by large, sumptuous homes of the wealthy and tract houses of the urban upper middle class. It is significant that in the face of overwhelming change influences stemming from urban Mexico and a resident North American retirement colony, the medical system of Ajijicans still retains many traditional features. It contains elements of both the modern and the traditional medical systems, physically juxtaposed in the community, and syncretically fused in the perceptual and behavioral health patterns of Ajijicans.

This paper will explore some features of Ajijican cognition and behavior with respect to obstetrics, that branch of medicine concerned with pregnancy and childbirth. Obstetrics, of course, represents part of the totality of health perceptions and practices in any cultural system. As such, it may be assumed to be a reflective subsystem of the total system, and therefore amenable to separate investigation.

The data for this paper were gathered during two visits to Ajijic, the first from January 1967 to June 1968, and the second from August to September 1973 (2). The descriptions of Ajijican obstetrical cognition are taken from many

From the *Anthropological Quarterly*, Vol. 48 (1975), pp. 38-56. Used by permission of the publisher and the author.

informal conversations with Ajijican women. The quantitative material presented later in the paper was obtained from a series of questionnaires administered to a sample of 41 mothers of families, and which were designed to elicit data on the circumstances of birth of all of the respondents' children.

Obstetrical Cognition

One problem of cognitive analyses is that of intracultural variation or diversity (Wallace 1970:109; Harris 1968:585). Diversity is especially evident in the domain of medicine with an esoteric or specialist component and an exoteric or lay component. The extent of cognitive similarity between and within these two components will vary from culture to culture and must be investigated and ascertained independently for each (Fábrega and Silver 1973; Erasmus 1952). Distinctions between medical specialist knowledge and lay knowledge will be made explicit in the following descriptions where possible.

A second problem that must be met in ethnoscientific approaches to a given cultural domain and which also deals with intracultural variation is the increase in cognitive diversity in acculturational situations. People of traditional societies undergoing change brought about by direct contact with, in most cases, representatives or sectors of modern, industrialized societies, experience modifications in their perceptual and behavioral patterns. The rate of modification will vary from individual to individual, although in a patterned way. It is likely that in such circumstances, perception and behavior, with respect to a given aspect of culture (medicine for example) will exhibit considerable heterogeneity (Broom, et al. 1954; Woods 1968). It should be kept in mind, then, that the material presented here represents idiosyncratic rather than collective cognition. While the core or universal elements of the following account of obstetrical knowledge are generalized in the community, the extent of individual variation in the superficial, alternative elements has not been determined (3). I identify as core knowledge elements of cognition that all persons in the study share. Alternative knowledge are cognitive elements that exhibit some variation from individual to individual.

There is variation of another order between medical perceptions and medical behavior or practices. The relationship may be described as dissonant in the sense that the latter have changed in response to modern medical influence to a much greater extent than have the former (4). With respect to obstetrics, both lay and specialist perceptions of conception and fetal development are less affected by modern medicine than are obstetrical practices, which incorporate modern medical materials and techniques with the existing corpus of traditional obstetrical practices. Thus, women utilize both Western physicians and traditional obstetrical specialists *(parteras)* for antenatal care, and may deliver in a hospital or at home under the supervision of a doctor or a partera. Similarly, parteras, while maintaining traditional perceptions of fetal development, utilize modern drugs and other medical paraphernalia in combination with elements from the traditional medical system in their professional activities.

The ensuing description of selected aspects of ethno-obstetrical knowledge is a preliminary analysis of perceptions of a process, that of fetal development and childbirth. The particular cognitive emphases that emerge, such as the distinction between male and female fetal development, were made by the women who acted as consultants. I made as few direct inquiries as possible in order not to bias the descriptions in favor of my own cognitive structure.

Conception
The source for the following description was a partera, and I have not ascertained whether the material should be regarded as core or alternative knowledge.

1. A male fetus is formed from the *naturaleza* (nature, essence) of the mother. A female fetus is formed from the naturaleza of the father. During sexual intercourse, the mouth of the uterus opens and if pregnancy is to occur, a drop of blood from the father "falls" and becomes the first substance of the female embryo. If the drop of blood falls from the mother, the first substance will be that of a male embryo. If the father should achieve climax first, the embryo will be female, and if the mother should achieve climax first, the embryo will be male.

2. As the embryo forms, it will migrate to its proper position within the uterus: a male embryo to the right, a female embryo to the left. The placenta forms to the left.

The behavioral concomitant to this perception is evidenced by the actions of the partera at parturition. She has already determined the sex of the child by its position. If it is male, she will massage from the right; if it is female, massage from the left. After the birth, she will then massage from the left to aid the expulsion of the placenta.

Fetal Development
The perceptual elements described in (1) below are core beliefs and were articulated by virtually all specialists and lay women in the study. Elements in (2), (3), and (4) are alternative. Sources of information are indicated in parentheses following each statement.

1. At forty days (5) the male fetus is completely formed, and resembles a miniature Christ figure on the cross, with arms extended and feet crossed. The female fetus however, does not completely form until five months. Until five months the female fetus is a small piece of tissue folded upon itself. Women who have experienced miscarriages say they can determine the sex of the fetus by its appearance.

2. Male embryos develop facing dorso-posteriorly with respect to the mother, and females ventro-posteriorly (partera).

3. The developing fetus breathes in the uterus through the mouth and

anus. The respiration is permitted by the open position of the mouth of the uterus. If it closes (from a variety of causes) the fetus will suffocate (partera).

A behavioral concomitant to this perception is that some women will refuse injections while pregnant in the belief that it will close the mouth of the uterus.

4. A first child requires nine months for development and subsequent children eight months and 20 days. Twins may require 11 to 12 months for complete development (6) (lay mother).

Interference with Fetal Growth

Preliminary data indicate that abortions, stillbirths, and all other abnormal births are attributed by both the esoteric and lay components of Ajijic to some external factor affecting either the mother or the fetus during the course of pregnancy. There is no articulated concept of congenital abnormalities in the sense of being genetically derived.

External Factors Affecting the Fetus

1. There are a variety of food taboos that are observed by Ajijican expectant mothers (McClain n.d.). The harm to the unborn child which may result from eating proscribed foods is apparent at birth or shortly after birth. Food taboos are heterogeneous but appear to be more extensive in traditionally-oriented women. These women tend to proscribe certain foods more than do modern-oriented women, while modern-oriented women tend to believe that certain foods should be eaten in greater amounts while pregnant because they are favorable to the healthy development of the unborn child. A core traditional perception is that an excess of "cold" (7) foods may cause illness in the neonate.

2. Jealousy on the part of the unborn child may cause the illness of the youngest of the postnatal siblings. Diagnoses of sibling jealousy, for which there is no consensual term in Ajijic, are made *ex post facto,* when a small child does not respond to treatment for other diagnosed illnesses.

3. Eclipses of the sun and the moon are extremely damaging to any life form in the process of growth or reproduction, including unborn children. This belief stems from pre-Conquest times and is described in Sahagun (1590) and the Badianus Manuscript (1552). Briefly, eclipses cause severe deformities in the developing fetus resulting in stillbirth or abortion. In Ajijic, a lunar eclipse will cause an excess of parts, such as fingers or toes, while a solar eclipse will cause incomplete development, and parts of the body which may be affected, such as the nose or the ears, are "eaten by the sun". The damaging effect of lunar and solar eclipses is core knowledge and is familiar to all Ajijicans, even those who may no longer subscribe to the belief. There is no variation in perceptual details between medical specialists and lay persons.

Women who are pregnant will wear a metal object such as a safety pin beneath their clothing to absorb the effects of an eclipse. For protection at night a metal object will be placed beneath the bed.

4. A father who drinks to excess will be the cause of weakness or deformities in neonates or will cause stillbirths. Again, *ex post facto* diagnoses are characteristic of this etiological category.

External Factors Affecting the Mother

1. *Susto* (fright), *coraje* (anger), or any other emotionally derived shock experienced by a woman during pregnancy constitutes potential harm in that the shock will be transmitted to the fetus *en utero* causing illness. Strong emotional experiences as etiological agents are core perceptions (3).

2. Certain herbs and substances ingested during early pregnancy may result in abortion through their effect on the mother. One obstetrical specialist claims knowledge of herbally based abortifacients. Lay women who are pregnant and do not wish to abort avoid certain substances which are believed to stimulate miscarriage. Quinine was mentioned by two lay mothers in the study as a substance to be avoided while pregnant. Quinine is also used intravaginally during intercourse as a contraceptive measure, according to a partera.

3. One partera and one lay mother articulate the following belief. Accumulated semen from sexual intercourse during pregnancy forms a substance *(tela blanca,* white film or tissue) which is expelled shortly before birth. It causes difficulty in labor because it is cold. In general, any prolonged contact with cold substances will endanger both the mother and the unborn child. This latter belief is part of the core perceptions of Ajijicans. A lay mother expressed the following associated belief. Women have three telas blancas. The first is broken at menstruation; the second is broken during a women's first sexual experience; and the third is broken upon the birth of her first child.

Childbirth (9)

The expectant mother in Ajijic, regardless of her cognitive orientation with respect to conception and pregnancy, may select from several available options for delivery. She may choose to have her child in a hospital, and if so, she may choose from a large number of hospitals which are available. Guadalajara, of course, offers the full range of hospital facilities, from small, expensive, private hospitals to large, state-operated hospitals which may charge a small fee or none at all. Closer to Ajijic is a federally subsidized hospital in Chapala, the Salubridad, and a private hospital in Jocotepec, 15 kilometers west of Ajijic. If a woman decides to have her baby at home, she may select one of three currently active parteras, or she may request the services of a locally based physician, several of whom consent to attend home deliveries. A few women have had babies at home without any form of traditional or modern professional assistance.

Table 1. Number and frequency of hospital and home deliveries for 41 Ajijican mothers before 1968 and between 1968 and 1973

| | 1968-1973 | | | Before 1968 | | | |
	Home	Freq.	Hospital	Freq.	Home	Freq.	Hospital	Freq.
1.	0		1	1	4	.66	2	.33
2.	0		0		6	.86	1	.14
3.	2	.5	2	.5	8	.88	1	.12
4.	0		0		1	.5	1	.5
5.	0		1	1	4	1	0	
6.	1	.5	1	.5	0		0	
7.	0		2	1	0		0	
8.	1	1	0		0		2	1
9.	0		0		4	.66	2	.33
10.	0		1	1	1	.5	1	.5
11.	0		1	1	0		3	1
12.	2	.66	1	.33	5	.83	1	.17
13.	2	1	0		4	1	0	
14.	0		0		8	.88	1	.12
15.	0		2	1	0		3	1
16.	0		5	1	10	1	0	
17.	4	1	0		0		1	1
18.	2	.66	1	.33	2	.66	1	.33
19.	2	1	0		14	1	0	
20.	0		0		11	1	0	
21.	0		2	1	2	.33	4	.66
22.	0		0		1	1	0	
23.	0		3	1	5	.83	1	.17
24.	1	.33	2	.66	0		0	
25.	0		0		3	1	0	
26.	1	.33	2	.66	3	1	0	
27.	4	1	0		3	.75	1	.25
28.	0		0		0		2	1
29.	0		1	1	2	.5	2	.5
30.	0		3	1	0		0	
31.	0		1	1	7	.77	2	.22
32.	1	.5	1	.5	0		0	
33.	0		0		2	1	0	
34.	2	.66	1	.33	0		1	1
35.	0		3	1	0		0	
36.	2	.66	1	.33	1	.33	2	.66
37.	0		4	1	0		0	
38.	1	.25	3	.75	6	.66	3	.33
39.	0		2	1	4	.8	1	.2
40.	0		3	1	0		3	1
41.	0		0		1	1	0	
Total	28	.35	50	.65	119	.74	42	.26

Table 1 presents the frequencies of hospital and home deliveries for all of the children of 41 Ajijican mothers of families. While there is an increasing tendency for women to have their children in hospitals (see Table 2), there is still consider-

Table 2. Frequency of hospital and home deliveries of 41 Ajijican women before 1968 and between 1968 and 1973

	Home	Hospital	Total
Before 1968	121	40	161
1968-73	30	48	78
Total	151	88	239

$x^2 = 30.40; p < .001$

able heterogeneity exhibited in delivery options. Of particular interest is the fact that an individual woman will not necessarily choose to have all of her children at home or all in the hospital. Discussions with the women who served as respondents in the study revealed that for each pending birth, separate considerations were made regarding the advantages or disadvantages of hospital or home deliveries for the coming child. A woman might decide to have her baby in the hospital because her husband is away on a trip. Another woman might decide to have her baby at home because the family lacks the money for hospital services. Another woman might decide to have her baby at home because her last child died within hours of delivery in a hospital, and she is afraid to have another child under the same circumstances. Regardless of individual motivation, and judging by the increasing frequency of hospital use, and the decreasing number of parteras available for traditional obstetrical services, childbirth at home will eventually disappear or become comparatively infrequent as an alternative to hospitalization.

It is impossible to make an objective evaluation of the comparative merits of the two opposing childbirth services. While hospital delivery might be advantageous in one respect, such as the availability of modern medical equipment in case of obstetrical emergencies, home delivery might be advantageous in another, such as the psychological benefits obtained by both mother and infant through close physical and emotional association during and immediately subsequent to the birth process. A gross estimate of the relative advantages however, may be evidenced by comparing the infant mortality figures for hospital and home deliveries. Infant mortality data were compiled from the questionnaires previously referred to. Of the total number of children born at home under the care of a partera, or without any professional assistance whatever, 7.63 percent died before the age of three months. Of the total number of children born in the hospital or at home under the care of a physician, 11.5 percent died before the age of three months. Clearly, it is at least as safe, and possibly safer, for Ajijican women to continue to have their children at home in the traditional manner.

The Partera

At the time of my first stay in Ajijic in 1967 and 1968, there were four practicing parteras, and one who had recently retired because of old age. At the time of my second field visit in 1973, two of the original four were still active, one had died, another had retired because of old age, and an additional woman had begun practice (this individual is the daughter of one of the other still active parteras). A sixth woman had been a partera when she was younger, but had given up the profession after a frightening experience. She had witnessed the murder of her brother-in-law and had been unable to withstand the sight of blood thereafter. She continues to be active as a health practitioner however, in that she administers injections.

A gross estimate of the trend in the number of parteras available to the potential clientele indicates that they may be dying out as an alternate form of health care delivery in the area of childbirth assistance, at least. In 1967 the population of Ajijic was approximately 4,500 and in 1973, approximately 7,700. In 1967, traditional obstetrical care was being provided by four parteras, and in 1973, by three. Clearly, fewer traditional practitioners are available for a larger potential clientele. In addition, two of the active parteras are older women, both well over 65. The third, who has only recently begun her professional career, is 28.

In order to define and describe some patterned features of the role of the partera, a short personal history of four of these women will be given. Subsequently, the results of interviews with each about the extent to which they utilize modern techniques and materials will be reviewed.

Doña Carmen

Doña Carmen emphasizes that although she doesn't know how to read, she does know how to cure. She was born in another village in the state of Jalisco and at the age of six came to Ajijic with her family to live At the age of 33 she began to practice medicine. She worked many years "with a doctor." She was married, gave birth to six sets of twins, was widowed, and presently makes her permanent home in Ajijic, although she travels a great deal to treat patients who have heard of her skills and have sent for her. She has traveled as far as Mexico City to bring patients back to Ajijic for extended treatment. Doña Carmen is a popular *curandera* in Ajijic. Obstetrics is only one of her medical specialties. She frequently makes trips across the small range of mountains behind Ajijic to treat patients and deliver babies in various semi-isolated *ranchitos* where many Ajijicans have relatives. Her house in Ajijic is located in the poorest and most traditional *barrio*. It is very modest, with only a few rooms, a dirt floor, and a small garden in which she keeps a few chickens and one or two pigs. Doña Carmen studied under a *yerbero* (herbalist) for five years. She believes herself to be divinely chosen for the curing profession. As a child she possessed special curing skills which were recognized by others, although she did not begin curing professionally until she was an adult.

Josefina

Doña Carmen's daughter Josefina, at age 28, is the youngest partera in Ajijic in well over 30 years. She began her professional career at age 25, having learned everything she knows from her mother. She is married, lives with her mother, and has children of her own, all of whom were delivered by her mother. She uses the same procedures and materials, both traditional and modern, as Doña Carmen, and at least thus far in her career, enjoys a good reputation. It is clear through many conversations with women in Ajijic that experience weighs heavily in the evaluation of a partera's skill, and Josefina's age and few years of experience might seem to work against her. However, in the course of the month I spent in the field in 1973, I never heard any criticisms of Josefina on account of her lack of experience. Josefina also specializes in *sobando,* the curing of certain illnesses by massage. Like her mother, then, she does not confine herself to midwifery.

Doña Josefa

Doña Josefa, a widow for many years, was born in Ajijic in 1904 and has two living children. At the time of my first field study she was living alone in the same small house which her husband had built many years before, and supported herself solely by her professional services as a partera and a curandera. When I returned in 1973 I found she had sold her house to Americans and moved to Chapala to a tiny stucco house her son had built for her. She is not happy in Chapala and misses Ajijic even though it is only six kilometers away. According to Doña Josefa she learned all she knows about medicine from her aunt and a doctor who lived in Chapala many years before. She became active as a partera at age 32. Like Doña Carmen, Doña Josefa does not limit herself to obstetrics but is very much the generalist. She cures children's diseases and massages in particular. Furthermore she is regarded as a specialist in infertility and birth control.

Unlike the other parteras described here, Doña Josefa has retired because of old age. It is curious that during my second field stay, Doña Josefa's reputation appeared to have suffered somewhat. I was told by some women that she was careless and not knowledgeable about childbirth. I found this somewhat of an enigma in view of the fact that she has delivered the majority of the children born in Ajijic in the last 25 years.

Doña Petra

Doña Petra was born and raised in San Juan Cosalá, a neighboring *pueblo.* She was born in 1900 and began practicing as a partera in 1920. Midwifery is her only specialty. She acquired her skills by heredity in the sense that her mother and older sister were both parteras, and her mother told her she was destined for the profession. In addition, as a young woman she was apprenticed under a doctor in Guadalajara for nine months and gained her earliest experience under his tutelage. At present she lives with her married son, a school teacher, and his family.

Doña Petra is proud of her record of never having lost a single patient. She strictly limits her practice to obstetrics, and regards herself as especially skilled in situations involving abnormal deliveries such as breech presentations, *placenta previa,* and puerperal infections. Like all of the parteras discussed here, she stresses that in certain, very difficult deliveries, she does not hesitate to send her patient to a hospital.

Doña Petra utilizes modern drugs and equipment (in this case, syringes and hypodermic needles) obtained from a pharmacy in combination with traditional herbal preparations and methods of delivery assistance. The other three parteras do also, but apparently to a lesser extent than Doña Petra. While Doña Petra is familiar with the effect of the drugs she administers, she conceptualizes these effects in traditional rather than modern terms. Thus, capsules of Compositrina (a trademark for a uterine contractant according to a local physician) are utilized by Doña Petra in combination with an herbal tea primarily for predictive purposes. If labor is true, the preparation will cause the contractions to continue, and if labor is false, it will cause the contractions to stop. She also administers injections before and after delivery, the first to stimulate contractions, the second to control uterine bleeding. Herbal remedies may be used for the same purposes.

From these brief personal histories, and from the data presented in Table 3, it is evident that all four midwives have certain professional features in common. With the possible but not probable exception of Doña Carmen, the role of partera was socially inherited from an older female relative who was also a partera.

In terms of training, another common feature emerges—a claimed formal relationship with a physician. This aspect of their medical training may have more to do with prestige than with acquisition of necessary skills, in that their techniques do not correspond with modern techniques apart from the incorporation of the use of certain modern drugs and paraphernalia. It is significant that of the four, Doña Petra has added modern elements to her methods to the greatest extent, and charges more than twice as much as any of the others (see Table 3). She also enjoys a higher socioeconomic position relative to the others. One might assume that she is able to charge higher fees because of popularity, but Table 4 shows that her professional services are not in that much demand in Ajijic compared to some of the other alternatives. Conversations with women in Ajijic indicate that Doña Petra's high fees inhibit them from requesting her care. Fortunately for Doña Petra, it is not imperative that she be in continual demand because she is not completely self-supporting. At age 73 she shows no signs of loss of alertness, vivacity or skill and does not plan on retiring in the near future.

Table 4 shows, for a sample of 41 women and a total of 239 babies born, under what conditions the deliveries took place. Dona Carmen has delivered only three of the children, but this number does not reflect her total professional load, because she does not confine her practice to Ajijic, but is frequently out of town treating patients and delivering babies elsewhere.

That Josefina has delivered only one baby for our sample reflects her recent entrance into the profession, and at a time when more and more women are opting to have their babies at a hospital.

Doña Josefa has delivered an easy majority of the children in the sample, even taking into account her decreasing activities prior to retirement and her inactivity for the past year. A total of 51 children in the sample were delivered by

Table 3. Comparisons of four parteras

	Doña Carmen	Josefina	Doña Josefa	Doña Petra
Recruitment	By God*	Social heredity	Social heredity	Social heredity
Training	Herbalist, doctor	Mother	Aunt, doctor	Mother, doctor
Other specialties	Yes	Yes	Yes	No
Age (as of 1973)	About 70	28	69	73
Years of practice	About 37	3	37	53
Socioeconomic level	Low	Low	Low	Middle
Professionally self-supporting?	Partial	Partial	Complete	Partial
Recommends patients to doctors?	Yes	Yes	Yes	Yes
Utilizes modern drugs & materials?	Yes	Yes	Yes	Yes
Average fees charged (in pesos)	1964, 50 1968, 70 1971, 60	1971, 80	Before 1948, 18-15 1948-52, 30-35 1953-57, 30-60 1958-62, 40-90 1963-67, 50-75 1968, 72, 65-150	1968-72, 200-300

*Whether Doña Carmen also received her profession by social heredity was not determined.

Table 4. Type of delivery for 41 Ajijican mothers

	Doña Carmen	Josefina	Doña Josefa	Josefina	Doña Petra	Other parteras	Home under Care of Doctor	Chapala Hospital	Jocotepec Hospital	Hospitals in Guadalajara	Other Hospitals	Home-Registered Midwife	Home- No Assistance
1.			1			3		3					
2.						3	3			1			
3.			2			2		2	1				6
4.							1			1			
5.			2			1				1		1	
6.								1					1
7.										2			
8.							1	2					
9.			1			2	1	2					
10.						1				2			
11.								1		3			
12.			4			3		1		1			
13.	1		1			4							
14.			4			1	3	1					
15.								3	2				
16.			10				1	1	2	1			
17.					4				1				
18.	1					2	1	1		1			
19.	1		15										
20.							2						10
21.						1		1		5			1
22.						1							
23.						5				4			
24.					1					2			
25.						2	1						
26.		1							1	1			
27.		5					2			1			
28.										2			
29.			1				1		1	1			
30.										3			
31.						7		2	1				
32.						1	1						
33.						2				1			
34.			1			1		2					
35.								2		1			
36.					2	1			1	2			
37.								4					
38.			1			5	1	5					
39.			2			2		3					
40.							1	3		2			
41.						1							

Total: 239 — Total at home: 151 — Total in hospital: 88

parteras other than the four under consideration here. Three of these other parteras were indigenous to Ajijic and delivered the majority of the 51 babies. Two of these women have died and the third is retired. A few other children were born at home in towns and villages other than Ajijic when their mothers were living elsewhere.

Twenty babies were delivered at home under the care of a physician (several cases in which a child was born in the office facilities of resident or visiting physicians in Ajijic were included in this category). This appears to be a quite viable intermediate alternative between home and hospital delivery. The family feels the mother and child are receiving the benefits of modern medicine in the person of the attending physician, but not the disadvantages of hospitalization. Combined with the fact that most hospital deliveries are performed by nurses rather than doctors, and the fact that the cost of home delivery is less (see Table 5), this alternative becomes even more attractive.

Home delivery under the care of a physician is another illustration of the manner in which Ajijicans maximize benefits from the continuum of health services offered. By selecting elements from both the traditional and the modern sector of health services available, persons are able to make both systems work concurrently in their favor.

Table 4 illustrates another pattern of childbirth care which requires explanation. Only one child in the sample was delivered at home under the care of a Western-trained registered midwife. I did not investigate the relative availability of this form of care, and think it inadvisable to speculate on the reason for its absence as an alternative method, considering the fact that Ajijic is so heterogeneous in its use of medical resources. There are, however, several possible explanations. Registered nurses may not be available, or they may compete at a disadvantage with either the partera or the doctor making home deliveries.

Eighteen children were born at home with no professional assistance whatever, traditional or modern. In both cases in which a woman had multiple unassisted births, she was the mother of many children, and one of the women in question was a curandera.

Finally, an examination of the dispersion of childbirth events represented in Table 4 shows the pattern of heterogeneity of Ajijicans in terms of medical resource use. Even though the trend is in the direction of continued and increasing use of hospitals for obstetrical care, traditional obstetrical care is still viable and will probably continue to be so for an inestimable period of time in the future, depending on many different factors in the local and national socioeconomic unfolding of Mexico.

Table 5 compares the cost of obstetrical care at different hospitals and at home under the care of a physician. The greatest variation in hospital cost is found in Guadalajara. Depending on the hospital and on one's economic standing, the cost may range from virtually nothing at the Hospital Civil to over 3,500 pesos at any number of private hospitals. The government hospital in Chapala was built in 1962 and is used by more Ajijican women than any other hospital. The doctors and staff are paid by the government. A set fee of 100 pesos is supposed to be charged

Table 5. Comparative costs of modern obstetrical care (in pesos) for a sample of
41 Ajijican women

	Chapala (2 hospitals)	*Jocotepec (1 hospital)*	*Guadalajara (many hospitals)*	*At Home under the Care of a Doctor*
1968-73	150-670	540-1000	0* 150-3,500	150-550
1963-67	150-450	800	0* 75-1,200	500
1958-62	**	**	0*, 350	275-300
1953-57				150-300
1948-52				125-150
Total number deliveries	41	5	42	20

*Some hospital services are free in two hospitals in Guadalajara; the Hospital Civil and the Cruz Roja.
**The hospitals in Chapala and Jocotepec were built after 1962.

to all maternity patients, but often, higher fees may in fact be charged. A second, private, hospital has been available for maternity care in Chapala since 1971, and fees at this hospital run regularly two or three times as much as in the Salubridad. The hospital in Jocotepec is consistently more expensive than either hospital in Chapala as can be seen by comparative figures in Table 5. It is utilized less by women from Ajijic than other hospitals, because of higher costs and because the two doctors who operate it have a rather dubious reputation, at least outside of Jocotepec.

Summary and Conclusions

The Ajijican medical system, as reflected in patterns of obstetrical perceptions and practices, is currently in dynamic flux. A descriptive analysis of obstetrical practices indicates that Ajijican women may and do choose from a selection of options in obstetrical services, ranging from purely traditional to purely modern. While the direction of change is obviously from traditional to modern, at present the obstetrical practices of both specialists and lay women are heterogenous, on an individual level and on a collective level. Thus, an individual woman may have some of her children at home under the care of a partera and some of her children at a hospital. On the collective level, Ajijican women may be located along a continuum of traditional to modern with respect to obstetrical practices. Some women have had all of their children at home (although they do not reject modern medical services for other purposes), while others have had all of their children at a hospital and would not even consider a home delivery. Traditional obstetrical specialists use modern medical drugs and equipment along with traditional herbally-based preparations and methods, and claim professional accreditation from both traditional and modern sources.

However, obstetrical perceptions, ideas and knowledge concerning conception and fetal development, continue for the most part to be traditionally based. I suggest that for descriptive purposes, perceptions may be usefully regarded as universal (shared by all members of the community) or alternative (idiosyncratic or showing variation from person to person). Irrespective of variations in beliefs about pregnancy, some of which have been outlined here, they have not been altered by the influence of modern medicine to the same extent as have practices. Whether and to what extent perceptions will also change as the modern medical system further entrenches itself in the community remains to be seen and should be the subject of additional research.

Whatever advantages traditional obstetrical care offers women and their children in Ajijic (and these may be considerable), they will be lost if it is completely displaced by modern hospital services. A partial compromise may be the alternative method of home delivery under the care of a physician.

Notes

1. This figure represents the number of residents in 1973. The town is growing rapidly because of a high birth rate and especially immigration from other parts of Mexico.
2. The first field study was financed by a grant from the Organization of American States. The second was financed by a fellowship from the Oregon State University Foundation.
3. The conceptual basis of the core or universal/alternative dichotomy is borrowed from Linton (1936:278-285).
4. In the sense that the medical perceptual orientation of Ajijicans will continue to change from traditionally-oriented to modern-oriented, and so "catch up" with contemporary medical practices, the concept of culture lag (Ogburn 1957) may apply descriptively to the relationship between the two.
5. Forty days is also the traditional length of postnatal behavioral restrictions of the mother. The medico-religious significance of the forty-day period apparently stems from sixteenth century Spanish medical contributions to the emerging syncretic medical systems of Indian and Mestizo communities all over Mesoamerica (Foster 1953b).
6. A belief in a longer gestation period for twins raises the question of the incidence of premature births of twins in different societies. Is it lower in traditionally-based societies than in modern societies, and if so, why?
7. The medical significance of the qualities of hot and cold in foods and other substances and bodily states is remarkably uniform throughout Mexico and Latin America (Foster 1953; Adams & Rubel 1967; Logan 1973; Simmons 1955).
8. As in the case of hot and cold imbalance, strong emotional experiences are viewed as causes of illness in many parts of Mexico and Latin America (Rubel 1964).
9. The material which follows is abstracted from my doctoral dissertation which is in preparation at the time of this writing.

David Landy

Role adaptation: traditional curers under the impact of Western medicine

The functions of the curer's role in a tradition-directed society facing the challenge of a technologically more powerful medical system may be studied from many points of view. This paper will be confined to a consideration of certain theoretical aspects in the adaptation of the curer's role to changes accompanying acculturation threats and opportunities. Data are taken from a variety of studies by anthropologists and others. My objective is to place the changing role of the curer into substantive and theoretical perspective and to contribute to a model for the study of role adaptation under conditions of culture change.

Anthropological Treatment of the Curer's Role

Much attention has been given in ethnographic reports to the curer's status and role. Until recently, however, relatively few studies furnished detailed descriptions of the process of becoming a curer, of recruitment to the role, or the articulation of the curer's role with the social system (except, usually, the religious system). Among conspicuous exceptions we may cite Gillin's (1956) account of "the making of a witch doctor," Hallowell's (1939, 1942, 1955, 1963) many studies of socio-cultural aspects of Ojibwa medicine, Handelman's (1967) account of "the development of a Washo shaman," Kluckhohn's (1944) classic study of Navaho witchcraft, Spiro's (1967) analysis of Burmese medical-religious beliefs and practitioners, Press' (1971) case-study analysis of the careers, practices, and variations among urban curanderos in Bogota, Colombia, and Turner's (1964) study of a Ndembu "doctor." Studies of the social control aspects of indigenous medical systems are now becoming available and these frequently relate the curer's role to the social structure, e.g., those in Kiev (1964) and Middleton (1967).

Scotch's (1963a) review of "Medical Anthropology" contains a brief section on "ethnomedicine" citing twelve studies of which fewer than half are concerned with the role of the curer. Polgar's (1962) comprehensive review of studies in health and human behavior has a helpful section on social and cultural conditions under which people in preindustrial and industrial societies make a choice of medical personnel and is relevant to the subject of interest here. Caudill's (1953) earlier

Reproduced by permission of the American Anthropological Association from the *American Ethnologist*, 1 (1), 1974.

review also contains several relevant sections. Paul's (1955) well-known volume of "public reactions to health programs" contains only three cases that deal incidentally with the indigenous healer's role. Goodenough's (1963) book on applied anthropology and culture change contains but a handful of passing allusions to the healer's role, and it is scarcely mentioned in Foster's (1962, 1969) books in the same field.

Perhaps the closest approach to our concern with adaptation of the traditional healer's role in acculturation appears in the work of Alland (1970:155-178) on the medical system of the Abron of the Ivory Coast; reference to Alland's material appears later in the present study. Several studies in the compilations of Kiev (1964) and Middleton (1967) deal in part with the problem, though not within the context of the concept of role adaptation or role theory.

Uses of the Role Concept in Anthropology

Social science has been concerned with concepts of the self at least since the writings of James in 1890 and Cooley in 1902 and with the notion of role since Simmel in 1920 and Park and Burgess in 1921 (Biddle and Thomas 1966:4 passim). Moreover, social and legal philosophers have examined what are now termed role relationships and the nexuses of social relationships to social systems for well over two centuries, as Banton (1965:21-24) has shown. The major interest of anthropologists in the concept began with the still influential work of Linton (1936) and received further stimulus from the work of Parsons (1951) in sociology and Nadel (1957). However, original theoretical contributions by anthropologists, as contrasted with sociologists and psychologists, until recently have been sparse. For the most part anthropologists seemed content either to take the concept for granted, using it uncritically without attempting further refinement, or simply to ignore it. This becomes the more remarkable when one notes a rare statement of appreciation such as that by Southall (1959:17): "Role theory may be said to mark the highest level of generalization about social phenomena that has as yet become in any sense operational." Thus Manners and Kaplan's (1968) sourcebook in anthropological theory contains a single selection (Kaplan, "Personality and Social Structure") dealing in part with role as it relates to a Parsonian notion of personality, and Harris' (1968) monumental *The Rise of Anthropological Theory* scarcely mentions the concept in its 800 pages.

However, in the past decade some anthropologists have returned to the idea and have begun to rethink the concept of role as providing an important key to what Goodenough terms the "cultural organization of social relationships" (Barth 1963, 1966; Banton 1965; Benedict 1969; Coult 1964; Freilich 1964, 1968; Goodenough 1965a; Keesing 1970; Southall 1959). Certain studies in political anthropology have focused on changing functions of chiefs and other political roles (e.g., Swartz, Turner, and Tuden 1966), and in economic anthropology on changing functions of entrepreneurs, traders, and other economic roles (e.g., Barth 1963, 1966; Belshaw 1955; Helm, Bohannan, and Sahlins 1965).

Among the more stimulating formulations, and most relevant to my notion of role adaptation, have been those explorations around the notion of the "cultural broker," beginning with the seminal paper by Wolf (1956a) on the mediating functions of the politician-broker role between local and national institutions in Mexico; Geertz's (1960) incisive analysis of the cultural broker role of the Javanese *kijaji* as Moslem religious teacher and nationalist politician; and the more recent work in Mesoamerica of Hunt (1968) and Press (1969a) to which subsequent reference will be made. It will be seen that in some ways the more adaptive traditional curer roles incorporate important aspects of the cultural broker's role, though in some respects the curer's role departs from the broker model.

Press' (1971) very useful study of curers in an urban South American city calls attention not only to basic differences in the curing role in rural and peasant communities as contrasted with urban ones, but the fact that the culture and multiplex social organization of cities provide opportunities for a wide variety of curers to flourish. While in complete agreement with Press' major points, it must be asserted that many rural and peasant cultures contain a fair degree of variation in curing roles, though not nearly as broad as in urban cultures. Reference in this paper to *the* curing role refers only to specific instances in specific societies and makes no assumption about either stereotyped role models or lack of variation in role types.

I do not pretend that the works just cited fully represent the important recent work in anthropology on role, though they do provide, in my opinion, a sample of seriously critical and potentially fruitful writings. Many refinements of the concept in these papers are not utilized herein, in part because that task is beyond the scope of this essay, and in part because much of the data on the curing role with which I am familiar will not permit the kind of fine-grained analysis these conceptual refinements require (cf. especially Goodenough 1965 and Keesing 1970 for reasons).

Conceptual and Theoretical Assumptions

The use of the role concept in social science has been primarily structural-functional (role performance, role-taking, role-modeling, role expectations, etc.), as recent comprehensive surveys clearly indicate (Biddle and Thomas 1966; Sarbin and Allen 1968). Processes of role change have been studied primarily as chronological modifications occurring, as in the socialization process, when the person assumes new roles as he reaches new age grades and therefore new social horizons. Research has also dealt with sex role changes due to status changes, as in the changing roles of women, or socialization into occupational roles in industrial organizations.

But in the case of role change in response to the stimulus of competing values and technology of another, economically more potent culture, this question has seldom been handled except in terms of conflict and strain, and these are seen as almost inevitably arising from culture contact. (Exceptions in economic and political anthropology were noted previously.) Indeed some writers seem to assume that a concomitant of acculturation will be personality disturbance, and by implication role conflict. It will be seen in the present essay that in the case of the curer the contact situation may be actually or potentially conflictual, but it may also possess possibilities for role adaptation insofar as elements of ideology and behavior patterns of the impinging culture are adopted to enhance therapeutic efficacy, and even to strengthen the curer's status in his own society. Some curers may resemble marginal men caught in an insoluble dilemma between the drag of the culture of orientation (what Belshaw [1955] calls the entrepreneur's "home group" culture) on the one hand, and the pull of the culture of reference—that of scientific Western medicine—on the other. But frequently the curer maintains his position strongly in his membership group while borrowing liberally from Western medicine, without necessarily identifying with the reference group, in which realistically he accepts the fact that the doors to membership are closed, and without losing his psychological and social stability through fruitless floundering between the two cultures.

We define role adaptation as the process of attaining an operational sociopsychological steady-state by the occupant of a status or status set through sequences of "role bargains" or transactions among alternative role behaviors. In situations of rapid culture change, alternative behavior possibilities, expectations, rewards, and obligations will originate both within and without the indigenous social system. All individuals in any sociocultural system are confronted with "overdemanding" total role obligations (Goode 1960:485 passim) but must manage to equilibrate role relationships and role sets through continual bargaining and consensuses with other actors in the system, and consequently reduce role strain. Therefore, the instance of the traditional curer's role under potential stress from the demands and temptations of the competing medical system represents an extension of Goode's theory of role strain (cf. also Banton 1965: Chs. 2, 3).

I make the following assumptions:

1. The curer's place in his society originally was relatively secure until threatened by the pressures of culture change. His personality may or may not have been in phase with the behavioral norms of his own sociocultural system, but his status was traditional and prescribed, though not invariably ascribed.

2. Prior to contact, in addition to ameliorating the effects of illness and disease, the curer's activities were oriented toward enhancing and/or reinforcing his social position. Although role prescriptions were traditional, he would still have to rationalize nonsuccess, and ordinarily he would have to compete with other curers in the number and profundity of his achievements. Admittedly the factor of competition among curers is not emphasized in most anthropological accounts, though many data suggest it. For example, Lévi-Strauss (1963:167-185) describes the acquisition of curing power by a Kwakiutl skeptic who then engages in competitive exhibitions with other shamans. Press (1971) emphasizes competition among curers in Bogota. I

hypothesize that the curer's status was at least as competitive as any other highly valued position in a given society.

3. Nevertheless, a measure of security was present in that role performance expectations were shared with other members of the society, and competition originated primarily from within the group and presented a relatively known range of possibilities. To some extent competing performances could be gauged, anticipated, and controlled. Sources of role strain probably were fewer than in the post-contact period, and possibilities for successful interpersonal transactions in the interest of reduction of role strain and achievement of role adaptation probably were greater (Goode 1960:491).

4. The curing role could be a full- or part-time one, but prestige in one role tended to be linked to prestige in others, so that status in any tended to reinforce the power of all (Goode 1960:491-493). This follows from the notions of role sets, status sets, and status sequences (Merton 1957).

Analysis of role adaptation of curers in selected societies undergoing acculturation has suggested a model of adaptation possibilities in which the data may be grouped into three categories: adaptive, attenuated, and emergent curing roles. We now proceed to examine the data in these terms.

Adaptive Curing Roles

Erasmus (1952) found in Quito, Ecuador, as has been discovered by many other investigators, that those illnesses thought to be supernaturally caused were referred to indigenous practitioners, those that had a mundane origin and were thought to respond to common remedies were treated at home, and certain others of non-supernatural origin such as tuberculosis and appendicitis were referred to the modern physician, "folk" practitioners agreeing that the latter referral was appropriate. Usually the victim of illness first tried home remedies, then a folk curer, and only when these two possibilities failed did he consult the physician. As Erasmus (1952:417) shows, a division of role responsibility has been arranged tacitly between the traditional curer and the physician:

> *It would appear that the folk look up to the doctor for his ability to cure serious illnesses for which their own remedies are less likely to be efficacious, independently of whether or not they understand or believe in his explanation of causes. Their acceptance of the doctor rests primarily upon empirical observation and experience.*

In the village of Sherupur in North India, Gould (1957) differentiated between what he called "village medicine" and "doctor medicine." He conceptualized these as two systems of treatment in constant interaction. Village medicine was used primarily to treat "chronic nonincapacitating dysfunctions" ("conditions manifesting drawn-out periods of suffering, sometimes cyclical in character, usually not fatal ... and only partially debilitating, enabling the sufferer to maintain a semblance of his daily routine" [Gould 1957:508]). Doctor medicine was solicited mainly for "critical incapacitating dysfunctions" ("ailments . . . involving sudden and often violent onset, and rather complete debilitation with reference to some aspects of the individual's routine" [1957:508]). The people tended to make choices on the basis of what Gould terms "folk pragmatism." Choice of scientific over folk medicine was related directly to "(a) economic well-being, (b) formal education, and (c) occupational and spatial mobility" (1957:515). Since there is a wide range of chronic nonincapacitating dysfunctions for which modern medicine can prescribe no specific remedy, and since many critical incapacitating dysfunctions may respond to different remedies, including the therapy of time, it seemed probable that native medicine would continue to thrive in a structure complementary to scientific medicine.

Nurge's (1958) study of an agricultural fishing village in eastern Leyte, Philippine Islands, differs somewhat in its conclusions from Erasmus and Gould, since "the relationship between a treatment and its effect is usually far from obvious, is often obscure, and at best is amazingly complex" (Nurge 1958:1170). She felt that neither Erasmus nor Gould could be certain that disease entities that they defined in Western scientific terminology were clearly apprehended by their subjects. As she stated the case for this Filipino village, "the individual does not grapple with a disease, but with a discomfort or malaise which he may describe as being itchy, disturbing, or painful. It is not measles or bronchitis or tuberculosis but an unhappiness and a disease which the patient brings to specialists and which the curer or physician defines for the patient" (Nurge 1958:1169-1170). She believes with Hsu (1952) that

> *Magic and "real knowledge" are often intertwined, may be indistinguishable, and . . . the individual oscillates between the two and resorts to both quite indiscriminately . . . . Such practice is not confined to primitives or to peoples of underdeveloped areas, but is part of the way of life of societies everywhere, although the proportions of magic and science in a given society vary (Nurge 1958:1169).*

Nurge describes the functions of five types of indigenous curers, and, like Gould and Erasmus, sees them functioning in a cultural system in effective interaction with modern medicine.

After additional fieldwork Gould (1965) elaborated on his earlier work by recasting his findings within the cognitive structure and world view of the indigenous culture. That people in Sherupur made pragmatic choices did not mean that they had achieved an understanding, let alone acceptance, of scientific medicine, but simply that they had availed themselves selectively of its technology. He appears to approach the view of his critic, Nurge, when he says, "the acceptance of scientific medicines . . . resulted in no material changes in basic folk cognitive structure. These experiences were filtered through the screen of this cognitive system and converted into meanings which did no violence to it" (Gould 1965:204).

The implications of Gould's findings for the role of the traditional curer coping with the competition of Western medicine are that

> *The more modern medicine becomes entrenched in, say, the domain of the critical incapacitating dysfunctions, the more indigenous practitioners stabilize their control over the treatment of chronic nonincapacitating dysfunctions. The latter even adopt the paraphernalia of modern medicine in order to intensify their psychological impact on their patients.... The routinized impersonality now so intrinsically a component of the modern professional role probably intensifies and helps promote the consolidation of this defensive reaction (1965:207-208).*

Gould has made a significant contribution to the study of comparative medical systems by indicating the need to differentiate the technical from the scientific since they do not necessarily coexist.(2) Thus, also, the traditional healer is seen not merely as passive receptor of modern science and technology,(3) but as incorporating technocultural agent and as creator of new technocultural syntheses. The curing role is not only changed, but resynthesized.

Many detailed descriptions are available of the role of Navaho singers, diagnosticians, and herbalists, as well as of the reactions of the Navaho to modern medical practice (Leighton and Leighton 1945). More recently in the work of Adair (1963) and others we are beginning to learn of the adaptation of traditional Navaho curers to contemporary scientific medicine. Rosenthal and Siegel (1959:148) pointed out that they have "often tried, unsuccessfully, to make new magical songs for the white man's tuberculosis, measles, influenza, and syphilis." Adair and the Leightons indicate that most Navaho still trust traditional curers even while selectively utilizing "white medicine," and occasionally they were permitted to hold a sing in a hospital or clinic, usually after Western medical treatment had been given (see also Kluckhohn and Leighton 1962). Adair (1963) reports that in the Many Farms community there were fifty-five curers or singers "among our clinic population—one for every two and one-half camps, or one for every forty-one people." Adair points out that Navaho curers respect White doctors, acknowledge their superiority in some areas, and cannot understand why their respect is not reciprocated. Diagnosticians (hand tremblers) are still usually the first professionals to be consulted and they in turn advise "their patients to go to the clinic in certain circumstances, rather than to the medicine men" (1963:246). After extensive interviewing and psychological testing of thirty Navaho informants, Adair (1963:248) concludes:

> *There was general agreement ... that both types of medicine were essential for Navaho health needs, and that it was best to follow the advice of the hand trembler. There are 73 diagnosticians in the area, more than one to every two camps.... This large number of diagnosticians reflects the important role they play in the Navaho society, as decision-makers between alternate means of curing.*

Adair points out that patients with injuries or suffering from acute, sudden disease attacks "are readily brought to the clinic," while those suffering from illnesses developing more slowly and less well-defined are assumed to have broken a taboo and usually are treated by the singer, a finding reminiscent of those of Erasmus and Gould.

The revitalization movement of Handsome Lake among the early nineteenth century Iroquois (Wallace 1956a, 1961a, 1961b, 1961c, 1966) seemed to be an effort to reinvigorate remnants of the indigenous culture by blending into it elements of the Quaker variant of Christian religion and by creating a new ideal personality type that would be rewarding through becoming the diametric opposite in most respects of the existing, somewhat anomic modal personality. This process required what Wallace (1956b) describes as "the association of rapid personality change with 'paranoid' cultural creativity" in the case of the leader-curer, and involved profound and dramatic behavioral transformations. Its effect on the Iroquois medical system, insofar as emotional disorder was concerned, transformed the aboriginal "cathartic" system of preventive and curative psychotherapy of the previous 200 or more years into a "control" system (Wallace 1958, 1959). The role of the religious leader-curer was that of a modified control agent, in which the major task was to repress traditional Dionysian-like, often violent types of activities and ceremonies which formerly had been expressed to appease dreams and "wishes of the soul" (Wallace 1958), and to create a type of modal personality and culture that would both preserve national cultural integrity and terminate internal and external conflict and frustration. The people did not wholly relinquish the old ethics and ceremonies but reworked them into a new synthesis in the Code of Handsome Lake. The role of curer was thus transformed and resynthesized.

Among the highly acculturated Cherokee Indians of the southeastern United States, Fogelson (1961) has found a strong persistence of traditional medical beliefs and practices compounded with many Christian elements, and the role of the conjurer-curer still surprisingly viable. The Cherokee syllabary, originally an instrument of progressive change in the early nineteenth century, has functioned as a conserving force, since it affords the conjurer a means of transcribing sacred formulas formerly transmitted orally through a priestly hierarchy. One result, strengthened by geographic isolation until comparatively recently, has been for an increase in secretiveness and interconjurer rivalry, and a rigidifying and freezing of practices and beliefs current in the early 1800s. As elsewhere, some functions and related artifacts have changed in modern times, with hunting, fishing, and agricultural magic fading out, but divination, sorcery, and curing by the conjurer persisting and being used simultaneously with scientific medicine by modern Cherokee. "The impact of Western medicine on Cherokee theory and practice can be seen to involve partial assimilation, the accentuation of differences where the two theories are irreconcilable, and an overall feeling that the two systems are complementary, rather than fundamentally contradictory" (Fogelson 1961:222).

A study of the medical system of a Philippine town (Lieban 1960, 1962) illustrates again the role of the curer as control agent and the process of cultural and role adaptation and resynthesis. Illnesses of supernatural origin remain in the province of the local curers, and while physicians may be consulted for illnesses of more earthly etiology, it is felt that treatment by them of supernaturally caused maladies actually may exacerbate them. The medical mythology is altered, so that the traditional chameleon-like, dangerous, illness-producing spirits called *ingkantos* that may be unpredictably invisible or exist in any organic or nonorganic form, including that of humans, have assumed new powers and functions.

> *To the people of the barrios, ingkantos appear to represent,* inter alia, *glittering and inaccessible wealth and power beyond the local community. The individual who sees and interacts with an ingkanto can, through fantasy, bring temptation within reach, or succumb to it. However, such experiences are considered hazardous and often are thought to lead to illness or death. This pattern of thought and behavior associated with beliefs about ingkantos and their influences appears to support social equilibrium in the community by dramatizing and reinforcing the idea that it is dangerous to covet alluring, but basically unattainable, wealth and power outside the barrios. In this way, the value of accepting the limitations of barrio life and one's part in it is emphasized. Furthermore, if someone has a relationship with a dazzling ingkanto and becomes ill, it is the manambal [indigenous healer], a symbol of barrio service and self-sufficiency, who restores the victim to health and reality (Lieban 1962:309).*

The local healer had always acted as an agent to control overly lusty appetites. To this traditional function is now added that of controlling the expression of newly acquired tastes as well. The healer represents the leveling pressures of the community so that "part of an individual's wealth is siphoned off to kinsmen and neighbors . . . . In this perspective illness attributed to *ingkantos* can be seen as helping to reconcile the individual to social reality by demonstrating that it is a mistake to overindulge personal desires" (1962:311). The healer frequently functions in a dual role as sorcerer and must be capable of the kind of cognitive adjustment that will smoothly incorporate both roles.

> *The contrastive roles of sorcerer and healer may be assimilated by scheduling each for the appropriate situation, whether that be service for health or service for "justice" [the rationalization underlying vengeance sorcery]. Even in situations where role contradictions are most sharply focused—when X, the healer, treats someone whose illness the same X, as sorcerer, was responsible for—the apparent discrepancy in behavior can be explained by resorting in turn to relevant values of the roles involved (Lieban 1960:132).*

This presents an interesting example of role adaptation of the curer, since he must operate in at least two different roles and clusters of ideas and behaviors that are cognitively dissonant (Rosenthal and Siegel 1959; Banton 1965:Ch. 7). He must adapt the apparently contradictory indigenous roles of healer and sorcerer while preserving and extending his status as healer and control agent in his contest with modern medicine.

In the southern Caribbean islands of Trinidad and Grenada, Mischel (1959) found that healing functions of the Shango cult curer operated within the context of a tendency for people to "affiliate themselves with several different religious organizations [and] many of them visit both the bush healer and the legitimate [*sic*] doctor in times of illness" (Mischel 1959:407). The Shango cult is itself "an amalgam of old Yoruba beliefs and New World Roman Catholicism" (1959:408), and cult leader-healers derive their powers directly from the gods, but resort to medications and advice derived in part from older cult members and in part from such sources as Napoleon's *Book of Fate*, prayer books, the Bible, and the *Home Physician's Guide*. Scientifically trained physicians and clinics are over-burdened, refer patients in "severe mental stress" to mental hospitals, and tend to treat only physical complaints. By contrast, the cult healer will treat any type of ailment using differential diagnosis and therapy; where he fails after several attempts he will "often refer his patient to an older or generally more prestigeful leader" (1959:411), and where ills appear for which he recognizes that the cult treatment has no cure, fractured limbs for example, he will refer the patient to a physician.

In Trinidad the physician feels modern medical facilities are available, dismisses the Shango healer as pagan, and will not refer patients to him. But in Grenada, with inadequate medical facilities, the physician frequently refers psychic or psychosomatic disorders to a cult curer. From the viewpoint of the people, the modern physician is perceived as a person of a different social class and culture whose financial and social prestige and technical abilities are recognized, but not his scientific knowledge. The "bush" healer is seen as a trustworthy sharer of one's own culture, with a direct tie to the spirit world, and a broad range of curing powers. The patient may be a passive participant in the curing process, and does not have to try to recover as is required of the European or American sick role (Parsons 1951; Parsons and Fox 1952). Especially in the case of lower-class Negroes whose channels of social advancement are blocked, the sick role becomes a source of social recognition, and "the longer the illness, the broader the symptoms, the more the patient may gain in the way of attention and unquestioning acceptance of his limitations with respect to work and other duties" (Mischel 1959:417). The indigenous curer thus serves, in contrast to the Philippine case, not so much to dampen newly acquired appetites as to assuage them in acceptable and unpunishing ways. And he assumes the major responsibility in the therapeutic relationship.

In Southern Ghana, despite some utilization of Western medicine and hospitals, indigenous healers are handling the bulk of ailments, physical and mental, in all social classes, and a differentiation cannot be made between literate and illiterate (presumably more and less acculturated) patients, either in kinds of medical problems or frequency of use of native curers. These inferences derive from a study by Jahoda (1961) and are strengthened because of the care with which he investigated sociocultural background factors of the clientele, as well as the nature of presenting symptoms and complaints. More men than women seem to consult and utilize services of indigenous healers, probably because the brunt of acculturative pressures is felt most poignantly in the demands placed on male role performance, and channels of social mobility and role enhancement are more open to men than to women. While complaints of a group of mental hospital patients contained a frequent overlay of "magical" problems such as "accidental contact with dangerous 'juju,' " most emotional problems centered around interpersonal conflicts at home and at work that seem directly related to the acculturative impact on role requirements.

Jahoda's study of 315 adult cases that were handled by his five healer informants reveals that 54 percent dealt with physical complaints of which more than half were concerned with venereal disease and gynecological problems, 12 percent were classified as "mental," 18 percent as "job, love, and marriage," and 16 percent as "protection and ritual (4)." It could be speculated that a large proportion of the latter two categories would be looked upon as emotional disturbance by Western-trained psychiatrists. The majority of cases under "job, love and marriage" concern problems connected with social and occupational mobility (5).

In addition to traditional healers, a new type has emerged "involving the adoption of some of the external trappings of the Western medical man and pharmacist" (Jahoda 1961:254), who dispenses herbal remedies in an affectively neutral manner and tends not to become as closely involved with the patient as the traditional healer. Furthermore, a number of healing churches have sprung up that cater to, and recruit on the basis of, a broad range of illnesses summarized by Jahoda as "barrenness, sickness, difficulties in life, worry caused by witches" (Jahoda 1961:255), and which approach the role of the traditional healer in the intensity and closeness of the therapist-patient relationship.

It is not clear whether these healing churches are to be placed in the same category as the shrines studied by Field (1960), but if we can assume that they are, then these instrumentalities are handling most illnesses in rural Ghana. A total of twenty-nine shrines were included in Field's study in the Ashanti area of Ghana alone, and these did not represent the total. The shrine priests are licensed by the government as "private practitioners of native medicine." On the basis of government registration records, Field estimated "at least ten thousand native practitioners in Ghana, *excluding* the Northern Territories" (Field 1960:91n), and these healing agencies are "seething with vitality whereas all the ancient supernatural sanctions are moribund . . ." (1960:87) (6).

Among the Fanti of Southern Nigeria, Christensen (1959) found that healer-priests still played a crucial and viable role, though many role modifications were taking place under the impact of European religion, education, and economics, with consequent weakening of indigenous religion, kinship, and family structure. Christensen feels that acculturation has resulted in a steep increase in anxiety, though not necessarily mental illness, among the Fanti, the individual and group being torn between the new and the old.

There has been an increasing emphasis on aids and nostrums to meet the needs of the modern world. Traditional charms to aid the traveler are now used by drivers and passengers on lorries; one priest claimed that he provided

*a charm to make people invisible to the police; a medicine formerly used to
"tie the tongue" of an opponent in a dispute heard in the traditional manner
before a chief is sometimes used by the plaintiff or defendant in adjudication
before the government court; students request assistance to develop acumen
or pass an examination; and one deity was reported to be particularly efficacious in causing the football teams from other towns to stumble when playing
the home team (Christensen 1959:272).*

Christensen also includes similar changes in the economic, political, and
technological spheres with respect to priestly medical functions. And among the
Fanti, as among the Ashanti, new shrine cults have arisen with healing as a major
function.

Alland's (1970) investigation of the Abron medical system and its several
curing roles compared their fate *vis-a-vis* Western medical practitioners. Major
Abron curing roles are those of the nonprofessional curer, essentially a lay herbalist
and user of charms; the *kparese,* a priest with powerful magico-religious curing
functions, who operates both as diviner-diagnostician who may refer a diagnosed
patient to a specialist, and as healer; the *sise,* a secular curer, employing magical and
empirical techniques, standing "halfway between the nonprofessional curer and the
kparese" (Alland 1970:167), working in symbiotic complementarity with the
kparese since the *sise* is not trained in divining and depends upon the *kparese*
for referrals; and the *sogo,* a Moslem sorcerer who is sometimes used and usually
feared. Facing this indigenous array of healers stand the Western trained physician,
few in number, not always accessible; the *médecin africain,* Africans with a two-
year special course in medicine at the University of Dakar, more numerous and
more accessible; the nurse, frequently accessible but with very limited training and
competence; and the missionary doctor. To the Abron, the *médecin africain,* the
physician, and the nurse are all classed as "doctor" which "further dilutes the
doctor role in the eyes of his Abron patient" (1970:178). The more analogous and
viable indigenous roles are those of the *sise* and *kparese,* the former because his
approach to medicine is similar to the Western approach, the latter because he is, as
the missionary doctor, priest, and curer rolled into one. Thus the *kparese* actually
may use the *médecin africain* and Western physician for referrals, but he feels
understandably threatened by the missionary, "a conflict," says Alland, "the
missionary welcomes." The Abron will use Western practitioners if available, but
do not hesitate to use their own practitioners, and, for magically-caused or prolonged illnesses, prefer them.

In the face of incessant pressures of immigration and social-cultural change,
the healing role of the Yemenite Jewish *mori* persists, though in a somewhat
narrowed orbit (Hes 1964). For centuries he functioned as "a teacher, a judge,
a religious leader, a ritual slaughterer, and a healer" (1964:364) but as the Jews of
Yemen slowly and resistantly adapted to life in Israel, with a curtailing of the traditionally authoritarian father's role (and expansion of the social importance of
wives and children), as schools displaced his role as teacher, courts took over his
function as judge, and physicians and clinics his role as healer, he adapted to these

losses, while maintaining his traditional roles as healer of supernaturally-caused disease, especially mental illness, and as counselor in times of emotional stress and social uncertainty. Indeed in these roles he has maintained his community status and not only older Yemenites but even acculturated, educated younger ones continue to use him to help cure emotional stress, or resort to him when the ministrations of medical psychiatry have failed. As Hes (1964:382) states it, "Although stripped of many of his traditional functions, the mori in Israel still provides an important source of psychotherapeutic help for persons suffering from emotional problems and troubles in living. This kind of help is adapted specifically to the needs of his fellow men and could not be easily supplied in more effective ways from any other source." Surrounded by ways of life they do not fully prefer and economic and social discrimination, the Yemenite Jews cling to their traditional beliefs, and only the *mori* understands them and knows how to negotiate the believer back to health within their terms.

Attenuated Curing Roles

As the powerful scientific medical and economic system spreads its influence, the curer may choose to continue in his traditional role and ignore the attrition in clientele due to competitive services. This implies, in effect, his voluntary acceptance of diminished prestige because he now yields his influence to more powerful competitors that threaten to render his own role completely obsolete. The social position of a Tuscarora curer with whom I lived was in part anchored to the fact that he was a clan chief and member of the tribal council (Landy 1958) and in part to the fact that he still prepared his remedies and performed his treatments, not only for many Indians, but for middle- and lower-class Whites from Niagara Falls and Buffalo. He charged modest amounts for his potions and services and did not depend upon them for a living (his wife owned a small store on the reservation) but he had resigned himself to only a moderate amount of prestige, no special powers beyond those of diagnosis and prescription, and to the reality of the state health clinic on the reservation and the physicians and hospitals in the city. He expressed deep discouragement over his inability to interest a younger man to train as his successor and predicted that the traditional role of curer would terminate with his death.

Among the Anang, an Ibibio group of southeastern Nigeria (Messenger 1959), traffic is heavy among native healers in patent medicines and other forms of treatment, but an increasing number of persons are visiting physicians and hospitals where, paradoxically, treatment is less expensive than among indigenous curers. Anang women, attracted by efficient obstetrical services, preceded men in changing their medical allegiance. Here the traditional curer would seem not to have been able effectively to adapt his role, and perhaps the most prevalent form of therapy is the sale of commercial remedies.

Bantu curers in South Africa of a variety of types, all of whom are called *izinyanga,* were studied in Durban and Johannesburg by Bloom (1964) and compared with lay Africans of varying degrees of literacy and urbanization. As in the West Indies, they refer difficult cases to presumably more qualified Bantu specialists, and as in many places, they handle a broad range of diseases, with special competence in the treatment of emotional and hysterical states. They were found to rely more heavily than most laymen on "traditional, hereditarian, magical explanations," and to serve as "a conservative force in African society and therefore as repositories of traditional beliefs" (Bloom 1964:66, 94). Bloom goes on to say, "The *izinyanga* respond to the pressures of urbanization largely by clinging to their traditional beliefs but also, paradoxically, by trying to incorporate into these certain elements derived from urban experience" (1964:69). Apartheid only seems to whet the appetites of the Bantu for Western ways and this author feels that as soon as racial restrictions are removed there will be "a complete assimilation of modern ideas and a withering away of traditional beliefs that are no longer functionally siginificant" (1964:94), and, one would conclude, consequent obsolescence of the traditional curer's role. Role adaptation here seems to have decreasing support because of rapidly changing beliefs among the laity and the curer's role is subject to much strain, uncertainty, and attenuation.

One type of parallel, but dependent, coexistence was the case of the Negro midwife in parts of the rural southern United States who took over many of the obstetrical accoutrements of the modern town physician, utilized his sponsorship as protection against the threat of dislicensing by public health agents, and for a long time enhanced and preserved her place in the indigenous social system (Mongeau, Smith, and Maney 1961). Her role after several decades, however, became weakened and decayed as recruiting into the apprenticeship system failed because younger female relatives acquired formal education and entered other occupations, as the older White town physicians who functioned as protectors and sanctioning agents died out, as contemporary physicians sought not to change but outlaw midwifery, and as hospitals and clinics grew in influence.

Still another type of marginal coexistence is the kind of parallel but competitive role of the subprofessional nurse or *tsukisoi* in Japan, a combination domestic and mother-figure who ministers to, and sleeps in with, the mental patient (Caudill 1961). Caudill sees the *tsukisoi* role as directly reflective of the mother's function in the Japanese family and social structure, as in conflict with the nurse and psychiatrist, though her role is legitimated by both professionals, as therapeutic but also possibly maltherapeutic, and probably slated for drastic change.

Emergent Curing Roles

While some curers have adapted their roles successfully to the demands of acculturation and others have become so battered as to be attenuated and in danger of extinction, the contact situation may stimulate new, emergent roles. This happened among the Manus, a technologically primitive people of New Guinea when first observed by Mead (1930), with no special curing roles who treated most injuries and illnesses by family members within the household but referred some to the "doctor boys" appointed by the administration of the Australian Trust Territory. By the time of Mead's (1961) restudy doctor boys were being used as agents of control by the central government, and the efforts of the charismatic, Western-oriented leader, Paliau, to encourage the use of modern medicine by setting up his own hospitals and "screening" presenting symptoms were interpreted by physicians and government officials as hiding patients and therefore "subversive" (Mead 1961:264-265). Nevertheless, some individuals had apparently become part-time local practitioners

> *who collect huge fees for using counter-magic. . . . The tendency to blame disease, whenever it is intractable, on a source wholly external to the society, and to reserve tractable and curable diseases for confession, reform, and medicine, may well grow. These attributions of sorcery to work boys from other areas are justified on the grounds that other peoples may not have "thrown everything away yet," and by the statements of the inability to help made by European physicians and employers who send hopeless cases home to their villages to die (1961:286).*

Thus, in a sociocultural system in which apparently there had been no traditional curing specialists, the impact of Western medicine in fact seemed to give rise to them. In this formerly preindustrial but rapidly acculturating society, medical system and curing role thus resemble only in part solutions reached in other spheres of culture. A new synthesis both of sociocultural system and of curing role begins to appear, with Western medicine fertilizing, rather than starving, the emerging practitioner's role.

Another new medical role, emerging side-by-side with both the still strong traditional curing roles on the one hand, and those of the scientific medical system on the other, is that the Navaho health worker or health visitor (Adair 1960; Adair and Deuschle 1957; Deuschle and Adair 1960; McDermott et al. 1960). This role was created by the Cornell University health project as a way of contacting isolated Navaho and mediating, linguistically and medically, between them and the clinic. The role seems to have fallen mainly to Navaho who were more or less marginal to local groups, either because of formal education and high aspiration levels, or because they had been away in White society and were out of touch with the native culture. Unfortunately we are not told whether the role was ever filled by indigenous curers, but it proved strategic in securing increased acceptance of modern medicine by the people.

A healer may invent or discover a revolutionary new medical method that places him in a potently competitive position *vis-a-vis* modern medicine. In McCorkle's (1961) brief study of chiropractic we learn that the method was discovered by one D. D. Palmer in rural Iowa in 1895. Palmer, "a sometime general storekeeper and magnetic healer," cured the hearing impairment of a man by snapping a displaced vertebra back into place. He extended this curing technique to others with great success, and thereby evolved a single-cause disease theory that all ailments are due to obstructions between the brain and body organs, the spine being the principal transmission tract. As McCorkle (1961:22) describes it,

> *Healing is by manual "adjustment" of the spine, supplemented by massage, and by advice as to diet and rest, the latter defined as proper amounts of sleep, not as taking to one's bed. All medicines are denounced as "drugs" and therapy may involve "withdrawal" from "drugs" formerly used by the patient. Surgery and preventive medicine are rejected as violations of the sanctity of the human body. Appeals, delivered verbally and through pamphlets written to relate chiropractic theory to specific diseases and ailments, are to the "common sense" of the mechanically minded Midwestern patient.*

The widespread and continued success of this emergent indigenous healer appears to be due to the precision with which he fitted his theory and practice into the existing social structure and value system. Especially in the Midwestern family-type farm, the major relevant characteristics are: extensive mechanization, frequent injuries, and "aches and pains" (perhaps related to working in all kinds of weather), work as a primary value, pragmatic world view (a thing is good if it works), deep belief in "the good work of God and in the sanctity of the human body," the healing power of the laying on of hands, and belief in natural remedies. The role of the chiropractor, therefore, has been not simply competitive, but parallel in its development and spread to modern medicine. McCorkle does not describe the prestige and power of these healers in their communities but it is likely they are rewarded with both trust and wealth.

Finally, we may see an instance of an emergent curing role that involves aspects and functions of several preceding roles, that of the Puerto Rican spiritist medium. Rogler and Hollingshead (1963) found widespread belief in spiritism and utilization of mediums in all urban social strata, being most pervasive in the lower class, and rationalized in scientific terms in the upper class. For the former, especially, beset by "the intimate trials, strife, and personal turmoil that enmesh the members of a socially and economically deprived stratum . . . its function is to discharge the tensions and anxieties generated in other areas of social life" (Rogler and Hollingshead 1961:654). These investigators believe that most lower-class schizophrenics will receive group therapy from a spiritist medium before, during, after, or instead of seeing a psychiatrist, and they see this emergent curing role in competition with modern medicine as having many assets.

> *In addition to the presumed advantages of group psychotherapy as practiced in clinical settings, spiritualist sessions are coterminous with the values, beliefs, aspirations, and problems of the participants. No discontinuity in social contacts is required for participation. Little social distance separates the afflicted person from the medium, but, in contrast, visiting a psychiatrist involves bringing persons together who are separated by a vast social gulf. The others in the session are often neighbors, and so the spiritualist and her followers form a primary group where problems are discussed in a convivial*

> *setting, classified, interpreted, and rendered understandable within a belief system that is accepted even by those who profess not to believe in it. . . . Participation in a spiritualist group serves to structure, define, and render behavior institutionally meaningful that is otherwise perceived as aberrant (1963:657-658).*

These authors claim that the spiritist also serves a protective function since going to a clinic or psychiatrist places the person in the category of *loco*, which is stigmatized and highly feared, while anyone may visit the medium regardless of the severity of his affliction (see also Landy 1965:42-44 passim; Seda Bonilla 1969).

Interpretation and Discussion

We have considered the role of the indigenous curer confronting the demands and possibilities of his own often rapidly changing society on the one hand, and those of the intrusive Western medical system on the other. Studies have been examined in many parts of the world in which Western beliefs, practices, and technology in medicine, as in most life-spheres, are impinging with ever-increasing velocity upon preindustrial societies. Used as a conceptual framework was Goode's theory of role strain from which I have derived the concept of role adaptation in order to consider the special instance of the curing role under acculturation and change. If the studies selected for analysis are partially representative of the world range of acculturation situations in which the traditional curing role is being critically confronted in some fashion, and I believe they may be, then we have presented a crude nonrandom sample of acculturative contexts and types of curing role adaptations.

In any society the process of healing involves to some degree what Freidson (1959, 1960, 1961b, 1970b) has conceptualized as the interaction of the lay referral system with the professional medical system. Freidson postulates that the process by which a case for curing reaches beyond the stage of home treatment involves a concentric series of decision-making diagnoses by the patient himself, by family members, friends, and then, in ever-widening circles of referral, various types of lay, religious, and medical agents. Even in New York City where Freidson's studies took place, the process could be short-circuited at the door of an indigenous ethnic curer before reaching a physician or clinic. Only at that point did the lay system come into contact with the professional medical system. The indigenous medical role may carry as much and at times more, power, prestige, and responsibility as the medical role in Western society (Sigerist 1951:161-180). Therefore the label of "professional" should not be confined to scientifically-trained personnel, though obviously the ideology, technology, and recruitment of personnel of scientific medicine are different in many respects from that of nonscientific medicine. In culture contact and change, then, the formulations of Freidson can be extended to include two potentially contesting medical systems in contact with each other and with the indigenous lay referral system.

We have seen that the indigenous medical system frequently contains its own professional referral system, as in the instance of the Ecuadorian urban folk curer, the Bantu *izinyanga,* the Abron *kparese,* the Navaho hand trembler, or the West Indian Shango religious curers, and that sometimes the indigenous professional referral system maintains a degree of cooperative interaction with the scientific professional referral system, and sometimes it does not, as in the relatively independent activities of the Yemenite *mori,* the Japanese *tsukisoi,* and the curers in the Leyte fishing village. Such factors as numbers, cost, and location of Western medical services, as well as ability to recognize and tolerate the indigenous medical system, undoubtedly set the limits and conditions permitting such cooperative interaction. Primarily it is the local curer who borrows elements from Western medicine rather than vice versa, although many "primitive" botanicals have been incorporated or synthesized.

In his role adaptations to culture change, the traditional healer not only incorporates, but elaborates, Western elements. Furthermore, resynthesis flows in the other direction when customary ceremonies and fetishes become used for new functions, especially to relieve some of the tensions and anxieties of acculturative pressures, as in West Africa, for example, the Fanti, Anang Ibibio, and Ashanti.

The indigenous curing role may exist in complementarity to the scientific medical system in a variety of ways, from almost complete isolation to almost total interaction. In endeavoring to strengthen his role relationships, the traditional curer may make grudging or happy accommodations to as many Western medical elements as he feels he must. Generally this means, as in most instances cited herein, that he becomes, or remains, an advocate of conservative beliefs, and if change is sharply accelerated, may find himself perhaps fatally lagging his lay fellows. When this occurs, his role adaptations have become ineffective since the basis for his prescribed role relationships is broken, and it is likely that his role is slated for oblivion, as in the instance of the Tuscarora curer. Furthermore, even if a dependent relationship is worked out under the protection of the scientific medical system, as the Southern rural Negro midwife had evolved under the town physician, when the external supports are removed (the dying out of the older physicians as patrons, the attack of public health and medical authorities) and the internal means of recruitment to the role dry up (young women preferring other careers), the role soon crumbles away.

Another possibility is that at the bidding of the donor culture (Manus doctor boys, Navaho health workers) a new medical or quasi-medical role is created, usually in order to bring about change and acceptance more quickly and efficiently, though, as among the Manus, new indigenous healers also may arise. Still another possibility is that a new role is created, due to the ingenuity of native practitioners or laymen (Midwest U.S. chiropractor, Puerto Rican spiritist, many varieties in urban Bogota), which operates completely independently of, and offers vigorous competition to, the scientific medical system. I do not know whether the point has been investigated, except by Adair (1960), but it is likely that such powerful, emergent curing professions contain many practitioners who utilize this occupational channel to circumvent blocked mobility, and that some of these individuals possess capabilities that, given education and training, might equip them for entering the scientific medical system.

Although he may be a change agent and innovator, the effect of any of the role adaptations we have cited nevertheless places the traditional curer in the position of a cultural conservative. Not only is he a conserver of old ways, but his social control functions in a situation of culture change seem largely to be those of assuaging or holding the lid on rising aspirations and containing the discontent of his people, as the Filipino *barrio* and Shango curers. This may not be his intent, but it appears to be a consequent of his role imperatives. Hunt (1968) has made a strong case for the basically conservative role functions of the cultural broker in Mexico.

> *We attempt to document the following propositions: (a) the mestizos in the rural areas of Oaxaca form an important group of cultural brokers [Hunt uses the Spanish term* agentes *as a preferred equivalent]; (b) these brokers act mainly as promoters of the status quo, that is, they are conservatives and do not induce change in the indigenous segment [the Indian culture]; and (c) the functions of these mestizo brokers are not so much to maintain open interaction among the [cultural] segments as to preserve cultural distance (Hunt 1968:600; translation mine).*

In a sense, the curer, even more than such cultural brokers as teachers, entrepeneurs, and politicians, has a crucial stake in the maintenance of the indigenous culture, for the more closely it begins to approximate the donor culture, the more vulnerable his role becomes. Adaptation for role preservation consists in selecting only those changes that will preserve his role while at the same time minimally disturbing his already intruded culture. A possible exception might be the case of the leader-curer Handsome Lake in the revitalization of nineteenth century Iroquois culture. Even here, however, he was interested not so much in changing his culture to approximate White, Christian, capitalist culture as in remaking it in an image that would allow a greater probability of survival against the thrusts of White society while at the same time strengthening those components which had become frayed under acculturative pressures, and returning to his people a sense of pride and ethnic identity (Wallace 1966:31-33, 211-213 passim, 1961b).

On the psychological level it may be assumed that if role adaptation to cultural stress is to be achieved, it must be accompanied by cognitive change or by what Wallace (1956a, 1956b, 1956c, 1957, 1961a, 1961b, 1961c, 1966) terms "mazeway resynthesis." Depending upon the pace of culture change, the curer may have to undergo continual adaptation, not only socially in seeking constant realignment of interpersonal relationships, but psychologically in assimilating or redirecting the ever-increasing flow of new ideas, values, and technology, in learning rewarding paths in the changing external maze, and in repressing some paths in his internal mazeway while adding on others. His personality inventory would include a tolerance of cognitive dissonance, a capacity to "compartmentalize" (Goode 1960) dissonant values and role requirements. In applying his theory to the case of the individual facing a suddenly catastrophic change in his environment following such disasters as tornadoes, floods, fire, or bombardment, Wallace (1957:26) says

There is first of all a considerable reluctance ("drag") to changing the old way, because of its symbolic satisfying value. As the old way, however, leads to less and less reward, and as frustrations and disappointments accumulate, there are set in motion various regressive tendencies, which conflict with the established way and are inappropriate to the existing maze. The individual can act to reduce his discomfort by several means: by learning a new way to derive satisfaction from the maze; by encapsulating the regressive strivings in a fantasy system; and by reifying to himself his current way and maze, regarding a major portion of it as dead, and selecting (from either traditional or foreign regions, or both) part of the existing mazeway as vital, meanwhile mourning the abandoned (or abandoning) portion.

The traditional curer who achieves a viable role adaptation not only retains the indigenous community as his major membership group but also retains it as his basic reference group, as in the examples of the curers of Sherupur and the Cherokee conjurer-curer. It is from the culture of his membership group that he draws his sanction as healer, and from the maintenance of its values and practices that he retains the legitimation of his role. We may speak of the scientific medical system as representing only his secondary reference culture, since his identification with its values is partial and he draws upon its practices only insofar as his clientele may demand them or he may safely select those that augment his therapeutic repertory without diminishing his charisma. He may even enhance his diagnostic capabilities by utilizing the scientific system for referral of those cases he clearly recognizes to be beyond his capabilities. Insofar as such cases may be identifiably terminal, the apparent failure of the modern medical system to alter the course of death actually may enhance his position in the local community while discrediting his competitor.

The curer's status does become attenuated, however, when the expectations of his community are such that the technology, if not the values, of scientific medicine is perceived by them as so clearly superior that they distinctly prefer it to their own, as the Anang women who prefer scientific obstetrics, or the Tuscarora who increasingly use the state clinic. Role strain and role conflict follow, and the curer's status may become so hopelessly compromised that role adaptation is impossible of fulfillment and the status of curer becomes marginal and headed for extinction. Since only viable or partly viable curing roles are most readily perceived by the anthropologist, we do not, unfortunately, have very much or very useful data on circumstances under which the role becomes marginal or obsolete, and this process is little understood. I suggest the following alternatives (and others could be hypothesized as well):

  1. The curer accepts a marginal status, though perhaps maintaining some recognition and gratification through hostile means, such as sorcery.
  2. The curer attempts to denigrate scientific medicine by associating it

with an oppressor group. If this occurs in a period of rising nationalism, his efforts may succeed since his medicine may not seem as potent as scientific medicine, but it will be associated with "good" values and the other with "bad" ones.

3. The curer surrenders or radically modifies his status and attempts to capture a substitute status, perhaps even as an adjunct to the Western physician or clinic. This has occurred with mutual benefit in Western Nigeria where native healers may be called in as adjunctive therapists in difficult cases of psychoneuroses (Lambo 1956; Leighton, Lambo, et al. 1963).

4. The curer becomes unable, or unwilling, to adapt to a marginal role and his sufferings from status deprivation may drive him not only to alienation from his traditional role but from the society which has rejected that role. The result may be behavioral deviance, including the possibility of neurosis or psychosis, or even self-exile as he in turn rejects the society. At least in part these alternatives, and others as well, could be cast into the framework of alternative modes of deviance suggested by Merton (1957) in his essay on "Social Structure and Anomie," though I suspect the model would have to be modified.

As for the new emergent curing or quasi-medical roles, it may be predicted that they also are likely to be thrust into competitive stress and strain with their analogues within the Western medical system, especially such paramedical roles as those of nurse, attendant, medical technician, etc. Structural strains certainly seem characteristic of all paramedical roles in Western medical systems. In urban settings where population size and heterogeneity encourage many variations in role performance and technique, curers may compete with each other (Press 1971).

A well-established general principle of sociocultural change is that those values and practices will be most easily transferred which are most consonant with the ideology and behavioral standards of the host culture. Proceeding from this premise, Alland (1970:157 passim) hypothesizes that those impinging new roles for which "analogue roles" exist in the host culture will be most easily accepted. His example, to which we earlier alluded, was that of the missionary doctor and his analogue, the Abron *kparese.*

The process of change is influenced not only by the relationship between new elements and existing theories and the reward value of certain behavior, but also by similarities and differences between role systems in donor and receptor populations. When analogous roles exist in two different behavioral systems, change need only involve a shift in the content of existing roles. When no such analogues exist, change may require the adoption of an entirely new role or set of roles. What I am suggesting is that analogue roles act as templets for behavior and have the effect of facilitating and directing change (Alland 1970:157-158).

The *kparese* was most threatened by the missionary doctor's role and seemed most vulnerable to displacement precisely because his role was pervasive, encompassing "the entire religious life of the Abron" and not only the medical system, so that the missionary is predicted by Alland to "have much greater success [than the secular physician] in the long run in the introduction of Western medical practice in Abron culture" (1970:178). Although the *sise* (secular curer) provides an analogue to the secular physician's role, his role is likely to be retained since it is semantically classed with that of the doctor, *médicin africain,* and nurse as "doctor" (see earlier discussion), and many critical substances considered essential in curing are not obtainable in the Western medical system. However, Alland does not suggest that the *kparese's* role is slated for complete obsolescence and one could wonder what might happen to a *kparese* who adopted Christianity and parts of the Western physician's technical and pharmacological repertory. Perhaps it should also be assumed that those roles that provide no, or a negative, analogue to the Western medical roles stand the greatest chance of survival and are least in need of change in the interest of adaptation, for example, that of the Moslem sorcerer.

Press (1969a) suggests in the instance of the cultural broker role of a teacher in Yucatan that his role-set is strengthened as it embodies larger numbers of mutually dependent roles from both cultures, thus rendering his "total configuration" "the more ambiguous" (1964:214). Press seems to be saying that in such a case role viability, and by implication role adaptability, are strengthened by the incumbent taking on visible, essential, and needed roles or role characteristics, of both the host and the contacted culture. He suggests that "As the bicultural passes from one behavioral complex or role-set to another . . . it is possible that he is clearly identified at one time or place, and viewed ambiguously at another" (1969a:216) and that this very ambiguity increases role adaptability. Thus, insofar as the indigenous curer attempts to innovate, adopting elements of Western medicine, he increases the ambiguity of his role but also the possibility of its adaptation to the acculturation situation. Indeed he could increase what is already fundamentally ambiguous in his traditional role, since it has been recognized that the medical role in Western medicine (Davis 1960; Parsons 1951), and, I assume, in non-Western medicine, is fraught with ambiguity precisely because the healer in any society deals with "real" uncertainty in scientific and clinical knowledge, with the uses to which uncertainty is put by the healer and his patient, and by the fact that such uncertainty derives from the basic ambiguities inherent in all serious phenomena that threaten life, such as disease and illness.

Associated with the uncertainty and ambiguity of the phenomena with which the curer deals are the factors of unpredictability and uncontrollability. As Aberle (1966:221 passim) has shown

> *it is through the unpredictable and uncontrollable that man most experiences power, whether in the world of nature or of man, that he endows with power that which or those who help him cope with the helplessness that results from these experiences, and . . . due consideration of amounts and kinds of un-*

predictability and uncontrollability may help to order a variety of beliefs and acts relating to supernatural power.

The curer's role is endowed with power precisely because it stands at the interstices of religion, magic, and the social system. As Aberle (1966:228-229) further states:

Magic is a technique used to try to achieve empirical ends when empirical techniques provide inadequate prediction and control; religion is action that deals with the inevitable, unpredictable, and uncontrollable gap between the normative and the existential order; charismatic figures are unpredictable, do things other people cannot do, and force decisions in spite of lack of information; divinatory techniques use the unpredictable to predict the unpredictable.

As the course of disease becomes more controllable (prevention, public health measures), more predictable (medical intervention with miracle drugs, scientific surgery) and less uncertain, the curer's role faces its greatest challenge. Its survival, of course, is heavily dependent in the acculturation situation on the ability of its incumbents to increment their power through adoption of what might, in indigenous terms, seem to be Western "magic." But he soon learns that most serious diseases may still be essentially unpredictable and uncontrollable, and in this basic uncertainty lies the probability of successful role adaptations. For he should come to know that uncertainty is often no less for his scientific competitors than for himself.

There are many relevant questions that could not be handled in this paper. Thus, it is apparent that the ultimate usefulness of the notion of role adaptation will depend upon the clarity with which future investigators may be able to define the social and cultural conditions under which role adaptation will succeed or fail. The relationship of this concept to new ways of conceptualizing the notion of role, for example in the works of Goodenough (1965) and Keesing (1970), should be examined. I am aware, for example, of the point that both of these scholars make regarding the social identity component of role, and the fact that, because a role is operative mainly in terms of the various alters with which a particular ego interacts, it is misleading to speak of *the* curing role, or even *a* curing role. A curer necessarily enacts his role differently with each class of alters (men, women, children, nurses, other curers, chiefs, etc.). Another important factor completely ignored here is that of the "impression management" aspects of role, since, as Goffman (1959) has shown, this is basic to defining and understanding the way in which roles are in fact effectively negotiated.

The relationship of role adaptation to the notion of cultural broker also needs further exploration. Most, though not all, instances of cultural brokers, especially in Mexico (Wolf 1956a; Hunt 1968; Press 1969), are those of bicultural Mestizos, who in a basic sense stand outside the indigenous (in this case, Indian) culture, while the curer is indigenous to his cultural system. Furthermore, especially for shamans and other religious curers (some are mainly empirical lay practitioners), there is a strong element of a calling and of religiosity in the curing role which is of course completely absent from those teachers, entrepreneurs, and politicians who frequently are the focus of analyses in terms of the cultural broker concept. It is also clear that field studies in depth of role adaptation of the curer confronting the Western medical system need to be undertaken to a much greater extent than they have been heretofore.

In his essay on role Southall (1959:17) has said. "What is required is a type of theoretical formulation applicable to the analysis of highly heterogenous situations, influenced alike by the ubiquitous international exchange economy and by the presence of persons from markedly contrasting social matrices, Western and industrial on the one hand, nonliterate, peasant and 'folk' on the other." I propose role adaptation as one such formulation. As I have attempted to use it here, I believe it permits the possibility of more fully understanding the changing role of the traditional curer in the confrontation between the "markedly contrasting social matrices" mentioned by Southall. I suggest also it may be applied usefully as well to other changing roles in traditional societies moving toward industrialization and what many, perhaps ethnocentrically, have called "modernization."

Notes

1. A quite different version of this paper was presented to the Society for Applied Anthropology, San Juan, Puerto Rico in 1964. The present one is the last of many redrafts since that time. Oral presentation of an early draft benefited greatly from comments of my former colleagues at the University of Pittsburgh, especially Leonard Kasdan (now Michigan State University), Edward A. Kennard, George Peter Murdock, Arthur Tuden, Alexander Spoehr, and Otto von Mering (now University of Florida), and a sociological colleague, Paul N. Geisel (now University of Texas, Dallas). I am also grateful to Golamreza Fazel (University of Massachusetts, Boston) and to Robert Hunt (Brandeis University) for calling my attention to the citations by Barth and Belshaw (Fazel) and by Banton and Keesing (Hunt). Responsibility herein is entirely mine.

2. For example, in such complex preindustrial societies as those of ancient India and China, huge areas of culture were highly technological, as the superbly developed Indian surgery and the Chinese irrigation systems, but they rested upon a substructure of essentially empiricist and spiritual beliefs regarding the nature of man and the universe.

3. Polgar (1963:411-412) has suggested this crucial fact from another point of view when he defines four fallacies of Western health personnel in contacts with non-Western societies. One is "the fallacy of the empty vessels," that is, the assumption that new values and technology are to be poured into the "empty" receptacles of the cultural receivers, oblivious to "the fact that clients already have established health customs."

4. I made these extrapolations by converting percentages in Table 1 of Jahoda (1961:248) back into whole numbers and taking means of the rows.

5. Scotch's (1963:49) review of this study includes a misinterpretation of Jahoda's conclusions when he says, "These findings contrast strongly with the expectations of experts in the area of mental health who maintain that rapid culture change is a fertile area in the pathogenesis of psychopathology (e.g., Leighton)." Jahoda does not question this assumption and indeed his data would lead to the conclusion that Ghanaians under acculturative stress experience psychic disturbances severe enough to be diagnosed as mental illness in Western terms, though we have no evidence from any study that these are

more, less, or the same in quantity and distribution as before the contact situation. Scotch's (1963:49) point that "The traditional healers, as well as the healing churches, function to prevent occurrence of serious breakdowns, and thus keep the mental hospitals, which Jahoda also studied, from being overwhelmed by a flood of cases," indicates that Field's (1960) inference of a heavy rate of mental illness in Ghana *may* be correct, but see note 6.

6. Bohannan (1961) has praised Field's study as "far and away the best book on mental illness among Africans." While in many respects this may be true by comparison with previous studies, I find myself, with a few exceptions, in agreement with most of the criticisms of Field's work voiced by Opler (1963), and I hope that the book will not be accepted uncritically by anthropologists. The case histories and description of healing shrines on the whole are excellent, but the book suffers from the absence of a summary chapter so that the findings are not brought together, from a vagueness on Field's part in identifying the sources of many of her findings and assertions, and from the frequent admixture of unsubstantiated generalizations and evaluative statements regarding Africans and Europeans. The following is not untypical:

In our own society there has always been a proportion of good-for-nothings—tramps, work-shy, slum-makers, poachers and (abroad) beachcombers and "poor whites," unemotionally resisting all redemptive efforts or, if they accept it, always shambling back to their old ways. It is now recognized that most of them are either mentally defective or schizophrenic. In the East (I do not know the East) I suppose their counterparts become beggars. In West Africa they stay with their kinsmen, drink palm-wine and trap "bush-meat" (Field 1960:447).

John M. McCullough

Human ecology, heat adaptation, and belief systems: the hot-cold syndrome of Yucatan [1]

The importance of thermal stress to man is based on well-known facts. For example, man's normal cranial temperature of 37°C is less than 5°C below a lethal limit; yet men live and work in many world areas where heat stress may push the cranial temperature toward the lethal limit. As part of a larger study of responses to thermal stress in Ticul, Yucatan, Mexico (McCullough 1972) some time was spent collecting data concerning these responses.

Climatic conditions in rural Yucatan can reach a daily high of 38° or 39°C in the shade during the dry season, with radiant temperatures commonly exceeding

Reprinted by permission of the *Journal of Anthropological Research*, Vol. 29, No. 1, pp. 32-36, 1973.

60°C. The ensuing wet season usually cools to a daily high of only 36°C but with moderate to high relative humidities. In this climate men have grown maize and other staple crops, built pyramids, and now live a peasant life economically based upon hand methods of cultivation. Obviously, heat stress is an important factor of Yucatec life. Morphological and physiological factors of adaptation to heat in Yucatan have been discussed elsewhere (McCullough 1972), and attention here is drawn to behavioral adaptation to heat as influenced by a series of local beliefs, or rules, known as the "hot-cold" (2) syndrome (Currier 1966).

The "hot-cold" syndrome is essentially a categorization of objects and processes, especially those related to foods and health, into "hot" and "cold" types, with an insistence on balancing the "hot" and "cold" in the body. The syndrome is known for many world areas and has been viewed by various cultural anthropologists as health-related (Bonfil Batalla 1962), a physiological principle (Redfield and Villa Rojas 1934), a cultural rationalization of psychological reality (Currier 1966), or simply as a cultural and historical phenomenon (Foster 1953, 1960; Rubel 1960; Ingham 1970). I suggest here that the syndrome is an important factor in behavioral adaptation to heat among the Maya of Yucatan, even if native rationalizations for the behavior do not appear to have a physiological base. A cultural description of the "hot-cold" syndrome among the Yucatec Maya is given elsewhere (McCullough 1969; Bonfil Batalla 1962; Redfield and Villa Rojas 1934) and will not be repeated here.

Central to the "hot-cold" syndrome are the concepts of "hot," "cold," *cuch,* and balance of forces. However, as Ingham (1970) insightfully points out, "hot" and "cold" elude definition. They do not directly relate to temperature conditions measured by conventional thermometry, as perusal of food categories discloses (Redfield and Villa Rojas 1934; Bonfil Batalla 1962). Nor do they relate to a culturally definable "coldness" or "hotness." Reasons for a particular categorization rest upon individual perception, for instance, of how a particular food "feels" in the body. Tubers are "cold" foods because they feel "cold" and because they grow in the ground in "cold" soil.

The term *cuch* really has two meanings. People are thought to have a *cuch,* or thermal set-point, and as such are intrinsically "hot" (*chokó u cuch*) or "cold" (*siis u cuch*). However, this set-point is thought to vary during the day so that a man is temporarily "colder" in the morning, or he can be made "colder" by contact with "cold" substances or by simple inactivity. This second use of the term *cuch* is closer to the physiological meaning of the term, "load," as in heat load. The load must not be too great; a balance is absolutely essential. Becoming too "hot" or too "cold" may lead to illness and possibly to death because the body cannot tolerate imbalance. The balance is maintained by regulation of activity level and by contact with various substances, including food and water.

The importance of the "hot-cold" syndrome in behavioral adaptation to heat stress rests upon three basic rules; together, they form the conceptual background for the behavioral adaptation. These are:

1. The water-salt rule. Men working in the fields are thought to have a very "hot" *cuch* from the sun and the work itself. The inevitable thirst requires water, but water, a "cold" substance, is thought to be dangerous. Taking a small amount of salt, a "hot" substance, with the water is felt to diminish the dangerous effect of the "cold" water on the man and to result in a more balanced *cuch*.

2. The cold exposure rule. Work and the sun make the *cuch* "hot." A man returning from the fields is therefore "hot" and sweaty, and thought to be surrounded by disease-bearing winds (*ik'*) that abound in the woods. He must sit down outside the house in the house-lot to "cool" after returning. As he "cools" and the sweat evaporates, the "cold" winds are thought to leave. By entering the house immediately, where it is "cold," the man himself would sicken and bring the winds, and illness, to other members of his family. Likewise, while cooling outside the house, neither liquids nor a shower, both "cold," may be taken, for they would make the man susceptible to the winds.

3. Pacing rule. All work is consciously paced to avoid overexertion and overheating; these would imbalance the *cuch* to the "hot" end of the dichotomy. Men tend to pace themselves by time and distance, using familiar landmarks; a *legua* (league) is an hour's walk and 4 kilometers. This pace can be maintained for 2 to 4 hours at a time, even in the rainy season. While walking, men are cautioned not to stop and rest lest the *ik'* (winds) cling to the "hot" sweaty body and bring illness. Work in the fields is paced on an individual basis. In one way or another most farmers have worked in fields since early childhood and have developed their own pace in cutting, planting, weeding, and harvesting. Only the most general of rules is followed, allowing individuality in expression; avoidance of overexertion and overheating is primary.

These rules may be considered descriptions of prophylactic measures against dangerous effects of heat. Most of the common, medically-defined heat disorders discussed by Leithead and Lind (1964) are uncomfortable rather than dangerous. Illnesses such as heat syncope, heat edema (deck ankles, Colombo Flop), rolling mill gonorrhea, and tropical neurasthenia most often afflict the unacclimatized; rarely serious, they are generally self-terminating. However, there are two disorders found in many tropical or industrial settings which are excruciatingly painful and can be fatal even with adequate medical care. These disorders are heat cramps and heatstroke (heat hyperpyrexia).

Heat cramps are characterized by painful spasms of voluntary muscles following hard physical labor in a hot environment (Leithead and Lind 1964:170-177). Onset is sudden, and it generally strikes the acclimatized, especially manual laborers. Cramps begin after midday, seldom before. The necessary prodromal circumstances for severe muscle cramps are salt depletion with inadequate replacement, accompanied by adequate or excessive water intake, or water intoxication, with extracellular fluid at normal levels or above. Other factors which may precipitate cramps are exposure to cold air or cold water, as in a shower, and drinking cold liquids after work or other heavy exercise. The most effective treatment for heat cramps is intravenous injection of saline or, lacking that, oral administration of salt. Heat cramps are most easily prevented by increased salt intake or reduction of nonsalted liquids during work, and by restrictions immediately after work on exposure to cold surroundings or foods.

Heatstroke is a state of thermoregulatory failure, usually of sudden onset, following exposure to a hot environment. It is characterized by disturbance of the central nervous system, a rectal temperature above 40.6°C and often anhidrosis (Leithead and Lind 1964:195-236). Heatstroke is fatal without adequate and prompt medical attention. The three most common predisposing conditions appear to be cessation of sweating, continuation of manual labor in excessively hot conditions, and failure to appreciate the dangers of heat stress. Treatment of heatstroke consists of administering ice baths, ice-water baths, water or alcohol spray, and ice-water enemas. These techniques are dependent upon rapid transportation and modern medical facilities only recently available anywhere. The most efficient methods of preventing heatstroke are adequate fluid and electrolyte intake, regulation of exercise level to within tolerable limits for the environmental conditions, and recognition of the seriousness of environmental conditions (Minard *et al.* 1957).

It is apparent that the preventive measures against both these incapacitating or lethal disorders coincide well with the "hot-cold" syndrome rules. Yucatec farmers are cautioned to take water while working, but only with salt, to avoid exposure to "cold" liquids or "cold" ambient conditions for a while after work, and to pace themselves to avoid overexertion and overheating. Although specific physiological experiments must be done in the future to empirically test the effectiveness of the "hot-cold" syndrome in prevention of heat-related morbidity and mortality, the hypothesis is appealing. Incomplete knowledge of the "hot-cold" syndrome among other New World subtropical or tropical groups makes generalizing beyond the Yucatec situation dangerous. Although research is lacking, heat stress is probably much less severe among the highland Mexican peoples.

The "hot-cold" rules would appear to be important for epidemiological and evolutionary reasons. Effective behavioral observance of the "hot-cold" rules may result in decreased incidence of heat casualties among the farmers whose daily activities place them in stressful circumstances. Also, because walking speed affects relationships between morphology and physiology under conditions of heat stress (McCullough 1972), it is possible that the "hot-cold" syndrome rules governing pacing of work may influence the operation of natural selection on body components which are important to heat regulation.

Notes

1. This research was supported by National Institute of Mental Health Predoctoral Fellowship 5 F01 MH34661-03 and accompanying research grant MH14193-01. This paper was presented in a different form at the 14th Annual Conference, Rocky Mountain Social Sci-

ence Association, 28 April 1972, Salt Lake City. I would like to express my thanks to Frederick Sargent, II, Alfredo Barrera Vásquez, Herman W. Konrad, Richard A. Thompson, Bela C. Maday, and the patient and tolerant people of Ticul. Christine S. McCullough was a valuable critic of the manuscript in its many manifestations.

2. The words "hot" and "cold" within quotation marks designate the opposing qualities of the syndrome. The same words without quotation marks refer to their normal scientific meanings. Italics indicate words used in the Maya language, regardless of their origin.

Culture and
Mental Health

This section, which examines cultural aspects of mental health, again portrays a theme of universality and diversity. All societies recognize forms of deviant or abnormal behavior and have systems by which such behavior is explained and treated. This becomes particularly clear in the opening paper by Jane Murphy. From her comparative study of the labeling and prevalence of mental illness, it is learned that certain disorders are equally common in diverse societies and are viewed and treated in similar ways. Some illnesses supersede cultural boundaries, while other conditions, for example anxiety and pain tolerance, seem to be strongly influenced by variations in culture.

The article by Carl O'Nell and Henry Selby, and the following paper by Mark Zborowski, focus specifically on this problem. In each study differences in illness-related behavior are explained culturally. The work of O'Nell and Selby employs an epidemiological approach in the analysis of anxiety and adoption of sick-role. Their conclusions have significant implications for studying the etiology and prevalence of a large range of disorders, both somatic and psychosomatic in nature. The Zborowski article complements the previous study in its use of cultural variables to explain data. Persons of different cultural backgrounds have learned to perceive and to react toward pain in different ways.

This finding is highly important to the clinician treating patients of foreign cultural heritage, a subject discussed by Tseng and Hsu in the closing paper of this section. There is great need for the therapist and the patient to be fully aware that cultural factors have an effect on the success of treatment in mental illness. Even the most acculturated individuals adhere to ethnic attitudes toward pain, disease etiology, and what constitutes meaningful and appropriate therapy. Conservatism in health attitudes has repeatedly been encountered by medical anthropologists in pluralistic communities, as is illustrated by the papers in section V.

Jane M. Murphy

Psychiatric labeling in cross-cultural perspective

In recent years labeling (or societal reaction) theory has aroused strong interest among people concerned with mental illness. From the perspective of labeling theory, the salient features of the behavior patterns called mental illness in countries where Western psychiatry is practiced appear to be as follows: (i) these behaviors represent deviations from what is believed to be normal in particular sociocultural groups, (ii) the norms against which the deviations are identified are different in different groups, (iii) like other forms of deviation they elicit societal reactions which convey disapproval and stigmatization, (iv) a label of mental illness applied to a person whose behavior is deviant tends to become fixed, (v) the person labeled as mentally ill is thereby encouraged to learn and accept a role identity which perpetuates the stigmatizing behavior pattern, (vi) individuals who are powerless in a social group are more vulnerable to this process than others are, and (vii) because social agencies in modern industrial society contribute to the labeling process they have the effect of creating problems for those they treat rather than easing problems.

This school of thought emerged mainly within sociology, as an extension of studies of social deviance in which crime and delinquency were originally the major focus (1). It is also associated with psychiatry through, for example, Thomas Szasz and R. D. Laing (2). These ideas have come to be called a "sociological model" of mental illness, for they center on learning and the social construction of norms. They began to be formulated about 25 years ago (3), commanded growing attention in the late 1960's, and have been influential in recent major changes in public programs for psychiatric care, especially the deinstitutionalization which is occurring in a number of states (4, 5).

Several aspects of the theory receive support from a study reported in *Science* by David Rosenhan (6), based on the experiences of eight sane subjects who gained admission to psychiatric hospitals, were diagnosed as schizophrenic, and remained as patients an average of 19 days until discharged as "in remission." Rosenhan argues that "we cannot distinguish insanity from sanity" (6, p. 257). He associates his work with anthropological considerations" and cites Ruth Benedict (7) as an early contributor to a theme he pursues, which is that "what is viewed as normal in one culture may be seen as quite aberrant in another" (6, p. 250). He indicates that the perception of behavior as being schizophrenic is relative to context, for "psychiatric diagnosis betrays little about the patient but much about the environment in which an observer finds him." He argues that, despite the effort to humanize treat-

From *Science*, Vol. 191, pp. 1019-1028, 12 March 1976. Copyright 1976 by the American Association for the Advancement of Science.

ment of disturbed people by calling them patients and labeling them mentally ill, the attitudes of professionals and the public at large are characterized by "fear, hostility, aloofness, suspicion, and dread." Once the label of schizophrenia has been applied, the "diagnosis acts on all of them"—patient, family, and relatives—"as a self-fulfilling prophecy. Eventually, the patient himself accepts the diagnosis, with all of its surplus meanings and expectations, and behaves accordingly" (6, p. 254).

The research to be described here presents an alternative perspective derived from cross-cultural comparisons, mainly of two widely separated and distinctly contrasting non-Western groups, Eskimos of northwest Alaska and Yorubas of rural, tropical Nigeria. It is concerned with the meanings attached to behaviors which would be labeled mental illness in our society. I interpret these data as raising important questions about certain assumptions in the labeling thesis and therefore as casting doubt on its validity as a major explanation of mental illness, especially with respect to schizophrenia. These cross-cultural investigations suggest that relativism has been exaggerated by labeling theorists and that in widely different cultural and environmental situations sanity appears to be distinguishable from insanity by cues that are very similar to those used in the Western world.

The Labeling Orientation

As Edwin Schur (8) points out, if labeling theory is conceived broadly it is the application of George Herbert Mead's theories about self-other interactions to a definition of social deviance extended to include human problems ranging from crime to blindness. Labeling theory emphasizes the social meanings imputed to deviant behavior and focuses on the unfolding processes of interaction whereby self-definition is influenced by others. Further, "it is a central tenet of the labeling perspective that neither acts nor individuals are 'deviant' in the sense of immutable, 'objective' reality without reference to processes of social definition." Schur states that "this relativism may be viewed as a major strength" of labeling theory (8, p. 14).

Edwin Lemert's concept of secondary deviance (9) is of critical importance in linking self-other considerations to deviations. Secondary deviation occurs when a person learns the role and accepts the identity of a deviant as the basis of his lifestyle. It is a response to a response; negative feedback from significant others reinforces and stabilizes the behavior that initially produced it. Applied to criminality, this idea has created general awareness of a process whereby a young person on being labeled a juvenile delinquint may enter a network of contingencies that lead ultimately to his learning criminal activities and "hardening" as a criminal rather than to the correction of behavior.

In *The Making of Blind Men*, Robert Scott points to a similar process regarding a very different type of deviance (10). If a person is labeled blind by certain administrative criteria he is likely to become enmeshed in care-giving agencies that encourage him to accept a definition of himself as helpless and to learn to play the role of the blind man. These experiences may even inhibit the use of residual vision.

Scott shows that institutions for the blind vary in the degree to which they encourage acceptance or rejection of the deviant role and that these differences are related to differences in the life-style of blind men. Insofar as the labeling concept has been employed in this way I believe it is sound and has disclosed new and valuable information.

The application of labeling ideas to mental illness has tended to take a different course (11) and has aroused considerable controversy, as indicated, for example, in the continuing exchange between Thomas Scheff and Walter Gove *et al.* (12-15). One question in this controversy is whether mental illness should be considered a "pure case" of secondary deviation or a more complex case. Lemert's formulation of the concept of secondary deviation was influenced by his investigation of stuttering, and he suggests that stuttering represents the pure case: "Stuttering thus far has defied efforts at causative explanation. . . . It appears to be exclusively a process-product in which, to pursue the metaphor, normal speech variations, or at most, minor abnormalities of speech (primary stuttering) can be fed into an interactional or evaluational process and come out as secondary stuttering" (9, p. 56).

The important point here is that primary deviance is considered to be normal variation or only "minor abnormalities," and the influence of societal reactions is considered genuinely causative. Societal reactions "work on" and "mold" normal variations of speech to "create" stuttering. For mental illness the labeling theorists have tended to use the "pure case" model rather than the more complex model represented by blindness, where lack or loss of sight is primary deviance and the role of blind man is secondary deviance.

Scheff has provided the most systematic theoretical statement regarding labeling and mental illness, and in his formulation the primary deviations that are fed into interactional processing to come out as mental illness are described as "amorphous," "unstructured," and "residual" violations of a society's norms (11, pp. 33, 82). Rosenhan suggests that the behaviors labeled schizophrenic might be " 'sane' outside the psychiatric hospital but seem insane in it . . . [because patients] are responding to a bizarre setting" (6, p. 257). Lemert says that social exclusion can "create a paranoid disposition in the absence of any special character structure" (9, p. 198). Further, many have posited that behavior we call mental illness might be considered normal in a different culture or in a minority social class. Thus, the primary deviations of mental illness are held to be for the most part insignificant, and societal reactions become the main etiological factor.

This view is reminiscent of ideas about human plasticity, cultural determinism, and cultural relativism which were prominent in what used to be called the culture-personality studies of anthropology. In fact the influence of culture-personality on labeling theory is explicitly stated by Lemert, who was trained jointly in sociology and anthropology and who has drawn on non-Western studies throughout his career. The influence is equally acknowledged by Rosenhan (6). It seems to me that numbers of proponents of labeling theory assume that the expanding body of data from non-Western areas has supported the relativist propositions put forth by Benedict and others in the 1930's and '40's (16). Indeed, it was my own assumption when I began anthropological work with Eskimos. I thought I would find their conception of normality and abnormality to be very different, if not opposite, from that held in Western Culture. This did not prove to be the case, and my experience is not unique. Anthropologists who have been conducting field research in recent years using more systematic methods but continuing to work on the relations between individual behavior and cultural context tend to hold a greatly modified view of the extent of individual plasticity and the molding force of culture (17, 18).

It would be misleading on my part to imply that all theory building and investigation regarding the relation of labeling and mental illness have followed the pure-case model. In their studies on mental retardation Robert Edgerton and Jane Mercer use moderate labeling ideas and show that social reactions are related to differences in the ways subnormal individuals are able to function both in and outside of institutions (19). A growing number of studies of alcoholism, many of them influenced by labeling views, have demonstrated that social attitudes and the variable meanings attached to drinking are correlated with marked differences in alcoholism rates in various cultural groups (20). There are, in addition, numbers of studies of the social pathways leading to hospitalization, the impact of hospitalization, attitudes toward discharged mental patients, and so on which reveal important outcomes for the mentally ill without imputing to societal reactions the degree of significance given them in the more deterministic formulations.

Most labeling studies of mental illness have been carried out in the United States and the United Kingdom. Variations in the definition and tolerance of mental illness have mainly been studied in groups at different social class levels in industrialized society (21). Since cultural relativism is one of the main elements of the orientation, it seems useful to put some of the basic labeling questions to non-Western data. As background for this, I quote from four contributors to labeling theory: Scheff, Erving Goffman, Theodore Sarbin, and David Mechanic. These references do not encompass the breadth and elaboration of each contributor's own approach to the problem of mental illness, but they do reflect the view of cultural relativity which runs throughout the labeling orientation.

Scheff says that "the culture of the group provides a vocabulary of terms for categorizing many norm violations" (11, pp. 33, 82). These designate deviations such as crime and drunkenness. There is a residual category of diverse kinds of deviations which constitute an affront to the unconscious definition of decency and reality uniquely characteristic of each culture. Scheff posits that the "culture provides no explicit label" for these deviations but they nevertheless take form in the minds of societal agents as "stereotypes of insanity." When people around a deviant respond to him in terms of these stereotypes, "his amorphous and unstructured rule-breaking tends to crystallize in conformity to these expectations." Scheff further suggests that these cultural stereotypes tend to produce uniformity of symptoms within a cultural group and "enormous differences in the manifest symptoms of stable mental disorder between societies."

It has been pointed out that there appears to be a contradiction in one aspect of Scheff's theory (12, p. 876; 22). It is difficult to accept that a socially shared image of behavior that can influence action and has the concreteness of a stereotype should lack a name. It is possible Scheff meant that in the evolution of language a label for insanity was the last to emerge because it refers to a residue of norm violations. The dating of words is beyond the scope of the data to be presented here, but it will be possible to see whether an explicit label currently exists in the two cultures studied, a hunting-gathering culture (Eskimo) and an agricultural society (Yoruba), neither of which developed a written language. If a word for insanity occurs we can then investigate the kinds of behaviors therein denoted.

Regarding our own society, Goffman stresses that the "perception of losing one's mind is based on culturally derived and socially engrained stereotypes as to the significance of symptoms such as hearing voices, losing temporal and spatial orientation, and sensing that one is being followed" (23). He further indicates that there is cultural variation in this kind of imagery and differential encouragement for such a view of oneself. This makes it appropriate to ask whether hallucinations, delusions, and disorientations are present or absent from the conception of losing one's mind in Yoruba and Eskimo cultures, assuming they have a stereotype of insanity at all.

Labeling theorists express considerable dissatisfaction with the concept of mental illness, pointing out that it is a vague and euphemistic methaphor and ties together phenomena that are neither "mental" nor "illness." They argue that mental illness is a myth developed in Western societies, that the term represents an abortive effort to improve the treatment of people previously called lunatics, that in the name of this myth we continue to incarcerate, punish, and degrade people for deviating from norms. Sarbin suggests that defining behavioral aberrations as illness occurred in medieval Europe as a way to relabel people who might otherwise have been burned at the stake as witches (24). He further suggests that it was during this phase of Western history that the concept of mind came into being. It was used as a way to explain perplexing behavior that could not be related to occurrences external to the person. It is "as *if* there are states of mind" that cause these patterns of conduct. The "as if" was transmuted into the myth that the mind exists as a real entity and can therefore be sick or healthy.

In the data to be given, it will be possible to ask whether the idea of an inner state that influences conduct is found in these non-Western groups and, since both groups believe in witchcraft, whether a stereotype of insanity is associated with the conduct of witches. Everywhere that witchcraft has been systematically studied the role of the witch involves deviances that are heavily censured. The witch carries out practices that are believed to harm people through supernatural means. If the insane person and the witch are equated in the beliefs of non-Western groups, it would appear to follow that in those groups mental illness is thought of as social deviance; and this would be a telling point for labeling theory.

Mechanic makes the point that "although seemingly obvious, it is important to state that what may be viewed as deviant in one social group may be tolerated in another, and rewarded in still other groups" (25). He emphasizes that the social response may influence the frequency with which the deviant behavior occurs. It has been hypothesized by a number of researchers that holy men, shamans, or witch doctors are psychotics who have been rewarded for their psychotic behavior by being made incumbents of highly regarded and useful roles (26). This is the obverse of the possibility that the insane are thought of as witches. The role of the healer carries great power and approval. The idea of social rewards for mental illness underscores the lengths to which relativity can be carried, for it suggests that the social definition of one kind of behavior can turn it into such opposing roles as the defamed witch or the renowned shaman. Mechanic's points make it appropriate, therefore, to ask whether the shamans in Eskimo culture and the healers in Yoruba culture are thought by the people to be mentally ill and whether the rates of such mental illness in these groups are similar to or different from those in the West.

Scheff, Goffman, Sarbin, and Mechanic share the view that in our society the appellation "mentally ill" is a "stigmatizing" and "brutalizing" assessment. It robs the individual of identity through profound "mortification" and suggests that he is a "non-person." It forces him into an ascribed role, exit from which is extremely difficult. Thus another question is posed: If Eskimos and Yorubas have a stereotype of insanity, are they less harsh than we with those defined as insane?

To illustrate the model I have in mind for exploring these questions I will first describe a non-Western event which suggests that certain aspects of labeling theory are valid. It does not concern mental illness but it demonstrates the use of labels as arbitrary social definitions in the labeling theory sense. The case is reported by W. H. R. Rivers in connection with his analysis of the concept of death among the Melanesians (27):

Some persons who are seriously ill and likely to die or who are so old that from the Melanesian point of view they are ready to die are labeled by the word *mate*, which means "dead person." They become thereby subjects of a ceremonial live burial. It can be argued that the Melanesians have a concept of death which is a social fiction. It embodies what they arbitrarily agree to define as death and is a distortion of reality as seen by most cultural groups. The label *mate* involves a degradation ceremony in which an elderly person is deprived of his rights and is literally "mortified." He is perceived "as *if* dead" and then buried. The linguistic relativist might even say that this use of the word *mate* shows that the Melanesians do not perceive death by means of the indicators of vital functioning applied in Western society (28).

Rivers's own conclusion is that the Melanesians view death the way we do and are cognizant of the difference between biological and social *mate*. Biological *mate* is by far the commoner phenomenon. In their practice of live burials the Melanesians in fact take close note of two typical precursors of death—old age and illness.

It seems clear, however, that socially sanctioned acts based on symbolic meanings, such as those involved in social *mate*, are powerful in influencing the course of human affairs. They can be treacherously abused and lead to what we think of as cruel outcomes. Rivers says that the practice is not conceived to be cruel or degrading by the Melanesians because in their meaning the burial relieves the person of a worn-out earth-life so that he can enter the higher status of the spiritual afterlife. By our standards the Melanesian interpretation would nevertheless be considered a collective rationalization of "geronticide." Whatever the intent, the socially defined death of elderly Melanesians is a myth and serves as a model of what I understand the labeling theorists to mean by the "myth of mental illness." Thus a final question: Do the Eskimos and Yorubas subscribe to such fictions about mental illness through which they perpetrate inhumanity and degradation?

Method of Study

The data to be presented derive mainly from a year of field work, in 1954-55, in a village of Yupik-speaking Eskimos on an island in the Bering Sea, and an investigation of similar length, in 1961 and 1963, among Egba Yorubas. I also draw on shorter periods of field work in Gambia, Sudan, and South Vietnam.

Some of the Eskimo data came from a key informant, who systematically described the life experiences of the 499 Eskimos who constituted a total village census over the 15 years previous to and including the year of investigation. In addition, a dictionary of Eskimo words for illness and deviance was developed. Extended life histories of a small number of Eskimos were gathered. Also daily observations and comments from Eskimos about Eskimos (both in their own village and in other areas known to them) were recorded for the purpose of understanding their conceptions of behavior (29).

The approach among the Yorubas was different in that I worked with a group of three native healers and a member of an indigenous cult. Interviews were directed toward understanding Yoruba concepts of behavior in the abstract and centered on actual people only to the extent that acquaintances and patients were brought into the discussion as illustration (30).

The Eskimo data served as the base for an epidemiological study of the village in 1955, and the Yoruba data constituted one of the first phases of a larger epidemiological study carried out with a group of Nigerian and U.S. colleagues in which we studied 416 adults, of whom 245 constituted a representative sample from 14 villages (31).

In *The Social Meanings of Suicide*, a study affiliated with the labeling tradition, Jack Douglas has shown the weakness of official statistics as a basis for judging the social significance of behavioral phenomena in groups (32). The Eskimo and Yoruba studies reflect a similar orientation about the inadequacies of mental hospital statistics for the purposes at hand. As has been done in many labeling studies, I relied on participant observation and interviewing about microcultural events. The focus was on indigenous meanings. These meanings were then used as a basis for counting similar behavior patterns, so that they were defined from within a cultural group rather than by imposed criteria.

In these studies I have considered language to be the main repository of labels. Insofar as there is a counterpart to the official recognition of mental illness involved in hospital commitment in a Western society, it resides in what Eskimos and Yorubas say are the kinds of people treated by shamans and native healers.

Labeled Behavior Patterns

The first specific question is: Do Eskimos and Yorubas have labels for psychological and behavioral differences that bear any resemblance to what we mean by mental illness? These groups clearly recognize differences among themselves and describe these in terms of what people do and what they say they feel and believe. Some of the differences lead people to seek the aid of healers and some do not, some differences arouse sympathy and protection while others arouse disapproval, some are called sickness and others health, some are considered misconduct and others good conduct. Some are described by a single word or nominative phrase. Some that seem to have common features are described in varying circumlocutions and sentences. If a word exists for a complex pattern of behavior it seems acceptable to assume that the concept of that pattern has been crystallized out of a welter of specific attributes and that the word qualifies as an explicit label.

Of major importance is whether or not the Yorubas and Eskimos conceptualize a distinction between body and mind and attribute differences in functioning to one or the other. The first indication of such a distinction arose early in the Eskimo census review when a woman was described in these terms: "Her sickness is getting wild and out of mind . . . but she might have had sickness in her body too." The Eskimo word for her was *nuthkavihak.* It became clear from other descriptions that the word refers to a complex pattern of behavioral processes of which the hallmark is conceived to be that something inside the person—the soul, the spirit, the mind—is out of order. Descriptions of how *nuthkavihak* is manifested include such phenomena as talking to oneself, screaming at someone who does not exist, believing that a child or husband was murdered by witchcraft when nobody else believes it, believing oneself to be an animal, refusing to eat for fear eating will kill one, refusing to talk, running away, getting lost, hiding in strange places, making strange grimaces, drinking urine, becoming strong and violent, killing dogs, and threatening people. Eskimos translate *nutkavihak* as "being crazy."

There is a Yoruba word, *were,* which is also translated as insanity. The phenomena include hearing voices and trying to get other people to see their source though none can be seen, laughing when there is nothing to laugh at, talking all the time or not talking at all, asking oneself questions and answering them, picking up sticks and leaves for no purpose except to put them in a pile, throwing away food because it is thought to contain *juju,* tearing off one's clothes, setting fires, defecating in public and then mushing around in the feces, taking up a weapon and suddenly hitting someone with it, breaking things in a state of being stronger than normal, believing that an odor is continuously being emitted from one's body.

For both *nuthkavihak* and *were* indigenous healing practices are used. In fact, among the Yorubas some native healers specialize in the treatment of *were* (33, 34).

The profile of *were* behaviors is based not only on what the healers described in the abstract but also on data concerning two members of the sample identified as *were* by the village headman and a group of 28 *were* patients in the custody of native healers and in a Nigerian mental hospital. The profile of *nuthkavihak* is built from information about four individuals within the 15-year population of 499 persons and six Eskimos from earlier times and from a related Eskimo settlement in Siberia.

Of paramount significance is the fact that *were* and *nuthkavihak* were never used for a single phenomenon such as hearing voices, but rather were applied to a pattern in which three or four of the phenomena described above existed together. It is therefore possible to examine the situations in which a person exhibited one or another of the listed behaviors but was not labeled insane.

The ability to see things other people do not see and to look into the future and prophesy is a clearly recognized and highly valued trait. It is called "thinness" by Eskimos. This ability is used by numerous minor Eskimo diviners and is the outstanding characteristic of the shaman. The people called "thin" outnumber those called insane by at least eight to one. Moreover, there were no instances when a "thin" person was called *nuthkavihak*.

When a shaman undertakes a curing rite he becomes possessed by the spirit of an animal; he "deludes" himself, so to speak, into believing that he is an animal. Consider this description (35):

> The seance is opened by singing and drumming. After a time the shamaness falls down very hard on the floor. In a while, the tapping of her fingers and toes is heard on the walrus skin floor. Slowly she gets up, and already she is thought to "look awful, like a dog, very scary." She crawls back and forth across the floor making growling sounds. In this state she begins to carry out the various rites which Eskimos believe will cure sickness, such as sucking the illness out of the body and blowing it into the air. Following this the shamaness falls to the floor again and the seance is over.

Compare this to the case, reported by Morton Teicher, of a Baffin Island Eskimo who believed that a fox had entered her body (36). This was not associated with shamanizing but was a continuous belief. She barked herself hoarse, tried to claw her husband, thought her feet were turning into fox paws, believed that the fox was moving up in her body so that she could feel its hair in her mouth, lost control of her bowels at times, and finally became so excited that she was tied up and put into a coffin-like box with an opening at the head through which she could be fed. This woman was thought to be crazy but the shamaness not. One Eskimo summarized the distinction this way: "When the shaman is healing he is out of his mind, but he *is not crazy*" (37).

This suggests that seeing, hearing, and believing things that are not seen, heard, and believed by all members of the group are sometimes linked to insanity and sometimes not. The distinction appears to be the degree to which they are controlled and utilized for a specific social function. The inability to control these processes is what is meant by a mind out of order; when a mind is out of order it will not only fail to control sensory perception but will also fail to control behavior. Another Eskimo who was asked to define *nuthkavihak* said that it means "the mind does not control the person, *he is crazy*." I take this to mean that volition is implicated, that hearing voices, for example, can be voluntary or involuntary, and that it is mainly the involuntary forms that are associated with *were* and *nuthkavihak*.

In cultures such as Eskimo and Yoruba. where clairvoyant kinds of mental phenomena are encouraged and preternatural experiences are valued, something similar to what we might call hallucinations and delusions can probably be learned or simulated. A favorable audience reaction is likely to stabilize the performance of the people who fill the roles of fortune-teller and faith healer. For example, the shamaness described above was unable to keep her patient alive but her performance was considered to have been well executed; she was said to have done "all her *part, acting* like a dog." The Eskimos believe that a person can learn to be a shaman. Their view of *nuthkavihak* is something that befalls the person, a pattern of behavioral processes that can appear and disappear, lasting a long time with some people and a short time with others.

A number of researchers in the field of cross-cultural psychiatry take the position that the underlying processes of insanity are the same everywhere but that their specific content varies between cultural groups (38). A psychotic person, it is thought, could not make use of the imagery of Christ if he had not been exposed to the Christian tradition and he could not elaborate ideas about the *wittiko* cannibalistic monster if not exposed to Cree and Ojibwa Indian traditions (39). It would seem that if a culture-specific stereotype of the content of psychosis exists in a group it might have the kind of influence suggested in labeling theory. If the content stereotype were applied to the unstructured delusions of a psychotic his thought productions might be shaped and stabilized around the theme of that stereotype.

There have been several attempts to study phenomena such as *wittiko* and *pibloktoq*, the former being thought of as the culturally defined content of a psychotic process in which the person believes himself to be a cannibalistic monster and the latter as a culture-specific form of hysteria found in the arctic (40, p. 218; 41). The evidence of their existence comes from early ethnographies. It has been difficult in the contemporary period to locate people who have these illnesses (42). If the availability of a content stereotype has the effect one would expect from labeling theory, the stereotype should have sustained the pattern, but in fact these content patterns seem to have disappeared.

Prominent in the descriptions of the images and behavior of people labeled *were* and *nuthkavihak* were cultural beliefs and practices as well as features of the natural environment. Eskimo ideation concerned arctic animals and Eskimo people, objects, and spirits. The Yoruba ideation was based on tropical animals and Yoruba figures. The cultural variation was, in other words, general. There was no evidence that if a person were to become *were* or *nuthkavihak* he would reveal one specific delusion based on cultural mythology. In this regard I reach the same conclusion as Roger Brown did when he set out to see how far labeling ideas would aid his understanding of hospitalized schizophrenics: "Delusions are as idiosyncratic as individual schizophrenics or normals. . . . There seems to be nothing like a standard set of heresies, but only endless variety" (15, p. 397).

The answer to the first specific question, whether Eskimos and Yorubas have labels for psychological and behavioral differences resembling what we call mental illness, is to my mind a definite yes. The expanding ethnographic literature on this topic indicates that most other non-Western groups also have such labels [in addition to the papers already cited see (43)] . From this broad perspective it appears that (i) phenomenal processes of disturbed thought and behavior similar to schizophrenia are found in most cultures; (ii) they are sufficiently distinctive and noticeable that almost everywhere a name has been created for them; (iii) over and above similarity in processes, there is variability in content which in a general way is colored by culture; and (iv) the role of social fictions in perceiving and defining the phenomena seems to have been very slight.

Unlabeled Behavior Patterns

The questions of this section are: Do phenomena labeled mental illness by us go unlabeled elsewhere, and if so what are the consequences? Are there natural experiments of culture which allow us to gain some understanding of the effects of not labeling? From the linguistic relativist's viewpoint, if phenomena are not named they are screened out of the perception of the people who speak that language; thus not only would mental illness go unrecognized if unlabeled but also the negative effects of labeling could not pertain.

Although one cannot speak of mental illness without reference to insanity and psychoses, most people in our culture mean more by the term and include some or all of the phenomena described in a textbook of psychiatry. Elsewhere I have presented data about Eskimo and Yoruba terms, lack of terms, and levels of generalization for mental retardation, convulsions, and senility (30, 44). According to the healers with whom I worked, the Yorubas have no word for senility but they recognize that some old people become incapable of taking care of themselves, talk to themselves, are agitated, wander away and get lost. In such cases they are watched, fed, and protected in much the same way as might be done in a nursing home. The lack of an explicit label seems to make little difference in how they are treated.

In contemporary Western society psychoneurotic patterns are thought of as one of the main types of mental illness, yet neurosis has a minor role in the labeling theory literature (45). Since labeling theory is addressed to the concept of mental illness per se, one feels it ought to apply to the neurotic as well as the psychotic.

In working with the Eskimos and Yorubas I was unable to find a word that could be translated as a general reference to neurosis or words that directly parallel our meaning of anxiety and depression. On the other hand, their words for emotional responses that we might classify as manifestations of anxiety or depression constitute a very large vocabulary. The Yoruba lexicon includes, for example, words for unrest of mind which prevents sleep, being terrified at night, extreme bashfulness which is like a sense of shame, fear of being among people, tenseness, and overeagerness. The Eskimo terms are translated as worrying too much until it makes the person sick, too easy to get afraid, crying with sadness, head down and rocking back and forth, shaking and trembling all over, afraid to stay indoors, and so on. The point is that neither group had a single word or explicit label that lumped these phenomena together as constituting a general class of illness by virtue of their underlying similarities or as a pattern in which several components are usually found in association (46). In the terms of this article, these symptoms are unlabeled but they do exist. People recognize them and try to do something about them. Some of them are conceived as severely disabling and cause people to give up aspects of their work (such as being captain of a hunting boat); others appear to be less serious. Some of them are transient; others are life-long characteristics.

Of special significance to the problem at hand is the fact that most of these emotional phenomena are definitely thought of as illnesses for which the shaman and witch doctor have effective cures. The number of people who exhibit these phenomena is considerably in excess of those labeled *were* and *nuthkavihak*. Among the Yorubas the ratio is approximately 12 to 1 and among the Eskimos 14 to 1. In the clientele of a typical shaman or healer a large proportion would be people who came with symptoms such as "unrest of mind that prevents sleep" or "shaking and trembling all the time."

The answer to the question whether phenomena we label mental illness go unlabeled elsewhere is thus also yes. These Eskimos and Yorubas point out a large number of psychological and behavioral phenomena which we would call neuroses but which they do not put together under such a rubric. The consequence is not, however, a reduction in the number of persons who display the phenomena or great difference in how they are treated. The fact that these peoples cannot categorically define someone as "a neurotic" or that the Yorubas do not talk about "a senile" appears mainly to be a classification difference, and I am led to conclude that the phenomena exist independently of labels.

Evaluation of Behavior Patterns

Do non-Western groups evaluate the labeled behaviors of mental illness negatively or positively? Are they more tolerant of deviance than we are? I shall consider first the related institutional values of the culture, its roles and ceremonies, and then the noninstitutionalized actions and attitudes toward the mentally ill.

As pointed out earlier, it has been proposed that the shaman role is a social niche in which psychopathology is socially useful and that therefore mental disorder is positively valued. Since the Eskimos do not believe the shaman is *nutkavihak*, it cannot be insanity that invests the role with prestige in their eyes. It could be, however, that some other form of mental illness, possibly a neurotic disorder like hysteria, is considered essential to what a shaman does and therefore is accorded the same respect that the role as a whole commands.

Among the 499 Eskimos 18 had shamanized at some time in their lives. None was thought to be *nuthkavihak*. No other personality characteristic or emotional response was given as typical of all of them, and in these regards the shamans seemed to be a random sample of the whole. The only feature I was able to determine as common to the group was that they shamanized, and they did that with variable success.

The Yoruba healer has not been described in the literature as a mentally ill person, though some of the Yoruba healing cults consist of individuals who have been cured and thereafter participate in curing others. The healers known to me and my conversations with Yorubas about their healers gave no evidence that mental illness was a requisite. Thus as far as the groups reported here are concerned, mental illness does not appear to be venerated in these roles. If the shaman is to be considered either psychotic or hysterical it seems to require that a Western definition be given to the portion of behavior specific to shamanizing.

If not institutionalized in an esteemed role, is mental illness institutionalized in a contemptible role? Both the Yorubas and the Eskimos have a clearly defined role of witch as the human purveyor of magically evil influences. Though feared, the man or woman who is believed to use magic in this way is held in low esteem.

Is insanity or other mental illness prima facie evidence that a person is a witch? If one tries to answer this by identifying the people labeled *were* or *nuthkavihak* and then the people labeled witches and comparing the two groups to see how much they overlap in membership, as I did regarding the shamans, a serious problem arises. The difficulty is in identifying the witches. Unlike shamanizing, which is a public act, the use of evil magic is exceedingly secretive. I did note, however, that there was no correspondence between the group of Eskimos said to have been insane at some point in their lives and the six people named as *auvinak* (witch) by at least one Eskimo.

In the more generalized information from the Yoruba healers it was evident that insanity was often believed to result from the use of evil magic but an insane person was rarely believed to use it against others. Thus my interpretation of whether mental illness is built into the role of witch is similar to the view presented about the role of healer. Some insane people have probably been accused of being witches, but it has been by happenstance, not because witching and insanity are considered to be the same thing and equally stigmatized.

In these regards the Eskimos and Yorubas seem to have much in common with the Zapotecs studied by Henry Selby (47, pp. 41-42). His work focuses on witchcraft as a major form of social deviance, and he interprets his information as supporting labeling ideas (48), especially the vulnerability of outsiders to labeling. He found that accusations of witchcraft are more likely to be leveled at someone outside the immediate group of kin and neighbors than at a group member. However, after "talking about deviance for months" with his Zapotec informants, Selby realized that he had no information on mental illness. He explored this topic separately and "found out that there were people who were 'crazy' " and that the condition was defined as having "something to do with the soul and was symptom-ized by agitated motor behavior, ataraxia, violent purposeless movement, and the inability to talk in ways that people could readily understand." Clearly, the Zapotecs have a conception of insanity, and, like Eskimos and Yorubas, they do not classify it in the same frame of reference with such norm transgressions as witching, envy, stinginess, and adultery.

Another way in which a culture might institutionalize a negative view of men-tal illness is through a degradation ceremony or ritual slaying, as in the case of the Melanesian social *mate*. Ceremony is a preservative of custom, and there is volumi-nous information on ceremonies for healing, ceremonies for effecting fertility of land, animals, and humans, and rites of passage, as well as ceremonies in which various forms of human sacrifice are carried out.

In view of the wide elaboration of customs whereby groups of people enact their negative and positive values, it is perhaps surprising that no groups seem to have developed the idea of ceremonially killing an insane person in the prime of life just because he is insane. Infanticide has sometimes been conducted when a child was born grossly abnormal in a way which might later have emerged as brain damage, and senility may have been a contributing factor in live burials. Also there is no doubt that insane people have sometimes been done away with, but that is different from ritual sacrifice. There is no evidence as far as I can determine that killing the insane has ever been standardized as a custom. There are, on the other hand, numerous indications from non-Western data that the ceremony appropriate for people labeled mentally deranged is the ceremony of healing (34, 36, 38, 43). Even the word "lunatic" associates the phenomena with healing, since it was usual-ly the healer who was believed to have power over such cosmic forces as the lunar changes which were thought to cause insanity.

Regarding informal behavior and attitudes toward the mentally ill it is diffi-cult to draw conclusions, because there is evidence of a wide range of behaviors that can be conceptualized as audience reactions. Insane people have been the objects of certain restrictive measures among both the Eskimos and the Yorubas. The Eskimos physically restrain insane people in violent phases, follow them around, and force them to return home if they run away; and there is one report of an insane man's being killed in self-defense when, after killing several dogs, he turned on his family. In describing the Chukchee, a Siberian group known to these Bering Strait Eskimos, Waldemar Bogoras reports the case of an insane woman who was tied to a pole during periods of wildness (49). Teicher describes, in addition to the coffin-like box mentioned earlier, the use of an igloo with bars across the opening through which food could be passed (36). This is again similar to Selby's observa-tions of Zapotecs who barred the door of a bamboo hut as a way of restraining a psychotic man (47).

The Yoruba healer of *were* often has 12 to 15 patients in custody at one time. Not infrequently he shackles those who are inclined to run off, and he may use various herbal concoctions for sedation. In Nigeria, where population is much denser than in the arctic, it was not uncommon to see *were* people wandering about the city streets, sometimes naked, more often dressed in odd assortments of tattered clothing, almost always with long, dirt-laden hair, talking to themselves, picking up objects to save. In studying a group of such vagrant psychotics Tolani Asuni noted that they usually stayed in one locale, that people fed them generously, allowed them to sleep in the market stalls, teased them mildly or laughed at them for minor deviations, and took action to control them only if the psychotics became violent (50).

A case I encountered in Gambia illustrates the complexities of the situation and indicates that compassion and rejection are sometimes both engaged. The case is of a man, identified as insane, who lived some 500 yards outside a village. The villagers lived in thatched mud houses. The madman lived on an abandoned anthill. It was about 2.5 meters long and 1.5 meters high and the top had been worn away to match the contours of his body. Except for occasional visits to the village, he remained on this platform through day and night and changing weather. His behavior was said to have become odd when he was a young man, and when I saw him he had not spoken for years, although he sometimes made grunting sounds. In one sense he was as secluded and alienated from his society as patients in back wards are in ours. On the other hand, the villagers always put food out for him and gave him cigarettes. The latter act was accompanied by laughter, because the insane man had a characteristic way of bouncing several leaps into the air to get away from anyone who came close to him, and that was considered amusing. Once a year someone would forceably bathe him and put new clothes on him.

If one defines intolerance of mental illness as the use of confinement, restraint, or exclusion from the community (or allowing people to confine or exclude themselves), there does not appear to be a great deal of difference between Western and non-Western groups in intolerance of the mentally ill. Furthermore, there seems to be little that is distinctively cultural in the attitudes and actions directed toward the mentally ill, except in such matters as that an abandoned anthill could not be used as an asylum in the arctic or a barred igloo in the tropics. There is apparently a common range of possible responses to the mentally ill person, and the portion of the range brought to bear regarding a particular person is determined more by the nature of his behavior than by a preexisting cultural set to respond in a uniform way to whatever is labeled mental illness. If the behavior indicates helplessness, help tends to be given, especially in food and clothes. If the behavior appears foolish or incongruous (in the light of the distinctive Eskimo and Yoruba views of what is humorous), laughter is the response. If the behavior is noisy and agitated, the response may be to try to quiet, sometimes by herbs and sometimes by other means. If the behavior is violent or threatening, the response is to restrain or subdue.

The answer to the question posed at the beginning of this section seems to be that the patterns these groups label mental illness (*were* or *nuthkavihak*) are not evaluated in either a starkly positive or starkly negative way. The flavor and variability of the audience reactions to mental illness suggest the word "ambivalence." Two recent studies in the United States also indicate that stigma is not automatically and universally applied to mental illness and that complex responses are typical in our society as well (51).

Norm Violations

If these Eskimos and Yorubas are ambivalent about mental illness, do they strongly condemn any behaviors at all? Both groups have words for theft, cheating, lying, stinginess, drunkenness, and a large number of other behaviors which they consider to be specific acts of bad conduct. These, like the practice of witchcraft, are thought of as transgressions against social standards and are negatively sanctioned.

In addition, the Eskimos have a word, *kunlangeta*, which means "his mind knows what to do but he does not do it." This is an abstract term for the breaking of many rules when awareness of the rules is not in question. It might be applied to a man who, for example, repeatedly lies and cheats and steals things and does not go hunting and, when the other men are out of the village, takes sexual advantage of many women—someone who does not pay attention to reprimands and who is always being brought to the elders for punishment. One Eskimo among the 499 was called *kunlangeta*. When asked what would have happened to such a person traditionally, an Eskimo said that probably "somebody would have pushed him off the ice when nobody else was looking." This suggests that permissiveness has a limit even in a cultural group which in some respects, such as attitude toward heterosexual activity, is very lenient. The Yorubas have a similarly abstract word, *arankan*, which means a person who always goes his own way regardless of others, who is uncooperative, full of malice, and bullheaded.

There are parallels between *kunlangeta* and *arankan* and our concept "psychopath"—someone who consistently violates the norms of society in multiple ways. Also, some of the specific acts of wrongdoing which Eskimos and Yorubas recognize might in our society be called evidence of "personality disorders." In Western psychiatry, this term refers to sexual deviations, excessive use of drugs or alcohol, and a variety of behaviors that primarily cause trouble for other people rather than for the doer.

It is of considerable interest that *kunlangeta* and *arankan* are not behaviors that the shamans and healers are believed to be able to cure or change. As a matter of fact, when I pressed this point with the Yoruba healers they specifically denied that these patterns are illness. Both groups, however, believe that specific acts of wrongdoing may make an individual vulnerable to illness or other misfortune. For example, Eskimos hold to a hunting ethic which prescribes ownership and sharing of animals; cheating in reference to the hunting code is thought of as a potential cause of physical or mental illness. The social codes among the Yorubas are somewhat different, but they also believe that breaking taboos can cause illness. It has been recognized by anthropologists for nearly half a century that among peoples who believe in magic there is remarkable similarity in the explanations of illness, and that transgression as well as witchcraft ranks high in the accepted etiology of many non-Western groups (52). Believing that transgression causes illness is nevertheless quite different from believing that transgression *is* illness.

Thus the answer to the question of this section appears to be that these groups do have strong negative sanction for a number of behaviors. A difference between their opinions and those embodied in Western psychiatry is that the Eskimos and Yorubas do not consider these transgressions symptomatic of illness or responsive to the techniques used for healing.

Prevalence

Is the net effect of a non-Western way of life such that fewer people suffer from something they label mental illness than is the case in the West? In view of the focus on *were* and *nuthkavihak*, attention will mainly be directed to this pattern of behavior and it will be compared with schizophrenia.

There are available now a number of epidemiological studies of mental illness in different countries and cultures. Warren Dunham has compared prevalence rates for schizophrenia from 19 surveys in Europe, Asia, and North America; Table 1 is adapted from tables he presents (53). Like several others who have studied these

Table 1. Compilation of prevalence rates for schizophrenia, from Dunham (53)

| | | | | Cases | |
| | | | | No. | Rate per 1000 |
Investigator	*Date*	*Place*	*Population*		
Brugger	1929	Thuringia, Germany	37,546	71	1.9
Brugger	1930-31	Bavaria, Germany	8,628	22	2.5
Stromgren	1935	Bornholm, Denmark	45,930	150	3.3
Kaila	1936	Finland	418,472	1,798	4.2
Bremer	1939-44	Northern Norway	1,325	6	4.5
Sjogren	1944	Western Sweden	8,736	40	4.6
Böök	1946-49	Northern Sweden	8,931	85	9.6
Fremming	1947	Denmark	5,500	50	9.0
Essen-Möller	1947	Rural Sweden	2,550	17	6.6
Mayer-Gross	1948	Rural Scotland	56,000	235	4.2
Uchimura	1940	Hachizo, Japan	8,330	32	3.8
Tsugawa	1941	Tokyo, Japan	2,712	6	2.2
Akimoto	1941	Komoro, Japan	5,207	11	2.1
Lin	1946-48	Formosa, China	19,931	43*	2.1
Cohen and Fairbank	1933	Baltimore, U.S.	56,044	127	2.3
Lemkau	1936	Baltimore, U.S.	57,002	158	2.9
Roth and Luton	1938-40	Rural Tennessee, U.S.	24,804	47	1.9
Hollingshead and Redlich	1950	New Haven, U.S.	236,940	845†	3.6
Eaton and Weil	1951	Hutterites, U.S.	8,542	9*	1.0

*Inactive as well as active cases.
†Cases treated six months or more.

figures, Dunham concludes that the prevalence rates "are quite comparable" despite the fact that some are based on hospital data and some on population surveys, despite differences in definitions and methods, and despite the cultural variation involved.

The rates of *were* and *nuthkavihak* can be compared to rates of schizophrenia in two Western surveys, one in Sweden and one in Canada. The Swedish study was carried out by Erik Essen-Möller and colleagues in two rural parishes for which a population register existed. Each member of the population was interviewed by a psychiatrist. A prevalence rate of schizophrenia is reported, with figures for cases in the community and cases in a hospital during a specific year (54). This design is similar to the one I used among the Eskimos, where a census register provided the base for determining the population, and each person was systematically described by at least one other Eskimo. Focusing on the people living in the specified year reduces the Eskimo population studied from 499 to 348.

The Canadian study, in which I was one of the investigators, was based on a probability sample of adults in a rural county (55). We designed the Yoruba study to explore the possibilities of comparing mental illness rates, and so used similar sampling procedures. The rates in these two surveys are based on compilations of interview data with selected respondents as well as systematic interviews about those respondents with local physicians in Canada and local village headmen in Nigeria.

The results of comparing these studies is that the proportion of people who exhibited or had at some time exhibited the pattern of behavior called schizophrenia, *were*, or *nuthkavihak* appears to be much the same from group to group (Table 2). At the time these studies were carried out, mental hospitals existed all

Table 2. **Rates of nonhospitalized schizophrenia in two Western samples and of indigenously defined insanity in two non-Western samples. Rates are per 1000 population after adjustment by the Weinberg method (58).**

			Cases	
Group	Date	Size	No.	Rate per 1000
Swedish	1948	2550	12	5.7
Eskimo	1954	348	1	4.4
Canadian	1952	1071	7	5.6
Yoruba	1961	245	2	6.8

over the world. The Canadian and Swedish populations are similar to the United States in having a sizable number of large mental hospitals. The Eskimo population was considered to be in the catchment area served by a mental hospital in the

United States, and the Yoruba villages were in the vicinity of two mental hospitals (56). For the Canadian and Yoruba studies we do not know the number of people who might otherwise have been in the communities but were hospitalized during the period when prevalence was surveyed. The Swedish and Eskimo studies, by virtue of starting with census registers, provide information on this point. The age-adjusted prevalence rate in the Swedish survey is 8.1 per 1000 when hospitalized schizophrenics are included and the Eskimo rate of *nuthkavihak* is increased to 8.8 when the one hospitalized case is added.

The number of schizophrenics, *were*, and *nuthkavihak* in a population is small, but this comparison suggests that the rates are similar. With a broader definition of mental illness which I have explained elsewhere (it includes the neurotic-appearing symptoms, the senile patterns, and so on) the total prevalence rates for the three groups I have studied are: Canadian, 18 percent; Eskimo, 19 percent; and Yoruba, 15 percent (57).

The answer to the last question above seems thus to be that the non-Western way of life does not offer protection against mental illness to the point of making a marked difference in frequency. The rates of mental illness patterns I have discussed are much more striking for similarity from culture to culture than for difference. This suggests that the causes of mental illness, whether genetic or experiential, are ubiquitous in human groups.

Summary and Conclusions

Labeling theory proposes that the concept of mental illness is a cultural stereotype referring to a residue of deviance which each society arbitrarily defines in a distinct way. It has been assumed that information from cultures that are markedly different from Western society supports the theory. This paper presents systematic data from Eskimo and Yoruba groups, and information from several other cultural areas, which instead call the theory into question.

Explicit labels for insanity exist in these cultures. The labels refer to beliefs, feelings, and actions that are thought to emanate from the mind or inner state of an individual and to be essentially beyond his control; the afflicted persons seek the aid of healers; the afflictions bear strong resemblance to what we call schizophrenia. Of signal importance is the fact that the labels of insanity refer not to single specific attributes but to a pattern of several interlinked phenomena. Almost everywhere a pattern composed of hallucinations, delusions, disorientations, and behavioral aberrations appears to identify the idea of "losing one's mind," even though the content of these manifestations is colored by cultural beliefs.

The absence of a single label among Eskimos and Yorubas for some of the phenomena we call mental illness, such as neuroses, does not mean that manifestations of such phenomena are absent. In fact they form a major part of what the shamans and healers are called upon to treat. Eskimos and Yorubas react to people they define as mentally ill with a complex of responses involving first of all the use of healing procedures but including an ambivalent-appearing mixture of care giving and social control. These reactions are not greatly dissimilar from those that occur in Western society. Nor does the amount of mental illness seem to vary greatly within or across the division of Western and non-Western areas. Patterns such as schizophrenia, *were*, and *nuthkavihak* appear to be relatively rare in any one human group but are broadly distributed among human groups. Rather than being simply violations of the social norms of particular groups, as labeling theory suggests, symptoms of mental illness are manifestations of a type of affliction shared by virtually all mankind.

References and Notes

1. H. S. Becker, *Outsiders* (Free Press, New York, 1963), reprinted in 1973 with a new chapter, "Labelling theory reconsidered."
2. T. S. Szasz, *The Myth of Mental Illness: Foundations of a Theory of Personal Conduct* (Hoeber-Harper, New York, 1961); R. Laing and A. Esterson, *Sanity, Madness, and the Family* (Basic Books, New York, 1964).
3. Notably in E. Lemert's distinction between primary and secondary deviance, which appeared initially in his book *Social Pathology* (McGraw-Hill, New York, 1951).
4. "In California, labeling theory itself contributed to the formulation of the Lanterman-Petris-Short act, a law which makes it difficult to commit patients to mental hospitals, and still more difficult to keep them there for long periods of time" (5, p. 256).
5. T. Scheff, *Am. Sociol. Rev.* 40, 252 (1975).
6. D. Rosenhan, *Science* 179, 250 (1973).
7. R. Benedict, *J. Gen. Psychol.* 10, 59 (1934).
8. E. Schur, *Labelling Deviant Behavior: Its Sociological Implications* (Harper & Row, New York, 1971).
9. E. Lemert, *Human Deviance, Social Problems and Social Control* (Prentice-Hall, Englewood Cliffs, N.J., 1967).
10. R. Scott, *The Making of Blind Men* (Russell Sage Foundation, New York, 1969).
11. T. Scheff, *Being Mentally Ill: A Sociological Theory* (Aldine, Chicago, 1966).
12. W. Gove, *Am. Sociol. Rev.* 35, 873 (1970).
13. _____ and P. Howell, *ibid.* 39, 86 (1974); W. Gove, *ibid.* 40, 242 (1975); R. Chauncey, *ibid.*, 248; T. Scheff (5, 14). In addition to the Rosenhan study (6), Scheff (14) evaluates the following six investigations as strongly supporting labeling: J. Greenley, *J. Health Soc. Behav.* 13, 25 (1972); A. Linsky, *Soc. Psychiatr.* 5, 166 (1970); W. Rushing, *Am. J. Sociol.* 77, 511 (1971); M. Temerlin, *J. Nerv. Ment. Dis.* 147, 349 (1968); W. Wilde, *J. Health Soc. Behav.* 9, 215 (1968); D. Wenger and C. Fletcher, *ibid.* 10, 66 (1969). For several articles unfavorable to labeling theory see W. Gove, Ed., *The Labelling of Deviance, Evaluating a Perspective* (Wiley, New York, 1975). Also not favorable are R. Brown (15); N. Davis, *Sociol. Q.* 13, 447 (1972); J. Gibbs, in *Theoretical Perspectives on Deviance*, R. Scott and J. Douglas, Eds. (Basic Books, New York, 1972), p. 39; S. Kety, *Am. J. Psychiatr.* 131, 957 (1974); R. Spitzer, *J. Abnorm. Psychol.* 84, 442 (1975); D. Ausubel, *Am. Psychol.* 16, 69 (1961).
14. T. Scheff, *Am. Sociol. Rev.* 39, 444 (1974).
15. R. Brown, *Am. Psychol.* 28, 395 (1973).
16. R. Benedict, *Patterns of Culture* (Houghton Mifflin, Boston, 1934); M. Mead, *Sex and Temperament in Three Primitive Societies* (Morrow, New York, 1935); *Male and Female* (Morrow, New York, 1949).
17. W. Caudill, in *Transcultural Research in Mental Health*, W. Lebra, Ed. (Univ. Press of Hawaii, Honolulu, 1972), p. 25; R. Edgerton, in *Changing Perspectives in Mental Illness*, S. Plog and R. Edgerton, Eds. (Holt, Rinehart & Winston, New York, 1969), p. 49; R. Levine, *Culture, Personality and Behavior* (Aldine, Chicago, 1973); M. Field, *Search for Security, An Ethno-*

psychiatric Study of Rural Ghana (Northwestern Univ. Press, Chicago, 1960); A. Wallace, *Culture and Personality* (Random House, New York, 1970); B. Whiting and J. Whiting, *Children of Six Cultures* (Harvard Univ. Press, Cambridge, Mass. 1975).

18. J. Honigmann, *Personality in Culture* (Harper & Row, New York, 1967).

19. R. Edgerton, *The Cloak of Competence* (Univ. of California Press, Berkeley, 1967); J. Mercer, *Labeling the Mentally Retarded* (Univ. of California Press, Berkeley, 1973).

20. R. Jessor, T. Graves, R. Hanson, S. Jessor, *Society, Personality and Deviant Behavior* (Holt, Rinehart & Winston, New York, 1968); J. Levy and S. Kunitz, *Indian Drinking* (Wiley, New York, 1974); H. Mulford, in *The Mental Patient: Studies in the Sociology of Deviance*, S. Spitzer and N. Denzin, Eds. (McGraw-Hill, New York, 1968), p. 155; D. Pittman and C. Snyder, *Society, Culture and Drinking Patterns* (Wiley, New York, 1962).

21. S. Spitzer and N. Denzin, Eds., *The Mental Patient: Studies in the Sociology of Deviance* (McGraw-Hill, New York, 1968).

22. C. Fletcher and L. Reynolds, *Sociol. Focus* 1, 9 (1968).

23. E. Goffman, *Asylums: Essays on the Social Situation of Mental Patients and Other Inmates* (Aldine, Chicago, 1962), p. 132.

24. T. Sarbin, in *Changing Perspectives in Mental Illness*, S. Plog and R. Edgerton, Eds. (Holt, Rinehart & Winston, New York, 1969), pp. 11, 15, 19.

25. D. Mechanic, *Ment. Hyg.* 46, 68 (1962).

26. G. Devereux, in *Some Uses of Anthropology: Theoretical and Applied*, J. Casagrande and T. Gladwin, Eds. (Anthropological Society of Washington, Washington, D.C., 1956), p. 23; A. Kroeber, *The Nature of Culture* (Univ. of Chicago Press, Chicago, 1952), pp. 310-319; R. Linton, *Culture and Mental Disorders* (Thomas, Springfield, Ill., 1956), pp. 98, 118-124; J. Silverman, *Am. Anthropol.* 69 (No. 1), 21 (1967).

27. W. Rivers, *Psychology and Ethnology* (Harcourt Brace, New York, 1926), pp. 38-50.

28. B. Whorf, *Language, Thought and Reality* (Technological Press of MIT, Cambridge, Mass., 1956).

29. J. Hughes [Murphy], thesis, Cornell University (1960). The recording of Eskimo words was conducted by Charles C. Hughes. The spelling given here follows the principles used in C. Hughes (with the collaboration of J. Murphy), *An Eskimo Village in the Modern World* (Cornell Univ. Press, Ithaca, N.Y., 1960). The census of 1940 which served as a baseline was prepared by Alexander Leighton and Dorothea Leighton. The extended statements by Eskimos and Yorubas which appear in quotation marks in the text are taken from my unpublished field notes, 1954-55, 1961, 1963. Most of the Eskimo and Yoruba phrases are also taken directly from these sources. In a few instances I have needed to paraphrase for intelligibility and therefore I have not used quotation marks for phrases.

30. A. Leighton and J. Murphy, in *Comparability in International Epidemiology*, R. Acheson, Ed. (Milbank Memorial Fund, New York, 1965), p. 189.

31. A. Leighton, T. Lambo, C. Hughes, D. Leighton, J. Murphy, D. Macklin, *Psychiatric Disorder among the Yoruba* (Cornell Univ. Press, Ithaca, N.Y., 1963).

32. J. Douglas, *The Social Meanings of Suicide* (Princeton Univ. Press, Princeton, N.J., 1967).

33. Prince found that *were* was defined for him in terms almost identical to those I present here; he studied 46 *were* specialists (34, p. 84).

34. R. Prince, in *Magic, Faith, and Healing*, A. Kiev, Ed. (Free Press of Glencoe, New York, 1964).

35. J. Murphy, in *Magic, Faith, and Healing*, A. Kiev, Ed. (Free Press of Glencoe, New York, 1964), p. 53.

36. M. Teicher, *J. Ment. Sci.* 100, 527 (1954).

37. In looking through a magazine with me, an Eskimo pointed to a picture and said that it resembled the shaman in seance; Fig. 1 is a photograph of that picture retouched to eliminate garments which the Eskimo said were irrelevant to the similarity.

38. A. deReuck and R. Porter, Eds., *Ciba Foundation Symposium: Transcultural Psychiatry* (Churchill, London, 1965); A. Kiev, *Transcultural Psychiatry* (Free Press, New York, 1972).

39. S. Parker, *Am. Anthropol.* 62, 603 (1960).

40. Z. Gussow, in *Psychoanalytic Study of Society*, W. Muensterberger, Ed. (International Univ. Press, New York, 1960), p. 218.

41. M. Teicher, *Windigo Psychosis* (American Ethnological Society, Seattle, 1960).

42. Gussow (40) provides a description of *pibloktoq* based on 14 recorded cases, mainly from explorers and ethnographers in the area from Greenland to the west coast of Alaska during the first part of this century. Recently a serious attempt was made to study *pibloktoq* properly and measure its prevalence. Ten cases were located from a population of 11,000 Innuit Eskimos. These cases were found on further study to be exceedingly heterogeneous: "Several subjects had epilepsy; several were diagnosed as schizophrenic; most had low normal serum calcium levels; one had hypomagnesemia and possible alcoholism" [E. Foulks, *The Arctic Hysterias of the North Alaskan Eskimo* (American Anthropological Association, Washington, D.C., 1972), p. 117]. This information suggests that *pibloktoq* is and may always have been a rare and ill-defined phenomenon. Regarding *wittiko* my assessment of the evidence is similar to Honigmann's when he says, "I can't find one [case] that satisfactorily attests to someone being seriously obsessed by the idea of committing cannibalism" (18, p. 401).

43. M. Beiser, J. Ravel, H. Collomb, C. Egelhoff, *J. Nerv. Ment. Dis.* 155, 77 (1972); M. Micklin, M. Durbin, C. Leon, *Am. Ethnol.* 1, 143 (1974); H. Kitano, in *Changing Perspectives in Mental Illness*, S. Plog and R. Edgerton, Eds. (Holt, Rinehart & Winston, New York, 1969), p. 256; R. Edgerton, *Am. Anthropol.* 68, 408 (1966); the following in *Magic, Faith, and Healing*, A. Kiev, Ed. (Free Press of Glencoe, New York, 1964): S. Fuchs, p. 121; K. Schmidt, p. 139; M. Gelfand, p. 156; B. Kaplan and D. Johnson, p. 203; M. Whisson, p. 283.

44. J. Murphy and A. Leighton, in *Approaches to Cross-Cultural Psychiatry*, J. Murphy and A. Leighton, Eds. (Cornell Univ. Press, Ithaca, N.Y., 1965), p. 64.

45. A. Rose, in *Human Behavior and Social Processes*, A. Rose, Ed. (Houghton Mifflin, Boston, 1962), p. 537.

46. Western society also lacked a comprehensive concept of neurosis prior to Freud's influence, but at the present time neurotic patterns hold a firm position in the official classifications of Western psychiatry; see *Diagnostic and Statistical Manual of Mental Disorders* (American Psychiatric Association, Washington, D.C., 1968).

47. H. Selby, *Zapotec Deviance, The Convergence of Folk and Modern Sociology* (Univ. of Texas Press, Austin, 1974).

48. Much of the support for labeling theory which Selby finds in his evidence stems from the following statement: "To the villagers, witches have an objective reality 'out there'. To me, they do not. I, the sociologist-anthropologist, do not believe that there are people in the world who have the capacity to float foreign objects through the air, insert them into my body, and make me sick or kill me" (47, p. 13). He concludes, "*We* create the deviants; they are products of our minds and our social processes." It seems to me this is a mistaken conclusion. I agree that the people who use witchcraft do not actually kill their victims by their incantations, burning effigies, boiling nail parings, and so on. The question, however, is whether some people actually carry out these maliciously intended acts. My work with Eskimos and Yorubas suggests that the idea of witchcraft is widely available to these groups just as the idea of lethal weapons is to us and that a few people in such groups really do conduct the rites that they believe will harm others (the artifacts of witchcraft attest to this), that they are genuinely deviant in these practices, and that they are the brunt of strong disapproval because of them. In this regard witchcraft involves real acts. It just happens that because these acts are by definition secret they give rise to distortions, false accusations, and misidentifications.

49. W. Bogoras, in *The Jesup North Pacific Expedition*, F. Boas, Ed. (Memoir of the American Museum of Natural History, New York, 1904-1909), p. 43.

50. T. Asuni, in *Deuxième Colloque Africain de Psychiatrie* (Association Universitaire pour le Développement de l'Enseignement et de la Culture en Afrique et à Madagascar, Paris, 1968), p. 115.

51. W. Bentz and J. Edgerton, *Soc, Psychiatr.* 6, 29 (1971); H. Spiro, I. Siassi, G. Crocetti, *ibid.* 8, 32 (1973).

52. F. Clements, *Primitive Concepts of Disease* (Univ. of California Publications in American Archeology and Ethnology, Berkeley, 1932).

53. W. Dunham, *Community and Schizophrenia, An Epidemiological Analysis* (Wayne State Univ. Press, Detroit, 1965), pp. 18, 19. Dunham indicates that 21 cases of schizophrenia were discovered in the Essen-Möller study. I use 17 of these (those for whom the author had high confidence that the pattern was schizophrenia). For comparability between Tables 1 and 2, I recalculated the rate for this one study. See also T. Lin, *Psychiatry* 16, 313 (1953), for a similar use and interpretation of several of the studies cited here.

54. E. Essen-Möller, *Individual Traits and Morbidity in a Swedish Rural Population* (Ejnar Munksgaard, Copenhagen, 1956). The rates for schizophrenia in the community and in the hospital were calculated from information on pp. 85-86.

55. A. Leighton, *My Name is Legion* (Basic Books, New York, 1959); D. Leighton, J. Harding, D. Macklin, A. Macmillan, A. Leighton, *The Character of Danger* (Basic Books, New York, 1963).

56. T. Lambo, in *Magic, Faith, and Healing*, A. Kiev, Ed. (Free Press of Glencoe, New York, 1964), p. 443; T. Asuni, *Am. J. Psychiatry* 124, 763 (1967).

57. J. Murphy, in *Transcultural Research in Mental Health*, W. Lebra, Ed. (Univ. Press of Hawaii, Honolulu, 1972), p. 213.

58. W. Weinberg, *Arch. Rassen. Gesellschaftsbiol.* 11, 434 (1915). The Weinberg method of adjusting the rate of mental illness for the probable age period of susceptibility is useful when the age distributions of the populations compared are different. Comparison of Western and non-Western populations particularly need such adjustment. The age of susceptibility for schizophrenia is assumed by Weinberg to be 16 to 40 years; I used 20 to 40 years because that age breakdown is available in the four studies compared.

59. The Eskimo and Yoruba studies which form the core of this paper, and the Canadian study used for comparison, have been carried on as part of the Harvard Program in Social Psychiatry directed by Alexander H. Leighton and supported by funds from the Social Science Research Center of Cornell (for the Eskimo studies), the National Institute of Mental Health, the Ministry of Health of Nigeria, and the Social Science Research Council (for the Yoruba studies), the Carnegie Corporation of New York, the Department of National Health and Welfare of Canada, the Department of Public Health of the Province of Nova Scotia, the Ford Foundation, and the Milbank Memorial Fund.

Carl W. O'Nell
Henry A. Selby

Sex differences in the incidence of susto in two Zapotec pueblos: an analysis of the relationships between sex role expectations and a folk illness[1]

Susto is a name frequently given to an illness widely reported in Hispanic America. Because of its obvious affinity to specific cultural patterns and because the condition falls beyond the pale of orthodox medical practice, susto is classed as a folk illness (Rubel 1964). In dealing with the phenomenon we have chosen susto in preference to other terms (e.g., espanto, miedo, pasmo, desasombro) largely because of its rather general usage in anthropological literature. Susto has been richly described by numerous authors writing on Hispanic American cultures, among the more recent being Carrasco (1960), Clark (1959), Foster (1953), Gillin (1948), Guiteras Holmes (1961), and Rubel (1960).

Although widely distributed in Hispanic America, the distribution is by no means uniform, and there are local variations in assumed causalities, symptomatologies, diagnoses, and treatment processes (Kelly 1965). Nevertheless, the consistencies in ethnographic reports of this condition for various groups are strong enough to warrant the description of a basic syndrome (Gillin 1948; Rubel 1964). In wakefulness, the susto sufferer is listless, depressed, and timid, usually exhibiting a loss of interest in his customary affairs, and frequently complaining of poor appetite and loss of strength. In sleep, the patient is restless, often complaining of troublesome dreams or other manifestations of sleep disturbance. One of the more consistently encountered folk beliefs is that the asustado (sufferer from susto) has lost his soul to a malignant spirit and that the patient's cure rests upon the recovery of the soul through specific treatments or rites performed by a curing specialist (2).

The majority of anthropological contributions to the subject of susto have been descriptive. Recent work (Clark 1959; Foster 1959; Gillin 1948) suggests that the condition probably serves a psycho-social function in certain cultural settings. The contribution of Rubel (1964) is particularly valuable, not only because it attempts an orderly description of the phenomenon—its symptomatology and folk etiology—but especially because it presents an array of hypotheses which can be considered for empirical research.

Reprinted by permission from Ethnology, 7:95-105, 1968.

Having learned in the course of our field work in two Zapotec communities in Oaxaca, Mexico, that *susto* was commonly experienced in both villages, we were encouraged to undertake a collaborative study of this folk illness as a psycho-social phenomenon. Using Rubel's work as a point of departure, we developed an hypothesis linking sex role performance to the incidence of *susto*. Each of us worked independently, collecting the necessary field data in his selected village, O'Nell in San Marcos Tlapazola and Selby in Santo Tomas Mazaltepec.

The Villages

The villages are each about one hour's drive by automobile from the city of Oaxaca. San Marcos Tlapazola lies to the southeast and Santo Tomas Mazaltepec to the northwest of the capital. Both are old foundations. Santo Tomas Mazaltepec is clearly pre-Columbian in origin, and it appears in the list of towns originally allotted to Cortez (Iturribaria 1955:75). The antiquity of San Marcos Tlapazola is not as clearly documented, although Spanish archives currently stored in the local *palacio*, dealing with civil and religious administrative affairs, support the probability that it was a settled community at the time of the arrival of the Spaniards.

The pre-conquest histories of the two pueblos are divergent, evidenced by the fact that San Marcos Tlapazola speaks a Valley dialect, and Santo Tomas Mazaltepec a Sierra dialect. Events since the Spanish conquest have tended to produce convergence. The two villages share approximately the same ecological conditions, subsistence patterns, social organization, and general cultural form. Despite their proximity—they are about 42 kilometers from each other (3)—there is no direct contact between them. For our purposes, then, they represent two independent cases within the same cultural area.

In describing their experiences with or knowledge of *susto*, the people in San Marcos Tlapazola and Santo Tomas Mazaltepec evidenced close agreement. Reports of symptomatology, folk etiology, and courses of treatment were essentially consistent between the two communities. Commonly reported symptoms closely approximated those making up the syndrome described by Rubel (1964).

A few variations will illustrate regional and individual differences which conceivably could be of importance in cross-regional studies of *susto*. These variations tended to be in the nature of additional symptoms, i.e., unexpected complaints offered in addition to, rather than in place of more commonly reported symptoms. Loosely ranked in order of the frequency with which they were reported, these symptoms were fever, muscular pains, complexion changes, nausea, other stomach or intestinal upsets, and vertigo. One person gave intense thirst as a *susto* symptom; another listed rectal bleeding.

There is also a widespread and interesting belief that in stubborn cases the assistance of a *medico* (orthodox medical practitioner) may be efficacious. Strongly implicit in this belief, however, is the notion that the powers of the native curer are paramount in soul recovery and that the medical doctor assists only in strengthening the body by supplying vitamins and other medicines. Also deserving of mention, because it is consistent with similar beliefs elsewhere in Hispanic America, is the belief that unless cured, *susto* culminates in death.

The Psycho-Social Function of *Susto*

Developing an hypothesis relating sex role expectations to the reported incidence of *susto* in each of the villages seemed the most feasible approach we could take in this study. Because of anticipated sampling difficulties and the reduced likelihood of obtaining sufficient data to specify variables, we excluded the study of age role expectations. And because of the gross social and cultural similarities between the villages, we focused the study on sex role differences rather than intervillage differences.

Following Rubel (1964), we made the basic assumption that *susto* represents an important culturally and socially sanctioned avenue of escape for an individual suffering from intra-culturally induced stress. *Susto* was assumed to be the result of an individual's self-perceived failure to meet a set of culturally established expectations in a role in which he had been socialized. Although not fundamental to the design of our study, we made the further assumption that the *susto* experience provides a person and his social group with mechanisms for the eventual social reinstatement of the individual.

Once a person is labeled *asustado*, an important shift obviously occurs in his relationship to others. Normal role expectations are relaxed to a greater or lesser extent and a new repertoire of behavior becomes appropriate. The *asustado* becomes temporarily what Goffman (1958:95-96) would call a "non-person"–a person who by virtue of his relaxed social situation can act without reference to the detailed codes that normally bind his behavior. The disease condition provides a psychological respite–a moratorium in normal role performance. This shift in role is conceived to be the basic function of *susto* as a psycho-social phenomenon. The culture provides a channel of escape for the relief of psychological stress engendered within the cultural framework.

Of no less importance, either to the individual or society, are the processes of rehabilitation and reintegration which ultimately will reunite the individual to his group (Parsons and Fox 1948). The treatment of the sufferer involves a temporory change of status which of itself may signal the beginning of rehabilitation. By village standards, considerable time and money are expended upon the *asustado*. More importantly, perhaps, he frequently becomes the focus of a great deal of sympathetic understanding, especially within his own extended family group. The treatment thus constitutes a form of reassurance that the sufferer is, in fact, an important member of the extended family.

From Bateson's (1958) point of view, the development of *susto* constitutes a signal that schism within the extended family had gone too far for the affected individual to tolerate. Treatment is the process whereby the schism is resolved and the sufferer is reincorporated into the group.

We do not, of course, assume that *susto* represents the only mechanism of escape in the face of stress generated through self-perceived role inadequacy. General health conditions, temperamental tendencies, personality traits, situational variables, and other factors conceivably must all be assumed to have a bearing upon whether a given person develops *susto* when confronted with role stress or whether some other avenue of relief from stress becomes manifest. Our assumption is merely that, once it is developed, *susto* presents us with a measure of role stress.

Cognizant of all the preceding assumptions, but focusing upon the assumption that *susto* is the result of emotional stress engendered through a self-perceived failure to meet a set of social expectations regarding sex role performance, we have formulated the following hypothesis: *The sex which experiences the greater intra-cultural stress in the process of meeting sex role expectations will evidence the greater susceptibility to susto.*

Sex Role Differences

Male-female sex role differences hinge fundamentally upon the differential socialization of boys and girls. Parents in the two communities often indicate that boys are more delicate than girls in infancy with the observable result that boys are more freely indulged. The factual basis for this alleged delicacy is difficult to validate with our data, but it agrees with findings in our own and other cultures that male infants are subject to higher mortality rates than are female infants (Scheinfeld 1958). It may simply reflect a prevailing tendency to prefer male offspring to female offspring.

From some point early in childhood girls learn that they are more restricted than boys. A small sample of mothers in Santo Tomas Mazaltepec (N = 6) indicated that boys require greater indulgence than girls because they are eventually due to experience greater liberty. Although parents in San Marcos Tlapazola were less explicit on this point, very young boys were more frequently observed moving about freely in the *calles* near their homes than were young girls.

In middle childhood both sexes are expected to perform certain simple duties, such as carrying small bundles and running errands. Observation seems to indicate that boys frequently escape punishment for dalliance on errands, whereas girls may be severely reprimanded or punished for similar dalliance. Responsibilities of child care are preponderantly allotted to girls, although boys do not escape such duties, especially if there are no girls in the household.

Young boys are permitted, even encouraged under certain conditions, to manifest aggressive behavior, whereas girls rarely exhibit aggressive tendencies and run the risk of punishment if they do exhibit them. This is particularly evident in teasing behavior and the maltreatment of small animals.

Prepubescent and adolescent girls are expected to learn and master many tasks the counterparts of which occur much later for boys. At an age when a boy is just learning how to direct a plow and drive oxen, a girl may be married, pregnant, and responsible for an adult woman's tasks of food preparation.

These differences in socialization are but reflections of the differential sexrole expectations of mature men and women. A woman should be constantly at work caring for her house, her children, her mother-in-law, her husband, or tending to her pottery making. In contrast, a man is expected to rest periodically because his work is deemed to be harder. If a woman appears idle she is suspected of being a gossip. Except for infidelity, this is the worst offense a woman can commit since it tends to disrupt communal harmony.

A woman is expected to control herself. In Santo Tomas Mazaltepec a woman's loss of composure is associated with temporary possession of *mal de ojo* (evil eye). In San Marcos Tlapazola it may indicate that the woman is incapable of presenting a proper spiritual defense against malignant forces which may harm her or her family. In either circumstance an angry mother is frequently held accountable for illness in her children. The ideal woman is enduring and patient. Men, too, are expected to control themselves, but if a man seriously loses his temper it is often assumed that he is justified in doing so.

A woman must be submissive and give no indication of rebelliousness (actually women learn to get their way by the practice of guile). Ideally, men do not rebel either, but they have at their disposal many more ways of making their wishes known or effecting their own plans.

The Zapotec woman in these communities is allowed virtually no freedom of sexual expression, and she must tolerate her husband's infidelities as long as he does not publicly proclaim a rupture in their marital relations. Men, on the other hand, enjoy a distinct sexual advantage in being able to exploit women other than their wives. Cognizant of the intricacies of this situation, men show extreme jealousy of their wives. The slightest suspicion of infidelity grants a man license to beat his wife. Unaccompanied women do not move about freely in either village. Men frequently say, "Women have no vices because they do not go out in the streets." It would be more correct to say, "Women do not go out in the streets so that there will be no suspicion of vice."

Residential patterns after marriage also complicate a woman's sex role expectations compared to those for men. In both Santo Tomas Mazaltepec and San Marcos Tlapazola it is customary for the young bride to move to her husband's family. In Santo Tomas Mazaltepec residence is 75 per cent patrilocal, i.e., with the husband's parents. In San Marcos Tlapazola it is 78 per cent patrilocal (4).

Currently some girls marry as early as fourteen years of age (5). Although the vast majority of marriages are contracted within the village, girls move into a new extended family setting. The emotional effect of changing residential patterns at marriage may be considerable. The new bride is subject to the authority not only of her husband but also of his mother and father, and in fact she may find that she has to obey many other persons as well. To be sure, the authority of her father-in-law or husband's older brother may be indirect, it is nevertheless felt and in actuality may outweigh the authority of her husband.

The mother-in-law is usually the key figure with whom the new bride has to contend. The young girl may literally be under the surveillance of her mother-in-law from dawn until dusk. The prevailing ethic brooks no disrespect or disobedience to the mother-in-law, and neither beatings, tongue lashings, nor "sweat-shop" work conditions constitute grounds for noncompliance. Ordinarily mothers-in-law are strict, much stricter than mothers. Boys continue to work with their fathers and brothers even after marriage. Young men, married or unmarried, have considerable freedom of movement and in their leisure meet with friends in the *calles* or the *cantinas*.

Children represent a positive value in these communities. Sterility is regarded as a very unfortunate condition and is feared by married couples since it means that in old age they will not have the assistance of adult children. The major responsibility of any married woman is the bearing and rearing of children. If the union is sterile, the onus of sterility is commonly placed on the woman, although some people realize that men as well as women can be sterile. Child mortality in the two villages is high—conservatively estimated at about 40 per cent of all births. Stillbirths are frequent, and in such cases little if any public recognition is given to the fact that pregnancy has even occurred. For children who have survived the first year of life, however, death is viewed as a tragic occurrence, and someone, nearly always the mother, is held responsible for the tragedy. (In neither village did we observe the resignation to the death of young children which has been reported for other parts of Meso-America.) The grave responsibilities associated with having children and the uncertainties which surround it constitute a potential source of deep emotional stress weighing more heavily upon women than upon men.

It seems quite clear that women must conform to a tighter set of role expectations than men. Moreover, they have fewer ways of reducing anxiety over role performance. The role expectations of the male more readily allow him to shift responsibility from his shoulders than is true for the female. If his crops do poorly, he may blame the weather or a malevolent agent, but if the woman fails in her household tasks or in the care of children she alone is to blame. Similarly men are freer than women to engage in strategic retreat from uncomfortable situations. A man under emotional stress may relieve his anxieties by going to his *milpa* (corn field) for a day, on a trading expedition for a week, or, if necessary, to the *fincas* (plantations) in the hot country for a prolonged period of work. Women, with extremely few exceptions, cannot practice comparable forms of social withdrawal. Finally, men can retreat into an approved state of irresponsibility, the most frequent and obvious being that of drunkenness. The *borracho* (drunk), even when he proves to be a nuisance, is treated with exceptional tolerance. People are also willing to concede that he may have his reasons, and there are many situations in which this method of escape is socially sanctioned.

Young women are effectively barred by community pressures from using drunkenness as an escape from responsibility. And older women, who enjoy increased status (6) and greater freedom from restraint in their use of alcohol, find the occasions which they can use alcohol with impunity fewer in number and kind than those open even to younger males.

Two additional measures of differential sex role expectations support our other ethnographic observations. The first of these measures freedom of social participation; the second measures cognitive evaluation.

In Santo Tomas Mazaltepec drunken fiestas lasting three to five days are customarily celebrated in honor of a person's saint's day (called *cuelga* or *dia del onomastico*). These are socially sanctioned occasions when participants are permitted relatively free expression of aggression and affective feelings. We interpret them as opportunities for the relief of emotional stress. The frequency of *cuelga* attendance by men and women, obtained from a sample of 55 individuals in Santo Tomas Mazaltepec, revealed a statistically significant difference between the sexes (see Table 1).

Table 1. Reported attendance at cuelgas in Santo Tomas Mazaltepec: differential response by sex

	Attend	*Do Not Attend*	*Total*
Men	26	4	30
Women	12	13	25
Total	38	17	55

Result: $x^2 = 7.2$; $p < 0.01$ (1df).

If our assumption about the *cuelga* as a sanctioned means of stress relief is correct, it appears that men are significantly freer to avail themselves of this avenue of escape than women are. However, one must be cautious in making the broad assumption that the *cuelga* operates uniformly as a mechanism for relief from stress for the two sexes. It may be that young married women find attendance at *cuelgas* stressful (7).

The second measure is one of the cognitive evaluation of comfort in the life situation. Fifty individuals in San Marcos Tlapazola—25 men and 25 women—were asked which sex, in their opinion, finds life more comfortable. The results are reported in Table 2.

Table 2. Differential response by sex concerning which sex experiences greater comfort in the life situation (San Marcos Tlapazola)

	Men Do	*Women Do*	*Both Equal*	*Total*
Men	13	5	7	25
Women	16	2	7	25
Total	29	7	14	50

Both men and women agree that life is more comfortable for men than it is for women. We find the agreement between the sexes on this matter interesting in view of the fact that it supports descriptive ethnographic data gathered largely by observation with data of an evaluative type from a sizable sample of informants.

Differential Susceptibility to *Susto*

Since women appear to experience greater intra-cultural stress than do men in the process of meeting sex-role expectations in both San Marcos Tlapazola and Santo Tomas Mazaltepec, our hypothesis would lead us to anticipate that they would reveal greater susceptibility to *susto* than men. Susceptibility to *susto* is defined as the relative proportions of individuals of each sex reporting *susto*.

The data were gather first in San Marcos Tlapazola from a sample of 30 individuals—fifteen males and fifteen females. They were commonly sought in context with other data, the rationale being that people might not respond readily if confronted by direct questions regarding their experiences with *susto*. In the course of gathering other data, respondents were asked about their personal experiences with *susto* when it seemed convenient to do so. The questions followed a generalized pattern, though they were not always phrased in exactly the same terms for all respondents. They were first presented in Spanish in most cases but frequently had to be repeated in Zapotec. The respondent was first asked whether or not he had experienced *susto* at any time in his life. Then his approximate age at the time of each experience and its duration were recorded. If they wished to do so, respondents were allowed to give details of their experiences concerning symptoms, precipitating causes, etc., but such data were not actively solicited. The ethnographer indicated an equal interest in negative and positive responses to guard against bias.

It was found that most people showed no obvious reluctance to answering questions about their experiences with *susto*. Consequently some persons—both men and women—were approached directly with these questions. In such cases the investigator made it known that he was interested in various health problems in the village and would appreciate any help the respondent might give him by answering a question or two about his experiences with *susto*.

For each individual it was noted whether or not he or she had experienced *susto*. The case was considered positive if an individual reported having had such an experience, regardless of the number and intensity of the experiences reported. An individual was regarded as a negative case if he reported no such experience. A chi square (x^2) test was made of the individual responses. The x^2 difference between men and women was 2.14 (1 df.) Though not significant at the .05 level, this result was encouraging; 67 per cent of the women reported some experience with *susto* as compared to 40 per cent of the men.

Two modifications were made in the method for Santo Tomas Mazaltepec. First, it was felt that a random sample was necessary to control for latent bias. Second, it was decided to take a slightly larger sample. Accordingly, a sample of 40 persons—twenty males and twenty females—over twenty years of age was

Table 3. Relative proportions of males and females reporting *susto* in San Marcos Tlapazola

	One or More Times	Never	Total
Men	6 (40%)	9 (60%)	15
Women	10 (67%)	5 (33%)	15
Total	16	14	30

Result: $x^2 = 2.14$; $p > 0.10$ (1 df).

randomly made of the entire native population of Santo Tomas Mazaltepec. Each respondent was asked directly, i.e., not in connection with other data, whether or not he or she had ever experienced *susto*. The number of experiences, the ages at which they had occurred, and the duration of each were recorded for each respondent.

A chi square (x^2) test was run on these data, and the result $x^2 = 5.22$ (1 df) was significant, $p < 0.025$. In Santo Tomas Mazaltepec 55 per cent of the women sampled indicated that they had experienced *susto* at some time in their lives as compared to 20 per cent of the men (see Table 4).

Table 4. Relative proportions of males and females reporting *susto* in Santo Tomas Mazaltepec

	One or More Times	Never	Total
Men	4 (20%)	16 (80%)	20
Women	11 (55%)	9 (45%)	20
Totals	15	25	40

Result: $x^2 = 5.22$; $p < 0.025$ (1 df).

Conclusions

We feel that these two independent tests of our hypothesis serve to support our basic assumption that *susto* represents an important culturally and socially sanctioned mechanism of escape and rehabilitation for persons suffering from intra-culturally induced stress resulting from failure in sex-role performance. The ethnographic evidence encountered in the two villages indicated that women stand the greater likelihood of experiencing role stress both because their sex roles are more narrowly defined than are those for men and because fewer outlets for escape from stress are open to them in this culture. Consistent with this is our evidence on differential susceptibility, indicating a markedly higher incidence of *susto* among women than among men.

The fact that the percentages of men and women who experienced *susto* were greater in San Marcos Tlapazola than in Santo Tomas Mazaltepec may possibly reflect unanalyzed differences between the two communities. On the other hand, they may be only a reflection of differences in method. If this is the case, the data collected in Santo Tomas Mazaltepec, because of the use random sampling, may be presumed to represent the situation in that community more accurately than would be true of the data collected in San Marcos Tlapazola.

Ethnographic work on *susto* has largely tended to be descriptive. Valuable as this has been for many purposes, it is limited in the understandings it provides of the cultural, social, and psychological underpinnings of folk illnesses such as *susto*. We agree with Rubel (1964:269) who writes:

> *In the absence of precise chronological, social or cultural parameters it is hazardous to attempt to infer rates of prevalence or incidence of a folk illness, much less the relationships which obtain between these rates and such demographic variables as age, sex or marital status. Yet it is precisely from such inferences and associations that we may hope to gain an understanding of the nature of folk illness.*

Notes

1. We wish to express our gratitude to Robert A. Le Vine of the University of Chicago and to Arthur J. Rubel of the University of Notre Dame for their interest in and comments upon this paper, but any short-comings it may have are our own.
2. Either male (*curanderos*) or female (*curanderas*) curers are sought to alleviate this condition in various places in Oaxaca. However, residents of San Marcos Tlapazola insist that only women are effective as curers of *susto* in their community. This preference was not noted for Santo Tomas Mazaltepec.
3. Estimated from a map of Oaxaca produced by Cecil R. Welte (Mapa de las localidades del Valle de Oaxaca, segun el censo de poblacion de 1960, Oaxaca, 1965).
4. These percentages were higher in the past (cf. Murdock 1960:13). In San Marcos Tlapazola, however, 35 per cent of all households are nuclear family residential units.
5. A small number of informants in Santo Tomas Mazaltepec reported marriages at from six to eight years of age, and the customary age for the marriage of girls in previous generations was reported to be from ten to twelve years of age. When this occurred it meant that the young girl, still immature, went to live with her husband's family. Such a girl slept with her mother-in-law until she was sufficiently developed to sleep with her husband. During this maturation period the young girl was socialized in her wifely role under the close supervision of her mother-in-law. Older informants who had experienced this pattern reported that they went to their husbands' houses ignorant of sex, nervous at leaving their family of orientation, feeling abandoned, exploited, and intimidated. Young husbands during the same period of maturation neither changed their residence nor were they so closely supervised. Older and freer than their wives, they were permitted the adolescent license of running with a *palomilla* (gang) and gaining such sexual experience as could be found.
6. Upon becoming a *suegra* (mother-in-law) a woman's status changes appreciably in both communities. The status of mother-in-law brings with it not only respect, deference, and obedience from daughters-in-law but also some relaxation of the disabilities and restrictions associated with the feminine role. At its fullest expression it brings with it a privi-

lege of drunken license and ribaldry approximating that of a senior male.
7. Women who attend these fiestas in Santo Tomas Mazaltepec may actually be subjected to increased stress by the fact of their attendance. Although older women may participate rather freely in the festivities, younger women are expected to remain in the background, sitting discreetly to one side if not working in the kitchen. If a man wishes to dance with a woman other than his wife, he requests this privilege of her husband. Women fear such requests because they may raise suspicion and ire in their husbands. The wife of a jealous man is in danger of a beating on such an occasion.

Mark Zborowski

Cultural components in responses to pain 1

This paper reports on one aspect of a larger study: that concerned with discovering the role of cultural patterns in attitudes toward and reactions to pain which is caused by disease and injury—in other words, responses to spontaneous pain.

Some Basic Distinctions

In human societies biological processes vital for man's survival acquire social and cultural significance. Intake of food, sexual intercourse or elimination—physiological phenomena which are universal for the entire living world—become institutions regulated by cultural and social norms, thus fulfilling not only biological functions but social and cultural ones as well. Metabolic and endocrinal changes in the human organism may provoke hunger and sexual desire, but culture and society dictate to man the kind of food he may eat, the social setting for eating or the adequate partner for mating.

Moreover, the role of cultural and social patterns in human physiological activities is so great that they may in specific situations act against the direct biological needs of the individual, even to the point of endangering his survival. Only a human being may prefer starvation to the breaking of a religious dietary law or may abstain from sexual intercourse because of specific incest regulations. Voluntary fasting and celibacy exist only where food and sex fulfill more than strictly physiological functions.

Thus, the understanding of the siginificance and role of social and cultural patterns in human physiology is necessary to clarify those aspects of human experience which remain puzzling if studied only within the physiological frame of reference.

Reprinted by permission of the *Journal of Social Issues,* Vol. 8, No. 4 (1952), pp. 16-30.

Pain is basically a physiological phenomenon and as such has been studied by physiologists and neurologists such as Harold Wolff, James Hardy, Helen Goodell, C. S. Lewis, W. K. Livingston and others. By using the most ingenious methods of investigation they have succeeded in clarifying complex problems of the physiology of pain. Many aspects of perception and reaction to pain were studied in expermental situations involving the most careful preparation and complicated equipment. These investigators have come to the conclusion that "from the physiological point of view pain qualifies as a sensation of importance to the self-preservation of the individual (2). The biological function of pain is to provoke special reactive patterns directed toward avoidance of the noxious stimulus which presents a threat to the individual. In this respect the function of pain is basically the same for man as for the rest of the animal world.

However, the physiology of pain and the understanding of the biological function of pain do not explain other aspects of what Wolff, Hardy and Goodell call the *pain experience*, which includes not only certain "associated feeling states" (3). It would not explain, for example, the acceptance of intense pain in torture which is part of the initiation rites of many primitive societies, nor will it explain the strong emotional reactions of certain individuals to the slight sting of the hypodermic needle.

In human society pain, like so many other physiological phenomena, acquires specific social and cultural significance, and accordingly, certain reactions to pain can be understood in the light of this significance. As Drs. Hardy, Wolff and Goodell state in their recent book, ". . . the culture in which a man finds himself becomes the conditioning influence in the formation of the individual reaction patterns to pain . . . A knowledge of group attitudes toward pain is extremely important to an understanding of the individual reaction" (4).

In analyzing pain, it is useful to distinguish between self-inflicted, other-inflicted and spontaneous pain. Self-inflicted pain is defined as deliberately self-inflicted. It is experienced as a result of injuries performed voluntarily upon oneself, e.g., self-mutilation. Usually these injuries have a culturally defined purpose, such as achieving a special status in the society. It can be observed not only in primitive cultures but also in contemporary societies on a higher level of civilization. In Germany, for instance, members of certain student or military organizations would cut their faces with a razor in order to acquire scars which would identify them as members of a distinctive social group. By other-inflicted pain is meant pain inflicted upon the individual in the process of culturally accepted and expected activities (regardless of whether approved or disapproved), such as sports, fights, war, etc. To this category belongs also pain inflicted by the physician in the process of medical treatment. Spontaneous pain usually denotes the pain sensation which results from disease or injury. This term also covers pain of psychogenic nature.

Members of different cultures may assume differing attitudes towards these various types of pain. Two of these attitudes may be described as pain expectancy and pain acceptance. Pain expectancy is anticipation of pain as being avoidable in a given situation, for instance, in childbirth, in sports activities or in battle. Pain acceptance is characterized by a willingness to experience pain. This attitude is manifested mostly as an inevitable component of culturally accepted experiences, for instance, as part of initiation rites or part of medical treatment. The following example will help to clarify the differences between pain expectancy and pain acceptance. Labor pain is expected as part of childbirth, but while in one culture, such as in the United States, it is not accepted and therefor various means are used to alleviate it, in some other cultures, for instance in Poland, it is not only expected but also accepted, and consequently nothing or little is done to relieve it. Similarly, cultures which emphasize military achievements expect and accept battle wounds, while cultures which emphasize pacifistic values may expect them but will not accept them.

In the process of investigating cultural attitudes toward pain it is also important to distinguish between pain apprehension and pain anxiety. Pain apprehension reflects the tendency to avoid the pain sensation as such, regardless of whether the pain is spontaneous or inflicted, whether it is accepted or not. Pain anxiety, on the other hand, is a state of anxiety provoked by the pain experience, focused upon various aspects of the causes of pain, the meaning of pain or its significance for the welfare of the individual.

Moreover, members of various cultures may react differently in terms of their manifest behavior toward various pain experiences, and this behavior is often dictated by the culture which provides specific norms according to the age, sex and social position of the individual.

The fact that other elements as well as cultural factors are involved in the response to a spontaneous pain should be taken into consideration. These other factors are the pathological aspect of pain, the specific physiological characteristics of the pain experience, such as the intensity, the duration and the quality of the pain sensation, and finally, the personality of the individual. Nevertheless, it was felt that in the process of a careful investigation it would be possible to detect the role of the cultural components in the pain experience.

The Research Setting

In setting up the research we were interested not only in the purely theoretical aspects of the findings in terms of possible contribution to the understanding of the pain experience in general; we also had in mind the practical goal of a contribution to the field of medicine. In the relationship between the doctor and his patient the respective attitudes toward pain may play a crucial role, especially when the doctor feels that the patient exaggerates his pain while the patient feels that the doctor minimizes his suffering. The same may be true, for instance, in a hospital where the members of the medical and nursing staff may have attitudes toward pain different from those held by the patient, or when they expect a certain pattern of behavior according to their cultural background while the patient may manifest a behavior pattern which is acceptable in his culture. These differences may play an important part in the evaluation of the individual pain experience, in dealing with pain at home and in the hospital, in administration of analgesics, etc. Moreover, we expected that this study of pain would offer opportunities to gain insight into related attitudes toward health, disease, medication, hospitalization, medicine in general, etc.

With these aims in mind the project was set up at the Kingsbridge Veterans Hospital, Bronx, New York (5), where four ethno-cultural groups were selected for an intensive study. These groups included patients of Jewish, Italian, Irish and "Old American" stock. Three groups—Jews, Italians, and Irish—were selected because they were described by medical people as manifesting striking differences in their reaction to pain. Italians and Jews were described as tending to "exaggerate" their pain, while the Irish were often depicted as stoical individuals who were able to take a great deal of pain. The fourth group, the "Old Americans," were chosen because the values and attitudes of this group dominate in this country and are held by many members of the medical profession and by many descendants of the immigrants who, in the process of Americanization, tend to adopt American patterns of behavior. The members of this group can be defined as White, native-born individuals, usually Protestant, whose grandparents, at least, were born in the United States and who do not identify themselves with any foreign group, either nationally, socially or culturally.

The Kingsbridge Veterans Hospital was chosen because its population represents roughly the ethnic composition of New York City, thus offering access to a fair sample of the four selected groups, and also because various age groups were represented among the hospitalized veterans of World War I, World War II and the Korean War. In one major respect this hospital was not adequate, namely, in not offering the opportunity to investigate sex differences in attitude toward pain. This aspect of research will be carried out in a hospital with a large female population.

In setting up this project we were mainly interested in discovering certain regularities in reactions and attitudes toward pain characteristic of the four groups. Therefore, the study has a qualitative character, and the efforts of the researchers were not directed toward a collection of material suitable for quantitative analysis. The main techniques used in the collection of the material were interviews with patients of the selected groups, observation of their behavior when in pain and discussion of the individual case with doctors, nurses and other people directly or indirectly involved in the pain experience of the individual. In addition to the interviews with patients, "healthy" members of the respective groups were interviewed on their attitudes toward pain, because in terms of the original hypothesis those attitudes and reactions which are displayed by the patients of the given cultural groups are held by all members of the group regardless of whether or not they are in pain although in pain these attitudes may come more sharply into focus. In certain cases the researchers have interviewed a member of the patient's immediate family in order to check the report of the patient on his pain experience and in order to find out what are the attitudes and reactions of the family toward the patient's experience.

These interviews, based on a series of open-ended questions, were focused upon the past and present pain experiences of the interviewee. However, many other areas were considered important for the understanding of this experience. For instance, it was felt that complaints of pain may play an important role in manipulating relationships in the family and the larger social environment. It was also felt that in order to understand the specific reactive patterns in controlling pain it is important to know certain aspects of child-rearing in the culture, relationships between parents and children, the role of infliction of pain in punishment, the attitudes of various members of the family toward specific expected, accepted pain experiences, and so on. The interviews were recorded on wire and transcribed verbatim for an ultimate detailed analysis. The interviews usually lasted for approximately two hours, the time being limited by the condition of the interviewee and by the amount and quality of his answers. When it was considered necessary an interview was repeated. In most of the cases the study of the interviewee was followed by informal conversations and by observation of his behavior in the hospital.

The information gathered from the interviews was discussed with members of the medical staff, especially in the areas related to the medical aspects of the problem, in order to get their evaluation of the pain experience of the patient. Information as to the personality of the patient was checked against results of psychological testing by members of the psychological staff of the hospital when these were available.

The discussion of the material presented in this paper is based on interviews with 103 respondents, including 87 hospital patients in pain and 16 healthy subjects. According to their ethno-cultural background the respondents are distributed as follows: "Old Americans," 26; Italians, 24; Jews, 31; Irish, 11; and others, 11 (6). In addition, there were the collateral interviews and conversations noted above with family members, doctors, nurses and other members of the hospital staff.

With regard to the pathological causes of pain the majority of the interviewees fall into the group of patients suffering from neurological diseases, mainly herniated discs and spinal lesions. The focusing upon a group of patients suffering from a similar pathology offered the opportunity to investigate reactions and attitudes toward spontaneous pain which is symptomatic of one group of diseases. Nevertheless, a number of patients suffering from other diseases were also interviewed.

This paper is based upon the material collected during the first stage of study. The generalizations are to a great extent tentative formulations on a descriptive level. There has been no attempt as yet to integrate the results with the value system and the cultural pattern of the group, though here and there will be indications to the effect that they are part of the culture pattern. The discussions will be limited to main regularities within three groups, namely, the Italians, the Jews and the "Old Americans." Factors related to variations within each group will be discussed after the main prevailing patterns have been presented.

Pain Among Patients of Jewish and Italian Origin

As already mentioned, the Jews and Italians were selected mainly because interviews with medical experts suggested that they display similar reactions to pain. The investigation of this similarity provided the opportunity to check a rather popular assumption that similar reactions reflect similar attitudes. The differences between the Italian and Jewish culture are great enough to suggest that if the attitudes are related to cultural pattern they will also be different despite the apparent similarlity in manifest behavior.

Members of both groups were described as being very emotional in their responses to pain. They were described as tending to exaggerate their pain experience and being very sensitive to pain. Some of the doctors stated that in their opinion Jews and Italians have a lower threshold of pain than members of other ethnic groups, especially members of the so-called Nordic group. This statement seems to indicate a certain confusion as to the concept of the threshold of pain. According to people who have studied the problem of the threshold of pain, for instance Harold Wolff and his associates, the threshold of pain is more or less the same for all human beings regardless of nationality, sex or age.

In the course of the investigation the general impressions of doctors were confirmed to a great extent by the interview material and by the observation of the patients' behavior. However, even a superficial study of the interviews has revealed that though reactions to pain appear to be similar the underlying attitudes toward pain are different in the two groups. While the Italian patients seemed to be mainly concerned with the immediacy of the pain experience and were disturbed by the actual pain sensation which they experienced in a given situation, the concern of patients of Jewish origin was focused mainly upon the symptomatic meaning of pain and upon the signifiance of pain in relation to their health, welfare, and eventually, for the welfare of the families. The Italian patient expressed in his behavior and in his complaints the discomfort caused by pain as such, and he manifested his emotions with regard to the effects of this pain experience upon his immediate situation in terms of occupation, economic situation and so on; the Jewish patient expressed primarily his worries and anxieties as to the extent to which the pain indicated a threat to his health. In this connection it is worth mentioning that one of the Jewish words to describe strong pain is *yessurim*, a word which is also used to describe worries and anxieties.

Attitudes of Italian and Jewish patients toward pain-relieving drugs can serve as an indication of their attitude toward pain. When in pain the Italian calls for pain relief and is mainly concerned with the analgesic effects of the drugs which are administered to him. Once the pain is relieved the Italian patient easily forgets his sufferings and manifests a happy and joyful disposition. The Jewish patient, however, often is reluctant to accept the drug, and he explains this reluctance in terms of concern about the effects of the drug upon his health in general. He is apprehensive about the habit-forming aspects of the analgesic. Moreover, he feels that the drug relieves his pain only temporarily and does not cure him of the disease which may cause the pain. Nurses and doctors have reported cases in which patients would hide the pill which was given to them to relieve their pain and would prefer to suffer. These reports were confirmed in the interviews with the patients. It was also observed that many Jewish patients after being relieved from pain often continued to display the same depressed and worried behavior because they felt that though the pain was currently absent it may recur as long as the disease was not cured completely. From these observations it appears that when one deals with a Jewish and Italian patient in pain, in the first case it is more important to relieve the anxieties with regard to the sources of pain, while in the second it is more important to relieve the actual pain.

Another indication as to the significance of pain for Jewish and Italian patients is their respective attitudes toward the doctor. The Italian patient seems to display a most confident attitude toward the doctor which is usually reinforced after the doctor has succeeded in relieving pain, whereas the Jewish patient manifests a skeptical attitude, feeling that the fact that the doctor has relieved his pain by some drug does not mean at all that he is skillful enough to take care of the basic illness. Consequently, even when the pain is relieved, he tends to check the diagnosis and the treatment of one doctor against the opinions of other specialists in the field. Summarizing the difference between the Italian and Jewish attitudes, one can say that the Italian attitude is characterized by a present-oriented apprehension with regard to the actual sensation of pain, and the Jew tends to manifest a future-oriented anxiety as to the symptomatic and general meaning of the pain experience.

It has been stated that the Italians and Jews tend to manifest similar behavior in terms of their reactions to pain. As both cultures allow for free expression of feelings and emotions by words, sounds and gestures, both the Italians and Jews feel free to talk about their pain, complain about it and manifest their sufferings by groaning, moaning, crying, etc. They are not ashamed of this expression. They admit willingly that when they are in pain they do complain a great deal, call for help and expect sympathy and assistance from other members of their immediate social environment, especially from members of their family. When in pain they are reluctant to be alone and prefer the presence and attention of other people. This behavior, which is expected, accepted and approved by the Italian and Jewish cultures often conflicts with the patterns of behavior expected from a patient by American or Americanized medical people. Thus they tend to describe the behavior of the Italian and Jewish patient as exaggerated and over-emotional. The material suggests that they do tend to minimize the actual pain experiences of the Italian and Jewish patient regardless of whether they have the objective criteria for evaluating the actual amount of pain which the patient experiences. It seems that the uninhibited display of reaction to pain as manifested by the Jewish and Italian patient provokes distrust in American culture instead of provoking sympathy.

Despite the close similarity between the manifest reactions among Jews and Italians, there seem to be differences in emphasis especially with regard to what the patient achieves by these reactions and as to the specific manifestations of these reactions in the various social settings. For instance, they differ in their behavior at home and in the hospital. The Italian husband, who is aware of his role as an adult male, tends to avoid verbal complaining at home, leaving this type of behavior to the women. In the hospital, where he is less concerned with his role as a male, he tends to be more verbal and more emotional. The Jewish patient, on the contrary, seems to be more calm in the hospital than at home. Traditionally the Jewish male does not emphasize his masculinity through such traits as stoicism, and he does not equate verbal complaints with weakness. Moreover, the Jewish culture allows the patient to be demanding and complaining. Therefore, he tends more to use his pain in order to control interpersonal relationships within the family. Though similar use of pain to manipulate the relationships between members of the family may be present also in some other cultures it seems that in the Jewish culture this is not disapproved, while in others it is. In the hospital one can also distinguish variations in the reactive patterns among Jews and Italians. Upon his admission to the hospital and in the presence of the doctor the Jewish patient tends to complain, ask for help, be emotional even to the point of crying. However, as soon as he feels that adequate care is given to him he becomes more restrained. This suggests that the display of pain reaction serves less as an indication of the amount of pain experienced than as a means to create an atmosphere and setting in which the pathological cause of pain will be best taken care of. The Italian patient, on the other hand, seems to be less concerned with setting up a favorable situation for treatment. He takes for granted that adequate care will be given to him, and in the presence of the doctor he seems to be somewhat calmer than the Jewish patient. The mere presence of the doctor reassures the Italian patient, while the skepticism of the Jewish patient limits the reassuring role of the physician.

To summarize the description of the reactive patterns of the Jewish and Italian patients, the material suggests that on a semi-conscious level the Jewish patient tends to provoke worry and concern in his social environment as to the state of his health and the symptomatic character of his pain, while the Italian tends to provoke sympathy toward his suffering. In one case the function of the pain reaction will be the mobilization of the efforts of the family and the doctors toward a complete cure, while in the second case the function of the reaction will be focused upon the mobilization of effort toward relieving the pain sensation.

On the basis of the discussion of the Jewish and Italian material two generalizations can be made: (1) *Similar reactions to pain manifested by members of different ethno-cultural groups do not necessarily reflect similar attitudes to pain.* (2) *Reactive patterns similar in terms of their manifestations may have different functions and serve different purposes in various cultures.*

Pain Among Patients of "Old American" Origin

There is little emphasis on emotional complaining among "Old American" patients. Their complaints about pain can best be described as reporting on pain. In describing pain, the "Old American" patient tries to find the most appropriate ways of defining the quality of pain, its localization, duration, etc. When examined by the doctor he gives the impression of trying to assume the detached role of an unemotional observer who gives the most efficient description of his state for a correct diagnosis and treatment. The interviewees repeatedly state that there is no point in complaining and groaning and moaning, etc., because "it won't help anybody." However, they readily admit that when pain is unbearable they may react strongly, even to the point of crying, but they tend to do it when they are alone. Withdrawal from society seems to be a frequent reaction to strong pain.

There seem to be different patterns in reacting to pain depending on the situation. One pattern, manifested in the presence of members of the family, friends, etc., consists of attempts to minimize pain, to avoid complaining and provoking pity; when pain becomes too strong there is a tendency to withdraw and express freely such reactions as groaning, moaning, etc. A different pattern is manifested in the presence of people who, on account of their profession, should know the character of the pain experience because they are expected to make the appropriate diagnosis, advise the proper cure and give the adequate help. This tendency to avoid deviation from certain expected patterns of behavior plays an important role in the reaction to pain. This is also controlled by the desire to seek approval on the part of the social environment, especially in the hospital, where the "Old American" patient tries to avoid being a "nuisance" on the ward. He seems to be, more than any other patient, aware of an ideal pattern of behavior which is identified as "American," and he tends to conform to it. This was characteristically expressed by a patient who answered the question how he reacts to pain by saying, "I react like a good American."

An important element in controlling the pain reaction is the wish of the patient to cooperate with those who are expected to take care of him. The situation is often viewed as a team composed of the patient, the doctor, the nurse, the attendant, etc., and in this team everybody has a function and is supposed to do his share in order to achieve the most successful result. Emotionality is seen as a purposeless and hindering factor in a situation which calls for knowledge, skill, training and efficiency. It is important to note that this behavior is also expected by American or Americanized members of the medical or nursing staff, and the patients who do not fall into this pattern are viewed as deviants, hypochondriacs and neurotics.

As in the case of the Jewish patients, the American attitude toward pain can be best defined as a future-oriented anxiety. The "Old American" patient is also concerned with the symptomatic significance of pain which is correlated with a pronounced health-consciousness. It seems that the "Old American" is conscious of various threats to his health which are present in his environment and therefore feels vulnerable and is prone to interpret his pain sensation as a warning signal indicating that something is wrong with his health and therefore must be reported to the physician. With some exceptions, pain is considered bad and unnecessary and therefore must be immediately taken care of. In those situations where pain is expected and accepted, such as in the process of medical treatment or as a result of sports activities, there is less concern with the pain sensation. In general, however, there is a feeling that suffering pain is unnecessary when there are means of relieving it.

Though the attitudes of the Jewish and "Old American" patients can be defined as pain anxiety they differ greatly. The future-oriented anxiety of the Jewish interviewee is characterized by pessimism or, at best, by skepticism, while the "Old American" patient is rather optimistic in his future-orientation. This attitude is fostered by the mechanistic approach to the body and its fuctions and by the confidence in the skill of the expert which are so frequent in the American, in that the body is often viewed as a machine which has to be well taken care of, be periodically checked for dysfunctioning and eventually, when out of order, be taken to an expert who will "fix" the defect. In the case of pain the expert is the medical man who has the "know-how" because of his training and experience and therefore is entitled to full confidence. An important element in the optimistic outlook is faith in the progress of science. Patients with intractable pain often stated that though at the present moment the doctors do not have the "drug" they will eventually discover it, and they will give the examples of sulfa, penicillin, etc.

The anxieties of a pain-experiencing "Old American" patient are greatly relieved when he feels that something is being done about it in terms of specific activities involved in the treatment. It seems that his security and confidence increase in direct proportion to the number of tests, X-rays, examinations, injections, etc., that are given to him. Accordingly, "Old American" patients seem to have a positive attitude toward hospitalization, because the hospital is the adequate institution which is equipped for the necessary treatment. While a Jewish and an Italian patient seem to be disturbed by the impersonal character of the hospital and by the necessity of being treated there instead of at home, the "Old American" patient, on the contrary, prefers the hospital treatment to the home treatment, and neither he nor his family seems to be disturbed by hospitalization.

To summarize the attitude of the "Old American" toward pain, he is disturbed by the symptomatic aspect of pain and is concerned with its incapacitating aspects, but he tends to view the future in rather optimistic colors, having confidence in the science and skill of the professional people who treat his condition.

Some Sources of Intra-Group Variation

In the description of the reactive patterns and attitudes toward pain among patients of Jewish and "Old American" origin certain regularities have been observed for each particular group regardless of individual differences and variations. This does not mean that each individual in each group manifests the same reactions and attitudes. Individual variations are often due to specific aspects of pain experience, to the character of the disease which causes the pain or to elements of the personality of the patient. However, there are also other factors that are instrumental in provoking these differences and which can still be traced back to the cultural backgrounds of the individual patients. Such variables as the degree of Americanization of the patient, his socio-economic background, education and religiosity may play an important role in shaping individual variations in the reactive patterns. For instance, it was found that the patterns described are manifested most consistently among immigrants, while their descendants tend to differ in terms of adopting American forms of behavior and American attitudes toward the role of the medical expert, medical institutions and equipment in controlling pain. It is safe to say that the further is the individual from the immigrant generation the more American is his behavior. This is less true for the attitudes toward pain, which seem to persist to a great extent even among members of the third generation and even though the reactive patterns are radically changed. A Jewish or Italian patient born in this country of American-born parents tends to *behave* like an "Old American" but often expresses *attitudes* similar to those which are expressed by the Jewish or Italian people. They try to appear unemotional and efficient in situations where the immigrant would be excited and disturbed. However, in the process of the interview, if a patient is of Jewish origin he is likely to express attitudes of anxiety as to the meaning of his pain, and if he is an Italian he is likely to be rather unconcerned about the significance of his pain for the future.

The occupational factor plays an important role when pain affects a specific area of the body. For instance, manual workers with herniated discs are more disturbed by their pain than are professional or business people with a similar disease because of the immediate significance of this particular pain for their respective abilities to earn a living. It was also observed that headaches cause more concern among intellectuals than among manual workers.

The educational background of the patient also plays an important role in his attitude with regard to the symptomatic meaning of a pain sensation. The more educated patients are more health-conscious and more aware of pain as a possible symptom of a dangerous disease. However, this factor plays a less important role than might be expected. The less educated "Old American" or Jewish patient is still more health-conscious than the more educated Italian. On the other hand, the less educated Jew is as much worried about the significance of pain as the more educated one. The education of the patient seems to be an important factor in fostering specific reactive patterns. The more educated patient, who may have more anxiety with regard to illness, may be more reserved in specific reactions to pain than an unsophisticated individual, who feels free to express his feelings and emotions.

The Transmission of Cultural Attitudes Toward Pain

In interpreting the differences which may be attributed to different socio-economic and educational backgrounds there is enough evidence to conclude that these differences appear mainly on the manifest and behavioral level, whereas attitudinal patterns toward pain tend to be more uniform and to be common to most of the members of the group regardless of their specific backgrounds.

These attitudes toward pain and the expected reactive patterns are acquired by the individual members of the society from the earliest childhood along with other cultural attitudes and values which are learned from the parents, parent-substitutes, siblings, peer groups, etc. Each culture offers to its members an ideal pattern of attitudes and reactions, which may differ for various sub-cultures in a given society, and each individual is expected to conform to this ideal pattern. Here, the role of the family seems to be of primary importance. Directly and indirectly the family environment affects the individual's ultimate response to pain. In each culture the parents teach the child how to react to pain, and by approval or disapproval they promote specific forms of behavior. This conclusion is amply supported by the interviews. Thus, the Jewish and Italian respondents are unanimous in relating how their parents, especially mothers, manifested over-protective and over-concerned attitudes toward the child's health, participation in sports, games, fights, etc. In these families the child is constantly reminded of the advisability of avoiding colds, injuries, fights and other threatening situations. Crying in complaint is responded to by the parents with sympathy, concern and help. By their over-protective and worried attitude they foster complaining and tears. The child learns to pay attention to each painful experience and to look for help and sympathy which are readily given to him. In Jewish families, where not only a slight sensation of pain but also each deviation from the child's normal behavior is looked upon as a sign of illness, the child is prone to acquire anxieties with regard to the meaning and significance of these manifestations. The Italian parents do not seem to be concerned with the symptomatic meaning of the child's pains and aches, but instead there is a great deal of verbal expression of emotions and feelings of sympathy toward the "poor child" who happens to be in discomfort because of illness or because of an injury at play. In these families a child is praised when he avoids physical injuries and is scolded when he does not pay enough attention to bad weather, to drafts or when he takes part in rough games and fights. The injury and pain are often interpreted to the child as punishment for the wrong behavior, and physical punishment is the usual consequence of misbehavior.

In the "Old American" family the parental attitude is quite different. The child is told not to "run to mother with every little thing." He is told to take pain "like a man," not to be a "sissy," not to cry. The child's participation in physical sports and games is not only approved but is also strongly stimulated. Moreover, the child is taught to expect to be hurt in sports and games and is taught to fight back if he happens to be attacked by other boys. However, it seems that the American parents are conscious of the threats to the child's health, and they teach the child to take immediate care of any injury. When hurt the right thing to do is not to cry and get emotional but to avoid unnecessary pain and prevent unpleasant consequences by applying the proper first aid medicine and by calling a doctor.

Often attitudes and behavior fostered in a family conflict with those patterns which are accepted by the larger social environment. This is especially true in the case of children of immigrants. The Italian or Jewish immigrant parents promote patterns which they consider correct, while the peer groups in the street and in the school criticize this behavior and foster a different one. In consequence, the child may acquire the attitudes which are part of his home-life but may also adopt behavior patterns which conform to those of his friends.

The direct promotion of certain behavior described as part of the child rearing explains only in part the influence of the general family environment and the specific role of the parents in shaping responses to pain. They are also formed indirectly by observing the behavior of other members of the family and by imitating their responses to pain. Moreover, attitudes toward pain are also influenced by various aspects of parent-child relationship in a culture. The material suggests that differences in attitudes toward pain in Jewish, Italian and "Old American" families are closely related to the role and image of the father in the respective cultures in terms of his authority and masculinity. Often the father and mother assume different roles in promoting specific patterns of behavior and specific attitudes. For example, it seems that in the "Old American" family it is chiefly the mother who stimulates the child's ability to resist pain, thus emphasizing his masculinity. In the Italian family it seems that the mother is the one who inspires the child's emotionality, while in the Jewish family both parents express attitudes of worry and concern which are transmitted to the children.

Specific deviations from expected reactive and attitudinal patterns can often be understood in terms of a particular structure of the family. This became especially clear from the interviews of two Italian patients and one Jewish patient. All three subjects revealed reactions and attitudes diametrically opposite to those which the investigator would expect on the basis of his experience. In the process of the interview, however, it appeared that one of the Italian patients was adopted into an Italian family, found out about his adoption at the age of fourteen, created a fantasy of being of Anglo-Saxon origin because of his physical appearance and accordingly began to eradicate everything "Italian" in his personality and behavior. For instance, he denied knowledge of the Italian language despite the fact that he always spoke Italian in the family and even learned to abstain from smiling, because he felt that being happy and joyful is an indication of Italian origin. The other Italian patient lost his family at a very early age because of family disorganization and was brought up in an Irish foster home. The Jewish patient consciously adopted a "non-Jewish" pattern of behavior and attitude because of acute sibling rivalry. According to the respondent, his brother, a favored son in the immigrant Jewish family, always manifested "typical" Jewish reactions toward disease, and the patient, who strongly disliked the brother and was jealous of him, decided to be "completely different."

The analysis of cultural factors in responses to pain is tentative and incomplete. It is based upon only one year of research which has been devoted exclusively to collection of raw material and formulation of working hypotheses. A detailed analysis of the interviews may call for revisions and reformulations of certain observations described in this paper. Nevertheless, the first objectives of our research have been attained in establishing the importance of the role of cultural factors in an area relatively little explored by the social sciences. We hope that in the course of further research we shall be able to expand our investigation into other areas of the pain problem, such as sex differences in attitudes toward pain, the role of age differences and the role of religious beliefs in the pain experience. We hope also that the final findings of the study will contribute to the growing field of collaboration between the social sciences and medicine for the better understanding of human problems.

References and Notes

1. This paper is based upon material collected as part of the study "Cultural Components in Attitudes toward Pain," under a grant of the U. S. Public Health Service.
2. James D. Hardy, Harold G. Wolff and Helen Goodell, *Pain Sensations and Reactions.* Williams and Wilkins Company, 1952, p. 23.
3. *Ibid.*, p. 204.
4. *Ibid.*, p. 262.
5. I should like to take the opportunity to express my appreciation to Dr. Harold G. Wolff, Professor of Neurology, Cornell University Medical College, Dr. Hiland Flowers, Chief of Neuropsychiatric Service, Dr. Robert Morrow, Chief of Clinical Psychology Section, Dr. Louis Berlin, Chief of Neurology Section, and the Management of the hospital for their cooperation in the setting up of the research at the Kingsbridge Veterans Hospital.
6. Italian respondents are mainly of South Italian origin; the Jewish respondents, with one exception, are all of East European origin. Whenever the Jews are mentioned they are spoken of in terms of the culture they represent and not in terms of their religion.

From W.-S. Tseng (ed.), J. F. McDermott and T. W. Maretzki, *People and Cultures in Hawaii* (1974), pp. 90-93. Reprinted by permission of the Transcultural Psychiatry Committee, University of Hawaii School of Medicine.

Wen-Shing Tseng

Jing Hsu

Suggestions for intercultural psychotherapy

Intercultural psychotherapy refers to psychotherapy in which the therapist and the patient have different cultural backgrounds so that the interaction of cultural components is involved in addition to the ordinary process of psychotherapy. In a sense, every person has his own unique cultural background, associated with his own personal experience, family situation, and social environment, which constantly affects the process of ordinary psychotherapy. However, such influence is not

From W.-S. Tseng (ed.), J. F. McDermott and T. W. Maretzki, *People and Cultures in Hawaii* (1974), pp. 90-93. Reprinted by permission of the Transcultural Psychiatry Committee, University of Hawaii School of Medicine.

overt or easily determined unless the cultural backgrounds of therapist and patient are very distinct.

The influence of cultural factors in the process of such psychotherapy will be discussed in the areas of communications, diagnosis, therapist-patient relations, therapeutic model, and goal of treatment. Suggestions will be made for dealing with such intercultural psychotherapeutic work.

From the moment the therapist begins to make contact with a patient of different cultural background, there immediately occurs the problem of communication between them. The situation is more difficult when they speak different languages. An interpreter should be called in without hesitation so that they can communicate with each other at least to some extent. The therapist should be aware of the limitation of such interpretation. It is fairly easy to translate something which has concrete meaning, it is much more difficult to interpret emotion or something which is symbolic in nature. Furthermore, many of the same words were used to express different emotions in the different cultures.

The difficulty occurs not only in the area of verbal communication, but also in nonverbal communication, such as by facial expression, gesture, or behavior. It is necessary for both of them to constantly check the meaning of such nonverbal communication.

The problems of communication do not happen only at initial contact but may continue to exist throughout therapy. This is true even at a time when both should presumably have become better acquainted with each other's cultural system. Both the therapist and the patient should be constantly aware of the existence of such cultural differences and communication difficulties. They should make every effort to actively inquire as to meanings within the cultural context. Both of them should keep checking on what kind of message has been sent out and how it has been received, so that misunderstandings can be minimized. This is sometimes very hard for the patient who may have difficulty in relating well with reality and in communicating with others, such as in organic brain cases, borderline cases of paranoia and schizophrenia. It is also difficult for a person who does not appreciate cultural differences and who tends to interpret things only in terms of his own culture without being aware that other interpretations exist.

Clearly related to the problem of communication is the issue of proper diagnosis. The boundaries of normality and pathology have not been well defined in the area of behavioral science and social psychiatry. In the work of transcultural psychiatry it has been recognized that there are at least two kinds of abnormality which should be distinguished, i.e., psychiatric abnormality and sociocultural deviance. Psychiatric abnormality is by virtue of its nature abnormal and is universally recognizable in terms of symptom criteria that are culture-free and generally applicable. For example, some manifestations of psychiatric symptoms, such as hallucination, talking to oneself, or silly laughing, can be easily recognized by any psychiatrist who knows how to inquire about the presence of such symptoms. However, for other symptoms, such as delusion, "incoherent" speech, or "bizarre" behavior, the psychiatrist needs information about the sociocultural environment, the "reality" on which to base his diagnosis—to what extent it is abnormal. Otherwise he will be unable to tell what is distorted from reality, incoherent, or bizarre. Sociocultural deviance is situationally determined and is relative to the norms of a given community. Therefore, it should be considered and judged within the context in which the behavior occurs.

As every person has his own individual way of expressing his emotional behavior according to his personal pattern, so also do groups of people, according to their group pattern—cultural style. It is important for the therapist to distinguish the patient's *individual* style of coping mechanism and his *cultural* style of dealing with problems so that the meaning of such response can be more clearly understood. Even the way of expressing emotional problems should be checked and evaluated carefully. For example, if a patient manifests a suicidal wish to a therapist, the latter should clarify the meaning of such a complaint—is it his cultural way to get attention from others, or his individual style in asking for help, etc.?

During the process of intercultural psychotherapy, the therapist should make an effort to obtain knowledge not only about the norms and value system of the patient's cultural environment, but also about the usual stresses members of his culture must meet and the customary psychiatric reaction pattern that is manifested within such a cultural context. This will certainly help the therapist to make a more appropriate and accurate diagnosis of the patient. Making judgments just from the therapist's point of view and measuring by scales useful in the therapist's own cultural background should be avoided.

The issue of therapist-patient relationships should be carefully watched and handled in the situation of intercultural psychotherapy, as it is more complicated than in ordinary psychotherapy. The attitudes toward authority and the relationships with authority vary widely among different cultural groups. Patients who come from a background where authority tends to be autocratic will expect the therapist to be active, instructive, and responsible in the session; while other patients who are used to relating with authority in a more democratic way will prefer a more equal relationship and expect the therapist not to manipulate them even though their unconscious motivation for seeking therapy is to get help from the authority.

The matter of transference can be defined in a broad sense as the transfer to the therapist of the patient's relationship with someone in his past, i.e., mother or father, or of a projected stereotype such as the ethnic identity of the therapist. In the course of intercultural psychotherapy, the transference situation is complicated: the patient does not only put the therapist in the place of someone from his individual past experience, but also projects the customary cultural image of the therapist's role onto the therapist, regardless of whether it is true or not. This applies to the counter-transference situation also—the therapist displaces his customary image of the patient's background onto the particular patient without realizing whether it is true or not.

Therefore, both the therapist and the patient have to develop awareness of their stereotyped beliefs about each other, particularly if it is distorted from the reality. In the meanwhile, the therapist should be consciously aware of what kind of therapist-patient relationship is culturally relevant so that both the therapist and the patient can relate to each other with greater ease and in a more therapeutic way.

Psychotherapy can be defined in broad terms as a therapeutic process of psychological interaction which takes place between the therapist and the patient, the latter who in his suffering consults the former with the aim of seeking relief from his problems. Due to the different sociocultural backgrounds, experience, and theory, there are numerous different models of psychotherapeutic activities—some are so-called indigenous while others are modern, etc. In the situation of intercultural psychotherapy, the issue of attitude, understanding, and familiarity toward a certain kind of treatment model may arise. For some people, it may be taken for granted that treatment is a contract between the therapist and the patient to work on regular sessions for a certain period of time for the patient to work out his problems; while others may view treatment as a kind of service through which a person can get service from the authority at any time when he drops in. The basic understanding and attitude toward the treatment should be clarified as soon as possible so that any misunderstanding can be minimized to influence the process of treatment.

The basic process of psychotherapy involves the series of processes which involve revealing to the patient the causes and dynamics of his disorder, giving advice for better adjustment, and giving support for behavior change. The technique of interpretation usually varies according to the condition of the patient, and the goal of the therapeutic effort. In intercultural psychotherapy an effort should be made to ensure that the explanation is relevant to the patient's cultural background. The best language and concepts to be used are those familiar to the patient so he can receive the explanation with ease and will find it meaningful.

The therapist usually formulates advice for the patient based not only on his professional knowledge of psychiatry and psychology, but also on his own personal experience and social knowledge, although the latter work in subtle ways. When a therapist is facing the task of helping a patient who is living in a very different social environment, the therapist will feel handicapped in his ability to find and formulate sound and adequate advice for his patient, as he does not know the patient's assets in terms of the environment in which he lives and kinds of mechanisms available there. This is a disadvantage that the therapist must overcome in the course of intercultural treatment.

The therapist should be free to talk with his patient and to ask his cooperation in searching together for the most suitable way for the patient to cope with his problems. Sometimes the therapist, as an outsider, may have some objective and new idea, while the patient, as an insider, may have some "expert" suggestions. After all, it is the aim of psychotherapy for the therapist and the patient to work together.

The purpose of comprehensive treatment does not only include removing existing emotional symptoms and alleviating disturbed patterns of behavior, it also embraces promoting positive personality growth and development. The concept of a "normal" person or a "mature" personality implies a mental condition of creative self-fulfillment, a productive attitude toward life, gratifying relationships with people, etc. This concept is considered to be the final goal aimed for in the ordinary process of psychotherapy, and it is accepted as such without question when both therapist and patient belong to the same cultural background and share the same value system and concepts of normality and maturity. However, in the situation of intercultural psychotherapy it becomes very necessary to always question what is meant by "normal" and what "mature" implies within a particular cultural environment.

For example, for a group of people it may be ideal to be self-directed and independent in life, to emphasize work and socialization, to have a problem-solving approach to life's conflicts; it may be better for another group of people to be mutually dependent, to learn rational control over emotion and desire, and to be harmonious with others and with nature. Therefore, it is very important for the therapist to consider the patient's prior life, what kind of cultural environment he is going to live in, and then to discover with the patient what can improve his ability to function.

In intercultural psychotherapy it is better to maintain the open system model in which the therapist reveals his opinion, attitude, values, and expectations as does the patient: from the ongoing mechanism of feedback interaction, a higher state of organization evolves. It is not a matter of imposing values, but rather of searching for and developing a new value system for the patient to follow.

In summary, in the situation of intercultural psychotherapy, there is great need for the therapist and the patient to be fully aware of the fact that cultural factors may have an effect in the practice of treatment. The therapist should be active in seeking the meaning of the facts the patient expresses and to be open to learning from the patients. His technique should be flexible so that it is always congruent with the patient's expectations and needs. Awareness of the limitations as well as the handicaps and the ability to compensate for them by responding to the patient with a warm and supportive relationship throughout the course of therapy are both essential.

Modernization, Cultural Pluralism, and Health Care

Recently traditional cultures throughout the world have been affected by the paired expansion of modern political organization and scientific health care. The resulting pluralism between traits native and introduced has created settings of considerable complexity, as have immigrations of rural peoples to larger, more affluent cities and nations. In these settings effective health education and clinical treatment rest very heavily on cultural factors binding those in a pluralistic society. Repeatedly health programs fail, and for a multiplicity of reasons. Patients many times misunderstand or ignore prescribed medical procedure. Others may choose not to use modern clinical services, relying instead on local remedies and curers. Frequently the ill will simultaneously employ both modern and ethnomedical resources. The culture and bureaucracy of scientific health care also present serious obstacles to effective delivery. A major objective in medical anthropology is to provide the data and procedural guidelines needed to achieve maximum success in health care delivery in pluralistic settings. The articles in this section describe and collectively illustrate the importance of applied anthropology in nursing, nutrition, family planning, drug abuse, medicine and other related fields.

George Foster, a leading figure in the anthropological study of health, opens this section with a discussion of international health planning. In reviewing the history and difficulties of cross-cultural medical care, Foster defines several criteria which affect the overall success of health programs. His paper provides a background from which the other articles in this section can be interrelated and used to further exemplify his points concerning the practical significance of medical anthropology.

Antoinette Ragucci, for example, explores the uses of anthropological re-

299

search in nursing. The paper by Gretel Pelto and Norge Jerome adds a similar perspective, although one focusing on nutrition. Steven Polgar and John Marshall, in their study of fertility regulation, emphasize that the acceptability of family planning rests on cultural characteristics of both the recipient or target population and the donor or delivery group. This point is made equally clear in several papers, including the one on drug abuse programs by William Aron, Norman Alger and Ricardo Gonzales. Their work is relevant for improving the design of many types of health programs.

Coexistence, blending, and competition commonly occur between traditional and modern forms of medicine, as shown in the article by Clarissa Scott and the article by Hessler, Nolan, Ogbru, and New. Similar findings are presented by Michael Logan in a study of peasant acceptance or rejection of modern medicine. An interesting contrast to these articles is provided by Irwin Press, who explains why nationalization of health care in Spain has served to virtually eliminate folk or traditional medicine from Spanish society.

Because the success of health education and delivery programs hinges so closely on cultural factors, including those of both target and donor populations, there is a definite need to include anthropology in the teaching and training curricula of medical schools. This need is defined and traced historically, as well as exemplified, in the article by Ethel Nurge.

The closing paper by Pertti and Gretel Pelto is useful for integrating the previous works in this section. By discussing various perspectives taken by medical anthropologists in studying cross-cultural aspects of health, the Peltos establish a series of highly relevant criticisms concerning anthropological assumptions, research strategies, and selection of research topics. Medical anthropologists can more meaningfully contribute to health education and medical care if they progressively improve their methods and subjects of research. Through improvement the anthropologist gains increasing interest and cooperation among health care personnel in all fields, a necessary step toward successful realization of mutual goals.

Hopefully the materials in this book have illustrated the importance of recognizing that culture, the proper domain of anthropology, is a crucial variable in the etiology, control, and treatment of human diseases and related health problems.

George M. Foster

Medical anthropology and international health planning

Introduction

On a number of occasions and in various settings during the last generation the Agency for International Development (and predecessor organizations) has brought together health personnel and behavioral scientists to explore the ways in which knowledge about the social organization and cultural forms of "target" groups, the recipients of health services, can assist in the planning and operation of these services. As early as 1951 the Institute of Inter-American Affairs contracted with the Smithsonian Institution for behavioral science assistance in a six-month long team evaluation of the first ten years of United States-assisted health programs in Latin America (Anonymous 1953; Servicio 1953). Subsequently the "Health Advisory Committee" of the Foreign Operations Administration included behavioral scientists as well as medical and administrative personnel. Over the years many formal and informal meetings have been held, all concerned with the problem that brings us together today: the ways in which knowledge of the social, cultural, and psychological factors in traditional societies that influence change can be used to improve health service planning and operations, including the search for new ways to make the most efficient use of scarce health resources.

A Sequence of Premises

While it may seem discouraging that the interrelationships between sociocultural and medical-health behavior phenomena are in danger of being rehashed once more, the terms of reference for this meeting are challenging in that they reflect a broader and more flexible approach to the basic problems than has been found in many earlier conferences. In order better to appreciate this flexibility it will be helpful briefly to review the changing premises, the underlying assumptions, that have characterized American-aided health programs in developing countries. Three major premises have appeared in chronological order:

1. **The institutional forms and clinical practices of the medical systems of technologically-advanced nations are the appropriate models for the development of health services in all countries.**   In early American attempts to help developing countries provide better health services for their citizens, program planners and

Reproduced by permission of the Society for Medical Anthropology from *Medical Anthropology Newsletter* 7 (3), 1976.

field personnel operated on the basis of two seemingly obvious (to them) assumptions: First, the best and most advanced American preventive and curative medical practices, *and* the institutional framework that provides these services, are absolutes that work equally well in all sociocultural and economic settings; and, second, the people in developing countries will immediately perceive the advantages accruing to them if they give up old medical practices and adopt new ones. (One wonders if smallpox immunization was taken as the universal model, for here indeed is a medical technique whose efficacy does not depend on culture; willingness to be vaccinated is, of course, another matter, and that *does* depend on cultural factors.)

These ethnocentric assumptions represented the prevailing view that American civilization was superior in all ways to other societies, and that given the opportunity people in "less fortunate" countries would clamor to adopt our ways. In the past, Western medical personnel have been, if anything, even more ethnocentric than the general public about the superiority of scientific medicine in all its ramifications, finding it difficult to believe that all peoples would not quickly accept it. Consequently, early workers in international health programs saw their task in simplistic, easily definable terms: transplant the American models, and health goals will be achieved. This philosophy underlay the work of the Rockefeller Foundation in its attempts to eradicate hookworm in Ceylon, 1916-22, and it was implicit in much of the work of the Institute of Inter-American Affairs beginning in 1942. Even today more than a few traces of this point of view are found in international health programs.

2. Medical and public health programs in developing countries will be more successful if in design and operation they take into consideration the social, cultural, and psychological characteristics of the target group. By about 1950, American international health specialists began to realize that the successful delivery of improved health services required more than the silver platter approach. They began to appreciate that modernization is a social as well as a technological phenomenon, and that the people who modernize have cultures and values that strongly influence their decisions in accepting or rejecting innovation. Small numbers of anthropologists came into international public health during the years following 1950, and they played an important role in promoting the "human factors in technological development" point of view, which postulates that the major problems in the development of traditional communities (including health services) are embedded in the society and culture of the target group. These people, it was now assumed, are anxious to enjoy better health, and they are willing to change their health behavior if they understand better the advantages in new ways. If the cultural, social, and psychological "barriers" that inhibit acceptance of new health programs could be identified, it was reasoned, health programs could be designed and presented in ways that conform to cultural expectations. Recognition of the importance of understanding sociocultural factors in designing and carrying out health programs represented a great step forward, and much progress has been made in the delivery of health services as a consequence of this awareness. Still, the fact that we are assembled here indicates that this assumption alone, valid as far as it goes, is insufficient to the task.

3. **The most successful medical and public health programs in developing countries require knowledge about the social, cultural, and psychological factors inherent in the innovating organizations and their professional personnel.** In other words, major "barriers" to improved health programs also are found in the cultures of bureaucracies, the assumptions of the medical profession, and in the psychological makeup of the specialists who participate in these programs. This assumption, regrettably, appears not to be widely accepted; it is, in fact, stoutly resisted by many. The second premise—that the principal barriers are in the target group—was easily accepted by international health personnel. It seemed to offer quick and easy answers to many problems that had seemed insoluble, and it defined the problem as "out there," among the people who were to be helped. The implications of premise three are, however, disquieting; it is much harder to point the finger at oneself and say, "A lot of the difficulty is right here."

Nevertheless, I am increasingly struck by the fact that many of the apparent resistances to acceptance of health services commonly attributed to villagers' apathy' and their cultural barriers, are, in fact, the result of administrative and professional inadequacies. International health programs made significant strides when the importance of social, cultural and psychological factors in target group cultures was recognized. The next opportunity for comparable progress lies, first, in recognizing (or admitting) the limitations in present bureaucratic forms, and in many professional and individual assumptions found in all health programs; and second, in being willing to face up to these problems, even at the cost of professional discomfort.

Innovation in Health Behavior

Let us now ask a pair of questions that stem from premises two and three: (1) What have we learned about the sociocultural and psychological factors in traditional populations that enable us better to understand the process of accepting scientific medicine, and that suggest leads in future program planning? and (2) What do we know about health bureaucracies and health personnel, or what must be learned about them, in order to design and carry out more effective health programs?

In early analyses of the sociocultural factors that seemed to inhibit acceptance of scientific medicine by traditional peoples, anthropologists developed an "adversary" model to explain the resistances that occurred. It was postulated that scientific and traditional medicine were locked in battle, each trying to win (or hold on to) the allegiance of the community. The model postulated that traditional peoples divided illness into two categories: those that medical doctors understood and could cure; and those medical doctors did not know about, much less understand, and which therefore they could not treat. Acute, infectious diseases—those yielding to antibiotics—quickly fell into the first category; the medical doctor's competence here was easily demonstrated. Chronic illnesses, those with major psychological components, and those "magical" in nature (e.g., the evil eye)—illnesses marked by vague and shifting symptoms—tended to remain the provenience of the traditional curer. The task of the anthropologist was to help medical personnel find ways to demonstrate the superiority of scientific medicine, which little by little would move the illnesses in this second category into the first one, the illnesses routinely brought to the medical doctor.

This model is not without merit: independently it has been worked out in Latin America, South and southeast Asia, and other places as well. It was through this model that we learned the *pragmatic* quality of traditional reasoning processes, that if peasant and tribal peoples could *perceive* advantages resulting from changed behavior, they were willing to drop old and cherished beliefs and practices by the wayside. This dichotomous model—illnesses medical doctors can cure, and those they cannot cure—has proven to be simplistic, as will be pointed out a little farther along.

Obviously there are social, cultural, and psychological barriers to the full acceptance of modern medicine that are found in every traditional community. It would be foolish to deny the importance of these factors, examples of which are known to all of us. In parts of Latin America there is great resistance to withdrawal of blood for laboratory analyses, or for blood transfusions, because of the belief that blood is a non-renewable substance, and that a person is weakened permanently by such withdrawals (Adams 1955:446-447). In Africa where the belief in witchcraft is strong, resistance to the use of sanitary latrines has been noted. People are reluctant to concentrate their feces for the convenience of witches who may wish to work their magic on them (Kark 1962:26). In India it has often been reported that villagers are reluctant to vaccinate against smallpox because of the belief that this is a "sacred" disease sent by a Mother Goddess whose will should not be contravened. In other countries, pregnant women have given as their reason for refusing hospital delivery the fear that the placenta will not be given to the family for ritual disposal. All of these, and countless more examples, can be given of real "barriers" to full acceptance of available medical services.

Yet I am increasingly convinced that *economic* and *social costs* are more important in determining the use or nonuse of scientific medicine than is the belief-conflict between traditional and modern medicine. I now believe that the adversary model is appropriate for the initial contact period when traditional peoples for the first time have the alternative of consulting medical doctors. But the evidence is overwhelming that in countries where traditional peoples have had access to modern medicine for a generation or longer, and where this medicine has been of reasonably good quality, the battle has been won, and scientific medicine is the victor.

The first decision-making model to account for choice of medical help, worked out by anthropologists for developing countries, was a three-stage sequence: (1) home remedies, (2) indigenous curer, and (3) the medical doctor, but only after the first two choices failed to produce results. In 1945, this was true in

Tzintzuntzan, Mexico, a peasant community I have studied since that date. Today, however, the sequence is the same as that followed by many Americans: (1) home remedy, (2) medical doctor, and (3) indigenous curer (or faith healer in the United States) only after the first two choices fail to produce results.

It may be argued that relatively few countries in the developing world have the resources of Mexico, and that general acceptance of scientific medicine will not come so readily in the rest of the world. Yet the evidence suggests the contrary. In India, Banerji and his colleagues have carried out studies that show the same trend. In a fairly extensive study they were surprised to find

> *that the response to the major medical care problems is very much in favour of the western ... system of medicine, irrespective of social, economic, occupational and regional considerations. Availability of such services and capacity of patients to meet the expenses are the two major constraining factors (Banerji 1974:6; emphasis added).*

Further, while Banerji found numerous examples of consulting practitioners of indigenous or homeopathic medicine,

> *Among those who suffer from major illness, only a very tiny fraction preferentially adopt these practices by positively rejecting facilities of the western system of medicine which are more efficacious and which are easily available and accessible to them (1974:7).*

The picture is the same in Thailand where, in a major study of doctor-patient relationships, it was found that "The decision to go to a hospital depends less on the gravity of the disease than on financial resources" (Hinderling 1973:74). The same study revealed that, while in rural areas far from hospitals physicians are sometimes seen as a last resort, in cities the order is reversed: "The modern doctor is the first to be consulted, and [only] if he is not successful, one of the quite fashionable [traditional] healers will be called upon" (Boesch 1972:34).

The Basis for Acceptance of Scientific Medicine

We now turn to the motivations and processes underlying innovation in medical practice. The first thing we note is that they are essentially the same as those that underlie innovation in all areas. I suggest that people will change traditional behavior, i.e., innovate:

1. if they perceive personal economic, social, psychological, health, or other advantages in so doing;
2. if they perceive change as a realistic possibility for them;
3. if the economic costs are within their capabilities;
4. if the social costs do not outweigh the perceived advantage.

In other words, people are remarkably pragmatic in evaluating and testing new alternatives, including health services. One can almost speak of a cost-benefit mode of analysis. When, on the basis of empirical evidence, traditional peoples see that scientific medicine is more effective than their own, and when they can have scientific medicine on terms they deem acceptable, they happily turn to it. Speaking of the acceptance of curative medicine in Ecuador, Erasmus, many years ago pointed out that, as far as tradition was concerned, "folk beliefs in themselves are offering no resistance to modern medical practices *in so far as those practices may be judged by the folk on an empirical basis*" (Erasmus 1952:418; emphasis added). In contrast Erasmus found that preventive medicine was resisted because its comprehension is essentially theoretical, not lending itself to easy empirical verification.

The evidence clearly indicates that, as far as individual decision making is concerned, curative medical services are embraced much more readily than preventive services. The reason is obvious: the results of scientific curative medicine are much more easily demonstrated than the results of preventive medicine. Few people suffering from yaws or other dangerous infections which have been cut short by an injection of an antibiotic question that this is indeed a miracle medicine much superior to any they have previously known. Cause and effect are easily comprehended when serious illness gives way to no illness in a few hours or days. Cause and effect are less easily seen when, as in the case of immunization and environmental sanitation programs, no disease is followed by no disease. The implications that must be drawn from this evidence is that the traditional American separation of most clinical from most preventive medical measures is, in other parts of the world, counter-productive. Experience suggests that preventive measures are more apt to be accepted if they are "blanketed in" with, or sold as a part of a "package deal" along with curative medicine, whose advantages are so much more easily demonstrated.

But, however pragmatic people may be, this quality is of little value unless innovation is seen as a realistic aspiration for the individual. A peasant farmer may be persuaded that hybrid rice sown on a heavily fertilized irrigated field is agriculturally advantageous, but if his marginal lands do not lend themselves to this intensive approach, or if credit facilities are inadequate, his planting practices are unlikely to change. Similarly, changing health practices may be perceived to be desirable but if for any one or combination of reasons a person feels the goal is unrealistic, change motivation will be lacking.

"Free" Services

When traditional peoples attempt to determine whether contemplated changes in their health practices are in fact realistic, economic factors appear to be the most important of all variables. While on the one hand token fees for medical services have often been reported to confer value on these services, and hence may be desirable policy in some situations (e.g., Foster 1973:136-138), most improved medical services for village peoples will have to be provided by the state, at little or no cost to the consumers. Increasingly this is recognized, and more and more "free" services are offered. "Free" services, unfortunately, are often expensive by village standards. Ndeti, for example, in a study of tuberculosis control in Kenya found that the bus fare kept a large number of patients from coming to the clinic (Ndeti 1972:408).

In Indonesia, family planning services, "free" in the strict sense of the word, are sometimes underutilized because of social customs requiring expenditures. Most mothers are interested in birth control only after they have had four or five children. Often they have no one with whom to leave these children so that when, in response to the urging of a family planning worker, they decide to visit a clinic, at least the younger children must trail along. This usually means a bus fare for all. But a trip on a bus is, by definition, an "outing," and on such occasions people buy food snacks, to which Indonesians are much addicted. So a mother with three or four small children may well spend a day's income on a simple visit to the "free" family planning clinic.

Other kinds of costs may also make "free" family planning services prohibitively expensive. In a village near Bandung, in western Java, at the bottom of a steep valley reached only by a poor dirt road, a woman seeking family planning help has to ascend to the health center in a truck or old bus that requires nearly an hour for the five-mile trip, paying 100 rupiahs fare each way. There she finds that, prior to being given pills or fitted with an IUD she must take a pregnancy test, which carries a laboratory fee of 150 rupiahs. The woman is asked to return three days later—again at a cost of 200 rupiahs for transportation—to learn the laboratory results. If the 200 rupiahs lost by absence from work for two days are added in, it costs a woman 750 rupiahs—more than a week's income—simply to find out if she is eligible for family planning. Small wonder that few of these women are interested in this kind of service (author's field notes).

Social Costs

Finally, we must take note of the "social" costs often involved in changing health behavior. A young woman may be convinced that the government health center in or near her village that offers pre- and post-natal care, and delivery services by a doctor and nurse-midwife team, is a more desirable alternative than is delivery with the aid of a village midwife. But if the midwife is her mother's sister, failure to turn to the aunt may be seen as a personal rejection, an act that may cause major family rifts. This kind of a "social" cost is sometimes seen by traditional peoples as too high a price to pay for perceived advantage. Major behavioral changes almost always produce, or require, major restructuring of traditional and valued social relationships. When the "social" costs of this restructuring—the conflict potential—are seen as outweighing the potential advantage, the decision will be against change.

Bureaucracies in Relation to Health Innovation

We now turn to the (frequently) unrecognized barriers to the best possible health services that are inherent in bureaucratic structures and in the premises of their personnel. The term "Bureaucracy" is used here, not in a pejorative sense, but rather to refer to an organization, an administrative structure, whose manifest functions are to meet formally defined societal needs. As a university professor, I see myself as much a bureaucrat as is a medical adviser sent abroad by AID. My manifest function is to contribute to higher education and research, formally defined as a societal need.

My argument here is that if we are fully to appreciate the dynamics of the planned change process, in health practices and in all other fields, it is essential to study administrators, planners, and professional specialists as individuals and as members of professions and bureaucracies, in the same ways and for the same reasons that we study traditional societies or any other client group—for bureaucracies and their personnel can be studied in essentially the same fashion as a peasant village or the urban neighborhood served by a public health center. A bureaucracy, in its structural and dynamic aspects, is very much like a "natural" community such as, for example, a peasant village, in that it is a real society with a real culture. And, like a peasant village, most bureaucracies include members of both sexes of widely varying ages, organized in a hierarchy of authority, responsibility, obligations, and functional tasks. Bureaucracies have social structures that define the role relationships and statuses of their members, and they have devices to change these relationships, through promotion, horizontal shifts, by-passing manoeuvers and—rarely—demotion. Like all people in social units, the personnel of bureaucracies, and the bureaucracies themselves, operate on the basis of implicit and explicit assumptions which can be analyzed just as can those assumptions found in natural societies. Many of these assumptions are influential in the planning of developmental programs, as the following examples will show.

A bureaucracy, as we have seen, ostensibly exists to fulfill a need or needs in society; the manifest functions of bureaucracies are expressed in their charters or enabling legislation, and it is expected that they will fulfill these functions, normally defined in terms of a client group. Yet we all know that, in practice, the primary concern of every bureaucracy and of its personnel is the corporate survival and, if possible, the growth of the organization, and the simultaneous protection of the position of staff members. Only when these concerns are taken care of can a bureaucracy turn full attention to its client group; and on those occasions when corporate or individual survival are threatened, this group may receive short shrift.

A second premise characterizing most bureaucracies is that the convenience of personnel, their likes and dislikes, has priority over the convenience of clients. This is seen particularly clearly in hours of service. I speak from experience: in setting my major university lectures at eight o'clock in the morning I have uppermost in mind my own convenience. I realize this hour is not the choice of most members of my client group, the students, whose needs I am supposed to serve. They would prefer the more popular hour of ten o'clock; and were I to lecture at that time my client group would double. Similarly, hours of service of government offices, including health departments, in this country and in developing countries, are set for the convenience of personnel and not for clients. We have all observed instances where the services of government clinics have been badly underutilized, largely because official hours from eight in the morning until two in the afternoon are the least convenient time for village women. Moreover, frequent failure of health personnel to be available at these stipulated times means that long and expensive trips by patients may be in vain. Such casual attention to the needs and feelings of patients is at least as much a "barrier" to adoption of better health practices as are beliefs in the efficacy of traditional medicine, or the fear of disrupting family relationships by adopting new health customs.

Social Costs of Changes in Bureaucracies

The social cost of bureaucratic flexibility, of responsiveness to changing needs, are at least as great as are the social costs of new behavior in traditional communities. The problem lies in the inevitable changes in role relationships—changes that threaten the position of some of the members of the group—that accompany major restructuring in any society, a bureaucracy included. The societal needs that a major bureaucracy should meet are not static; over time they change and evolve. Innovative programs and pilot projects designed to meet these changing definitions of purpose and need require that new skills and professional specialties be brought into the organization. Simultaneously the talents of some staff members which were of critical importance during an earlier period, or in the context of projects now closed out, may become less essential. To put it briefly, new priorities mean that new roles must be created, and some old roles given added importance, while other old roles diminish in importance, with loss of relative rank, authority, and privilege to the incumbents occupying these latter roles. But, just as the first concern of a bureaucracy is to ensure its survival and to protect itself against inroads from competing organizations, so is the first priority of the professional to protect his or her position within the organization. Like people in "natural" communities, we professionals jealously guard our traditional perquisites and privileges; we do not willingly surrender something except in exchange for something as good or better. All of us, as bureaucrats, rationalize our resistance to change that may leave us in a less desirable position by arguing—and usually genuinely believing—that what is good for us is also best for our institution, and for its clients. Consequently, we may go to extreme lengths, including back-biting, in-fighting, and bickering in effort to protect ourselves. The resulting social costs—lowered morale and intra-organizational friction—often seem to outweigh the advantages of greater responsiveness to new needs, and consequently most bureaucracies change very slowly.

Medical Role Perceptions as Barriers to Change

The underlying assumptions of medical personnel about their roles, responsibilities, and the structure of medical services sometimes constitute barriers to the development of health services best suited to the needs of developing countries. The traditional American division of health services into preventive and curative fields, for example, which developed in response to a variety of pressures and vested interests inherent in the American way of life, was assumed in early programs to be the "norm" for overseas development. The Rockefeller anti-hookworm campaign in Ceylon was very strictly a preventive program, and field personnel repeatedly were cautioned not to become involved in curative services. Yet one reason the project failed to eradicate hookworm was that to the Ceylonese the rationale of environmental sanitation to the exclusion of *their* health priorities made little sense.

> *Some villagers were irritated by the concentration on hookworm disease in view of their other overwhelming medical needs . . . The villagers were more interested in having their wounds and abscesses dressed and their miscellaneous acute illnesses attended than continuing in the dull routines of anti-hookworm work (Phillips 1955:289).*

Despite the home-office warnings not to scatter their energies by engaging in curative activities, field directors found they had to treat all kinds of complaints in order to gain support for the hookworm work.

Institute of Inter-American Affairs programs in Latin America in the 1940s also emphasized prevention rather than curing. This medical assumption has, in the past, proven to be one of the most serious of all barriers in building better health services in developing countries. Fortunately, few if any such countries today are planning their health services on other than a combined basis.

The mode of definition of health problems frequently limits medical organizations in searching for the most efficient ways of meeting health needs. As John Bryant has pointed out, a health problem is what is defined by the medical establishment (headed by medical doctors) as a health problem; consequently health priorities set by "medically qualified" people are the appropriate priorities. In exploring this phenomenon, we find that we are dealing not alone with the traditional wisdom of the medical profession, but also—frequently—with the ego structure of individual specialists. As professionals we are proud of our skills, and we derive satisfaction in demonstrating our competences to ourselves and our colleagues, *and* in having these competences acknowledged. If we are honest with ourselves, we must admit that we crave recognition. Consequently, our ego-needs not infrequently motivate us to search out and concentrate on special problems that are important, not so much to our client group as to ourselves, because of the opportunity they offer to demonstrate to our peers our exceptional capacities. All too often we confuse our psychological needs with the needs of our clients, and we assume that our personal priorities must also be those of the people we serve. In the planning and operation of health programs we must acknowledge that personal interests—even research hobbies—play an enormously important role in the final form of a service.

Finally, we must note an assumption of many medical doctors that is crucial to one of the main themes of this workshop, the possible role as sub-professional workers of indigenous medical personnel. John Bryant, in *Health and the Developing World,* has put the matter succinctly and sympathetically. A part of the greatness of the good physician, he says, is his acceptance of responsibility to give unstintingly of himself to those who need his help. But this is also the basis for his traditional reluctance to share his activities with others, to relinquish some of his tasks to less thoroughly trained personnel. To admit that many of the professional tasks he has been trained to perform can be carried out equally well by less well trained people apparently threatens the ego of many medical practitioners.

> *A curious side of this concept [that only the physician can provide quality care] is the value the physician places on the particular acts of diagnosis and prescription of treatment. Physicians are anxious to use every level of health worker in furthering a health program . . . but the words "diagnose" and "prescribe" evoke the strongest feelings of professional possessiveness (Bryant 1969:141-142).*

The concept that the physician must attend personally to his patients actually determines the form of most health services, says Bryant, and it can obstruct efforts to change the design of health systems.

> *Thus while logic tells us that the physician's role should be determined by the health needs of the entire population, implementation of this logic is obstructed by the insistence of the medical profession that only physicians can evaluate and treat the sick. This stand of the medical profession has a paralyzing effect on the design and implementation of health services and is one of the most serious obstacles to the effective use of limited health resources" (1969:143).*

Bryant's warning leads to my final point: possible roles for traditional healers in national health services.

Possible Roles for Traditional Healers

Paradoxically, the growing acceptance of Western medicine is creating a crisis in most developing countries. There are not now, nor will there be in the foreseeable future, sufficient fully-trained health personnel to meet all health needs. Auxiliary health workers have been and will continue to be used in almost all countries. In the former British and French colonies, local men were trained as "dressers" or *"infirmier auxiliaries"* to staff rural clinics and, depending on level of training, to perform a variety of therapeutic duties including simple laboratory analyses. Among the Navaho Indians the "health visitor" works under the supervision of the public health nurse, significantly extending her capacity to fulfill her role. In contemporary China, rural "barefoot doctors" offer a primary level of treatment in a referral system which sends seriously ill patients to more highly trained health personnel.

In these, and in other comparable instances, the subprofessional worker is (or was) a member of the formal health establishment, trained by qualified teachers, and paid by, and formally incorporated into colonial, tribal, or national health services. Because of the relative success of this approach in helping to solve health problems, and in the face of (almost certainly) permanent shortages of highly trained personnel, the question periodically is asked, should indigenous healers also be recognized as having something important to offer? Should they, in some way, be incorporated into the health services of a country? In the development of national health programs based on Western medicine official attitudes toward traditional healers have ranged from neglect to outright opposition: they have been looked upon by most medical doctors as undesirable competitors, if not outright enemies to be vanquished. Only occasionally, as with Ayurvedic medicine in India, has an indigenous medical system and its practitioners been formally encouraged by government. Even in India the vast substratum of "folk" medicine not recognized as Ayurvedic is ignored by the government.

The question of recognition of traditional healers is important because, in addition to the manpower problem, the fact remains that no scientific medical system completely satisfies all health needs of a nation. Even in countries with highly developed health care systems many people, under certain conditions, will turn to non-establishment forms of medical help such as faith healers, herbal doctors and the like. "Alternate" forms of medical care fill social, psychological, and perhaps organic health needs which, at least for some people, remain unmet by physicians and associated care services. With respect to a formal policy, the answers are not easy. Viewing particularly the supportive sociopsychological functions of the indigenous curer, anthropologists have been impressed with the positive aspects of non-Western medicine. Medical doctors, on the other hand, point out that some traditional remedies are definitely dangerous, and that at the very least treatment by traditional curers may delay referral to medical doctors until routine treatment such as an appendectomy becomes vastly more complicated.

Harrison, in discussing the possible role of non-Western medical personnel in Nigeria found that most government personnel were skeptical of their value.

> *One government official told me that they are untrainable because of their superstitious beliefs and because their practice is secret and difficult to evaluate. They view the delivery of babies as a supernatural process. Mothers are discouraged from using traditional healers because there are so many quacks among them (Harrison 1974-75:12).*

This negative evaluation is reflected in most other countries.

In spite of this prevailing view, successful efforts have been made to incorporate indigenous midwives into formal medical services. Since most births are "normal," it is reasoned, the primary problem is (1) to encourage the midwife to practice hygienic methods and (2) to refer difficult cases to government health services. Since at least the early 1950s village midwives in El Salvador have been recognized and trained by government personnel, and among the Navajo Indians similar training has reduced infant and maternal mortality. More recently there are reports of this kind of training for indigenous midwives in Tanzania (Dunlop 1974-75:138) and Liberia (Dennis 1974-75:23).

Mental illness is a second area in which formal recognition of traditional healers seems potentially promising. Since patient expectation is an important element in therapy, it seems reasonable to expect that in the absence of organic dysfunction mental stress and illness can be alleviated by curers whose treatments have been seen to be successful in the past. Torrey believes that, in spite of the anecdotal nature of the evidence on the efficacy of therapists in other cultures, "It is almost unanimous in suggesting that witchdoctors get about the same therapeutic results as psychiatrists do" (Torrey 1973:119). In Nigeria, Maclean appears favorably impressed by many aspects of traditional treatment of mental illness, and not the least by rituals enacted to symbolize recovery at the end of a period of treatment. Dressed in the clothing worn during his illness, the patient is taken to a river where a dove is sacrificed over his head, and he is washed in its blood. Then his old clothing is removed and, with the carcass of the bird, thrown into the stream and carried away, while the priest-curer chants:

As the river can never flow backwards,
So may this illness never return.

The former patient now dresses in new clothes and meets his relatives who have assembled for a feast in honor of his newly recovered health. Both patient and family benefit from this ritual: the former is reassured that his relatives welcome him back to his usual role, while the latter has the priest's assurance that he can be counted on to carry on with his normal activities. This is in striking contrast, says Maclean, to Western society where a former mental patient leaves the hospital with a stigma which may never disappear (Maclean 1971:79-80).

Whatever the potential merit of making formal use of the medical talents of indigenous curers, the idea has made little progress in practice. Perhaps the question will never need to be resolved, for it erroneously assumes that traditional healers will continue to be produced in the same numbers and with the same skills as in the past. But social, economic, and educational change is coming with such speed in all the world that most of tomorrow's traditional healers probably will have been trained in medical schools, schools of nursing, and other government health institutions. Consequently, I suspect that any increase in the formal use of traditional healers in the context of national health services will be at best no more than a transitional step, and that after relatively few years, the question of their possible utility will be moot.

Antoinette T. Ragucci

The ethnographic approach and nursing research

In utilizing the ethnographic approach for the investigation of cultural phenomena related to health, the method of participant–observation, used by anthropologists to study peoples of non-Western cultures, was adapted for the investigation of cultural continuity and change in the concepts of health, curing practices, and ritual expressions of women living in an ethnic enclave of a large American city.

The focal point of the research described here centered on the discovery of "conceptual models" of health and illness of peoples who represent variants of Western and Eastern European civilization. Attention was directed toward the identification of so-called "folk" health systems, usually associated with an agrarian mode of life, as viable and functional entities within an urban milieu. The scope of interest, then, was similar to that of anthropologists who engage in research in the more recently developed areas of the science of man—medical and urban anthropology.

A concomitant interest focused upon the delineation of intra- and intercultural variations in cultural beliefs and practices about health. Most comparative studies that deal with behavioral differentials in response to illness of ethnic groups residing in American urban centers disregard or minimize the differences which may be present not only between generations but also within generations. Some studies do not specify the generational depth nor control adequately for the generation variable. A truncated sample results if the first or immigrant generation is not taken sufficiently into account. Valid generalizations about cultural differences and persistence and change in health beliefs and associated practices require adequate sampling of at least three generations, the first or foreign-born established as the base line. At present, progress in the development of a comparative frame of reference for the study of cultural differences in response to illness is impeded by the lack of descriptive data about specific subcultural groups residing in America.

Ethnographies, empirically descriptive of the real world, provide the chief analytic instruments by which valid cross-cultural comparisons are made. For example, 862 sample societies, classified in the *Ethnographic Atlas*, are sufficiently described so that they may be used for cross-cultural comparisons (Murdock, 1967). However, only 15 appear to be samples of Western or Eastern European societies.

A Naturalistic Approach

The ethnographic approach is a naturalistic comparative method aimed at studying human behavior and attitudes through observations in the natural setting. Ethnographic study or community study is a method in which "a problem or problems in the nature, interconnections or dynamics of behavior and attitudes is explored against or within the context of other behaviors and attitudes of the individuals making up the life of a particular community" (Arensberg and Kimball, 1965, p. 29). Community study is a method of observation, exploration, comparison, and verification. It is an observational rather than a statistical or experimental method.

The task of the anthropologist is to describe specific cultures adequately. The rules for the collection of cultural data using the naturalistic field research approach were explicated by Malinowski in 1922. Radcliffe-Brown (1935) and Malinowski (1922), identified with the school of functionalism, were among the first to advocate the study of cultures as functional wholes by the use of field techniques.

The basic assumption underlying the functionalist view of culture is that everything in the life of a community has a function, and what appears to be the same social usage in two or more societies may actually have different functions in each. According to Radcliffe-Brown, the acceptance of the functional hypothesis results in the recognition "of problems for the solution of which comparative studies of diverse societies and intensive study of a single society are required" (pp. 399-400).

A more recent development in ethnographic methodology is referred to as the "new ethnography" or ethnoscience. The suffix "science" is not used in the usual sense. It refers to classification or taxonomy. When used with the prefix "ethno-," ethnoscience refers to the systems of cognition typical of a given culture (Sturtevant, 1968, p. 475). Hence, ethnobotany—folk taxonomy of plants; ethnohistory—a conception of the past shared by the people of a culture; ethnomedicine—folk medical classifications or folk conceptions of phenomena associated with illness or disease.

Goodenough at a roundtable in 1957 proposed that ethnography be conceived as the discovery of the conceptual models with which a society operates. According to this view:

> *A society's culture consists of whatever one has to know or believe in order to operate in a manner acceptable to its members . . . It is the form of things that people have in mind, their models for perceiving, relating and otherwise interpreting them. . . . Ethnographic description . . . requires methods of processing observed phenomena such that we can inductively construct a theory of how our informants have organized the same phenomena. It is the theory, not the phenomena alone, which ethnographic description aims to present (Goodenough, 1964, p. 36).*

The ethnoscientific approach facilitates intracultural as well as cross-cultural comparisons. Anthropologists have borrowed the concepts of *etic* and *emic* as used by linguists for the study of native or folk classificatory systems. Derived from the word phonetic, etic refers to units or classifications not validated in native reactions to the behavior in question (Pike, 1964; Hymes, 1964, p. 14). Etic features are common to more than one culture, that is, they are "culture-free," and, therefore, can be utilized for cross-cultural comparative purposes. On the other hand, emic classifications are culture-bound or culture-specific. An emic approach is an attempt to "discover and describe the behavioral system of a given culture in its own terms" (French, 1963, p. 398).

The "new ethnography" raises the standards of reliability and validity in ethnography. It employs rigorous methods for the intensive study of selected cultural domains. Ethnoscience requires the specification of the discovery procedures and the validity of the descriptions depends upon the discovery procedures (Sturtevant, 1968, p. 483).

The old and new approaches are not mutually exclusive. Both methods may be utilized in the same field experience. Frake (1961), for example, discovered that effective communication with the Subanun people depended upon the anthropologist's mastery of the terminology of folk medicine and botany before he could proceed to a systematic study of other cultural and structural elements.

The concept underlying ethnoscience is not a new idea. Malinowski expressed a similar view 50 years ago:

> *The final goal of which the Ethnographer should never lose sight . . . is briefly to grasp the native's point of view, his relation to life, to realize his vision of his world (Malinowski, 1954, p. 25).*

The size and complexity of American communities have been cited as obstacles for attaining the ethnographic ideal of studying cultures as wholes. However, the study of one aspect, for example, health, within the context of the community will allow the investigator to gain an understanding of its spatial or ecological patterns and social and cultural processes. For example, in my study (Ragucci, 1971) of the health beliefs and practices of women in an Italian-American enclave, the structure of social relationships at the level of kin, ritual kin and neighborhood were analyzed according to the functional nature of the social links in events concerned with illness and death. In like manner, the dominant value orientations were studied according to their fit with cultural behavior during periods of crisis.

The Participant-Observation Method

A strategy was devised to insure the researcher's maximum exposure to a number of situations in which the beliefs and behaviors about health and healing were more likely to be expressed. The method of participant-observation is synonymous with the ethnographic approach. The observation process itself is part of what Nagel (1961) referred to as "controlled investigation" (p. 452).

Scientific observation is deliberate search, carried out with care and fore-thought, as contrasted with the casual and largely passive perceptions of everyday life. It is this deliberateness and control of the observation process which is distinctive of science, not merely the use of special instruments (Kaplan, 1964, p. 126).

The major instrument for the collection of data is the investigator himself. Thus, the successful employment of the method of participant-observation is predicated upon one's ability to establish rapport and relationships of mutual trust and respect with his informants. The way in which the investigator defines his role may facilitate or hinder his entry into the community. For example, in collecting data for my study of the cognitive orientations and basic premises about health held by women in an Italian-American enclave, the decision about the role in which I wished to be perceived was made prior to my initial reconnaissance in the community to rent an apartment. The role had to be congruent not only with the type of research questions that I intended to ask, but also with the residents' expectations of those who occupy the role. After much deliberation, I decided that the most plausible explanation for my presence in the community was that of a graduate student who was interested in studying health and the "old traditions" and customs associated with health and curing. This definition was congruent with the role I assumed for the 15-month period of residence in the enclave.

The type and location of living quarters, too, determined the quantity and quality of primary or face-to-face relationships. I rented modest living quarters in an apartment complex which had a larger number of units than the typical tenement. After moving into the community, I discovered my decision had been a fortunate one. Rental of a cold water flat, one of the choices, would have lowered my status with my neighbors. On the other hand, occupancy of a remodeled luxury-type apartment rented to middle-class professionals considered "outsiders" by the older residents would have increased social distance.

The time table and circumstances relative to entry in the social world of the women varied according to generation. Four months elapsed before I was accepted as a neighbor and friend. Some factors which facilitated acceptance by the women in the oldest age class, the established base line group, were my identity as a second-generation Italian who could communicate in the native tongue and the ascription of the role of "literati" by those women who lacked literary and language skills in English. The strategy of using the quotations of Italian proverbs, the repositories of folk wisdom, was particularly effective in establishing rapport with women who were initially resistant to the researcher's attempts to elicit information about their traditional and contemporary customs and beliefs. This resistance might be viewed from the perspective of women who probably were sensitive to the criticism of their children for holding "superstitious" ideas.

Status differentials delayed entry into the social world of second-generation women. The problems associated with social distance decreased as I immersed myself in neighborhood and community activities. The establishment of a symmetrical dyadic relationship with a neighbor was probably the most important single factor for my eventual acceptance within the established neighborhood social structure. In the community, the principle which defined the social relationships of the first- and older second-generation women, for example, those above 50 years of age, was that derived from the model of the dyadic contract. According to Foster (1961), this model is consistent with the form of interpersonal relationships which prevail in some European Mediterranean peasant societies. Reciprocity is the basic integrative principle of the implicit dyadic contract which serves to link a person to certain relatives, neighbors, or friends to the exclusion of others who occupy the same status (Foster, p. 1174).

Age differentials limited participation in the social activities of the women of the third generation. To counteract this, data were collected by means of unstructured interviews and unobtrusive observations of mothers who brought their children to the weekly well-child conference. At this time I had the opportunity to check out observations made in my interactions with the older women during the week. Contact with these women continued through the period of time required for the completion of their children's immunization program. Casual meetings in neighborhood stores and markets and at social functions provided additional contacts.

Primary relationships were established with ten first-generation women, 12 second-generation, and three in the youngest age group. These women, in turn, introduced me to a wider circle of their relatives and friends who resided in different sectors of the enclave.

Small Group Structure
The anthropological ideal of collecting data within the context of the natural setting was accomplished mainly through the medium of the small group structure prevalent in the enclave. During the summer months we sat in front of the tenement, and in the winter we moved to the warmth of the kitchen. Current ailments, deaths, or hospitalization of neighbors and friends would invariably appear as topics for discussion. Some visits were specifically oriented to fulfill one's obligations to the sick and ailing. The neighbors customarily gathered at the homes of hospitalized persons when family members returned from the afternoon or evening hospital visiting hours. A veritable mine of data was collected on these occasions. The family members would report their perceptions of the progress of the hospitalized person, the perceived rationale of the prescribed treatment and, very often, their perception of the quality of medical and nursing care administered to the relative.

In the later phase of field work, efforts were directed toward reaching women who were marginal to the established neighborhood social systems. These women, many of whom were economically marginal, were dependent upon various formal community organizations for meeting their social and recreational needs. Data were collected by means of informal interviews during the social hours which followed the regular programs.

A retired visiting nurse, who had ministered to the health needs of the enclave for over 30 years, was instrumental in introducing me to women emigrants of a region in Italy whose folklore of health and healing had been documented at the turn of the century (Pitrè, 1871-1913, 1896). This provided the opportunity to assess the persistence and change in beliefs and practices of this variant group utilizing an historical source for base line information.

Unobtrusive observations at such diverse social occasions as wakes and picnics yielded a wealth of pertinent data. Wakes provide a setting where folk or laymen's theories about the etiology of disease and cause of death are more likely to be expressed. An opportunity to assess the current usages of herbal remedies by members of the first and second generation occurred during a combined picnic and pilgrimage to a religious shrine located in a rural area. Elderly women used this occasion to replenish their supply of herbs, and the researcher was able to elicit the people's beliefs about the curing properties of these substances. On the other hand, unobtrusive observations at the local pharmacies enabled the researcher to determine current usages of patent medicines. By means of unstructured interviews, additional data about the layman's use of pharmaceutical preparations were obtained from the pharmacists.

Data Classification
The data collected by means of this essentially qualitative inductive approach were organized and recorded in several ways. Field notes, life histories, and a personal diary constituted the chief records of the field research; 35mm. slides of the public events and rituals associated with the patron saint societies were made. Data were processed according to the categories listed in *The Outline of Cultural Materials* (Murdock *et al.*, 1967), a tool developed for the Cross-Cultural Survey at the Institute for Human Relations at Yale University.

A typology, "Traditional Folk Medicine" and "Contemporary Folk Medicine," was constructed to serve as a heuristic device for the organization and analysis of data along the generational dimension. The theoretical bases for the typology were: Redfield's (1947) construct of the folk-urban continuum and his concepts of the "great" and "little" traditions; Ackerknecht's (1942, 1946) theories on the nature of primitive and folk medicine; Lévi-Strauss' (1966) "Science of the Concrete"; and Freidson's (1961a) differentiation of modern medical and layman's knowledge. The users of "Traditional Folk Medicine" focus upon the concrete qualitative aspects of the substances employed for cure or prevention of illness. This type exhibits correspondingly more features embedded in a magical-religious frame of reference than the contemporary. The pharmacopoeia consists mainly of elements found in nature. Cultural or medical lag is revealed by the presence of traits similar to those held by older medical traditions, i.e., Greek-Roman or early twentieth-century medicine.

"Contemporary Folk Medicine" consists of elements which have filtered down from modern medicine and which have been reinterpreted by the layman. Magical-religious conceptualizations do not occupy a prominent role in the curing system, and the pharmacopoeia consists largely of manufactured or patent remedies.

The accumulating field record was reviewed at frequent, usually daily, intervals. The regularly recurring behaviors or events were noted, and patterns or configurations were isolated. Tentative or working hypotheses were formulated as guides for future inquiry. Significant events and interactions were recorded according to two categories, "act meaning" and "action meaning." As used here, "act meaning" refers to the people's explanation or definition of an event or behavior, that is, the semantic explanation. "Action meaning" refers to the meaning of the event or behavior from the perspective of the investigator, that is, the theoretical explanation of the event (see Kaplan, 1964, pp. 358-363).

The personal diary functioned as a "dialogue with self." It provided a means by which observations were insulated by focusing attention upon those factors which might have interferred with the achievement of the necessary detachment or objectivity. Most notations dealt with problems associated with value conflicts between those being observed and the observer, overidentification with the group, doubts about the ethical validity of collecting data by means of an essentially indirect and unobtrusive method, and conflicts relative to the exploitation of relationships as means to an end not always fully understood by my informants. One of the most problematic issues was the role conflict engendered by the constraints imposed upon a health professional when incorrect or irrelevant health beliefs or practices were noted. Deliberate and planned intervention occurred when the occasion demanded it, that is, when a belief or practice was known to be potentially or actually harmful.

These records of field research provide the raw materials from which data are selected for the ethnography. A qualitative inductive method of data collection presents a formidable challenge for the organization of the final account. The task of separating interpretations from descriptions is difficult, and the report of findings does not always yield elegant explanations.

Uses for Ethnography

However, the advantages in the use of this method outweigh its costs. The ethnographic approach is most effective for the study of groups whose members do not have the literary and language skills characteristic of the dominant white middle-class culture. The method of participant-observation permits entry into cultures which would otherwise be inaccessible by reason of their marginality or style of life. For example, the child psychiatrist, Robert Coles (1970), adapted the methods of the social anthropologist for the study of the early life of migrant workers. The method of participant-observation allows the investigator to look beyond reports of behavior and to observe the behavior itself so that he can assess the correspondence or the discrepancy that exists between the real and the ideal cultural statements. Finally, prolonged residence in a community and the continuing relationships provide more opportunity to check the reliability of informants.

The ethnographic study of urban communities will probably best be accomplished by means of the coordinated efforts of a research team. In the division of labor within the fields of medical and urban anthropology, the basic task of the nurse-anthropologist appears to be that of the ethnographer of the "health cultures" of the various subcultural groups which make up the population of large urban centers.

The investigation of the functional relationships and the interconnections of health, social structure, and culture need not be restricted to the community. Ethnographies of the natural settings in which behaviors and attitudes related to health and illness are more likely to be expressed—namely, the hospital, the clinical division, the health center, or the nursing home—need to be compiled. The ethnography of these samples of social and cultural systems should be written from the point of view of the people who are recipients of health services.

An alternate approach, the ethnoscientific, will enable the nurse-ethnographer to describe adequately the phenomena associated with health and illness according to the conceptual systems of the people she is studying. Having identified a culture's or a patient's model for perceiving, relating, or otherwise interpreting health phenomena, she can inductively construct a theory of how her informants or patients have organized the same phenomena (see Goodenough, 1964).

The ethnoscientific method is most effectively used within the context of the natural setting. In the study of the women residents of an ethnic enclave, I constructed theories of how people perceived health and illness by listening to their conversations and eliciting information within the context of situations specifically oriented to illness experiences.

An interesting area of ethnoscientific exploration is ethnophysiology, a domain which refers to the classification of human physiology by the folk or laymen. Because I hold an appointment as associate in nursing, I can explore this area while engaging in the administration of nursing care on the medical-surgical clinical divisions. The ultimate objective is to devise a method which can be replicated for the study of intracultural and intercultural similarities and differences in the classification of the same phenomena. The use of a three-generation design in this area may pose formidable problems in eliciting information from non-English-speaking people because the introduction of a translator will change the natural research setting. A more immediate problem concerns the framing of the research questions. Therefore, I am currently concentrating on the task of phrasing the eliciting questions without the imposition of my own preconceived categories of human physiology.

The ethnographic is an appropriate methodological approach to the study of the cognitive and affective orientations of diverse urban subcultural groups and the mode of their responses to the processes of acculturation considered within the perspective of health and medical systems. It has a place in nursing science. For, the final goal—of which the nurse-ethnographer should never lose sight—is to grasp the patient's point of view, his relation to life, to realize his vision of the phenomena of health and illness.

Gretel H. Pelto

Norge W. Jerome

Intracultural diversity and nutritional anthropology

Historically, cultural anthropologists have been remarkably uninterested in the nutritional systems of the communities they study. Ethnographers usually describe food procurement under the general heading of "economics," but food preparation, dietary patterns, and eating habits have received less systematic treatment. Assessment of nutritional quality and quantity is rarely, if ever, a subject of general ethnographic research. A few striking exceptions to this general lack of anthropological attention to diet do exist, most notably Audrey Richard's *Hunger and Work in a Savage Tribe* and the work of Margaret Mead and her collaborators in their research during World War II on food consumption habits of the American public.

Of course, applied anthropologists have been working in public health and nutrition programs, but the lack of more widespread interest in their work is surprising given the long-term anthropological concern with integrating social and biological aspects of human behavior. The study of nutrition is a biocultural issue, par excellence. The consequences of food intake are biological; that is, individual biological functioning is directly and continuously affected by food intake over the course of a lifetime. But the nature of food intake—what people eat, how, when, where, and how much—is heavily influenced by social, political, and cultural processes. From assessment of nutrient distribution at the national level to analysis of nutrient distribution within communities and families, social variables are an integral part of nutritional outcomes.

There are, however, both methodological and theoretical barriers to a successful integration of the social and biological aspects of nutritional research. A brief review of the major types of research by nutritionists and anthropologists should serve to demonstrate the nature of the problem.

Research within nutritional science usually takes one of the following forms:

> 1. Studies by biochemists of the physiological functions of some nutrient. Frequently such research examines the relationships of different levels of a nutrient (vitamin, mineral, lipid, and so forth) to metabolic behavior, some aspects of growth, or disease process. Methodologically this type of research involves collecting data from individual subjects (human or

animal), with or without experimental manipulation of some of the relevant parameters. Relationships among the selected variables are then analyzed in order to generalize about human physiological processes.

2. Large-scale surveys of populations using biochemical and clinical assessments to determine nutritional status and/or interview techniques to elicit data on food intake, dietary patterning, and nutritional adequacy of diet, or some combination of each. In this type of research the data are collected from individuals to create descriptive generalizations about a population, which may be as small as a community or as large as a nation. Results are frequently presented in terms of percentages of the population characterized by particular nutritional states (for example, serum levels of vitamins and minerals), food consumption levels, or nutritional adequacy of diet.

3. Food habit surveys. Foods consumed by individuals, families, households, or ethnic and economic subgroups of communities are recorded for a given period of time (using twenty-four-hour recall, three-day records, seven-day inventories) and are used to determine dietary habits and nutritional composition of food ingested. However, such surveys generally minimize the cultural and socioeconomic forces influencing dietary practices.

Anthropological Studies

In sociocultural anthropology research design is quite different. An older research style, uncommon today, sought to describe the cultural system of a people, often identified as a tribe or ethnic group. Descriptions of groups such as "the Navajo" or "the Nuer" were often generated from research in a particular community, with special focus on a few trusted key informants who provided verbal information about "the way we do things" or "the way we used to do things."

More recently, a typical research style involves fieldwork in a community to describe its cultural patterns. The focus tends to be on normative description—of values, beliefs, and symbolic meanings of particular practices—as well as on descriptions of the usual way of carrying out subsistence activities, child training, and so on. Often the research concentrates on some particular aspect of community life, such as conflict resolution, economic exchange, and kinship relations.

The research methods associated with much of cultural anthropology (whether problem-oriented or aimed at ethnographic description) utilize a mixture of observation and interviews of a carefully selected sample of the community. A great deal of variability exists in the systematizing of data collection. Yet, with rare exceptions, the anthropologist produces a more or less generalized description of typical or normative cultural patterns.

These problems with methodology have limited the integration of the biological and social aspects of nutrition in anthropological research. We can begin to see why there have been serious problems in trying to relate the data of nutrition to those of cultural anthropology. Nutritional data are not easily articulated because anthropologists and nutritionists use different units of analysis and seek different kinds of generalizations. (We might add that similar problems exist within anthropology, where the disjunction between the methods and data of physical and cultural anthropologists have been a barrier to the development of a true biocultural anthropology.)

Of course, it is stating the obvious to suggest that disciplines differ in their units of analysis and theoretical constructs. The real issue in interdisciplinary research is whether units of analysis in one discipline can be identified with or articulated into units of analysis in another. Thus, the data of macrobiology (for example, animal ecology) are not easily articulated with research in chemistry, but when biologists focus on characteristics of individuals (on particular components of blood, hormones, and so forth) then collaboration with chemists becomes meaningful. The growth of research on human biochemistry demonstrates how effective interdisciplinary collaboration can be when the data can be articulated.

What is required to bring cultural anthropology and nutrition into similar congruity? From the anthropological side, we must shift from an interest in normative description to a focus on intracultural diversity of behaviors and beliefs. We must describe societies in terms of the ranges of variation that are the realities of human life. For example, economic and political structures must be described not only in general terms but also in terms of the way they are reflected in individual behavior. Just as the value of biological parameters is measured for individuals, so the social and cultural variables must be measured for individuals. When anthropologists work in this way, their data can be readily linked with the data of nutritionists.

From the nutrition side must come recognition that social processes are every bit as complex as biological processes and that their measurement is as difficult. Too often, for example, nutritional researchers have assumed that simply asking people about their income is a sufficient measure of socioeconomic status or that respondents' description of the composition of breakfast provides ample data for determining nutritional adequacy of that meal. Again, residence in particular economically marginal neighborhoods or villages is sometimes considered sufficient to identify low income status. Both verbal reports and place of residence can miss altogether the subtle but significant differences in families' economic situations that may strongly affect nutrient intake. Just as biological measures are powerfully affected by the choice of the measurement technique, so too are social variables. The methodological sophistication required to measure sociocultural factors is no smaller than that required to produce valid biological data. Therefore, in addition to congruence of units anthropologists and nutritionists also need an appreciation of each others' theoretical constructs and methodological problems.

Recently, some researchers have tried to resolve some of the methodological problems in cultural anthropology and human nutrition by trying to account for diversities in food consumption, nutritional adequacy, and nutritional status of individuals in communities.

In our work we have found that a research strategy that assumes intracultural diversity is very useful for understanding the relationships of food consumption to other social and cultural factors. For example, Jerome carried out intensive research with twenty-three black households in Milwaukee, Wisconsin as part of a larger project on food-consumption patterns of low income black families. The twenty-three households did not present a homogeneous picture. Rather they exhibited a variety of eating and food preferences. What explains the differences? It was found that national and racial indices of socioeconomic status were not very useful in classifying the respondents (Jerome 1968). In terms of education, occupation, and income, most of the families could be placed at the bottom of the tripartite class structure. The characteristics that did make a difference in food consumption patterns included family background and length of residence in the South, time of migration and length of residence in the North, as well as home ownership, church membership, and several other sociocultural factors. By focusing on the difference within the community and systematically collecting data on individual and family characteristics, it was possible to delineate the major variables that affected food consumption and to examine the adaptation in progress. The research in Milwaukee reveals how people discard old modes of food consumption as they learn to use the resources of a new environment.

In research in a Mexican community DeWalt and Pelto (in press) studied factors that contribute to dietary complexity. Within the community there were impressive differences in the varieties of food consumed, ranging from diets of mainly tortillas, beans, and chilis to those that were well-balanced and varied. Analysis of data on social status and beliefs suggests that in this community people's beliefs about the characteristics of particular foods have relatively little to do with the frequency of their consumption. Dietary complexity is, apparently, much more strongly affected by household composition, access to land, and occupation. As in the research in Milwaukee, an approach to the community that focused on normative patterns would have failed to discover such relationships.

In an interesting study in a neighboring community in Mexico, Miriam Muñoz de Chávez and her colleagues (1974) studied differences in families of malnourished and well-nourished children. Excluding families at both upper and lower ends of the economic spectrum, the researchers focused on families of farmers— thirty-six families with well-nourished children and thirty-seven families with children who showed unequivocal signs of malnutrition. Among the variables that differentiated the two groups were: (1) differences in the ratio of children to adults within a household; (2) sex differences (68 percent of malnourished children were girls; 62 percent of well-nourished children were boys); (3) diet of mother; and (4) weaning history of the child. The researchers felt that the interpretation of these results and other findings should be approached cautiously because of the complexity of the data. They did not find any minor variations in feeding practices or in child care that might cause large differences in the physical state and health of the children. What was found was a spider's web of facts that needed to be proven (1974).

We should add to the comments by Muñoz and colleagues that in that part of Mexico, as elsewhere, even among seemingly homogeneous communal-land farmers there can be significant differences in economic status, based on access to paying jobs, differences in agricultural productivity, and number of wage earners in the household. Time and again we have found that assumptions about the same social stratum are not warranted when households are examined more closely.

In the sociocultural system of the United States there has been a good deal of discussion recently about the health food movement, vegetarianism, and so-called food faddism. These phenomena are often discussed in general terms, suggesting that vegetarians are all pretty much alike and people know a food faddist when they see one. But a closer look at the health food people shows a fascinating diversity in their complex networks. Even though articulation among the diverse groups is maintained to some extent through magazines, books, and other publications, as well as by traveling food evangelists, there are notable differences among macrobiotic enthusiasts, followers of Guru Maharaji, *Diet-for-a-Small-Planet* vegetarians, and various meat-eating health food people (Kandel and Pelto, in press). This research demonstrated the importance of social networks in affecting individual food consumption patterns.

A recent multivariate study of factors affecting malnutrition was carried out by the economist F. James Levinson and associates (1974) in a rural area of the Punjab in northern India. The study sample comprised 496 children, including both the Jats (an economically and socially dominant group) and the Ramdasias (landless agricultural laborers). Data included relatively short interviews with the children's mothers, examination of stool samples, and height, weight, and health measures. Nutritional status was determined from height, weight, and age according to the well-known Harvard standards. Nutrient intake was estimated for each child through the use of the twenty-four hour recall method. Roughly three times as many of the Ramdasia children as Jat children were categorized as having third-degree malnutrition.

It is perhaps not surprising that the sex of the child was a major variable in predicting malnutrition in this Punjab population. Severe malnutrition appeared to be about seven times as frequent among female children as among males. Levinson concluded that sex, income of parents, age of child, disease status, and reported caloric intake were the major predictors of nutritional status and that the health and nutrition beliefs of the childrens' mothers contributed to the prediction of caloric intake. Concerning programmatic recommendations, he suggested that because of large differences in economic position of the two groups "most interventions which did not in some way augment real income would have a far greater positive effect on the Jat child that on the Ramdasia" (1974:62).

Thomas Marchione (in press) has recently studied factors related to different nutritional status of infants in a Jamaican community using data on the interrelationships among economic, social, and cultural variables. Through factor analysis he was able to identify a series of significant variables, including a "nuclear-family-solidarity" factor as well as "caretaker-maturity" and "dependency-ratio" factors. As in other recent studies, it was found that an infant is subjected to greater risk of malnutrition if there are other small children in the household. A "rural-subsistence-dependency" factor was a significant predictor as well, reflecting the marginality and inadequacy of the small plots available to people for food cultivation in the outlying areas.

Although Marchione's data leave a considerable portion of total variance unexplained, his statistical analysis goes farther than most other community studies in identifying the inputs of different social and economic factors in predicting variations in nutritional status within a community. Such a study does not, of course, tell us much about what to do about Jamaica's marginal position with regard to food sources, but it aids in the identification of nutritional risk factors in on-going community health programs.

These studies delineating intracultural diversity move us further in the direction of formulating theories and developing methodologies that capture the realities of dietary adequacy in relation to sociocultural and biological variables. DeWalt and Pelto's research demonstrates that relationships between belief and behavior are not as simple as was formerly assumed. Jerome takes us one step further to demonstrate how these selection patterns parallel nutritional adequacy of diet in various subgroups. Levinson's and Marchione's work show how belief patterns, food choice patterns, and dietary adequacy culminate in differential nutritional status within the community.

Summary and Conclusion

We will briefly outline here some of the major ideas that emerge from analysis of these methodological trends in food and nutritional systems research.

At the most general level, research that focuses on individuals, from both the biological and the sociocultural dimension, can greatly enhance our understanding of the complexities linking nutritional status, disease, and other health measures with income, family cultural patterns, households structures, and other variables in adaptational systems.

Some of the more recent and more sophisticated research is beginning to provide ways to sort out the relative strengths and predictive power of various social and cultural factors. In some cases income alone may be a powerful predictive factor in determining nutritional status. In other instances, the complex interactions of other intervening variables may disguise the effects of economic variables.

Controlling a research design for economic factors, we have yet to demonstrate how and when beliefs and attitudes play significant roles in affecting people's health and nutritional behavior. When do adequate economic means lead to health, when to obesity and illness? People's support networks—their social systems—have strong effects on their adaptational styles and on their chances of success in coping with challenges to health and well-being. These support networks are very difficult to fit into research operations even with the most complicated interview schedules. The rich, qualitative data of participant observation sometimes fail to do justice to this sociocultural dimension. Much more work is needed to get a richer expression of this dimension into our predictive, theoretical frameworks.

Sophisticated multifactor studies in nutrition and health can contribute significantly to general anthropological theory and to nutritional science; at the same time, they can aid in solving some of the practical health and nutritional problems of human communities. The point is that intracultural research strategies, focusing on individuals and households as units of analysis, permit the specification of predictive models by means of which "at-risk" subpopulations within communities can be identified. At the same time major barriers to the implementation of nutritional programs, counseling, and other efforts can be identified, as well as the places most responsive to intervention by well-informed community and regional health efforts.

Anthropologists working in the areas of nutrition and food consumption have significant contributions to make, especially in connection with conceptualizing, making operational and measuring the effect of social, economic, and cultural variables. After all, that is what we are supposedly trained to do best. But sociocultural data will not advance multidisciplinary research unless we shape research strategies and conceptual units to be in conjunction with the data and theoretical constructs of our colleagues on the nutritional, biochemical side of the research enterprise. This paper is intended to further those research efforts.

Steven Polgar
John F. Marshall

The search for culturally acceptable fertility regulating methods

There seem to be two quite different views on the ease with which technical innovations can be transferred across cultural boundaries. A number of anthropologists have concluded that items of material culture are borrowed from one society by another more readily than forms of social organization, value emphases, or cognitive patterns—a process known as spontaneous or undirected culture change. Case studies of deliberate efforts to introduce items from Western, industrial societies to peasant or tribal groups, however, often conclude by stressing the cultural barriers that thwart these "technical assistance" programs, rather than the ease of diffusion of material culture. Failures to persuade non-Western peoples to

Reprinted by permission from S. Polgar and J. F. Marshall (eds.), *Culture, Natality, and Family Planning*, Monograph 21 (Chapel Hill, North Carolina: Carolina Population Center, 1976), pp. 204-218.

adopt pit latrines, boiled drinking water, new types of cooking stoves, European-style agricultural implements, or other technical innovations have been a major topic of analysis for several generations of applied anthropologists.

Possible reasons for this discrepancy in views might lie in the fundamental differences between self-determined and programmed culture change, in the inadequacy of the generalization about objects diffusing more readily than nonmaterial items, or in the nonrepresentativeness of the instances of directed change studies by anthropologists. Part of the explanation, we think, is that in many of the instances where material culture is borrowed spontaneously, the transfer occurs between neighboring societies which do not differ greatly in motor habits, value systems, division of labor, or cognitive maps. In Western-directed culture change, however, the program staff may not only have an exaggerated view of the superiority of the new gadgets they bring, but also a tendency to ignore the many ecological and sociocultural variables that can differ significantly between the new setting and the industrial country where the innovation was developed.

This chapter reports on recent efforts intended to fit technology to people, rather than fitting people to technology. The material innovations at issue are new and improved fertility regulating methods, and the research efforts—centered in the World Health Organization Task Force on Acceptability of Fertility Regulating Methods (part of the Expanded Programme of Research, Development, and Research Training in Human Reproduction)—are intended to help guide biomedical scientists who are exploring new means for controlling human fertility.

Modern fertility regulation technology has diffused in a most uneven pattern from Western to non-Western societies, a phenomenon largely explained by three interacting factors which vary considerably between and within populations:

1. Interest in avoiding or postponing births
2. The quality of the delivery system for fertility regulating methods and the accessibility of services and information
3. The suitability of the particular methods (i.e., of the available technology for fertility regulation)

Improved technology—improved, that is, in terms of increasing its compatibility with the life circumstances and preferences of potential users—seems unlikely, by itself, to lead to change from non-use to use, certainly not by people who see substantial advantages in having more children. But increasing the sociocultural fit of fertility regulating methods is clearly one part of the equation that results in providing couples with real choices in determining their reproductive future.

Point of Interference in Reproduction

Technology for human fertility regulation is not new, but it has recently begun to focus on different points of intervention in the reproductive process. Ethnological and archeological evidence indicates that infanticide was perhaps the earliest method of fertility regulation. During the gathering and hunting stage of human evolution, abortion was also practiced (Polgar 1968, 1972; Dumond 1975).

In figure 1 infanticide is postpartum, while abortion occurs during gestation. It is possible that behavioral, mechanical, and chemical means of blocking the

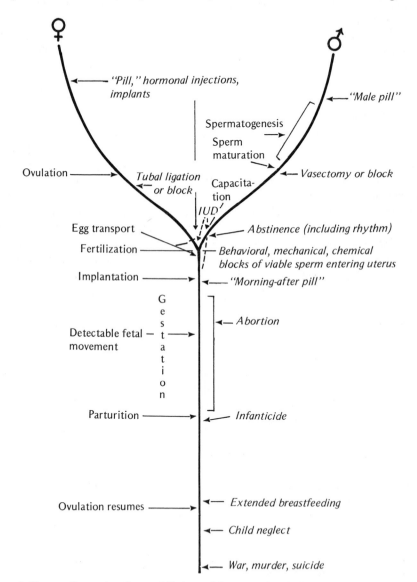

Figure 1. Human Reproduction and Points of Intervention in It

ascent of viable sperm through the cervix were also invented before the change from the gathering-hunting to the agricultural mode of existence. Reports of plugs made from vegetable materials inserted into the vagina, attempts to block the ejaculate from escaping the penis, coitus interruptus, douches, and the like, however, are much more common from agricultural people than gatherer-hunters. The distribution of long postpartum periods of sexual abstinence also favors an origin after the transition to food production.

Much of the effort of improving birth control in the period of industrialization centered on mechanical interference with the entry of sperm into the uterus, particularly with the condom, diaphragm, and cervical cap. The improvements in knowledge about ovulation, in the meantime, led to development of the rhythm method which in a sense represents a refinement of the old methods of postpartum, magical, religious, and life-stage-connected periods of abstinence from sexual intercourse. Even the Grafenberg intrauterine device was reportedly an accidental by-product of experiments with a mechanical barrier, which was to be kept in place over the cervix by a stem extending into the uterine cavity.

Since we do not classify castration as a cultural means for fertility regulation, the advent of surgical sterilization can be regarded as relatively recent. While progress was slow in refining techniques for mechanically interrupting the vas deferens and the Fallopian tube, until recently it was more marked for the former than the latter. By contrast, development of hormonal methods for interfering in sperm production and capacitation has lagged acutely behind attempts to influence female reproductive physiology.

Attributes of Fertility Regulating Methods

Although a great deal of clinical experience and common sense was used by biomedical scientists in developing new technology, little research has been devoted specifically to the relative acceptability of fertility regulating methods from the viewpoint of potential users. This neglect is curious in light of the importance of this variable in helping to explain differential rates of adoption of various methods in the past. It has been persuasively argued, for example, that the Lippes IUD failed in India largely because it led to an unexpected increase in the amount and irregularity of menstrual bleeding. Such changes in menstrual patterns were usually not considered biomedically unacceptable, but in many cases they did exceed thresholds perceived as tolerable by Indian women who were potential users of the technology. Also, those doing the insertions seldom gave adequate warning of what might happen.

There are many aspects of fertility regulating technology that affect its "fit" into a cultural setting. In the example of the unsuccessful attempt to gain wide acceptance for the first-generation plastic IUD in India, the attribute apparently responsible for its limited diffusion was its side effects. In the case of the rapid and widespread diffusion of Depoprovera in Northern Thailand, the relevant attribute is probably the method's route of administration: injections are consonant with the existing cultural patterns of the population (McDaniels and Tieng 1972; Cunningham 1970). Vasectomy is unattractive in many societies because it is not reversible, and the diaphragm, among other reasons, because it is coitus connected and demands manipulation of the genitalia. A brief look at several attributes of existing and potential fertility regulating methods illustrates what is involved in attempts to design safe and effective technology that is consonant with societal values, beliefs, preferences, and material conditions.

Duration of Fertility Regulating Action and Frequency of Use

Infanticide will obviously eliminate at least one child (more if the birth is multiple) and reduce the effective reproductive period of the woman by about 14-18 months (counting three to five months for the conception wait, nine for pregnancy, and two to four annovulatory months postpartum). The effects of prolonged breast-feeding may vary in accord with the nutritional status of the woman, and are not likely to increase the interpartum interval by more than 12-16 months. Abortion has less of an effect than infanticide, reducing the reproductive period by nine to 15 months, depending on how late in the pregnancy it is performed.

Most of the methods interfering with the entrance of sperm into the cervical canal are "one coitus" methods, representing a very high behavioral cost—each use reducing the reproductive span by no more than a few days. Rhythm used in the incorrect way—abstention just before or after the menses (which is in accordance with medical notions before Knauss' and Ogino's findings became accepted)—may in fact reduce the waiting time for conception rather than the total reproductive period.

The pill in its most widespread current form requires even more frequent contraceptive action than the coitus-connected methods, but its great advantage lies in this action being independent of sexual intercourse. The fact that "morning-after'" treatments do not share this feature may make them less or more attractive for general use than hormonal methods applied every day, week, month, six months, or year, regardless of coital timing.

Much of recent research on fertility regulating methods has concentrated on lengthening the effect of a single contraceptive act. The cervical cap, the Grafenberg device, and Ota's rings are early attempts in this direction, and the current generation of IUDs its most prominent manifestation. The IUD is not only coitus independent, but one insertion can reduce the reproductive period for several years.

Some of the IUD's advocates would count as an added advantage the fact that removal of some forms requires the help of a qualified person other than the patient—hence the debate concerning the advantages of tailed versus tailless devices. That it must also be *inserted* by a qualified person other than the patient is usually recognized as a distinct drawback.

Sterilization goes farther than the IUD, both in the length of its effect and its requirement of technical personnel and facilities. Many commentators have advocated more research on techniques of reversible sterilization, recognizing that the death of one or more children, a new marital union, and similar contingencies, would inhibit the acceptance of a "permanent" method. Malthusian extremists, on the other hand, might tend to encourage methods which leave patients powerless to exercise choice over adoption and continuation.

Side Effects

Physicians and biologists make a three-fold distinction among the influences which a fertility regulating method has on the human body: (1) effectiveness in influencing reproductive functions; (2) safety; and (3) side effects. The first is relatively clear: How reliably does a certain intervention interfere with or promote reproduction? The second and third are distinguished more empirically than logically. Occasional inter-menstrual bleeding may be regarded by the biomedical community as a side effect—troublesome but not a medically serious condition; but once the bleeding has been shown to affect the hemoglobin level in a population where anemia is a widespread condition, it moves over to the safety category.

For the clients, these distinctions may be quite beside the point. Alterations in biological, psychological, and social functioning seen as related to the fertility regulating method will be evaluated by criteria relevant to their culture. If bleeding through the vagina entails prohibitions on praying, cooking, coitus, and being in the vicinity of men, the amount of blood lost (and one's hemoglobin level) may be of less immediate consequence than the frequency with which days with *any* noticeable blood loss occur.

While condoms in most societies have the undesirable effect of reducing sexual satisfaction, in some groups the possibility of prolonging the part of the sex act before ejaculation may be an advantage. One should obviously be alert, then, to positive as well as negative side effects. Humorist Art Hoppe (1963) illustrates the complexity of the situation that would ensue if a pill were marketed for men which —in a synergistic effect with alcohol—turned the eyes red:

> *Actually, when you stop to think about it, there's nothing inherently wrong with red eyeballs. Not that a little good promotion work wouldn't cure. Ads: "Are your Eyeballs Pale, Tired, Colorless?" Drinks: "The New Red Eye Highball." Contests: "Mr. Red-Blooded American Eyeball."*
>
> *Of course the ladies would take a bit of convincing. You know how they are. We might start by planting a few pointed articles in the ladies' magazines. Such as* True Confessions: *"There We Were, Eyeball to Eyeball—And His Were White!"*
>
> *Eventually, I'm sure, we'd convince them of the undeniable advantages of such a method. I mean there you are, an attractive young lady. You walk into a cocktail party crowded with handsome young bachelors. Half have red eyeballs, half don't. Which . . . Well, I don't want to go into details. But we'd soon separate the ladies from the girls. And most bachelors will, I know, agree that's an undeniable advantage right there.*
>
> *Oh, I can hear you saying you don't care. You still don't like red eyeballs. Well let me tell you this is no time for petty aesthetic prejudices. All present methods require diligence or sacrifice. Join your local Red Eyeball League today. And remember our slogan:*
>
> *"Better Red Than Bred!"*

Routes of Administration

Actions to promote health and cure disease in different medical traditions use a variety of routes to influence the human body. The mouth is primary, but other orifices may be used. The skin may be heated or cooled, rubbed dry or with some liquid or powder, or it may be punctured superficially or deeply; muscles and other body parts can be massaged; and so forth. In fertility regulation, materials may be inserted through the vaginal opening or used to sheathe the penis; abortion may be attempted by manipulating the uterus or engaging in violent exercise.

To discover what routes of administration may be most suitable for new fertility regulating methods it is not only advisable to see what routes are commonly used for other medicinal or hygienic purposes and what routes are generally avoided, but it is also important to increase our knowledge of ethno-anatomy and ethno-physiology in a number of cultures. Some traditions—such as the humoral theory and the hot-cold distinction—are very widespread around the world, and are influential even in countries where Western scientific medicine has been practiced for some time (although often accessible mostly to well-to-do urban populations).

In a study of contraceptive decision making in a rural village in North India, Marshall (1972) suggested that the most acceptable fertility regulating method for the people would be a blue substance injected by hypodermic needle into the arms of women. In a subsequent paper, Marshall (1973) explained the proposal that an injection would be the most acceptable route of administration:

> The ideal method of application would be by hypodermic injection, for several reasons. First, because of years of exposure to antibiotics and vaccinations, an injection is an entirely acceptable medical procedure in the village. Indeed, a villager who was not given a shot during a visit to a doctor felt himself somehow cheated. Second, an injection in the arm avoids both the mortifying experience of exposing one's genitals to medical scrutiny, and the necessity of handling one's genitals demanded by the condom, diaphragm, foam, or jelly. Not only is an injection coitus-independent, but like the oral pill, it is genitalia-independent, a highly desirable attribute in a culture in which modesty is imperative and privacy rare. Third, an injection can be given in the village, even in one's home, thus obviating the need to visit a threatening and inconvenient hospital or clinic. Finally, unlike a loop insertion, which requires a female doctor, or a vasectomy, which requires a male doctor, an injection in an arm can be given by either a male or a female.
>
> The injected substance would be a distinctive color—perhaps blue—primarily to differentiate it visibly from other kinds of injectable medicines. This anticipates the probability that some villagers, in need of antibiotics but firmly opposed to the idea of contraception, would suspect unscrupulous doctors of trying to enforce population control by sneaking the contraceptive substance into the hypodermic needle. Such a belief could lead to the avoidance of all injections, as in a neighboring village the belief that vitamin pills were abortifacients led to the shunning of all pills. If it were widely known that the contraceptive liquid—and only the contraceptive liquid—was always blue, a villager could assess for himself that he was, or was not, getting what he wanted.

Moreover, some colors tend to connote certain inherent qualities of substances, and a color should be selected that indicates the injected substance is not dangerously "hot" or "cold." It is likely that the injection would be perceived as being cold. Most hypodermic injections were thought to operate in much the same way as the pill, by decreasing the heat of the genital area below the threshold at which conception can occur. The knowledge that the substance would remain in her body for six months, together with the belief that hot or cold foods and medicines can be dangerous in certain pathological states, might lead a woman to avoid the injection in apprehension of succumbing to one of these states. If a color could be found that connotes warmth but not heat, it would probably lead to a more acceptable contraceptive. Furthermore, to make the substance acceptable to vegetarians, it must not contain any components derived from meat or eggs; therefore a color should be selected, if possible, that does not connote flesh or blood.

Gender of User

Many innovations which have come into prominence in the twentieth century—including the diaphragm, vaginal spermicides, hormonal pills, and plastic IUDs—have been closely connected with the feminist emphasis given to the family planning movement by Margaret Sanger and her allies. The stress on freeing women from "compulsory" childbearing had the correlate that men supposedly did not care a great deal about the burdens that pregnancy imposed on women, or indeed saw frequent childbearing as a means to keep them in bondage. However, research done in the 1940s and 1950s showed that in European cultures fertility regulating methods used by males—withdrawal and condoms—accounted for the bulk of contraceptive practice. Nowadays the widespread use of the pill and the IUD have helped to swing the pendulum the other way, and feminists ask (with considerable justice) why so little research has been done on developing new male methods.

In studying systematically the attributes of methods, the distinction between male and female methods is likely to be too simple. In some cases where the woman's body is the only one affected, it may be her husband who keeps the pills and gives one to her to take when appropriate. Withdrawal and condom may be called male *participating* methods, since the pulling away before ejaculation may be done by both partners or even the woman primarily, and it is not unheard of by any means for the woman to be the one to put the condom on the man's penis for him.

While we have some inkling that in many societies it is the males who have a dominant role in deciding whether another pregnancy is or is not wanted, we know little about the acceptability, say, of daily pills or monthly injections for men.

The Mix of Attributes

Table 1 lists selected attributes of fertility regulating methods. Because it is not the

Table 1. Some attributes of existing and potential fertility regulating methods

General Attribute	Specific Attributes
Gender of user	Male, female, both
Main action	Prevents conception, prevents birth, determines gender of offspring, promotes conception
Mode of action	Chemical, mechanical, surgical
Organs/systems involved	Penis, testicles, vas deferens, vagina, cervix, uterus, endometrium, Fallopian tube, endocrine system
Route of administration	External—e.g., over penis Internal—*implant* (subdermal); *injection* (subdermal, intramuscular, intravenous; in arm, thigh, shoulder, etc.); *oral ingestion* (as solid, liquid, powder, etc.; alone or combined with other substances); *insertion* (vaginal, anal, nasal)
Administration	Self, other (if other, degree of professional skill required)
Frequency of use	Daily, weekly, whenever coitus occurs, annually
Circumstances of use	Coitus-related, coitus-independent
Effectiveness	100 percent, 90 percent, etc.
Duration of fertility regulating effect	Temporary, long-acting, permanent (if permanent, reversibility is easy, difficult, impossible)
Side effects	Changes in bleeding (amenorrhea or spotting); changes in weight, skin pigmentation, breast size, libido/sexual pleasure; causes pain, weakness, etc.
Long-term safety	Certain, doubtful
Client convenience in obtaining	Can be obtained in local shops, from vending machine, only in hospitals, etc.
Client convenience in using	Demands collateral equipment; interferes with spontaniety; requires storage space; etc.
Familiarity to client	Well-known or new procedure or substance
Cost of method	Expensive, moderate, inexpensive, etc.
Physical properties of method as perceived by client	Color, texture, taste, odor, size

attractiveness of a single attribute, but of the total configuration of attributes which determines the acceptability of any particular method, the problem of providing cultural specifications to biomedical scientists becomes complex. This is perhaps best illustrated when the effectiveness of a contraceptive method is considered in conjunction with other characteristics. All other things being equal, it is probable that most people prefer a method that is 100 percent reliable rather than one of uncertain effectiveness. But if the 100 percent effective method is not reversible, while the method of uncertain effectiveness is easily reversible, the users' evaluation of the methods' acceptability is more complex. As other attributes (such as amount of weight gain, whether the methods are coitus-connected or coitus-independent, et cetera) are added to the equation, assessing the relative acceptability of the two methods becomes difficult—for the researcher as well as the potential user.

It becomes clear that the search for culturally acceptable fertility regulating methods will not lead to a single answer; societies, and cultural preferences, differ. Moreover, it is clear that there are significant variations in preferences not only between but within cultures, on the basis of gender, marital status, health, stage in the domestic cycle, and other subgroup differences. Within a single extended family in a North Indian village, for example, a recently married woman will likely have very different specifications for acceptable methods than the mother-in-law into whose house she has been brought. The younger woman, assuming she wished to postpone her next birth, would probably prefer a method easily reversible and coitus-independent; effectiveness may be a lower priority, since she anticipates having more pregnancies soon, anyway. The older woman, for whom another pregnancy is considered socially inappropriate, would probably prefer a method completely effective, even if it were coitus-connected and irreversible. Perhaps a range of "first-line" contraceptive technology should be developed, methods which are culturally acceptable though less than 100 percent effective, supplemented (in those populations where it is acceptable) with safe methods of early abortion.

The WHO Acceptability Task Force

The World Health Organization has recently established a Task Force on Acceptability of Fertility Regulating Methods. The main objective is to conduct research on perceptions of and attitudes toward specific methods of regulating fertility, in order to provide guidance to biomedical scientists engaged in developing new and improved methods. The Acceptability Task Force operates in the context of the WHO Expanded Programme of Research, Development, and Research Training in Human Reproduction—a predominantly biomedical international effort to stimulate and coordinate research which will lead to new technology.

Current research in the Acceptability Task Force is divided into:

> 1. Studies in conjunction with clinical trials of the most recently developed fertility regulating methods
> 2. Studies exploring particular attributes of potential technology—projects not necessarily connected with clinical trials of existing methods
> 3. Studies intended to lead to new methodological instruments with which to assess acceptability

In addition, the Acceptability Task Force has established a nine-month nondegree research training program for social scientists interested in undertaking acceptability research, and maintains an on-going bibliographic review of relevant research findings.

A current study of the acceptability of male fertility regulating methods illustrates one Task Force approach. The purposes of the project, involving social scientists in Korea, India, Iran, Fiji, Mexico, and the United States, are twofold: (1) to determine the acceptability of male methods relative to female methods, and (2) to determine the acceptability of attributes of existing and potential methods for men. In each site the study begins with a survey of "knowledgeable sources," involving informed physicians, social scientists, and family planning field workers. This information is used to help develop the survey research instruments, which are pretested, modified, and implemented on a stratified quota sample. The same research strategy is being used in a 12-country study of patterns and perceptions of menstrual bleeding. Other multinational projects of this type are being developed to investigate the acceptability of various routes of administration, the relative acceptability of reversible and irreversible sterilization, and other topics.

As new fertility regulating methods are developed, they are subjected to rigorous clinical trials to assess safety and effectiveness. Although the men and women participating in these trials do not represent a random sample of the local population, the clinical studies provide an opportunity for social scientists, working in collaboration with biomedical scientists, to explore the acceptability of new methods. Such studies can help lead to modifications of the methods to increase their attractiveness, and can help identify new approaches in fertility regulation which justify intensified biomedical efforts. The Task Force is currently investigating, or planning to investigate, the acceptability of such methods as three-month injectable contraceptives, medicated vaginal rings, subdermal implants, potentially self-administered vaginal suppositories to induce abortion, and intra-cervical devices.

Conclusion

The search for acceptable fertility regulating methods involves research providing a profile of cultural specifications, like a blueprint, to help guide biomedical scientists and those who support the development of contraceptive technology. If social scientists can provide these cultural specifications, and if these guidelines can be translated into new technology, is it reasonable to assume that the diffusion of the innovation will be more rapid and widespread? The answer, we think, is a qualified yes.

Potential users of fertility regulating methods vary greatly in their interest in avoiding or postponing the next birth. For persons who, for whatever reasons, have a very high desire to bring forth a child (or another child) as soon as possible, improved methods will be as uninteresting as existing ones, and new technology will be unlikely to influence the occurrence of their next pregnancy. Couples at the other end of the continuum, those who are firmly resolved to avoid another birth, are in many cases already employing some method to regulate fertility. For this group, safer, more effective, and more acceptable methods (if made accessible) would replace such "high cost" or high risk methods as abstention or clandestine abortion, and thus have a favorable effect on health and welfare, as well as reducing the number of contraceptive failures. The influence on demographic patterns, however, may not be very large.

In all populations, however, there is also a group of people who are uncertain whether or not to avoid or postpone their next birth. In this uncertain state, the existence of safe, effective *and attractive* technology may represent the critical factor in the decision-making process, and lead to (at least) tentative adoption. This idea is congruent with at least two different models for the adoption process, and in fact the two authors of this chapter subscribe to somewhat different conceptual approaches.

One of us (Marshall), while agreeing that the provision of more acceptable fertility regulating technology would hasten the diffusion of the innovation, sees this factor (improved methods) as essentially independent of the other two factors (desire to avoid or postpone the next birth, and adequacy of the delivery and service systems) which comprise the fundamental equation leading to adoption by people in this uncertain stage. For widespread diffusion, improved fertility regulating methods may be necessary, but are not sufficient; a basic reorientation of the potential users' values and beliefs regarding the necessity of having additional children is the critical factor. Improved technology is an independent factor in the equation, important in its own right, but having no effect on the need to have children. Beliefs and values regarding the desirability of avoiding or postponing the next birth will be changed only by real changes in the world surrounding the decision maker; a recognized drop in child mortality, for example, and the provision of functional equivalents for children will create a situation in which people are *able* to consider adopting improved fertility regulating methods.

A second view (to which Polgar subscribes) is that the technology of modern contraception or abortion may be adopted as a substitute for earlier, widespread methods of birth spacing, for example, by many of the large number of couples who are not committed to having another pregnancy start as soon as possible after the last delivery. Such behavior can—if it does successfully prevent conception for a while—permit embarking on new, rewarding activities that are conditioned on not being pregnant, and, in turn, reinforce continuation of fertility regulation and further delaying another pregnancy (Polgar 1972). In other words, behavior initiated under one set of circumstances can bring about dispositions and cognitive evaluations that under another set of circumstances would not be expected from a "means-ends" decision-making model. This view of culture change stresses long term behavioral tendencies that have feedback relationships with processes of mental justification and affective states, rather than regarding each action as separate and consequent upon a summation of positive and negative predispositions.

Research concerning the acceptability of fertility regulating methods bears on the broader anthropological question about the ease of diffusion of material culture. In spontaneous or undirected culture change, the borrowed items are those which, through a kind of Darwinian process of selection, are compatible with the material conditions, beliefs, and values of the borrowing society. Too frequently directed or planned culture change implies the promotion of foreign items which are perceived by significant segments of the host society, in weighing the attributes and consequences of the novelty, as essentially incompatible with their well-being.

It is possible that the distinction between spontaneous and planned change is relatively unimportant for the diffusion of many material innovations. The question of cultural acceptability has to be examined apart from the difference between internal *versus* external impetus for the diffusion of the new item of material culture. Attempts to modify technology in such a way that it will "fit" the material interests, cognitions, and values of a host society are not incompatible with a philosophy of anthropology that attempts to divorce itself from economic and cultural (as well as—in the present instance—a demographic) imperialism.

William S. Aron
Norman Alger
Ricardo T. Gonzales

Chicanoizing drug abuse programs

This article will focus on the problem of drug addiction and its antecedent conditions in a Chicano (1) population. We shall also examine several therapeutic interventions suggested by these conditions and show how they might be incorporated into a drug abuse treatment program designed to meet the needs of Chicano drug addicts.

In Mexican-American culture, as in all cultures, there is a wide range of variation in attitudes and behavior. We must therefore be careful to avoid simplistic cultural stereotypes. Instead of generalizing about Mexican-American culture, we shall focus on a specific community, that of La Colonia (in the city of Oxnard, Ventura County, California). La Colonia has been chosen for examination because (1) there is a high concentration of Mexican-Americans, (2) there is a high incidence of drug addiction, and (3) there are reliable statistical data available (Gutierrez 1972).

1. **Population concentration of La Colonia.**   The city of Oxnard contains approximately one-third of the Mexican-American population of Ventura County, and La Colonia contains nearly 40% of the Mexican-American population of the city of Oxnard in which it is located. The population density of La Colonia is 11,524, with 90% of its residents being Mexican-American (U.S. Department of Commerce 1972).

2. **Drug addiction in La Colonia.** The "Preliminary Report of Crime and Demographic Profile for Ventura County" (Public Safety System, Inc. 1973) notes that while Ventura County ranks 12th in population of California's 58 counties, it ranks fourth in the frequency of adult opiate arrests and second in the frequency of juvenile opiate arrests. Only 19.6% of the population of Ventura County is Mexican-American, yet, 69% of all drug-related arrests in Ventura County involve Mexican-Americans. The same report indicates that of the adult offenders arrested for burglary in Ventura County during 1972, 75% had a history of previous narcotics involvement; for Mexican-Americans, the percentage was 88.6% (2).

Broomes (1971) estimates that 28% of the residents of the Colonia area are addicted to heroin, barbiturates, or (to a lesser extent) amphetamines. This estimate appears to us to be unreasonably high, but nevertheless, it is safe to say that the area has a very serious drug problem (see also Ozaetta and Gonzales 1972; Bidwell 1973).

The city of Oxnard is commonly referred to as "Hype City" on the streets and in the press, and is the center for buying and selling heroin in Ventura County. A recent newspaper feature quoted the Oxnard police chief as saying that La Colonia is the heroin center for Oxnard (Bidwell 1973).

3. **Poverty in La Colonia.** Poverty is a fact of day-to-day living for many of the Mexican-Americans of Ventura County. According to the 1970 Census (U.S. Department of Commerce 1972), 38% of the population in low-income families in Ventura County are Mexican-Americans. This simple statistic does not give a complete picture of the poverty experienced by many Mexican-Americans in Ventura County. Gutierrez (1971:43) reported that 71.3% of the families in the Colonia area had annual incomes of less than $5,000; this figure gives a better picture of poverty than the standards set by the Social Security Administration, which really only allow for the barest subsistence level. Other data gathered from this survey further serve to document this poverty.

(1) No major purchases (of more than $100) had been made by 55.5% of the families in the Colonia area in the last year. (2) In spite of the fact that much of our population carries some form of health insurance, 77.6% of the families in the Colonia area did not do so. (3) Vacations are a normal part of the lives of most Americans, but 56% of the families surveyed had never taken a vacation. (4) 76.4% of the families surveyed had never obtained a bank loan. (5) Not only were bank loans rare, but 71.6% of the families surveyed did not have savings accounts.

Many of the Mexican-Americans in the Colonia area, and elsewhere in the county, are suffering from what John Kenneth Galbraith (1969) calls "Insular Poverty." Insular poverty results when an area (such as the Colonia area) becomes isolated from the general stream of economic progress and a cycle of poverty results: slum living, poor health, poor educational facilities, ignorance of opportunities elsewhere, and an inability or unwillingness to take advantage of opportunities, if known. This cycle of poverty guarantees further isolation and further poverty unless it can, in some manner, be broken.

During the month of August 1971, the unemployment rate in the county was 7.7%, but in the Colonia area at the same time the unemployment rate was 20.8% for Mexican-Americans (Public Safety System, Inc. 1973).

One of the causes of poverty common to many Mexican-Americans in Ventura County is a lack of education which often leaves them unqualified for occupations with higher earnings. Gutierrez (1971:50) found that the average length of education for both males and females is only 6.8 years, that only 6.8% have finished high school, and only 2.2% have any college education.

These figures only indicate years of formal education completed and give no indication of the quality of education received. The California State Committee of the US Commission on Civil Rights reported in the Star Free Press: "There is still evidence that racism and indifference are continuing problems among staff, and that too many teachers regard Mexican-American students as devoid of a positive cultural heritage, less capable of academic achievement and less deserving of a good education." The attitude toward Mexican-Americans in this district is "representative of many rural communities found throughout the Southwest." As a result, the report also said, the schools "prepare Mexican-American students for roles as second-class citizens in society" (Star Free Press 1973:A-6). The second-rate education offered many Mexican-Americans not only leaves them underqualified for many jobs, but also reinforces their poor self-image.

Another major factor that influences the Mexican-American student's self-image is the prohibition against using Spanish in school. Unless the student is fluently bilingual, it is difficult for him to adequately express himself and to fully understand others in his second language. A feeling of inferiority is often the result. This point was made in another way by a NEA-Tucson Survey group, when they commented:

> In telling him that he must not speak his native language, we are saying to him by implication that Spanish and the culture which it represents are of no worth. Therefore (it follows again that) this particular child is of no worth. It should come as no surprise to us, then, that he develops a negative self-image and an inferiority complex (National Educational Association 1966:11).

The residents of La Colonia are thus caught in a cycle of poverty, lack of education, and discrimination. These conditions then tend to create in the population a negative self-image. It is common for groups caught in such a predicament to resort to the use of illicit drugs as a means of escape.

Therapeutic Intervention

In dealing with Chicano drug addicts from communities such as La Colonia, there are two conditions discussed in the preceding section which are open to therapeutic intervention: (1) a negative self-image and (2) a lack of education with an attendant high unemployment rate.

1. **Negative self-image.**   This is intimately connected with the cultural discrimination that Chicanos have experienced. The means to the improvement of the Chicanos' self-image, therefore, must first be the development and then the strengthening of a positive image of the Mexican-American cultural heritage. In mental health terms, "pride in one's cultural heritage appears functional for reducing identity and role conflict" (Derbyshire 1968:43). Members of cultural minorities are best suited for competition in the majority culture if they first acquire a strong identity with their own minority culture. We therefore feel that a positive reinforcement of this cultural heritage and identification should be basic to any program for Chicano drug addicts.

There is, thus, a need for a separate drug addiction treatment program for Chicanos—one which is oriented toward the Mexican-American culture. In Ventura County, most Chicano addicts do not avail themselves of the existing drug addiction rehabilitation programs. At the Camarillo State Hospital Detoxification Center, in 1972, approximately 40% of the 1,666 patients were Mexican-American; but of the 40 addicts who have completed the residential therapeutic community program at the hospital, only one has been a Chicano. By his own admission, he is not a "typical" Chicano, as most of his life has been spent in Anglo culture. Only two more Chicanos of the many that have gone through the drug detoxification program at Camarillo State Hospital have even gone on to try the rehabilitation program. The Chicanos who chose not to go through the rehabilitation program all gave as their reason for not doing so the fact that they considered the program only for Anglos. It did not relate to Chicanos or to the Chicano lifestyle. However, about 50% of them did indicate a willingness to go through a rehabilitation program if it were run by Chicanos and oriented toward Chicano culture.

If drug programs are open to anyone, they will probably become Anglo dominated; they will then not be able to deal with the special needs of Mexican-Americans. There is a reason why Anglos are likely to dominate such a group; verbal skills are essential to group therapy, which is the principle therapeutic agent of drug programs. Because verbal skills are so important, those who are the most articulate and the most aggressive are likely to be the most successful. The "art of talking," in the sense that it is used in therapy (i.e., intellectualizing, thinking abstractly, and verbalizing), is a culture-specific skill. In any drug program the individuals who possess these skills are likely to dominate the group, be successful, and thereby insure that the characteristic culture of the group is their own. Thus, if drug programs are open to anyone, the chances are that members of the dominant culture will possess these skills and thereby determine and dominate the characteristic nature of the therapy group. In addition, once a group forms a character or personality of its own, it is extremely difficult to change or modify its substance. Fischmann makes the point well when he describes the therapeutic group as being "an organized social system that develops its own characteristic culture, tends to be self-perpetuating, is relatively unaffected by the coming and going of individual members, and even differs from the sets and patterns characterizing individual members prior to their integration into the system" (1968:115).

2. Rehabilitation.   To be drug free is clearly not enough; nor is it sufficient to be "clean" and self-enlightened through the therapeutic experience. A major problem that both ex-addicts and ex-convicts have is of being placed in low-paying jobs or in training programs for which they have little incentive to do well. We have talked extensively with residents of La Colonia and their feelings are very clear: unless there is something to be rehabilitated for, it is not worth the bother. Invariably, that "something" is described as a "skill" with which to maintain self-respect, a decent livelihood, and a family. It is not really rehabilitation that is needed; rather it is habilitation.

There is, thus, a need for separate drug addiction treatment programs for Chicanos; programs whose definitions, concepts, practices, and language are grounded in the Chicano culture, and whose staff are mostly Chicano, perhaps ex-addicts, who share an identification with the Mexican-American heritage. The rationale for such a separate program is twofold. First, Chicano addicts prefer to have their own programs. Second, the cultural heritage of any individual is an important aspect of his definition of himself in place and in time. It is largely from within the context of this cultural heritage that the Chicano drug addict can begin to define for himself a new image and a new place in society.

Notes

1. The terms "Chicano," "Mexican," and "Mexican-American" will be used interchangeably. There is a greater preference for the term "Chicano" shown here because this is the preference of the age group in which the majority of addicts is to be found. The term "Anglo," as used here, refers to non-Chicanos.
2. Chambers et al. (1970) points out that while Mexican-Americans make up only 2% of the population of the United States they account for 10% of the population of drug addicts in this country. Also, based on his observations of addicts at the Fort Worth and Lexington U.S. Public Health Service Hospitals, he found that the arrest record for Chicano addicts is higher than that of any other ethnic group in the United States.

Clarissa S. Scott

Competing health care systems in an inner city area

Preliminary findings of a research project (1) at the University of Miami School of Medicine indicate that five local ethnic populations (Bahamian, Cuban, Haitian, Puerto Rican, and southern United States Black) are combining the use of orthodox and traditional systems in different ways and to different extents according to the individual ethnic group.

This communication reviews hypotheses which attempt to explain this variable use of folk and orthodox health care systems in order to point up the need for intensive research into the underlying factors involved in making choices between or among therapies and healers in competitive situations.

Several commonly accepted reasons have been put forth to explain preferential use of folk health care systems or the use of them in tandem with the orthodox health system. Frequently cited are language and transportation difficulties, the "social distance" (2) factor and lack of health cultural "fit" between specific beliefs and practices. In addition, these groups attribute certain symptoms and conditions to social/interpersonal conflict and supernatural activity; "everybody knows" that medical doctors generally are incapable of curing these illnesses.

Although preliminary data suggest that the five Miami ethnic groups have unique patterns for utilizing orthodox and traditional health care systems, one characteristic cuts across the five individual patterns: the use of different therapies or healers serially or concurrently. Evident in our study are four types of competition within and among systems. In each of these, the remedies and/or healers are utilized one after another or at the same time: (1) competition among healers and therapies within the orthodox system; (2) competition among healers and therapies within a folk system; (3) competition between healers and therapies in two different folk systems; and (4) competition between healers and therapies in a folk system and in the orthodox system.

Given the wide variety of healers and therapists in competition with each other in Miami, we cannot be content to note only the above mentioned factors of a practical or obvious nature which influence choice. Those factors which motivate an individual to accept or reject the orthodox health system, such as poor transportation or a poor health cultural "fit," provide us with only partial answers to the problem of selection. Elements which are specific to each group's health behavior add to, but do not complete the picture. We must search for deeper, more com-

Reproduced by permission of the Society for Applied Anthropology from *Human Organization*, 34 (1), 1975.

pelling motives which underlie the selection of a particular therapy or healer.

Schwartz, describing her health research in the Admiralty Islands, recapitulates earlier statements that in the process of cultural change, "universals are replaced by others but there is a period in which the new is added to the old in competitive alternativity until a new universal emerges" (1969:205). She also described Erasmus' notion that "where medical treatment is quickly effective, dramatic and evident, it will prevail over others" (1969:208). Acknowledging the validity of these but suggesting that they are not the complete answer, she proposes another explanation for the underlying motivation toward a particular therapy or healer. Schwartz hypothesizes that alternative modes of curing are arranged in hierarchies of resort, with different alternatives being used as the illness progresses without cure, and according to the particular phase in the individual's or group's acculturative process (Schwartz 1969:205).

An additional theoretical explanation for the motivational factors underlying the choice of alternatives in life crisis situations (such as illness) is suggested by Bryce-Laporte (1970). Two of his hypotheses relating to plural societies which manifest asymmetrical relations are relevant to the Miami context: (1) the subordinate minority will tend to observe the norms of the official superordinate culture as well as the subordinate culture; and (2) their choice of alternatives will relate to the degree of assimilation or perceived appropriateness of the institution, e.g., health institution.

The Miami study data indicate that the five local ethnic populations are bicultural in their choice and utilization of therapies/therapists, as Bryce-Laporte suggests will be the case when subordinate groups are only partially assimilated within a dominant culture.

Simmons (1955), speaking of Mestizo communities in Peru and Chile, proposes an additional explanation of health-seeking patterns. He notes that "modern cures have supplemented rather than replaced their popular (i.e., folk) counterparts . . ." and suggests that the reason is to be found in beliefs concerning etiology (Simmons 1955:64-70). In these cultures, a malady which "falls into the etiological categories of severe emotional upset, ritual uncleanness, and bad air" must be treated with at least one magical curing technique. Until there is an acceptance of modern etiological explanations, this pattern of utilizing folk cures along with modern therapies with demonstrated value will continue.

Gonzalez' work in Guatemala (1966) supports Simmons' speculation above and notes the similar theme of Gould and Erasmus. These writers suggest that the type of disease is crucial in influencing the individual's choice between seeking "doctor medicine" and "folk medicine" (Gonzalez 1966:125). In her study of the health beliefs and practices in three Guatemalan cultures, Gonzalez found that an ill person very often seeks relief from *symptoms* from a medical doctor while looking to the folk therapist to remove the *cause* of the disease.

A final theoretical stance to be discussed developed out of Egeland's health study of the Amish (1967). In order to gain a better understanding of the fundamental relationships between general cultural values and the subsystem of health,

Egeland administered the Kluckhohn and Strodtbeck Value Profile (1961) to her Amish sample. The resulting statistical analysis of her data demonstrates that one clear dominant value system cuts through all main areas of Amish life activities *except* that of health. In this *one* life situation, it appears that the Amish not only tolerate, but actually seek out more than one solution to a health problem.

Egeland's hypothesis, the only one which is readily testable by means of a standardized instrument (i.e., the Kluckhohn and Strodtbeck Value Scale), is that in the particularly crucial area of life and death, reliance on only one therapist or therapy or system of health care may be too precarious. In order to shed further light on this hypothesis, the Health Ecology Project in Miami is replicating this part of the Amish study on Bahamians, Cubans, Haitians, Puerto Ricans, and southern United States Blacks.

The fields of medical and urban anthropology badly need more comparative studies such as this in which the same instruments are utilized in conjunction with the standard ethnographic approach. Increased research of this type, called for by Scotch (1963a), Polgar (1962), and Weidman and Egeland (1973), should move us toward a more refined theory and methodology. Gropper (1967) has not only recognized the need for cross-cultural fieldwork and data but has attempted, herself, to establish a set of "medical categories of etiology and therapy universally applicable through time and space" (1967:5).

The scientific health care system must be modified in order to become more central to the health-seeking behavior of the multiethnic populations in urban areas today. Practical considerations such as language and transportation problems cannot be disregarded. Neither can the problem of lack of cultural "fit" between health consumers and providers. However, the central issue of choice has not been sufficiently explored. It is imperative that we understand the deeper, *underlying* motives which compel the ill person to select particular therapies or therapists. Without this understanding, we cannot begin to suggest the changes necessary to make the orthodox system more attractive to ethnic minorities.

Notes

1. The Health Ecology Project is supported by a grant from the Commonwealth Fund of New York. Its Principal Investigators are James N. Sussex, M.D., Professor and Chairman of the Department of Psychiatry, and Hazel H. Weidman, Ph.D. Janice A. Egeland, Ph.D. is serving as Primary Consultant.
2. "Social distance" is used here to indicate the discomfort felt by members of an ethnic group who must interact with members of a different ethnic or cultural group. In this case, it is the distance between ethnic "consumers" and health "providers" who subscribe to a different set of values.

Richard M. Hessler
Michael F. Nolan
Benjamin Ogbru
Peter Kong-Ming New

Intraethnic diversity: health care of the Chinese-Americans

This paper reports on a study of the types of medical care received by Chinese-Americans residing in Boston's Chinatown. It is within the context of dual medical care institutions in Chinatown—the Chinese traditional and the Western scientific—that we analyze the medical care patterns of Chinatowners in order to clarify an issue in the literature regarding the relationship between ethnic status and health-seeking behavior.

Behavioral scientists have studied the effects of ethnicity on patients' responses to pain (Zola 1963; Zborowki 1958); on health care consumership (Clark 1959; Mechanic 1963; Suchman 1965; Croog 1961; Saunders 1954; Srole 1962); on voluntary associations (Teele 1969); and education (Jensen 1969). While this research has had impact on the development of middle-range theories concerning the relationships between ethnicity and behavioral patterns, especially illness behavior (Twaddle 1969), the studies assume a degree of cultural homogeneity. For the most part, members of the ethnic or racial group studied are treated, theoretically, as if they possess a relatively uniform set of attitudes, values, beliefs, and behaviors. This is particularly true for studies of ethnic groups which are highly visible due to their distinct racial characteristics and tenacious pursuit of separateness. In this regard, Chinese, Japanese, Mexicans, and Blacks serve as good examples. Attitudes, values, and beliefs are considered major independent variables for explaining behavior or they are studied as dependent variables in their own right as correlates of ethnicity (Granberg 1973). The critical point is that the ethnic group is treated as if it were uniform, homogeneous, and undifferentiated.

It is fairly clear that cultural differences in behavior, be it illness behavior or otherwise, are important to a large extent. This is especially true for research on illness behavior and pathways to care. Nevertheless, we argue that the assumption of cultural homogeneity is an unwarranted stereotype which can produce misleading results, particularly when studying ethnicity and its relationship to patterns of behavior.

In this paper we present data from a survey of 200 households in Boston's

Reproduced by permission of the Society for Applied Anthropology from *Human Organization*, 34 (3), 1975.

Chinatown, with which we attempt to show that there is intraethnic diversity in health-seeking behavior. More specifically, we believe that variations in health-seeking behavior are great within the Chinese-American sample.

Because there is a tendency in the literature on social science and medicine to confuse the concept of ethnicity with the concept of race, we treat ethnicity as ethnic solidarity and define this concept as the extent to which individuals identify with Chinese culture. Ethnic solidarity is treated as one of four independent variables indicative of the hypothesized diversity. In short, four groups of independent variables (see Figure 1) are studied individually and collectively in terms of their

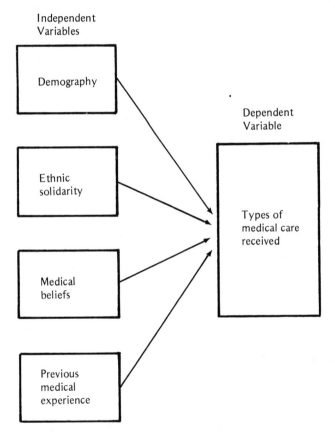

Figure 1. Effect of Ethnic Diversity on Ability to Discriminate Between Types of Medical Care Received

ability to discriminate between the types of medical care received, the dependent variable. We hypothesize that structural factors (demographic variables), medical beliefs, ethnic solidarity, and previous medical experience will discriminate between the types of health-seeking behaviors of the Chinese-Americans studied.

The Research Design

In 1970 a survey of 200 households in Boston's Chinatown was conducted to determine the patterns of health care consumership through the experiences and perceptions of the residents themselves. Our questions focused on patterns of seeking primary and preventive medical care in both Western and Chinese medical care systems. The study was a cross-sectional survey; while we have a great deal of prospective data on aspects of medical care for Chinatown, the data are based on a single interview with each of 200 Chinatowners.

It was decided that a face-to-face interview would maximize the probabilities of obtaining valid and reliable information. The interview situation was best suited for allowing one the flexibility so necessary for asking questions and determining whether they were clear and understood given the complex language situation. Furthermore, the interview allowed for exchanges between interviewer and respondent.

The schedule contained a combination of open-ended and fixed-category questions worded in a manner congruent with the Chinatown idiom. An English version of the interview schedule was typed and Chinese words were added where translation was difficult. The interviews were conducted mainly in Chinese and translation into English was done by the Chinese interviewer.

Entry into the Community

Entry into the community was our most difficult problem. Chinatowners are rightfully suspicious of research and they pose difficult questions to the potential researcher such as, "What will we get out of this study? What's in it for us to cooperate?" or "What harm will come to us from the data collected?" Entry was eased through an exchange process whereby a research committee consisting of Chinatown residents was established to make all of the research decisions associated with the study (Hessler and New 1972).

Interviews were conducted by one full-time Chinese interviewer, who spoke the Cantonese and Toisanese dialects and who knew the community well enough to establish rapport with its residents. The interviewer's working class background was quite helpful in conducting the interview.

The research committee decided that the respondent should be that person in the household considered the most knowledgeable regarding the affairs of the household. In the Western interview situation, this person would most probably be referred to as the head of the household. Where two or more single, unrelated males or females were living in a single room (considered a household), the interviewer would interview the person most available at the time. Usually, in these situations, the person who answered the door ended up as the respondent. Except where indicated, all of the data reported refer to 200 respondents. It was decided to do 200 interviews simply because that was all our budget would allow. To do these, we approached every door in Chinatown. Using the publicly published police listing of names and phone numbers as indicative of the total number of households in Chinatown, we were unable to contact persons in 114 households. These were not outright refusals, but were cases where no one was home or the dwelling unit appeared vacant. There was no pattern to these 114 households and they were scattered throughout Chinatown. Nevertheless, our sample of 200 is not a probabilistic sample although it is our feeling that a pure random sample would have netted the same or similar respondents, given the apparent randomness of the "unable to contact" cases.

Chinatown: A Demographic Description

Although geographically quite small, Chinatown contains one-fourth of Boston's Chinese population and is the cultural, social, and economic hub for the 20 to 30 thousand Chinese persons living in Boston and greater New England.

Historically, the housing which exists in Chinatown today is for the most part the same as that built and occupied by the first wave of middle-class settlers. The original residents of Chinatown (late 1840s) were mainly Anglo-Saxon native Americans who remained for 15 or 20 years at which point deteriorating housing conditions and increasing industrialization drove them out of the area. The 1860s saw a wave of Irish immigrants settle in Chinatown only to leave and be replaced 20 years later by European Jews and Syrians. Twenty years later, the Syrian community began to leave and for the past 85 years, the Chinese have established and maintained a rather stable community.

The median age of the respondents was 48.2 years. Occupationally, Chinatown men and women are basically locked into two tracks, both of which are dead ends in terms of significant advances in salary and position. For men, work means a job either waiting on tables, cooking, or washing dishes in a Chinese restaurant. Restaurant work demands little knowledge of English and consequently it provides scant opportunity to learn English, a prerequisite for getting a better job. Chinatown women work in the declining garment industry on the fringes of Chinatown primarily as stitchers or seamstresses.

Less than half of the Chinatowners surveyed reported working full-time, and unemployment was 15.7%. This reflects the economic crunch that Chinatowners are experiencing as they are caught between a declining labor market (e.g., the garment industry is in the process of closing shop and the recession has hit the restaurant business heavily), the steady increase in Chinese persons seeking work, and the inability to move vertically or horizontally into other occupations. However, for those who do work, the hours put in on the job are incredibly long. Fifty-two percent of all persons working, including part-time workers, put in 60-80 hours a week.

The median income was $5,037, which is considerably lower than the median family income for the city ($7,540), and somewhat lower than the official poverty target areas in Boston. According to our data, only three of the respondents admitted to being on welfare, whereas 52 indicated that they were receiving social security (out of 64 respondents 65 years and older). Only eight of the respondents indicated that they were registered for medicaid. However, 56 said they were registered for medicare.

Regarding place of birth, we found that 90% of the Chinatowners surveyed were born in Kwangchow, China. The mean years that the Chinatowners have lived in the U.S. was found to be 20.4, but 50% have lived in the U.S. 10 years or less, and 38% have lived here for five years or less. These data reflect the extent of the recent immigration of Chinatowners to the U.S. while at the same time pointing to the fact that many Chinatowners are also relatively long-time residents of the U.S.

The median years of formal education for the respondents is 5.9 years. Since only 15 respondents went to school in the U.S. (129 went to school in mainland China, nine in China and the U.S., one in Brazil, and the rest in Hong Kong), one must not fall into the taxonomic error of attempting to compare the educational level of Chinatowners to that of other ethnic and racial groups in Boston. Six years of education in China is quite simply not comparable to six years in the U.S.

Only a handful of the respondents indicated that they were able to speak and understand English fluently and even fewer were fully literate. There are several dialects of Chinese spoken by Chinatowners and 108 (54%) respondents speak both Cantonese and Toisanese.

Most of the respondents reported that they are currently married. Only 119 respondents stated that they were living with their wives and/or children which indicates that at least 25 Chinatowners are in the U.S. without their spouses and/or children. Finally, only 53 (26.5%) of the Chinatowners surveyed are U.S. citizens, while the vast majority (143 or 71.5%) have "permanent resident" status.

Type of Medical Care: Dual Systems

Chinatowners utilized two very distinct medical care systems for their health needs: (1) Western medicine and (2) Chinese medicine. Before analyzing the specific pathways to medical care in Chinatown, the problem of describing the Chinese medical care system must be dealt with.

Frameworks which delineate healers and health care systems into primitive, folk, and scientific categories are not applicable to Chinese medicine in Chinatown. For example, Rodney Coe defined primitive medicine as "basically nonscientific medicine where its causal roots are located in beliefs and practices which are founded in tradition and magic, lending a moral imperative to its credence" (Coe 1970). Chinatown medicine is not primitive according to this definition since it is not founded on magic, but rather harks back to a long tradition of scientific medical practices on mainland China and in Hong Kong.

Furthermore, Coe defines folk medicine as "medicine of the people—a set of beliefs and behaviors shared and practiced by everyone—which may be based on theories either nonscientific or quasi-scientific in nature. It is to be sharply distinguished from the specialized and more or less codified medicine practiced by specialized healers" (Coe 1970). He goes on to argue that folk medicine persists alongside Western "scientific medicine," for example in an urban setting, when the consumers of folk medicine do not come into contact with "scientific" medicine.

Again, Chinatown medicine does not fit this description exclusively, since all Chinatowners do not adhere to its beliefs and behaviors. Furthermore, one cannot distinguish Chinatown medicine from "specialized" or more or less-codified medicine practiced by specialized healers. Chinatown medicine exists alongside the Western medical care system, which is perhaps the most advanced in the country, and there is considerable contact between Chinatowners and Western medical care.

Chinese Medicine

Basically, the Chinese medical care system is grounded in the ancient principle of hot and cold forces (Yin-Yang) in which a balance of heat and cold must be maintained within an organism to insure good health. Foods and herbs are characterized as hot or cold as well as specific bodily disorders, real or anticipated, and a counterbalance of food and body is sought to prevent or cure illness. This dialectic, when translated into forces of hot and cold, represents the traditional Chinese system of palliative and preventive medical care (Basil and Lewis 1940). Specialized Chinese medical practitioners or healers serve as physicians for this system of medical care. Minor illnesses are treated through the use of Chinese medicine. Two aspects of Chinese medicine are involved: (1) the use of Chinese doctors, and (2) the use of Chinese medicine for illnesses (Allen 1973).

Within the Chinese system of Yin-Yang, preventive care is viewed from a "hot" and "cold" perspective by both the Chinese herb doctor or specialist and the Chinese consumer. The body must be balanced, which means avoiding conditions where the body is excessively hot or excessively cold. There are Chinese foods and herbs that have "hot" and "cold" value and these are used to keep the body balanced or to correct an imbalance.

If one's body is too "cold," one takes "hot" foods and/or herbs, and vice versa. Most minor problems of the body, like minor colds or sore throat, are considered to be due to too much heat in the system and hence, one would use "cold" foods and/or herbs to counteract this situation. The most common types of herbs we found to be taken are described below.

Dong Kuei—angelica sinesis (Diels)—which is a root used to make a soup with chicken fruit flesh (*longan*). Also there is *gay tse* which women usually take because it reportedly builds blood lost during menstruation. This herb is commonly taken after a woman has given birth.

The equivalent of *dong kuei* for men is *look mai ba* (deers tail) but men take this herb less frequently than women take the *dong kuei*.

Another herb is *buck kay fong dong suin*. This is a stimulant which helps one gain energy. It is a combination of two herbs, *buck kay* and *fong dong suin,* and is usually made in a soup with pork or other meats. Also, *wak san, lin tze,* and *bak hap* are three herbs used for cleaning the lungs and keeping them clear. They are usually made with chicken in a soup.

Foods like winter melon soup, beef broth, certain fruits, and vegetables are also used as folk medicine to prevent illness. Herbs, when taken alone or out of the context of soup, are very bitter to the taste. However, the taste is quite pleasant when they are made with soup.

There are basically two categories of Chinese doctors. There is the doctor who treats such illnesses as colds, flu, diarrhea, and so forth, by prescribing Chinese medicine. He is analogous to the Western medical doctor who treats problems in a clinic setting. Also, there is the "chiropractic" doctor who treats bone fractures, dislocations, sprains, and other muscular problems. His treatment typically includes use of his hands to feel and massage and straighten the affliction by manipulation. This technique is held in high esteem by Chinatowners mainly because confining casts are not used by Chinese doctors, a distinct advantage from their perspective.

Analysis and Findings

The dependent variable is types of health care received (Chinese Medicine and Western Scientific Medicine) and there are four groups of independent variables: (1) demography (age, income, education, length of stay in the United States, citizenship status, marital status, employment status, and number of children); (2) medical beliefs (attitudes toward giving and receiving blood, the worth of flu shots, chest x-rays, and yearly physical exams); (3) ethnic solidarity (send money to China, membership in family association; personnel in local Western hospitals); and (4) previous medical experience. Instead of using Suchman's (1965) causal sequence model of patient pathways to care, we chose to analyze the discriminatory power of each of the four types of variables taken singly and ultimately considered together. This model enables one to test the discriminatory power of a specific set of ethnic coordinates in addition to other factors which may be indicative of intraethnic diversity. Finally, causal sequencing of the variables is rejected primarily because such an ordering would be purely arbitrary given the dearth of empirical findings on the problem of variation within ethnic groups vis-à-vis the type of care received. We treat the variables as both active and reactive in the sense of symmetrical relationships.

It is hypothesized that Chinatown residents utilize the Chinese and Western medical care systems in a complex fashion which reflects intraethnic diversity. We feel that these utilization patterns can be explained by combinations of demographic, ethnicity, belief, and medical experience variables.

Multiple discriminate analysis was the technique chosen for classifying the sample into user groups based on the independent variables of our theoretical model. We categorized the dependent variable into four types of health care utilizers: (1) Nonpure Western; (2) Nonpure Chinese; (3) Pure Chinese; and (4) Dualists. Four variables indicating use of the Chinese medical care system and four variables indicating the same for Western medicine form the basis for the categorization. The eight items were scaled and the four categories of users were derived by comparing the Western and Chinese medicine scale scores. Thus, the nonpure Western users are those who have a high score on the Western scale and a low score on the Chinese scale. They use both health care systems but favor Western medical care in their patterns of use. The nonpure Chinese consumers have high scores on the Chinese scale, and low scores on utilization of Western medicine. The pure Chinese group uses only Chinese medicine and the dualists are those who have equal scores on the Western and Chinese medicine scales. Interestingly, no one in the sample used Western medicine exclusively.

In using multiple discriminate analysis, our purpose generally was like that of multiple regression. In other words, we were attempting to determine which of the criterion variables (independent) is the most important for predicting types of health users. As its name implies, multiple discriminate analysis is a statistical technique designed to discriminate between groups of individuals. It is most commonly used as a classification method and, as such, discriminate analysis enables one to find out whether there is a compound score of the independent variables that differentiates optimally between the groups being considered, and as well to find out how far this score can be used to decide which subgroups an individual properly belongs to. Thus, one of the results from a discriminate analysis is a predicted group membership like the estimated y obtained in multiple regression (Van de Geer 1971; Hallberg 1971).

A test to determine the extent to which the Western scale and Chinese scale are independent was performed, and significant differences between the scales when controlling for Citizenship and the nonpure Western and Chinese categories were found. On the other hand, as expected, the dualist category is a synthesis of identical scale scores on the Western and Chinese medicine scales, a finding which is verified by the identical mean scores for this category. We conclude that Chinese and Western scales are relatively independent within the context of the four categories of health care consumer patterns.

The remainder of the analysis consists of three parts. First, analysis was done on the four subgroups of variables as well as a composite run for all variables for the total sample of Chinatown residents. Second, controlling for sex, separate runs essentially replicating what was done for the total sample were done. This was based on the assumption that the community may be stratified traditionally along sex lines, with sex playing a role in determining those factors which influence health care usage.

Discriminate Analysis for Total Sample
Only three of the demographic variables (employment status, age, and sex) proved to be good discriminators (1). As Table 1 indicates, when these three variables were used as the only predictor, 34% of the sample was correctly classified into one of the four user groups. The best classification records were for the Dualist category with 52% of the respondents classified correctly and the nonpure Western group with 43% of the respondents classified correctly. Neither the nonpure Chinese nor the pure Chinese group had over 30% of the respondents correctly classified.

The ethnic solidarity variables were reduced to three with the variable, "send money back to China," eliminated because of its lack of discriminatory power. The variables remaining were family association, language fluidity, and favorable-

Table 1. Discriminate analysis on three subgroups of variables and all variables for the total sample of Chinatown residents showing percentage classified correctly and direction of the relationship by group*

	Nonpure Western (N=73–76)	Nonpure Chinese (N=53–60)	USER CATEGORY Pure Chinese (N=26–28)	Dualist (N=22–25)	All classes (N=174–189)
			Percent Classified Correctly		
Demographic variables	43	17	29	52	34
Age (2.75)	+	++	-	--	
Employment status (2.64)	++	+	-	--	
Sex (2.23)	--	-	+	++	
Ethnicity variables	43	51	50	8	41
Family Association (4.79)	+	--	-	++	
Language fluency (4.43)	--	+	++	-	
Chinese personnel (2.73)	+	-	++	--	
Beliefs	29	63	54	0	39
Physical exams (4.98)	--	-	++	+	
Flu shots (3.85)	++	--	-	+	
All variables	42	45	62	27	44
Language fluency (5.02)	--	+	++	-	
Flu shots (4.71)	-	--	+	++	
Age (3.48)	++	-	-	--	
Employment status (3.01)	++	-	--	+	
Family Association (2.33)	++	--	-	+	
Sex (2.29)	--	-	++	+	

*Figures in parentheses are F values

ness toward having Chinese personnel work in the local hospital. These three varia-bles classified 41% of the sample correctly. However, in contrast to the demograph-ic variables the worst prediction record was for the Dualist group with only eight percent of the respondents classified correctly and the best prediction was in the nonpure Chinese and the pure Chinese groups with 51% and 50%, respectively, classified correctly.

The only two belief variables to emerge unscathed from the initial discrimi-nate analyses were the helpfulness of flu shots and the worth of physical exams. The two variables correctly predicted 39% of the sample. They were most effective in placing individuals in the nonpure Chinese category and the pure Chinese category and were quite ineffective in classifying the Dualists.

Finally, when all eight of the above variables were put in the discriminate function simultaneously, two were eliminated because they failed to achieve the minimum discriminatory power. These were the physical examination variable and the favorableness toward having Chinese personnel in local medical establishment variable. For the remaining variables, 44% of the respondents were correctly classi-fied, most successfully for the pure Chinese group (62% classified correctly), and least successfully for the Dualists (only 27% classified correctly).

The plus and minus signs in Table 1 indicate the direction of the relationship. Two pluses or minuses means that there was a consistent direction to the relation-ship for all comparisons (e.g., comparing nonpure Western versus nonpure Chinese, nonpure Western versus pure Chinese, and nonpure Western versus Dualists). For this to occur, the sign for the discriminate coefficient (function) for all three com-parisons would have to be the same. If only one plus or minus was reported it means that the relationship held for only two of the three comparisons and is hence a weaker relationship.

For the total sample then, nonpure Westerners tended to be employed, fe-male, fluent in English, favorable to physical exams, and did not think flu shots were particularly important. To a lesser extent they were older, not a member of a family association, and did not feel that Chinese personnel in the local medical center was important.

The nonpure Chinese tended to be older, a member of a family association, favorable to flu shots, to a lesser extent employed, female, not fluent in English, favorable to Chinese personnel in the medical center, and favorable to physical exams.

The pure Chinese was characterized as not being fluent in English, not favor-able to Chinese personnel in the medical center, unfavorable to physical exams, and to a lesser extent younger, unemployed, male, a member of a family association, and favorable to flu shots.

Finally, the Dualists were younger, unemployed, male, not a member of a family association, favorable to Chinese personnel in the medical center, and, to a lesser extent, fluent in English and unfavorable to physical exams and flu shots.

Overall, there are some interesting comparisons for the total sample. Different groups of variables have different discriminatory utility. This is true for the demographic variables which were most effective in classifying the nonpure Western and the Dualist types correctly whereas the other two sets of variables were much better at classifying the nonpure Chinese and the pure Chinese correctly. It is also worth noting that all the variables measuring previous medical experience proved to be totally without value in the discriminate analysis and were eliminated.

Discriminate Analysis by Sex
When sex was introduced as a control variable, many changes occurred. Of all the demographic variables considered for males, only age and marital status were found to be good discriminators. These variables classified 37% of the males correctly into one of these four groups, with the best classification occurring for the nonpure Chinese group and the Dualist group. This stands in contrast to the analysis of the demographic variables for the total sample, where the best classification was on the nonpure Western and the Dualists.

The results for the ethnicity variables were equally intriguing. Three variables (language fluency, member of family association, and desirability of Chinese personnel in medical centers) were able to classify 50% of the males correctly in one of the four user categories. This was the highest percentage correctly classified. However, for the males, the ethnicity variables proved to be best in classifying the nonpure Western group although they were also able to classify over 50% of the respondents correctly for the nonpure Chinese and the pure Chinese groups. This is in part a reversal of what occurred for the total sample.

The only belief variable that proved a good discriminator was the variable assessing the favorableness of the respondent to chest x-rays. This variable by itself was able to classify 42% of the respondents correctly and was particularly good at classifying the nonpure Western users correctly, with 85% of them so classified. This is what one might expect given the fact that the chest x-ray is a Western medical technique.

When all of these variables were considered together in a discriminate function, the family association variable ceased to be a good predictor and was dropped. The remaining variables classified 48% of the males correctly. The best discriminating category for all these variables was the pure Chinese group with 56% of the cases correctly classified.

For males, the nonpure Western users were single, fluent in English, not favorable to Chinese personnel, favorable to a yearly chest x-ray, and to a lesser degree younger, and a member of a family association. The nonpure Chinese were older, married, a member of a family association, favorable to Chinese in the medical center, and to a lesser extent not fluent in English and favorable to a yearly chest x-ray. The pure Chinese tended not to be fluent in English and to a lesser extent were married, younger, not a member of a family association, not favorable to Chinese in the local medical center, and not favorable to chest x-rays. Dualists were younger, members of a family association, not favorable to chest x-rays, and to a lesser degree single, fluent in English, and favorable to Chinese personnel in the medical center.

Table 2. Discriminate analysis on three subgroups of variables and all variables for the *male* sample of Chinatown residents showing percentage classified correctly and direction of relationship by group*

	Nonpure Western (N=38–41)	Nonpure Chinese (N=32–37)	USER CATEGORY		Dualist (N=13–17)	All classes (N=99–116)
			Pure Chinese (N=16–20)			
			Percent Classified Correctly			
Demographic variables	17	68	0		65	37
Age (2.75)	–	++	+		– –	
Marital status (2.75)	++	– –	–		+	
Ethnicity Variables	60	53	53		0	50
Language fluency (5.19)	– –	+	++		++	
Family Association (3.61)	–	– –	+		++	
Chinese personnel (2.78)	++	– –	+		–	
Beliefs	85	0	0		63	42
Chest x-rays (8.07)	– –	–	+		++	
All variables	58	50	50		46	53
Chest x-rays (6.69)	– –	–	+		++	
Marital status (3.39)	++	– –	–		+	
Age (3.27)	+	++	–		–	
Language fluency (2.81)	– –	+	++		– –	
Chinese personnel (2.46)	++	–	+		– –	

*Figures in parentheses are F values

The females presented quite a contrast to the males. The only demographic variable which proved to be of discriminatory usefulness was the number of children under age 16 the respondent had. This variable, for females, enables one to predict 37% of their health care usage category correctly, with the best prediction occurring for the nonpure Chinese and the pure Chinese users.

The ethnic solidarity variables had absolutely no discriminatory utility for the female group. This is in striking contrast to the males. The only belief variable found useful was that which assessed favorableness toward flu shots. This correctly classified 49% of the females, with the greatest percentage occurring for the nonpure Chinese group. These two variables, when combined, classified 45% of the females correctly and, as might be expected, the greatest number correctly classified were in the nonpure Chinese category.

For females, the nonpure Western users were not favorable to flu shots and to a lesser degree had a small number of children. The nonpure Chinese had a small number of children and were in favor of flu shots while the pure Chinese had large families and to a lesser extent did not favor having flu shots. The few female Dualists sampled tended to have a large number of children and favored flu shots.

A final observation on the discriminate analysis is in order. While it is true that our analysis came nowhere near correctly classifying all 200 Chinatown residents sampled, this may have been too much to expect. Discriminate analysis undoubtedly works best when the groups to be discriminated are clearly different from each other. It is well at this point to recall that the groups we used were constructed by us, not by the respondents themselves. In this sense we have only one "pure type," the pure Chinese group, and it might be that the best discrimination would have occurred between this group and a pure Western group if that group had in fact existed. It did not exist and, thus, the other types of usage that we observed—the nonpure groups and the Dualist groups—were in one sense an amalgam of people. Any attempt to categorize them might not be overly successful. Consequently, we were pleased that the discriminate analysis did as well as it did in terms of classifying nearly half of the respondents correctly.

Discussion

It is interesting to note, first of all, the extent to which alternative types of care were utilized by Chinatowners. In analyzing the diverse patterns of medical care utilization, we were able to locate individuals within one of four types of users. The only "pure" type (Chinese medical care only) contained relatively few cases (N = 24) while the remaining types consisted of Chinatowners who used both Western and Chinese medical care systems to a greater, lesser, or equal extent respectively. This in itself suggests that no one pattern of usage can be used to characterize the illness behavior of the Chinese-Americans studied. Furthermore, one cannot assume that the normative structure of the community is simple enough to allow one to predict a common utilization pattern knowing specific ethnicity, beliefs, and demographic factors. In other words, Chinatowners partici-

Table 3. Discriminate analysis on two subgroups of variables and all variables for the *female* sample of Chinatown residents*

	Nonpure Western (N=35-36)	Nonpure Chinese (N=22-25)	USER CATEGORY		All classes (N=73-76)
			Pure Chinese (N=7-8)	Dualist (N=9)	
			Percent Classified Correctly		
Demographic variables	29	56	57	0	37
Number of children (3.12)	–	– –	++	+	
Beliefs	53	82	0	0	49
Flu shots (2.47)	++	– –	+	–	
All variables	34	77	57	0	45
Number of children (2.88)	–	– –	++	+	
Flu shots (2.78)	+	– –	++	–	

*Figures in parentheses are F values

pate in a complex multifaceted pattern of illness behavior.

Of equal interest is the finding that different combinations of the independent variables are of varying predictive importance in terms of correctly placing Chinatowners in one of the four user categories. When all eight independent variables accepted by the discriminate model were analyzed together, a different discriminatory utility was achieved. The demographic variables were most effective in classifying the nonpure Western and Dualists correctly whereas the other variables were more useful for predicting nonpure and pure Chinese utilization.

Perhaps the most interesting result was the interaction between sex and the other independent variables in terms of their importance in predicting user types. For females, only two variables were found to have predictive power even though they were quite important. The number of children (demographic) was quite significant for predicting female illness behavior but was not important for male usage. In contrast age and marital status were significant predictors for males but not for females. Of greatest interest substantially was the ethnic solidarity variables which were quite important for male usage but not for female.

The above difference in discriminatory power tends to offer support to the concept of intraethnic diversity and variation, even within a tight-knit and exclusive ethnic community such as Chinatown. Perhaps research on illness behavior and ethnicity should, at the conceptual level, begin with theoretical models based on the premise of diversity. Based on the sexual division of labor alone in Chinatown, traditional female roles include major responsibility for childrearing. Furthermore, ethnic solidarity is a male institution, at least as far as we have operationally defined the concept, where males become the link between family and family association, and assume a principal leadership role in the Chinatown community. Therefore, it is understandable that ethnic solidarity would be quite important as a predictor for males whereas females do not find these factors important in determining the nature of their health care utilizations. However, there is no ready explanation as to why age and marital status exerted such importance for males' usage but not for females.

Thus, we conclude that earlier research which explicitly or implicitly posits cultural or ethnic homogeneity in studying an ethnic group's illness behavior appears to be problematic. Uniformitarianism of this order can lead to one's neglecting to appreciate and consider the complex network of independent variables and the extent to which the dependent variable, illness behavior, varies within a seemingly homogeneous ethnic group. The extent to which explanatory variables differ for males and females suggests that sex is an important factor for understanding illness behavior. It suggests that sex roles permeate the basic structure of society to exert a much greater effect on attitudes and behavior than ethnicity per se.

On the broadest level of generality, the social structure of ethnic groups is related in a complex fashion to individual medical response or behavior. If we are to advance our knowledge of social organization and pathways to health care, it is important to begin to design theories and studies which take into account the rich sources of intraethnic diversity. This can probably be done most effectively through research which is linked to health care policy for ethnic groups in this country. Rather than designing innovative organizational forms which assume cultural uniformity and reflect, accordingly, modes of operation relevant to a minority of the ethnic group members, health care organizations could be based on research which takes into account the multiple and diverse networks of factors associated with types of medical care received. In this position we can use our research to reach out with new medical care concepts and techniques vested with the compelling authority and power of cultural traditions and tuned to the complex and diverse social order of ethnic survival.

Note

1. Arbitrarily an F value of 2.0 or more was used to decide if a variable should remain in the discriminate function.

Michael H. Logan

Humoral medicine in Guatemala and peasant acceptance of modern medicine

Many Indian and Ladino peasants of highland Guatemala classify foods, medicinal plants, illnesses, and now modern medicines according to a conceptual scheme of opposition between the qualities of hot and cold. Belief in the humoral scheme of medicine influences an individual's selection and assessment of medical treatment. When prescribed treatment ignores the humoral concept, or creates unacceptable contradictions between modern and native philosophies of health, such treatment is likely to be less effective than if native concepts were incorporated into the prescribed therapeutic program.

The concept of humoral medicine has received considerable attention in the anthropological study of folk cultures. The history and diffusion of humoral medicine has been dealt with adequately (Foster 1953; Hart 1969); methodological procedure for recording data on humoral classifications has been outlined (Foster and Rowe 1951); and descriptive accounts of the humoral theory of disease are present in the ethnomedical literature of Mexico (Currier 1966; Foster 1967; Ingham 1970; Lewis 1960; C. Madsen 1966; W. Madsen 1955; Mak 1959; Redfield and Park 1940), Guatemala (Adams 1952; Cosminsky 1972; Douglas 1969; Gillin 1951;

Reprinted from *Human Organization*, 32 (4), 1973.

Gonzales 1969; Woods 1968), Costa Rica (Orso 1970; Richardson and Bode 1971); Puerto Rico (Landy 1959; Mintz 1956; Wolf 1956b); South America (Gillin 1947; Reichel-Dolmatoff and Reichel-Dolmatoff 1961; Simmons 1955; Valdizan 1922; Wellin 1955); Latin Americans in the United States (Clark 1959; Kiev 1968; W. Madsen 1964; Padilla 1958; Rubel 1960; Saunders 1954); the Philippines (Hart 1969); Burma (Spiro 1967); India (Opler 1963); and England (Tillyard 1944). Although anthropologists have concerned themselves with describing the humoral theory of disease, "the direct implications of this theory for understanding and and treating patients who subscribe to it have rarely been examined" (Harwood 1971:1153).

In this presentation I will discuss (1) the history and structure of humoral medicine; (2) the function of humoral medicine among the peasantry of Guatemala; (3) the cognitive system underlying humoral classifications; and (4) how commitment to humoral medicine can impede effective medical treatment. From my discussion and comparison of data with those collected and reported by Dr. Alan Harwood in the *Journal of the American Medical Association,* I hope to present conclusions from which I will be able to provide useful and practical suggestions for those interested in the ethnomedicine and public health of Latin American culture areas.

The majority of the data presented in this report are derived from materials collected in 1971 and 1972 during field research in highland Guatemala, where I resided for nine months in the Department of Chimaltenango. There, I had the opportunity to interview patients and resident medical personnel at the Behrhorst Clinic and Hospital. The three peasant populations included in this research, and referred to specifically in this presentation, are the Cakchiquel and Tzutuhil Maya, and the monolingual Spanish-speaking class of Ladinos (1).

History and Structure of Humoral Medicine

The science of treating illness and maintaining health by prescribing elements or foods with the qualities of hot and cold first appears in the writings of Greek scholars, notably Hippocrates. It is interesting to note, however, that the striking similarities between the Hippocratic doctrine and the centuries older Yin-Yang philosophy of ancient China might suggest a center of origin other than that of the Mediterranean area (cf. Hart 1969; Lessa 1968).

Humoral science diffused from Greece and Rome to the Arabic world and was introduced into Iberia with the Moorish occupation of that region (Foster 1953). Expansion of the Spanish empire during the sixteenth century brought the doctrine to aboriginal America, and through acculturation in the conquest and colonial periods, humoral medicine was incorporated into Indian and Mestizo world views of health and, to this day, humoral medicine remains an integral part of peasant culture.

According to the Hippocratic theory, "there were four primary and opposite fundamental qualities, the hot and the cold, the wet and the dry . . . these met in binary opposition to constitute the Essences or Existences which entered in varying proportions into the constitution of all Matter" (Singer 1928:33). The four humors—blood, phlegm, black bile, and yellow bile—possessed these fundamental qualities. Each humor had its complexion: blood, hot and wet; yellow bile, hot and dry; phlegm, cold and wet; black bile, cold and dry (Foster 1953:202). The health or "complexion" of an individual could only be maintained as long as the body's natural and requisite equilibrium between hot and cold, wet and dry was not upset.

The humoral qualities of hot and cold do not refer to actual temperature changes produced by cooking nor to pungent tastes as found in peppers. Similarly, the terms wet and dry do not pertain to water content. They refer, rather, to the constitutional essence or innate character of a given item or personal state of being. Natural objects, foods, and illnesses possess these symbolic qualities and can alter the health of an individual through contact, consumption, or contagion. For example, overconsumption of hot foods increases the body's normal content of heat and, if excessive, provokes ailments thought to be hot in nature. Treatment, therefore, would call for equalizing the body's temperature balance and restoring neutrality by consuming principally cold foods and medicines.

In the New World, the Hippocratic theory of humoral medicine was simplified as a result of cultural trait selection. The qualities of moisture became less significant in diagnosis and treatment, while the temperature dichotomy grew in importance and came to dominate the Latin American version (2).

Function of Humoral Medicine in Guatemala

The assumption that one's life is affected by the ever-present qualities of hot and cold is widely held in Guatemala, and the peasant's belief in the reality of the humoral qualities serves as a principle guiding his daily behavior. The natural world and its elements possess these qualities and continuously threaten to upset the individual's internal balance between hot and cold. It is believed that the body is a self-regulating system which strives to maintain its temperature balance, but if exposed to sources of heat and cold of an intensity or duration which it is incapable of handling, illness or death will develop as a result of temperature imbalance.

Children are particularly susceptible to extremes in temperature. In one village, for example, the death of a six-month-old infant was attributed to the "coldness" of penicillin given the infant by her godparent (*padrino*). The child's mother, an Indian, in an attempt to aid her daughter asked the child's godparent, a Ladino from a neighboring town, to help in any way he could. Responding to the mother's plea, the godparent purchased penicillin and a syringe, and unknowing to the parents of the child, injected the infant with 2 c.c. of penicillin (probably 100,000 units) and afterwards instructed the parents to give the child several pills which he had also purchased. That night, only hours after the injection and first series of tablets, the child died. The godparent, upon returning to visit the household the following morning, was shocked to hear of the child's death and explained to the despondent mother that he had given the child an injection of penicillin in hope of saving the child's life. (The remaining tablets, along with the empty syringe, were presented to me by the mother. The pills contained penicillin.) Although the godparent acted in good faith, the amount of the drug given was excessive and it is likely that the child was allergic to penicillin. This fact, however, was never realized by the parents of the deceased. They maintained that it was the additional cold produced by the penicillin that brought death to their child, who had been suffering from severe diarrhea for over two weeks. All agreed that the child was simply too weak to combat the excessive cold created by both the penicillin and diarrhea. Maintaining an even balance between hot and cold is an essential prerequisite for health; a prerequisite rarely sustained.

Heat may "overwhelm" the body as a consequence of strenuous labor, radiation from a cooking fire, emotional or sexual excitement, intoxication, exposure to "evil eye," overconsumption of hot foods, or from contracting an illness regarded as being "heat induced," for example, fever. Cold may overtake the body from careless use of cold medicines, foods and beverages, exposure to "evil winds," bathing while one is hot, or from having an illness with symptoms of diarrhea or chills, both of which are "cold induced."

It would be inappropriate for a patient suffering from fever to employ a medicine known locally to be hot. The equal qualities of heat existing between the illness and the medicine would not only make the medicine ineffective, but harmful. On several occasions, as reported to me by staff members at the Behrhorst Clinic, hospitalized patients running high fevers refused to take the prescribed vitamin and protein supplements given to them daily. Rather, the patients hid the pills under their pillows or secreted them elsewhere in the room. Upon questioning, a few confessed that it would be best not to use vitamins at that time because vitamins, like their fever, are *katan,* or very hot. Taking or continuing to use a hot medicine in this case would worsen the patient's condition, supposedly by increasing the level of heat in his body. Therefore, the only appropriate choice of remedies, according to the patient's frame of reference, would be those consisting of medicines and foods cold in nature. Vitamins were temporarily rejected by patients as long as their fevers continued, because vitamins were not considered to be an appropriate medicine for treatment of fever.

Commitment to the humoral philosophy functions as a directive of behavior, and the effect upon behavior is relative to the degree of commitment. Most significantly, belief in this system of disease etiology influences the individual's diagnosis of illness and choice of diet and medical treatment.

Cognitive System of Humoral Classification

Patterns of hot-cold classification vary considerably throughout Meso-America (Adams and Rubel 1967; Currier 1966; Foster 1953, 1967; Ingham 1970; Lewis 1960; Redfield 1934, 1940) (3). The cognitive system underlying various classifications, however, remains constant and is universal. It is based on the assumption that elements exist naturally in a state of binary opposition and the effect of one

Table 1. Important symptoms in native illness classification

Symptoms	Symptom Classification		Prescribed Treatment	Treatment Classification		Expectable Behavior	
	Guat.	*P.R.*		*Guat.*	*P.R.*	*Guat.*	*P.R.*
Chills	C	C	Penicillin	C	H	Reject	Accept
Fever	H	H	Penicillin	C	H	Accept	Reject
Chronic cough (no blood)	C	—*	Penicillin; tetracycline	C	—	Reject	—
Chronic cough (blood)	H	—	Penicillin; tetracycline	C	—	Accept	—
Common cough	C	C	Citrus fruits	C	C	Reject	Reject
Nonproductive cough	H	—	Penicillin; citrus fruits	C	—	Accept	—
Productive cough	C	—	Penicillin; citrus fruits	C	—	Reject	—
Sinus pains	C	C	Menthol	H	—	Accept	—
Hoarseness	C	C	Gargle (hot salt water)	H	—	Accept	—
Wheezing	C	—	—	—	—	—	—
Rash	H	H	Creams	C	—	Accept	—
Black urine	H	—	Aspirin; no alcohol	H	H	Reject	—
White stools	C	—	Aspirin; no alcohol	H	H	Accept	—
Diarrhea (no blood)	C	H	Entero-leina	H	—	Accept	—
Diarrhea (blood)	H	H	Entero-leina	H	—	Reject	—
Constipation	C	H	Fruits; greens	C	C	Reject	Accept
Indigestion	H	C	Alka-Seltzer	C	—	Accept	—
Menstrual pain	C	C	Aspirin	H	H	Accept	—
Urinating pain	H	—	Penicillin	C	H	Accept	—
Penis discharge	H	—	Penicillin	C	H	Accept	—
Joint and body pains	C	C	Vicks Vapor Rub	H	H	Accept	Accept
Paralysis	C	C	Aspirin	H	H	Accept	Accept
Vomiting	C	—	Alka-Seltzer	C	—	Reject	—
Heartburn	H	—	Alka-Seltzer	C	—	Accept	—
Weakness	C	—	Vitamins; sucros	H	H	Accept	—
Sweating	H	—	Cold compress	C	—	Accept	—
Fainting	C	—	Vitamins; sucros	H	—	Accept	—
Burns	H	H	Creams	C	C	Accept	Accept
Cuts	H	H	Creams	C	C	Accept	Accept

*Dashed lines indicate data not available.

Table 2. Diseases recognized by natives and medical doctors

Disease	Disease Classification		Prescribed Treatment	Treatment Classification		Expectable Behavior	
	Guat.	P.R.		Guat.	P.R.	Guat.	P.R.
Common cold*	C	C	Citrus fruits	C	C	Reject	Reject
Influenza*	H	—**	Penicillin	C	H	Accept	—
Tuberculosis (no blood)	C	—	Penicillin	C	H	Reject	—
Tuberculosis (blood)	H	—	Penicillin	C	H	Accept	—
Whooping cough*	C	—	—	—	—	—	—
Bronchitis*	C	—	Penicillin	C	H	Reject	—
Pneumonia*	C	—	—	—	—	—	—
Laryngitis*	C	C	Gargle (hot salt water)	H	—	Accept	—
Asthma*	C	—	Ethedrine	—	—	—	—
Measles*	H	H	Aspirin; vitamins	H	H	Reject	—
Chicken pox	H	H	Aspirin, vitamins	H	H	Reject	—
Hepatitis	H	—	Alcohol and spices prohibited	H	H	Accept	—
Tenesmus	H	C	Diuretics; potassium (fruits)	C	C	Accept	Reject
Dysentery*	H	H	Penicillin; tetracycline	C	H	Accept	Reject
Intestinal worms*	C	—	Lombiz-sante (T.M.)	H	—	Accept	—
Rheumatic fever	—	C	Penicillin	C	H	—	Accept
Rabies*	H	—	—	—	—	—	—
Typhoid	H	—	Penicillin	C	H	Accept	—
Syphilis	H	—	Penicillin	C	H	Accept	—
Rheumatism*	C	C	Aspirin; Vicks	H	H	Accept	Accept
Meningitis	C	—	Penicillin	C	H	Reject	—
Ulcers	H	—	Milk; bread	C	C	Accept	—
Malnutrition (with diarrhea)	C	—	Vitamins; sucros	H	H	Accept	—

*Diseases recognized by natives.
**Dashed lines indicate data not available.

element upon the other equalizes the valence of each. Taken as such, this theorem is simplistically understood. One must ask: What conceptual criteria segregate elements into opposing qualities? How are new elements defined and incorporated into preexisting structures?

In an attempt to answer these questions, I start with a "given": categorization is based upon binary opposition. Logically, then, each element must fulfill specific, culturally known criteria by which it is defined as being either hot or cold. Therefore, if the definitional criteria underlying classification can be successfully elicited and tested empirically, then our current understanding of the effect of humoral medicine upon modern therapeutic programs will be significantly improved.

I find that the following criteria are operative in the binary classification of foods and medicinal plants: color, sex, origin, nutritive value, physiological effect, and medical use. It should be added that the first criterion, color, is significant only in reference to foods, the domain here used to briefly illustrate the suggested criteria.

Color: Generally speaking, darker colored flesh, for example, beef, is hot, but lighter toned meats, such as pork and fish, are cold.

Sex: Female items are hot, while males are cold. Thus, hens are hot but roosters are not (4).

Origin: A by-product typically retains the temperature quality of its source—flour and bread are cold because their source is cold. Moreover, aquatic products, like most subterranean animals and low-lying plants, are cold, whereas organisms more exposed to the direct heat of sunlight are generally hot.

Nutritive value: Most fruits and vegetables are cold, although those believed to be unusually nutritious, such as avocados and peanuts, are hot.

Physiological effect: Foods that affect an individual by producing an allergic response are thought to be hot, and so is the disease. Hives, for example, is classified as being hot; but those foods which consistently provoke symptoms of diarrhea or other cold reactions are defined as being cold.

Medical use: Dietary items traditionally consumed to treat a cold ailment are typically hot; and those used to treat a hot ailment are typically cold. Thus, chocolate for chills and lemonade for fevers.

Definitional criteria involved in classifying illnesses include: etiology, therapeutic prescription, individual sensation, and affected organs and body substances.

Etiology: When etiology is known, the ailment is equal in temperature to that of the cause. One "overcome" by evil eye, for example, will manifest an illness also hot in nature.

Therapeutic prescription: Instructing a patient to omit hot foods from his diet—say peppers and liquor—inadvertently isolates a temperature quality for the illness equal to that of the restricted foods. In this case, the illness would be hot because the forbidden foods are hot.

Individual sensation: In general, when a patient has a sensation of being "chilled" or "heated" due to abnormal metabolic temperature, his condition is categorized equally to that of his sensation. If chilled, the condition is cold; if feverish, the condition is hot.

Affected organs and body substances: Lastly, illnesses affecting specific organs or body substances are of the same temperature quality of the organ or substance. Hepatitis, for example, is hot because it involves a pathogenic condition of the liver, which also is thought to be hot.

Temperature classification of modern medicines is based upon a single, dominant criterion: establishing contrast with illness. Regardless of the color, physical properties, or means of administration, a medicine is classified opposite to the culturally known temperature quality of the illness or symptoms for which it is to be employed. Aspirin is hot because it is believed to be highly effective in treating cold-induced ailments, such as head colds or rheumatism; but Alka Seltzer is cold because it is preferred for treating fever and stomach inflammation, both of which are hot.

Medicines not yet known to a patient will, upon introduction, be classified according to the above assumption that a medicine, if it is to be effective, must be of an opposite quality of the known disorder, because equal qualities between illness and medicine only aggravate a patient's condition. Furthermore, this assumption also holds true for classifying an unknown illness. For example, if a culturally known medicine is prescribed to treat an unknown illness, the illness will be classified in the opposite temperature grouping of the prescribed medicine. Therefore, the use of Aspirin defines "migraine" as being cold.

Term-frame test questions (Goodenough 1965b) were used in 40 of the several hundred informant interviews to test the validity of the contrasting illness-medicine criterion. While frame components and given terms (known) were addressed in the informant's language, test-terms were pronounced in English and occasionally were fictitious to insure their "unknown" character. Examples are:

Question: En mi país, los médicos usan la *Anhydrocine* (unknown and fictitious) para curar la *Fiebre* (known). Esta medicina, Anhydrocine, es caliente ó es fría?

Response: Es fria porque la fiebre es caliente.

Validation: Sería buena la Anhydrocine para curar la diarrea?

Response: No, porque la diarrea es tambien fria.

Question: En mi país, los médicos usan la *Penicilina* (known) para curar la *Spirochetosis* (unknown and not fictitious). Esta enfermedad, Spirochetosis, es caliente ó es fría?

Response: Es caliente porque la Penicilina es fria.

Validation: Sería buena la Anhydrocine para curar la Spirochetosis?

Response: Sí, porque la Anhydrocine es fria y la Spirochetosis es caliente.

Use of the term-frame method established sufficient data to now conclude that modern medicines are classified opposite to the temperature quality of the illnesses for which they are to be used.

The Humoral Concept and Improving Medical Treatment

When physicians or medical aides prescribe medicines or dietary regimens that conflict with a patient's belief in the humoral concept, the successful treatment of that patient can be adversely affected. Comparison of data from Puerto Rican patients in New York City (Harwood 1971) shows significant similarities in patient behavior between Guatemalans and Puerto Ricans.

Guatemalan and Puerto Rican patients display almost equivalent behavioral patterns in response to treatment of specific disorders. That is, when a conflict arises between the temperature qualities of a patient's condition and the prescribed medication, the patient will typically reject the medication. For example, in both Guatemalan and Puerto Rican samples, vitamins are rejected in treatment of illnesses producing high fevers. Fruit juices rich in citric acid are rejected in treatment of the common cold. On the other hand, preferential use of foods in accordance with humoral theory may prove beneficial, as with selecting a restricted diet of hot foods like chicken-broth and peanuts to treat infant diarrhea, a frequent symptom of malnutrition (Logan 1972).

To illustrate behavioral patterns for patients who adhere to the humoral concept, two charts have been constructed giving (1) the temperature classification for various symptoms, diseases, and treatment regimens and (2) expectable patient behavior or reaction to prescribed treatment. The Guatemala data were elicited from intensive interviews with field informants and from consultation with patients and medical personnel at the Behrhorst Clinic. Data were verified by employing various methods, namely, term-frame construction (Goodenough 1965b), named information-slips (Berlin 1968), paired comparisons (Berlin 1968), and triads test (Romney and D'Andrade 1964). The data presented here concerning Puerto Ricans were extracted from Harwood's study. His data were derived from three sources (1971: 1154): observations of medical practices in 64 Puerto Rican households; responses to a questionnaire concerning postpartum practices, and infant care administered to 27 mothers; and anecdotal reports from medical personnel at the Martin Luther King, Jr., Neighborhood Health Center.

When patient behavior differed in the two study groups—as with selection of medication to treat fever—it is found that this variation is caused by a difference in the way the two groups classify the medicine prescribed in therapy. Fever is classified as a hot illness by both groups. Puerto Ricans also consider penicillin to be hot and, therefore, will not take this medicine to treat fever but instead will use cold substances in therapy. Guatemalans, on the contrary, judge penicillin to be a cold medicine and therefore accept this drug for treatment of fever. Similarly, we find that Puerto Ricans reject penicillin when employed to treat diarrhea, because both the illness and the medicine are hot. Guatemalans, however, accept penicillin as treatment for dysentery (presence of blood) because the temperature quality of the illness is hot while that of the medicine is cold. Although their treatment-behavior varies at times, as we have seen, it is, nonetheless, predictable and consistent to humoral theory.

From the above data it becomes obvious that patient behavior is predictable as long as, and to the degree with which, the appropriate temperature qualities are known for both the patient's illness and the prescribed medicine. By knowing these, a physician would be capable of forecasting expectable patient behavior and therefore devising a therapeutic program suitable to the patient's medical and ideological needs. This can be done by (1) selecting medicines and foods of the opposite temperature quality of that of the patient's condition, but if this cannot be done without jeopardizing the clinical effectiveness of treatment, then by (2) "neutralizing" the essential medicines and foods by jointly prescribing "placebo" elements of an appropriate temperature category to restore the necessary opposition between the patient's condition and essential medication.

In treating cases of malnutrition, for example, adequate sources of protein and vitamins can usually be derived from either hot- or cold-classified foods. Care should be given to select a therapeutic diet consisting of foods opposite in temperature to the dominant symptom. If diarrhea is persistent, hot foods are appropriate; if symptoms of fever or skin rash are manifest, then cold foods are preferable. Several medical students from Columbia University, who were participating in the Behrhorst program in Guatemala, confessed to me that they could not understand why patients, including those who were not hospitalized, refused to eat some of the foods prescribed in therapeutic diets. At times, vegetables or fruits were left on the plate, while beef, beans, and coffee were consumed. Invariably, these patients displayed symptoms reported to be cold. When patients had symptoms confessed to be hot, a reverse in eating patterns was observed.

Foods and medicines may be "neutralized" by combining elements of opposing temperature qualities. Guatemalan peasants recognize the principle of neutralization and use it to their advantage, as do Puerto Ricans (Harwood 1971). Frequently I observed individuals adding sugar (*panela*) to fruit juice recommended to them by physicians. When asked why sugar was added, the predominant reply was "to heat the juice," and therefore render it safer to drink when afflicted with a cold illness. Similarly, vitamins, sugar water, chocolate, or Incaparina might be used to "heat" penicillin, thus making it more acceptable to the patient to treat general diarrheal symptoms resulting from enterobacterial infection. Harwood reports several cases where the neutralization of foods and medicines resolved the contradiction of opposing temperature qualities. Postpartum mothers, for example, added tea and barley water to "cool" evaporated milk formula and therefore protect their infants from the "heat" of this prescribed food (Harwood 1971:1156).

Suggestions for Medical Personnel

Contact between modern and traditional forms of medicine is characteristically marked by discrepancies and contradictions in theories of health specific to each form of medical knowledge. Physicians working with patients from cultures other than their own must realize that discrepancies and contradictions left hidden, or patently ignored, hinder optimal therapeutic success. Ethnographic examples abound that illustrate how ineffective modern therapeutic programs can be when medical personnel fail to gain a thorough understanding of the principles and concepts of traditional medicine that govern the behavior of their patients.

Coexistence of modern and folk systems of medical practice is a persistent feature of peasant societies undergoing acculturation in the expansion of western science and culture. Acculturation in medical beliefs, however, frequently has not kept pace with changes that have occurred in other aspects of folk society. As a result, patients may overtly appear to be "progressive" in dress and speech, but in respect to basic premises of health, they often adhere to traditional beliefs. The general pattern that prevails, then, at least in much of Latin America, is that modern medicine does not replace or significantly alter patterns of folk medicine, but serves as an additional system employed concurrently with traditional forms of medical practice (Douglas 1969; Gonzales 1966; Holland 1962; Press 1971; Simmons 1955).

The probability of a physician changing a patient's belief in humoral medicine in the course of often infrequent and impersonal treatment sessions is exceedingly low. It is far more productive, in a pragmatical sense, to accept and work within the existing system of humoral beliefs than to simply impose modern medicine upon native concepts and trust that patients will comply to prescribed medical regimens despite contradictions arising between the different forms of medical theory.

To improve the efficiency of patient care under the present conditions of health services in Guatemala and elsewhere in rural Latin America, physicians are urged to continue employing medicines and dietary regimens known to be clinically effective, while at the same time, attempting to construct therapeutic programs sympathetic to, and compatible with, their patients' belief in the humoral doctrine.

For optimal success in achieving this goal, I feel the following conditions must be met: (1) the physician should gain an understanding and appreciation of local ethnomedical theories; (2) the physician should interview the patient concerning his humoral classification of foods, illnesses, and medicines; (3) the physician should then determine if the patient's beliefs undermine the prescribed treatment; and if so, (4) the physician should try to construct a medical regimen which is agreeable to both the physician and the patient.

Finally, it should be noted that many other investigators have demonstrated convincingly that folk theories of health often challenge, and sometimes cancel, the general effectiveness of modern therapeutic programs (Paul 1955). The commitment of Guatemalan peasants to the humoral concept illustrates the usefulness of incorporating the patient's theory into the doctor's practice.

Appendices

Appendix A. List of Foods According to Temperature

Spanish: Hot (*Caliente*); Cold (*Frio, Fresco, Congelado*); Neutral (*Templado*).
Cakchiquel and Tzutuhil: Hot (*Katan*); Cold (*Teoh*); Neutral (*Templado*).

Hot	*Neutral*	*Cold*
Beef	⁀Tortilla	Pork
Goat	Frijoles	Fish
Hen	Squash	Rooster
Rabbit	Potatoes	Turkey
Squirrel	Rice	Lard
Deer	Bread	Potatoes
Tortilla*		Rice
Frijol de suelo		Frijol de milpa
Bread*		Milk*
Eggs*		Cheese*
Peppers		Lemons
Chocolate		Onions
Honey		Green beans
Peanuts*		Tomatoes
Peaches		Squash
Apples		Carrots
Sugar		Beer
Distilled drinks and wine		Soda pop

*Considerable idiosyncratic variation

Appendix B. List of Common Medicinal Plants* According to Temperature

Hot
Pericon: *Tagetes lucida.* Antidiarrheal
Altamisa: *Ambrosia cumanensis.* Antidiarrheal
Vuelveteloco: *Datura stratimonium.* Rheumatism
Cacao: *Theobroma cacao.* Pneumonia
Raiz de Valeriana: *Choptalia nutans.* Intestinal parasites

Cold
Te de Limon: *Cymbopogon citratus.* Hangover; tonics
Hierba Buena: *Lippia reptans.* Stomach acidity
Quilete: *Solanum sp.* Anemia
Piñon: *Jatropha curcas.* Dysentery (presence of blood)
Caña Fistula: *Cassia fistula.* Measles

*In Indian communities the above plants are known by their Spanish names.

Appendix C. List of Common Proprietary and Prescribed Medicines According To Temperature

Hot	*Cold*
Aspirin	Alka-Seltzer
Vick's Vapor Rub	Sal Andrews
Vitamins	Vegetal oils
Kaopectate	Sulfa
Sucrose	Milk of Magnesia
Alcohol	Penicillin
Lombriz-Sante (Piperacine anhydrate)	Tetracycline
Entero-Leina (Oxyquinoline)	*Carbanato* (bicarbonate of soda)

Notes

1. The term "Ladino" refers to a "person no longer identified culturally as Indian and, in Guatemala, includes many individuals genetically Indian as well as those representing various degrees of European-Indian racial mixtures who are Mestizos in the customary sense" (Scrimshaw and Tejada 1970:203).
2. Although the quality of moisture is of negligible significance in present day folk diagnosis, remnants of the concept are found in the classification of minor respiratory ailments, where a tight or dry cough (*Tos Seco*) is different from a loose or wet cough (*Tos Flujo*). Here, dryness denotes a hot quality and wetness a cold quality.
3. A third and newly emerging category of "neutral" is being employed by some acculturated Maya and well-to-do Ladino peasants. Neutral elements are neither hot nor cold and have no effect upon the body's temperature balance. Included in this category are most dietary staples and some illnesses and modern medicines. Perhaps the emergence of a neutral category reflects a reduction in anxiety concerning food and disease among acculturated persons who experience higher standards of living in comparison to less-acculturated individuals.
4. Sex as a defining criterion is most significant among Mayan informants. Chicken, beans, and some medicinal plants are thought of having female and male representatives; female being hot and male being cold. Frijol de Suelo (*Phaseolus sp.*) is hot but Frijol de Milpa (*Phaseolus sp.*) is cold; Agalia Embra (*Algalia hembra*) is hot while Agalia Macho (*Algalia varon*) is cold.

Irwin Press

Bureaucracy versus folk medicine: implications from Seville, Spain [1]

Literature on folk medicine offers many examples of contact and conflict between modern and folk health complexes. By and large, the resiliency and dominance of folk medical practice is stressed. Data thus far suggest that the mere presence of medical practitioners and facilities, whether it be in tribal, peasant or urban milieux, may not be sufficient to seriously threaten a strong folk medical complex. Difficulties in establishing private medical practices or comprehensive low cost clinics have been demonstrated in rural India (Marriott 1955), Mexico (Lewis 1955), New Mexico (Saunders 1954) and Colorado (Saunders and Samora 1955) to mention but a few examples. In each case, medical "competence" of the facility is subordinate to social-cultural differences between the competing complexes.

Even in cities, where modern medical facilities are numerous and "official," folk medical practitioners and treatments may continue with vigor (Clark 1959; Kelly 1965; Maclean 1966; Lieban 1967). Press has indicated the complex manners in which city patients may simultaneously or sequentially utilize both physicians and curers (1969), and the manner in which urban curers may ensure their continuity through stylistically reflecting social characteristics of the urban milieu (1971).

It is important to note that existing accounts of curer versus modern medical use—whether in Tepoztlan, Cebu City, Bogota or Los Angeles—are accounts of rural dwellers with a full-blown folk medical system, or of lower class urbanites, most of whom are migrants (or migrants' children) from areas where folk beliefs are dominant. In any case, to the patients in question, the modern medical complex is the "foreign" element.

Modern medicine may be "foreign" for a variety of reasons. At a more surface level, the healer-patient interaction situation offers many potential problems. Physicians and patients may view different symptoms as meaningful; they may use different terms to describe ailments; they may have diverging views as to the healer's proper role behavior; they may differ in defining the degree of privacy and participation of others required by the healing situation; they may differ in the assignment of causality. Many more examples can be added.

These differences are not insurmountable, however. Physicians and other health personnel can ostensibly be trained to accommodate to local sub-cultural definitions of the healing interaction. Far less resolvable is the deeper divergence

Reprinted by permission of Plenum Publishing Corporation from I. Press, "Bureaucracy versus Folk Medicine: Implications from Seville, Spain," *Urban Anthropology,* 2:232-247, 1973.

in *function.*

Folk illness and curing may fill a wide range of psycho-social and cultural needs. In Mexico alone, illness has been shown to serve functions of: economic leveling; control of antisocial behavior; aggression release; explanation of failure to conform; dramatization of role stress; and cultural identity maintenance. In its approach to illness, modern medicine accommodates few of the functional ramifications so common to folk medicine. These ramifications are often of systemic proportions. The more enmeshed the individual in this kind of system, the more difficult to leave it, or to admit to the utility of elements outside it.

Anthropological research has so stressed these functions and their systemic nature, it stands to reason that where modern medicine fills a range of functions wider than the simple amelioration of symptoms, it can compete seriously with folk medicine.

This hypothesis does not require that the modern medical system offer comparable functions of social control, identity maintenance, etc., in order to compete. There is no reason why any body of inter-related functions will not do, so long as these enmesh the individual in a system from which deviation is impractical or undesirable.

To test this, we focus upon a modern medical-welfare system which does offer such an array of functions. Spain, with its pervasive social security, socialized medicine, sindicalism and rent control, offers insight into the manner in which a bureaucratic system may make impractical the recourse to "unofficial" sources of healing. In that modern services tend to be most concentrated and efficient in the urban milieu, we concentrate upon health in the city and province of Seville.

Seville and Its Modern Medical System

Seville, a city of 600,000, is the cultural center of Andalucia—the area which provided a large part of the Spanish influence upon Latin America. Seville is highly urban in terms of literacy, residence pattern, and services. Economically and socially, however, the city has changed little over the past half century. The bulk of the lower classes, though presently living in highrise condominia, were socialized in semi-communal "casas de vecinos," in which up to a hundred families live in single rooms surrounding a common courtyard. Industry is still minimal, skill requirements low and patronism or personal contact the only means to jobs at all levels. Provincialism is high. There is not a single "foreign" restaurant in Seville. Local fiestas and customs, which elsewhere in Spain have disappeared or become "modernized," still flourish. Seville, in other words, is *not* an industrial city with a tradition of universalistically based interpersonal relationships.

Folk medicine has had a long tradition in Seville and its province. Many of the medical forms of Andalucia were transposed to the Spanish New World. Indeed, a veritable museum of old Andalucian medical forms can be seen in Latin America today (2). Formal medicine in Seville was still but an alternative to folk practice until well into the 20th century. Around the turn of the century, *promesas* (promises to saints) and curer-use was utiquitous among the city's lower classes (Montoto 1883:88). Most Sevillanos feared the hospital, which was viewed as a last resort for the ailing.

"Formal" medicine in Spain also has a long tradition, keeping rough pace with developments elsewhere in Europe. This contrasts strongly with the course of modern medical development in Spanish colonial areas. Both the great language gaps and the scarcity of physicians in Latin America and the Philippines, for example, led to a subsequent lag in diffusion of European medical concepts throughout these areas (Hart 1969:67). "In view of the relative lack of doctors," comments Foster, "priests and other educated [though medically unsophisticated] individuals were called upon to help the sick to a degree probably not characteristic of Spain" (1953b:204). As late as 1573, Quito (Ecuador) "had neither physician nor apothecary" (Haring 1947:233). In 1847, only one year after the development of general anesthetic, Spain was not only testing ether, but offering a prize for the best scholarly paper on its use (Garcia 1946:641). General anesthesia was not used in Ecuador, however, until almost thirty years later (Paredes 1946).

The "medical lag" in Latin America encouraged wholesale reliance upon "un-official" health recourses. In Spain, continual contact with the centers of medical development allowed modern health practices to evolve steadily and undiluted, thus offering a continual alternative to folk medicine. This "separate but equal" co-existence continued until the Spanish civil war.

The modern health system is essentially a post-civil war phenomenon. There is no doubt that the war importantly influenced receptivity to universalistic services. During the conflict, the ability of families to fill basic physical and social needs was severely disrupted. In the cities, particularly, those who had had to survive on precariously low wages found cheap medical care, sick pay, old age disability and pensions, union job guarantees, rent control, and unemployment compensation to be of very real and immediate utility.

Spain's social welfare programs essentially began with the founding of the *Instituto Nacional de Prevision* (I.N.P.) in the second decade of this century. Most benefits, however, were developed in the six year period 1938-1944. National health insurance began in 1942 (Instituto Nacional de Prevision 1944:20-21) and today, under the *Seguro Social* (Social Security) branch of the I.N.P., enrolls most of Spain's salaried employees. All lower income salaried workers (excepting farm labor) belong—compulsorily—to the service, which embraces both health and welfare benefits. Approximately 8% of the worker's salary is deducted for all of these benefits. Employers contribute an even greater percentage.

The average worker enjoys the following benefits from the Instituto Nacional de Prevision:

    1. "Cost-free" medical, emergency, hospital and maternity care for the worker and his or her dependents;

    2. Approximately 85% discount on prescription medicines at any pharmacy;

3. Sick pay of 50% of salary for illness and 75% for accident;

4. A monthly cash subsidy for being married and for each child;

5. Old age pension;

6. Gift or loan for health needs such as eyeglasses, orthopedic devices, etc.

7. Unemployment compensation of 75% of last earned salary.

A typical urban Spaniard may have 400 pesetas monthly deducted from his pay for all I.N.P. benefits. However, being married and having, say, two children, he receives 700 pesetas monthly in subsidy "points." He thus *nets* 300 pesetas cash monthly (equivalent to a lower class daily wage) *in addition* to health and all other benefits.

Though the salaried employee's deductions actually go to the parent I.N.P., workers invariably refer to these deductions as going for "social security"–the health-oriented sub-agency.

As with any low-income workers whose paychecks are diminished by health insurance deductions (and quite regardless of the "point" money which they also receive), Sevillanos feel strongly that they are paying for their medical care and want to "get their money's worth." This accounts for much of the abuse or overuse of the health system. "Almost fifty per-cent of my patients come with sniffles or hangnail," complains a Social Security doctor in a lower class barrio. "And then there are the mothers whose daughters are 'too thin,' in need of some 'tonic.' " Doctors, however, are so often inundated with patients during allotted short office hours, that little more than cursory examinations can be made. Patients state their major symptoms and almost inevitably the hard-pressed physician immediately prescribes some medicine or injectible. To a considerable degree, the patient thus controls the diagnosis and subsequent prescription.

No Social Security patient may judge his own inability to work. Only the "baja" (the "low") or official permission to take sick leave (issued by his GP) will allow the worker to stay home from the job. While on the "baja," the individual receives sick pay. The state distrusts the worker, however. Random visits by inspectors force him to stay close to his bedside. Violation of the baja may lead to loss of sick pay and permission to remain away from the workplace.

This has both advantages and disadvantages. The individual's freedom is somewhat curtailed, particularly in cases where he is not necessarily bedridden. On the other hand, a "baja" is not difficult to obtain. The necessarily cursory examination made by the general practitioner encourages reliance upon patient claims of suffering and invalidity. Sevillanos accept the baja at face value, however. One is reluctant to suggest that someone else is not ill enough to warrant it. It is, in other words, a readily accessible and universally accepted sick role permit. At a somewhat lower "level," any doctor's prescription is also proof of illness. Indeed, the bureautop jumble of bottles, medicine boxes and old prescriptions is an almost ubiquitous symbol of the Social Security-insured worker.

The "baja" granted by the Social Security physician has other advantages, however. Many lower class Sevillanos are, in fact, willing to accept half their meagre salaries by feining illness. They then use this income to supplement a full salary obtained in clandestine work. Numerous employers, particularly in the construction industry, are more than happy to take on unofficial, unlisted workers, in that they need not pay any social security (42% of a worker's salary) to the government for such nonexistent employees.

Though the vast majority of Sevillanos will never see a curer, and whereas those who do almost invariably see a physician first, physicians are not always seen upon onset of symptoms. In an effort to save money and time Sevillanos will almost invariably first treat themselves with left-over medicines which have been prescribed for maladies with similar symptoms. If no such medicine is around the house, close neighbors or conveniently located kin will be contacted. Indeed, exchange of used prescription medicines is the rule in such dwelling types as the "casa de vecinos" where ten to fifty or more families live in close proximity around a single courtyard. The gift of otherwise expensive prescription drugs (generally "slightly used") is a common method by which less well-to-do wage earners can reciprocate favors of better-off entrepreneurial kin who do not qualify for Social Security.

Social Security is not the only medical service available to Sevillanos. For provincial and municipal employees and low income indigents, there is the *Padron Benefica* or municipal medical service. Scattered clinics throughout the city provide emergency and outpatient services. For the indigent, medical care, prescriptions, and hospitalization in the provincial-municipal hospital are free. Once investigated by the police, vouched for by the parish priest, and certified needy, the indigent receives an official *Padron Benefica* card, which functions as an insurance ID card at any *Padron* center. This obviates the necessity of repeated investigation and potential embarrassment. Any indigent person in the province who is of rural or town origin is eligible for *Padron.* As with SS, a permanent general practitioner is assigned each individual. For hospitalization, all must use the large municipal hospital of Seville, which is no more than two or three hours from any point in the province.

Associated with the hospital is the medical school, whose outpatient clinic offers the services of the top specialists in Seville. These services are free to *Padron* patients, and minimal charges are made of anyone else, regardless of income. If one is thus willing to wait in line, the famous heart specialist whose private office fee surpasses 1000 pesetas can be seen for 75 before noon at the school clinic. No referral is required for consultation with specialists, and patients are thus allowed the opportunity of preliminary self diagnosis through free access to all specialists.

Operating privately, though in a similar fashion, is the Red Cross, with two hospital-clinics in Seville. Physicians both donate and rent their time, and while poor patients may be treated without cost, only minimal charges are made of anyone else wishing to receive medical care.

For self-employed Sevillanos there are a number of private health plans. These, not unlike experiments in the U.S. (see, for example, Freidson 1961a) provide all medical services (except medicines) for a set annual premium. As with

Social Security and the *Padron Benefica,* their service is "direct" in that they maintain a staff of part-time physicians and offer a choice of sanitoria should hospitalization be required. The insured are assigned GPs, as in SS and *Padron.*

Finally, many of the physicians who staff the Social Security, *Padron,* private insurance groups and Red Cross also hold private office hours in the late afternoon.

Most of the facilities mentioned, though naturally concentrated in the urban zone, are available in full or part to rural dwellers. Social Security and *Padron Benefica* both maintain (or contract for) rural clinics. Frequently these consist simply in the local physician's office. Patients may be—and usually are—referred (without additional cost, of course) to the major facilities in Seville (or Cadiz, Cordoba, Granada, etc.).

Regardless of the medical plan with which they are associated, Sevillanos regularly "shop around" within the overall system. Due to the commonly expressed desire for more personal attention, there is hardly a Social Security member who has not seen a private physician at least once during the year. On any given day approximately *half* the patients at the medical school clinic or Red Cross are Social Security members seeking intensive examination by a specialist of their choice. (Patients are not allowed such choice within SS.)

Each of the medical entities operates within a distinct bureaucratic milieu and offers distinct services or qualities of service. Thus, overall, the Sevillano feels he has a choice. The fact that the Sevillano shops first *within* the official medical system, exhibits his deep commitment to it (most individuals, in fact, *never* leave the system for curers). The Sevillano's medical vocabulary reflects this commitment. He is conversant with the relative advantages of a wide variety of antibiotics, medicines and treatments. He can generally name the top man in each of the city's major medical specialties. The most illiterate of Sevillanos may speak of "intramuscular injections" rather than "shots" (*pinchazos*).

It is not surprising that the salaried employee of Seville exhibits such commitment. He is forced to participate in a system which requires that he accept health care, medicines, sick-role validation, sick pay, therapeutic aids, extra monthly cash, O.A.B. and unemployment compensation from a single bureaucratic entity. The health care division (Social Security) occupies but a suite of offices in the large Instituto Nacional de Prevision building. To the Sevillano, however, all of these benefits are linked conceptually. Moreover, they are all referred to popularly as "Social Security" benefits, and thus linked terminologically with health and its administration.

With what does this system compete?

Folk Illness in Seville

Folk medical beliefs in Andalucia in general appear to be ubiquitous yet weakly developed and of little major behavioral significance. That is, while many "believe in" evil eye, sorcery and other "folk" illness, and many have "heard of" someone who suffered from such phenomena, few actually "know of" an individual who has so suffered, let alone suffered themselves. There is little behavior, therefore, which reflects concern for folk medical concepts in terms of preventive acts or conscious and observable caveats in interaction with others.

Pitt-Rivers most specifically concludes that folk medical beliefs "show no logical consistency" in rural Alcala de la Sierra (1961:199), and this observation seems to hold for Andalucia as a whole. Evil eye, for example, may vary from community to community. Few have suffered it personally. In Cantillana, some twenty kilometers north of Seville, people speak of evil eye as an unconscious force. Those who have it may make a child sick with an admiring glance. It is not malicious. It can be cured by orations only, and one townswoman is known to perform these. On the other hand, a suburban Seville folk curer claims that evil eye can be cured only by having the person who caused it tweak the skin of the affected child. In Corria de Rio, some twenty kilometers west of Seville, evil eye is viewed by some as synonymous with sorcery; "Something of the gypsies"; something a malicious person consciously "puts" on an enemy. In Alcala, some hundred kilometers south, evil eye is possessed by women only. It can be either intentional or not and its cure is apparently not familiar to the general public (Pitt-Rivers 1961: 198). In other words, few are ever bothered by it or adjust their behavior to it.

Sorcery is similarly "known," often "believed in," yet behaviorally an unimportant phenomenon in Andalucia. It too is generally a "thing of the gypsies." Beliefs in rural Alcala, for example, vary considerably. The source may be a living individual who uses "poltergeists" or "spirits." Or the source may be "ghostly," rather than human (Pitt-Rivers 1961:96). Reasons for engaging in sorcery also vary, but appear to stem from jealousy due to absolute deprivation (direct competition for an inheritance or a woman, for example) rather than relative deprivation as in Foster's concept of the "limited good." Menstrual magic as described by Pitt-Rivers in Alcala appears to be little more than a belief in the general negative affect which menstruating women involuntarily may have upon things in their vicinity (1961: 197). In Seville, on the other hand, curers and laymen alike say that women may *use* powdered menstrual blood to make husbands oblivious to adultery. This however, is clearly a phenomenon of *explanatory* (post facto) nature which does not in itself *generate* behavior such as preventive action or seeking professional help.

Other forms of "folk illness" similarly appear to be of minimal importance in Andalucia. Among residents in and around Seville hot and cold distinctions are absent. *Envidia* makes the envier sick. Other conditions may or may not be recognized from town to town and include such infrequently encountered phenomena as "culebrina" (shingles—still not readily curable by modern medicine) which "certain women" are "said" to cure. In most larger towns, only few people would know who these women might be.

To reiterate, folk medical beliefs in Andalucia appear to represent the vestige of a formerly stronger complex. These beliefs are widespread in Andalucia and are familiar to Sevillanos. The general inconsistency of many of these beliefs, however, indicates the lack of a widespread self-reinforcing behavioral complex. We must therefore be wary of equating *belief* with *practice.* The behavioral weakness of folk illness is further seen in an examination of the folk healer.

Curers

Rarely are Seville's curers confronted with "folk illness" per se. Rarely do curers or patients speculate about cause. The concern, rather, is overwhelmingly with remission of symptoms. In Seville and vicinity, *most* people (whether rural or urban) *never* visit curers. Those who do will almost always see a physician first. Pitt-Rivers notes a similar pattern in Alcala. Though he does not go into the matter it is apparent that when Alcalanos do visit a curer it is after having seen the local physician in the first place. That a curer is seen at all may be due to the inconvenience of journeying to a town with more sophisticated modern facilities.

Data are sparce on the relative quantity of curers in Andalucia. Pitt-Rivers notes that Alcala has two, neither full time. Both are "generalists," dealing with a variety of symptoms as well as divining, predicting, finding thieves or lost objects. Other individuals are "known" to specialize in particular ailments such as broken bones, boils, etc. (Pitt-Rivers 1961:190-194).

It is likely that a number of communities (certainly not all) contain similar personnel. There are few general curers near Seville itself, though in some communities there may be individuals who "are said" to cure a specific ailment (such as cancer, shingles or breaks). Few residents are able to identify them, however. Within thirty kilometers of the city, in fact, there are but two well-patronized general curers (perhaps three, if the city's sole naturopath be included). One curer lives in a suburb of Seville, the other in a town to the north. Aside from the naturopath there are no professional or semi-professional curers in the city itself (though of course in every neighborhood there are individuals known to be familiar with home remedies). A quite limited quantity of medicinal herbs are sold by condiment and seed dealers in Seville's market places, but such venders do not generally diagnose or know much about plant medicine. One old woman sits with her few herbs on a curb some twenty meters from Seville's largest seed shop, where, in fact, she purchases her stock. She claims that her few customers would be embarrassed by publicly purchasing medicinal herbs in the crowded shop across the street. The bulk of her sales are of condiments for pickling olives.

The two curers are also called *sabios* because of their ability to divine, foretell the future and diagnose at a distance (3). They both diagnose in a trance-like state and obtain their powers through the grace of a saint. Both claim to cure any illness. In their early fifties, both make much of their inability to read and write. They are married, kindly and white-haired, presenting an appearance of paternal concern. Andres "el Sastre" ("the tailor") who operates in the Seville suburb of Panoleta, receives patients in his bedroom. Seated before the patient, he begins by reciting Catholic prayers. After several minutes he suddenly stiffens. With violent gasps and eye rolling he is possessed by a saint (sometimes S. Martin de Porres, sometimes, S. Francisco de Ignacio) who then speaks through his mouth (no voice change, however), asks questions and gives advice. Andres specializes in clairvoyance and counsel. Afraid of arrest, he is reticent about discussing his curing abilities. More people come to him for advice than cures.

Juan, the famous sabio of the town of Cantillana, is exclusively a curer. He diagnoses while in a darkened room with eyes closed. He claims to "see" (with a "red x-ray beam") into the depth of the patient. No ailment escapes his scrutiny. Then the proper treatment appears before his eyes.

Both sabios cure in much the same way. They may have patients drink plain tap water into which they had gazed (and thus given grace).

The Cantillana sabio prescribes only patent medicines which are available at most pharmacies. The suburban Seville sabio usually prescribes patent medicine though he will on occasion recommend or prepare a simple herbal. Neither takes much interest in the etiology of illnesses brought to them. Thus, *de facto,* the question of natural versus supernatural causality does not enter into consultations. The sabios almost never discuss illness in terms of folk concepts; rather they attempt to describe the patient's pathology in medical or pseudo-medical terms—such as "growths on the throat" or "duodenal mucosity." Sessions involve a limited number of questions—such as *who* the patient is (often the patient remains at home while a kinsman or spouse represents him), where the pain is and who (meaning physicians) the patient has seen previously. Though the sabios are invariably paternal and pleasant, sessions rarely last longer than five or ten minutes. Neither charges a fee, yet relies instead upon donations (which have ranged from a few pieces of fruit to an automobile).

Both are full-time practitioners. Andres "the tailor" may see a dozen patients daily. Juan's courtyard is generally packed with patients from all parts of Andalucia. He may see dozens daily. By refusing to set a fee, the sabios (who are well known) minimize the likelihood of being denounced and arrested as profit-seeking quacks. Juan of Cantillana has nonetheless faced quackery charges four times in the past three years. On each occasion he has been freed following glowing testimonials of former patients. Only recently the College of Surgeons of Seville vigorously denounced a local newspaper for presenting a feature article on him. ("Patients have come to see me from as far as Notre Dame, Indiana, in the United States," he was quoted as boasting.)

There is but one homeopath left in Seville, an eccentric old man who sees but a patient or two monthly. He is known throughout the city. Sockless, in split shoes, with a wild and sparce grey beard, he wanders the streets of Seville's famous Arab quarter in a tattered suit that is half cloth, half patches. He is, in reality, comfortably well off and owns a home within this expensive *barrio.* The tattered old man provides a clear view of homeopathy's demise in Spain. "When social security was formed after the civil war, homeopathy was not included as a branch of medicine. So, the official—the mandatory—thrives, and the unofficial dies. Separated from official medicine, we couldn't survive." Though ostensibly allied with modern medicine, homeopaths are viewed as distinct by their patients. To the patient, the "anicitos" or little candy-like medicinals of the homeopath are the essence of his therapy and thus quite unlike modern medications.

In addition to the homeopath, there is one practicing naturopath in the city. Upon entering his office, the patient is immediately confronted with framed graduation certificates and a large sign proclaiming "I am not a medical doctor." In his use of iris diagnosis (4), in his search for a cause which generally results in discovery of "bad" dietary habits, in his vegetarian regimens, in his prescription of unknown herbs in numbered packets, and in his lectures on the necessity for cleansing the body, he is, perhaps, even less "orthodox" than the patent-medicine oriented sabios with their saint-bestowed grace. Unlike the sabios, both homeopath and naturopath (or "naturist") are legally licensed to practice and charge a set fee, comparable to that of a private GP. There is apparently insufficient demand for the naturist's services to warrant full-time practice, however. As a result, he divides his month between Malaga, Cordoba and Seville, maintaining offices in each. He may see a dozen or more patients on each consulting day.

The curers of Seville fall within Press' model of "urban curandero" (1971b). Their approach is impersonal, and they spend little time with patients. They take no interest in social etiology. They classify illnesses in medical symptomal jargon rather than according to folk categories such as "aires," "sustos," sorcery, etc. Not only does their paucity in numbers and overall style reflect the lack of behavioral importance of folk medicine in the area, but as the *only* widely known general curers they clearly influence (and limit) local concepts of unofficial illness and cure.

Though the number of curers has been declining in Seville, the number of *non*-curing "sabios" has increased. Perhaps half a dozen are plying a part- or full-time trade in the city. They specialize in advice and prognosis. Many individuals come to them for confirmation of diagnoses made by physicians, and for an idea as to what the course of their illness will be like (i.e., "Is my tumor malignant?"; "Will my child recover from his surgery?"; etc.). Such practitioners are supplemental to modern medical practice, not an alternative or back-up. They offer hope and prognosis where modern medicine is either impersonal or uncertain.

With exception of the naturist's clients (who all find they suffer from poor dietary habits), curer patients are little concerned with cause. When pressed, Sevillanos in general attribute illness to poverty, and/or "excess" of food, drink, work or play.

Almost invariably, curer patients attend a physician first for any given ailment. And patients who utilize curers have previously entered the formal sick role through diagnosis by a physician. Most patients are of two types: (1) Those either medically incurable, impatient after lengthy medical treatment with little result, or chronically ill; (2) those seeking an alternative to a long, costly or anxiety-producing course of medical treatment recommended by their physicians. The old homeopath, for example, stated that some of his patients came simply because "they were afraid of shots." A typical patient of the Catillana sabio was a young man with a heart problem necessitating some 3000 pesetas in diagnostic procedures. He was visiting the curer in hopes of being quickly healed and spared the larger expense. A young man at the naturopath's office said that physicians had diagnosed a lesion on his left lung and prescribed two months of bed rest. He could not afford to remain idle that long. So he seeks another opinion and treatment which will allow him to continue his normal routine. One woman interviewed at the home of suburban Andres said she had come to obtain "reassurance" that Social Security would release X-rays of her son to a private physician they had just engaged.

Overall, the visit to a curer reflects a reaction to specific bureaucratic or non-intrinsic methodological aspects of modern medical practice, rather than against the modern medical process or philosophy in general. Curer patients by no means view medical and curer systems as "separate but equal." Primacy is clearly granted the medical.

Discussion and Conclusions

The weakness of folk medicine reflects both the minimal functional importance of folk illness and the increasing pervasiveness of the modern health-related bureaucracy. It is likely that the latter has had a strong influence upon the former.

Some of the more familiar traditional functions of folk illness find no structural bases in Seville and vicinity. While conformity to dress, respect, friendship interaction and sex role requirements are stressed in all barrios of the city, economic accumulation or social mobility are viewed as an individual's prerogative. Envy of the better-off is certainly universal, yet not viewed as leading to punitive action. The leveling function of witchcraft or envy is thus unnecessary (c.f. Foster 1960-61). Lieban (1967:144-148) has attributed lower incidence of sorcery cases in Cebu City (as compared with the rural hinterland) to the weakening of personal interdependencies and the "image of limited good." In terms of social control, Whiting (1959), Adams and Rubel (1967:354) and others suggest that witchcraft may function as a mechanism of control where "superordinate punitive authority" is weak. Such "superordinate" authority has been conspicuously *present* in both rural and urban Spain. The local priesthood, police and the highly respected and feared Guardia Civil exercise quite efficient control. Less formally, "verguenza" (shame, precepts of "proper" behavior) forces conformity by threat of gossip or ridicule.

In a similar manner, cultural identity maintenance is of little importance to the Sevillano or recent migrant to Seville. Most are Andalucians, of similar dialect and values. Governmental rent control makes intra-city mobility disadvantageous for the lower class of rentors, in that landlords are entitled to establish new (and much higher) rents for new tenants. Public housing in the city is strictly limited to subsidized condominium apartments, in which the lower class tenant becomes a mortgaged owner. Thus, rural migrants find their kin scattered throughout the city in highly stable situations, rather than in high-mobility, rurally oriented peripheral barrios. There is neither opportunity nor reason for a linguistically distinct or rurally oriented sub-culture to develop. Folk illness is thus not needed to maintain an "us versus them" orientation in the face of urban threat to "traditional" cultural values (c.f. Rubel 1960; Madsen 1964).

Curanderismo in Seville reflects its peripheral functional importance. The full-time healers do not compete with modern medicine. Nor are they compartmentalized into a "separate but equal" category. By and large, curanderismo is a second choice and last resort. In its focus upon symptoms rather than socio-moral etiology, and in its concern with modern patent medicines, medical jargon and (more recently) in its near total shift to supportive prognosis, curanderismo reflects its patients' shifting commitment to the primacy of official over folk medicine and economic-somatic over social consequences of illness.

The modern medical system offers a range of minimally psycho-social functions, filling needs specific to life in the urbanizing, wage-dependent society. Quite apart from the coerciveness of the health-welfare bureaucracy (participation is mandatory for salaried workers), it is pervasive in terms of benefits and controls over the individual (5).

Medicines, health care, sick pay, sick leave, family "point" money, O.A.B., etc., are but part of the picture. The pervasiveness of the Spanish bureaucracy goes further still. The government controls all rents. It subsidizes the construction of all public housing. It makes down-payment loans available. It allocates apartments. Through the sindicates (unions), the central government sets *all* wages and benefits, and maintains strict control over employee rights.

In terms of health alone, few wage earners can afford even partial reliance upon another (folk medical) system. The modern medical complex has become significantly systemic in the extent of non-medical behaviors which it affects. To rely upon the curer is simply downright disadvantageous.

Certainly a number of elements in the present case are specific to the special historical and cultural configuration of Seville. Such "local" factors always make generalization difficult. Cautiously, therefore, we conclude that systemic involvement appears to be crucial to commitment to, and continuing use of modern medical facilities. The wider the range of functions the health-linked bureaucracy can service, the more likelihood of its competing successfully with traditional health systems.

Notes

1. The author wishes to thank Professor Steven Kertesz and the Western European Studies Program of Notre Dame for financial support.
2. However, such well known phenomena as *envidia*, soul-loss (*susto*) and hot-cold food beliefs have no counterpart today in Spain (Foster 1953; Currier 1966), and likely developed independently in the new world.
3. Sevillanos have also heard of, and patronized, several other famous Andalucian *sabias* (in this case, females) over a hundred kilometers distant. Descriptions of these curers by their patients indicate that they differ minimally from the two *sabios* herein described.
4. Iris diagnosis is a well-known technique wherein striations of the iris reflect the condition of body parts.
5. See Etzioni (1965) for an enlightening discussion of "pervasiveness" and "coerciveness" among large scale organizations.

Ethel Nurge

Anthropological perspective for medical students

In these days when we are training more anthropologists than the country is ready to employ, we need to explore what function we can perform in fields other than the traditional. Concern about the contracting market for employment of anthropologists has led to many meetings and discussions (Leacock et al. 1974). One field which anthropologists have been entering in increasing numbers is the health field. The circulation of *Medical Anthropology Newsletter* and the size of the membership of the Society for Medical Anthropology mirror the interest of those in the field, if not necessarily the numbers employed. I am an anthropologist of traditional social anthropological training, trained before there was a specialty of medical anthropology, and I have been in a medical school for six years.

The struggle for a student's time in medical school is an interdisciplinary matter and the behavioral scientists are gradually making some headway, but still the exposure of the medical students to the teachings of anthropology is so minimal as to be discouraging. However, many students do get some exposure to the concepts of society and culture; indeed some students enter medical school using "culture" in the anthropological sense. But no required course designed specifically to teach the cultural and social aspects of medicine and health to medical students has gotten past the curriculum committee in my school and our best hope is in electives. Student interest in American Indians is very high and through capitalizing on that interest two of us have established an elective that is proving very attractive indeed. A pediatrician and I offer a course called "Blended Clinical Experience and Cultural Study of Certain Ethnic Minority Groups" for one or more elective periods. Electives had been six weeks long in what is called a module; the module is now only four weeks in duration. Of the students who have chosen the course thus far, none have chosen just one module; most of them opt for two or more to run serially. Thus, they are on location for two or three months at least. I have to emphasize the shortness of the stay and also to make a point that it is an achievement to have students for fieldwork for that length of time.

The location for the fieldwork is the Checkerboard Area Health System (CAHS), northwestern New Mexico. The CAHS began in 1971 when local health planners responded to the need for a rural health delivery system. Planning to build a model to supply health care in a distressed area in New Mexico, they applied for funds to the Social and Rehabilitation Services of HEW. Money for three years was granted and the project began November 1, 1971. The applicants proposed a system emphasizing primary care and prevention and planned for the training of native

Reproduced by permission of the Society for Applied Anthropology from *Human Organization* 34
    (4), 1975.

New Mexicans as allied and paraprofessionals. The state of New Mexico was named the grantee and the agency named to provide the services was the Presbyterian Medical Services (PMS). PMS is a voluntary, community-based, nonprofit health care corporation which operates two general hospitals, four diagnostic and treatment centers, and seven clinics in a nine-county rural area. The PMS has 12 physicians and six dentists, and numerous allied health personnel: for example, nurses, physicians' assistants, family, pediatric, and perinatal nurse practitioners, child health associates, home health workers, and emergency medical service technicians. All PMS locations have transportation services and a VHF radio system to connect the cars, ambulances, hospitals, and clinics.

The PMS clinic that our students go to is in Cuba, New Mexico. Cuba is 90 miles northwest of Albuquerque on Highway 44. To say it is on a "highway" is misleading for it is a small town in an underpopulated area. About 2,500 people are in and around Cuba, but the Checkerboard Area Health System as a whole can be considered to be 3,000 square miles with about 10,000 inhabitants. The CAHS name refers to the fact that land ownership is checkerboarded in patterns familiar in the West. Portions of the land are owned by individual Navajos, some of it is still Navajo reservation land, and other inhabitants are Spanish Americans and Anglos. The population distribution is approximately three to five persons per square mile. In addition to the community of Cuba, there are three outlying areas known as Coyote (Spanish American), and Torreon and Nageezi (both Navajo). Eighty-nine percent of the people at Coyote and Nageezi and 56% of the people at Torreon do not speak English, but in Cuba only 23% of the population do not. These figures come from a socio-demographic survey made by the CAHS in August of 1973. From the same survey we get the figures on ethnicity shown in Table 1.

Table 1. Ethnicity of checkerboard area health system (Cuba, New Mexico)

	Cuba	Coyote	Nageezi	Torreon	Total
Indian	0	1%	95%	99%	48%
Spanish	76%	92%	0	0	42%
White	24%	7%	4%	1%	10%

Factors other than ethnicity and language limit the use of the health facilities and one of these is difficulty of access. The percentages of those surveyed not having access to a telephone were 22% in Cuba, 57% in Coyote, 95% in Nageezi, and 99% in Torreon. Between 70 and 85% of the people in the outer areas lived over four miles from the outer area clinics. In Cuba 42% live within one mile and 30% over four miles from the clinic. Lack of paved roads, lack of vehicles, and weather also contribute to the difficulty of reaching the clinics. From 1970 Census data we learn that the houses are crowded, and most are without flush toilets or running water. There is a high percentage of below poverty and borderline poverty families: 85 to 90% of the people in the Indian areas are below the Office of Economic Opportunity poverty level. Cuba is the most affluent area; still 30% of the people are below the poverty line.

The state of New Mexico has insufficient funds for public assistance and approximately 50% of the Indian families receive assistance from the Bureau of Indian Affairs. Not all apply for the benefits due them. In the Checkerboard area, of 287 people over the age of 65, only 187 had registered to receive Medicare.

Geographically the area is dry, has problems of a clean and adequate water supply, road construction and maintenance, and, of course, economic development. What limited employment opportunities there are include copper mining, logging, a saw mill, a natural gas company, ranching, the school system, and highway maintenance. Half a dozen churches include both Catholic and Protestant denominations. Community activities, some of them church related, are an important part of the Cuba community: there are school ball games, dances and rodeos; and there is a Lion's Club and a Cuba Women's Club.

Into the Checkerboard Health Area System and the Presbyterian Medical Service we send medical students, sometimes singly, sometimes with a spouse, but not a pair have been sent yet who are both medical students. The big question is: What can instructors do in such a limited period to alert medical students to cultural and social factors relevant to sickness and health? A first approach to this problem is the impetus behind this article. We have adopted as a text Adair and Deutschle's *The People's Health* (1970) and we have a short selected list of readings and source bibliographies. Lacking was something focal to tie the students' medical interests in to social and cultural factors. Dr. W. K. Ng, an epidemiologist from the University of Singapore, was visiting out department for a year and he and I began work on materials that might stimulate the students' interests and alert them to the cultural context.

When a student goes into another cultural setting to learn as much as he or she can about the social and environmental factors affecting health, one is tempted to say all, everything, is important. And in a large sense, it is true: All is important. Still the time to be spent in another cultural setting is limited and the student must have some signposts, some indicators, as to what are the circumstances and conditions he should look for which are pertinent.

One goal of the course "Blended Clinical Experience and Cultural Study" is to sensitize students to environmental, familial, and social factors as they intersect with disease. It seemed strategic to adopt a disease orientation as a beginning point because disease and pathology are the focal concern of medical students. That is what they spend the most time on; correct diagnosis is what they are proud of; and public health is taught in separate public health schools, not in medical schools. Another observation on medical education is that students are taught to think in terms of "systems" and to make system reviews when they take a medical history. Taking all of these factors into consideration we sought to organize knowledge and present it in the form of a table. This would provide rapid reading and easy reference—features valued by students. For the table, information is organized vertically in terms of infectious diseases, nutritional deficiencies, and diseases by organ systems and "other diseases" including alcoholism and drug addiction. That was one axis, the vertical. Listing disease categories is a good beginning but equally helpful is naming the agent and the mode of transmission. Disease, agent, and mode of transmission became columns one, two, and three in Table 2. We thought of disease, agent, mode of transmission, and environmental factors (natural setting and man-made artifacts such as buildings) as being one division of data: disease and environmental factors which might be balanced by attention to familial and social factors.

It is important to alert the student to look for conditions of sanitation and infection in terms of inter- and intrapersonal relations relevant to infection, and, also, it is necessary to sensitize him to definitions of illness and health and the cultural experience of being ill. The scheme presented in the table is simplified to an extent which necessarily omits distinctions important and perhaps necessary to the anthropologists. The simplification is justified for the audience it is intended for—medical students who will have no opportunity for further anthropological study. The last three columns, then, are factors divided into three categories: (1) environmental, including the natural setting and man-made artifacts; (2) biological and social arrangements in the family; and (3) beliefs and behaviors relating to a state of well-being, illness, and therapy. These are the categories which form the bulk of the knowledge which we put on a table on a horizontal axis.

For an example of the use of the chart, let us consider that many of the diseases which are common among Third World and economically undeveloped populations are preventable. For instance, when there is a preponderance of infectious disease, knowledge of the conditions permitting and perpetuating the incidence of this disease is necessary in order to be successful in an effort to prevent or treat it. Of the infectious diseases, measles, chicken pox, and diphtheria, note that the environmental factors important for all of them concern space, light, ventilation, and density of occupation. Translating these environmental factors into social or cultural ones, we would ask, what is the common type of house. Taking the Navajo as a case in point, we note that they traditionally lived in a hogan, a rounded or eight-sided building with an earthen floor, a smokehole, and a door facing east. Many adaptations of the hogan exist today but the basic structure makes it difficult to maintain the sanitary conditions necessary for the prevention of infectious disease. Today the Navajo have two other house types, a frame structure indistinguishable from millions of others in America, and house-trailers or mobile homes which the Navajo are beginning to buy and use. In using the last, they make a quantum leap to a new life style because they acquire an interior furnished and equipped with modern appliances. The point is that the hygienic measures possible and the level of cleanliness probable differ with different house types. Of course, the water supply and water supply problems are independent of the house, but in a hogan there is no way to introduce and control running water. On the other hand, a trailer comes with a water hookup, a sink, and a tank for heating water, and the

Table 2.

	Disease and Environmental Factors			Familial and Social Factors	
Disease	Agent	Mode of Transmission	Environmental Factors: Natural Setting, Man-Made Artifacts	Biological Factors and Social Arrangements in the Family	Beliefs and Behaviors Relating to State of Well-Being, Illness, and Therapy
I. *Infectious diseases*					
Measles	Virus	Respiratory	House type, size and room arrangements, number of persons per room or house; sleeping arrangements; presence or absence of recreation areas; ventilation.	Family size, type, and composition, age-sex distribution. Economic status. History of previous attacks. Siblings and adults with disease in home. Availability and accessibility of immunization. Immunization rate.	Amount and kind of contact in household, outdoors, at school, religious ceremonies and large gatherings. Attitude toward immunization. Are shots valued? To be avoided? Ideas about the disease. Deliberate exposure? Home remedies. Different treatment for men and women?
Chicken pox	Virus	Respiratory			
Diphtheria	Bacteria	Respiratory			
Tuberculosis	Bacteria	Respiratory			
Typhoid fever	Bacteria	Oral	Is general environment clean and sanitary? Water supply and source clean? What system of refuse disposal? Flies? Excreta disposal adequate? Purification of water? Pipes, electricity.	Same as above	Patterns of water ingestion. Care of cooking utensils and implements. Methods of cooking and serving food. Ideas about feces. Magical use of feces.

Disease	Agent	Mode			
Dysenteries Amoebic Bacillary	Protozoa Bacteria	Oral Oral	Distance between latrines and water supply, storage vessels for water, ladles, how is water drawn? Agencies involved in testing and purifying. Halazone pills? Fuel for boiling?	Same as above except immunization. Other sources of contamination: rotting foods; baby or animal feces. In fruit season, is fruit exposed to dust and flies? Disposal of excreta. Who prepares food for whom? Wife or mother serves and cleans up? Whose task is it to get water?	Food preparation, service, storage and reuse. Hygiene of food handlers. Use of untested or impure water. Ideas about water and sewage. Defecating in designated areas, i.e., bushes, bamboo grove, latrine.
Trachoma	Virus	Contact	Involved are the house and water supply. Overcrowding. What are the bathing facilities? Is the body dried with a towel used by several people? Personal hygiene good? Are dirt and dust raised by wind or excavation?	Family size, type, and composition, age-sex distribution. Economic status. Hygiene of mother, father, child, etc. Blindness in family. Concomitant eye ailments. Availability and accessibility of treatment facilities.	Minor infections are not considered disease or worthy of note. Swimming in polluted rivers, streams, or lakes. Beliefs about eyes, vision, and disturbances to same.
Dermatitis Bacterial Fungal	Bacteria Fungi	Contact Contact	Same as measles. Dirt and dust in the environment. Flies and irritating insects. Personal hygiene, especially nails.	Economic status, nutritional status, education, pattern of play or work in dusty environments. Availability, accessibility and use of simple treatments such as antiseptics.	Sores common and not considered a disease, thought an evitable part of child raising. Belief that it will heal by itself. Beliefs about the etiology of the sore. Indigenous therapy.

Hookworm Ascariasis	Helminth Helminth	Contact Oral	Water supply, system of excreta disposal; adequacy and use of latrines. Areas contaminated by defecation habits. Dense population, communal living, multiple activities under one roof with inevitable contamination of soil.	Children crawl on the floors, bare feet for all age groups, use of human excreta as fertilizer. Alert to possibilities of contamination?	Beliefs about hookworm and ascariasis—its etiology, symptomatology, and therapy.
Syphilis	Spirochetes	Sexual Contact	Water supply, general sex hygiene and care. City, urban differences.	Pre- and extramarital intercourse, several sexual partners, prostitution, mobility of occupation.	Beliefs and rationale for prescriptions and proscriptions about sex.
Gonorrhea	Bacteria	Body	Same as above	Same as above. Connected with alcoholism or drug addiction? Connected with social life outside of the family, or recreation?	Same as above. Attitudes toward family planning and sex education for the young. Beliefs about folk medicine and home remedies.
II. *Nutrition deficiency diseases*					
	Iodine deficiency	Lack of food and nutrients	Hill and mountains with iodine deficiency. Scarcity of food. Soil inadequate for agriculture. Natural resources inadequate for good diet.	Goiter is in the community. What is the distribution among adult, children and old people? Are the incomes adequate? Are there priorities in feeding?	Is goiter recognized as a disease? What are the beliefs about it?

| Malnutrition Protein-calorie deficiency | Nutrient deficiency, poverty and hunger | Soil deficiencies. Inadequate resources for balanced diet. Absence of vitamin C. Absence of balanced diet in some seasons. Inadequate protein source. Natural calamities and disasters. Problems with transportation because of terrain. Lack of a cash crop. | Single unit (family) feeding vs. communal feeding. Daily diet vs. festivity diet. Is protein given in greater quantity to male? What are infants and young children fed? When are they weaned? Is there restriction of food in pregnancy, lactation, menstruation, during or after illness or before for rituals? Are vegetables and legumes consumed disproportionately? Is there induced vomiting? | Beliefs about the origin of different foods, their nature, how they must be treated, prepared, consumed, and disposed of. Are there sacred foods? Starvation foods? Forbidden edibles in the environment, etc. |

whole can be connected easily to a running water supply.

For another example, a patient suffering from gastroenteritis who has reached the hospital system, either as an inpatient or an outpatient, should initiate thought in the physician and/or the nurse about a train of circumstances relevant to gastroenteritis. Without considering these circumstances, it is not possible to give sensible care to the patient, the family and the community. The patient may be one of the many members of her family or community currently infected with disease. She may have drunk from a communal water supply, used shared sanitary facilities, and eaten from a common pot—or, at least, shared food. The physician and nurse should be aware of these factors in order to consider other household members who may be ill and also to suspect other diseases which may be present, either in the patient or her family. Health personnel should ask, why has this particular patient come to the hospital while others have not? Perhaps it is considered unmanly to be sick. Perhaps women are considered "by nature" to be weak and sickly. Therefore, it is appropriate that they go to a clinic.

The diversity and intensity of symptoms from a particular disease necessary to motivate a person to seek medical care differ. The significant others who influence a person to stay home, or try home remedies or to seek help in the hospital need to be investigated and understood in local cultural terms. It is helpful to know the attitudes of peers, nuclear family, and more distant relatives before we can intuit who may not be in the clinic but who may be ill and who ought to be in the clinic. It is helpful to know who in the family or kin group is likely to be giving advice, home treatments, or urging the sufferer to go to the clinic. Finally, the patient's values, level of education, and store of information are other important factors both in determining his health status and influencing him when he seeks medical care. Of course, with the nutritional diseases, extensive inquiry into diet, food choice, food preparation, storage, distribution, and consumption are rewarding avenues of inquiry.

In Table 2, which covers infectious and nutritional diseases, it was possible to relate the disease, the agent, and the mode of transmission to environmental, familial, and social factors, but for disease by organ systems the agent is not singular and the modes of transmission are complex. Therefore, we continue with a simplified chart, omitting the agent and the mode of transmission.

With rare but notable exceptions, modern medicine does not take into account the patient's conception of the world; world view takes an added significance when dealing with illness among ethnic or cultural minorities. Traditionally, little attention is paid to how patients of differing cultural origin perceive their symptoms, what they believe about the etiology of illness, and how they define the nature of sickness and appropriate treatment or therapy. In Western medicine a series of symptoms are grouped together and called a certain disease. There is very little chance that the same grouping of symptoms will have a similar meaning to the members of another culture, and more significantly, that they can and will accept any explanation of their illness which is too far removed from their culturally taught understanding. Physicians too often dismiss perceptions and beliefs as "ignorance" or superstition. By failing to learn what are the culturally conditioned beliefs and practices of any patient, they may misinterpret what they are told about symptoms and also fail to help patients by prescribing treatment slated to be disregarded because it is misunderstood, incongruous, meaningless, or contraindicated in the patient's world view.

To add to the difficulties of a Western physician practicing in a non-Western setting, what is therapeutically relevant is culturally determined. What is therapeutically relevant in Western medicine is a theory based on the existence of bacteria and viruses and the proper functioning of body systems. However, for the Navajo medicine man, illness is caused by an infraction of the rules of human conduct. For example, washing of hands before eating is a necessary part of hygiene in Western culture. It is irrelevant to the Navajo. Moral conduct is not important to the Western physician; it is very important to the Navajo medicine man.

A physician in Western culture begins by taking a medical history, by asking questions. This basic approach puts him in an unfavorable light in the eyes of many Navajo, whose two classes of therapeutic practitioners are a hand trembler diagnostician; and the medicine man or singer who is the therapist. When the Navajo go to the hand trembler, he studies the patient and his situation and awaits an intuition as to what the problem is. He does not ask questions. The Indian, on the basis of lifelong experience in his own culture, expects a diagnostician to know what is wrong with him by looking at him and the M.D. appears as less than able if he asks questions, as indeed, he must and does.

If Western healers have had the handicap of working through a screen of cultural distortion, they also have had the benefit of advanced knowledge and sophisticated technology in diagnosis and therapy in their own culture; they have some special abilities and these become obvious to members of other cultures despite disparate expectations of behavior and performance. That the White man brought his own diseases (tuberculosis, for example) to indigenous cultures is a truism in anthropology but it is also documented that Indians note that the M.D. is successful in curing tuberculosis while the medicine man is not. While Navajo singers do not agree with physicians on the cause for tuberculosis, they do know that they (the singers) cannot cure tuberculosis and they send tuberculosis patients to the White medicine man. The referral system, whereby practitioners of "free enterprise," Western style medicine refer a patient to another physician when his ailment is outside of their province, is unofficially at work.

Very frequently what is practical and sensible to Western medicine brings unexpected problems and unacceptable solutions to the Navajo. For instance, see Table 3 and the skeletal system entry, and then consider the problem of congenital hip. Congenital hip disease may be present at birth and is characterized by an acetabulum that does not securely grasp the head of the femur. Consequently, the femur may move completely out of the socket, or it may be seated insecurely within the socket and predispose the joint to later excessive trauma. Sometime between the ages of 30 and 50, the man so afflicted may develop a painful, refractory, traumatic osteoarthritis in the joint. He begins to walk with a limp and

Table 3

Disease	Disease and Environmental Factors — Environmental Factors: Natural Setting and Man-Made Artifacts	Familial and Social Factors — Biological Factors and Social Arrangements in the Family	Beliefs and Behaviors Relating to State of Well-Being, Illness and Therapy
III. *Disease by Organ System*			
G.I. System	Housing, water, food animals, and existing disposal system.	Food sharing. Portions and content for father, mother, children, and baby. Time and place for eating.	Patterns of food procurement, preparation, distribution and consumption. Daily, ceremonial, and therapeutic diet. Theory of digestion and home remedies for digestive ailments.
Cardiovascular System Renal System	Quality of water and use of water supply. Presence and excessive use of salt in the environment. Stress to survive such as in hilly terrain.	Age. Sex. Previous infection. Hereditary or congenital. Cholesterol intake. Amount of physical exertion. Worry and anxiety. Amount of fat in the diet.	Beliefs about salt or fat intake, work, and exertion in sport. Salt as an aphrodisiac. Home remedies.
Genital System Trichomonas Moniliasis	No or poor facilities for washing or douching. Presence or absence of family planning, diagnostic, and treatment facilities.	Contraceptive use. Age at menarche and menopause. Menstruating women isolated, use Kotex, or what? Use sweat bath? Role of mother and grandmother regarding sex relations.	Attitudes: toward menarche, menstruation, menopause. Are women's ills no concern of men? Are women shy, isolated, uninformed? Ideas about infertility and sterility.
Skeletal System Congenital hip Accidents	The physical environment connected with daily life. Uneven terrain, cliffs, crevasses, rivers, bogs, accident traps, unsafe houses, and other structures. Wild animals. Stock on the road. Snakes.	Males may run, climb, rappel, gallop horses, drive fast, or hunt wild animals. Women work in hazardous conditions. Lack of knowledge of hazards and rules of safety. Care of injured, crippled, or paraplegic.	Stoic attitude. Ideas about bravery, courage, success and manhood. Bronco riders. Fast car drivers. Pain thought of as penance, necessary to receive grace or to merit attention from guardian spirit. Safety not an ideal.

IV. *Others* Alcoholism	Rural or urban. Presence of substance to make alcohol from native materials. Ease of purchasing commercial alcohol.	Anxiety, worry, old age, sexual frustration, poor economic status. Manufacture of native alcohol. Pattern of use: sporadic, continuous, or excessive. Do children and women drink? Ceremonial drinking?	Drunkenness believed manly, drunken behavior talked about admiringly. Drunken euphoria valued.
Drug Addiction	Presence of tobacco, peyote, marijuana, aspirin, tranquilizers, etc. Facilities for procurement or purchase.	Anxiety, worry. Age and sex differences in use. Presence of technology to manufacture drugs. Social occasions for drug use.	Behavior under drugs valued for diagnostic, prophetic purposes, or achieving a high. Drugs used in religious ceremonies or in native curing.
Psychological Stresses Nervous Suicide	Sparsity and scarcity of necessities of life. Harsh environment. Minimal resources. Terrain difficult to impossible to farm.	Family is nonsupportive and source of conflict and strain. Absence or shortage of necessities increases discontent, disharmony, frustration, and conflict with neighbors and others.	Reasons for suicide, buffers against suicide, power base of community, pressures to suicide like in Japan.

eventually has severe arthritis for which nothing can be done. Good preventive medicine depends on early diagnosis and treatment (Adair and Deuschle 1970:131-35) and this used to mean surgery which resulted in a strong but nonflexible hip joint. Many of the families on the reservation still live much of their life without modern furniture. Having no tables or chairs, the families sit on the floor to take their meals and for their informal socializing. When a child has had surgery to correct a congenital hip, he is stiff-legged as a result and it is no longer possible for him to sit cross-legged or to squat on the floor. He cannot ride horseback. He has become a trouble to everyone in the family as well as to himself. It is no wonder that many patients do not accept surgery as a treatment or a solution. They are not disturbed, while still young, by the possibilities of the trouble they will have with a congenital hip disease when they are forty, anymore than our young smokers will think about cancer, emphysema, or other disorders related to smoking, which will not become noticeable for two, three, or four decades. Fortunately, in regard to congenital hip disease, surgery has now been developed which does not result in an inflexible leg.

With the Tables and other examples such as have been given in the text, we hope to sensitize the student to social factors relevant to sickness and health. We try to teach that, at every level of sickness and treatment behavior, culture interposes a screen of perception and interpretation. We have taken examples from the Navajo experience of how differing interpretations of the same phenomenon can affect the course of sickness and treatment. Perhaps the examples given have been sufficient to give an indication of the complexity and variability of cultural factors to which the student needs to be sensitized.

Now as to some of the limitations in tabulating knowledge: all the factors in the Tables are not intended to, and, indeed, cannot be exhaustive. It is not possible with such a reductionist technique to include many details. Also the entries in the Tables are not determinative. We have not arbitrarily listed conditions which inevitably lead to disease; rather we sought to indicate possible connections. We expect that the student will add to the list of relevant factors as his observations prolong and experience accumulates. Indeed as he continues his residence with and deepens his understanding of a different ethnic group, we expect that he may add to the knowledge of the cultural aspects of sickness and health in the particular community in which he works and early evidence indicates that this is so. Students return to the medical school elated and excited by what they have experienced and learned. Several have stayed on at the clinic beyond their coursework and some have announced their intention to work among minorities when their training is completed.

Pertti J. Pelto
Gretel H. Pelto

Medicine, anthropology, community: an overview

Much discussion and debate in medical anthropology focuses on the relation-ships of anthropology to medicine and to the community. The definition of an appropriate relationship varies depending on whether a person is primarily identi-fied with medicine, with a community, or with anthropology (1).

Medicine as Conceptual Field and as Social System

There are several different ways in which medical anthropologists relate to the medical establishment or modern medicine (2). For some researchers the impor-tant idea is scientific medicine as a cultural system. For example, Fábrega and associates have been concerned with "linking native conceptual traditions about illness with Western scientific medical knowledge" (Fábrega, 1974:7). In a similar vein the focus of discussion in recent papers on the "hot-cold syndrome" has been on the cultural assumptions involved in "contact between modern and traditional forms of medicine" (Logan, 1973:392).

The concepts of modern medicine are generally embodied in the medical practitioners, often identified in anthropological research literature as physicians or medical personnel. For example, George Foster, in discussing aspects of medical anthropology in applied contexts, refers to situations in which "medical personnel asked the anthropologists: what can you tell us about cultural and social factors that will help explain the attitude of people toward health centers?" (Foster 1969: 25). Although perhaps too many discussions have focused on the physician as the central figure representing medical personnel, quite a number of studies have also referred to public health nurses, health aides, and others involved in health care.

The physician in medical anthropological discussions often turns out to be the psychiatrist. As a matter of fact, the major developments linking medicine and social/cultural anthropology, especially from about 1920 to the 1950s and 1960s, have reflected the affinities between psychiatry and anthropology. These affinities early in the period found expression in culture-and-personality studies, which gained new momentum with the rise of the community mental health movement of the early 1960s (Hochstrasser and Tapp 1970).

It is interesting to note that during the late 1940s and throughout the 1950s anthropologists increasingly developed ties with schools of public health. For ex-ample, several of the applied projects in medical anthropology to which Foster refers were carried out in cooperation with public health people who were working in community-based sanitation and disease-control programs (cf. Foster 1969). Similarly, Margaret Clark's study, "Health in the Mexican-American Culture" (1959), makes a number of references to public health nurses, medical social workers, and other community-oriented personnel in California public health departments.

Ties and collaboration between anthropologists and public health professionals came about to a considerable extent because of a common focus on communities (including those in developing countries). Public health people frequently encountered resistance to sanitation measures, vaccinations, prenatal clinics, and other programs, and anthropologists were in a position to explain the "cultural barriers" to acceptance of modern health care.

However, anthropologists became aware of the limitations inherent in collaboration with public health personnel. As Hochstrasser and Tapp have pointed out, "public health has evolved basically into a governmental and largely preventive form of social medicine. . . . Most of its major centers of research, teaching and practice are now stationed outside or in a satellite relationship to the mainstream of American medicine." In effect, Hochstrasser and Tapp argue, many anthropologists have been allied with a segment of the medical system that is "a very small, usually marginal and often ineffectual activity in most medical schools throughout the country" (1970:255).

We now come to a central problem in the relationship of anthropology to the medical system. Anthropologists have been too slow in recognizing and in analyzing the complexities, especially the different distributions of power, in the many sectors of the medical establishment. Too often anthropologists have referred to doctors or medical personnel as if they were a monolithic bloc in terms of power and privilege, with homogeneous views and common assumptions about health care.

Rather significant changes are taking place in the medical system, especially within the United States, as federal legislative enactments move us slowly toward some system of national health insurance. New medical schools have been established which have proposed new definitions of the relationship between medical people and social and/or behavioral scientists. Hospitals are still the central bastions of health care and medical training, but current trends in health care place greater emphasis on ambulatory care, home care, and facilities and services outside the hospital.

Anthropologists have paid too little attention to the drift of these developments and to the divergences of behavior, attitudes, and characteristics of various types of medical personnel. Also, they have not been sufficiently aware of the importance of certain trends in medical education. During the late 1960s medical students took matters into their own hands and pushed some medical activities into economically deprived communities. Such student activism has subsided somewhat, but behind that movement is another, less heralded development. In a growing number of medical schools departments of community medicine have been established that attempt to bridge the gaps between clinical medicine and health-care needs in communities.

With the rapid expansion of community medicine, beginning in the 1960s, a significant new dimension has been added to the medical system—one that will hopefully develop new links between medical schools, health practitioners in communities, and social and/or behavioral scientists. A strong and growing movement within medical schools seeks to push the focus of attention into communities through research on health-care systems and placement of medical students in community-based training experiences.

We suggest that anthropologists pay much more attention than they have to the currents of change within medicine and try to establish lines of collaboration with people in community medicine in order to participate in new developments in medical student training as well as to help build research and action programs in community-oriented health-care systems. This is not to say that anthropology's older relationships with psychiatry and public health are unproductive. Far from it. Without going into detail, we should note that the public health sector, itself, has shifted away from a long-time concentration on infectious disease to tackle the very difficult areas of chronic illness, where sociocultural factors loom large as major contributors. We are emphasizing community medicine here because it is one of the significant new developments and because medical personnel, like anthropologists, are now focusing on the community as the major arena of activity.

The Community

The community has been the favorite haunt of anthropologists ever since Robert Redfield developed the community study, beginning with his memorable research in Tepoztlán (1930). The focus in this type of research is on finite communities, different from other communities in the vicinity. They share similar cultural backgrounds but create distinct cultural styles in a particular microecological context.

Anthropological research in communities is characterized by participant observation, informal interviewing, and other flexible and ofttimes nearly undefinable data-gathering techniques. As a result anthropologists have been rather closely attuned to the health needs and aspirations of the people they study and have come to identify with them and to accept indigenous health beliefs and practices as efficacious and commendable. This favorable attitude toward indigenous health and curing practices has, in our view, made a significant contribution to the efforts of anthropologists in coordinating traditional and modern health systems.

On the other hand, some anthropologists working in applied health programs appear to have taken the view that modern medicine is much more efficacious than indigenous practices and that every effort should be made to spread Western medicine to all peoples. As anthropologists came to be involved in various forms of community activism in the late 1960s and early 1970s, one goal was to make modern health care facilities more accessible to those people on the economic and social margins of society. Anthropologists were caught somewhat in a bind, for part of the radical attack on anthropology during this period took the view that the focus on the beliefs and aspirations of minority enclaves in the United States avoided inaccessibility of the benefits of modern health facilities to these groups. On the other hand, community mental health outposts, particularly those based on the established medical models, were criticized for participating in the alienation of people from their folk medical practices and thus indirectly reducing medical alternatives (Ayala 1975).

Although the locus of anthropological research and effort has most often been the community, its primary conceptual focus has been on culture, usually defined as the concepts, beliefs, and norms characteristic of particular, identifiable ethnic groups. Intracommunity diversity of culture has been salient only when a particular community contained more than one identifiable ethnic group—for example, in "mixed" communities with black, Chicano, Puerto Rican, and European ethnic groups. The cultural patterns within each of these ethnic groups has been assumed to be definable in relatively homogeneous or uniform terms.

However, the uniformist or homogeneic treatment of cultural norms and beliefs, especially in relation to matters of health and disease, has come under increasing scrutiny and challenge (3). The sociologists Hessler and New have recently published an analysis of intraethnic diversity among the Chinese in Boston (see Chapter VI-8). Logan and Morrill (1977) have examined intracommunity diversity with respect to the "hot-cold syndrome" among Guatemalans. Woods and Graves (1973) have demonstrated significant differences in health-seeking behaviors in another Mayan group in Guatemala, and Schensul (1973) has commented on variations in behavior and attitudes among Chicanos in a Chicago community. Furthermore, the work by Woods and Graves offers some statistical evidence that cultural beliefs are not necessarily the major factors influencing people's health behavior. A paper by DeWalt and Pelto (in press) makes the same point with regard to food consumption patterns in a Mexican community. In both the Woods-Graves and DeWalt-Pelto studies, economic factors appear to be more significant than ideational ones in influencing relevant behavior.

From the perspective of some of this newer research, the community cannot be simply described in terms of cultural norms or a social system. People in communities are as complex in their health beliefs and behaviors as are the people in that amorphous system we refer to as the medical establishment.

Anthropology

Anthropologists have usually been identified with the community in need of health care. That is presumably why, in the case described by Foster, the medical personnel asked the anthropologists about the cultural and social factors affecting a people's reception of health programs. Thus, in many instances of applied work, the role of the anthropologist has been that of the culture broker (Weidman 1974; and others). Anthropologists can deal with the discrepancies and misunderstandings between the community cultures and the cultural system of the medical establishment that can lead to problems of communication. Anthropologists can negotiate understandings and behavioral interactions between medical people and community people. This model of the anthropologist's role often assumes that the problems of getting effective health care to the people arise from misunderstandings. Often it is necessary for health workers to learn to use the people's health concepts in congruence with their own concepts of modern medicine.

There is logic in the culture broker model, and it has a great deal of appeal because it makes anthropologists communications experts in a complex process. Unfortunately, in practice there are often some serious problems with the model. Both anthropologists and medical people have frequently been too simplistic in accepting a uniformist view of health-care behavior that stresses cultural norms. Anthropologists have led medical people to expect clear-cut answers to questions about the community. Yet the broker model can be a useful one, especially when it is based on more complex views of communities and medical systems.

However, there is another dimension to consider. The culture-broker model usually suggests some sort of equality of power between parties, but anthropologists are painfully aware of the differences in power, for people in the community often lack political and economic leverage compared to people in the health-care system and in government agencies. Consequently, some anthropologists have tried to identify ways to inject political power into their applied activities. Research on behalf of organized consumer groups may be one way in which some political and economic power can be mobilized (Marchione 1975).

Conclusion

As people in communities and medical systems go through the process of redefining their relationships to each other, anthropologists must also develop new models for their relationships to both groups. Certainly, the directions of change are not at all clear, and there are many competing views about what relationships between health-care providers and so-called consumers should be. Inevitably, anthropologists find themselves in disagreement as well about what part they and other social scientists can play in helping to forge more satisfying relationships between the medical establishment and consumer communities. Some anthropologists argue that better methdological and theoretical tools are needed if they are to play a constructive role. An approach to health-care issues focused on uniformist, cultural beliefs and an anecdotal, nonquantified style of research is inadequate for the complexities of all contemporary situations, either within the United States or in other parts of the world. One place for anthropologists to begin is to recognize that the credibility of their data depends, in part, on focusing on the range of variation within both communities and medical systems and on identifying interrelationships among them. From there they must find ways of making their data and insights useful for both the rapidly changing medical system and the communities of people seeking more effective health care.

Notes

1. We will be concerned mainly with cultural and/or social anthropology in this paper, at the same time recognizing that there are areas of physical anthropology that relate closely to medical concerns. However, the work of medically oriented physical anthropologists has not focused on community health systems as often as have the activities of cultural and/or social anthropologists. Any full treatment of medical anthropology must discuss the relationship of both physical and cultural anthropology to medical establishments and to the communities served by health-care systems.
2. The medical establishment or medical system refers to the social system(s) of modern or Western medicine, including hospitals and their personnel, health-center organizations, physicians, nurses, dentists, and other members of health-care teams, as well as to the medical and dental schools in which professionals are trained. It also includes various medical societies and other professional organizations.
3. Uniformist cultural theory refers to the tendency among anthropologists and others to describe a culture in terms of norms and standards thought to be essentially homogeneous or uniform for most well-socialized individuals of the given community or ethnic group.

Selected Source Materials Relative to Medical Anthropology

There is a vast and rapidly expanding literature on the interrelationships between culture and health. To assist students and professionals in their search for pertinent information, we have selected various review articles, abstracts and indexes, journals, bibliographies, and films that we feel are important both to research and teaching in medical anthropology.

Review Articles in Medical Anthropology

The reader who wishes to gain a synoptic view of the history of research in medical anthropology should be aware of the following works:

Caudill, W. 1953 Applied Anthropology in Medicine. *In* Anthropology Today. A. L. Kroeber, ed. Pp. 771-806. Chicago: University of Chicago Press.
Colson, A. C., and K. E. Selby 1974 Medical Anthropology. *In* Annual Review of Anthropology. B. J. Siegel, ed. Pp. 245-262. Palo Alto: Annual Reviews.
Fábrega, H., Jr. 1972 Medical Anthropology. *In* Biennial Review of Anthropology, 1971. B. J. Siegel, ed. Pp. 167-229. Stanford: Stanford University Press.
Lieban, R. W. 1973 Medical Anthropology. *In* Handbook of Social and Cultural Anthropology. J. J. Honigmann, ed. Pp. 1031-1072. Chicago: Rand McNally.
Polgar, S. 1962 Health and Human Behavior: Areas of Interest Common to the Social and Medical Sciences. Current Anthropology 3:159-205.
Scotch, N. 1963 Medical Anthropology. *In* Biennial Review of Anthropology, 1963. B. J. Siegel, ed. Pp. 30-68. Stanford: Stanford University Press.

Abstracts and Indexes

The sources listed below should be housed in most university libraries, and the reader is encouraged to consult with a reference librarian concerning the use of these and other related publications.

Abstracts in Anthropology
Biological Abstracts
Nutrition Abstracts and Reviews
Psychological Abstracts
Sociological Abstracts
Anthropological Index to Current Periodicals in the
    Library of the Royal Anthropological Institute
Author-Subject Indexes of the Peabody Museum of
    Archaeology and Ethnology, Harvard University
Social Science and Humanities Index
Social Science Citation Index
Excerpta Medica
Accumulated Index Medicus
National Library of Medicine Catalog
Medical Subject Headings
International Nursing Index

Journals

The following list of serial publications is, by necessity, highly selective, for there are literally thousands of scientific journals that regularly contain published reports of great interest to medical anthropologists. The purpose of this section is to inform the reader of some of the major sources that should be consulted frequently in pursuing research developments in medical anthropology and in allied fields. Many of the journals cited below have subject and author indexes.

American Anthropologist
American Ethnologist
American Journal of Physical Anthropology
American Journal of Sociology
American Psychologist
American Sociological Review
Anthropological Quarterly
Anthropos
British Journal of Preventive and Social Medicine
Current Anthropology
Ecology of Food and Nutrition
Economic Botany
Ethnology
Ethnomedizin
Human Organization
Journal of Anthropological Research
Journal of Chronic Diseases
Journal of Health and Human Behavior
Journal of Medical Education

Journal of Nursing Research
Medical Anthropology: Cross-Cultural Studies in Health and Illness
Medical Anthropology Newsletter
Psychiatry
Psychosomatic Medicine
Quarterly Journal of Studies on Alcohol
Social Forces
Social Science and Medicine
Urban Anthropology

Bibliographies

In addition to the many references contained in the present volume, the concerned reader may wish to consult the following bibliographies for additional research materials.

American Public Health Association (Variable dates) Current Bibliography of Epidemiology. New York: American Public Health Association.
Brown, R. E. 1972 Community Action Programs: An Annotated Bibliography. Monticello, Ill.: Council of Planning Librarians.
Burg, N. G. 1972 Physician's Assistants: A Health Manpower Planning Bibliography. Monticello, Ill.: Council of Planning Librarians.
Conklin, H. C. 1972 Folk Classification: A Topically Arranged Bibliography of Contemporary and Background References through 1971. New Haven: Department of Anthropology, Yale University.
Driver, E. D. 1972 The Sociology and Anthropology of Mental Illness: A Reference Guide. Amherst: University of Massachusetts.
Dunaye, T. M. 1971 Health Planning: A Bibliography of Basic Readings. Monticello, Ill.: Council of Planning Librarians.
Dyck, R. G. 1973 Comprehensive Health Planning Bibliography. Monticello, Ill.: Council of Planning Librarians.
Guerra, F. 1950 Bibliografia de la Materia Medica Mexicana. Mexico City: La Prensa Medica Mexicana.
Harrison, I. E., and S. Cosminsky 1976 Traditional Medicine: Implications for Ethnomedicine, Ethnopharmacology, Maternal and Child Health, Mental Health, and Public Health—An Annotated Bibliography of Africa, Latin America, and the Caribbean. New York: Garland Publishing.
Lee, D. H. 1972 A Selected, Annotated Bibliography on Aging and the Aged: 1968-1972. Monticello, Ill.: Council of Planning Librarians.
Litman, T. J. 1973 The Sociology of Medicine and Health Care: The First Fifty Years. Berkeley: Glendessary Press.
Litman, T. J. 1976 The Sociology of Medicine and Health Care: A Research Bibliography. San Francisco: Reference Book Department, Boyd and Fraser Publishing Company.
Logan, M. H. 1975 Selected References on the Hot-Cold Theory of Disease. Medical Anthropology Newsletter 6 (2):8-14.
Marshall, J. F., S. Morris, and S. Polgar 1972 Culture and Natality: A Preliminary Classified Bibliography. Current Anthropology 13:268-278.
Medical Readings, Inc. (Variable dates) Encyclopedia of Health Sciences, 12 vols. Stanford: Medical Readings.
National Institute of Public Health (Variable dates) Publications of The National Institute of

Public Health. Rockville, Maryland.

National Library of Medicine (Variable dates) Bibliography of Medical Reviews. Bethesda: National Library of Medicine.

National Library of Medicine (Variable dates) Selected References on Environmental Quality as It Relates to Health. Bethesda: National Library of Medicine.

National Library of Medicine (Variable dates) Monthly Bibliography of Medical Reviews. Bethesda: National Library of Medicine.

New, P. K. 1975 Chinese Medicine Bibliography. Medical Anthropology Newsletter 6 (3):13-14.

Pearsall, M. 1963 Medical Behavioral Science: A Selected Bibliography of Cultural Anthropology, Social Psychology, and Sociology in Medicine. Lexington: University of Kentucky Press.

Sargent, C., and A. J. Rubel 1976 Selected Literature on the Utilization of Indigenous Midwives in Health Delivery Systems. Medical Anthropology Newsletter 7 (2):13-16.

Seijas, H. 1967 A Preliminary Bibliography on Columbian Ethnomedicine. Etnoiatria 1 (2): 68-69.

Simmons, O. G. 1963 Social Research in Medicine and Health: A Bibliography. *In* Handbook of Medical Sociology. H. E. Freeman, S. Levine, and L. G. Reeder, eds. Pp. 493-581. Englewood Cliffs, N. J.: Prentice-Hall.

Simmons, O. G., and E. Berkanovic 1972 Social Research in Health and Medicine: A Bibliography. *In* Handbook of Medical Sociology. H. E. Freeman, S. Levine, L. G. Reeder, eds. Pp. 523-584. Englewood Cliffs, N. J.: Prentice-Hall.

Strauss, M., and L. Aronoff 1969 Bibliography of Periodicals for Health Planning. Monticello, Ill.: Council of Planning Librarians.

U. S. Department of Health, Education, and Welfare (Variable dates) N.I.H. Publications List. Washington, D.C.: U. S. Department of Health, Education, and Welfare.

U. S. Department of Health, Education, and Welfare (Variable dates) Catalog Publications. Washington, D. C.: U. S. Department of Health, Education, and Welfare.

Wilson, C. S. 1973 Food Habits: A Selected Annotated Bibliography. Journal of Nutrition Education 5 (1):41-72.

Films

The catalogs listed below provide useful information for professors who wish to use films for teaching medical anthropology. Of the five catalogs referenced here, we have decided to republish the annotated list of films on medical anthropology compiled by Baldwin, Dutt, and Teleki. Their catalog and film rental-purchase information can be obtained on request from:

Audio-Visual Services
17 Willard Building
The Pennsylvania State University
University Park, PA 16802
Telephone: (814) 865-6315

Important Film Catalogs

Baldwin, L., K. Dutt, and G. Teleki 1976 The Visualization of Anthropology. University Park: Pennsylvania State University.

Brewer, Ruth 1975 An Annotated List of Films on Aging and the Aged. Eugene: Librarian, Oregon Center for Gerontology, University of Oregon.

Hunt, G., and A. S. Mondell 1972 Social Factors in Health Care: An Evaluation of Selected Films and Videotapes. Baltimore: Department of Psychiatry, School of Medicine, University of Maryland.

Mason, E. A. 1973 Films on Death and Dying. New York: Educational Film Library Association.

National Library of Medicine 1970 Film Reference Guide for Medical and Allied Sciences. Bethesda: National Library of Medicine.

National Medical Audiovisual Center 1968 Motion Picture and Videotape Catalog. Atlanta: National Medical Audiovisual Center.

World Health Organization 1973 Films on Health for Public Education, Washington, D.C.: World Health Organization.

Selected Films on Medical Anthropology from Baldwin, Dutt, and Teleki (1976)

Acupuncture Anesthesia: Parts 1 and 2 (NBC) 1973 46 min. color 50304 $16.50 rental.
    Documentary filmed by U.N. delegation to the People's Republic of China. Eight operations performed in Peking hospitals using acupuncture as anesthetic. Development of electrical acupuncture.

Barefoot Doctors of Rural China (LI) 1974 50 min. color 50343 $28.00
    Unique and intimate view of life in the Chinese countryside, People's Republic of China. Examines China's efforts to provide adequate health care services for its agrarian population. Training and activities of peasant paramedics. (Diane Li.)

Big Problems for Little People (PSUPCR) 1975 23 min. color PCR-2274K rental $13.50 sale $276.00
    Relationship between poverty, malnutrition, environment, and sociocultural factors as they relate to human growth and development. Documents cases in the Phillippines, a rural tropical area. (G. and H. Guthrie.)

Care of the Sick Among Primitive Groups (MVNE) 1970 30 min. 31778 $11.00
    Basic needs of man; major problems of community health and solutions to health problems, including folk medicine, the nurse, occult practices, the shaman, and approved social customs. Lecture by Josephine A. Dolan, R.N.

Care of the Sick in Ancient Civilizations (Greek, Roman, Hindu, Chinese) (MVNE) 1970 30 min. 31777 $11.00
    Mythological and religious influences; prominent individuals; medical treatments. Lecture by Josephine A. Dolan, R.N.

Care of the Sick in Ancient Civilizations (Sumerian, Egyptian, Hebrew, Aztec) (MVNE) 1970 30 min. 31776 $11.00
    Historical indications of disease and medical care as seen in Egyptian wall paintings, Biblical accounts. Contributions of religion; influence of astronomy and astrology on medicine; hypnotherapy and healing. Early medical education. Lecture by Josephine Dolan, R.N.

Catfish: Man of the Woods (APPAL) 1974 26 min. color 32108 $14.00
    Portrait of Clarence Gray, a fifth generation herb doctor in the Appalachia mountains. He is outspoken about his philosophy of life and comments on sex, religion, and the way of the woods.

A Curing Ceremony (DER) 1966 8 min. 10857 $6.00
    In a !Kung Bushmen band, Sha//gai, a young woman about to have a miscarriage, is cured by /Ti!kay, who enters a mild trance without the stimulus of dancing. (J. Marshall.) From the !Kung and /Gwi Bushman series.

Death (FLMLIB) 1968 43 min. 40135 $14.00
   Follows terminal cancer patient, who faces death without deception, through his last days. Psychology of dying discussed by doctors. Produced by NET.

The Faces of "A" Wing: Parts 1 and 2 (PSUAVS) 1974 58 min. 60172 rental $14.00 sale $290.00
   An observational documentary, using minimal narration, designed to allow the viewer to experience life in one nursing home through a series of vignettes that focus on different people—staff, residents, and relatives—and how they relate on a personal and on an institutional level. The program introduces individuals ranging in age from eighteen to ninety-seven, each having his own perspective on life in a nursing home.

Geel: a Changing Tradition (UCEMC) 1967 40 min. color 40225 rental $19.50 sale $455.00
   Past, present and future of Geel, a Belgian town which is the oldest center of home care of the mentally ill in Europe. Attitudes of townspeople, caretakers of mental patients and young people.

Himalayan Shaman of Northern Nepal (IFB) 1968 15 min. color 21681 rental $10.00 sale $175.00
   Presents paraphernalia and methods of a paid shaman of the Inner Asian shamanic tradition. Shaman aids a client family by controlling spirits, foretelling the future, and sucking out intrusive objects. Shows self-induced possession trance. Demonstrates role of shaman in entertainment, curing, and intercaste communication.

Himalayan Shaman of Southern Nepal (IFB) 1968 14 min. color 21682 rental $10.00 sale $175.00
   Training, techniques, income, and practice of a curer in the southern portion of the Nepalese Himalayan section where the people are predominantly Hindu. He incorporates ideas of Western medicine and practices learned in travels in Tibet, India, and Nepal: taking the pulse and saying a spell, giving a potion and spirit contact during an auto-suggested trance together with cure by live animal sacrifice.

Hungry Angels (AIM) 1960 20 min. color 20021 $12.00
   True-to-life story of three Guatemalan children through the first years of their lives shows the dramatic fight for life when malnutrition results from ignorance and superstition. Dramatic music accompanies strongly moralistic tone of the film. No mention of overpopulation.

Japan: Answer in the Orient (IU) 1967 30 min. 31042 $11.00
   Interest of large Japanese industries in abortion and fertility control measures, and the trend among the Japanese to marry at a later age, have helped the Japanese people to balance births with deaths. Produced by NET.

Kwashiorkor (MRC) 1968 32 min. color 31448 $14.00
   Clinical and laboratory information from the Infant Malnutrition Clinic in Uganda. Both chronic and acute cases of kwashiorkor are shown and contrasted to marasmus. Studies food patterns, preparation, and serving habits in relation to development of disease. Value of paramedical personnel in disease control and eradication stressed. Narrated in English with Buganda musical background.

Ma'Bugi: Trance of the Toraja (UCEMC) 1974 19 min. 21800 $13.00
   Trance ritual and spirit possession in the Toraja highlands of Sulawesi, Indonesia.

Psychology and motivation for trance and such activities as the ascent of a ladder of knives and the supernatural curing of the chronically ill.

Magical Death (PSUPCR) 1973 28 min. color PCR-2248K rental $8.50 sale $125.00

Role of prominent political leader and renowned shaman, Dedeheiwä, among the Yanomamö Indians of the Orinoco River in South America. Film documents two-day ceremony during which Dedeheiwä and villagers launch magical attack on souls of children in distant village. Use of hallucinogenic snuff by shamans. Useful for courses relating religious activities to social and political organization. (N. A. Chagnon.) From the Yanomamö series.

Nature's Way (APPAL) 1974 22 min. color 21755 $12.50

Mountaineers care for their own ailments with help of herbs, home remedies, and Indian folklore. Several people explain their cures and remedies, and a midwife assists in the delivery of twins. Appalachia.

N/um Chai: The Ceremonial Dance of the !Kung Bushmen (DER) 1966 20 min. 21594 $8.50

The medicine dance is one activity in !Kung life that draws people together in groups that are not shaped by family, band, or close friendship. The dance is essentially a curing ritual but is not solemn; the !Kung take pleasure in music and dancing, and enjoy the sociability of the occasion. (John Marshall.) From the !Kung and /Gwi Bushmen series.

Nursing in Society series:

Care of the Sick Among Primitive Groups
Care of the Sick in Ancient Civilizations (Greek, Roman, Hindu, Chinese)
Care of the Sick in Ancient Civilizations (Sumerian, Egyptian, Hebrew, Aztec)
For descriptions see individual titles.

Paracelsus (IU) 1966 30 min. 31049 $11.00

Drawings illustrate medical practices of the late Middle Ages and quotations from the works of this legendary iconoclastic physician reveal his life and principles. Produced by NET.

Pomo Shaman (UCEMC) 1964 22 min. 21780 $9.50

Edited version of *Sucking Doctor.* Pomo Indian Shaman participates in healing ceremony. Shaman enters trance, locates and cures patient by aid of a spiritual instrument in throat used to suck out illness.

Question of Immunity (HAASF) 1973 13 min. color 21726 $10.00

Body mechanisms which identify and reject foreign intruders depicted through photomicrography and animation. White blood cells crawl through blood vessel walls to seek out and engulf disease organisms; antibodies are formed; vaccines prepare the body in advance against potential danger; activation of lymph system. Immunity response as obstacle to successful foreign tissue grafts and organ transplants. Produced by the National Film Board of Canada.

The Right to Die (CCMFI) 1974 51 min. color 60165 $24.00

Interviews with dying patients, ranging from a young boy to the elderly. Raises questions and confronts problem of the best means for families, medical personnel, clergy, and law to deal with dying.

Separations and Reunions: Parts 1-4 (STOKE) 1968 36 min. 31927 rental $10.00 sale $180.00
Reactions of four children, aged fourteen to twenty months, to hospitalization. In these separations from parents, complicated by illness, following behavior is noted: apathy, withdrawal, self-comforting, acute misery, dull unresponsiveness and varying responses to play with nurses. At reunion, hostility and resentment combine with joy and relief. In time, normal behavior returns. Frequent parental visits and "living in" by mother help alleviate anxiety. (H. Lowenstein and D. MacCarthy, Stoke-Mandeville Hospital, England.) SHOWINGS RESTRICTED.

Sickle-Cell Anemia (LEECC) 1972 18 min. color 21723 $15.00
Puerto Ricans, Latin Americans, many groups near the Mediterranean, and people of African descent are affected by sickle-cell anemia. Describes disease and its effects.

Spirit Possession of Alejandro Mamani (FLMLIB) 1975 27 min. color 32046 $13.50
Documentary on old age and mental stress in another culture—the Aymara Indians of Bolivia. Portrays an old man's problems—loneliness, feelings of rejection, grief at losing members of his generation. In addition, he believes he is possessed by "evil spirits." Follows his decline as he struggles with the spirits; the inability of his family to help; and his preoccupation with suicide. (English subtitles.)

Sucking Doctor (UCEMC) 1964 50 min. 50328 $15.50
Entire curing ceremony practiced by Kashia group of the southwest Pomo Indians. Illustrates element of trance; formalized use of a group of singers; and the sucking action used by shaman to remove patient's pain.

Terre Sans Pain (Land Without Bread) (MGHT) 1932 31 min. 31752 $12.00
Classic documentary on tragic struggle for survival of poverty-stricken Hurdanos, village dwellers of northern Spain. Also known as *Unpromised Land—A Study of Human Geography*, this is a film by surrealist filmmaker Luis Bunuel. Photographed by Eli Lotar.

Tibetan Medicine: A Buddhist Approach to Healing (HP) 1976 29 min. color 32072 $15.00
Tibetan medicine heals both the physical and the psychic being, treats the patient rather than the disease. Medicines of animal, vegetable and mineral substances, gathered in the surrounding mountains, as well as acupuncture and moxibustion, are used at the Tibetan Medical Center of the Dalai Lama. (Sheldon Rocklin.)

To Find Our Life: The Peyote Hunt of the Huichols of Mexico (UCLA) 1969 60 min. color 60142 $22.00
Documents the ritual journey of the Huichol Indians led by a shaman to obtain peyote. Included are curing rituals, the hunt of the peyote cactus with bow and arrow, communal eating of the peyote, all-night ceremonies, and the final ritual.

The Work of Gomis (WASHBF) 1972 48 min. color 50312 $22.00
Gomis, a doctor of southern Ceylon, practices methods of healing thousands of years old. Documents a thirty-hour series of ceremonies in which Gomis, with dancers and artists, attempts to exorcise a man's illness through ritual dances, dreams and prayers.

Yanomamö: A Multi-Disciplinary Study (USNAC) 1970 45 min. color 50259 $17.00 Biological-anthropological study of Yanomamö Indians of southern Venezuela and northern Brazil illustrates field techniques used by a team of specialists in human genetics, anthropology, epidemiology, dentistry, linguistics and medicine. (Timothy Asch, Napoleon Chagnon, and James Neel.)

Encyclopaedia Cinematographica Films

Brazil
E75 Tukurina. *Treatment of the sick by the medicine man.* 1950 color 2½ min. $6.80
E436 Kraho. *Treatment of the sick.* 1959 color 3 min. $6.80
E442 Javahe. *Blood letting by scratching the skin.* 1959 color 4½ min. $6.80

Africa
E1087 South Africa (Zulu). *Divination, oracle, and curative treatment of a medicine man.* 1965 color 9 min. $10.25
E222 Upper Volta (Nuna). *Morning children care with enema.* 1956 color 2 min. $6.80
E908 Central Sudan (Bideyat). *Lancing and dyeing of the gums.* 1963 color 7 min. $10.25
E909 Central Sudan (Bideyat). *Lancing and dyeing of the lips.* 1963 color 10 min. $10.25
E905 Kanem (Danoa). *Circumcision.* 1965 color 16½ min. $5.50
E960 South Wadi (Diongor). *Scarification of girls.* 1965 color 14 min. $13.25
E910 South Wadi (Hamar Arabs). *Excision.* 1963 color 10 min. $10.25
E1219 South Wadi (Hamar Arabs). *Circumcision.* 1963 color 6 min. $10.25
E458 Basse Koto (Banda). *Excision ceremonies.* 1959 color 9½ min. $10.25
E145 Tanzania (Mbunga). *Circumcision of a young man.* 1949 5 min. $5.50

Pacific and Insular Southeast Asia
E937 Gilbert Island (Nonouti). *Curing the sick (massage, tooth care).* 1963 color 5 min. $10.25
E187 New Guinea (Wantoat). *Curing of sick people by magic.* 1956/7 2 min. $5.50

Middle East
E1201 Arabia (Hadramaut). *Medical treatment with heated iron.* 1967 color 3 min. $6.80

Southeast Asia
E528 Burma (Kachin). *Dances and rites at the dispelling of death spirits.* 1962 color 13½ min. $13.25
E1276 Thailand (Tak, Meo). *Smoking of opium.* 1964/5 color 5 min. $6.80

References

Aberle, David F. 1966 Religio-Magical Phenomena and Power, Prediction, and Control. Southwestern Journal of Anthropology 22:221-230.
Ackerknecht, Erwin H. 1942a Problems of Primitive Medicine. Bulletin of the History of Medicine 11:503-521.
_____1942b Primitive Medicine and Culture Pattern. Bulletin of the History of Medicine 12: 545-574.
_____1943a Primitive Autopsies and the History of Anatomy. Bulletin of the History of Medicine 13:334-339.
_____1943b Psychopathology, Primitive Medicine, and Primitive Culture. Bulletin of the History of Medicine 14:30-67.

_____1944a White Indians. Bulletin of the History of Medicine 15:15-36.

_____1945a Primitive Medicine. Transactions, New York Academy of Sciences. Series 2, 8:26-37.

_____1945b Malaria in the Upper Mississippi Valley, 1760-1900. Supplement to the Bulletin of the History of Medicine, No. 4. Baltimore: Johns Hopkins Press.

_____1945c On the Collection of Data Concerning Primitive Medicine. American Anthropologist 47:427-432.

_____1946 Natural Diseases and Rational Treatment in Primitive Medicine. Bulletin of the History of Medicine 19:467-497.

_____1947 Primitive Surgery. American Anthropologist 49:25-45.

_____1948 Medicine and Disease among Eskimos. Ciba Symposia 10:916-921.

_____1949 Medical Practices of the South American Indians. *In* Handbook of South American Indians. J. Steward, ed. Vol. 5 Pp. 621-643. Washington: Smithsonian Institution.

_____1958 Primitive Medicine's Social Function. Mexico City: Paul River, Miscellanea.

_____1965 History and Geography of the Most Important Diseases. New York: Hafner.

_____1971 Medicine and Ethnology: Selected Essays. Baltimore: Johns Hopkins Press.

Acsadi, G., and J. Nemeskeri 1970 History of Human Life Span and Mortality. Budapest: Akademiai Kiado.

Adair, John 1960 The Indian Health Worker in the Cornell Navaho Project. Human Organization 19:59-63.

_____1963 Physicians, Medicine Men, and Their Navaho Patients. *In* Man's Image in Medicine and Anthropology. I. Galdston, ed. Pp. 237-257. New York: International Universities Press.

Adair, John, and Kurt Dueschle 1957 Some Problems of the Physicians on the Navaho Reservation. Human Organization 16:19-23.

_____1970 The People's Health: Anthropology and Medicine in a Navaho Community. New York: Appleton-Century-Crofts.

Adams, R. M. 1964 The Origin of Agriculture. *In* Horizons in Anthropology. S. Tax, ed., Pp. 120-131. Baltimore: Johns Hopkins Press.

Adams, Richard N. 1952 An Analysis of Medical Beliefs and Practices in a Guatemalan Indian Town. Guatemala: Instituto Indigentista Nacional de Guatemala.

_____1955 A Nutritional Research Program in Guatemala. *In* Health, Culture, and Community. B. D. Paul, ed. Pp. 435-458. New York: Russell Sage Foundation.

Adams, Richard N., and A. J. Rubel 1967a Sickness and Social Relations. *In* Handbook of Middle American Indians. R. Wauchope, ed. Vol. 6. Pp. 333-356.

_____1967b Sickness and Social Relations. *In* Handbook of Middle American Indians. R. Wauchope, ed. Pp. 333-355. Austin: University of Texas Press.

Aitken, R. T. 1930 Ethnology of Tubnai. Honolulu.I

Alajouanine, Th., and R. Thure 1945 Perte de Substance Cranienne Consécutive à un Traumatisme Fermé. Revue Neurologique 77:71-77.

Alland, A. 1966 Medical Anthropology and the Study of Biological and Cultural Adaptations. American Anthropologist 68:40-51.

_____1967 War and Disease: An Anthropological Perspective. Natural History 76:58-61.

_____1970 Adaptation in Cultural Evolution: An Approach to Medical Anthropology. New York: Columbia University Press.

Allen, E. J. 1973 Alternate Modes of Medicine in the Chinese Culture. Doctoral dissertation, Stanford University.

Allison, A. C. 1954 Protection Afforded by Sickle-Cell Trait against Subtertian Malarial Infection. British Medical Journal 1:290-294.

Alpers, M. P., D. C. Gajdusek, and S. G. Ono 1975 Bibliography of Kuru. Study of Child Growth and Development and Disease Patterns in Primitive Cultures. U. S. Department of Health, Education, and Welfare Publication, No. (NIH) 76-800.

Anderson, R. G. 1911 Some Tribal Customs in Their Relation to the Medicine and Morals of the Gore Peoples Inhabiting the Bahr-El-Ghazal. Tropical Research Laboratory. Vol. B. Pp. 239-278. Khartoum.

Angus, H. C. 1897-98 A Year In Azimba. Journal of the Royal Anthropological Institute of Great Britain and Ireland 27:324ff.

Anonymous 1953 Ten Years of Cooperative Health Programs in Latin America: An Fvaluation. Washington, D.C. Conducted by the Public Health Service, Department of Health, Education, and Welfare for the Institute of Inter-American Affairs.

Arensberg, C. M., and Kimball, S. T. 1965 Culture and Community. New York: Harcourt, Brace, and World.

Armelagos, G. J. 1967 Man's Changing Environment. *In* Infectious Diseases: Their Evolution and Eradication. T. A. Cockburn, ed. Pp. 66-87. Springfield, Ill.: Charles C. Thomas.

Armelagos, G. J., and J. Dewey 1970 Evolutionary Response to Human Infectious Disease. Bioscience 20 (5):271-275.

Armelagos, G. J., and A. McArdle 1975 Population, Disease, and Evolution. Population Studies in Archaeology and Biological Anthropology: A Symposium. A. C. Swedlund, ed. Memoir of the Society of American Archaeology, No. 30.

Audy, J. R. 1961 The Ecology of Scrub Typhus. *In* Studies in Disease Ecology. J. M. May, ed. Pp. 387-433. New York: Hafner Publishing Co.

———1971 Measurement and Diagnosis of Health. Environ-Mental. P. Sheppard, ed. Boston: Houghton-Mifflin.

Audy, J. R., and F. L. Dunn 1974 Health and Disease. Human Ecology. F. Sargent II, ed. North Holland Publishing Company.

Ayala, Felipe 1975 A Community-Based Health Training Program. Paper presented at the American Anthropological Association Annual Meetings, San Francisco.

Badgley, Robin F. 1963 Social Sciences and Public Health. Canadian Journal of Public Health 54:147-153.

Badgley, Robin F., and Samuel W. Bloom 1972 Sociology and Medical Education. *In* Study for Teaching Behavioral Sciences in Schools of Medicine, Vol. III. Pp. 182-214. Behavioral Science Perspectives in Medical Education, National Center for Health Services Research and Development, Department of Health, Education, and Welfare, Public Health Service.

Badianus Manuscript 1940 (1952) An Aztec Herbal of 1552, by Martin de la Cruz. Introduction, translation, and annotations by Emily Walcott Emmart. Baltimore: Johns Hopkins Press.

Bahnson, Claus B., et al. 1974 Behavioral Factors Associated with the Etiology of Physical Disease. American Journal of Public Health. 64:1033-1056.

Baker, P. T. 1974 The Implications of Energy Flow Studies in Human Populations for Human Biology. *In* Energy Flow in Human Communities. P. L. Jamison and S. M. Friedman, eds. Pp. 15-20. University Park, Pa.: Human Adaptability Coordinating Office, U. S. International Biological Program and Committee on the Biological Bases of Social Behavior, Social Science Research Council.

Baker, P. T., and J. Weiner 1966 The Biology of Human Adaptability. Oxford: Clarendon.

Balsdon, J. P. V. D. 1969 Life and Leisure in Ancient Rome. London: Bodley Head.

Bandelier, A. L. 1904 Aboriginal Trephining in Bolivia. AA, 6, 440 ff.

Banerji, D. 1974 Health Behavior of Rural Populations: Impact of Rural Health Services. A Preliminary Communication. New Delhi: Jawaharlal Mehru University, Center of Social Medicine and Community Health.

Banton, Michael 1965 Roles: An Introduction to the Study of Social Relations. New York: Basic Books.

Barr, J. 1970 The Assaults on Our Senses. London: Methuen.

Barrau, Jacques, ed. 1963 Plants and the Migration of Pacific Peoples. Honolulu: Bishop Museum Press.

Bartels, M. 1893 Die Medizin der Naturvölker. Leipzig.

Barth, Fredrik 1963 Introduction. *In* The Role of the Entrepreneur in Social Change in Northern Norway. Fredrik Barth, ed. Pp. 1-16. Oslo: Norwegian Universities Press.

_____1966 Models of Social Organization. Occasional Paper No. 23. Royal Anthropological Institute of Great Britain and Ireland.

Barton, J. 1923 Notes on the Kipsikis of Kenya. Journal of the Royal Anthropological Institute of Great Britain and Ireland 53:42-78.

Basedow, H. 1932 Diseases of the Australian Aborigines. Journal of Tropical Medicine and Hygiene 35:177-185.

Basil, G. C., and E. F. Lewis 1940 Test Tubes and Dragon Scales. Chicago: University of Chicago Press.

Bates, M. 1953 Human Ecology. *In* Anthropology Today. A. L. Kroeber, ed. Pp. 700-713. Chicago: University of Chicago Press.

Bateson, G. 1958 Naven. Second ed. New York.

Bateson, G., et al. 1956 Toward a Theory of Schizophrenia. Behavior Science 1:25.

Becker, Howard S., et al. 1961 Boys in White: Student Culture in a Medical School. Chicago: University of Chicago Press.

Belshaw, Cyril S. 1955 The Cultural Milieu of the Entrepreneur: A Critical Essay. Explorations in Entrepreneurial History 7:146-162.

Benedict, Burton 1969 Role Analysis in Animals and Men. Man 4:203-214.

Bennett, J. H. 1962a Population and Family Studies of Kuru. Eugenics Quarterly 9:59-68.

_____1962b Population Studies of the Kuru Region of New Guinea. Oceania 33:24-46.

Bennett, J. H., F. A. Rhodes, and H. N. Robson 1958 Observations on Kuru: A Possible Genetic Basis. Australasian Annals of Medicine 7:269-275.

_____1959 A Possible Genetic Basis for Kuru. American Journal of Human Genetics 11:169-187.

Bentley, F. 1971 Poisons, Pigments, and Metallurgy. Antiquity 45:138.

Berlin, B., D. Breedlove, and P. H. Raven 1966 Folk Taxonomies and Biological Classification. Science 154:273-275.

_____1968 Covert Categories and Folk Taxonomies. American Anthropologist 70:290-300.

Berndt, R. M. 1958 A Devastating Disease Syndrome: Kuru Sorcery in the East Central Highlands of New Guinea. Sociologus 8:4-28.

Best, E. 1924 The Maori. 2 Vols. Wellington.

Biddle, Bruce, and Edwin J. Thomas 1966 Role Theory: Concepts and Research. New York: John Wiley.

Bidwell, C. 1973 Heroin III: Oxnard is Hype City. News-Chronicle, Thousand Oaks, Calif., June 26:1-3.

Billington, B. P. 1960 The Health and Nutritional Status of the Aborigines. *In* Records of the American-Australian Scientific Expedition to Arnhem Land. C. P. Mountford, ed. Melborne: Melborne University Press.

Black, R. H. 1959 Haptoglobins and Haemoglobins in Australian Aborigines. Medical Journal of Australia 1959:175-176.

Blake, S. F. 1922 Native Names and Uses of Some Plants of Eastern Guatemala and Honduras Contribution of U.S. Natural Herbareum 24:87-100.

Bloom, Leonard 1964 Some Psychological Concepts of Urban Africans. Ethnology 3:66-95.

Bloom, Samuel W. 1973 Power and Dissent in the Medical School. New York: The Free Press.

Blum, H. F. 1961 Does the Melanin Pigment of Human Skin Have Adaptive Value? Quarterly Review of Biology 36:50-63.

Blumberg, B. S., and J. E. Hesser 1975 Anthropology and Infectious Disease. *In* Physiological Anthropology. A. Damon, ed. Pp. 260-294 New York: Oxford University Press.

Boesch, Ernst E. 1972 Communication between Doctors and Patients in Thailand, Part I. Saarbrücken: University of the Saar, Sociopsychological Research Center on Development Planning.

Bohannan, Paul 1961 *Review of* Search for Security, by M. J. Field. American Anthropologist 63:435-436.

Bolman, W. M. 1968 Cross-Cultural Psychotherapy. American Journal of Psychiatry. 124:1237-1244.

Bonfil Batalla, Guillermo 1962 Diagnóstico sobre el hambre en Sudzal, Yucatán: un ensayo de antropología aplicada. Mexico: Publicaciones del Departmento de Investigaciones Antropológicas, Instituto Nacional de Antropología e Historia 11.

Botting, D. 1968 Quest on the Upper Orinoco. Geographic Magazine 41:205.

Boyden, S. V. 1970 The Impact of Civilization on the Biology of Man. Toronto: University of Toronto Press.

_____1973 Evolution and Health. The Ecologist 3(8):304-309.

Bronte-Stewart, B., et al. 1960 The Health and Nutritional Status of the !Kung Bushmen of Southwest Africa. South African Journal of Laboratory/Clinical Medicine 6:187-216.

Broom, L., et al. 1954 Acculturation: An Exploratory Formulation. American Anthropologist 56:873-1000.

Broomes, L. R. 1971 The Camarillo Drug Abuse Program. Paper presented at the National Medical Association Convention, Philadelphia, Pa.

Brothwell, D., and P. Brothwell 1969 Food in Antiquity. London: Thames and Hudson.

Brothwell, D., A. T. Sandison, and P. H. K. Gray 1969 Human Biological Observations on a Guanche Mummy with Anthracosis. American Journal of Physical Anthropology 30: 333.

Brown, G. 1910 Melanesians and Polynesians. London.

Bruch, H. A., et al. 1963 Studies of Diarrheal Disease in Central America. American Journal of Tropical Medicine and Hygiene (July).

Bryant, John 1969 Health and the Developing World. Ithaca and London: Cornell University Press.

Bryce-Laporte, R. S. 1970 Crisis, Contraculture, and Religion among West Indians in the Panama Canal Zone. In Afro-American Anthropology. N. Whitten, Jr., and J. Szwed, eds. New York: The Free Press.

Bunzel, Ruth 1940 The Role of Alcoholism in Two Central American Communities. Psychiatry 3:361-387.

Burnet, Sir F. M. 1962 Natural History of Infectious Disease. England: Cambridge University Press.

Burnet, MacFarland, and D. O. White 1972 Natural History of Infectious Disease. Fourth ed. England: Cambridge University Press.

Cairns, John 1975 The Cancer Problem. Scientific American: 233(5):64-78.

Callen, E. O., and T. W. M. Cameron 1960 A Prehistoric Diet Revealed in Coprolites. New Scientist 8:35-40.

Carneiro, R. L. 1968 Cultural Adaptation. In International Encyclopedia of the Social Sciences 3:551-554. New York: Macmillan.

Carrasco, P. 1960 Pagan Rituals and Beliefs among the Chontal Indians of Oaxaca. Anthropological Records 20:87-117.

Carr-Saunders, A. M. 1922 The Population Problem: A Study in Human Evolution. Oxford: Oxford University Press.

Caseley-Smith, J. R. 1959 The Haematology of the Central Australian Aborigine, 11. Australian Journal of Experimental Biological and Medical Science 37:481-488.

Cassel, John 1955 A Comprehensive Health Program among the South African Zulus. In Health, Culture, and Community. Benjamin D. Paul, ed. Pp. 15-41. New York: Russell Sage Foundation.

Castaneda, Carlos 1968 The Teachings of Don Juan: A Yaqui Way of Knowledge. New York: Ballantine Books.

Castiglioni, A. 1947 A History of Medicine. Translated by E. B. Krumbhaar from Italian to English. London: Routledge and Kegan Paul.

Catlin, G. 1876 Illustrations of the Manners, etc. of the North American Indians. London.

Caudill, William 1953 Applied Anthropology in Medicine. In Anthropology Today. A. L.

Kroeber, ed. Pp. 771-806. Chicago: University of Chicago Press.

_____1961 Around the Clock Patient Care In Japanese Psychiatric Hospitals: The Role of the Tsukisoi. American Sociological Review 26:204-214.

Chambers, C. D., W. R. Cuskey, and A. D. Moffett 1970 Demographic Factors in Opiate Addiction among Mexican-Americans. Washington, D.C.: U.S. Government Printing Office.

Chang, K., and Co-workers 1949 Studies on Hookworm Disease in Szechwan Province, West China. Baltimore: Johns Hopkins Press.

Christensen, James Boyd 1959 The Adaptive Functions of Fanti Priesthood. *In* Continuity and Change in African Cultures. William R. Bascom and Melville J. Herskovits, eds. Pp. 257-279. Chicago: University of Chicago Press.

Clark, Margaret 1959 Health in the Mexican-American Culture. Berkeley and Los Angeles: University of California Press.

Clausen, John 1959 The Sociology of Mental Illness. *In* Sociology Today, Problems and Prospects. Robert K. Merton, Leonard Broom, and Leonard S. Cottrell, Jr., eds. Pp. 485-508. New York: Basic Books.

Cleland, J. B. 1928 Disease amongst the Australian Aborigines. Journal of Tropical Medicine and Hygiene. 31:53-59; 65-70; 141-145; 157-160; 173-177; 196-198; 232-235; 262-266; 281-282; 290-294; 307-313; 326-330.

Clements, F. E. 1932 Primitive Concepts of Disease. University of California Publications in Archeology and Ethnology 32(2):185-252.

Cockburn, T. A. 1963 The Evolution and Eradication of Diseases. Baltimore: Johns Hopkins Press.

_____1967a Infections of the Order Primates. *In* Infectious Diseases: Their Evolution and Eradication. T. A. Cockburn, ed. Pp. 38-107. Springfield, Ill.: Charles C. Thomas.

_____1967b The Evolution of Human Infectious Diseases. *In* Infectious Diseases: Their Evolution and Eradication. T. A. Cockburn, ed. Pp. 34-107. Springfield, Ill.: Charles C. Thomas.

_____1971 Infectious Disease in Ancient Populations. Current Anthropology 12(1):45-62.

Codrington, R. H. 1891 The Melanesians. Oxford.

Coe, M. D. 1962 Mexico. London: Thames and Hudson.

Coe, Rodney M. 1970 Sociology of Medicine. New York: McGraw-Hill.

Cohn, H. 1960 The Evolution of the Concept of Disease. Concepts of Medicine. B. Lush, ed. Oxford University Press.

Coleman, James S., Elihu Katz, and Herbert Menzel 1966 Medical Innovation: A Diffusion Study. Indianapolis: Bobbs-Merrill.

Coles, Robert 1970 Uprooted Children. New York: Harper and Row.

Colson, Anthony C., and Karen E. Selby 1974 Medical Anthropology. *In* Annual Review of Anthropology. Bernard J. Siegel, Alan R. Beals, and Stephen A. Taylor, eds. Vol. 3: Pp. 245-262. Palo Alto: Annual Reviews, Inc.

Conklin, H. C. 1954 The Relation of Hanunoo Culture to the Plant World. Ph.D dissertation in Anthropology, Yale University.

Cook, S. F. 1955 The Epidemic of 1830-1833 in California and Oregon. University of California Publication in American Archaeology and Ethnology Journal 43:303-326.

Coppoletta, J. M. and S. B. Wolbach 1933 Body Length and Organ Weights of Infants and Children. American Journal of Pathology 9:55-70.

Corlett, W. Th. 1935 The Medicine Man of the American Indian. Springfield.

Coser, Rose Laub 1962 Life in the Ward. East Lansing: Michigan State University Press.

Cosminsky, S. 1972 Decision Making and Medical Care in a Guatemalan Indian Community. Ph.D dissertation, Brandeis University.

Coult, Allan D. 1964 Role Allocation, Position Structuring, and Ambilineal Descent. American Anthropologist 66:29-40.

Cowgill, U. M., and G. E. Hutchinson 1963 Differential Mortality among the Sexes in Childhood and Its Possible Significance in Human Evolution. Proceedings of the National Academy of Science 49:425-429.

Croog, S. H. 1961 Ethnic Origins, Educational Level, and Responses to a Health Questionnaire. Human Organization 20:65-69.

Crotty, J. M., and R. C. Webb 1960 Mortality in Northern Territory Aborigines. Medical Journal of Australia 2:489-492.

Crump, T. A. 1901 Trephining in the South Seas. Journal of the Royal Anthropological Institute of Great Britain and Ireland 21:167.

Culwick, A. T., and G. M. Culwick 1935 Ubena of the Rivers. London.

Cunningham, Clark E. 1970 Thai Injection Doctors. Social Science and Medicine 4(1):1-24.

Currier, Richard L. 1966 The Hot-Cold Syndrome and Symbolic Balance in Mexican and Spanish-American Folk Medicine. Ethnology 5:251-263.

Czaplicka, M. A. 1914 Aboriginal Siberia. Oxford.

Darwin, C. 1859 On the Origin of Species. London: John Murray.

_____1873 The Descent of Man. London: John Murray.

Davis, Fred 1960 Uncertainty in Medical Prognosis: Clinical and Functional. American Journal of Sociology 66:41-47.

_____1963 Passage Through Crisis. Polio Victims and Their Families. Indianapolis: Bobbs-Merrill.

Davis, K. 1965 The Urbanization of Human Populations. Scientific American 213:40-54.

Deane, W. N. 1961 The Culture of the Patient: An Underestimated Dimension in Psychotherapy. International Journal of Social Psychiatry 3:181-186.

Deevey, E. W., Jr. 1960 The Human Population. Scientific American 208:48, 194-198.

DeKruif, P. 1926 Microbe Hunters. New York: Harcourt, Brace, and World, Inc.

Dembo, A., and J. Imbelloni 1938 Deformaciones intencionales del cuerpo humano de carácter étnico. Buenos Aires.

Demerath, N. S. 1942 Schizophrenia among Primitives. The American Journal of Psychiatry 98:703-707.

Dennis, Ruth E. 1974-75 The Traditional Healer in Liberia. In Traditional Healers: Use and Non-Use in Health Care Delivery. I. E. Harrison and D. W. Dunlop, eds. Pp. 17-28. East Lansing: Michigan State University.

Densmore, F. 1928 Uses of Plants by the Chippewa. Bureau of American Ethnology Report 44:275.

Derbyshire, R. L. 1968 Adolescent Identity Crisis in Urban Mexican-Americans in East Los Angeles. In Minority Group Adolescents in the United States. E. B. Brody, ed. Baltimore: Williams and Wilkins.

Deuschle, Kurt, and John Adair 1960 An Interdisciplinary Approach to Public Health on the Navajo Indian Reservation: Medical and Anthropological Aspects. Annals of the New York Academy of Sciences 84:887-904.

Devereux, George 1940 Primitive Psychiatry. Bulletin of the History of Medicine 8:1194-1213; 11:522-542 (1942).

_____1944 The Social Structure of a Schizophrenic Ward and Its Therapeutic Fitness. The Journal of Clinical Psychopathology. 6:231-265.

DeWalt, Kathleen, and Gretel H. Pelto (In press) Household Ecology and Dietary Complexity in a Mexican Village. In Nutrition and Applied Anthropology. T. Fitzgerald, ed.

Dieseldorff, E. P. 1939 Las plantas medicinales del Departamento de Alta Verapas. Anales Sociologia, Geografia, y Historia Guatemala 4:92-105.

Dimbleby, Phillip 1967 Plants and Archeology. London: John Baker.

Dixon, D. M. 1972 Population, Pollution, and Health in Ancient Egypt. In Population and Pollution. P. R. Cox and J. Peel, eds. Pp. 29-36. London: Academic Press.

Dobzhansky, Theodosius 1951 Genetics and the Origin of Species. Third ed. New York: Columbia University Press.

_____1962 Mankind Evolving. New Haven: Yale University Press.

_____1970 Genetics of the Evolutionary Process. New York: Columbia University Press.

Doi, L. K. 1964 Psychoanalytic Therapy and Western Man: A Japanese View. International Journal of Social Psychiatry (Special ed. No. 1) 13-18.

Doob, L. W. 1965 Psychology. *In* The African World. R. A. Lystad, ed. New York: Praeger.

Douglas, W. 1969 Illness and Curing in Santiago Atitlan. Ph.D dissertation, Stanford University.

Driberg, J. H. 1923 The Lango. Oxford.

_____1929 The Savage as He Really Is. London.

_____1930 People of the Small Arrow. London.

Dubos, Rene (1959) 1961 Mirage of Health, Utopias, Progress, and Biological Change. New York: Harper

_____1965 Man Adapting. New Haven: Yale University Press.

Duguid, C. 1963. No Dying Race. Adelaide: Rigby Limited.

Dumond, Don E. 1975 The Limitation of Human Population: A Natural History. Science 187 (28 February):713-21.

Dunlop, David W. 1974-75 Alternatives to Modern Health-Delivery Systems in Africa: Issues for Public Policy Consideration on the Role of Traditional Healers. *In* Traditional Healers: Use and Non-Use in Health Care Delivery. I. E. Harrison and D. W. Dunlop, eds. Pp. 131-139. East Lansing: Michigan State University.

Dunn, F. L. 1965 On the Antiquity of Malaria in the Western Hemisphere. Human Biology 37:385-393.

_____1966 Ecological Simplification, Parasitism, and Primate Evolution. American Journal of Physical Anthropology 25:205.

_____1968 Epidemiological Factors: Health and Disease among Hunter-Gatherers. *In* Man the Hunter. R. B. Lee and I. DeVore, eds. Pp. 221-228. Chicago: Aldine.

_____1972 Intestinal Parasitism in Malayan Aborigines (Orang Asli). Bulletin of the World Health Organization 46:99-113.

Duran, F. D. 1964 The Aztecs. The History of the Indies of New Spain. Translated, with notes, by Doris Heyden and Fernando Horcasitas. New York: Orion Press.

Eagan, C. J. 1963 Introduction and Terminology. Federation Proceedings 22:930-932.

Egeland, J. 1967 Belief and Behavior as Related to Illness. Unpublished Ph.D dissertation, Yale University, 2 vols.

Ehrenreich, P. 1891 Beitrage zur Volkerkunde Brasiliens. Berlin.

Eiseley, L. 1958 Darwin's Century. New York: Doubleday Anchor.

Ella, S. 1874 Native Medicine and Surgery in the South Sea Islands. The Medical Times and Gazette 1:50 ff. London.

Ellis, E. S. 1945 Primitive Anesthesia and Allied Conditions. London.

Ellis, W. 1853 Polynesian Researches. London.

Emin, Bey 1897 Reise von Mruli nach der Hauptstadt Unjoros. Petermann's Mitt. 25:179, 220, 338 ff.

Emmart, Emily, trans. 1940 The Badianus Manuscript. An Aztec Herbal of 1552. Baltimore: Johns Hopkins Press.

Erasmus, C. J. 1952 Changing Folk Beliefs and the Relativity of Empirical Knowledge. Southwestern Journal of Anthropology 8:411-428.

Etzioni, Amitai 1965 Organizational Control Structure. *In* Handbook of Organizations. James G. March, ed. Pp. 650-677. Chicago: Rand McNally.

Evans-Pritchard, E. E. 1937 Witchcraft, Oracles, and Magic among the Azandes. Oxford.

Fábrega, Horacio 1971 Some Features of Zinacantecan Medical Knowledge. Ethnology 10: 25-43.

Fábrega, Horacio, Jr. 1972 Medical Anthropology. *In* Biennial Review of Anthropology, 1971. Bernard Siegal, ed. Pp. 167-229. Stanford: Stanford University Press.

_____1974 Disease and Social Behavior: An Interdisciplinary Perspective. Cambridge: MIT Press.

_____1975 The Effect of Changing Social Organization on Infectious Diseases. *In* Impact of

Civilization on the Biology of Man. S. V. Boyden, ed. Canberra: Australian National University Press.

Fábrega, Horacio Jr., and Daniel B. Silver 1973 Illness and Shamanistic Curing in Zinacantan: An Ethno-medical analysis. Stanford: Stanford University Press.

Faris, R., and H. Dunham 1939 Mental Disorders in Urban Areas. Chicago: University of Chicago Press.

Felkin, R. W. 1884 Caesarean Section in Uganda. Edinburgh Medical Journal 29:928ff.

Field, M. J. 1960 Search for Security: An Ethno-Psychiatric Study of Rural Ghana. Evanston, Ill.: Northwestern University Press.

Firschein, I. L. 1961 Population Dynamics of the Sickle-Cell Trait in the Black Caribs of British Honduras, Central America. American Journal of Human Genetics 13:233-254.

Firth, R. 1951 Elements of Social Organization. London: Watts.

Fischer, A., and J. L. Fischer 1961 Culture and Epidemiology: A Theoretical Investigation of Kuru. Journal of Health and Human Behavior 2:16-25.

Fischmann, V. S. 1968 Drug Addicts in a Therapeutic Community. Psychotherapy and Psychosomatics 16:109-113.

Fletcher, A., and F. La Flesche 1911 The Omaha. Bureau of American Ethnology Report 27:15-672.

Flint, M. P. 1976 Does the Chimpanzee Have a Menopause? American Journal of Physical Anthropology 44:178-179.

Fogelson, Raymond D. 1961 Change, Persistence, and Accommodation in Cherokee Medico-Magical Beliefs. *In* Symposium on Cherokee and Iroquois Culture. William N. Fenton and John Gulick, eds. Bureau of American Ethnology Bulletin 180:215-225.

Foster, G., and J. H. Rowe 1951 Suggestions for Field Recording of Information on the Hippocratic Classification of Diseases and Remedies. Kroeber Anthropological Society Papers 5:1-3.

Foster, George M. 1952 Relationships between Theoretical and Applied Anthropology: A Public Health Program Analysis. Human Organization 11:5-6.

_____1953a What Is Folk Culture? American Anthropologist 55:159-173.

_____1953b Relationships between Spanish and Spanish-American Folk Medicine. Journal of American Folklore 66:201-217.

_____1960 Culture and Conquest: America's Spanish Heritage. New York: Viking Fund Publications in Anthropology 27.

_____1960-61 Interpersonal Relations in Peasant Society. Human Organization 19:174-178.

_____1961 The Dyadic Contract: A Model for the Social Structure of a Mexican Peasant Village. American Anthropologist 63:1173-1192.

_____1962 Traditional Cultures and the Impact of Technological Change. New York: Harper and Row.

_____1967 Tzintzuntzan, Mexican Peasants in a Changing World. Boston: Little, Brown.

_____1969 Applied Anthropology. Boston: Little, Brown.

_____1973 Traditional Societies and Technological Change. New York: Harper and Row.

_____1974 Medical Anthropology: Some Contrasts with Medical Sociology. Medical Anthropology Newsletter 6:1-6.

Fox, Renee 1959 Experiment Perilous. Pp. 139-181. Glencoe, Ill.: The Free Press.

Frake, Charles O. 1961 The Diagnosis of Disease among the Subanum of Mindinao. American Anthropologist 63:113-132.

Frazer, J. G. 1890 The Golden Bough. London.

Freeman, Howard E., Sol Levine, and Leo G. Reeder 1972 Present Status of Medical Sociology. *In* Handbook of Medical Sociology. Howard E. Freeman, Sol Levine, and Leo G. Reeder, eds. Pp. 501-521. Englewood Cliffs, N.J.: Prentice Hall.

Freeman, L. 1924 Surgery of the Ancient Inhabitants of America. Art and Archaeology 18:21-36.

Frei, E. 1975 Cancer Research—Controversy, Progress, and Prospects. New England Journal of

Medicine 293:146-147.

Freidson, Eliot 1959 Specialties without Roots: The Utilization of New Services. Human Organization 18:112-116.

_____1960 Client Control and Medical Practice. American Journal of Sociology 65:374-382.

_____1961 Patients' Views of Medical Practice. New York: Russell Sage Foundation.

_____1961 The Organization of Medical Practice and Patient Behavior. American Journal of Public Health 51:43-52.

_____1961-62 The Sociology of Medicine: A Trend Report and Bibliography. Current Sociology 10-11(3).

_____1963 The Hospital in Modern Society. New York: The Free Press.

_____1970a Professional Dominance: The Social Structure of Medical Care. New York: Atherton.

_____1970b Profession of Medicine: A Study of the Sociology of Applied Knowledge. New York: Dodd, Mead.

Freilich, Morris 1964 The Natural Triad in Kinship and Complex Systems. American Sociological Review 29:529-540.

_____1968 The Anthropological Use of Role. Paper presented to the American Anthropological Association meetings, Seattle.

French, David 1963 The Relationship of Anthropology to Studies in Perception and Cognition. *In* Psychology: A Study of a Science. Sigmund Koch, ed. Vol. 6. Pp. 388-428. New York: McGraw-Hill.

Fujii, T. 1934 Endemic Diseases in the Caroline Islands. Collection of Medical Essays 3. South Seas Government Office, Tokyo. (Translated) *In* The Micronesians of Yap and Their Depopulation. E. E. Hunt, N. R. Kidder, D. M. Schnieder, and W. D. Stevens, eds. Cambridge: Peabody Museum, Harvard University.

Gadjusek, D. C. 1963 Kuru. Transactions of the Royal Society of Tropical Medicine and Hygiene 57:151-166.

Gajdusek, D. C., and M. P. Alpers 1972 Genetic Studies in Relation to Kuru. Cultural, Historical, and Demographic Background. American Journal of Human Genetics 24:51-238.

Gajdusek, D. C., and C. J. Gibbs 1975 Familial and Sporadic Chronic Neurological Degenerative Disorders Transmitted from Man to Primates. *In* Advances in Neurology. B. J. Meldrum, and C. D. Marsden, eds. Vol. 10. Pp. 291-317. New York: Raven Press.

Galbraith, J. K. 1969 The Affluent Society. Boston: Houghton-Mifflin.

Gans, Herbert 1962 The Urban Villagers. New York: Free Press.

Garcia del Real, Eduardo 1946 Surgical Anesthesia in Spain. Journal of the History of Medicine 1:641-643.

Gardner, Lytt 1974 Deprivation Dwarfism. *In* Biological Anthropology Readings from Scientific American. S. Katz, ed. Pp. 284-290. San Francisco: W. H. Freeman and Company.

Garn, S. M. 1963 Culture and the Direction of Human Evolution. Human Biology 35:221.

Garrison, F. H. 1914 An Introduction to the History of Medicine. Philadelphia.

_____1933 Quackery and Primitive Medicine. New York Academy of Medicine Bulletin 9: 601ff.

Gavan, J. A. 1953 Growth and Development of the Chimpanzee. Human Biology 25:93-143.

Geertz, Clifford 1960 The Javanese Kijaji: The Changing Role of a Cultural Broker. Comparative Studies in Society and History 2:228-249.

Gelfand, M. 1964 Medicine and Culture in Africa. Edinburgh: Livingstone.

Gillin, J. 1947 Moche: A Peruvian Coastal Community. Washington: Publications of the Institute of Social Anthropology, Smithsonian Institution.

_____1948 Magical Fright. Psychiatry 11:387-400.

_____1951 The Culture of Security in San Carlos. Middle American Research Institute. Publication 16. New Orleans: Tulane University Press.

_____1956 The Making of a Witch Doctor. Psychiatry 19:131-136.

Glaser, Barney G., and Anselm L. Strauss 1967 The Discovery of Grounded Theory. Chicago: Aldine.

_____1968 Time for Dying. Chicago: Aldine.

Glaser, William A. 1968 Medical Care: II. Social Aspects. International Encyclopedia of Social Sciences 10:93-100.

Glasse, R. M. 1967 Cannibalism in the Kuru Region of New Guinea. Transactions of the New York Academy of Science 29(2):748-754.

_____1970 Some Recent Observations on Kuru. Oceanis 40:210-213.

Glasse, R. M., and S. Lindenbaum 1969 South Fore Politics. Anthropological Forum 2:308-326.

Gleiser, I., and E. E. Hunt, Jr. 1955 The Permanent Mandibular First Molar: Its Calcification, Eruption and Decay. American Journal of Physical Anthropology 13:253-284.

Goffman, E. 1958 The Presentation of Self in Everyday Life. Edinburgh.

_____1961 Asylums. Garden City: Anchor Books.

Goldstein, Marcus S. 1963 Human Paleopathology. Journal of the National Medical Association 55:100-106.

Gonzales, Nancy S. 1963 Some Aspects of Child-Bearing and Child-Rearing in a Guatemalan Latino Community. Southwestern Journal of Anthropology 19:411-423.

_____1966 Health Behavior in Cross-Cultural Perspective: A Guatemalan Example. Human Organization 25:122-25.

_____1969 Beliefs and Practices Concerning Medicine and Nutrition among Lower-Class Urban Guatemalans. In The Cross-Cultural Approach to Health Behavior. L. R. Lynch, ed. Rutherford: Fairleigh Dickinson University Press.

Goode, William J. 1960 A Theory of Role Strain. American Sociological Review 25:483-496.

Goodenough, Ward H. 1963 Cooperation in Change: An Anthropological Approach to Community Development. New York: Russell Sage Foundation.

_____1964 Cultural Anthropology and Linguistics. In Language in Culture and Society. Dell Hymes, ed. Pp. 36-39. New York: Harper and Row.

_____1965a Rethinking Status and Role: Toward a General Model of the Cultural Organization of Social Relationships. In The Relevance of Models for Social Anthropology. Max Gluckman and Fred Eggan, eds. A. S. A. Monographs 1:1-24. London: Tavistock.

_____1965b Yankee Kinship Terminology: A Problem in Componential Analysis. American Anthropologist 67:259-87.

Goodman, A., K. Jacobs, and G. J. Armelagos 1975 The Role of Infectious and Nutritional Diseases in Population Growth. Paper delivered at the 74th Annual Meeting of the American Anthropological Association, San Francisco.

Gorbach, S. L. 1975 Travelers' Diarrhea and Toxigenic *Escherichia Coli.* New England Journal of Medicine 292:933.

Gordon, J. E., M. Behar, and N. S. Scrimshaw 1964 Acute Diarrheal Disease. Guatemala: Boletin de la Oficina Sanitaria Panamericana.

Gould, Harold A. 1957 The Implications of Technological Change for Folk and Scientific Medicine. American Anthropologist 59:507-516.

_____1965 Modern Medicine and Folk Cognition in Rural India. Human Organization 24:201-208.

Graham, Saxon 1960 Social Factors in the Epidemiology of Cancer at Various Sites. Annuals of the New York Academy of Science 84(17):807-815.

_____1964 Sociological Aspects of Health and Illness. In Handbook of Modern Sociology. Robert E. L. Faris, ed. 310-347. Chicago: Rand McNally.

Granberg, D. 1973 Jewish-Nonjewish Differences on the Vietnam War: A Study of Social Psychologists. The American Sociologist 8:101-06.

Grandidier, A. and G. Grandidier 1908 Histore physique etc. de Madagascar. Paris.

Greenberg, D. S. 1975 Progress in Cancer Research—Don't Say It Isn't So. New England Journal of Medicine 292:707-708.

Griffin, J. B. 1960 Some Connections between Siberia and America. Science 131:801-812.

Grinnell, G. B. 1923 The Cheyenne Indians. New Haven.

Gropper, R. C. 1967 Toward a Universal Comparative Medicine. A working paper prepared for Folk Healthways Newsletter.

Guiard, E. 1930 La trépanation cranienne chez les néolithiques et chez les primitifs modernes. Paris.

Guiteras Holmes, C. 1961 Perils of the Soul. New York.

Guppy, N. 1964 Fishing with the Guiana Indians. Animals 3:234.

Gupta, P. N. S. 1953 Population Studies on Living Conditions of the Tribes in the Padam and Minyong Areas of Abor Hills (Assam). Bulletin of the Department of Anthropology, Calcutta 2:91.

Gutierrez, J. 1971 Colonia Family Living Study. Ventura County Neighborhood Youth Corps. Mimeo.

Hackett, L. W. 1937 Malaria in Europe. London: Oxford University Press.

Haddon, A. C. 1901 Headhunters, Black, White, and Brown. London.

Hagaman, R. M. 1974 Divorce, Remarriage, and Fertility in a Micronesian Population. Micronesia 10:237-242.

Hagen, B. 1899 Unter den Papuas. Wiesbaden.

Haldane, J. B. S. 1949 Disease and Evolution. Supplement to La Ricerca Scientifica 19:68-76.

_____1957 Natural Selection in Man. Acta Genetica et Statistica Medica (Basel) 6:321-332.

Hallberg, M. C. 1971 Multiple Discriminate Analysis for Studying Group Membership. Bulletin 755. Pennsylvania State University.

Hallowell, A. Irving 1934 Culture and Mental Disorder. The Journal of Abnormal and Social Psychology 29:1-9.

_____1935 Primitive Concepts of Disease. American Anthropologist 37:365-368.

_____1939 Sin, Sex, and Sickness in Saulteaux Belief. British Journal of Medical Psychology 18:191-197.

_____1942 The Role of Conjuring in Saulteaux Society. Philadelphia: University of Pennsylvania Press.

_____1955 Culture and Experience. Philadelphia: University of Pennsylvania Press.

_____1963 Ojibwa World View and Disease. In Man's Image in Medicine and Anthropology. I. Galdston, ed. Pp. 258-315. New York: International Universities Press.

Handelman, Don 1967 The Development of a Washo Shaman. Ethnology 4:444-464.

Hanson, F. Allan 1970 The Rapan Theory of Conception. American Anthropologist 72:1444-1447.

Harden, D. 1962 The Phoenicians. London: Thames and Hudson.

Haring, C. H. 1947 The Spanish Empire in America. New York: Oxford University Press.

Harley, George W. 1941 Native African Medicine. Cambridge: Harvard University Press.

Harris, Marvin 1968 The Rise of Anthropological Theory: A History of Theories of Culture. New York: Thomas Y. Crowell.

Harrison, G. A. 1966 Human Adaptability with Reference to IBP Proposal for High Altitude Research. In The Biology of Human Adaptability. P. T. Baker and J. S. Weiner, eds. Oxford: Clarendon Press.

Harrison, G. G. 1975 Primary Adult Lactase Deficiency: A Problem in Anthropological Genetics. American Anthropologist 77:812-835.

Harrison, Ira E. 1974-75 Traditional Healers: A Neglected Source of Health Manpower. In Traditional Healers: Use and Non-Use in Health Care Delivery. I. E. Harrison and D. W. Dunlop, eds. Pp. 5-16. East Lansing: Michigan State University.

Hart, D. V. 1969 Bisyan Filipino and Malayan Humoral Pathologies: Folk Medicine and History in Southeast Asia. Data Paper 76, Southeast Asia, Program, Department of Asian Studies, Cornell University.

Harwood, A. 1971 The Hot-Cold Theory of Disease: Implications for Treatment of Puerto Rican Patients. The Journal of the American Medical Association 216:1153-58.

Hasan, K. A. 1963 Applied Anthropology in History of Medicine. Journal of Social Research 6:71-78.

_____1964a Folk Concepts of Etiology and Illness in a North Indian Village. Kroeber Anthropological Society Papers, No. 30 (spring).

_____1964b The Anthropologist in a Health Education Bureau. The Antiseptic 61:39-43.

_____1964c Some Applications of Physical Anthropology in Forensic Medicine. Indian Medical Gazette 6:9-19.

_____1965 *Comment on* Alcohol and Culture, by David G. Mandelbaum. Current Anthropology 6:289.

_____1966a On Collecting Anthropological Data in a North Indian Village. Eastern Anthropologist 19:55-68.

_____1966b Physical Anthropology as Applied to Forensic Science. *In* Aspects of Indian Anthropology. P. C. Biswas and I. P. Singh, eds. Department of Anthropology, University of Delhi.

_____1967 The Cultural Frontier of Health in Village India. Bombay: Manaktalas.

_____1968 Anthropology and Medical History. *In* Applied Anthropology in India. L. P. Vidyarthi, ed. Allahabad: Kitab Mahal.

_____1971 The Hindu Dietary Practices and Culinary Rituals in a North Indian Village: An Ethnomedical and Structural Analysis. Ethnomedizin 1:43-70.

_____1973 Social Aspects of the Use of Cannabis in India. Paper presented at the Conference on Cross-Cultural Perspectives on Cannabis at the IXth International Congress of Anthropological and Ethnological Sciences, Chicago.

Hasan, K. A., and B. G. Prasad 1959 A Note on the Contributions of Anthropology to Medical Science. Journal of the Indian Medical Association 33:182-190.

_____1960 The Role of Anthropology in Social and Preventive Medicine. Journal of the Indian Medical Association 35:22-26.

_____1961 Place of Anthropology in Medical Education. Journal of Medical Education 36:940-942.

_____1962 Social Science Technique in Public Health Research. Antiseptic 59:303-309.

Hasan, K. A., B. G. Prasad, and M. R. Chandra 1961 Anthropological Paediatrics of Uttar Pradesh. Archives of Child Health 3:18-24.

Heger, F. 1929 Neue Formen von Aderlassgeräten. Festschr. F. Schmidt, p. 275ff. Wien.

Heinz, H. J. 1961 Factors Governing the Survival of Bushmen Worm Parasites in the Kalahari. South African Journal of Science 57:207-213.

Heizer, R. F. 1967 Analysis of Human Coprolites from a Dry Nevada Cave. Reports from University of California Archaeological Survey 70:1-20.

Helm, June, Paul Bohannan, and Marshall D. Sahlins, eds. 1965 Essays in Economic Anthropology. Proceedings of the American Ethnological Society. Seattle: University of Washington Press.

Henry, Jules 1949 Anthropology and Psychosomatics. Psychosomatic Medicine 11:216-222.

Hes, Jozef Ph. 1964 The Changing Social Role of the Yemenite Mori. *In* Magic, Faith, and Healing. Ari Kiev, ed. Pp. 364-383. Glencoe, Ill.: The Free Press.

Hessler, R. M., and P. K. New 1972 Research as a Process of Exchange. The American Sociologist 7:13-15.

Hessler, R., et al. 1975 Intracultural Diversity of Health Beliefs among Chinese Americans in Boston. Human Organization 35:253-262.

Hilferty, M. M. 1938 Analysis of the Vital Statistics of Guatemala: Official Data. *In* A Medical Survey of the Republic of Guatemala. Shattuck, ed. Pp. 7-32.

Hilton-Simpson, M. W. 1913 Some Arab and Shawia Remedies and Notes on Trephining in Algeria. Journal of the Royal Anthropological Institute of Great Britain and Ireland 43:706ff.

Hinderling, Paul 1973 Communication between Doctors and Patients in Thailand, Part III.

Saarbrücken: University of the Saar, Sociopsychological Research Center on Development Planning.

Hirsch, A. 1883-1886 Handbook of Historical and Geographical Pathology. London: New Sydenham Society.

Hoare, C. A. 1957 The Spread of African Trypanosomes beyond Their Natural Range. Z. Tropenmed. Parasitol. 8:1-6.

Hochstrasser, Donald L., and Jesse W. Tapp, Jr. 1970 Social Medicine and Public Health. *In* Anthropology and the Behavioral and Health Sciences. O. Van Mering and L. Kasdan, eds. Pittsburg: University Press.

Hogbin, H. T. 1930-31 Spirits and the Healing of the Sick in Ontong Java. Oceania I: 146ff.

Holdridge, L. R. 1965 The Tropics, a Misunderstood Ecosystem. Association for Tropical Biology Bulletin 5:21-30.

Holland, W. R. 1962 Highland Maya Folk Medicine: A Study of Culture Change. Ph.D dissertation, University of Arizona.

Holland, W. R., and R. G. Tharp 1964 Highland Maya Psychotherapy. American Anthropologist 66:41-52.

Hollingshead, August C., and Fritz Redlich 1958 Social Class and Mental Illness. New York: John Wiley and Sons.

Hoppe, Art 1963 Eyeball to Eyeball with Birth Control. San Francisco Chronicle (23 April).

Howell, F. C. 1964 The Hominization Process. *In* Horizons of Anthropology. S. Tax, ed. Pp. 49-59. Chicago: Aldine.

Hrdlicka, A. 1908 Physiological and Medical Observations among the Indians of the Southwestern United States and Northern Mexico. Bureau of American Ethnology Bulletin 34.

Hsu, Francis L. K. 1952 Religion, Science, and Human Crisis. London: Routledge and Kegan Paul.

Hudson, E. H. 1965 Treponematosis and Man's Social Evolution. American Anthropologist 67:885-901.

Hughes, Charles C. 1963 Public Health in Non-Literate Societies. *In* Man's Image in Medicine and Anthropology. Iago Galdston, ed. Pp. 157-233. New York: International Universities Press.

_____1965 Under Four Flags: Recent Culture Change among the Eskimo. Current Anthropology. 6(1):3-69.

_____1968 Ethnomedicine. International Encyclopedia of the Social Sciences 10:87-93.

Hunt, E. E., Jr. 1951 A View of Somatology and Serology in Micronesia. American Journal of Physical Anthropology 9:157-184.

_____1958 Anthropometry, Genetics, and Racial History. American Anthropologist 61:64-87.

_____1977 Some Evolutionary Comparisons of the Life Cycles and Demography of Chimpanzees and Human Beings. Occasional Papers in Medical Anthropology. (in preparation)

Hunt, E. E., N. R. Kidder, and D. M. Schneider 1954 The Depopulation of Yap. Human Biology 26:21-51.

Hunt, E. E., et al. 1949 The Micronesians of Yap and Their Depopulation. Cambridge: Peabody Museum, Harvard University.

Hunt, Robert 1968 Agentes culturales mestizos: Estabilidad y cambio en Oaxaca. America Indigena 28:595-609.

Hunt, V. R. 1975 Reproduction and Work. Signs 1:543-552.

Huntington, E. 1939 Mainsprings of Civilization. New Haven: Yale University Press.

Huxley, J. 1958 The Evolutionary Process. *In* Evolution as Process. J. Huxley, A. C. Hardey, and E. B. Ford, eds. New York: Collier Books.

Hyman, Martin D. 1967 Medicine. *In* The Uses of Sociology. Paul F. Lazarsfeld, William H. Sewell, and Harold L. Winensky, eds. Pp. 119-155. New York: Basic Books.

Hymes, Dell, ed. 1964 Language in Culture and Society. New York: Harper and Row.

Illsley, Raymond 1974 Plenary Address to the Fourth Social Science and Medicine Conference, Elsinore, Denmark.

Imperato, P. J. 1975 The Dubious Gamble Against Smallpox. Natural History 84(7):8-18.

Ingham, John 1970 On Mexican Folk Medicine. American Anthropologist 72:76-87.

Instituto Nacional de Prevision 1944 Los seguros sociales en Espana. Publication No. 593. Madrid.

Iturribaria, J. F. 1955 Oaxaca en la historia. Mexico City.

Jahoda, Gustav 1961 Traditional Healers and Other Institutions Concerned with Mental Illness in Ghana. International Journal of Social Psychiatry 7:245-268.

Jensen, A. R. 1969 How Much Can We Boost IQ and Scholastic Achievement? Harvard Educational Review 39:1-123.

Jerome, Norge 1968 Food Consumption Patterns in Relation to Life Styles of In-Migrant Negro Families. Discussion Paper, Institute for Research on Poverty, University of Wisconsin, Madison.

Johnson, Malcolm L. 1974 Medical Sociology and Sociological Theory. Paper presented at the International Conference on Social Science and Medicine, Elsinore, Denmark.

Johnston, James 1893 Reality vs. Romance in South Central Africa. New York.

Jolly, C. J. 1970 The Seed Eaters: A New Model of Hominid Differentiation Based on a Baboon Analogy. Man 5:5-26.

Joseph, Alice 1942 Physician and Patient: Some Aspects of Interpersonal Relations between Physicians and Patients, with Special Regard to the Relationship between White Physicians and Indian Patients. Applied Anthropology 1(4):1-6.

Junod, H. A. 1927 The Life of a South African Tribe. 2 Vols. London.

Just, Theodore 1959 Bibliography of American Paleobotany: 1932-1957. Lloydia 22:247-294.

Kandel, Randy F., and Gretel H. Pelto (In press) Vegetarianism and Health Food Use among Young Adults in New England. *In* Nutritional Anthropology. N. Jerome, R. Kandel, and G. H. Pelto, eds. Vol. 1.

Kaplan, Abraham 1964 The Conduct of Inquiry. San Francisco: Chandler Publishing Company.

Kaplan, David, and Robert Manners 1972 Culture Theory. Englewood Cliffs, N.J.: Prentice-Hall.

Kark, Sidney, and Emily Kark 1962 A Practice of Social Medicine. Chapter I in: A Practice of Social Medicine: A South African Team's Experiences in Different African Communities. S. L. Kark and G. E. Steuart, eds. Pp. 3-40. Edinburgh and London: E. and S. Livingstone.

Karstein, R. 1926 The Civilization of the South American Indians. London.

Katz, Solomon H., and Anthony F. C. Wallace 1974 An Anthropological Perspective on Behavior and Disease. American Journal of Public Health 64(11):1050-1052.

Keesing, Roger M. 1970 Toward a Model of Role Analysis. *In* A Handbook of Method in Cultural Anthropology. Raoul Naroll and Ronald Cohen, eds. Pp. 423-453. Garden City, N.Y.: Natural History Press.

Kelly, Isabel 1965 Folk Practices in North Mexico. Austin: University of Texas Press.

Kemp, W. B. 1971 The Flow of Energy in a Hunting Society. Scientific American 225(3):105-115.

Kennedy, A. G. 1931 Field Note on Vaitupu, Ellice Island. Memoirs of Polynesian Society 9. New Plymouth.

Kiev, Ari, ed. 1964 Magic, Faith, and Healing: Primitive Psychiatry Today. Glencoe, Ill.: The Free Press.

———1968 Curanderismo: Mexican-American Folk Psychiatry. New York: The Free Press.

Kingsley, M. H. 1899 West African Studies. London.

Kinzie, J. D. 1972 Cross-Cultural Psychotherapy: An Open System Model, the Malaysian Experience. American Journal of Psychotherapy. 26:220-231.

Kleiweg de Zwann, J. P. 1913 Die Heilkunde der Niasser. Haag.

Kluckhohn, Clyde 1944 Navaho Witchcraft. Papers of Peabody Museum of American Archaeology and Ethnology, Harvard University, XXII. (Republished by Beacon Press, Boston,
n.d.)

Kluckhohn, Clyde, and Dorothea Leighton 1962 The Navaho. Garden City, N.Y.: Natural
History Library, Doubleday.

Kluckhohn, F., and F. Strodtbeck 1961 Variations in Value Orientations. New York: Row,
Peterson and Company.

Koch-Grünberg, Th. 1923 Vom Roroima zum Orinoko. Stuttgart.

Kosa, John, Aaron Antonovsky, and Irving Kenneth Zola 1969 Poverty and Health. Cambridge: Harvard University.

Krieg, Margaret B. 1964 Green Medicine. New York: Rand McNally.

Kroeber, A. L., and C. K. M. Kluckhohn 1952 Culture: A Critical Review of Concepts and
Definitions. Papers of the Peabody Museum of Archeology and Ethnology 47(1). Cambridge: Harvard University Press.

Krogman, W. M. 1939 Medical Practices and Diseases of the Aboriginal American Indians.
CIBA Symposia 1:11-18.

Krzywicki, L. 1934 Primitive Society and Its Vital Statistics. Translated by H. E. Kennedy and
A. Truszkowski. London: Macmillan.

Kuhn, Thomas S. 1970 The Structure of Scientific Revolutions. Second ed. Chicago: University of Chicago Press.

Kunitz, S. J. 1974 Some Notes on Physiologic Conditions as Social Problems. Social Science
and Medicine 8:207-211.

Kunstadter, Peter 1972 Demography, Ecology, Social Structure and Settlement Patterns. *In*
The Structure of Human Population. G. A. Harrison and A. J. Boyce, eds. Pp. 313-351.
Oxford: Clarendon Press.

Lacaille, A. D. 1950 Infant Feeding-Bottle in Prehistoric Times. Proceedings of the Royal
Society of Medicine 43:565.

Lagercrantz, S. 1935 Fingerverstümmelung in Africa. Zeitscheif fur Ethnologic, p. 129ff.

_____1938 Zur Verbreitung der Monorchie. Zeitscheif fur Ethnologic 70:199ff.

Lambo, T. A. 1956 Neuropsychiatric Observations in the Western Region of Nigeria. British
Medical Journal 2:1388-1394.

_____1967 Mental and Behavioral Disorders. *In* Health of Mankind. G. Wolstenholme and M.
O'Conner, eds. London: Churchill.

Lambrecht, F. L. 1964 Aspects of Evolution and Ecology of Tsetse Flies and Trypanosomiasis
in Prehistoric African Environments. Journal of African History 5:1-24.

Landy, David 1958 Tuscarora Tribalism and National Identity. Ethnohistory 5:250-285.

_____1959 Tropical Childhood. New York: Harper and Row.

_____1965 Tropical Childhood: Cultural Transmission and Learning in a Puerto Rican Vil-
lage. New York: Harper and Row.

Lantman, G. 1927 The Kiwai Papuans. London.

Laubscher, B. J. 1937 Sex, Custom, and Psychopathology. London.

Laughlin, W. 1962 Primitive Theory of Medicine: Empirical Knowledge. Conference of Medicine and Anthropology, November 17-20, 1961. New York: Aiden House, Harriman.

_____1963 Primitive Theory of Medicine: Empirical Knowledge. *In* Man's Image in Medicine
and Anthropology. Iago Galdston, ed. Pp. 116-140. New York: International Universities Press.

_____1968 Hunting: An Integrating Biobehaviour System and Its Evolutionary Importance.
In Man the Hunter. R. B. Lee and I. deVore, eds. Chicago: Aldine.

Lave, L. B., and Seskin, E. P. 1970 Air Pollution and Human Health. Science 169:723-733.

Lawick-Goodall, J. van 1975 Cultural Elements in a Chimpanzee Community. *In* PreCultural
Primate Behavior. D. W. Menzel, ed. Basel: S. Karger.

Leacock, E., et al. 1974 Training Programs for New Opportunities in Applied Anthropology.
Washington, D.C.: American Anthropological Association.

Leavell, Hugh R., and E. G. Clark 1965 Primitive Medicine for the Doctor in His Community. New York: McGraw-Hill.

Lederberg, J. 1959 Genes and Antibodies. Science 129:1649-1653.

_____1963 Comments on A. Motulsky's Genetic Systems in Disease Susceptibility in Mammals. *In* Genetic Selection in Man. W. J. Schull, ed. Pp. 112-260. Ann Arbor: University of Michigan Press.

Lee, R. B. 1965 Subsistence Ecology of !Kung Bushmen. Unpublished doctoral dissertation, University of California.

Leechman, D. 1944 Trephined Skulls from British Columbia. Transactions of the Royal Society of Canada, Section II. Pp. 99-102.

Leighton, A. H. 1959 Mental Illness and Acculturation. *In* Medicine and Anthropology. I. Galdston, ed. New York: International Universities Press.

Leighton, Alexander H., and Dorothea C. Leighton 1941 Elements of Psychotherapy in Navaho Religion. Psychiatry 4:515-523.

_____1944 The Navaho Door. Cambridge: Harvard University Press.

_____1945 The Navaho Door. Cambridge: Harvard University Press.

Leighton, Alexander H., et al. 1963 Psychiatric Disorders among the Yoruba. Ithaca: Cornell University Press.

Leithead, C. S., and A. R. Lind 1964 Heat Stress and Heat Disorders. London: Cassell.

Lennard, Henry, 1971 Mystification and Drug Misuse. San Francisco: Jossey-Bass.

Leriche, R. 1944 La Chirurgie à l'ordre de la vie. Paris.

Léridon, H. 1973 Aspects biométriques de la fécondité humaine. Paris: Presses Universitaires de France.

Lessa, W. A. 1968 Chinese Body Divination: Its Forms, Affinities and Functions. Los Angeles: United World.

Levineson, F. James 1974 Morinda: An Economic Analysis of Malnutrition among Young Children in Rural India. Ithaca: Cornell/MIT International Nutrition Policy Series.

Levi-Strauss, Claude 1963 Structural Anthropology. New York: Basic Books.

_____1966 The Savage Mind. London: Wiedenfeld and Nicholson.

Lewis, Oscar 1955 Medicine and Politics in a Mexican Village. *In* Health, Culture and Community. Benjamin Paul, ed. Pp. 403-434. New York: Russell Sage Foundation.

_____1960 Tepotzlan, Village in Mexico. New York: Holt, Reinhart, and Winston.

Lieban, Richard W. 1960 Sorcery, Illness, and Social Control in a Philippine Municipality. Southwestern Journal of Anthropology 16:127-143.

_____1962 The Dangerous Ingkantos: Illness and Social Control in a Philippine Community. American Anthropologist 64:306-312.

_____1967 Cebuano Sorcery. Berkeley and Los Angeles: University of California Press.

_____1973 Medical Anthropology. *In* Handbook of Social and Cultural Anthropology. John J. Honigmann, ed. Pp. 1031-1072. Chicago: Rand McNally.

Lillico, J. 1940 Primitive Blood-Letting. Annals of Medical History Series 3, 2:133-139.

Lindblom, G. 1933 The Akamba. Upsala.

Linton, R. 1933 The Tanala. Chicago.

_____1936 The Study of Man. New York: Appleton-Century-Crofts.

_____1945 The Science of Man in the World Crisis. New York.

Little, M. A., and George B. Morren, Jr. 1976 Ecology, Energetics and Human Variability. Dubuque, Iowa: W. C. Brown.

Livingstone, F. B. 1958 Anthropological Implications of Sickle-Cell Gene Distribution in West Africa. American Anthropologist 60:533-562.

_____1960 Natural Selection, Disease, and Ongoing Evolution, as Illustrated by the ABO Blood Groups. *In* The Processes of Ongoing Human Evolution. G. W. Lasker, ed. Detroit: Wayne University Press.

_____1969 Gene Frequency Clines of the Beta Hemoglobin Involving Differential Selection. Human Biology 41:223-236.

Llewellyn, K. N., and E. A. Hoebel 1941 The Cheyenne Way. Norman, Oklahoma.

Loomis, W. F. 1967 Skin Pigment Regulation of Vitamin D Biosynthesis in Man. Science 157:501-506.

Logan, Michael H. 1972 Humoral Folk Medicine: A Potential Aid in Controlling Pellagra in Mexico. Ethnomedizin 4:397-410.

_____1973 Humoral Medicine in Guatemala and Peasant Acceptance of Modern Medicine. Human Organization 32(4):385-396.

Logan, M. H., and W. T. Morrill. Humoral Medicine and Informant Variability: An Analysis of Acculturation and Cognitive Change among Guatemalan Villages. Unpublished manuscript.

McArthur, J. 1964 The Age Incidence of Kuru. Annals of Human Genetics 27:341-352.

McClain, Carol n.d. Ethnomedicine in Ajijic. Unpublished manuscript.

McCorkle, Thomas, 1961 Chiropractic: A Deviant Theory of Disease. Human Organization 20:20-22.

McCracken, Robert D. 1971 Lactase Deficiency: An Example of Dietary Evolution. Current Anthropology 12:479-517.

McCullough, John M. 1972 A Physiological Test of the Bergmann and Allen Rules among the Yucatec Maya. Unpublished Ph.D dissertation, University of Illinois.

Maccurdy, G. G., 1923 Human Skeletal Remains from the Highlands of Peru. Journal of Physical Anthropology 6:218-329.

McDaniel, E. B., and Tieng Pardthaisong 1972 Acceptability of an Injectable Contraceptive in a Rural Population in Thailand. Paper presented at the First International Planned Parenthood Federation Southeast Asia and Oceania Regional Medical and Scientific Congress, 14-18 August 1972, Sidney.

McDermott, Walsh, et al. 1960 Introducing Modern Medicine in a Navaho Community. Science 131:197-205; 280-287.

Macdonald, G. 1965 On the Scientific Basis of Tropical Hygiene. Transcription of Royal Society of Tropical Medicine and Hygiene 59:611-620.

McKenzie, Dan 1927 The Infancy of Medicine. London.

Maclean, C. M. U. 1966 Hospitals or Healers? An Attitude Survey in Ibadan. Human Organization 25:131-139.

Maclean, Una 1971 Magical Medicine: A Nigerian Case-Study. Harmondsworth, Middlesex: Penguin Books.

McNair, P. K., R. R. Garison, J. H. Gilpin et al. 1949 Report of a Medical Survey of the Yap District of the Western Caroline Islands of the Trust Territory of the Pacific Islands. Hospital Corps Quarterly 22:5-19.

McNeill, W. H. 1976 Plagues and Peoples. Garden City, N.Y.: Anchor Press/Doubleday.

Madsen, C. 1965 A Study of Change in Mexican Folk Medicine. Middle American Research Institute, Publication 25. New Orleans: Tulane University Press.

Madsen, W. 1955 Hot and Cold in the Universe of San Francisco Tecospa, Valley of Mexico. Journal of American Folklore 68:123-39.

_____1964a The Mexican Americans of South Texas. Case Studies in Cultural Anthropology. New York: Holt, Rinehart and Winston.

_____1964b Value Conflicts and Folk Psychotherapy in South Texas. In Magic, Faith, and Healing. Ari Kiev, ed. Pp. 420-440. Glencoe, Ill.: The Free Press.

Maingard, J. F. 1937 Some Notes on Health and Disease among the Bushmen of the Southern Kalahari. In Bushmen of the Southern Kalahari. D. J. Jones et al., eds. Johannesburg: University of Wirwatersrand Press.

Mak, C. 1959 Mixtec Medical Beliefs and Practices. America Indigena 19:235-50.

Malcolm, L. W. G. 1934 Prehistoric and Primitive Surgery. Nature 133:200ff.

Malinowski, Bronislow. 1954 Argonauts of the Western Pacific. New York: E. P. Dutton and Company.

Mann, G. V., et al. 1962 Cardiovascular Disease in African Pygmies. Journal of Chronic Diseases 15:341-371.

Manners, Robert A., and David Kaplan, eds. 1968 Theory in Anthropology: A Sourcebook. Chicago: Aldine.

Marchione, Thomas 1975 Using Anthropology in Feedback from Community to Health Establishment. Paper presented at American Anthropological Association Annual Meetings, San Francisco.

_____(In press) Factors Affecting Nutritional Status of One-Year Olds in Jamaica. *In* Nutritional Anthropology Jerome, N., R. Kandel, and G. H. Pelto, eds.

Mariott, A. 1945 The Ten Grandmothers. Norman.

Marriott, McKim 1955 Western Medicine in a Village of Northern India. *In* Health, Culture and Community. Benjamin Paul, ed. Pp. 239-268. New York: Russell Sage Foundation.

Marshall, John F. 1972 Culture and Contraception: Response Determinants to a Family Planning Program in a North Indian Village. Ph.D dissertation, University of Hawaii.

_____1973 Fertility Regulating Methods: Cultural Acceptability for Potential Adopters. *In* Fertility Control Methods: Strategies for Introduction Gordon W. Duncan, et al., eds. New York: Academic Press.

Martin, P. S. 1967 Pleistocene Overskill. *In* Pleistocene Extinctions: The Search for a Cause. P. S. Martin and H. E. Wright, eds. Pp. 75-120. New Haven and London: Yale University Press.

Martinez, Maximino 1936 Plantas Utiles de Mexico. Mexico: Ediciones Botas.

Martius, K. Fr. Ph. V. 1844 Das Naturell, die Krankheiten, das Arztthum und die Heilmittel der Urbewohner Brasiliens. München.

Mathews, J. D., R. Glasse, and S. Lindebaum 1968 Kuru and Cannibalism. Lancet 1968i:449-452.

Mauksch, Hans 1969 The Organizational Context of Nursing Practice. *In* The Nursing Profession: Five Sociological Essays. Fred Davis, ed. New York: John Wiley and Sons.

May, J. 1958 The Ecology of Human Disease. New York: MD Publications.

_____1960 The Ecology of Human Disease. Annals of New York Academy of Science 84: 789-794.

_____1961 Studies in Disease Ecology. New York: Hafner.

Mayhew, Henry, 1861-62 London Labour and the London Poor. London: Griffin, Bohn, and Co.

Mead, George A. 1970 On the Improper Usage of Common Names When Giving Botanical Data. American Antiquity 35:108-109.

Mead, Margaret 1928 Coming of Age in Samoa. New York: Morrow.

_____1930 Growing Up in New Guinea. New York: Morrow.

_____1947 The Concept of Culture and the Psychosomatic Approach. Psychiatry 10:57-76.

_____1961 New Lives for Old: Cultural Transformation, Manus 1928-1953. New York: Mentor Books.

Means, Ph. A. 1931 Ancient Civilizations of the Andes. New York.

Mechanic, D. 1963 Religion, Religiosity, and Illness Behavior: The Social Case of the Jews. Human Organization 22:202-08.

_____1967 Medical Sociology. New York: The Free Press.

Merker, M. 1910 Die Masai. Berlin.

Merton, Robert K. 1957a Some Preliminaries to a Sociology of Medical Education. *In* The Student-Physician R. K. Merton, G. G. Reader, and P. L. Kendall, eds. Pp. 3-79. Cambridge: Harvard University Press.

_____1957b Social Theory and Social Structure. Revised. Glencoe, Ill.: The Free Press.

_____1967 On Theoretical Sociology. New York: Free Press.

Merton, Robert K., George G. Reader, and Patricia L. Kendall 1957 The Student Physician. Cambridge: Harvard University Press.

Messenger, John C., Jr. 1959 Religious Acculturation among the Anang Ibibio. *In* Continuity and Change in African Cultures. William R. Bascom and Melville J. Herskovits, eds. Pp. 279-299. Chicago: University of Chicago Press.

Metzger, D. G., and G. E. Williams 1966 Some Procedures and Results in the Study of Native Categories: Tzeltal Firewood. American Anthropologist 68:389-408.

Meyer, H. 1916 Die Barundi. Leipzig.

Middleton, John 1967 Magic, Witchcraft, and Curing. Garden City, N.Y.: Natural History Press.

Miklucho-Maclay, N. V. 1882 Bericht über Operationen Austral Eingeborener. Zeitschrift fur Ethnologie 12:526.

Mills, C. A. 1935 Dangers to Southerners in Northward Migration. American Journal of Tropical Medicine 15:1-9.

_____1938 Medical Climatology. Springfield, Ill.: Charles C. Thomas.

Milne, E. 1924 Home of an Eastern Clan. Oxford.

Minard, D., H. S. Belding, and J. R. Kingston 1957 Prevention of Heat Casualties. Journal of the American Medical Association 165:1813-1818.

Mintz, S. W. 1956 Canamelar: The Subculture of a Rural Plantation Proletariat. *In* The People of Puerto Rico. J. Stewart, ed. Urbana: University of Illinois Press.

Mischel, Frances 1959 Faith Healing and Medical Practice in the Southern Caribbean. Southwestern Journal of Anthropology 15:407-417.

Mongeau, Beatrice, Harvey L. Smith, and Ann C. Maney 1961 The Granny Midwife: Changing Roles and Functions of a Folk Practitioner. American Journal of Sociology 66:497-505.

Monod, J. 1971 Chance and Necessity. New York: Alfred A. Knopf.

Montagu, M. F. A. 1937 The Origin of Subincision in Australia. Oceania 8:193-207.

_____1957 Anthropology and Human Nature. Boston: Porter Sargent.

Montgomery, Edward 1973 Ecological Aspects of Health and Disease in Local Populations. *In* Annual Review of Anthropology. Barnard J. Siegel, Alan R. Beals, and Stephen A. Tyler, eds. Vol. 2. Pp. 30-35. Palo Alto: Annual Reviews, Inc.

Montoto, Luis 1883 Costumbres populares Andaluzas. *In* Biblioteca de las Tradiciones Populares Espanolas A. Machado y Alvarez, ed. Pp. 2-99. Seville: Francisco Alvarez y Company.

Moodie, R. L. 1917 The Influence of Disease in the Extinction of Races. Science 45:63.

_____1923a Palaeopathology: An Introduction to the Study of Ancient Evidence of Disease. Urbana: University of Illinois Press.

_____1923b The Antiquity of Disease. Chicago: University of Chicago Press Science Series.

_____1927 Injuries to the Head among the Pre-Columbian Peruvians. Annual Medical History 9:277ff.

Mooney, J. 1891 The Sacred Formulae of the Cherokees. Bureau of American Ethnology Report 7.

Morice, A. G. 1900-01 Déné Surgery. Transactions of the Canadian Institute. Pp. 15-28.

Moss, G. E. 1973 Illness, Immunity, and Social Interaction: The Dynamics of Biosocial Resonation. New York: John Wiley and Sons.

Motulsky, A. G. 1960 Metabolic Polymorphism and the Role of Infectious Diseases. Human Biology 32:28-63.

_____1963 Genetic Systems Involved in Disease Susceptibility in Mammals. *In* Genetic Selection in Man. W. J. Schull, ed. Pp. 112-260. Ann Arbor: University of Michigan Press.

Müller, F. 1928 Drogen und Medicamente der Guarani. Publicacion d'Hommage offerte au P. W. Schmidt. E. Koppers, ed. Wien.

Mumford, Emile 1970 Interns: From Students to Physicians. Cambridge: Harvard University Press.

Munoz de Chaves, Miriam, et al. 1974 The Epidemiology of Good Nutrition. *In* Ecology of Food and Nutrition 3:223-230.

Murdock, George 1959 Africa: Its People and Their Culture History. New York: McGraw-Hill.

_____1960 Social Structure in South East Asia. Chicago.

_____1967 Ethnographic Atlas. Pittsburgh: University of Pittsburgh Press.

Murdock, George, et al. 1967 Outline of Cultural Materials. New Haven: Human Relations Area File.

Nadel, S. F. 1957 The Theory of Social Structure. Glencoe, Ill.: The Free Press.

Nagel, Ernest 1961 The Structure of Science. New York: Harcourt, Brace, and World.

National Education Association 1966 NEA-Tucson Survey on the Teaching of Spanish to the Spanish Speaking. Washington, D.C.: U.S. Government Printing Office.

Ndeti, K. 1972 Sociocultural Aspects of Tuberculosis Defalutation: A Case Study. Social Science and Medicine 6:397-412.

Neal, E. 1948 The Badger. London: Collins.

Neel, J. V. 1958 The Study of Natural Selection in Primitive and Civilized Human Populations. American Anthropological Association Memoirs 86:43-72.

_____1962 Diabetes Mellitus: A Thrifty Genotype Rendered Detrimental by Progress? American Journal of Human Genetics 14(4):353-362.

Neel, J. V., et al. 1964 Studies on the Xavante Indians of the Brazilian Matto Grosso. American Journal of Human Genetics 16(1):52-140.

_____1970 Notes on the Effect of Measles and Measles Vaccine in a Virgin-Soil Population of South American Indians. American Journal of Epidemiology 91(4):418-429.

Nelson, Cynthia, and Virginia Olesen 1974 Preliminary Notes on Health Systems, Social Control and Articulation of the Moral Order. Paper presented at the Fourth International Conference on Social Science and Medicine, Elsinore, Denmark.

Neuhauss, R. 1911 Deutsch Neu Guinea. 3 Vols. Berlin.

Newman, L. F. 1972 Birth Control: An Anthropological View. Anthropology 27:1-21.

Nissen, H. W., and A. H. Riesen 1945 The Deciduous Teeth of the Chimpanzee. Growth 9:265-274.

_____1964 The Eruption of the Permanent Dentition of the Chimpanzee. American Journal of Physical Anthropology 22:285-294.

Nurge, Ethel 1958 Etiology of Illness in Guinhangdan. American Anthropologist 60:1158-1172.

Odum, E. P. 1959 Fundamentals of Ecology. Second ed. Philadelphia, London: Saunders.

Odum, H. T. 1971 Environment, Power and Society. New York: Wiley-Inter-Science.

Oesterreich, T. K. 1930 Possession, Demoniacal and Other. London.

Ogburn, William F. 1957 Culture Lag as Theory. Sociology and Social Research 41:167-174.

Olbrechts, F. R., and J. Mooney 1932 The Swimmer Manuscript. Bureau of American Ethnology Bulletin, No. 99. Washington.

Olesen, Virginia, and Elvi Whittaker 1968 The Silent Dialogue: The Social Psychology of Professional Socialization. San Francisco: Jossey-Bass.

Oliver, J. A. 1974 Air Pollution. *In* The Environmental Challenge. W. Johnson and W. Sleve, eds. New York: Holt, Rinehart, and Winston.

Opler, M. E. 1936 Some Points of Comparison and Contrast between the Treatment of Functional Disorders by Apache Shamans and Modern Psychiatric Practice. The American Journal of Psychiatry 92:1371-1787.

_____1941 An Apache Life Way. Chicago.

_____1963a The Cultural Definition of Illness in Village India. Human Organization 22:32-35.

_____1963b Cultural Definitions of Illness: Social Psychiatry Views Intercultural and Interclass Communication in Ghana. *In* Man's Image In Medicine and Anthropology. I. Galdston, ed. Pp. 446-473. New York: International Universities Press.

Orso, E. 1970 Hot and Cold in the Folk Medicine of the Island of Chira, Costa Rica. Working Paper, Institute of Latin American Studies. Baton Rouge: Louisiana State University.

Ozaetta, M., and R. Gonzales 1972 Consultation and Education Service Center Report. Mimeo.

Packard, F. 1901 History of Medicine in the United States. Philadelphia.

Padilla, E. 1958 Up from Puerto Rico. New York: Columbia University Press.

Pardal, R. 1937 Medicina aborigen americana. Buenos Aires.

Paredes Borja, V. 1946 Early History of Anesthesia in Ecuador. Journal of the History of

Medicine 1:657-661.

Parham, H. B. R. 1943 Fiji Native Plants with Their Medicinal and Other Uses. Polynesian Sociological Memoirs, No. 16. Wellington.

Park, W. F. 1938 Shamanism in Western North America. Evanston.

Parkinson, R. 1907 Dreissig Jahre in der Südsee. Stuttgart.

Parsons, Talcott 1951 The Social System. New York: The Free Press.

_____1958 Definitions of Health and Illness in Light of American Values and Social Structure. *In* Patients, Physicians, and Illness. E. C. Jaco, ed. Pp. 165-187. New York: The Free Press.

Parsons, T., and R. Fox 1952 Illness, Therapy, and the Modern Urban American Family. Journal of Social Issues 8:31-44.

Pattishall, Evan G., Jr. 1972 Organizational Forms for Medical Behavioral Science Programs. *In* Study for Teaching Behavioral Sciences in Schools of Medicine, Vol. III. Pp. 443-469. Behavioral Science Perspectives in Medical Education, National Center for the Health Services Research and Development, Department of Health, Education, and Welfare Public Health Service.

Paul, Benjamin D., ed. 1955 Health, Culture, and Community: Case Studies of Public Reactions to Health Programs. New York: Russell Sage Foundation.

_____1956 Anthropology and Public Health. *In* Some Uses of Anthropology. Washington, D.C.: Anthropological Society of Washington.

Paulitschke, P. 1896 Ethnographie Nordost Africas. Berlin.

Pellegrino, Edmund D. 1963 Medicine, History, and the Idea of Man. *In* Medicine and Society. J. A. Clausen and R. Straus, eds. The Annals of the American Academy of Political and Social Science 346:9-20.

Pflanz, Manfred 1974 Relations between Social Scientists, Physicians, and Medical Organizations in Health Research. Position paper at the Fourth International Social Science and Medicine Conference, Elsinore, Denmark.

Philips, Jane 1955 The Hookworm Campaign in Ceylon. *In* Hands Across Frontiers: Case Studies in Technical Cooperation. H. M. Teaf, Jr., and P. G. Franck, eds. Pp. 265-305. Ithaca: Cornell University Press.

Piggott, S. 1950 Prehistoric India to 1000 B.C. London: Penguin Books.

Pike, Kenneth 1964 Toward a Theory of the Structure of Human Behavior. *In* Language in Culture and Society. Dell Hymes, ed. Pp. 54-62. New York: Harper and Row.

Pitré, Giuseppe 1871-1913 Biblioteca delle Tradizione Popolare Siciliana. 25 vols. Palermo, Italy: L. Pedone-Lauriel de Carlo Clausen.

_____1896 Medicina Popolare Siciliana. Torino-Palermo, Italy: Pedone-Lauriel de Carlo Clausen.

Pitt-Rivers, J. A. 1961 The People of the Sierra. Chicago: University of Chicago Press.

Ploss, H., and M. Bartels 1899 Das Weib in der Natur und Völkerkunde. Leipzig.

Polgar, Steven 1962 Health and Human Behavior: Areas of Interest Common to the Social and Medical Sciences. Current Anthropology 3:154-205.

_____1963 Health Action in Cross-Cultural Perspective. *In* Handbook of Medical Sociology. Howard E. Freeman, Sol Levine, and Leo G. Reeder, eds. Pp. 159-205. New York: Prentice-Hall.

_____1964 Evolution and the Ills of Mankind. *In* Horizons of Anthropology. S. Tax, ed. Chicago: Aldine.

_____1969 Cultural Aspects of Natality Regulation Techniques. *In* Proceedings, 8th International Congress of Anthropological and Ethnological Sciences. Vol. 3. Tokyo: Science Council of Japan.

_____1972 Population History and Population Policies from an Anthropological Perspective. Current Anthropology 13:203-11.

Polunin, I. 1953 The Medical Natural History of Malayan Aborigines and Their Medical Investigation. Medical Journal of Malaya 8:55-174.

Post, P. W., F. Daniels, Jr., and R. T. Binford 1975 Cold Injury and the Evolution of White Skin. Human Biology 47:65-80.

Press, Irwin, 1969a Ambiguity and Innovation: Implications for the Genesis of the Cultural Broker. American Anthropologist 71:205-217.

_____1969b Urban Illness: Physicians, Curers and Dual Use in Bogota. Journal of Health and Social Behavior 10:209-218.

_____1971 The Urban Curandero. American Anthropologist 73:741-756.

Preuss, K. Th. 1890 Menschenopfer und Selbstverstümmlung in Amerika. Festschrift für Adolf Bastian. Berlin.

Price, D. L., et al. 1963 Parasitism in Congo Pygmies. American Journal of Tropical Medicine and Hygiene 12:383-387.

Price, W. A. 1939 Nutrition and Physical Degeneration: A Comparison of Primitive and Modern Diets and Their Effects. New York: Hoeber.

Price-Williams, D. R. 1962 A Case Study of Ideas Concerning Disease among the Tiv. Africa 32:123-131.

Public Safety System, Inc. 1973 Crime and Demographic Profile for Ventura County. Santa Barbara, Calif.: Public Safety System, Inc.

Pyke, M. 1968 Food and Society. London: Murray.

Radcliffe-Brown, A. R. 1933 The Andaman Islanders. Second ed. Cambridge: Cambridge University Press.

_____1935 On the Concept of Function in Social Science. American Anthropologist 37:394-402.

Ragucci, A. T. 1971 Generational Continuity and Change in the Concepts of Health, Curing Practices and Ritual Expressions of the Women of an Italian-American Enclave. Unpublished Ph.D dissertation, Boston University.

Rappaport, R. A. 1971 The Flow of Energy in an Agricultural Society. Scientific American 224(3):117-132.

Ray, S. G. 1917 The People and Language of Lifu, Loyalty Islands. Journal of the Royal Anthropological Institute of Great Britain and Ireland 47:239ff.

Reader, George, and Mary E. W. Goss 1959 The Sociology of Medicine. In Sociology Today, Problems and Prospects. Robert K. Merton, Leonard Broom, and Leonard S. Cottrell, Jr., eds. Pp. 229-246. New York: Basic Books.

Redfield, Robert 1930 Tepoztlan—A Mexican Village. Chicago: University of Chicago Press.

_____1934 Chan Kom, a Maya Village. Chicago: University of Chicago Press.

_____1947 The Folk Society. American Journal of Sociology 52:293-308.

Redfield, Robert, and Alfonso Villa Rojas 1934 Chan Kom: A Maya Village. Washington, D.C.: Publications of the Carnegie Institute of Washington.

Redfield, Robert, and M. Park 1940 The Treatment of Disease in Dzitas Yucatan. In Contributions to American Anthropology and History. Vol. 6. Pp. 49-81. Washington, D.C.: Carnegie Institution.

Rehse, H. 1910 Kisiba Land und Leute. Stuttgart.

Reichel-Dolmatoff, G., and A. Reichel-Dolmatoff 1961 The People of Aritama. Chicago: University of Chicago Press.

Reis, Siri von 1962 Herbaria: Sources of Medical Folklore. Economic Botany 16:283-288.

Richardson, M., and B. Bode 1971 Popular Medicine in Puntarenas Costa Rica: Urban and Societal Features. Middle American Research Institute, Publication 24. New Orleans: Tulane University Press.

Riesen, A. H., and E. F. Kinder 1952 The Postural Development of Infant Chimpanzees. New Haven: Yale University Press.

Riley, Matilda W. 1963 Sociological Research: A Case Approach. New York: Harcourt, Brace, and World.

Riopelle, A. J. 1963 Growth and Behavioral Changes in the Chimpanzee. Zeitschrift fur Morphologie und Anthropologie. 53:53-61.

Rivers, W. H. R. 1900 A Genealogical Method of Collecting Social and Vital Statistics. Journal of the Royal Anthropological Institute of Great Britain and Ireland 30:74-82.
_____1906 The Todas. New York and London: Macmillan.
_____1914a The History of Melanesian Society. 2 vols. Percy Sladen Trust Expedition to Melanesia. Cambridge: Cambridge University Press.
_____1914b Kinship and Social Organization. London School of Economics and Political Science, Studies No. 36. London: Constable.
_____1924 Medicine, Magic, and Religion. New York: Harcourt Brace.
_____1926 Psychology and Ethnology. London: Routledge; New York: Harcourt.
Rodriguez Rovanet, Francisco 1969 Practicas medicas tradicionales de los Indigenas de Guatemala. Guatemala Indigena 4:4-49.
Rogler, Lloyd H., and August B. Hollingshead 1961 The Puerto Rican Spiritualist as a Psychiatrist. American Journal of Sociology 67:17-22.
Rohl, A. N., et al. 1975 Exposure to Asbestos in the Use of Consumer Spackling, Patching, and Taping Compounds. Science 189:551-552.
Roig y Mesa, J. T. 1945 Plantas Medicinales, Auromaticos, y Veneosa de Cuba. Havana.
Romney, A. K., and R. G. D'Andrade 1964 Cognitive Aspects of English Kin Terms. American Anthropologist 66:146-70.
Roney, J. G., Jr. 1959 Paleopathology of a California Archaeological Site. Bulletin of the History of Medicine 33:97-109.
Roscoe, J. 1911 The Bazanda. London.
_____1921 Twenty-five Years in East Africa. Cambridge.
_____1923 The Banyankole. Cambridge.
_____1924 The Bagesu. Cambridge.
Rosebury, Theodor 1971 Microbes and Morals. New York: Viking Press.
Rosen, G. 1944 The Specialization of Medicine with Particular Reference to Ophthalmology. New York.
_____1958 A History of Public Health. New York: MD Publications.
Rosenthal, Theodore, and Bernard J. Siegel 1959 Magic and Witchcraft: An Interpretation from Dissonance Theory. Southwestern Journal of Anthropology 15:143-167.
Roth, Julius A. 1962 Management Bias in Social Science Study of Medical Treatment. Human Organization 21:47-50.
_____1963 Timetables. Indianapolis: Bobbs-Merrill.
Roys, Ralph 1931 The Ethno-Botany of the Maya. New Orleans: Middle American Research Institute, Tulane.
Rubel, Arthur J. 1960 Concepts of Disease in Mexican-American Culture. American Anthropologist 62:795-814.
_____1964 The Epidemiology of a Folk Illness: Susto in Hispanic America. Ethnology 3:268-283.
Sahagun, Bernardino de 1970 General History of the Things of New Spain. Translated from the Aztec by Arthur J. O. Anderson and Charles Dibble. Santa Fe: New Mexico School of American Research.
Samuels, R. 1965 Parasitological Study of Long-dried Fecal samples. In Contributions of the Weatherill Mesa Archaeological Project. Memoirs of the Society of American Archaeologists 19.
Sandison, A. T. 1967 Parasitic Diseases. In Diseases in Antiquity. D. R. Brothwell and A. T. Sandison, eds. Springfield: Charles C. Thomas.
Sapir, Edward 1916 Time Perspective in Aboriginal American Culture: A Study in Method. Ottawa: Government Printing Bureau. (Also reprinted in Selected Writings of Edward Sapir. David Mandelbaum, ed. Pp. 387-462. Berkeley: University of California Press.)
Sarbin, Theodore R., and Vernon L. Allen 1968 Role Theory. In The Handbook of Social Psychology, Vol. 1. Gardner Lindzey and Eliot Aronson, eds. Pp. 488-567. Reading, Mass.: Addison-Wesley.

Sarton, G. 1952 A History of Science: Ancient Science Through the Golden Age of Greece. New York: John Wiley and Sons.

Saunders, L. 1954 Cultural Differences and Medical Care: The Case of the Spanish-Speaking People of the Southwest. New York: Russell Sage Foundation.

Saunders, Lyle, and Julian Samora 1955 A Medical Care Program in a Colorado County. *In* Health, Culture, and Community. Benjamin D. Paul, ed. Pp. 377-400. New York: Russell Sage Foundation.

Schapera, I. 1930 The Khoisan Peoples of South Africa. London.

Schensul, Stephen L. 1973 Training the Applied Anthropologist: A Consideration of the Skills Needed in Action Research. Paper presented at the American Anthropological Association Annual Meetings, New Orleans.

Schneider, David M. 1947 The Social Dynamics of Physical Disability in Army Basic Training. Psychiatry 10:323-333.

———1955 Abortion and Depopulation on a Pacific Island. *In* Health, Culture, and Community. B. D. Paul, ed. Pp. 211-235. New York: Russell Sage Foundation.

Scheinfeld, A. 1958 The Mortality of Men and Women. Scientific American 198:22-27.

Schultes, R. E. 1962 The Role of the Ethnobotanist in Search for New Medicinal Plants. Lloydia 25:257-267.

Schultz, A. H. 1939 Notes on Diseases and Healed Fracture of Wild Apes. Bulletin of the History of Medicine 7:571ff.

———1940 Growth and Development of the Chimpanzee. Contributions to Embryology No. 170. Carnegie Institution of Washington Publication 28:1-63.

———1944 Age Changes and Variability in Gibbons. American Journal of Physical Anthropology 2:1-129.

Schwabe, C. W. 1964 Veterinary Medicine and Human Health. Baltimore: Williams and Wilkins.

Schwartz, L. R. 1969 The Hierarchy of Resort in Curative Practices: The Admiralty Islands, Melanesia. Journal of Health and Social Behavior 10:201-09.

Scotch, Norman A. 1963a Medical Anthropology. *In* Biennial Review of Anthropology. Bernard J. Siegel, ed. Pp. 30-68. Stanford: Stanford University Press.

———1963b Sociocultural Factors in Epidemiology of Zulu Hypertension. American Journal of Public Health 53:1205.

Scrimshaw, N. S. 1966 Ecological Factors in Nutritional Disease. *In* Chronic Disease and Public Health. Lilienfeld, A. M., and A. J. Gifford, eds. Pp. 114-125. Baltimore: Johns Hopkins Press.

———1968 Interaction of Nutrition and Infections. Geneva: World Health Organization.

Scrimshaw, N. S., and C. Tejada 1970 Pathology of Living Indians as Seen in Guatemala. *In* Handbook of Middle American Indians. Vol. 9. T. Dale Stewart, ed. Austin: University of Texas Press.

Sears, P. B. 1956 The Processes of Environmental Changes by Man. *In* Man's Role in Changing the Face of the Earth. W. L. Thomas, ed. Pp. 471-484. Chicago: University of Chicago Press.

Seda-Bonila, Eduardo 1969 Interacción social y personalidad en una comunidad de Puerto Rico. San Juan, Puerto Rico: Ediciones Juan Ponce de León.

Seligman, C. G. 1902 The Medicine, Surgery, and Midwifery of the Sinaugolo. Journal of the Royal Anthropological Institute of Great Britain and Ireland 32:297-305.

Selye, H. 1956 The Stress of Life. New York: McGraw-Hill.

Servicio 1953 Ten Years of Operation of the Bilateral Health Programs of the Institute of Inter-American Affairs. Public Health Reports 68:829-857.

Shapiro, H. L. 1927 Primitive Surgery. Natural History 27:266-269.

Shattuck, George C., ed. 1938 A Medical Survey of the Republic of Guatemala. Washington, D.C.: Carnegie Institute.

Sieroshewski, M. 1901 The Yakuts. Journal of the Royal Anthropological Institute of Great Britain and Ireland 31:61-110.

Sigerist, Henry E. 1933 Problems of Historical-Geographical Pathology. Bulletin of the History of Medicine 1:10-18.

_____1951 A History of Medicine: Primitive and Archaic Medicine. Vol. 1. New York: Oxford University Press.

Simmons, J. S., et al. 1944-1951 Global Epidemiology: A Geography of Disease and Sanitation. Philadelphia: Lippincott.

Simmons, O. C. 1955 Popular and Modern Medicine in Mestizo Communities of Coastal Peru and Chile. Journal of American Folklore 68:57-71.

Singer, M. T., and L. C. Wynne 1966 Principles for Scoring Communication Defects and Deviance in Parents of Schizophrenics. Psychiatry 29:260.

Sjoberg, G. 1965 The Origin and Evolution of Cities. Scientific American 213:55-63.

Smith, E. W., and A. M. Dale 1920 The Ila-Speaking Tribes of North Rhodesia. London.

Söderström, J. 1938 Die rituellen Fingerverstümmelungen in der Südsee und in Australien. Zeitschief fur Ethnologie 70:24ff.

Sontag, L. W., and E. L. Reynolds 1945 Fels Composite Sheet: Practical Method for Analyzing Growth Progress. Journal of Pediatrics 26:327-335.

Southall, Aidan 1959 An Operational Theory of Role. Human Relations 12:17-34.

Spiegelman, M. 1956 Recent Trends and Determinants of Mortality in Highly Developed Countries. In Trends and Differentials in Mortality. F. C. Boudreau and C. V. Kiser, eds. Pp. 51-60. New York: Milbank Memorial Fund.

Spier, L. 1928 Havasupai Ethnography. New York.

Spinden, H. J. 1908 The Nez-Percé Indians. Lancaster.

Spiro, M. E. 1967 Burmese Supernaturalism: A Study in the Explanation and Reduction of Suffering. Englewood Cliffs, N.J.: Prentice-Hall.

Srole, Leo, et al. 1962 Mental Health in the Metropolis: Midtown Manhattan Study. Vol. 1. New York: McGraw-Hill.

Standley, Paul C. 1926 Trees and Shrubs of Mexico. Contributions from United States National Herbarium, No. 23.

Standley, Paul C., and J. A. Steyermark 1946 The Flora of Guatemala. Vol. 24. Chicago: National History Museum, Fieldiana Botany.

Stanton, Alfred, and Maurice S. Schwartz 1954 The Mental Hospital. New York: Basic Books.

Star Free Press 1973 Ventura, California. January 23:A-6.

Stayt, H. A. 1931 The Bavenda. London.

Steinen, K. V. D. 1886 Durch Central Brasilien. Leipzig.

Stephen-Chauvet 1936 La medicine chez les peuples primitifs. Paris.

Stevenson, M. C. 1904 The Zuni Indians. Bureau of American Ethnology 23:1-634. Washington, D.C.

Stewart, J. H. 1955 Theory of Culture Change. Urbana: University of Illinois Press.

Stewart, O. C. 1956 Fire as the First Great Force Employed by Man. In Man's Role in Changing the Face of the Earth. W. C. Thomas, ed. Chicago: University of Chicago Press.

Stirling, M. W. 1938 Historical and Ethnographical Material on the Jivaro Indians. Bureau of American Ethnology Bulletin 117. Washington, D.C.

Stone, E. 1932 Medicine among the American Indians. New York.

Straus, Robert 1957 The Nature and Status of Medical Sociology. American Sociological Review 22:200-204.

Strickland, Stephen P. 1972 Politics, Science, and Dread Disease. Cambridge: Harvard University Press.

Sturtevant, W. C. 1968 Studies in Ethnoscience. In Theory in Anthropology. Robert A. Manners and David Kaplan, eds. Pp. 475-500. Chicago: Aldine.

Suchman, E. A. 1965 Social Patterns of Illness and Medical Care. Journal of Health and Human Behavior 6:2-16.

Sumner, W. G., and A. G. Keller 1927 The Science of Society. 4 Vols. New Haven.

Sussman, Marvin 1965 Sociology and Rehabilitation. Washington, D.C.: American Sociological

Association in cooperation with the Vocational Rehabilitation Administration, U.S. Department of Health, Education, and Welfare.

Swanton, J. R. 1928 Religious Beliefs and Medical Practices of the Creek. Bureau of American Ethnology Report 42:473-672. Washington, D.C.

Swartz, Marc, Victor Turner, and Arthur Tuden, eds. 1966 Political Anthropology. Chicago: Aldine.

Teele, J. E. 1969 Black Family, Voluntary Association and Educational Bureaucracy. Paper presented at the American Sociological Association meetings, San Francisco.

Teit, J. 1900 The Thompson Indians of British Columbia. New York.

Teleki, G. 1973 The Predatory Behavior of Wild Chimpanzees. Lewisburg, Pa.: Bucknell University Press.

Teleki, G., E. E. Hunt, Jr., and J.-H. Pfifferling 1976 Demographic Observations (1963-1973) on the Chimpanzees of Gombe National Park, Tanzania. Journal of Human Evolution.

Tello, J. C. 1913 Prehistoric Trephining among the Yautos of Peru. International Congress of Americanists, p. 75. London.

Temkin, Owsei 1963 The Scientific Approach to Disease: Specific Entity and Individual Sickness. *In* Scientific Change. A. C. Crombie, ed. Pp. 629-647. New York: Basic Books.

Tessman, G. 1934 Die Bafia. Stuttgart.

Thomas, R. B. 1973 Human Adaptation to a High Andean Energy Flow System. Occasional Papers in Anthropology 7:1-181. University Park: Pennsylvania State University.

———1976 Energy Flow at Altitude. *In* Man in the Andes: A Multidisciplinary Study of High Altitude. P. T. Baker, and M. A. Little, eds. Pp. 379-404. Stroudsburg, Pa.: Dowden, Hutchinson, and Ross.

Tillyard, E. M. W. 1944 The Elizabethan World Picture. New York: Macmillan.

Torday, E., and T. A. Joyce 1906 Notes on the Ethnography of the Ba-Yala. Journal of the Royal Anthropological Institute of Great Britain and Ireland 36:39ff.

Torrey, E. 1972 The Mind Game: Witchdoctors and Psychiatrists. New York: Emerson Hall Publishers.

———1973 The Mind Game: Witchdoctors and Psychiatrists. New York: Bantam Books.

Tseng, W-S, and McDermott, J. F., Jr. (In press) Psychotherapy: Historical Root, Universal Elements, and Cultural Variation. American Journal of Psychiatry.

Turnbull, C. M. 1965a The Mbuti Pygmies: an Ethnographic Survey. Anthropological Papers of the American Museum of Natural History 50(3):139-282.

———1965b Wayward Servants: The Two Worlds of the African Pygmies. Garden City: Natural History Press.

Turner, G. 1884 Samoa a Hundred Years Ago. London.

Turner, Victor W. 1964 An Ndembu Doctor in Practice. *In* Magic, Faith, and Healing. Ari Kiev, ed. Pp. 230-263. Glencoe, Ill.: The Free Press.

Twaddle, A. C. 1969 Health Decisions and Sick Role Variations: An Exploration. Journal of Health and Social Behavior 10:105-115.

Tylor, E. B. 1871 Primitive Culture. London: John Murray.

Underwood, J. H. 1973 The Demography of a Myth: Depopulation in Yap. Human Biology in Oceania 2:115-127.

United States Department of Commerce 1972 Census Tracts, Oxnard-Ventura, California Metropolitan Statistical Area: PC(1-155). Washington, D.C.: U.S. Government Printing Office.

Valdizan, H. 1922 La Medicina Popular Peruana. Lima: Imprenta Torres Aguirre.

Vallentine, H. R. 1967 Water in the Service of Man. London: Penguin Books.

Van De Geer, J. P. 1971 Introduction to Multivariate Analysis for the Social Sciences. San Francisco: W. H. Freeman.

Van Der Burgt, Y. M. M. 1903 Dictionnaire français Kirundi. Bois le Duc.

Vedder, H. 1923 Die Bergdama. Hamburg.

Vergiat, A. M. 1937 Moeurs et coutumes des Manias. Paris.

Villacorta, J. Antonio 1926 Monografia del Departamento de Guatemala.

Virchow, R. 1872 Untersuchung des Meanderthalschädels. Schriften für Ethnologie 4:157-165.

Vogel, V. J. 1970 American Indian Medicine. Norman: University of Oklahoma Press.

Volkart, Edmund 1957 Bereavement and Mental Health. *In* Explorations in Social Psychiatry. Alexander Leighton, John Clausen, and Robert N. Wilson, eds. Pp. 281-307. New York: Basic Books.

Wafer, L. 1934 A New Voyage and Description of the Isthmus of America (1680-88). Oxford.

Wallace, Anthony F. C. 1956a Revitalization Movements. American Anthropologist 58:264-281.

_____ 1956b Stress and Rapid Personality Changes. International Record of Medicine and General Practice Clinics 169:761-774.

_____ 1956c Mazeway Resynthesis. Transactions of the New York Academy of Sciences, Series 2, 18:626-638.

_____ 1957 Mazeway Disintegration: The Individual's Perception of Sociocultural Disorganization. Human Organization 16:23-27.

_____ 1958 Dreams and Wishes of the Soul: A Type of Psychoanalytic Theory among the Seventeenth Century Iroquois. American Anthropologist 60:234-248.

_____ 1959 The Institutionalization of Cathartic and Control Strategies in Iroquois Religious Psychotherapy. *In* Culture and Mental Health. Marvin K. Opler, ed. Pp. 63-96. New York: Macmillan.

_____ 1961a Culture and Personality. New York: Random House.

_____ 1961b Cultural Composition of the Handsome Lake Religion. *In* Symposium on Cherokee and Iroquois Culture. William N. Fenton and John Gulick, eds. Bureau of American Ethnology Bulletin 180:139-151.

_____ 1961c Religious Revitalization: A Function of Religion in Human History and Evolution. Paper presented at Eighth Institute on Religion in an Age of Science, Star Island, N. W.

_____ 1966 Religion: An Anthropological View. New York: Random House.

_____ 1970 Culture and Personality. Second ed. New York: Random House.

Warner, W. Lloyd 1937 A Black Civilization. New York.

Wax, Murray L. 1970 Sociology. *In* Anthropology and the Behavioral and Health Sciences. O. Von Mering and L. Kasden, eds. Pp. 39-51. Pittsburgh: University of Pittsburgh Press.

Webb, T. T. 1933-34 Aboriginal Medical Practice in East Arnhem Land. Oceania 4:91.

Weidman, Hazel H. 1974 Cultural Brokerage and Cultural Mediation: Emergent Strategies in Mental Health Care. Paper presented at the American Anthropological Association Annual Meetings, Mexico City.

Weinberg, E. D. 1972 Infectious Diseases Influenced by Trace Element Environment. Annals of the New York Academy of Sciences 199:274-284.

_____ 1974 Iron Susceptibility to Infectious Disease. Science 184:952-956.

Weiss, K. M. 1973 Demographic Models for Anthropology. Memoirs of the Society for American Archeology 27:1-186.

Wellin, E. 1955 Water Boiling in a Peruvian Town. *In* Health, Culture, and Community. B. Paul, ed. New York: Russell Sage Foundation.

Werner, David 1970 Healing in the Sierra Madre. Natural History (November):61-66.

Weyer, E. M. 1932 The Eskimos. New Haven.

Wharton, R. H., A. B. G. Laing, and W. H. Cheong 1963 Studies on the Distribution and Transmission of Malaria and Filariasis among Aborigines in Malaya. Annals of Tropical Medicine and Parasitology 57:235-254.

Whiting, B. B. 1959 Paiute Sorcery. New York: Viking Fund Publications in Anthropology No. 15.

Whiting, J. W. M. 1941 Becoming a Kwoma. New Haven.

Whiting, J. W. M., and Irvin L. Child, 1953 Child Training and Personality: A Cross-Cultural Study. New Haven: Yale University Press.

Williams, G. R., et al. 1965 Evaluation of the Kuru Genetic Hypothesis. Journal de Genetique Humaine 13:11-21.

Wisdom, Charles 1940 The Chorti Indians of Guatemala. Chicago.

Wisenfield, S. L. 1967 Sickle-Cell Trait in Human Biological and Cultural Evolution. Science 157:1134-1140.

Wolf, Eric R. 1956a Aspects of Group Relations in a Complex Society. American Anthropologist 58:1065-1078.

_____1956b San Jose: Subculture of a Traditional Coffee Municipality. *In* The People of Puerto Rico. J. Steward, ed. Urbana: University of Illinois Press.

Wölfel, D. J. 1925 Die Trepanation. Anthropos 20:1-50.

Wolman, A. 1967 Pollution of Water, Air, and Food. *In* Health of Mankind. G. Wolstenholme and M. O'Conner, eds. London: Churchill.

Woodburn, J. C. 1959 Hadza Conceptions of Health and Disease. *In* One Day Symposium on Attitudes to Health and Disease among Some East African Tribes. Kamapala, Uganda: East African Institute of Sociological Research, Makerere College.

Woods, Clyde M. 1968 Medicine and Culture Change in San Lucas Toliman: A Highland Guatemalan Community. Unpublished Ph.D dissertation, Stanford University.

Woods, Clyde, and Theodore Graves 1973 The Process of Medical Change in Highland Guatemala. Latin American Studies Center, UCLA.

Woolley, L. 1965 Beginnings of Civilization. History of Mankind. Vol. I, Part II. New York and Toronto: Mentor Books.

World Health Organization 1963 Conference on Medicine and Public Health in the Arctic and Antarctic. Geneva, 28 August-1 September 1962. Tecn. Report Series No. 253.

_____1968 Research on Human Population Genetic. Tecn. Report Series No. 387.

Wright, L. 1963 Clean and Decent. London: Routledge and Kegan Paul.

Wynne-Edwards, V. C. 1962 Animal Dispersion in Relation to Social Behavior. Edinburgh: Oliver and Boyd.

Young, F. B. 1931 Paleopathology. The Nebraska State Medical Journal 16:26-29.

Young, J. H. 1944 Caesarean Section. London.

Zborowski, M. 1958 Cultural Components in Response to Pain. *In* Patients, Physicians, and Illness. E. G. Jaco, ed. Glencoe, Ill.: The Free Press.

_____1969 People in Pain. San Francisco: Jossey-Bass.

Ziegler, Philip 1969 The Black Death. New York: Harper Torchbooks.

Zigas, V., and D. C. Gajdusek 1957 Kuru: Clinical Study of a New Syndrome Recalling Paralysis Agitans in Natives of the Eastern Highlands of Australian New Guinea. Medical Journal of Australia 2:745-754.

Zola, I. K. 1972 Medicine as an Institution of Social Control. The Sociological Review 20(4): 487-504.

_____1974 In the Name of Health and Illness: On Some Socio-Political Consequences of Medical Influence. Paper presented at the Fourth International Social Science and Medicine Conference, Elsinore, Denmark.

Zola, I., G. Davidson, and J. Stoeckle 1963 On Going to See the Doctor: The Contributions of the Patient to the Decision to Seek Medical Care. Journal of Chronic Diseases 16:975-85.